VALLABHĀCĀRYA
ON
THE LOVE GAMES OF KṚṢṆA

VALLABHĀCĀRYA
ON
THE LOVE GAMES OF KṚṢṆA

JAMES D. REDINGTON, S. J.

MOTILAL BANARSIDASS PUBLISHERS
PRIVATE LIMITED • DELHI

First Edition: Delhi, 1983
Reprinted: Delhi, 1990

ISBN: 81-208-0657-3

Also available at:
MOTILAL BANARSIDASS
Bungalow Road, Jawahar Nagar, Delhi 110 007
Chowk, Varanasi 221 001
Ashok Rajpath, Patna 800 004
24 Race Course Road, Bangalore 560 001
120 Royapettah High Road, Mylapore, Madras 600 004

UNESCO COLLECTION OF REPRESENTATIVE WORKS INDIAN SERIES.
This book has been accepted in the Indian Translation Series of the UNESCO collection of Representative books jointly sponsored by the United Nations Educational, Scientific and Cultural Organization (UNESCO).

PRINTED IN INDIA
BY JAINENDRA PRAKASH JAIN AT SHRI JAINENDRA PRESS, A-45 NARAINA INDUSTRIAL AREA, PHASE I, NEW DELHI 110028 AND PUBLISHED BY NARENDRA PRAKASH JAIN FOR MOTILAL BANARSIDASS PUBLISHERS PVT. LTD., BUNGALOW ROAD, JAWAHAR NAGAR, DELHI 110007.

To
My Parents

PREFACE TO THE SECOND EDITION

I am grateful to Messrs. Motilal Banarsidass for reprinting my book with such dispatch. I have made several small additions and corrections which I have either observed myself or received notice of from colleagues. I have also updated the Bibliography. Special thanks to Professors Frances A. Wilson and Noel Sheth for the very helpful corrections they have suggested, almost all of which I have incorporated here.

J.D.R.

Washington, D.C.
June 9, 1989

PREFACE

I have tried to treat all the matters which require explanation in the Introduction. But a few brief points remain. First, as to the question of how complete my translation of Vallabhācārya's Commentary is : it is complete, except for a few instances in which Vallabha glosses a word from the *Bhāgavata Purāṇa* with a synonym. As my translation of the *Bhāgavata* stanza concerned already embodies this help of Vallabha's, I do not repeat it in the Commentary unless I feel that an additional nuance or connotation is present.

Secondly, I am embarrassed, upon my final reading, by the overabundance of capital letters. Some of this is due to my own piety. But a number can also be attributed to the printer's misreadings of my hand-printed corrections. For these possible distractions I apologize.

Finally, the Sanskrit text which has been included as an Appendix is that of Telivala and Sankalia (cf. page 47, and Bibliography). But it had to be set in type anew. The proofs have therefore been diligently corrected, and the best is hoped for. Just one clarification : Viṭṭhala's interpolations into Vallabha's Commentary are parenthesized in the Sanskrit text.

In acknowledging the exceptionally effective help I received on this book, let me begin with my Advisor at the University of Wisconsin, Professor Frances A. Wilson, and with my chief teachers there : David Knipe, George Hart (now of Berkeley), Stephan Beyer, and the late, brilliant Richard H. Robinson. *Sine quibus, non...*

In India, the marvellous research-situation which yielded the book's first form was set up for me by Rev. Dr. Adolfo Esteller, S.J., tireless Professor Emeritus of Sanskrit of Saint Xavier's College, Bombay, and Rev. Dr. Joaquín Pérez-Remón, S.J., now of the Universidad de Deusto, Bilbao, Spain. To them, more thanks than I can say.

To the late Professor T.G. Mainkar, then Head of Bombay University's Sanskrit Department, and later Director of the Bhandarkar Oriental Research Institute, I owe much in the way of knowledge of Vallabhācārya, since we read and discussed thoroughly—how he could afford the time, I'll never know—Vallabha's Sixteen Verse-Treatises (*Ṣoḍaśagranthāḥ*), with their major commentaries. His kindness does not die.

And last, but by far most important, I express my loving thanks to Shri Shyam Goswamy, one of the Vallabha Sampradāya's keenest and most generous scholars, as had been his father, Shri Dikshitji Maharaj. Were it not that the mistakes in the book are entirely mine, Shri Shyam might even be listed as co-author. At least this is true for large portions of the work, especially : the entire sixth chapter, which, additionally, it was his idea to include; Viṭṭhala's long interpolation on Chapter I, stanzas 12-16; and a number of other difficult passages, as the reader will see. Shri Shyam also gave me a thorough overview of the teachings of Vallabha's system, thus helping significantly with the ideas presented in the Introduction. In addition, he provided the Sanskrit text which is the basis for the present volume's Appendix. Finally, in connection with Shri Shyam, who is its Administrator, I acknowledge very gratefully the subsidy given by the Shri Vallabh Vidyapith and Prabhucharanashram Trust to help support the publication of this book.

I am delighted to be able to thank also Mr. M.L. Sedat Jobe, of the Division of Studies and Dissemination of Cultures of UNESCO in Paris, and the Indian National Commission, for selecting this work for inclusion in UNESCO's Collection of Representative Works.

Delhi J.D.R.
1 June, 1983

TABLE OF CONTENTS

INTRODUCTION

Part I : Fundamental Themes of Kṛṣṇa's Love-Games

A. The Life of Kṛṣṇa as Fulfilment of Sanskrit Aesthetic Theory

Kṛṣṇa's love-games with the Gopīs—the divine dalliances of the Almighty in His childhood with the humble young girls and women of the cowherd-caste in Vraja—have constituted an inexhaustible source of wonder, of charm, and of inquiry for all who have read them with attention and concern, whether in India or elsewhere, and whether the person incline to the religious, the aesthetic, the ethical, the mythical, or what have you. In fact, right within the classical narrative of these games, in Chapters 29-35 of Book Ten of the Bhāgavata Purāṇa, we find the prototype of all the awestruck, charmed and inquisitive listeners in the form of King Parikṣit, the first to hear the story and the first to ask, and have answered for him, the questions that occur to all of us about its contents. Even the inspired answers given to inspired questions, however, have never been known to stop both frivolous and sincere readers from asking further questions. Hence the need of an introduction even to a great Commentary on the account of Kṛṣṇa's love-games.

Of the many possible viewpoints from which one might, indeed needs to, explain Kṛṣṇa's love-games, which are so uniquely beautiful in their constant joining of the vividly earthly with the genuinely divine, we might legitimately ask which was the main—the most explanatory—viewpoint for the learned founder/saint Vallabhācārya (c.1479-c.1531; hereafter called "Vallabha") in his Subodhinī (Commentary) on the Bhāgavata's account ? Was it the purely devotional, or, we might say, theological, since anyone who makes the Bhāgavata the prime scripture of the religious system he founds must certainly make these love-games central to his teachings, as they are central to the Bhāgavata itself? Or was Vallabha's viewpoint chiefly philosophical, seeking out answers to questions such as the nature and purpose of Kṛṣṇa's descent to the earth? Or did he take a fundamentally ethical approach, since no one can dispute that the ethical issues raised by these love-games are many and profound?

To put it briefly: Vallabha took all these viewpoints at different times in the account, as indeed he had to if he were going to comment faithfully on the story's major aspects, but none of these viewpoints formed, in my opinion, his overarching concern. The theological and philosophical problems are dealt with variously by Vallabha, one by one as they occur in the text. He unifies the major problems by tying them in with special doctrines which became central teachings of his system, largely because they explained this story. I will attempt to give a unified picture of some of these major doctrines in parts I-D and I-E of this introduction. The ethical concerns normally focus on groups of connected stanzas, and are thus already unified in the text and commentary themselves. This is true, for example, of the Gopīs' involved refutations of Kṛṣṇa's reasons why they should go home, rather than stay in the forest with Him, in stanzas 31-41 of Chapter I below. And it is true again for the highly important, supra-ethical justification of all Kṛṣṇa's actions which the Bhāgavata and Vallabha give in stanzas 30-36 of Chapter V.

But what does seem to me to be the fundamental viewpoint on these and all other "Games" of Kṛṣṇa's life, for both Vallabha and his son and co-founder Viṭṭhalanātha (hereafter Viṭṭhala) who, as we shall see, makes frequent interpolations into Vallabha's commentary, is the aesthetic viewpoint, both in the general and in a particular sense. First of all, the poetic beauty of the tenth book of the Bhāgavata as a whole, and especially of Kṛṣṇa's love-games, is universally recognized. The autumn, the moon, the river, the forest and the animals, and Kṛṣṇa as the paragon of male as well as the Gopīs of female beauty, all interact and address one another with a charm difficult to parallel in any scripture. And this is not by chance. For the particular sense of "the aesthetic viewpoint" which I mentioned above is that Vallabha and Viṭṭhala undoubtedly, and the Bhāgavata itself almost as certainly, see Kṛṣṇa's descent to earth as the coming of God to play the Games which He and His devotees wish. And this precisely in terms of the moods (Skt. *rasa*) and sentiments (Skt. *bhāva*) which had been developed by the masters of Sanskrit aesthetic theory (*alaṅkāraśāstra*). Thus, besides the recognized and continually delighting beauty of the poetry and persons and surroundings which we find in this account, we have a very particular and elaborate consciousness of aesthetic beauty at work here. The Bhāgavata itself is a sacred writing that demands thorough knowledge of Sanskrit aesthetic theory for its understanding. Perhaps it is the first such scripture in the Hindu tradition. And Vallabha and Viṭṭhala who might best be said to be developing an aesthetic theology, use there canons of aesthetic regularly, as we shall see.

The very beginning of the Bhāgavata indicates its aesthetic orientation. Its final invocation verse—Book I, Chapter, I, Stanza 3—gives us words which can leave little doubt of that. The stanza translates as follows :

> Drink, o you connoisseurs on earth who have a taste for the beautiful, drink again and again this nectar of mood which lasts right up to the world's dissolution, this Bhāgavata, this fruit which has dropped from the wishing tree of the Vedas, endowed with the flowing stream of nectar that comes from the mouth of Śuka.[1]

Three of the key Sanskrit words in this stanza come from Sanskrit aesthetics—two of them having no other usages but in aesthetics. These are the words *rasika* ("connoisseurs") and *bhāvuka* ("who have a taste for the beautiful"). The third is perhaps the key word in Indian aesthetics, the rich and manifold *rasa*. I have translated *rasa* by "nectar of mood," emphasizing

1. The stanza's Sanskrit runs : *nigamakalpatarorgalitam phalaṁ śukamukhādamṛtadravasaṁyutam / pibata bhāgavataṁ rasamālayam muhuraho rasikā bhuvi bhāvukāḥ. //* I follow Vallabha in interpreting *ālayam* as the prepositional phrase *ā layam*, "right up to dissolution," rather than as a noun. As a noun it would be quite difficult to construe, making an unpleasant, contradictory metaphor—something like : "drink . . . this Bhāgavata, this nectar of mood, this bountiful vessel." No matter which way *ālayam* is taken, however, the preponderance of deliberately aesthetic words in the stanza remains intact.

what I believe to be the intended two of its many meanings. "Nectar" because of the metaphor of drinking, and "mood" because of the aesthetic context. We will see the word *rasa* used almost innumerable times by Vallabha and Viṭṭhala in their commentary, in one or other, or, as above, in both these meanings, although it will become clear that the operative meaning is most often "mood," the aesthetic sense. Thus we have, right in the invocation of the Bhāgavata, a call to the aesthetically refined to understand the Bhāgavata precisely in terms of their favourite way of perceiving.

Another strong indication of the aesthetic nature of the Bhāgavata, specifically with regard to the person of Kṛṣṇa, is the number of stanzas which invite the reader to view Kṛṣṇa as the embodiment of many different moods and sentiments which are main features of aesthetic and aesthetic/devotional theory. Perhaps the best example of this is Bhāgavata X. 43.17:

> Then He (Kṛṣṇa) who is known to wrestlers as the thunderbolt, to men as the greatest of mortals, to women as the love-god incarnate, to the cowherds as one of their own, to evil kings as the Avenging Ruler, to His parents as a dear child, as death to king Kaṁsa, as Virāṭ (the Supreme Intellect) to the unknowing, as the Highest Reality to the Yogis, and the Supreme God to the Vṛṣṇis, entered the arena together with His elder brother.

Here Kṛṣṇa is perceived by the wrestlers in terms of the mood of terror (Skt. *bhayānakarasa*), by men in terms of the heroic mood (*vīrarasa*), by women in terms of the mood of love (*śṛṅgārarasa*), by the cowherds in terms of the sentiment of friendship (*sakhyabhāva*), by the kings in terms hatred (*dveṣabhāva*), by His parents in terms of parental love (*vātsalyabhāva*), by Kaṁsa in terms of terror, etc. Similar stanzas can be seen in Chapter One, Stanza 15 of this translation, as well as at Bhāgavata VII. 1.30. These verses stand very well by themselves as poetry and as unique religious teaching, but a strong degree of deliberate aesthetic consciousness seems to pervade them, enhancing rather than destroying their beauty.

There is further evidence of the reflective aesthetic nature of both the Bhāgavata—it says much for the genius of the author of Book Ten that his reflectiveness never robs his poetry of its spontaneity—and Vallabha's commentary. In fact, under close scrutiny the Bhāgavata proves to be not only a relatively late scripture, but in a certain sense a "secondary" one as well. Not secondary in importance—quite the contrary. But secondary in the sense that it draws upon other schools of thought, art and scholarship which are already well developed. We have already seen its consciousness of developed aesthetic vocabulary. But we might also cite, among others, the quoting in its very first stanza of one of the more important *Brahma-Sūtra-s*, and the late, fully developed Sāṁkhya-theory which Kapila teaches in the last several chapters of Book Three. In Book Ten, and in Vallabha's and Viṭṭhala's comments on it, this reflective and secondary quality comes across in the continual consciousness of the arts of the day, both performing and plastic, as perfect examples for making comparisons with what is happening in Kṛṣṇa's Games. This I find rather startling : that the archetypal Games Kṛṣṇa has come to play with His chosen devotees—Games meant to form the patterns for life and attitudes—should be compared to things so man-made as plays, paintings and musical performances. But it is constant, both for the Bhāgavata and for Vallabha. A few examples may illuminate matters here.

First of all, when commenting on the beginning of the Rāsa-dance, the high point of the love-games, Vallabha carefully tells us, although in this case the Bhāgavata had not, that Kṛṣṇa's divine Will was to order everything in such a way that this dance resembled a painting. The passage is from the commentary on stanzas 3-4 of Chapter V in our translation :

> "The sky all around" became crowded with a hundred heavenly chariots. For a dance that takes place underneath a canopy gives rise to the mood of love. Otherwise there would not be variety and attractiveness above (the dancers). For this reason "the sky was crowded with a hundred heavenly chariots." In just the same way men and women unite with one another in order to produce the mood of love, they assume different erotic positions, and are so pictured in a painting. For this reason the Blessed Lord has placed and ordered the gods and so forth here, in a way which resembles a

> painting. ...The Lord incited everyone and everything to act in this way, for the sake of His Game. Therefore, even in the context of the "ardent desire" of the gods, nothing happened except exactly what He wished. The gods' wives had come in order to partake of the mood of love, but the Blessed Lord's Wish was that they form part of the picture—the painting. Śuka describes how the gods in their heavenly chariots became part of the picture when he says : "containing the sky-dwellers. ..."

And the Bhāgavata itself, later in the same chapter, clarifies the nature of the autumn nights and their mood of love by pointing to the poetry on the subject : "And so the Lord...passed joyfully all these brightened-by-moonbeam nights, whose tales are told in the poetry of autumn and which are the refuge of the mood of the season" (Chapter V, Stanza 26 below). In the following chapter, Vallabha explains what he concludes must have been the way Kṛṣṇa made His eyebrows dance while He played the flute, since this was the way it was done on the stage. He says, quoting the relevant words from the Bhāgavata stanza: " 'Resting His left cheek on His left shoulder...His eyebrows dancing'. The eyebrow involved here is the right eyebrow, for that is precisely the way this is done in the theatre" (Comm. on Stanzas 2-3, Chapter VI). And in a sentence in which he speaks beautifully in the voice of the Gopīs, Vallabha compares the reactions of the cows, birds, trees and deer upon seeing Kṛṣṇa's Form to the responses of "a man of refined aesthetic taste", and he ends by having the Gopīs draw a conclusion for Kṛṣṇa :

> And yet if all these were embraced by the mood of love upon seeing the Blessed Lord's Form and hearing His song, so that their hair stood on end, and they thus manifested the qualities of a man of refined aesthetic taste, even though the Blessed Lord created them different from men, then it should be no surprise that we women have also shown some difference from our usual nature because of this sight (Comm. on Chapter I, Stanza 40).

And again, to finish with two brief examples from the Bhāgavata itself, Stanzas 4-5 of Chapter VI tell us how the cows are entranced by the playing of Kṛṣṇa's flute, and "they stood stock still...as if painted in a picture." And finally, in the most natural reference to the arts, since Kṛṣṇa is the flute-player par excellence, Stanzas 14-15 of Chapter VI tell us how Kṛṣṇa dazzles the greatest connoisseurs of music with His newly invented scales and compositions. The Gopīs are the narrators here : "When your Son, o faithful Yaśodā, setting His flute 'neath His lower lip...led forth the scales and kinds of sounds learned purely by Himself in His manifold playing of the flute, then the lords of gods, led by Indra, Śiva and Brahmā...these poet-sages, their necks bent and their minds bowed in appreciative homage, fell into a worried depression, no longer sure they knew all the elements of music." In all these examples we can see how both the Bhāgavata and Vallabha readily resort to the arts in order to clarify images, situations and emotions in Kṛṣṇa's Games. Thus the "secondariness," in the sense I have described above, and the dependence on the realm of the aesthetic, of both the Bhāgavata and its Commentary become quite clear.

But what is most important for us, in terms of our major contention thus far, is some proof that Vallabha and Viṭṭhala construe Kṛṣṇa specifically in terms of the Embodiment of all the moods elaborated by aesthetic theory, and as playing out His love-games in accordance with that theory's norms for producing the mood of passionate love (*śṛṅgārarasa*), which of course is the mood in question in the present chapters. Some of the technical terminology has already occurred in the passages we have quoted from Vallabha. But there are more explicit passages. The two most perfect passages for showing the doctrine that Kṛṣṇa is the Embodiment of all the moods come, as a matter of fact, from the pen of Viṭṭhala, not Vallabha. But Vallabha concurs in detail, as we shall see. I shall quote Viṭṭhala's first passage in full, since it is brief, and give the sense of the longer second passage, with perhaps a quotation from its conclusion. Near the end of his long interpolation on Stanzas 12-16 of Chapter I, Viṭṭhala says : "For the love-making that occurred after that (i.e., after the Gopīs had gone to Kṛṣṇa in the forest) was no more or less than His gift of the Joy of His own Form after the manner of the mood of love, for His own Form has the moods as its very

Essence, as holy scripture tells us in the words: 'Mood indeed is He' (*Taitt. Upan.* II. 7. 1)." This sentence is very thematic, for it explains in a nutshell nearly the whole of what Kṛṣṇa does in His love-games. The major philosophical point Viṭṭhala makes is that Kṛṣṇa is making love with the Gopīs in order to give them, from within Himself, the Joy (*ānanda*) which all souls, according to Vallabha's teaching, lost primordially, and which is the be-all and end-all that every person spends life searching to regain. The special privilege that Kṛṣṇa gave to the Gopīs, and to no one else at all, was that He filled them immediately with His own Joy. Thus the Gopīs did not have to take the normal religious means necessary for all other persons in order to reawaken the Joy which was once in themselves but had been lost due to the operation of Kṛṣṇa's Power of Ignorance (Skt. *avidyāśakti*) on all souls. This is obviously a teaching of crucial importance, but our direct concern here is with what Viṭṭhala goes on to say about how Kṛṣṇa gives the Gopīs His own Joy. The first point is that Kṛṣṇa does this "after the manner of the mood of love," i.e., in exact accordance with the norms of aesthetic theory, as well as of the treatises on erotic love (Skt. *kāmaśāstra*), for producing the fullness of the mood of love, in circumstance, in act, and in effect. And in Viṭṭhala's final clause comes the main point and the foundation-doctrine for the notion of Kṛṣṇa as the Embodiment of all the aesthetic theory's moods. "Mood indeed is He" (*raso vai saḥ*), says the Upaniṣad. And this means, as we shall see once more, in the translation, both that all the moods are in Kṛṣṇa (Skt. *sarve rasāḥ yasmin*) and that all the moods are from Kṛṣṇa (*sarve rasāḥ yasmāt*). This is, simply, the central perspective of Vallabha and Viṭṭhala for viewing the life of Kṛṣṇa on earth. To play His Games with His devotees in terms of the perfect expression of all the aesthetic moods is the only reason, ultimately, why Kṛṣṇa would descend in His full Form, according to Vallabha and Viṭṭhala, rather than in a partial form, as He does for all other purposes, such as removing a great burden from the earth. In another passage, as I have mentioned, Viṭṭhala expresses the same doctrine in a slightly different way, with two excellent examples. In an interpolation on our Chapter V, Stanza 17, he first makes the point that Kṛṣṇa had an absolutely unique experience of the mood of love with the Gopīs. It was different even from the mood of the love He experiences with His wife Ramā (Lakṣmī), because the Gopīs are not married to him. Next Viṭṭhala points out that Kṛṣṇa also acts in ways other than the Supreme Lord would act in His "charmingly confused" childhood Games. Finally Viṭṭhala tells us why, re-expressing the central doctrine :

> For He acted in this way, even though He has the fulness of Knowledge, because such was the nature of the mood of His childhood games. This is precisely the case here (with the Gopīs), too, for it is entirely valid to say that what is expressed in the words of holy scripture : "Mood indeed is He," is that all this is of the very essence of His Nature, since it falls within the purview of mood.

This could not be expressed more succinctly, so I'll spare the reader my belabouring the point. As I have already mentioned, Vallabha never, in the section of his Commentary I have translated, expresses the entire doctrine so succinctly in one place. But proofs that he concurs entirely—indeed gave Viṭṭhala the idea—are so numerous in the translation that no one could miss them. Perhaps the closest Vallabha comes to putting it all together—which he indicates he has done before—is in the lovely first sentence of his commentary on Chapter I, Stanza 47 : "The Blessed Lord, who, in the manner described above, has the power of granting the fulness of every mood and sentiment; Kṛṣṇa, who is eternal Joy—the embodiment of the final reward —has 'fulfilled all the desires' of the Gopīs."

There is also a good example of how Vallabha uses technical aesthetic theory to blend his themes and comment on a Bhāgavata stanza which has already alluded to aesthetic theory. The stanza concerned is the one we have already quoted, where the Bhāgavata pointed to poetry to explain autumn nights and their mood of love. Here is part, then, of Vallabha's commentary on Chapter V, Stanza 26 :

> Thus were all these nights passed, and the autumn, too, was passed. And the "stories told in poetry", too, came to pass.

> For He made love in the way described in poetry, and after the fashion narrated in the *Gītagovinda*, too. Śuka tells us the reason for this when he says that these nights "are the refuge of the mood of the season." The mood of passionate love, as is well known, belongs preeminently to these autumn nights. ...Or perhaps Śuka means that these nights find their refuge in the mood of the tales which appear in poetry which is describing autumn. These nights are not well known to the world; rather they are described only in poetry. For in poetry there is an absence of restrictions and obligations and the like—there is a singleness of delight, and no dependence on anything else; and other, like qualities as well. Just like this, Śuka means to tell us, were these nights of the Blessed Lord's Games.

And finally, it is very interesting to see just how bound by obligations to fulfil the requirements of aesthetic mood both Vallabha and Viṭṭhala consider Kṛṣṇa, whom they also consider to be absolutely and incomparably free. They do not consider Him absolutely bound, of course, but Vallabha's commentary and Viṭṭhala's interpolation on Chapter IV, Stanza 14, show how strongly obligated they take Him to be. The context is that an objector has viewed Kṛṣṇa's act of sitting on the seat the Gopīs had prepared for Him by laying their upper garments on the ground as an "improper manifestation of a mood" (Skt. *rasābhāsa*). Vallabha shows how concerned he is about the problem, first by making up the objection and putting it into his commentary at all, and secondly by answering it. He says that the Gopīs' upper garments were divine garments, specially created by Kṛṣṇa, and so it was most fitting that He sit down on them. Hence there is no improper manifestation of a mood here. It is Viṭṭhala, however, who examines all the angles of the objection more carefully and answers it fully :

> Or, we may answer the objection in this way. When Śuka uses the pronoun "this" (Mighty One), he intends to tell us that, since there was no improper manifestation of a mood at the time when the Gopīs had no clothes at all, when the Lord stole their clothes at the same time He was granting

> the favour they were praying for (cf. Bh. P. X. 22), how could there be such an improper manifestation in the present situation, when only their upper garments are missing ? If the person stretches his objection and says : "Well, isn't that ... also an improper manifestation of a mood ?", then Śuka's answer is : "Mighty One." For this Mightly One has the power to act, i.e., to do things. So, if a certain act were an improper manifestation of a mood, then He would not perform that act. But since He also has the power not to act, it is impossible for Him to leave the seat the Gopīs have specially given to Him, even for the reason that there is an improper manifestation of a mood involved. But since He has the further power to act in another way, He can produce a mood even by means of an improper manifestation of a mood. Therefore, Śuka's meaning is that there is nothing improper in the conduct described here.

I hope the reader will forgive my lengthy citation here. This is one of the texts, I believe, that does not yield its full value unless lifted partly out of the context of the specific stanza it explains and seen in terms of the broader question it also faces.

To sum up, then : we have seen in this section the aesthetic nature, both general—in referring often to the arts—and specific—in using the language of aesthetics and casting Kṛṣṇa as an example of many different moods and sentiments—of the Bhāgavata Purāṇa. And we have seen how Vallabha and Viṭṭhala take their cue from the Bhāgavata and from some famous sayings of the Upaniṣads, and portray Kṛṣṇa as the supreme possessor and bestower of the moods and sentiments developed by the pundits of aesthetics. We are now ready to consider the specific mood of the love games.

B. "*Eligibility*" *for the Mood of Love, and for Experiencing Kṛṣṇa in terms of any Mood*

So far we have been viewing things mainly from the side of Kṛṣṇa. He, we have found, is the Embodiment of all moods, and He is the Giver of the experience of the moods to others. Now we must consider the Gopīs, and find out why it was they who were the right women for Him to experience the mood of love with. In fact, we should raise the broader question of why and how any particular devotee becomes the right person for Kṛṣṇa to experience any of the particular moods or sentiments with. This question is put by Vallabha in terms of the "eligibility" (Skt. *adhikāra*) of a devotee (*bhakta*). And once we determine the requirements and *modus operandi* of eligibility, we will be able to discover that the Gopīs were eligible for the mood of love (*śṛṅgārarasa*). And the present translation is, of course, the story of their, and Kṛṣṇa's, experience of that mood.

The *locus classicus* for Vallabha's explanation of the normal Path of Devotion and for the "eligibility" that a devotee experiences in the higher stages of that Path, is his Commentary (*Subodhinī*) on Bhāgavata (normally abbreviated *Bh. P.*) III. 9.11. I will paraphrase some sections and quote others from this long, rich passage. Early in his comments Vallabha distinguishes between the Path of Devotion that proceeds "on the basis of the means of knowledge, i.e., Scripture" (Skt. *pramāṇabala*), and the Path that proceeds "on the strength of the Object of Knowledge—Kṛṣṇa" (*prameyabala*), i.e., purely and totally on the basis of what God's Grace is charming, and indeed forcing, the devotee to do. Vallabha says that Kṛṣṇa cannot be loved by the devotee in terms of "passion" (*kāma*, here = *śṛṅgāra*, "passionate love") and other similar sentiments when the devotee is on the scriptural path. He says : "In that (i.e., conceiving Kṛṣṇa in terms of passion, etc.) the strength of the Object of Knowledge (is operative), as we shall explain (in Book Ten)." Having made this important distinction, Vallabha goes on to explain what the Bhāgavata stanza says happens when love of Kṛṣṇa according to the scriptural path reaches its fulness :

> But those whose hearts are purified according to the prescribed (scriptural) course of love, i.e., if and when that love becomes natural to the heart, then that heart is called a lotus. That lotus alone, when it has bloomed in the water of love, is a worthy seat for the Blessed Lord ... And if that heart is continually freshened by love, the Lord sits there constantly.

Now we have reached the higher stages of love, and the question arises as to which form of Himself, since He "has infinite forms" (*anantamūrti*), Kṛṣṇa will take when He sits in the devotee's heart. The question is of paramount importance, as we shall see, for the Bhāgavata's and Vallabha's conception of the modes of Kṛṣṇa's relatedness with His devotees. Vallabha answers, following and explaining the Bhāgavata's words : "Whatever form of Yourself these devotees constantly think of You in, that very form, whether it be the form of Brahman, or the form of Vaikuṇṭha, or one of the forms in which You have descended to earth, that form alone is the one You make manifest to him." Therefore, Vallabha concludes, "what is fitting is what is according to the desire of the devotee." This last statement is crucial as well as logical, for the fact that Kṛṣṇa takes the form the devotee "constantly thinks of Him in," and consequently the form that is "according to the desire of the devotee," opens up the possibility that devotees will experience Kṛṣṇa in terms of each and every one of the moods and sentiments proper to human beings. And this is precisely what Vallabha teaches. When the devotee who has been following the path of scripture reaches the highest point of what Vallabha calls the "means-stage" (as opposed to the "reward-stage"), the point in love of God which Vallabha names, in Verse 3 of his verse-treatise *Bhaktivardhinī*, "addiction to" or "obsession with" Kṛṣṇa (Skt. *vyasana*), he begins to see everyone and everything as Kṛṣṇa Himself. He hallucinates Kṛṣṇa everywhere, as it were, sees nothing but Him, and, most important for our purposes, he sees Kṛṣṇa in a particular form. This is the stage at which, according to Vallabha, the restriction on the devotee's seeing Kṛṣṇa in terms of any mood whatsoever drops away. On the contrary, it is now of the utmost importance for the devotee to picture Kṛṣṇa precisely in terms of the mood he or she most desires to relate to Kṛṣṇa in terms of, whether as flute-playing boy, little baby, lover, warrior-chief, or what have you. The devotee is now completely "eligible" for experiencing Kṛṣṇa as the Embodiment of any mood, because his or her love has now become purified and completely transcendent of worldly love. This is Vallabha's path of carefully cultivated love of Kṛṣṇa according to the scriptural teachings, by means of which any devotee may come to experience Kṛṣṇa in terms of a particular mood.[2] Some classic scriptural examples of this would be the warrior/preceptor Bhīṣma, who related with Kṛṣṇa in terms of "the warrior-hero's mood" (*vīrarasa*), Arjuna in terms of "friendship" (*sakhyabhāva*), and Nanda and Yaśodā in terms of "parental love" (*vātsalyabhāva*). This, then, explains the "eligibility" of devotees in general.

But the Gopīs are a very particular case. They are eligible for the mood of love "on the strength of Kṛṣṇa, the Object of knowledge." That is to say, they are among the privileged few devotees whom the Grace of Kṛṣṇa chooses and will not let go. We know this because the Gopīs had not taken the scriptural path to love of Kṛṣṇa before the love-games, which are nevertheless, according to Vallabha, the "reward-stage" of their union of love with Him. Instead, it is in separation from Kṛṣṇa, after the love-games and indeed after He leaves Vraja, that the Gopīs must, as part of the "Game" which is their salvation, take the means necessary for their experience of love-in-separation, the lone remaining factor essential for fulness in their love of Kṛṣṇa. This reversal of the normal order of means-reward occurs only in the case of the Gopīs and the other devotees of Vraja. Vallabha also says the Gopīs are eligible to experience Kṛṣṇa in this way because of their "Total Love" (Skt. *sarvabhāva, sarvātmabhāva*), a phenomenon which I will explain later. But this is merely another way of saying that it was by the Grace of Kṛṣṇa's all-disposing Will that this happened, and for the very same reason : that the Gopīs had not taken the scriptural means, and Kṛṣṇa's special Grace is the only other way of achieving Total Love. Thus we have in the Gopīs a prime example of experience of Kṛṣṇa in terms of a mood "on the strength of Kṛṣṇa, the Object of knowledge" (*prameyabala*), the second of the two ways of achieving this, according to the passage of Vallabha which we explained. The other example of this explained in our translation is that of Śiśupāla, who experienced Kṛṣṇa in terms of hatred (Skt. *dveṣabhāva*), as Viṭṭhala teaches

2. Vallabha gives us a fine description of some aspects of this scriptural Path of Devotion in his Commentary on Chapter I, Stanza 27 *infra* (pp. 96-98).

near the beginning of his long interpolation on Chapter I, Stanzas 12-16. To summarize, then : there are two ways of becoming eligible to experience Kṛṣṇa in terms of a mood : in the final stages of the scriptural path, or simply by the Lord's special Grace. And once the devotees have attained eligibility, there is no longer a distinction between the two types, except in the case of the devotees of Vraja (including the Gopīs), who had to go through the means-stage, in terms of separation, afterwards. And so the operative conclusion for our present passage is that the Gopīs attained eligibility to experience Kṛṣṇa in terms of the mood of love on the strength of Kṛṣṇa, the Object of knowledge.

Let us see how Vallabha expresses himself on this topic in our translation. There are many times when he refers to this subject and treats it briefly. But in one place, he says practically all there is to be said on the question. The reader would do well to consult his Commentary on Chapter V, Stanza 2, in full. I will endeavour to gather here some of the key phrases and sentences of this passage, and to comment where necessary. In his Introduction to his commentary on the stanza, Vallabha says : "Kṛṣṇa began to do what He had to do." This means that Kṛṣṇa began to experience the mood of love with the Gopīs, which "He had to do" (Skt. *svakartavyam*) because the Gopīs were eligible for the mood of love. and Kṛṣṇa had come to earth precisely to experience this and other moods. Vallabha explains the obligatory nature of this later, in the commentary on the stanza :

> Śuka points out the suitability of the Gopīs for this mood when he mentions that they are "so devoted to Him." In other words, it is incumbent on the Lord to produce this mood in those who were so devoted in carrying out their vow concerning Him (cf. Bh. P. X. 22). And the Gopīs' lone intention is to do what the Blessed Lord intends.

Next, to the objection that this mood is "transcendent," and thus cannot be produced in "worldly people," Vallabha replies by pointing out with the Bhāgavata, that these Gopīs are "jewels among women". Vallabha then says : "Therefore by their Total Love of Him they are suitable women for Him to produce the mood of love in." Here, then, eligibility is predicated of the Gopīs on the basis of their graced Love of Kṛṣṇa. And finally, another objection surfaces, as to the dissimilarity of nature between Kṛṣṇa and the Gopīs. "If someone objects," says Vallabha, "that these Gopīs are human souls, while the Blessed Lord consists of pure Joy, and that consequently the desired mood cannot be produced because of this dissimilarity, Śuka's answer is : 'so joyful'. The Gopīs became like the Blessed Lord. Their joy was complete."

Lastly, we should point out that Vallabha has expressed, four times in his comments on the love-games, a specific and fascinating reason why Kṛṣṇa wished to experience the mood of love with these Gopīs, of all possible women. So far as I know, Vallabha is the only interpreter of the Bhāgavata who has discovered this rationale for the love-games, and I believe the passages which express it say much about Vallabha's general feeling that all Kṛṣṇa's Games are archetypal, but especially, of course, this one. Speaking in the voice of the Gopīs while commenting on Stanza 2 of Chapter III, which the Gopīs have sung, Vallabha says the following in order to explain the epithet, "Lord of love," by which the Gopīs have just addressed Kṛṣṇa (the reader should refer to the translation for the broader line of logic Vallabha follows; I am citing only the most direct words) :

> That is precisely why we address You as "Lord of love." For wherever there is love, in the form of sexual union, in this world, You are its Lord. And without Your command sexual love does not go forth into this world. Therefore we have been given to You, by Brahmā or Kāma (the gods of creation), as "hired slave-girls," in order for You to introduce sexual love into the world. ... If sexual love should remain constrained and locked up in the Blessed Lord alone, then the mood of love would not exist in the world. We have come here so that You may make this love spread from Yourself over the entire world through us. But bringing that to pass must be the farthest thing from Your mind, because instead of that You are killing us ! If this

> is so, then all the treatises on passionate love (Skt. *kāma-śāstra*) would be worthless, and the third of the four objects of human endeavour (i.e., *kāma*) does not even exist! Therefore You must by all means do what You have invited us here to do.

And so it is the Blessed Lord Kṛṣṇa who must introduce sexual love, and in the process its "mood", into the world. And the Gopīs have been specially created and designated to be the vehicles for its introduction. Vallabha could not have told us more clearly that these deeds are meant to be a mythical archetype for the origin and existence of all love, and, of course, its mood. And he refers back to this passage and its idea at least three times more, in stanzas 2, 10 and 24 of Chapter V (the first of which is the important passage we have explained immediately above), thus emphasizing its centrality to his way of viewing the love-games.

In this section, then, we have seen, first of all, that there are two possible ways for a devotee to gain "eligibility" to experience Kṛṣṇa in terms of his or her desired mood, and that the Gopīs attained their eligibility to experience Kṛṣṇa as their Husband/Lover on the strength of Kṛṣṇa's Grace, or, to put it in Sanskrit, *prameyabalena*. Next we saw that the Gopīs were "suitable", i.e., eligible, because of their "devotedness," because of the "Total Love" that Kṛṣṇa had graced them with, and because they, like Kṛṣṇa, possessed Joy. Lastly we found that Vallabha has discovered as Kṛṣṇa's reason for making love with the Gopīs the need, on a mythic/symbolic as well as real level, for introducing sexual love and its mood into the world.

C. The Meaning and Importance of the *Tāmasaphalaprakaraṇa*

Something I would have mentioned earlier, except that it would have required a complete explanation then and there, while we were exploring other topics, is that Vallabha names the section of his *Subodhinī* in which the love-games occur *Tāmasa-phalaprakaraṇa*, which means "The Treatise on the Reward of the Tāmasa-devotees." This gets us immediately into the terminology Vallabha uses in dividing up his Commentary on Book Ten of the Bhāgavata. Our translation consists of the fourth sub-division of the first major section of Vallabha's commentary on Kṛṣṇa's life. After treating the opening four chapters of Book Ten as the *Janmaprakaraṇa*—"The Treatise on Kṛṣṇa's Birth"—Vallabha divides the rest of the Book into four major sections, naming the sections with words relative to the three qualities of worldly existence (Skt. *guṇa*), viz., *tamas*, *rajas* and *sattva* (in ascending order of excellence). Thus the twenty-eight chapters which follow the Treatise on Kṛṣṇa's Birth are called the *Tāmasaprakaraṇa*; the next twenty-eight are called the *Rājasaprakaraṇa* ("Treatise on the Rājasa-devotees"); the following twenty-one are the *Sāttvikaprakaraṇa* ("Treatise on the Sāttvika-devotees"), and the final six are the *Nirguṇaprakaraṇa* ("Treatise on the Devotees who have transcended the Qualities of Existence").[3] Within the first two of these four sections, there are four sub-divisions, each consisting of seven chapters. These four sub-divisions are titled according to their order in the progression *pramāṇa* ("means of knowledge"), *prameya* ("object of knowledge"), *sādhana* ("means of attainment") and *phala* ("reward"). The reason the Treatise on the Sāttvika-devotees has only twenty-one chapters and three sub-divisions is that sāttvika-devotees are sufficiently advanced that they already possess knowledge, and thus have no need of the "means of knowledge" (*pramāṇa*). Thus Vallabha postulates, on a grand scale, a graded progression in which the devotees spoken of in Book Ten become more and more perfectly united with Kṛṣṇa as they pass through each subdivision of each major section. Hence a devotee will be spoken of in the Treatise on the Reward of one major division (say, Tāmasa) as being more advanced than he or she was in the Treatise on the Means of Knowledge of the same division. Likewise, of course, the devotees progress from being Tāmasa to Rājasa to Sāttvika, and finally, to Transcendence of the qualities. I know of no commentator on the Bhāgavata but Vallabha who has thought out such an elaborate and well-constructed scheme for understanding Book Ten, though one often doubts whether the author could have

3. Confer the first footnote in Chapter I for the reason why Vallabha's count of Chapters in Book Ten comes to only eighty-seven, while all the Bhāgavata texts have ninety chapters.

had all this in mind. Within this broad scheme, then, the story of the love-games of Kṛṣṇa and the Gopīs forms the "Reward" sub-division of the Treatise on the Tāmasa-devotees, the first major division.

This still does not tell us, however, what the word *tāmasa* means in this context. The best explanation I have seen of this question is that of Vallabha's seventeenth-century follower Lālūbhaṭṭa, in his *Prameyaratnārṇava*, perhaps the finest topic-by-topic treatment of Vallabhā's teachings—replete with quotations from the Bhāgavata, Vallabha, Viṭṭhala, and other scriptures and treatises.[4] Lālūbhaṭṭa's explanation would be generally acceptable to all Vallabha's followers, and Vallabha has never, so far as I know, treated this question concisely in one place. Lālūbhaṭṭa distinguishes three different usages of the word *tāmasa* in Vallabha's *Subodhinī*, the first of which is the usage which concerns us here (the second usage will be explained in Part Two of this Introduction). What Lālūbhaṭṭa initially says about the first usage is that *tāmasa* in our present sense is "a technical term" (Skt. *pāribhāṣikam*), having no necessary connection in meaning with its etymological root *tamas*. The tāmasa-quality denoted by this technical usage, continues Lālūbhaṭṭa, "embodies the means of attaining the experience of the mood of non-scriptural devotion."[5] The devotion that is not described in scripture, but is given purely by Kṛṣṇa's Grace—such as the hate-relationship Kṛṣṇa graced Śiśupāla with, or the fear-relationship He graced Kaṁsa with—is, of course, precisely what we are speaking of in the case of the Gopīs, as we have seen, since they are graced with the relationship of passionate love. This is one meaning of *tāmasa* in its technical usage. Lālūbhaṭṭa then goes on to discuss the more thematic, unified meanings of the technical term *tāmasa*. He says the tāmasa-devotees "have a special liking for those Games of the Blessed Lord which are similar to the world and

4. All my quotations, as well as the cited page-numbers, etc., will be from the text of *Prameyaratnārṇava* edited and translated into Hindi by Kedarnath Mishra. For further details on the book, cf. Bibliography under Mishra.

5. *avihitabhaktirasānubhavasādhanarūpam*, p. 164 Mishra's edition.

are according to their own desires." Here we come to the heart of the tāmasa-quality as Vallabha intends it in the Treatise on the Tāmasa devotees. These devotees are interested in doing their own will and doing everything the way they like, rather than in following the Lord's will and pleasure, which is a characteristic of sāttvika-devotees. Lālūbhaṭṭa specifies further, delightfully in spots, and completes for us the picture of a tāmasa-devotee : "For tāmasa-people are filled with impertinence, and whoever or whatever their stubbornness falls upon, it does not leave; they become bereft of knowledge and deluded, and precisely because they are bereft of knowledge they transgress the laws of the world and the commands of the Vedas. The devotees who lived in Vraja, too, were incredibly stubborn toward the Blessed Lord, and devoid of any knowledge except what was necessary for His Games, as we know from His saying : 'after you abandoned, as you did, for My sake the world, the Vedas, your very Selves and all that was yours' (Bh. P. X. 32. 21; Chap. IV, stanza 21 below)."[6] The Bhāgavata-quote with which Lālūbhaṭṭa ends is, of course, from the chapters we are concerned with, and describes the Gopīs as the exemplary tāmasa-devotees. Our picture, then, consists of a devotee who is very self-willed and stubborn, trying to force Kṛṣṇa to her own will rather than vice versa, and not caring whether she breaks all the conventional rules in order to play the game she wants with Kṛṣṇa. Lālūbhaṭṭa is clever enough to notice in addition, however, that this technical term is meant in a very complimentary sense, too. For he says : "The expression 'tāmasa' is used in the sense of a statement which has a hidden meaning (Skt. *parokṣavāda*)." This is because, even though the word is derived from the lowest of the three qualities of existence, *tamas*, it is used to describe the very highest devotees—the Gopīs. Here, as elsewhere, Vallabha delights in turning the tables on conventional usage. Finally, Lālūbhaṭṭa clarifies to whom, in fact, to whom alone, this kind of tāmasa-quality applies : "This tāmasa-quality is to be understood as applying to all the devotees who are in the *Tāmasaprakaraṇa*."[7] Our

6. This and the preceding quotation are also from op. cit., p. 164.
7. These last two quotations are from p. 165.

translation, then, is the Treatise on the Reward of the devotees who are *tāmasa* in this sense. This includes both the Gopīs and the other devotees who lived in Vraja.

As for the importance of the *Tāmasaphalaprakaraṇa,* there is first a prevailing misconception which must be cleared away concerning the teachings of Vallabha and his followers. A widespread impression exists, at least among Western readers, that the dominant emotional relationship of the devotee to Kṛṣṇa taught and practiced by Vallabha and his followers is that of "parental love" (*vātsalyabhāva*) toward Kṛṣṇa as a baby or little child. One source of this idea may be the fact that the most famous and popular Kṛṣṇa-images of the Vallabha Sampradāya (roughly, "Church"), such as the founding image, Śrī Nāthajī, which is by far the most popular, and Navanītapriyajī, which portrays the baby Kṛṣṇa stealing his mother's freshly-made butter, both portray Kṛṣṇa in His early years, before the love-games. The love-games, too, are childhood games of Kṛṣṇa, since they were played when He was about eight years old, but the difference is that they do not, nor are they meant to, lead to the emotion of parental love. And it may well be, although I do not know for certain, that, numerically speaking, more of the present-day devotees of the Vallabha Sampradāya worship Kṛṣṇa in terms of parental love than in terms of married or unmarried passionate love. But even if this is true, it should not cloud our perception of the fact that the love-games, inculcating as they do the mood of passionate love for those devotees who are eligible, are exalted high above the infancy and early childhood games of Kṛṣṇa by Vallabha, Viṭṭhala, and the great scholars and commentators of the Sampradāya. This can be seen from the very structure of the *Subodhinī,* which, as we have seen, is very deliberately ordered from lower to higher. Within the Treatise on the Tāmasa-devotees, then, all the games of Kṛṣṇa's infancy and early childhood are part of the sub-treatise on the Means of Knowledge or on the Object of Knowledge, while the love-games come later, in the sub-treatise on the Reward. This gradation becomes all the more important when we realize that, in the Vallabha Sampradāya, it is taught that only the Games of Kṛṣṇa which are played in Vraja (i.e., the Games described in the entire treatise on the Tāmasa-devotees) are to be imitated as "means of attainment" (*sādhana*) of devotion to Kṛṣṇa. This is because all devotees presuppose themselves to be *tāmasa*. Thus the love-games are the highest of the group of games which the devotees concentrate on and try to conform their attitudes to. And this also shows that the love-games are given pride of place not only by Vallabha, but by the ongoing teaching and practice of the Sampradāya. And finally, one has only to look at any significant portion of the writings of Vallabha, Viṭṭhala, or the great commentators Puruṣottama, Harirāya, Gokulanātha, and Lālūbhaṭṭa, to see how completely pervasive the influence of the love-games and of the Gopīs' attitudes and expressions of love toward Kṛṣṇa is. Vallabha makes the Gopīs the Gurus of renunciation on the Path of Devotion in verse 8 of his verse-treatise *Sannyāsanirṇaya.* And the love-games, along with the other passages where the Gopīs' attitudes toward Kṛṣṇa are expressed, are quoted far more frequently by all these authors than any other group of passages in the Bhāgavata or any other scripture.[8] Of course, it is only the devotees who become eligible in terms of the mood of love who will take the love-games passages as the sole model for their worship of Kṛṣṇa. But the fact that the Gopīs' attitudes of love are everywhere proclaimed as the most pure and ideal will of itself produce more and more devotees who become eligible in terms of this mood, since eligibility, as we have seen, depends on the devotees' desires as well as on Kṛṣṇa's Grace. And the Gopīs' attitudes strongly influence many other devotees as well. It is my own conclusion, then, that the love-games are of no less importance for Vallabha's Sampradāya than for any other Sampradāya of Hinduism, and that parental love is definitely not favoured over passionate love as a mood for relating to Kṛṣṇa except for beginners in devotion. I must also acknowledge my indebtedness, for some of the arguments and conclusions expressed on this question, to Shri Shyam Goswamy, one of the most learned present-day exponents of the teachings of Vallabha and his Sampradāya.

8. Cf., for example, the many commentaries on Vallabha's important short writings, *The Sixteen Verse-Treatises* (*Ṣoḍaśagranthāḥ*).

To sum up this section briefly, then : we have seen the elaborate structure of Vallabha's *Subodhinī*, and that the Tāmasa-devotees, within that scheme, represent the self-willed, stubborn type who want Kṛṣṇa to play their kind of game, but who also possess a very high degree of love, which their name is meant to signify in a hidden way. And lastly we saw the high place of the love-games in Vallabhite teaching and practice, and hopefully corrected the notion that parental love is the favoured attitude in the Vallabha-Sampradāya.

D. *Total Love* (*Sarvātmabhāva*) : *the Prerequisite for the Love-Games*

Now we come to one of the central doctrines of Vallabha and his followers, *sarvātmabhāva* (often shortened to *sarvabhāva* by Vallabha), which I have translated throughout his commentary on the love-games as "Total Love." The precise nature and emphasis of Vallabha's teaching on this point has occasioned the spilling of great deal of ink by the various scholars and commentators who have followed him, right up to the present day, because all concerned recognize the crucial place of the doctrine in Vallabha's system. But I do not propose to go into the many details of the argumentation, since it would be both out of place and out of my competence. Instead I will rely on the conclusions of the most recent study I know of, Shri Shyam Goswamy's exhaustive and excellent *Sarvātmabhāva kā Tulanātmaka Adhyayana*.[9]

The first thing which should be clarified in our explanation of this doctrine is the precise meaning of the word *bhāva* in the compound word *sarvātmabhāva*, for *bhāva* here has a particular, recognized and unchanging sense, while the other two words, especially *sarva*-, have, quite deliberately, more than one meaning. *Bhāva*, then, means "love", but love in the precise sense defined by Bharata in his *Nāṭyaśāstra*, a definition constantly quoted by Vallabha, Viṭṭhala, and their commentators : "The love which is directed toward a god, a guru, etc., is called *bhāva*."[10] *Bhāva* is therefore the love which proceeds from a soul towards a being who is both higher and religious. In the

9. For the full citation cf. the Bibliography under "Goswamy".
10. Skt. *devādiviṣayā ratirbhāva ityabhidhīyate*.

case of *sarvātmabhāva,* the object of the devotee's love is the Blessed Lord, Kṛṣṇa.

Now that we have two elements of the teaching, love, and the object of that love, the Blessed Lord, we can move toward explaining the primary and more frequent meaning of the term *sarvātmabhāva.* It is from the Bhāgavata, not surprisingly, that Vallabha gets the term, and I know of at least three occurrences of *sarvātmabhāva* there : IX. 4.21; X. 47.27; and XI. 12.15. In the first of these occurrences, where King Ambarīṣa is said to possess *sarvātmabhāva*, the Bhāgavata itself gives a perfect description of what Vallabha takes as the primary meaning of *sarvātmabhāva*, in the three stanzas which precede IX. 4.21, which stanza then gives the type of love just described the name *sarvātmabhāva.* I feel certain that this is the source of Vallabha's doctrine.[11] But he did not write a Commentary on Book Nine, so we don't have the benefit of his telling us so. Instead, Vallabha picks a stanza in Book Ten which, even though it does not specifically use the word, gives him a perfect opportunity to express the doctrine. The stanza is the one in which the Gopīs describe Kṛṣṇa as "the reward of everything which has eyes" (Bh. P. X. 21. 7), and the passage in which Vallabha explains *sarvātmabhāva* consists of the third through seventh Verses (*kārikā*) of his Subodhinī on the stanza. The verses translate as follows :

> Conversing with the Blessed Lord, seeing Him, embracing Him when we meet Him, as well as worshipping Him

11. The stanzas in question (*Bh. P.* IX. 4. 18-21) translate as follows : "He (Ambarīṣa) directed his mind to Kṛṣṇa's lotus feet, his speech to describing the glories of Vaikuṇṭha, his hands to the sweeping and cleaning of Hari's temples, his ears to hearing the sacred stories about Acyuta, his eyes to seeing the places where Mukunda's image dwells, his bodily contact to touching the limbs of the Lord's servants, his nose to the fragrance of Blessed Tulasī on Kṛṣṇa's lotus feet, his tongue to the food offered to the Lord, his feet to travelling to Hari's sacred places, his head to reverencing Hṛṣīkeśa's feet, and his passion (Skt. *kāma*) to service, without any indulgence of lust—a love like that which characterizes Uttamaśloka's own people. Thus at all times making a Total Love of the entire range of his actions to the Supreme Adhiyajña, the Blessed Lord Adhokṣaja, he ruled this earth under the direction of the brāhmaṇas who were devoted to him."

> and in that way touching Him; kissing the nectar of His lips, enjoying Him sexually, and the thrilling of the hair as well; hearing the sounds He makes when speaking, singing or playing the flute, as well as smelling His fragrance everywhere; moving constantly to be near Him, and meditatively imagining Him at all times : this alone is the reward of all who have senses—even liberation, if it is other than this, is not the proper reward, just as abiding forever in darkness can never be the reward of the eye! Thus even liberation is never the reward for beings endowed with senses and other faculties. For when the devotee abandons all the obstacles and takes up the proper means, liberation will not happen to him.

The beauty of this passage could and probably should delay us for a long time. But what is of interest here, besides the beauty, is the fact that Vallabha refers back to this passage in his Commentary, on X. 47.27, where the word *sarvātmabhāva* has occurred in the stanza, and points out that this is the place where he has explained *sarvātmabhāva*. And what has been explained here, we should note, is the worship of Kṛṣṇa with all the sense-faculties, motor-organs, and mental faculties. This is the key; this is the primary meaning of *sarvātmabhāva*. In this sense, the Sanskrit compound is resolved as follows : *sarvair* (*i.e., indriyādibhir*) *ātmano* (*bhagavati*) *bhāvaḥ*, or, in English : "The love of the soul for the Blessed Lord with (or "by means of") all the senses, motor-organs, life-breath, mind, heart and understanding." Hence *sarvātmabhāva* means "Total Love." Vallabha describes Total Love once more, with similar fullness and precisely the same meaning, in verses 17-19 of his verse-treatise *Nirodhalakṣaṇam*. There he is speaking of it (although, as here, he doesn't mention it by name) as the supreme means for attaining *nirodha* ("constraint"), the next topic of this Introduction, and he is describing the way it should be experienced by present-day devotees, just as, in the passage we quoted, he was describing mainly, though certainly not exclusively, the Gopīs' experience of Total Love. We should note for future reference the fact that both passages speak of Total Love as a means, though the passage quoted here speaks of it mainly in terms of a reward. This peculiarity of being both means and reward is a very important aspect of Total Love. Lastly, this principal kind of Total Love can, as Shri Shyam Goswamy has lately rediscovered and explained, be experienced in union with or separation from Kṛṣṇa.

Now to the second—and secondary according to Shri Shyam Goswamy, but still important—meaning of *sarvātmabhāva*. This type of Total Love can be experienced only in separation from Kṛṣṇa. And in this type, the compound-word is resolved as follows : *sarvatra ātmano (bhagavati) bhāvaḥ*. "The love of the soul for the Blessed Lord in everyone and everything." Or, to provide a very meaningful connotation for the word-*ātma*-, the compound may also be resolved, in the present meaning, as above, but with the following interpretation : "The love that is characteristic of the Self (i.e., the devotee loves Kṛṣṇa as intimately and non-dualistically as he loves his own Self) for the Blessed Lord in everyone and everything." Vallabha indicates this sense of *sarvātmabhāva* in his Subodhinī on Bh. P. X. 87. 27. He is relating his comment to the context of worship, which is the subject of the stanza he is explaining :

> The genitive case of the word "Your" means that whatever object they worship is connected with You. But *sarvātmabhāva* is required there, because we know from the scriptural passage : "He attains the supreme death who sees any difference here" (*B. Ā. Upan.* IV. 4 19), that he who sees any difference at all will be conquered by death.

It is perfectly clear that the primary sense of *sarvātmabhāva* cannot be meant here. Rather, it is the love of Kṛṣṇa in everything—the seeing of Kṛṣṇa as totally non-different from the things with which one worships Him, that is meant. The reference is not to the use of one's own faculties to love and worship the Lord, but to seeing that the Lord is the thing which one worships and it is He. This refers principally, of course, to the devotee's clay or stone "Kṛṣṇa-for-worship" (cf. p. 37), which must not be seen as merely symbolic. This is the second meaning of Total Love, and we will be seeing this meaning again.

The question that now arises is at which point on the path to perfect love and permanent union with Kṛṣṇa Total Love can be expected to dawn. We saw, in our section on eligibility, that the devotee can begin experiencing Kṛṣṇa in terms of the mood he or she desires only when he or she reaches the stage of "addiction to" or "obsession with" Kṛṣṇa (*vyasana*). Not illogically, it is also immediately after reaching this stage of obsession that the devotee begins experiencing Total Love for Kṛṣṇa. This is because, as noted before, the characteristic of "obsession" is that one begins seeing Kṛṣṇa everywhere. Kṛṣṇa is seen as everything, and everything as Kṛṣṇa--a remarkable state of ecstatic love. But this is precisely the experience of Kṛṣṇa in terms of the second type of Total Love : everyone and everything is loved as Kṛṣṇa. And a remarkable thing about this Total Love, when it is experienced on the Path of Devotion rather than the Path of Knowledge, is that the devotee does not see God in His creatures, i.e., he does not see the worldly things first, and then God in them; this is the insight of the Path of Knowledge. Rather, the nature of the devotee's perception is that he loves God first, and through Him as curtain or door he sees everything else. He is so obsessed with Kṛṣṇa that if he happens to look at an ordinary object he sees, and loves, only Kṛṣṇa. The ecstatic devotee, then, sees creatures through God, rather than vice versa.

Thus it is Total Love in our second meaning, loving everything in Kṛṣṇa and Kṛṣṇa in everything, that dawns initially. Then the primary type of Total Love takes over as its more permanent manifestation, and we love Kṛṣṇa totally, with all our senses, faculties, mind and heart, whether united with Him or separate from Him. The devotee still experiences occasionally the second type of Total Love, when in separation, but the primary type is the more permanent and dominant. This is the "Total Love stage" (*sarvātmabhāvadaśā*) which Vallabha and his followers teach as the stage intermediate between means (*sādhana*) and reward (*phala*) on the path to union with Kṛṣṇa. For "obsession," as we recall, marks the high point and end of the "means-stage," and the permanent union, without even occasional separation, of the "reward-stage" has not yet begun. Thus Total Love is both means and reward, and yet it is also above the one and a foretaste of the other. This intermediate nature of Total Love gives it both its uniqueness and its centrality as a doctrine of Vallabha's system, and it is crucial to remember this when Vallabha begins speaking of the Total Love of the Gopīs. It is also essential to remember that Total Love, coming where it does on the Path, immediately consequent upon its necessary condition, "obsession," is the final requirement and proof of "eligibility". Once Total Love is present, the reward can be, indeed must be, conferred by Kṛṣṇa, according to the mood the devotee desires. Now we have a context for understanding the Gopīs' Total Love.

I will note just a few of the more important examples of Total Love which occur in the translation. It will be the reader's delight to find and understand the rest of them. Interestingly, in our section of the Subodhinī, Vallabha never uses the full Sanskrit form we have described, *sarvātmabhāva*, very likely because the Bhāgavata text does not use it. Rather, he uses the terms *sarvabhāva* (again, "Total Love") and *sarvabhāvaprapatti* ("the surrender based on Total Love"). But in all cases except one (cf. Intro. to stanza 46, Chapter I), it is very clear from the context and from his commentators' assurances here and elsewhere, that Vallabha means "Total Love" in the sense I have explained. Viṭṭhala also uses two terms here, *sarvātmabhāva* itself and *sarvabhāvaprapatti*, and again it is perfectly clear that he means them in our sense. It seems that it is only in the later tradition that *sarvātmabhāva* became the consecrated phrase for the phenomenon of Total Love. Whether the consecrated phrase is used or not, however, the Gopīs' attitudes, words and actions prove them *the* paradigm of Total Love, as we shall see.

The first and perhaps clearest example of Vallabha's thinking on the question of Total Love as the prerequisite for experience of the reward of the mood of love (often also expressed as "the Joy of worshipping the Lord through love"—*bhajanānanda*) comes when Vallabha is explaining why Kṛṣṇa is sending back the married Gopīs, who, along with the virgin Gopīs, had come to Him in the forest (Kṛṣṇa had invited only the virgin Gopīs, according to Vallabha, because He had already seen their Total Love). He is commenting on stanza 17 of Chapter I :

> Since they (the married Gopīs) were still subject to someone other than the Lord, they were not fit to worship the Lord through love. This game of the Lord's which was about to begin requires of its participants that complete surrender to the Lord which is characterized by Total Love of Him.

But, a few stanzas later, Vallabha lets the married Gopīs off the hook. Speaking in the voice of Kṛṣṇa to explain Kṛṣṇa's realization, expressed by the stanza, that all the Gopīs who have come have Total Love of Him, Vallabha says (on Chap. I, stanza 23) :

> Those women who have 'intense love for Me', and who make their love total and exclusive, so that their hearts are compelled by that Total Love — if you have come here because You are that kind of woman, then that is fitting and right.

It is "fitting and right," then, according to Vallabha, that women who have Total Love should experience the reward—the Joy of worshipping Kṛṣṇa through love.

A second, extended example of the nature and place of Total Love in the love-games is provided by Viṭṭhala's long interpolation on stanzas 12-16 of Chapter I. In this passage Viṭṭhala argues, with very convincing logic, against his father Vallabha's position that the Gopīs who stayed at home, rather than going to Kṛṣṇa in the forest, did not possess Total Love. There is no need to quote from Viṭṭhala's comments here, because Total Love is the main, though not the only, topic of his interpolation, and the reader will be able to derive his own conclusions. Suffice it to say that this substantial difference of opinion makes both father's and son's comments on stanzas 12-16 all the more interesting.

The third example is even more extended, and—the reader will be happy to know—even less amenable to being quoted, because it takes in the major part of two chapters. I am speaking of Chapters II and III of the love-games. It seems to me — and I realize I may be stretching things a bit here, but I think not—that the entire section of Chapter II in which the Gopīs replay the Games of Kṛṣṇa, participating by playing the different parts, is a long, thorough and magnificent example of Total Love in the primary sense, in which all the senses and limbs, mind, heart and entire person become so absorbed in love of Kṛṣṇa that some of the Gopīs actually think they are Kṛṣṇa, while others offer their bodies completely to playing the part of an insentient object in His Game, still others become the demons whom He kills, and so forth. Actually, two sections of Chapter II are involved here : stanzas 2-3, where the Gopīs re-enact Kṛṣṇa's love-play with them; and stanzas 15-23, the charming and famous passage in which the Gopīs play again Kṛṣṇa's most celebrated childhood Games. What more perfect acting out of Total love could there be than the loving imitation of Kṛṣṇa, His friends and His enemies, in the sacred Games He has played (and, according to the teaching, is still and will eternally be playing in Vaikuṇṭha) ? This *has* to be what Vallabha means by Total Love. And, in a way less easy to see, but nevertheless profoundly true, it seems to me that in Chapter III, the famous "Song of the Gopīs" (*gopikāgīta*), the Gopīs are actually praying to Kṛṣṇa to worship them with Total Love ! The clue for this is, I think, the highly important stanza 31 of Chapter I, where the Gopīs beg Kṛṣṇa : "Return our loving worship" (repeated in Chapter III, stanza 6). They want Kṛṣṇa to fulfil what He has said in *Bhagavad-Gītā* IV. 11 about loving His devotees in return in exactly the same way as they have surrendered themselves to Him, as Vallabha points out. And, since the Gopīs have worshipped Kṛṣṇa with Total Love, they pray in Chapter III that He will fulfil His promise and return their worship in kind, with Total Love.[12] The Gopīs never say this in so many words, but this is exactly what they imply, and indeed they express it fully in words which mean the same thing. For in Chapter III they pray that Kṛṣṇa look at them with His eyes, touch their heads and breasts with both His hand and His feet, show them His face, kiss them, speak to them, and so forth and so on. What else is this but a prayer that He worship them with Total Love ? The entire logic of the story, and the words of the prayers themselves, tell us so.

12. The topic of worship and return of worship is treated fully and definitively in stanzas 16-22 of Chapter IV.

And just as Kṛṣṇa tells the Gopīs, in stanzas 20-22 and commentary of Chapter IV, that He cannot return their worship because "true worship ... is an attribute that can belong only to souls (and not to the Lord)" (Vallabha on stanza 22), so is Total Love an attribute that can belong only to souls, since only souls possess a composite relationship with bodies, minds, sense-faculties, etc. At any rate, to return to our point, the whole of Chapter III is expressed in terms of Total Love.

And finally, Vallabha, in finishing his commentary on Stanza 15 of Chapter I, writes a passage which richly intermingles both the meanings of Total Love. And, as is not unusual for him at the end of a commentary on a given stanza, he seems to be addressing not merely the story and subjects of the love-games, but the wider audience of his devotees, to instruct them specifically. The passage consists of the final three sentences of the commentary, and two verses which Vallabha adds on :

> It is by constantly imagining and fantasizing (Skt. *bhāvanā*) Him that the perception bursts upon us that this entire world has Him as its Self. This (i.e., a change of perception) will happen if our eyes have been coloured by passion. How much more will it happen when Hari is our very Self ? Therefore, these persons come to have Him alone as their Self, because the Blessed Lord appears in everything.
>
> *Two Verses* : Let the person so imagine Hari, through passionate desire, anger and so forth, that Hari is in his soul and his mental faculties, in his life-breaths, his senses and his body, in external objects, in his home and his possessions, his children and others, with the result that, just as the former world melts away completely in the sage's realization of truth, so will it melt away for this person.

Need I say that, once again, Vallabha has not used the specific phrase "Total Love" even in describing it ? But I think we can recognize it clearly enough. And if we can, it is time for me to stop writing on the subject.

Something more should be said, however, about how Vallabha thematizes the Gopīs' role in the love-games—on the issue, for example, of whether they are "responsible", in the ethical sense, for what happens between them and Kṛṣṇa. Vallabha and Viṭṭhala make comments on this theme in many places, but, as I think the reader will be able to see, their viewpoint boils down to the following. The Gopīs, by renouncing entirely all worldly things, everything that was theirs, and even their very Selves (Kṛṣṇa alone becomes their Self), made themselves a *tabula rasa* on which Kṛṣṇa could write whatever He wished. There was literally nothing left of the Gopīs as persons— they had made themselves mere instruments for Him to do what He wished with—and thus the possibility of ethical responsibility is precluded. Some of the language Vallabha and Viṭṭhala use in presenting this idea may be helpful here. First, Vallabha tells us, commenting on stanza 30 of Chapter I, how the Gopīs' renunciation of all had reduced their Selves to a single desire, which was the sole basis of their continued existence : "Because He is the only desire that remains for them. The Gopīs concluded that, if this desire were not present, their very selves would disappear." Farther on, the Bhāgavata itself tells us, in stanza 21 of Chapter IV, that the Gopīs abandoned and lost even their Selves. Unaccountably, Vallabha does not give this meaning of the stanza, even though it fits perfectly with his logic. So Viṭṭhala fills the gap with an interpolation whose logic and interpretation of Sanskrit can scarcely be disputed :

> But in truth the word *sva* in the stanza (which Vallabha interprets as "all—everyone and everything—that was yours") means "their very Selves." Otherwise, since the abandonment of one's husband, children and so forth is already included in the abandonment of the world and the Vedas, the word *sva* would be meaningless. Likewise one abandons one's Self only when one cannot consider the object of love to be one's own Self. The meaning is that, since the Blessed Lord is the object of the Gopīs' love because He is their be-all and end-all, they have abandoned their Selves and all else.[13]

13. Skt. *evam madarthojjhitalokavedasvānām hi vo mayyanuvṛttaye 'balāḥ | mayā parokṣam bhajatā tirohitam māsūyitum mārhatha tatpriyam priyāḥ ||.*

And so the Gopīs, after reducing their Selves to a single desire, abandoned their Selves totally to Kṛṣṇa's use. And Vallabha consequently teaches that it was Kṛṣṇa who was the fully responsible party, in his commentary on stanzas 23 and 25 of Chapter V, where Kṛṣṇa is portrayed as the bull elephant who bursts the dams of right conduct.

We might say that this is the "special" explanation given by Vallabha and Viṭṭhala concerning the Gopīs' conduct. Actually, the "general" explanation of Vallabha's system on the question of the ethical responsibility of any and all souls (persons) would have sufficed, by extension, to cover the Gopīs. For all souls are, in Vallabha's system, completely determined in their thoughts, feelings and actions by Kṛṣṇa, who dwells within each soul in His aspect as "Inner Controller" (Skt. *antaryāmin*). Kṛṣṇa, in Vallabha's system, is the only Agent, and the only One who causes actions (*kartā kārayitā hariḥ*). This central doctrine of determinism by the Inner Controller is much too big a topic for us to cover here, but the reader will get an idea of it at several points in our text. The most direct and simple statement of the idea comes in Vallabha's commentary on Stanza 13 of Chapter I, where he is addressing the question of how Śiśupāla attained ultimate freedom even though he hated Kṛṣṇa :

> And besides, there was no fault on his (Śiśupāla's) part at all. For hatred and the other faults are caused by the Blessed Lord alone. And so Śuka next says : "Hṛṣīkeśa (Kṛṣṇa)," i.e., "Lord of the senses." For the Blessed Lord is the instigator of our sense-faculties, and He produces in us whatever emotions He pleases.

Like Śiśupāla, then, the Gopīs would have been free from blame on this score, too. But the Bhāgavata and Vallabha give the deeper and more satisfactory reason that they literally lost themselves in Total Love, and, as is said repeatedly, Kṛṣṇa alone became their Self. Vallabha gives a beautiful summary reason for all this when commenting on stanza 24 of Chapter I : "By the very nature of things the Blessed Lord is the husband of all souls. And those souls who have become embodied as women must worship and serve the Blessed Lord alone in order to be free of infidelity." Had they not worshipped Kṛṣṇa, Vallabha even goes so far as to say, the Gopīs would have been unfaithful.

Finally, "Kṛṣṇa as Lover" is probably the main topic of our text, and so on that subject I would be doing the readers an injustice if I didn't let them draw their own conclusions from the wealth of its expressions. I would, however, like to point out three ideas which I think are especially important to Vallabha. First, the idea that Kṛṣṇa was "free from passion" as He played His love-games is expressed in Vallabha's second set of Verses on stanza 42 of Chapter I. Secondly, the notion that Kṛṣṇa is fundamentally "the One who delights in Himself" (Skt. *ātmā-rāma*), even when He is making love with others, is expressed most perfectly in Vallabha's comments on stanza 34 of Chapter II; it is also discussed on stanza 42 of Chapter I and stanza 17 of Chapter V. Third and last, Vallabha's comments on stanzas 30-36 of Chapter V form a detailed treatise on the doctrine that Kṛṣṇa (and indeed certain others) is above ethics.

E. *Constraint* (*Nirodha*) : *Kṛṣṇa's Salvific Intent*

Now we come to the concept which the Bhāgavata announces as the subject-matter of its Tenth Book, and which is the central soteriological doctrine of Vallabha's system. In stanza one of the tenth and final chapter of its Second Book, the Bhāgavata, dividing according to subject-matter its remaining ten Books, tells us that *nirodha* ("constraint") is the topic of Book Ten, the Life of Kṛṣṇa. A few stanzas later (Bh. P. II. 10. 6), the Bhāgavata indicates the meaning it wants to give "constraint" in this context, and of course this definition has great importance, since it would be almost impossible not to consider Book Ten the key book of the Bhāgavata. Unfortunately, however, the definition is not without its ambiguities, and different commentators on the Bhāgavata have come up with different interpretations of its meaning. One of the most widely-followed commentators, Śrīdhara, for example, disagrees with Vallabha on this point (or vice versa, since Vallabha wrote after Śrīdhara). But, rather than go into the details of the disagreements, I think our task here is to determine Vallabha's interpretation as exactly as possible, since his interpretation colors and dominates, as it should, his entire Subodhinī on Book Ten.

The definition, then, is : *nirodho 'syānuśayanamātmanaḥ saha śaktibhiḥ*. And Vallabha's interpretation of the definition, in a verse which appears twice in his writings,[14] translates as follows: "For 'constraint' is defined as the '*anuśayana*', that is, the Game-playing in the world, 'of this' Hari, along with and by means of the inconceivable 'Powers' of Kṛṣṇa." Kṛṣṇa is, of course, the full Form of Hari Who has limited His manifold Game-playing to this world. Vallabha uses the two names Hari and Kṛṣṇa to answer the definition's two words *asya* and *ātmanaḥ*. "Constraint", then, according to Vallabha, is the term which the Bhāgavata uses to refer to the descent to earth (Skt. *avatāra*) in which Kṛṣṇa brought all His Games and all his Powers here, rather than to His Vaikuṇṭha-Heaven or anywhere else. Thus Vallabha finds the definition a perfect description of the contents of Book Ten, which indeed it should be but which not all the commentators equally recognize. The first aspect of the meaning of *nirodha* for Vallabha, then, is Kṛṣṇa's abiding here on earth together with all His powers, His "constraint" or limiting of Himself from all the possibilities He could be fulfilling to the possibilities of one particular time and place. In short, as said above, it is Kṛṣṇa's "playing of His Games here in this world."

But Kṛṣṇa never constrains Himself without a purpose, according to Vallabha, and that purpose is always the salvation of souls. This is the second aspect of the meaning of *nirodha*, and it is inseparably connected with the first. Vallabha expresses the two-sidedness of constraint in the following, typically concise verse : "The combination (of elements) which goes by the name of 'the birth' of Hari endowed His Games, as well as His devotees' forgetting of the world and attachment to Him, (is 'constraint',) because of the joining (of the two ideas, represented by the prefix *ni-* and the noun-form *rodha*)."[15] So, the other

14. In Kārikā 9b-10a of Subodhinī on Bh. P. X. 1. 1, and in Kārikā X. 14b-15a of the *Bhāgavatārthaprakaraṇa* of his *Tattvārthadīpanibandha*. The Sanskrit is as follows : *nirodho 'syānuśayanaṁ prapañce krīḍanaṁ hareḥ | śaktibhir durvibhāvyābhiḥ kṛṣṇasyeti hi lakṣaṇam ||*

15. Skt. *samudāyo janmavācī krīḍāyuktasya vai hareḥ | prapañcavismṛtiḥ saktirbhaktānām cāpi yogataḥ ||* Kārikā X. 15 of the *Bhāgavatārthaprakaraṇa*.

side of the coin is the devotee, who is the object of Kṛṣṇa's constraining action. Kṛṣṇa constrains Himself in order to bring about in the devotee one necessary negative effect, "forgetting of the world" (*prapañcavismṛti*), and one positive effect, "passionate attachment to the Blessed Lord" (*bhagavadāsakti*; this is the phrase Vallabha and his followers use much more often, as on stanza 26 of Chapter VI below, than *sakti*, the word used in the above verse). To put it briefly : Kṛṣṇa constrains Himself so that the devotee becomes constrained away from the world to Him alone. The force of Kṛṣṇa's Grace charms the devotee away from all else. The Vallabha Sampradāya distinguishes the two aspects by calling Kṛṣṇa's Self-constraint "the constraint that is the means" (*sādhananirodha*) and the devotee's constraint by Kṛṣṇa "the constraint that is the reward" (*phalanirodha*). And it is very interesting to note that the constraint spoken of here is not that of a Yogī or a striver on the Path of Knowledge, both of whom deliberately constrain their senses and other faculties away from the world as an integral part of their spiritual path. Rather, we are dealing here with devotees, who are comfortable in the everyday world, who moreover use the things of the world for all their acts of worship, and on whom the idea of renouncing or forgetting the world has no reason to dawn. That is precisely why it is Kṛṣṇa who has to take the initiative and constrain Himself in order to try to attract these devotees away from the world to Himself. It is because the devotees are initially worldly, with ordinary, worldly views and sentiments, that Kṛṣṇa does not, at first, appear to them as God at all, but as someone particularly charming on purely worldly grounds. This is demonstrated time and again in all the Vraja-Games of Book Ten. He is simply the beautiful child of Nanda and Yaśodā, and whenever He gives one of them a glimpse of His divinity, He immediately uses His Power of Māyā to delude them once mor. into their sentiment of ordinary parental love, charming them along a little further and only gradually revealing His divinity as they grow ready. And we will see in our present passage that, at least for the Gopīs who could not leave their homes to go to Him, He was simply their illicit lover, according to Vallabha, and only His special Grace made things become different (of course, all constraint is His special Grace). The devotees, therefore, do not consciously exclude or forget the world. And so Kṛṣṇa must descend to their level to make them ascend. They *may* recognize Him as God early on, but they need not.

The immense love of Kṛṣṇa for His devotees, according to the teachings of Vallabha and his followers, is thus obvious. And this is just as true for present-day devotees as it was for the people of Vraja. Kṛṣṇa constrains Himself for each and every one of His chosen. Vallabha expresses Kṛṣṇa's constraining love beautifully in the deservedly famous eleventh verse of his verse-treatise "The Definition of Constraint" (*Nirodhalakṣaṇam*). He does this by turning the tables on the ordinary Hindu religious terminology, which glorifies those who are "liberated" or "set free". Vallabha tells us that things are not thus with Hari : "Those souls whom Hari set free have become sunk in the ocean of existence. But those whom He has constrained, and they alone, experience joy day and night in singing His praises and meditatively imagining Him."[16] Thus the persons whom Hari "set free," or, what would be an even better translation of Skt. *vinirmuktās*, "let go" at creation become entangled in Saṁsāra, while those whom He loves He "constrains" and presses to Himself. Kṛṣṇa's Grace is not a matter of choice for its recipient, but of irresistible charm. This, too, is very much in tune with the aesthetic nature of Vallabha's religion.

The present-day devotee's constraint takes place largely through the special presence of Kṛṣṇa in the *sevya svarūpa* (the "Kṛṣṇa-for-worship") which the devotee is given at his initiation. Vallabha tells us why the Kṛṣṇa-for-worship is the most effective object for the devotee's salvation, even though all things are Kṛṣṇa, when he says : "Having said to Himself: 'I will save this person,' Kṛṣṇa has become manifest in the form of clay or stone."[17] The Kṛṣṇa-for-worship, then, is the only object in which Kṛṣṇa makes Himself present with the specific intention of sav-

16. Skt. *hariṇā ye vinirmuktāste magnā bhavasāgare / ye niruddhāsta evātra modamāyāntyaharniśam //*

17. Skt. *enamuddhariṣyāmīti tadā mṛdādeḥ prādurbhūtaḥ. Prakāśa* on 228 of the *Sarvanirṇayaprakaraṇa* of *Tattvārthadīpanibandha*.

ing the devotee. It is through the clay or stone Kṛṣṇa-for-worship that Kṛṣṇa works out His salvific intent of constraining the devotee. This, then, is how Kṛṣṇa, in the present day, constrains Himself to play His Games with each individual devotee, gradually making him forget the world and become passionately attached to Him.

These aspects of the doctrine of constraint will hopefully give us enough information to interpret the frequent occurrences of the word and its allied concepts in the love-games. A few examples, however, may help familiarize us. Vallabha announces, early in the love-games (on stanza 4 of Chapter I): "Constraint in Him had to be brought about in all the Gopīs. And so all the Gopīs came to Him." This shows us, as we might have expected, that the constraint which is the main topic of the love-games, as of all the other games of Book Ten, is chiefly directed in these particular chapters to the Gopīs who were eligible to worship Kṛṣṇa in terms of the mood of love. And for the present-day devotees who have this same eligibility, these chapters, along with the Kṛṣṇa-for-worship, will be the special means Kṛṣṇa uses to bring about their constraint. In pursuing this theme, Vallabha expresses an important universal truth about constraint : that in order to constrain all, Kṛṣṇa must imitate all. The notion is expressed with specific application to the main topic—the constraint in terms of the mood of love—on stanza 34 of Chapter II. Commenting on the stanza's assertion that Kṛṣṇa, by His mode of love-making with the Gopī He chose especially, "showed the bankruptcy of worldly lovers," Vallabha says:

> For worldly lovers are a pitiable lot. As Kālidāsa says : "For those who are afflicted by passion lose their discrimination." It is these people that the Lord imitates here. If He did not, these people would never be able to achieve constraint in Him.

Therefore, to constrain a person, Kṛṣṇa goes right to the type of activity the person most loves, and acts out that kind of endeavor in an infinitely more perfect, and charming, way. By imitating the action and showing His superiority, Kṛṣṇa attracts the devotee to Himself. Vallabha makes a very revealing remark along these same lines on stanza 37 of Chapter V : "For without the entry of each and every one of His attributes into His devotees, each and every one of their faults would not be removed." Since the entry of Kṛṣṇa's attributes into the Gopīs is a very frequent topic of the love-games, no further explanation of this statement is needed here, except to say that it applies to all devotees, not just the Gopīs.

In stanza 20 of Chapter IV, the Bhāgavata and Vallabha give us a perfect example of how Kṛṣṇa brings about "forgetfulness of the world" (*prapañcavismṛti*) and "passionate attachment to the Blessed Lord" (*bhagavadāsakti*). What is especially interesting here is that Kṛṣṇa tells us He leads devotees to salvation by a kind of negative Grace—that of refusing to return the devotees' worship ! In the stanza, Kṛṣṇa says to the Gopīs ; "But I, dear friends, do not worship even those creatures of mine who worship Me, in order to change their attitude of mind, so they will become like a poor man who got rich and then lost all his wealth, so that now his anxiety over the wealth he lost lets him know no concern for anything else." The key portion of Vallabha's comments on this stanza reads as follows :

> The sum and substance of His teachings here is that His non-worship is precisely for the sake of loving devotion. And the Blessed Lord tells the Gopīs how His attitude and practice of non-worship will succeed by the example which begins : "like a poor man . . ." When a man is poor to start with and later becomes rich—if he then loses his wealth, he is consumed with anxiety about it, and is so intent on and immersed in that anxiety alone that he knows nothing else. This situation is well known in the world. In this way, the Gopīs, too, might first be bereft of the Blessed Lord, And if they attained Him, and He then disappears, from that time their minds become fixed on and immersed in Him alone, so that they will forget the outside world completely.

Thus Kṛṣṇa uses both positive and negative graces to lead the

Gopīs, and all His other devotees, to the constraint that is salvation.

We have already seen the necessary closeness of the concepts of Grace (Skt. *anugraha*) and constraint in Vallabha's system. But there is a passage which brings the two themes together in a particularly intimate manner, and joins them with a third major theme of the love-games : "the Joy of worshipping Kṛṣṇa through love" (*bhajanānanda*). And further, it gives us insight into the mode of constraint not only of the Gopīs, but also the Gopas, and even the cows! The passage is from Vallabha's commentary on stanzas 22-23 of Chapter VI, significantly near the end of the Treatise on the Reward :

> The herd of cows which the Blessed Lord is now leading to the cowpens, He leads by His Grace. Otherwise, even if they had been involved in only one game (cf. stanzas 4-5), they would already be liberated. The same is true for the Gopīs. But, by His Grace alone, He acts as He does in order that both these may experience the Joy of worshipping Him through love...And Kṛṣṇa makes not only the Gopīs successful and happy in attaining what they desire, but the Gopas (cowherd-boys) as well. It is to tell us this that the Gopīs have described the hymn of praise the Gopas sang : "His Game praised in song by His followers." "His followers" means His worshipful servants. By this we are told that the Gopas, too, sang of Him at night, just as the Gopīs do during the day. Otherwise the constraint of all would not come to pass. Precisely to tell us that Kṛṣṇa alone knows the effect of such activity and constraint, and He alone produces it, the Gopīs have used the word "joy" !

An interesting revelation of this passage is that Kṛṣṇa does not liberate the devotees He most loves by having them participate in just one Game, as is normally the case. Rather, He takes them beyond mere liberation to His highest reward, "Entry into His Eternal Game" (Skt. *nityalīlāpraveśa*), by gracing them with repeated participation in His Games on earth and thus leading them to complete constraint.

And finally, as is only right, the commentary on the very last stanza (stanza 26, Chapter VI) of the Treatise on the Reward of the Tāmasa-devotees, which is, of course, also the final stanza of the entire Treatise on the Tāmasa-devotees, takes "constraint" as its main, and almost exclusive, topic, in perfect accord with its being the main topic of Book Ten as a whole. Thus the reader should consult that passage in full. Vallabha mentions in introducing the stanza that the constraint of not only the Gopīs, who are the chief subjects of this particular sub-treatise, but of all the devotees who appear in the Treatise on the Tāmasa-devotees, i.e., all the devotees of Vraja, has come to pass. And, farther on, he writes his classic definition of "the constraint that is the reward," i.e., the constraint of the devotee by Kṛṣṇa, and says that this is what has been described as happening to the Gopīs, whose "abundance of good fortune," in terms of Grace, has been "overwhelming."

But I cannot finish this topic without mentioning that Vallabha, at a point much earlier in his Subodhinī (on stanza 16 of Chapter I), quotes the Bhāgavata's own beautiful summation of the "constraint" Kṛṣṇa accomplished during His descent to earth. The stanzas are Bh. P. XI. 1. 6-7, fittingly near the end of the account of Kṛṣṇa's life, and I will let Vallabha introduce them:

> Śuka's final words in this stanza ("For through Him this entire world attains freedom") mean that, either by Himself visibly present or by His succession of teachers, the Lord will free all people. He will tell us this explicitly later in this scripture, in the two stanzas which say : "After charming away the eyes of men with His own form, whose beauty far surpasses all the world's loveliness; and stealing with His words the minds and hearts of those who remember them; and attracting with His holy feet the actions of all those who gaze upon them; and after spreading far and wide a Fame which all praise; certain that now, by this form of His, all will swiftly and surely cross beyond the Darkness, the Lord returned to His own place."

Part II. Notes on the Translation

A. The Structure and Style of Vallabha's Commentary

My object in this section of the introduction is merely to inform the readers of some technical and stylistic points they will need to know for a fruitful reading of Vallabha's presentation of the love-games. So this will be simpler and briefer than my explanation of the main doctrines. The first point the reader will notice is that there are four different headings under which the text-material falls : "Introduction to a Stanza", "Stanza," "Commentary", and "Verses". The "Introduction" is simply my translation of Vallabha's word *ābhāsa*, the part of his commentary in which he sums up what has been said in the previous stanza and sets the stage for the next. "Stanza" is the stanza of the Bhāgavata Purāṇa which is to be commented on; so this is the only matter not written by Vallabha (or Viṭṭhala, whose "Interpolations" I will treat later). The "Commentary" is Vallabha's Subodhinī on each stanza, which naturally forms the bulk of our text. And the "Verses" are the Kārikā-s, written in the *anuṣṭubh* metre in Sanskrit, with which Vallabha introduces each Bhāgavata-chapter, marks the changes of subject within the chapter, or which he simply writes when he feels inspired to. The matter under the three headings apart from the "Stanzas" is collectively called "Subodhinī."

The second important point is the particular chapters involved in our presentation. "The Treatise on the Reward of the Tāmasa-devotees" encompasses seven chapters of Book Ten of the Bhāgavata: Chapters 29-35, according to the ordinary numbering. Of these I have translated only six. Chapter 34 is much less directly concerned with the love-games of Kṛṣṇa and the Gopīs. Consequently, I have omitted this chapter. The seventh chapter, Chapter 35 (the *Yugalagīta*), however, is of extreme importance both in the Bhāgavata and for Vallabha. For Vallabha, this chapter is the expression of that internal union of the Gopīs with Kṛṣṇa which he describes as "the supreme reward" (Skt. *param phalam*) in Verse 5 of the verses introducing our Chapter I (i.e., introducing the entire topic of the love-games). Another way of expressing this is to say that this chapter shows what the Gopīs do in separation from Kṛṣṇa, i.e., during the day. It is also the chapter in which the "constraint" of the Gopīs is completed, as we have already seen. So it is absolutely necessary to add this onto the traditional "Rāsapañcādhyāyī" (Chaps. 29-33), if we are going to make a complete presentation of Vallabha's teachings on the love-games. Consequently, our Chapters I-V correspond to Bhāgavata-chapters 29-33, and our Chapter VI is Bhāgavata-chapter 35.

Finally, a few stylistic points. Both Vallabha and Viṭṭhala have a tendency to be concise, elliptical, and, occasionally, downright opaque in their use of Sanskrit. This style has its good points as well as its bad, however. It makes their Commentary an extremely "live" piece of literature, in that new connotations and connections keep popping out upon every reading. This makes the Subodhinī extremely stimulating and delightful to read and re-read. It also produces passages, though, which are so tight-knit that they cannot, in my experience, be understood unless initially read two or three times. This is true in two very important passages I can think of : the first five pages or so of Viṭṭhala's long interpolation on stanzas 12-16 of Chapter I; and the whole of Vallabha's commentary on stanzas 16-22 of Chapter IV, where the topic of worship by devotees and return of worship by Kṛṣṇa is treated. It is very fulfilling to catch Vallabha's minimally-indicated connotations, and perhaps his effect couldn't have been achieved had he written out everything he meant in long form. Viṭṭhala is, if possible, even more concise. The second stylistic point is that Vallabha often (and Viṭṭhala occasionally) speaks in the voice of Kṛṣṇa or the Gopīs in his commentary, sometimes even creating conversations which aren't indicated in the Bhāgavata-stanza (usually, though, they are closely connected). This adds a charming intimacy and dramatic quality to the commentary, as I'm sure the reader will find. Sometimes the intimacy is so great that it is impossible to determine from the Sanskrit whether Kṛṣṇa, the Gopīs, or Vallabha is speaking.

Special Note : Viṭṭhala's Interpolations

The reader will find, scattered throughout the Subodhinī, interpolations, some short, some very long, which Vallabha's son and co-founder Viṭṭhala wrote into the text of his father's commentary. The Vallabha Sampradāya considers both Vallabha's and Viṭṭhala's words infallible. But the further distinction operative here is that the Sampradāya considers the interpolations Viṭṭhala wrote into the Subodhinī-text to be Subodhinī, while the "footnotes" (Skt. *ṭippaṇī*) Viṭṭhala also wrote on the

Subodhinī are not part of the Subodhinī. So, since the Vallabhite tradition in general considers both Vallabha's words and Viṭṭhala's interpolations to be equally and together Subodhinī, I have translated all Viṭṭhala's interpolations, marking their beginnings and endings in my translation.

Concerning the content of Viṭṭhala's interpolations, they can be said in general to point out further meanings and "suggestions"(Skt. *dhvani*) which Viṭṭhala saw in the Bhāgavata-stanza under consideration. There are important places, too, however, where Viṭṭhala disagrees with and/or endeavors to correct Vallabha. His long interpolation on stanzas 12-16 of Chapter I expresses an important disagreement and reinterpretation; another disagreement is aired at length in his interpretation of stanzas 10-11 of Chapter VI. And an important correction, or, we might say, drawing out of the true implication of Vallabha's line of thinking, can be found in Viṭṭhala's short interpolation on stanza 21 of Chapter IV. In general it can be said that, as we might expect, Viṭṭhala's writings show a secondary, and therefore more reflective and technical—but also often more devotional—level in the developing system.

B. *The Three Constituents of Existence : Sattva, Rajas and Tamas, and their Derivative Attitudes*

We have already seen, in the section where I explained the general "plan" of Vallabha's Subodhinī on Book Ten (Part I-C of this Introduction), Vallabha's dependence on the names of, or names derived from, the three "qualities" or "constituents" (Skt. *guṇa*) of material existence, those very elastic metaphysical/moral concepts introduced in early Sāṁkhya speculation and made famous by the Bhagavad-Gītā and practically every scripture thereafter. As Vallabha will be referring to these three "qualities" constantly, as well as basing his psychological typology of souls upon them, I feel it necessary to clarify my treatment of them in this translation. The Sanskrit words for these three qualities—*sattva*, *rajas* and *tamas*, to name the qualities in descending order of excellence—each bring to the mind of the reader of Sanskrit not a single, neat concept, but an entire range of similar (but far from identical) ideas. *Sattva*'s range of meanings includes goodness, knowledge, light, subtlety, purity, an inclination to introspection; *rajas* signifies activism, extroversion, initiative, the kingly virtues, the materially creative forces, but also, frequently, passion and/or confusion; *tamas* signifies darkness, dullness, ignorance, inertia, and also stubbornness, wilfulness, impudence. If one insists on a one-word English translation for each of the three, which it is obvious would be inadequate, the generally accepted words would be "goodness" for *sattva*, "activity" for *rajas*, and "darkness" for *tamas*. But a good example of the danger of so doing can be seen by translating the sentence *sattvāt sañjāyate jñānam* (*Bh. Gītā* XIV. 17; quoted by Viṭṭhala early in his long interpolation on stanzas 12-16 of Chapter I) as "Knowledge is born of goodness." This is not what the sentence means, and would be downright misleading, especially for a reader inclined to compare Indian and Western philosophical teachings. The words *sattva*, *rajas* and *tamas*, then, are ambiguous even in Sanskrit, and authors like Vallabha deliberately play upon their ambiguities. I am convinced that it is much better to let them be ambiguous in their native tongue than to compound the ambiguity by "translating" them into English. Therefore these words remain *sattva*, *rajas* and *tamas* in my translation.

Likewise, and for the same reasons, I will not translate the names of the nine categories, derived from the three qualities, which Vallabha uses to make his psychological typology of souls. The names used here are *sāttvika*, *rājasa* and *tāmasa*, and the three are joined in all the possible combinations of two (e.g., *sāttvika-sāttvika*, *rājasa-sāttvika*, etc.; *sāttvika-rājasa*, etc.; and *sāttvika-tāmasa*, etc.) to make nine different types. We should be careful to point out here, however, that the terms *sāttvika*, *rājasa* and *tāmasa* do not have the same meaning in our present context as they do when Vallabha uses them in the titles of the major divisions of his Subodhinī. This latter is the "technical usage" of the terms which I have explained above. And in this technical sense, all the devotees in the "Treatise on the Tāmasa-devotees" are *tāmasa*, all those in the "Treatise on the Rājasa-devotees" are *rājasa*, and so forth. What we are dealing with here is a second usage of these terms. This second sense, as Lālūbhaṭṭa recognizes and explains (*Prameyaratnārṇava* pp. 165-66), is the usage of these three words as *bhāvaviśeṣa*, literally, "particularities of emotion," but, to translate it into real English, "personality-traits." There are nine different types of personality-trait, derived from the three "qualities", then, which Vallabha sees in the Gopīs of Vraja. From observation I think I can generalize that a *tāmasa*-type in this sense is characterized by a sort of "aggressive nastiness" (cf., for example, the Gopī who sings stanza 2 of Chapter III), a *rājasa*-type by "agitated confusion" (cf. stanza 11, Chapter III), and a *sāttvika*-type by "firm knowledge" (cf. stanza 8, Chapter III). But it is rare for Vallabha to designate a Gopī by only one of these names. As mentioned above, he almost always uses a combination of two, one dominant and the other secondary (indeed this more realistically reflects the variety in human personalities). Therefore we will find that a Gopī who is designated *rājasa-sāttvika* (the secondary characteristic is listed first, the dominant second),[18] possesses knowledge and goodness as her basic traits, but they are colored by a tendency to flurried confusion. A *sāttvika-sāttvika* Gopī would be all sweetness and light. But dynamite couldn't move a *tāmasa-tāmasa* Gopī ! The reader will be able to see how each of these personality-types speaks and acts many times throughout the translation. And the final point to remember is that, since this second usage of *sāttvika*, *rājasa* and *tāmasa*, as personality-trait, is different from the first, technical usage of the words as titles for Vallabha's major divisions of his commentary, there is no contradiction, or even problem, with a *sāttvika-sāttvika* Gopī appearing in the

18. There is confusion in the writings of Vallabha's followers as to whether the proper order in listing these personality-types is "secondary-dominant" (e.g., *rājasa-sāttvika* for a person whose *sāttvika*-quality is dominant) or "dominant-secondary" (e.g., *sāttvika-rājasa* for the same person). I have found that this confusion seems to stem from the writings (perhaps garbled in transmission) of Vallabha himself, because in designating the two types of married Gopī who sang stanzas 12 and 17, respectively, of Chapter III, he uses the name *rājasatāmasa* for both, whereas his intention would have been to make the two different, one probably being the reverse of the other. At any rate, though the confusion still exists nearly five hundred years later, the form that Vallabha most uses in his writings seems to be the "secondary-dominant" designation, and so that is the one I have used.

Treatise on the Tāmasa-devotees, or with a *tāmasa-rājasa* Gopī appearing in the Treatise on the Sāttvika-devotees.

I should also note that, for Vallabha's tenth personality-type, the Gopī (or devotee) "who is free of the three qualities of worldly existence" (Skt. *nirguṇa*), I have simply translated their designation as "transcendent," since that is precisely what *nirguṇa* means. In this case there is no ambiguity or language-difficulty.

C. *Text-Critical Note*

It did not prove practicable, in the preparation of the present work, to make a manuscript-study of Vallabha's Subodhinī. This made the text-critical aspect of my work simpler, but still vexing at times. The latter was because I was using the volume of *Shrī Subodhinī Granthamālā*—containing a Sanskrit text, and a Hindi translation by Fatehchand Vasu (cf. Bibliography)—which contains the Treatise on the Tāmasa-devotees. This is one of the only printed editions of the Subodhinī available now, but unfortunately the Sanskrit text of at least this volume is absolutely riddled with printing errors. I was lucky enough, however, to be able to obtain the printed edition of Subodhinī on which my error-filled text was based—the one published by the yeoman editors of the Vallabha Sampradāya in recent times, M. T. Telivala and D. V. Sankalia (cf. Bibliography), in 1924—and thus to make all the corrections in my Sanskrit text. The Telivala-Sankalia text is the only reliable printed edition of Subodhinī which I know of (though most unfortunately now out of print !), and, so far as I know, all the editions available now are reprints of it. The Telivala-Sankalia text, too, has a few doubtful readings. These I have either emended and explained in footnotes, or let stand for want of a probable alternative.

CHAPTER I

(Bhāgavata Purāṇa Book X, Chapter 29)

Verse 1 : Now that Lord Kṛṣṇa has separated the devotees of Vraja from their experience of the joy of Brahman, that game of His which is perfectly suited for uniting them with the Joy of worshipping Him through love is narrated in this fourth and final section.[1]

Verse 2 : This Joy of worship is brought to perfect fulfilment in ordinary women;[2] and it is by means of them that it may come to a man. For the suitability of such women to experience Kṛṣṇa's Joy has also been described.

1. As has been explained already, the seven chapters which form the subject-matter of our study constitute, for Vallabha, the fourth and final, and the "highest" (in terms of the importance of the subject-matter and the teachings) section of the first major sub-division of Vallabha's commentary on the Bhāgavata's account of the life of Kṛṣṇa. The first subdivision as a whole is entitled "The Treatise on the Tāmasa-Devotees" (*tāmasa-prakaraṇam*); and the present section is entitled "The Treatise on the Reward of the Tāmasa-Devotees" (*tāmasa-phala-prakaraṇam*). We should also note that in *Verse* 8 of the present group, Vallabha refers to the present chapter as the "twenty-sixth chapter", whereas in the normal count of the Bhāgavata's tenth book, it is considered Chapter Twenty-Nine. This is because Vallabha considers the three chapters which are normally counted as Chapters 12-14 to be interpolations—not originally part of the Bhāgavata's text (although he considers them as authoritative as other Purāṇa texts). Therefore he does not assign numbers to these chapters, but simply refers to them as "the interpolated chapters" (*prakṣiptādhyāyāḥ*). Consequently, for every chapter subsequent to these three, Vallabha's number for a chapter comes to three less than the normally accepted number. There is, by the way, a good deal of internal and external evidence that the three chapters concerned are interpolations.

2. In Verses 2 and 3 and the first sentence of Verse 4, Vallabha uses the most general possible word (*striyaḥ*) in referring to "women". It is only in the subsequent verses that he is quite clearly and specifically referring to the Gopīs of Vraja. I think it would be an error for us to try to be more specific than Vallabha's Sanskrit is.

Verse 3 : Therefore the Joy of worshipping Kṛṣṇa through love becomes established perfectly in women. Men will come to experience it through them, and in no other way.

Verses 4-7 : For women alone can taste this Joy, and then a man can taste it in women. This is why the Blessed Lord Kṛṣṇa delighted in love with women day and night. This He did in two ways—internally and externally—but the internal is the supreme reward. Subsequently, that flawless game which consists of words is described (our Chapter VI). Therefore, Kṛṣṇa's love-games are said to be of five kinds, involving five of His multiplicity of forms. The first kind of game He plays with the Self; next (OR : higher), is the game He plays with the mind. The third game is with speech and life-breath; the fourth (OR : next and higher still), is with the senses. The game with the body is called the fifth. With these five games (our first five chapters) is He Himself fully revealed and established.

Verses 8-9 : In this twenty-sixth chapter Hari Himself first brings great Joy to the persons described, if they have dedicated themselves entirely to Him;[3] and then the means for attaining this dedication is demonstrated. Only to the extent that a person's entire Self has been surrendered to Him does Hari play His love-game with that person. And, united with the heart of His beloved, Hari disappears from sight.

Introduction to Stanza 1 : The narrator, Śuka, in order to begin his account of the first kind of the Joy of worshipping Kṛṣṇa through love (i.e., "with the Self") tells us that Kṛṣṇa desired to make love with the Gopīs because in that way His own Joy could be established in them. And so Śuka begins by saying :

Stanza 1 : When the Blessed Lord noticed that on these very nights the jasmine-flowers reached their full autumn bloom, even He made up His mind to begin His love-play, relying on Yogamāyā.

Commentary : The Blessed Lord, who had said to the Gopīs : "On these very nights you will enjoy my love" (Bh. P. X. 22. 27), realized that those nights which He had given

3. "That is, if they have Total Love For Him," says Viṭṭhala in a Footnote (*ṭippaṇī*) on these words.

them in answer to their prayer and fasting, as the nights on which He would make love with them, had arrived. And so He superimposed divine nights (i.e., the nights of His Eternal Game in Vaikuṇṭha) upon all these earthly nights, making the moon full because of the fulness of these divine nights, making the season Autumn, since Autumn causes the flowers to bloom, and carefully providing all the effects which serve to awaken the mood of love. And after this, He produced in Himself that mind which is the grandfather of love,[4] and which reveals His own Joy, in order to make love. And the decision of all the Gopīs to make love to Him, too (which is caused by the Lord's decision to make love to them), must be explained here. In this whole process the flute will be of assistance. And after this will come the description of passion (Skt. *kāma*). The sense of Śuka's words : "even He (the Blessed Lord) made up His mind" is this. Kṛṣṇa decided right at the start that, even though He can communicate His own Joy to another without the medium of a flute or anything else, He would deliberately allow the ordinary laws to apply to Him, too.

Now to someone who objects that, if all this were so, and the Lord's own Joy were to leave its original place and go elsewhere, it would suffer a loss in its essential form,[5] Śuka replies : "relying on Yogamāyā." For Yogamāyā can take what is in one place and transfer it to another, just as she transferred Saṅkarṣaṇa from one womb to another.[6] For the sake of this

4. The "decision" or "intention" (Skt. *saṁkalpa*) to make love (Skt. *kāma*) is the father of love. And "the mind" (*manas*) is the father of intention. Hence the mind is "the grandfather of love" (*kāmapitāmaha*).

5. The Hindi translator, Mr. Fatehchand Vasu, points out that the "ordinary laws" which Kṛṣṇa allowed to be applied to Himself in this context are the laws of the Treatises on Aesthetics (Skt. *rasaśāstra* or *alaṅkāraśāstra*). According to those laws, if Kṛṣṇa allowed His Joy to leave Him and go to someone or something else, He would suffer a loss or deterioration (Skt. *vikāra*) in His essential form (*svarūpa*). Thus He would become like an ordinary soul (*jīva*), since He would have "Being" (*sat*) and "Consciousness" (*cit*), but would no longer have "Joy" (*ānanda*), which makes Him Kṛṣṇa.

6. Yogamāyā's transfer of Saṅkarṣaṇa (i.e., Balarāma) from the womb of Devakī to the womb of Rohiṇī is narrated in Bh. P. X. 2. 6ff.

game She is taken along by Kṛṣṇa right at the start. And this is nothing new, for just as Balabhadra (Kṛṣṇa's brother Balarāma) is useful to the Lord in matters of scriptural justification and protection, so Yogamāyā is needed for the successful accomplishment of a given task. Yogamāyā is essentiál to this game in another way, too—in that she can transfer a means of knowledge (Skt. *pramāṇa*; this also means "the Scriptures") from one place or person to another, and likewise transfer one person's Joy to another. Therefore the Path which is not based on scriptural knowledge (Skt. *pramāṇātiriktamārga;* such as the Paths of Passion or Anger, in stanza 15 of this chapter) and the Path of Devotion will both be treated in detail below. The nights that He created for love alone—those nights are the only ones the Lord has seized upon here. Otherwise, had He chosen ordinary nights, his Joy would be shared by anyone and everyone. It is in the season of autumn that the jasmine-flowers bloom at night. When He saw them, He set his mind on love. And He relied on Yogamāyā and kept her near Him.

Introduction to Stanza 2 : Since this new mind of the Lord's did not yet have a presiding deity, and since no endeavor will succeed unless a god presides over it, Lord Kṛṣṇa brought forth the moon as its presiding deity, as the next stanza indicates.

Stanza 2 : Then that exalted king of the stars, using his cooling, refreshing beams as hands to paint the face of the East a glowing red, arose. And he removed the burning pain of the Carṣaṇī-powers, as does a lover when, after a long separation, he gazes at the beloved.

Commentary : The moment Kṛṣṇa set his mind on love, the moon, the deity which presides over the mind,[7] "arose." Though the Lord saw all these nights simultaneously, they actually came one by one, in order. And because it was the deity which was to preside over the mind of the Blessed Lord Himself, that king of the stars arose full—spotless and perfect.

7. In order to make the connection between Kṛṣṇa's mind and the moon more intelligible, we should recall that in the *Puruṣasūkta*—probably the most important creation-hymn of the Hindu tradition—the moon is said to have been born of the Ādipuruṣa's mind (*candramā manaso jātaḥ*, Ṛgveda X. 90, 13).

When the Lord's mind became manifest, so did the moon, and when the Lord's game ceases, the moon will disappear. It rises as far as the middle of the sky, but it never sets. By calling the moon "that king of the stars", Śuka also represents Kṛṣṇa's mind as the moon, and the minds of the Gopīs as the stars—His mind is the protector of their minds. Since this moon has arisen for the very first time, Śuka makes it clear that it rises in the East. As has been said : "It is the direction of the gods." Indra is the deity and overlord of that direction. But now the Blessed Lord alone is Indra, and therefore the moon, which represents His semen,[8] has arisen in the East. Therefore that exalted one (the moon) arose, and "painted the face"—the middle part—of the East "with his hands"—his beams. The face of the East was not red, because it is the face of the West, her rival, which is red because of her association with the sun. Therefore (to soften her jealousy of the West), the East's face is reddened by the moon's hands, which are like saffron. If the moon did not redden the face of its own direction, then the Blessed Lord's mind would not inflame the minds of women with passion. The hands (the moonbeams) are very beneficial, since their coolness takes away the heat. And their tinging everything with red makes them extremely helpful, for red is the color of passion. And when a man touches passionately, then only does his beloved feel joy.

But if the moon were meant to serve merely as the presiding deity, then it would arise in the mind alone. And if its function were to drive away the darkness, the Blessed Lord could have dispelled that by Himself. Or if it were meant to excite the proper mood, the Blessed Lord could have cared for that by Himself, too. Therefore, since the special function of the moon must be explained, Śuka has said : "he removed the burning pain of the Carṣaṇī-powers." "The Carṣaṇī" are powers who

8. The moon represents Kṛṣṇa's semen, according to Shri Shyam Goswamy, because it causes the arousing of *kāma*—"passion"—and sexual love generally. There is an Upaniṣadic identification of the moon with *vīrya*—"virility, semen". But there seems to be no more systematic or elaborate Tantric connotation here.

wander everywhere.[9] But even though they have roamed everywhere they have never attained union with Supreme Joy. Even if some soul should attain liberation, these powers do not join themselves to him, because right from the start they stay away from such a soul (since liberation is not their goal). Consequently their sorrow remains. Or, the sorrow of all the souls associated with these powers of wandering remains. Only now has their sorrow ended—that is to say, the sorrow of all those who have this capability has ended—for their experience of Supreme Joy is about to be described. In general, the people of that time had this power. And they were certain that when this moon rose, the experience of Supreme Joy would inevitably occur. Since this was so, there were three reasons for the moon's rising : to freshen the face of the presiding deity of the eastern sky, to dispel the sorrow of the carṣaṇī-powers, and to drive away the darkness and so forth. In order to illustrate two of these reasons in a single example Śuka says : "as does a lover, when, after a long separation, he gazes at the beloved." For after he has been gone for a long time, the loving husband returns and completely dispels the grief of his beloved and faithful wife and freshens her face by inflaming it with passion. This aim could not be accomplished in any other way.

Introduction to Stanza 3 : Now, after speaking of the arising of this mind and of its presiding deity, Śuka's next concern is to describe the arising of the Gopīs' decision (to go to Kṛṣṇa). And so, he explains how the sound of the Lord's flute arose when He saw the moon, and that sound caused the Gopīs to decide to go to Him :

Stanza 3 : When He saw the moon, that perfect orb which brings joy to the earth, gleaming like the face of Lakṣmī, red with fresh saffron (Skt. *navakuṅkumāruṇa*), and the forest

9. Vallabha will here elucidate the doctrine that the most highly-graced souls generally have a dynamic power, called *carṣaṇī-śakti*, which drives them in every direction, not allowing them to rest until they find Supreme Joy. Vallabha's commentator, Kākā Vallabhajī, illuminates this passage further in his *lekha*, which points out that the moon, the presiding deity of the mind, is the husband of *carṣaṇī-śakti*, which is a power of the mind.

dappled red by the gentle moon-beams, the Lord began to play that soft, indistinct tune that steals the hearts of fair-eyed women.

Commentary : The moon (Skt. *kumudvat*) is called "that which brings (*vat*) joy (*mud*) to the earth (*ku*)" because it has spread joy to every part of the earth. The moon has the power to do this because, being full, it is a "perfect orb"— a circle in which there are no gaps or imperfections. And the phrase "gleaming like the face of Lakṣmī" is used to indicate that the moon is a scenic effect which serves to produce the mood of love. He is Lakṣmī's brother, and his face, like hers, is here said to be resplendent. Moreover, his face has a red color like that of fresh saffron, just as Lakṣmī's face had at the time of her wedding. And because of this the moon arouses fresh love. Besides this, the forest also fosters the mood of love. It, too, is suffused everywhere with red "by the gentle moonbeams," i.e., by the small shafts of moonlight. (Here begins an interpolation by Viṭṭhala; he is explaining the connotations of the stanza's word *go*, which here means "rays of light" or "moonbeams", but which usually means "cow"—yet can, in addition, mean "sense faculty".) The moonbeams yield the milk of the mood of love. And to indicate that they must be fostered and kept in the forest alone, the word *go* ("cow") is used. And Śuka wants to indicate by the previous comparison of the moon's face with Lakṣmī's, that just as her fresh, lively glances cause love to arise, so do these moonbeams cause such love. The word *go* also signifies "sense-faculty", which means that at this moment, only the arising of love (in the sense-faculties) has occurred. But Śuka indicates, by using the word "gentle" (*komala*) to modify *go*, that the preservation and strengthening of this love will come later, with the arrival of the Svāminīs (an honorific name for the Gopīs) and the other events that are about to happen. And, inasmuch as the moon reddened the whole forest, too, how could he fail to redden (i.e., inflame with passion) those for whose sake he had arisen in the first place ? (End of Viṭṭhala's interpolation.) And so, since once the resolve to love has been made everything that needs to be done to arouse the passion of others will follow, "the soft, indistinct tune" came to the Lord's mind, and He "began to play." And the song of His flute "steals the hearts of fair-eyed women," i.e., of women whose eyes are beautiful. For, as Scripture says : "That is why women love a singer". By this song all the Gopīs were summoned. But if He were to play a distinctly beautiful song, the Gopīs, upon hearing it, would stay, stunned, right where they were. Also, the women whose eyes and seeing (both literally and figuratively) were not the very best were not invited.

Introduction to Stanza 4 : Now Śuka tells us how, upon hearing the sound of His flute, all the Gopīs came to Kṛṣṇa :

Stanza 4 : The women of Vraja, whose minds had been captivated by Kṛṣṇa, heard the music that made the love-god, Anaṅga, grow stronger within them. And, their movements unknown to one another, they hurried to the place where their Love was, their earrings swinging back and forth in their haste.

Commentary : Although the Blessed Lord had invited only the young, unmarried Gopīs (when He had said : "On these very nights you will enjoy my love"), his present calling of them sounded the same to everyone. And besides, constraint in Him[10] had to be brought about in all the Gopīs. And so all the Gopīs came to Him. The tune the Blessed Lord was playing makes the love-god, who has no body (*anaṅga*), grow, but it destroys the (earthly) body. Thus this newly arisen love-god led them on. Even before this, "the women of Vraja" had been the Blessed Lord's very own, for Kṛṣṇa alone had captivated their minds. And so "they hurried to the place where their Love was." By saying this Śuka indicates that only those virgin Gopīs who were invited came, at first, since, for them alone, He was the greatest love. For that very reason they did not notice each other's movements, because each of them individually claimed the Blessed Lord as her husband. And it is he who has been first claimed that is one's love. Śuka shows that the Gopīs paid no attention even to their bodies when he says : "their earrings (were) swinging back

10. This is the first mention, in the section of the Bhāgavata which we are considering, of Vallabha's very important doctrine of "constraint" (Skt. *nirodha*), which, according to Vallabha, is the central topic of the Bhāgavata's Tenth Book—The Story of Kṛṣṇa. Confer our introduction for an extended treatment of this doctrine of Vallabha's.

and forth in their haste," thus pointing out that they were unmindful of the pain to their ears. These women are from Gauḍadeśa.[11] From there alone did the virgin Gopīs come. Previously earrings were surely worn by the village women from around Mathurā, too. Or perhaps what are called "earrings" here are the ear-ornaments called "Tāṭaṅka" (Hindi *bālā*).

Introduction to Stanza 5 : Now Śuka tells us how other Gopīs, too (i.e., besides the unmarried Gopīs whom Kṛṣṇa had invited), took the occasion to come :

Stanza 5 : Some Gopīs had been milking, but in their great eagerness they left their milking and rushed to Him. Others had just put milk over the fire to boil, but they left it. Still others left without removing the wheat-porridge which they were cooking over the fire. And all of them went to Him.

Commentary : These Gopīs were preoccupied with their normal activities. The Gopīs who now came were not part of the group of sixteen thousand unmarried Gopīs, and they were of nine types, or rather, ten. Nine types because of the three-fold nature (with its nine different variations) of the qualities, or constituents, of material existence; and one other type which is made up of those who transcend the three qualities of material existence.[12] Within this classification three of the types are said to be concerned with caste duties, three are concerned with

11. Gauḍadeśa is the modern Bengal—which, of course, is a long, long way from Vraja. Vallabha's teaching on this point is probably to be explained in something like the following fashion : these same Gopīs refer to themselves in a future stanza as *śulkadāsikā*, i.e., "bought maid-servants" or, we would be accurate in saying, "slave-girls" (cf. Bh. P. X. 31.2; our Chapter III, stanza 2). This practice was rare in ancient India, but not un-known. Presumably, in Vallabha's opinion, Nanda, Kṛṣṇa's foster-father and the chief of Vraja, had purchased these young girls from Bengal to serve the members of his household and Vraja generally.

12. Here we have Vallabha's first reference, in this section of his commentary, to the three "qualities" or "constituents" (Skt. *guṇa*) of material existence, as well as to the souls who are "transcendent" (*nirguṇa*) of these three qualities. Please refer to our introduction for an explanation of the meaning of the three qualities and the ten types of soul, whom Vallabha here classifies into nine types who are affected by the qualities, and a tenth type who transcend the qualities.

family duties, and three concentrate on proper worldly conduct. In this context, the women of the cowherd caste are concerned with milk and milking. The three types of cowherd women who care for the origin, preservation and destruction of milk, respectively, are mentioned first (i.e., in this stanza). It is in order to speak of them by group, since they are made up of more than one type, that Śuka always refers to these women in the plural number. Now Śuka tells us that some of these women were milking, and right in the middle of the act of milking they stopped what they were doing and rushed to the presence of the Blessed Lord. The cow and its calf were tied together, and the milkpail was half-full—it was precisely the time when one cannot leave what she is doing, but right then they came straight to Him. The reason they came to Him was "their great eagerness"—they were very anxious, asking themselves question like : "Who knows where the Blessed Lord will go in the very next moment ?" Some other Gopīs had just put some milk over the fire, and they, too, left it and went to Him. The word "wheat-porridge" tells us that grains of wheat were being cooked in milk for the evening meal. If this mixture is burnt, it is, of course, destroyed completely. The word "wheat-porridge" also tells us that the mixture was at the point of being fully cooked. But these women, without even removing the kettle from the fire, rushed to the Lord. The word "others" (in "still others" above) shows us that each person's nature is differentiated from every other person's nature by the three qualities of existence. The three types of Gopī described here are *rājasa* (i.e., they have as their dominant characteristic the second quality of material existence, *rajas*: these three types, in the order in which they are described in this stanza, are, respectively : *rājasa-rājasa*, *sāttvika-rājasa* and *tāmasa-rājasa*).

Introduction to Stanza 6 : Śuka now describes the *sāttvika* Gopīs :

Stanza 6 : Some Gopīs were serving their husband his meal, and they left that. Some were giving milk to their babies, and they left that. Some were being obedient to their husbands, and they left that. Still others were eating their own meal, and they left that.

Commentary : It is the wife's duty to serve her husband and children. Her very rule of life is to serve her husband—with regard to his meals and with regard to lying with him—as well as to breast-feed her children when they are babies. To serve her husband his meals is like creation, for his seed is produced from food. And to breast-feed her children is like maintenance of the universe. And the third action described is like the other (destruction). And Śuka tells us that each woman abandoned entirely the duty she was doing. Besides these three types of Gopī,[13] Śuka describes still other Gopīs in this stanza. Thus he begins his description of the *tāmasa* Gopīs with the words : "Still others were eating their own meal, and they left that," and he continues to describe these Gopīs in the next stanza.

Stanza 7 : Some of the Gopīs were anointing their bodies, others were rubbing themselves with oils, and a few were decorating their eyes with collyrium. These last, in their haste, put on their clothes and jewelry upside-down or backwards. Of all these Gopīs, some reached the presence of Kṛṣṇa.

Commentary : "Anointing" means applying an ointment to the body. "Rubbing" means massaging the body with oils. Or perhaps the words refer to "treating or smearing" the floor and walls of the house, and "rubbing and polishing" one's jewelry or household utensils. Here again we see three types of Gopī, listed in the same order as before (therefore these are the *rājasa-tāmasa*, *sāttvika-tāmasa* and *tāmasa-tāmasa* Gopīs, respectively). The service (Skt. *sevā*) of one's body is less important than the service of the cows, but the latter is less important than the service of one's husband. The Gopīs who "were decorating their eyes with collyrium" have transcended the three qualities of material existence. Therefore by the phrase

13. The *sāttvika* Gopīs' concern with family duties places them above the *rājasa* Gopīs, who were preoccupied, as we saw in the last stanza, with their caste duties. And in the present stanza the order of the three types of *sāttvika* Gopīs is as follows : the *rājasa-sāttvika* Gopīs are concerned with creation, which is associated with *rajas*, "activity, extroversion"; the *sāttvika-sāttvika* Gopīs are those concerned with maintenance and preservation, which is associated with *sattva*; and the *tāmasa-sāttvika* Gopīs are concerned with destruction—presumably of the male seed—and destruction is associated with *tamas*.

"a few (were decorating) their eyes," Śuka indicates that the level of eligibility of these women is very hard to attain. Their transcendence of the three qualities consists in the fact that they purify (i.e., study, investigate) the Path of Knowledge. When these Gopīs are coming to the Lord, they are not even aware of their bodies. How much more, then, will they ignore the disarray of their clothing and jewelry, which are external even to the body ? This is what Śuka means when he says : "These last, in their haste, put on their clothes and jewelry upside-down or backwards." These Gopīs' clothes and jewelry were on backwards, or crosswise, or upside-down. Thus the effort of all the Gopīs is described as similar (i.e., they all attempted to go to Kṛṣṇa). Some interpreters say the passage means that their clothes fell into disarray as they went along the path. But aside from this, Śuka tells us that "some" of these Gopīs "reached the presence of Kṛṣṇa," while others did not. The Gopīs who depended on the words of their husbands and other relatives, even though they tried eagerly, did not come to Kṛṣṇa. But the Gopīs who had abandoned dependence on words were free from all dependence, and so naturally their clothes, which were mere attributes of their bodies, fell into disarray as they rushed straight to the Blessed Lord.

Introduction to Stanza 8 : Śuka next tells us the reason why not all the Gopīs came :

Stanza 8 : These Gopīs were forbidden to go by their husbands or their fathers, their sons or relatives, but their minds and hearts had been stolen away by Kṛṣṇa, and, stupefied, they did not turn back even when commanded.

Commentary : "When a woman is young, her father should protect her; when she has married, her husband; and in her old age, her son. When there are none of these, their relatives should protect her—never should a woman have to depend on herself alone." This is what the Treatise on Duty says about the four protectors of a woman (*Manusmṛti* IX. 3). Therefore some of the Gopīs were forbidden to go by their husbands, some by their fathers, and some by their sons or relatives—i.e., each was forbidden by the man entrusted with her welfare. For these men, even though they had become constrained in the Lord, were insensitive to the proper mood of the ultimate reward, since their sole preoccupation was with the means. They thought that these women could worship the Lord only through them, and never independently. Nevertheless, the Gopīs' very selves, that is to say, their minds and hearts, had been stolen away by Govinda. For (the men's) prohibition was heard (by their ears), but the Blessed Lord was the mover (of their hearts). And people are dependent on their hearts. For some ones shouting "Stop! Stop!" will never make a boat stand still when it is being carried away by a raging flood! Śuka explains the fact that the Gopīs had no fear and ignored all their duties by telling us that they were "stupefied". If they could not go straight to Kṛṣṇa, they would faint, as it were, and die. (Here begins an interpolation by Viṭṭhala.) What Śuka intends to teach us here is that the Lord made known to the inhabitants of Vraja the fact that these Gopīs were coming to Him in order to indicate to these men, precisely at this time, the fact that the Gopīs possessed Total Love for Him. If this were not so, then why would the Lord not have made them unaware of the Gopīs' coming right now, in the beginning, just as, later on, in the passage that says "each and every one of them thought that his wife was staying right at his side" (Bh. P. X. 33. 38), He does make them ignorant of the fact that the Gopīs are in the forest ? For, in line with the proverb : "It is far better not to step in the mud than to have to wash it off," it would be better for Him not to have made this known to the men at all than to have to remove all the evils that arise from it once it has been made known (end of Viṭṭhala's interpolation).

Introduction to Stanzas 9-11 : Śuka has thus described how these ten types of Gopī came to the Lord's presence. The only obstacle for them was the time it took them to reach Him. But those Gopīs who, even before this, had worshipped the Lord with Devotion, and yet were prevented now from going to Him, attained the reward of merging into Him (Skr. *sāyujya*) even though they did not experience the Joy of worshipping Him through love. Śuka tells us how this happens in the following three stanzas:

Stanza 9 : Some Gopīs stayed in their houses because they were unable to leave. They meditated on Kṛṣṇa, their eyes closed, by picturing Him to themselves.

Stanza 10 : All their evil actions were burnt away by the scorching fire of their unbearable separation from their loved one. And the bonds of their good actions, too, were broken by the intense joy of the embrace of Acyuta, which they attained in meditation.

Stanza 11 : They attained union with Him, the Supreme Self, even though they thought of Him as their illicit lover. Immediately all their bonds were shattered, and they abandoned the body which is made up of the three qualities.

Commentary : As fate would have it, some of the Gopīs stayed in their homes. After all, they were only cowherds' wives, and knew nothing of cleverness and deceit. Shy girls—most of them just recently married—they clung to their husbands, who were their only protectors. And so they were unable to leave. Therefore, in order to overcome the obstacle of their absence from Him, "they meditated on Kṛṣṇa," but "by picturing Him to themselves" with this thought in mind : "The Blessed Lord is my illicit lover, and I am the mistress hurrying to meet Him." Otherwise (i.e., if they had not thought of their relationship with Kṛṣṇa in this way) there would not be an obstacle. Thinking in even this way, then, they closed their eyes and meditated on the Blessed Lord, and through this method they attained ultimate freedom. Now to someone who objects that it is impossible for these women to have attained ultimate freedom since they had neither knowledge, nor the kind of devotion taught in the scriptures, nor the Blessed Lord's physical presence, Śuka replies that they attained ultimate freedom because the bonds of their past actions were destroyed, and he tells how the destruction of these bonds occurred in the stanza which begins : "All their evil actions were burnt away..." This intolerable separation from their loved one was a great fire—its searing heat burnt deeply. By that fire the evil actions of their past were removed, destroyed, burnt away, and, finally, reduced to ashes. For no one will dispute the fact that one's past actions are destroyed and no longer have an effect after their fruits have been experienced. Now someone who is separated from the Blessed Lord for just an instant suffers as much agony as someone who roasts in the fires of the Kumbhīpāka Hell for millions of aeons. In this agony of separation one experiences the fruits of all one's evil deeds. And Śuka tells us how all the bonds of these Gopīs' good actions were destroyed in the verse which begins : "And the bonds of their good actions, too..." For after all their evil actions had been destroyed they attained the Blessed Lord in meditation. "Acyuta" (Kṛṣṇa) is the Supreme Self.[14] This means that Kṛṣṇa did not come to them in the form of an illicit lover; for if that had been the case, these Gopīs would have some actions remaining which had not borne fruit. Rather the embrace with which He embraced them brought them intense joy, and the joy shattered the bonds of their good actions. Someone who is embraced by the Blessed Lord for just an instant feels just as much joy as someone who enjoys the fruits of his good actions in Svarga or one of the other heavenly worlds for millions of aeons. And so, in this ecstasy all the bonds of their good actions, too, were destroyed. Śuka indicates that it was because of this that these Gopīs attained ultimate freedom when he says : "They attained union with Him, the Supreme Self..." Although these women first embraced the Lord for the sake of enjoying the results of their good actions, even when they had experienced this enjoyment they were not separated from Him again, because evil

14. Vallabha here suggests, and in the remainder of this passage makes it clear, that even though these Gopīs were meditating on Him as their illicit lover (Skt. *jāra*), He did not come to them in that form. If He had done that, they would have remained affected by the earthly qualities, specifically lust (*kāma*), and could not have attained ultimate freedom. Instead, He graced them by manifesting Himself in the form of "the Supreme Self" (*paramātman*)—His most pervasive and interior form—the form that is most dear to, because nearest to, all living beings, as the Upaniṣads tell us (Cf. *B.Ā. Upan.* II. 4.5ff. and IV. 5.6ff.). This form is as remote as is possible from the very specific, external form of Kṛṣṇa as lover. Vallabha's identification of the name Acyuta with the name Paramātman here is not at all controversial, since Śuka himself tells us in the next stanza that it was with Paramātman that these Gopīs attained union.

actions, which are the cause of separation, were absent. And so they remained constantly united with Him. But their bodies, since all the past actions which had caused them were extinguished, (simply) fell down. If they had not embraced the Blessed Lord, then their souls would have entered other bodies, and experienced the fruits of the good and evil actions of those bodies. But since the Blessed Lord was their sole preoccupation, they attained ultimate freedom. This is what Śuka means when he says : "Him, the Supreme Self." Even if at first they attained union with Him with the thought that He was their illicit lover, still (i.e., since He manifested Himself as the Supreme Self, and they attained union with Him in that form) they abandoned the body which is made up of the three qualities because the bonds of their actions had been broken. If at that time any lack of knowledge or incorrect knowledge remain, they endure for no more than three instants and do not constitute an obstacle, since they neither cause separation from the Lord nor do they produce another body (as remaining actions would). But Ignorance (Skt. *avidyā*) does remain, since it is a power of the Blessed Lord. But It, too, has been removed here, since Ignorance is never allowed to delude a person who has attained union with the Blessed Lord. Śuka's meaning is that as a result of this these Gopīs attained ultimate freedom (Skt. *mukti*).

Introduction to Stanza 12: At this point King Parikṣit voices his suspicion that the Scriptures have been contradicted in these last few stanzas :

Stanza 12: King Parikṣit said : "These Gopīs, o wise one, knew Kṛṣṇa as their greatest love, but not as Brahman. How, then, could the flow of the qualities of earthly existence stop for them, since their minds were dominated by those very qualities?"

Commentary : In the scriptural passage : "It is by knowing Him alone that one passes beyond death—for that journey there is no other path" (*Śvet. Upan.* III. 8), knowledge alone is taught as the means of attainment. Then again, we see the passage : "Devotion alone pleases Viṣṇu completely : nothing else at all accomplishes this. He alone grants ultimate freedom, and devotion is the cause of that gift." And the two paths are construed together in the passage which says: "The discipline of knowledge which has Me as its basis and transcends the three qualities of existence is the characteristic of devotion. And the teaching that the object of both these paths is one is the characteristic of the Blessed Lord's teachings" (*Bh. P.* III. 32. 32). And the Blessed Lord has also said: "By devotion does he know Me completely" (*Bh. Gītā* XVIII. 55). Therefore on the Path of Limitations ultimate freedom comes through knowledge alone, while on the Path of Grace freedom comes either through loving devotion or through knowledge.[15] But neither of these two are present in these women. For their loving devotion possesses the qualities of material existence, and so does their knowledge, and, what's more, both these are *tāmasa* in the case of these Gopīs. So how can there be ultimate liberation on the basis of these? These are the grounds for the King's objection. Hence the king says: "These Gopīs knew Kṛṣṇa as their greatest love." Now a woman's "love" (Skt. *kānta*) may be either a husband or an illicit lover, "but these women did not know Kṛṣṇa as Brahman." The king calls Śuka "wise one" here because he wishes to know in full the sage's considered opinion. The contradiction that Parikṣit has pointed out is evident — that these Gopīs' minds were affected by the qualities of material existence both when they looked upon the Blessed Lord and when they looked upon themselves. And the mind which has its vision affected by the qualities is the root-cause of the continual flow of the qualities. If this were not so, then all the scriptures and treatises which

15. With regard to souls who are destined for salvation (Skt. *daiva jīva*; cf. Bh. Gītā XVI. 5-6), a salvation which may consist either of liberation (*mukti*) or of entry into Kṛṣṇa's eternal Game (*nityalīlāpraveśa*), Vallabha's most critical distinction is between the Souls who travel on the Path of (Scriptural) Limitations (*maryādāmārga*) and those on the Path of Grace (*puṣṭimārga*). The difference between these two Paths is that, on the Path of Limitations, Kṛṣṇa's Grace is given to those who have followed the rules and taken the means described in the scriptures, while on the Path of Grace, Kṛṣṇa's Grace overcomes all limitations, scriptural or other, and reaches straight to the soul, even if the soul has real deficiencies of knowledge, devotion, karmic eligibility, or what have you.

teach precisely how to overcome the domination of the mind by the qualities would be pointless. Further, it is impossible for us to presuppose that the Gopīs possessed the Vedic view (e. g., that the person who knows Brahman becomes Brahman).[16] How, then, can the flow of the qualities stop in these Gopīs, whose "minds are dominated by those very qualities," i. e., whose mental vision is affected by the qualities?

Introduction to Stanza 13-15 : Śuka makes his answer to the king in the next four stanzas :

Stanza 13 : Śuka said : I described to you earlier how Śiśupāla accomplished the ultimate goal even though he hated Hṛṣīkeśa (Kṛṣṇa). How much more, then, do those who love Adhokṣaja (Kṛṣṇa) attain it ?

Stanza 14 : It was for the ultimate happiness of all people, O king, that the Blessed Lord, the Unchanging and Immeasurable, who is free of the three qualities and yet is their very Self, manifested Himself (on earth).

Stanza 15 : Those who direct constantly to Hari either their passionate desire or their anger, their fear or their love, their striving to become one with Him or their friendship, become totally absorbed with Him.

Commentary on Stanza 13 : The story of how Śiśupāla attained ultimate freedom has already been told in the seventh book of this scripture (cf. Bh.P. VII, Chap. 1). The two kinds of scripture teach the path of devotion and the path of knowledge as means of attainment, but the manifestation of the Blessed Lord in His full form is also a means. For the Blessed Lord has come down to earth, i.e., He has made Himself manifest in the fulness of His Being, Consciousness and Joy, precisely to give the gift of ultimate freedom. Therefore any person who attains a close relationship with the Blessed Lord by any means at all becomes completely free. Normally knowledge and/or devotion are necessary to bring about a manifestation of the Lord. But if this manifestation has already been accomplished in another way, there is no need for knowledge or devotion. Here the Blessed Lord has become manifest of His

16. This is because women were not allowed to study the Vedas.

own accord, in order to grant ultimate freedom to all alike (OR : by being equally manifest to all. Skt. *sarvasādhāraṇyena*). For no one and nothing else control the Lord's will. And so He makes Himself manifest in three ways : by His own will, by devotion, or by knowledge. These two, knowledge and devotion, are the only causes for His self-manifestation at times when He has not descended to the earth. But when the Blessed Lord has come down to earth, these two are not necessary conditions for His manifestation. But these two are still useful, just as in the rainy season, even though water is easy to get anywhere, no one doubts the usefulness of wells and rivers.

Śuka said : "earlier," i.e., in the seventh book, he had narrated Nārada's description of "how Śiśupāla accomplished the ultimate goal," i.e., merging into the Blessed Lord. And this "even though he hated," i.e., though he actively hated. Although the evil results of hatred form a definite obstacle, those evil results were removed by his constant remembrance of the Lord (cf. Bh.P. VII. 1. 29), and so he attained the reward of merging into Him. And besides, there was no fault on his part at all. For hatred and the other faults are caused by the Blessed Lord alone. And so Śuka next says : "Hṛṣikeśa (Kṛṣṇa)", i.e., "Lord of the Senses." For the Blessed Lord is the instigator of our sense-faculties, and He produces in us whatever emotions He pleases. Since even hatred is therefore a means for attaining ultimate freedom, how much more must we say that those who love Adhokṣaja gain this same freedom !

Commentary on Stanza 14 : Śuka brings forth his main proof when he says : "It was for the ultimate happiness of all people..." The Blessed Lord manifested Himself solely in order to give ultimate freedom to living beings as such. Therefore, this manifestation was only for the sake of their ultimate happiness. Otherwise He would not have manifested Himself, since there was no special reason for His doing so. When His motive is to relieve the earth of a heavy burden, or something of the sort, He manifests Himself in another form. Therefore it was solely for the sake of the ultimate happiness of all people that the Blessed Lord made Himself manifest. And here Śuka says : "O king" to indicate that sometimes a king has to go somewhere in the same way (i.e., personally and not through his representatives) as the Lord does here. In order to point out that no full manifestation of such a person (i.e., either the king himself or the Blessed Lord in His full form) would occur in any other way, Śuka enumerates the Blessed Lord's attributes. First of all, "the Blessed Lord" possesses absolute sovereignty. He depends on no one and nothing. He is the Controller of time, actions, and the natures of all individuals. He has absolutely no needs. Why, then, would He come down to the earth ? Besides, if someone says : "Granted, He would not come for His own sake, but might He not come for the sake of others ?", Śuka rules out that possibility by saying that the Lord is "Unchanging, Immeasurable, Free of the three qualities, and yet their very Self." Only a thing which is attainable by action or by knowledge can be useful to others. But the Blessed Lord cannot be attained by (i.e., cannot be the proper object of) actions since He is "Unchanging," i.e., He undergoes no diminishment at all (and "action"—*kṛti*—implies "diminishment"—*vikṛti*). And He cannot be attained by knowledge since He is "Immeasurable." And if someone says : "Well surely He can be worshipped by the worship we perform with our bodies, our wealth, and so forth," there too the answer is no, because He is "Free of the three qualities," i.e., the three qualities which constitute material existence are not in Him. It is only where the three constituents of material existence are present that there is usefulness or applicability of an "other", just as when there is hunger, the gift of food is useful, and when there is passion, a woman is useful, and when sense-faculties exist, they must have their objects. Therefore the Blessed Lord does not even need to be worshipped, because there is no part of Him which needs to be completed by His servant who worships. Moreover, even if He needed anything for the sake of His games, everything belongs to Him alone, since He alone, as Śuka says, is the Self of all the qualities of material existence. And so He does not need to use others even as means for attaining His own ends (viz., playing His games).[17] Therefore since His motivation

17. To sum up Vallabha's argumentation briefly : the Blessed Lord (Skt. *bhagavān*) is not "usable by" or "useful to" others, because He is simply not attainable or reachable by the actions or knowledge of these

(for manifesting Himself) is neither for Himself nor for others, then if He did not come to grant the ultimate freedom which requires no means of attainment, His manifestation on earth would have no motive at all.

Commentary on Stanza 15 : Since all this is so, that person who gains a close relationship with Him by any means at all surely attains ultimate freedom. This is what Śuka teaches in the stanza that begins : "Those who direct constantly to Hari..." "Passionate desire" and the other five are the means of attaining a close relationship with the Blessed Lord. Among these passionate desire is the characteristic means of the women, and anger, of His enemies. Fear characterizes those whom Kṛṣṇa must kill, and love is the characteristic of His relatives. Striving to become one with Him is the trait of the sages who have mastered the Path of Knowledge, and friendship is the characteristic means of His devotees. Only in these last is friendship with Him accomplished. In the present circumstances there is no need of previous accomplishment in knowledge or devotion. According to the law of these two paths, the Lord must make an independent manifestation of Himself (to the sage or the devotee). But here we must conclude that, according to the law of plurality of application, by which a single ritual functions both obligatorily and optionally, the Lord's manifestation here serves as both an independent, occasional manifestation (for those on the Paths of Knowledge and Devotion) and as a manifestation motivated by His Will alone (to grant ultimate freedom to souls who have no means of attainment)[18].

One connotation of Śuka's use of the word "or" (Skt. *vā*) in this stanza is that he is dissatisfied with the idea that these six means exhaust all the possible means. "Or", he implies,

"others". And contrariwise, He has no need of others to help Him play His games, because everything everywhere is His. And so it cannot be said, in any ordinarily meaningful sense, that His present manifestation on earth is "for others."

18. The Mīmāṁsā law of plurality of application (Skt. *saṁyoga-pṛthaktvanyāya*) refers to a situation in which the sacrifice one desires to perform (*kāmya*) and the sacrifice one is obliged to perform (*nitya*) coincide. Thus the single ritual fulfils both obligation and desire.

there may be some other means, but it must be practiced constantly, otherwise, in accordance with the statement : "Where his mind is at the time of death, it is there that he goes" (compare *Bh. Gītā* VIII. 6), the person will fall under the domination of someone or something other than Kṛṣṇa. By the force of his past actions he will fail to remember the Blessed Lord at the time of death, and will remember someone or something else. For the Blessed Lord and the world are mutually contradictory. Therefore "those who direct to Hari (their passionate desire, etc.)... become totally absorbed with Him." Someone may ask how, if while one is exercising passion or some other emotion toward Kṛṣṇa, he is overwhelmed by some other suffering, it is possible to exercise that first emotion constantly ? Śuka answers this with the phrase : "to Hari." For He is the Remover of all suffering.[19] It is by constantly imagining and fantasizing (Skt. *bhāvanā*) Him that the perception bursts upon us that this entire world has Him as its Self. This (i.e., a change of perception) will happen if our eyes have been colored by passion. How much more will it happen when Hari is our very Self ? Therefore, these persons come to have Him alone as their Self, because the Blessed Lord appears in everything.

Two Verses : Let the person so imagine Hari, through passionate desire, anger and so forth, that Hari is in his soul and in his mental faculties, in his life-breaths, his senses and body, in external objects, in his home and his possessions, his children and others, with the result that, just as the former world melts away completely in the sage's realization of truth, so will it melt away for this person.

Introduction to Stanza 16 : In the next stanza, Śuka wonders why the king is so surprised that, here in the beginning of the account, these Gopīs attained ultimate freedom, since as the story proceeds many others will attain the same freedom :

Stanza 16 : You should not be so amazed at the Unborn, the Blessed Lord Kṛṣṇa, who is Lord even of the greatest Yogīs. For through Him this world (of Vraja) attains freedom.

19. This is based on the etymology of the name Hari which derives the name from the verb-root *HṚ*, "to bear (away), to remove."

Commentary : Then Śuka said : "You should not be so amazed," meaning that King Parikṣit should not express the kind of amazement that claims what Śuka is saying is impossible, because, as a rule, the mind which thinks something is impossible sees it as different from what it really is when it occurs (i.e., it conceives the thing falsely when it occurs). For, after all, we are speaking here of the Blessed Lord, and whatever means, knowledge or anything else, is necessary for ultimate freedom, all that is present in the Blessed Lord alone. And if someone should claim that ultimate freedom is impossible without knowledge, then since the Lord's knowledge is perfect, He will grant that knowledge to the person. Besides, even if some other person should express his doubts by saying that he had never seen the Blessed Lord's surpassing greatness, still you should have no such doubts, since you saw His glory even when you were in the womb.[20] Furthermore, everything is possible for one who is free from all defects. The source of all defects is birth, and when there is no birth, there are no defects. So the Lord is completely free of defects since He is "unborn." But all others are born, and it is impossible for them to attain ultimate freedom with each other's help, because they are all equal. Besides, it is the person who concentrates on a means of attainment that is liberated. In this context a "means of attainment" consists of a mind constrained away from all other things. This is achieved likewise through Yoga, and, as Śuka says, the Blessed Lord alone is the Controller of Yoga. Should ultimate liberation come to another person, too, it would come by the Blessed Lord's Will alone, for Yoga and all the other means of attainment are controlled by Him. Moreover, the Blessed Lord who is eternal Joy is Himself the final reward, and anyone at all who attains ultimate freedom will attain Him alone. Therefore the means of attainment, too, are meant to reach Him alone. And so there is nothing unsuitable in saying that the Lord, on His own initiative, becomes closely

20. The reference is to the incident in which Kṛṣṇa saved Parikṣit, who was still in his mother's womb, from being killed by Aśvatthāman, the implacable enemy of the Pāṇḍava family. This story is told in Bh. P. I.8.7-16.

related here with these Gopīs. And besides, as Śuka says, this visible world (i.e., the world of Vraja) in its entirety will attain ultimate freedom through Him. Śuka has said these things either through imagining meditatively that he himself was in Gokula at this time, or through the vision of knowledge. Śuka's final words in the stanza mean that, either by Himself visibly present, or by His succession of teachers, the Lord will free all people. He will tell us this explicitly later in this scripture, in the two stanzas which begin : "After charming away the eyes of men..."[21]

Viṭṭhala's Interpolation on Stanzas 12-16[22] : Or, alternatively: here, in stanza twelve, King Parikṣit is voicing a doubt about the consistency of the argument. "These Gopīs knew Kṛṣṇa as their greatest love," he says, "but not as Brahman. How, then, could the flow of the qualities of earthly existence stop for them ?", i.e., how is this consistent ? The meaning is as follows. The knowledge of Kṛṣṇa as Brahman is scriptural in nature, and scriptural knowledge should derive from (the quality) *sattva*. This we know from the Lord's own statement : "Knowledge is born of *sattva* (*Bhagavad-Gītā* XIV. 17)." But these Gopīs had their minds entirely taken up with the handsomeness and the other qualities of Him who is full of infinite qualities, who is present to their minds, whose hands, feet, face, stomach and all else are made up of nothing but Joy, and who utterly transcends the three qualities of earthly existence. So, since He transcends the qualities, how is a cessation of the flow of these

21. The two stanzas referred to, Bh. P. XI. I. 6-7, translate as follows: "After charming away the eyes of men with His own form, whose beauty far surpasses all the world's loveliness; and stealing with His words the minds and hearts of those who remember them; and attracting with His holy feet the actions of all those who gaze upon them; and after spreading far and wide a Fame which all praise; certain that now, by this form of His, all will swiftly and surely cross beyond the Darkness, the Lord returned to His own place."

22. This is the most extensive interpolation Viṭṭhala makes on the *Rāsalīlā* section of the *Subodhinī*, and by far the most important. This as well as all Viṭṭhala's other interpolations on the *Subodhinī* are considered by the Vallabha-Sampradāya to be equal in authority with the words of Vallabha himself. Consequently I have translated the interpolation in full.

earthly qualities consistent with the knowledge of Him (since only transcendent knowledge can perceive transcendent qualities)? For (in a relation, in the philosophical sense) only what is a referent can be negated, and here cessation, since it is a form of negation, requires a referent (i.e., an existing flow of the earthly qualities).[23] The king addresses Śuka as "wise one" in order to confirm through Śuka's own experience that knowledge never arises except where pure *sattva* is present. Śuka answers him in the next three stanzas (cf. Stanzas 13-15). Before this, says Śuka, in the Seventh Book of this scripture, we saw such statements as : "the Gopīs (attained Him) through passionate desire, Śiśupāla and the other kings through hatred" (Bh. P. VII. 1. 30). This means the following. Just as Śiśupāla, as well as others, was described as *tāmasa* by reason of his hatred, even though his mind was completely preoccupied with the transcendent Blessed Lord alone, so these Gopīs too, it seems to us, partake of the earthly qualities by reason of their thinking

23. Here Viṭṭhala is explaining the philosophical basis of Parikṣit's suspicion that Śuka's line of reasoning is inconsistent. Śuka, in saying that there was a cessation of the flow of the earthly qualities in these Gopīs, is positing a relation of absence or negation (Skt. *abhāva*) between the flow of the earthly qualities (the "referent" in the relation—Skt. *pratiyogī*) and these Gopīs (the "relatum" in the relation—Skt. *anuyogī*). In order to clarify these terms, perhaps it will be useful to cite one of the classical Indian examples of the negative relation : "There is an absence (relation of negation; *abhāva*) of a pot (referent; *pratiyogī*) on the ground (relatum; *anuyogī*) (Skt. *bhūtale ghaṭo nāsti*). Now the present relation presupposes that its referent—the flow of the earthly qualities—exists in the Gopīs, because the negation of a non-existent referent would be meaningless. Parikṣit's implied point, however—which Viṭṭhala is here bringing to light —is that the flow of the earthly qualities would not have existed in these Gopīs. For if it had, these Gopīs could not be grasping through knowledge the *transcendent* (Skt. *nirguṇa*) qualities of Kṛṣṇa, which Śuka clearly says they are doing. This is because it is an accepted principle that the object of knowledge colors both the act of knowledge and the knower. Therefore, since the object of knowledge (Kṛṣṇa) completely transcends the earthly qualities, so does the act of knowing His transcendent qualities, and so do the knowers themselves, these Gopīs, transcend the earthly qualities. So, for Śuka to speak of a cessation of the flow of the earthly qualities in these Gopīs is inconsistent and indeed meaningless, since these earthly qualities did not exist in them.

of the Lord as their illicit lover, even though their minds are completely preoccupied with Him who is transcendent. And their particular mood of love can be attained only by the surrender that is based on Total Love. For the surrender that is based on Total Love does not exist in the mind that thinks of the Lord as an illicit lover. Because all that is needed for that latter attitude to arise is the desire to fulfil one's passion. And here, since partaking of the earthly qualities is an obstacle, then just as Śiśupāla, as well as others, upon the death of his earthly body in his own particular fashion (i.e., his being killed by the Lord's discus while he thought of the Lord in terms of hatred), attained the Lord's feet in his own particular fashion, so these Gopīs, too, when they die in their own particular fashion, then, since their partaking of the earthly qualities has ceased, they worship Him as their own husband by the surrender based on Total Love alone. In this there is no inconsistency.[24]

24. Viṭṭhala's argumentation runs thus : first of all, these Gopīs have indeed transcended the earthly qualities, since they are contemplating the transcendent qualities of Kṛṣṇa. To reach this transcendent level, their surrender to Kṛṣṇa must be the surrender based on Total Love (*sarvabhāva, sarvātmabhāva*), just as is the case with the Gopīs who have gone out to meet Kṛṣṇa. But it is Kṛṣṇa's will to grace these Gopīs, in addition to their transcendent status based on their surrender in Total Love, with the sentiment of love for Him as their illicit lover (*jāra*)—a sentiment that partakes of the earthly qualities because of its involvement with passion (*kāma*). In the same way, Kṛṣṇa had graced Śiśupāla with implacable hatred of Him (that this was grace is shown by its results : complete preoccupation with Kṛṣṇa and ultimate liberation in Him; and that Śiśupāla had also, in previous lives, worshipped Kṛṣṇa with Total Love was made clear when his history was narrated in Chapter One of Book Seven). The grace of hatred given to Śiśupāla, of course, partook of the earthly qualities, since hatred is born of *tamas*. And just as Śiśupāla got rid of his involvement with this attitude and these earthly qualities only when his earthly body was killed by Kṛṣṇa, so these Gopīs will stop concentrating on Kṛṣṇa as their illicit lover only upon the departure of their bodies, with their earthly qualities. At that point, these Gopīs' surrender based on Total Love will be all that remains, and so they will achieve the reward proper to that surrender—the love-worship of Kṛṣṇa as their own husband in the Vaikuṇṭha Heaven. And so, by Kṛṣṇa's grace, they die here and go to that reward, while the other Gopīs, who have the surrender based on Total Love without the earthbound attitude of Kṛṣṇa as illicit lover, take part in the love-worship of Kṛṣṇa here on earth.

And if this were not the case, then the scriptural promise which the Lord Himself has made : "In just the same way as they surrender themselves to Me, so do I love them in return" (*Bhagavad-Gītā* IV. 11), would be broken. It is with this in mind that Śuka has said : "I described to you earlier how Śiśupāla accomplished the ultimate goal" (Stanza 13). King Parikṣit might object : "Nonetheless, how could the reward that is attained only by surrender in Total Love be granted merely on the basis of Śiśupāla's or these Gopīs' kinds of surrender ?" To this Śuka answers : "even though he hated Hṛṣīkeśa." Here is what Śuka means. Śiśupāla had no desire for the happiness of ultimate freedom—in fact he did something precisely contradictory to it : he indulged in hatred. And just as Kṛṣṇa granted him the kind of ultimate freedom that is scarcely ever attained even by sages, so did He grant these Gopīs that type of reward, on the basis of their kind of surrender. By saying this Śuka is indicating that, just as there is a difference between ultimate freedom and hatred, so is there a difference between worship of Kṛṣṇa which is subordinate to something else (here, the very idea of having an illicit lover) and the particular mood of love which these Gopīs possessed.

But you may raise the following objections : "But since Gokula was accepted as entirely suitable for the Blessed Lord's games, in that it transcended entirely the three qualities of existence, how is it that these Gopīs are said to partake of these qualities ? And furthermore, if the Blessed Lord wishes to give, later on, the reward that is attainable only by Total Love, then why didn't He produce this same Love in these Gopīs now—beforehand ?" To this we answer : in order to indicate that even the bodies of all those Gopīs who were to enjoy union with the Blessed Lord visibly and physically manifest, and who were to adorn the circle of the Rāsa-dance, transcended the earthly qualities completely, the Blessed Lord Himself caused the bodies of a certain number of Gopīs to be made of the three qualities. And to indicate that the love, too, of the Gopīs who went to Him transcended the three qualities, the Lord produced in the Gopīs who stayed at home a love that partook of the qualities. And to show that He Himself is also the only one who can bring to an end this type of earthly love for Him, He Himself terminates it (by appearing to these Gopīs in meditation, and so forth). And finally, to make it clear that the joy of union with Him and the sorrow of separation from Him which those Gopīs will later experience are not the results of their past actions, the Lord causes these Gopīs to attain Him precisely by destroying the bonds of all their actions. And my boast is that it is my own Lord who has done all this ! Since Kṛṣṇa has here accepted these Gopīs onto the Path of Grace, all arguments as to impropriety from the viewpoint of the Path of Limitations stand refuted simply because they are out of context. Therefore our entire argument is valid. The reason why Śuka has also said : "they abandoned the body which is made up of the three qualities" (Stanza 11), is that he intends to tell us later that these Gopīs obtained bodies which transcend the three qualities. But he has explicitly spoken here merely of the abandonment of their earthly bodies, and not of their attainment of transcendent bodies, because he wants to save that matter for a point later in the story.[25] Otherwise there would be no point to his specifying "the body which is made up of the three qualities," rather than simply "the body."

"But how can we be sure," someone may object, "that Kṛṣṇa did this merely to indicate what you have just said, since we have no supporting argument for that?" Śuka gives his argument in the passage that begins : "It was for the ultimate happiness of all people..." (Stanza 14). The meaning is as follows. In Kṛṣṇa's game and among the devotees who are involved in it, and all the more among the Gopīs who take part in these Rāsa-games, the mind which views these matters as ordinary is tantamount to a mentality which accuses them of fault. Rather, it is ordinariness itself which becomes a fault when it is applied to the Gopīs, in whom the ordinary, earthly qualities do not exist; and the logical extreme of this would be that even the Blessed Lord Himself, and His games as well, would partake of the ordinary earthly qualities ! If this were so, the Lord's game would be nothing but an obstacle to ultimate freedom, not a cause of it. If the above objection were

25. For example, when Parikṣit's (and the reader's) level of eligibility (Skt. *adhikāra*) will be high enough for him to understand this.

true, the Lord's purpose in coming down to earth would be contradicted. So we have spoken in this way because of the impossibility of explaining the Lord's actions in any other way. And we, in our turn, should conclude that this (the above explanation) alone was the purpose of the Lord's bringing these things to light in the way He did. But my explanation (as opposed to my above contextualization) of Stanza 14 is the same as Vallabhācārya's.

"But," the objector persists, "the conclusion that the above-mentioned fault (i.e., that it was an obstacle to liberation) is present in the game which the Lord has played up until now, with the Gopīs who partake of the earthly qualities, is inescapable." Śuka answers this objection by stating the Lord's purpose in playing the previously described game (i.e., the game with the Gopīs who stayed at home) when he says : "Those who direct constantly to Hari either their passionate desire or their anger..." (Stanza 15). For the words : "Those who direct constantly...come to have Him as their very Self" are said with universal application (to all Kṛṣṇa's games of all kinds), and not solely with reference to the cowherds' wives. It is for that very reason that anger, etc., are also mentioned. Otherwise, since these other attitudes would be out of context here, it would have been pointless to mention them. And in the same vein, the reason I said above that Śuka is here explaining the purpose of Kṛṣṇa's playing this first game was to indicate that, even when someone worships Kṛṣṇa with an attitude affected by the worldly qualities, the Blessed Lord grants that worshipper a reward that accords with His nature, not the world's nature. If this were not true, then, since all other people would know that only those on the topmost heights of spiritual eligibility attain the Blessed Lord, ultimate freedom would be lost as a goal of human striving, since ordinary people would not apply themselves to it. And as a consequence, the scriptures would have no *raison d'etre*, since those who are advanced in spiritual matters apply themselves of their own accord. But neither Kṛṣṇa Himself (Skt. *svarūpa*) nor His Games ever partake of the worldly qualities, because they bring about transcendence of the qualities even in those objects of His games which did partake of the worldly qualities. For the medicine which removes an ailment does not contract that ailment when it is applied to the sick person. If it did, it couldn't cure the ailment. If the rule of sameness of kind applied between Kṛṣṇa's game and its object, then His constraint of both kinds of devotee—those with worldly qualities and those who have transcended them—by means of any single game such as the flute-playing game, would be improper. We should realize that the mention of anger and the others is also meant to indicate the inferiority of that attachment, too, which is conditioned by passion, just as the attitudes of anger, etc., are inferior. And Śuka's words : "(they) come to have Him as their very Self" mean exactly that they attain transcendence.

"But," King Parikṣit might say, "when these Gopīs actually came into physical contact with the Blessed Lord Himself, how could the very nature of the thing possibly allow the continuation of their partaking of the earthly qualities ? It would be as if a piece of cotton were thrown into a fire, but still remained cotton ! This is amazing indeed. And that women who were attached to Him with a mere worldly passion could make love with the Transcendent One is a second cause for amazement. What's more, that people whose attitude to Him was one of anger or fear and so on did not experience the reward of their attitudes, but attained the Blessed Lord instead, is a third source of perplexity. Further, that these people experienced the same reward as those who love Him also astonishes me. Besides, these Gopīs loved the boy who was Yaśodā's son, and the fact that they attained him by meditation—in their homes—when he was off somewhere in the forest, is still another baffler. And isn't it bewildering that, when they attained Him in meditation, they obtained bodies which transcend the worldly qualities, when they were entirely without means for attaining such bodies ? And my seventh and last cause for amazement is : experience of the game the Lord will soon play is limited to those who have Total Love for Him; then how can it possibly be that those who do not have Total Love for Him can experience His other games ?" Realizing that the king is utterly perplexed by the occurrence of so many amazing things, Śuka refutes each of his doubts in order by enumerating the reasons why the people who had these different attitudes toward

Him attained the Blessed Lord, in the stanza which begins : "You should not be so amazed..." (Stanza 16).

To remove the king's first source of amazement, Śuka says simply : "You." The meaning is as follows. First of all, the Lord protected "you", while you were still in the womb, from even Brahmā's arrow, against which there is no defense—because this was His purpose. But now "you" yourself are experiencing that it is not His purpose to protect you from the curse uttered by the sage's child (cf. Bh. P. I. 18). So far as this goes, there is surely no meanness in 'the very nature of the thing'. All His Powers (such as Protection) are dependent on His Power of Will, for that Power is greater than all the others. For it is not correct to say that fire's power to burn has left it simply because a fire is not burning when its burning is being prevented by a sacred spell. In the matter under discussion, too, "you", instead of being "amazed", should realize that the Blessed Lord acted as He did in order to fulfil the purposes explained above by us in the passage that began : "To this we answer..." Śuka is saying in other words that someone else, who has not directly experienced the Lord's majesty and power, might be amazed at this, but "you" should not be.

Śuka refutes the king's second, third and fourth perplexities with the words : "(amazed at) the Blessed Lord." For, as these words tell us, Kṛṣṇa is the powerful Lord who is the Supreme Enjoyer of all moods, as holy scripture tells us in the passage : "(He...possessing all works, possessing all desires, possessing all odors,) possessing all moods..." (*Chānd. Upan.* III. 14.2)[26]. For the mood of passion can be experienced most

26. Skt. *sarvarasaḥ*. This adjectival compound is interpreted by Vallabha's tradition as having a double meaning : Kṛṣṇa "possesses all moods" in two senses. The first is : "in whom are all moods" (*sarve rasāḥ yasmin*), and the second : "from whom are all moods (bestowed or received)"—*sarve rasāḥ yasmāt*. There can be no doubt, from both the immediate context and from the system in general of Vallabha, Viṭṭhala and their followers (and, almost certainly, from the viewpoint of the Bhāgavata Purāṇa itself) that *rasa* is meant here to be taken as "mood," in the sense taught by Bharata in his *Nāṭyaśāstra* and elaborated by the long tradition of Sanskrit aesthetics (*alaṅkāraśāstra*). I must aver, however, that I am not convinced that the word *rasa* carried this elaborated connotation in the earlier Upaniṣads, which antedate the explicitation of these

strongly with women who are more inclined to illicit love. For this is exactly what the treatises on erotics have taught. And so this action of His should not cause you to be amazed at the One who possesses Lordly Power (Skt. *aiśvarya*). Similarly, because of the extreme fierceness of the Blessed Lord's heroic Strength (Skt. *vīrya*), which accomplishes what is impossible to accomplish by other means, Hari is able to wipe out completely, with His heroic Strength, even that anger and those other, similar faults which other warriors have found impossible to defeat. So you have no reason to be amazed on that score. And the Blessed Lord's Fame (*yaśas*, alternatively *kīrti*) is unique and extraordinary, so it comes into play when there is an extraordinary action. If He were to grant ultimate liberation only to those who love Him, and not to those who hate Him, then since this attribute would be one common to others as well, His Fame would not be unique. But when He grants even to those who fear Him, hate Him and so forth, the same reward He grants to those who love Him, then surely the extraordinary nature of such an act makes His Fame absolutely unique. And in the same vein, no amazement should be

theories by so many centuries. From an admittedly cursory glance at the usages of the word *rasa* in the Upaniṣads, I find three major meanings : *rasa* is used frequently in the sense of "a liquid or fluid"; next, *rasa* in the sense of "taste", the proper object of the sense faculty of taste; and finally, *rasa* in the sense of "essence" or "pith". It is the second sense of *rasa* that I think is more probably meant in the present quote from the Chāndogya Upaniṣad, especially since its occurrence comes immediately after the word *sarvagandhaḥ*, "possessing all odors." And it is the third sense of *rasa*, as "essence," which I think is meant, rather than "mood", in such passages as Chānd. Up. I. 1.2 & 3, and Taittirīya Upan. II. 2.1 and II. 7.1. In the latter occurrence—the famous saying *raso vai saḥ*, a passage crucial for Vallabha's system—I think the meaning : "The essence (of all existence—*tat sukṛtam sat*) surely is He" is more probable than : "Mood indeed is He." But I do not exclude the possibility of the latter meaning being contained in embryo, in this as well as the passage Viṭṭhala has quoted above. This is the position which Shri Shyam Goswamy, a learned representative of the Vallabha tradition, takes. And certainly Vallabha and Viṭṭhala have firmer ground to stand on than my doubts, namely the Bhāgavata, which they firmly believe—in a way common with but superior to all the other Purāṇas, which are also believed to have this function—has as its role "the confirmation and strengthening of the Vedas" (*śrutyupabṛṁhaṇatvam*).

expressed at the fact that in Hari, of whose nature such Fame is a part, the attributes that clearly reveal the existence of such Fame are also completely natural. And His Splendor (Skt. *śrī* —the Blessed Lord's fourth great quality) is Lakṣmī. She has such great love for Him that, even though She has attained a permanent dwelling-place on His chest, She craves only the dust of His feet so that, whenever He comes down to earth, She comes down after Him.[27] And Hari, since Lakṣmī has such love for Him at all times, is well aware of the mood of love. Thus He rightly bestows the gift of Himself on those who have this love. The "striving to become one with Him" (Stanza 15) occurs on the Path of Knowledge. And since Hari possesses Knowledge (Skt. *jñāna*), it is likewise right to grant the reward of unity to them. "Friendship" (Stanza 15) with Him exists when there is real intimacy. And this occurs when the interests, habits, and even the addictions of the two are the same. The Blessed Lord Himself has said such things as : "I do not desire Myself or even the infinite Śrī, O brahman, apart from My beloved, perfect devotees, whose Supreme Refuge I am. Those beloved, perfect ones are My heart, and I am theirs as well. They know nothing else but Me, and I know not even the least thing but them" (Bh. P. IX. 4. 64). As the Blessed Lord is devoid of love (Skt. *rāga*) for anyone or anything but His devotees, and He loves His devotees alone, He possesses the quality of Detachment (Skt. *vairāgya*). And His devotees display the same quality in loving no one and nothing but the Blessed Lord. Thus Kṛṣṇa grants friendship to those who are suited to be His friends. And since they possess the same Detachment mentioned above, the Lord's acting in this way with them is perfectly right.

It is in order to remove Parikṣit's fifth bewilderment, expressed above in the sentence that began : "Besides, these Gopīs loved the boy who was Yaśodā's son...", that Śuka has said : "(You should not be so amazed at) the Unborn." There would be room for doubt in this matter if the Blessed Lord

27. Cf. infra, X. 29. 37, X.31.1 (i.e., Chapter I, stanza 37, and Chapter III, stanza 1), and Vallabha's commentary on both stanzas, for further elaboration of these ideas.

had been born, like an ordinary person, in some particular place (Yaśodā's womb). Then, if He were present somewhere else—outside—how could He have come here—into these Gopīs' hearts ? He would either be present there—outside—or not. But there is no room for doubt, because there was no birth. Just as, by His Will, He ripped away the curtain of Māyā and manifested Himself in Yaśodā's house, so He manifested Himself in the forest, and so also in the hearts of these Gopīs. Therefore there is no reason to be amazed at "the Unborn."

In order to remove the grounds for the king's sixth puzzlement, Śuka says : "Who is Lord even of the greatest Yogīs." For Yogīs, on the strength of their Yoga, create all at once, in the twinkling of an eye, many bodies for their own enjoyment. And Yoga is an adventitious attribute of theirs. And the Blessed Lord, who is both the Creator of such an attribute in them and the Giver of its reward, so that He is "the Lord even of them"—that He, whose very Nature has countless and limitless powers, should do no more than create transcendent bodies for these Gopīs—this should be no cause for puzzlement.

And to remove Parikṣit's last source of amazement, Śuka says merely : "Kṛṣṇa." From the famous saying which analyzes His name : "*Kṛṣ* has been explained as expressing 'Being', and *ṇa* as expressing 'Joy'",[28] we know that Kṛṣṇa is the Blessed Lord whose very Form is Being and Joy, and who possesses the fulness of perfect (i.e., transcendent) qualities. From this it is certain that, because of the defectiveness of anything considered in itself—apart from Kṛṣṇa—there is surely defectiveness in a person who looks upon such a faulty thing as the cause of his well-being. And Śuka's meaning is that since the game the Lord will play, which will embody the Joy of His very Form, will be

28. I can't trace the source of this śloka, which is used frequently by Vallabha's followers—nor could Kedarnath Mishra trace it in his edition of Lālūbhaṭṭa's *Prameyaratnārṇava*, p. 48. The full form of the śloka runs as follows: *kṛṣir bhūvācakaḥ prokto, ṇaśca nirvṛtivācakaḥ | tayor aikyam param brahma kṛṣṇa ityabhidhīyate ||*. Shri Shyam Goswamy suggests the śloka is to be found either in the Kṛṣṇa Upaniṣad or the Gopālatāpanīya Upaniṣad.

of such a nature (that those whose knowledge is defective will see only the things in themselves—apart from Kṛṣṇa), there is no reason for you to be amazed that those who do not possess Total Love for Him (by which they would see Him in everything) are not fit to experience this game.

Besides, these Gopīs were using as a means the love which was described earlier. But even Gokula, though it was completely devoid of means, as Brahmā pointed out when he said : "But Gokula went about its business by day, and slept by night" (Bh. p. II. 7. 31), still at each and every moment Gokula dwelt in and was absorbed in His Form. But the Blessed Lord separated out Gokula again and again (from its unconscious absorption in Him), in order for it to experience the mood of the successive games that He was playing, and He caused Gokula to experience that inconceivable, boundless Power of His.[29] Śuka intends to point out that this was no exceptional miracle when He says : "For through Him this world (of Vraja) attains freedom." Śuka has said the word "this" here and now because he is not thinking of any other game, as Vallabhācārya noted when he commented thus on this passage : "(Śuka has said these things) through imagining meditatively that he was in Gokula at this time." And Śuka has used the present tense in the verb "attains freedom" because he is experiencing this game and no other. Therefore this explanation is quite acceptable.

But someone might raise a doubt as to whether it would not be better to say precisely the opposite. "For", he would say, "look at it this way. Even these Gopīs are in no way really different from the Gopīs described before them. Therefore when Śuka

29. "That inconceivable, boundless Power of His" must refer, it seems to me, to Kṛṣṇa's Power of Māyā, particularly the special *vaiṣṇavī māyā* by which He normally kept Gokula under the delusion that He was an ordinary boy, and returned it to that normal delusion after He had displayed some aspect of His real nature to some inhabitants of Gokula. For an excellent explanation of this *vaiṣṇavī māyā* , cf. *Prameyaratnārṇava*, pp. 166-67 in Mishra's edition. The reference here may, however, be to Kṛṣṇa's Power in general. This present passage of Viṭṭhala's describes the process by which even those who did not possess Total Love for Kṛṣṇa nevertheless experienced other games of His than the upcoming Rāsa-game. Thus it solves Parikṣit's last puzzlement.

told us (in Stanza 8) that those Gopīs didn't turn back even when their husbands commanded them to—something the world would consider utterly impossible—then how is it right that these Gopīs did stay back? In order to squelch this doubt Śuka said: "Some Gopīs stayed in their houses because they were unable to leave" (Stanza 9). His meaning is as follows. In the case of the first Gopīs, the prohibition was merely verbal. Since that was the case, their obeying the prohibition would consist in their own act of turning back. But that action was far from possible for certain of their counterparts, because these latter Gopīs, since they were forcibly prevented by the actions of their husbands, brothers, and so forth, abandoned the bodies which were being obstructed by their men, and attained union with the Blessed Lord! And likewise those Gopīs who were first described were of this same type, and so their not turning back was proper. And besides, since the word *tad* ("them") in the phrase *tadbhāvanāyuktā* ("these Gopīs, at one with the meditative imagining of them")[30] always refers to a word mentioned previously, and because the love (*bhāva*) of the first-mentioned Gopīs has also been expressed above, it should be concluded that the love, too, of those Gopīs is of the same kind as the love of these presently-described Gopīs. By this the fact that all the qualities present in these Gopīs are present in those Gopīs is also proved. But liberation was granted to these Gopīs alone, and that was not possible without their being prevented. For thus has Śuka described the situation. But it was not so with those Gopīs (i.e., those Gopīs were not to be liberated), and so they are not described as being prevented."

Ah, how hardened and inveterate is your stupidity, since you think you have a treasury full of doubts! Because of this your mind has gone haywire from the wounds sustained in your headlong plunge into a chasm of the mountain called "association with the wicked" and "distraction to external things," which has left you without eyes to see, so that you do not even examine what another has said! For here is how things are. Concerning

30. The objector here interprets quite differently the phrase of Stanza 9 which I, and, I think, Śuka and Vallabha, intend to mean: "by picturing Him (*tad*) to themselves."

this Story of Kṛṣna, which has come down to earth precisely to allay such doubts, and concerning its purpose as just interpreted by you, we ask you the following question. Was this story merely fabricated for the sake of the purpose you give to it, or is it recounting something which truly happened ? And if you claim this last doubt you expressed is true, then on that matter, too, we ask you : What was the cause of these Gopīs' being prevented from going to Kṛṣṇa ? And if you answer that even these Gopis, who are His very own loved ones, were prevented from going by Hari Himself, in order to make it known that those other Gopīs partook of the worldly qualities, we say : "Shame on you for thinking that way, and we can't understand why your heart doesn't burst into a hundred pieces !" For even that faith which is directed towards worship on the Path of Devotion according to Scriptural Limitations transcends the worldly qualities. And here you come saying that these Gopīs, who have had bodily contact with the Blessed Lord physically manifest, partake of the worldly qualities ! Besides, it is the Lord who has said such things as : "These women, with their minds on Me, with Me as their very lifebreath, have renounced all bodily things for My sake..." (*Bh. P.* X.46.4). And Uddhava has expressed sentiments such as the one which begins : "But these women, who have bodies..." (*Bh. P.* X. 47. 58). So that even he who was praised by the Blessed Lord with words like: "Uddhava is not even an atom lesser than I" (*Bh. P.* III. 4.31) has sung the praises of the Gopīs after praying for the dust of their feet ! Where is there room for the slightest trace of doubt in this ?

And if you persist in objecting by saying that Śuka has spoken the way he has because those Gopīs' love was conditioned by worldly passion, I say : "No !" For, if the Gopīs' love were of that type, then their saying : " (we) who have renounced all things (—"objects"; Skt. *viṣaya*) completely" (Chap. 29, Stanza 31) would be unsupported, because they would have thought of the Blessed Lord, too, as a sex-object, and would have come to Him for that object alone. Neither can it be said that the Gopīs are repeating, in that passage, the fact which Kṛṣṇa already knew – that they had abandoned all objects except Him—in order to convey that the Blessed Lord was their lone object.

For assigning that meaning to those words would contradict what they say in the words immediately following the ones just quoted : "and have attained Your feet." For women filled with passion do not speak like that—only loving devotees do !

What's more, the reason the Gopīs performed rituals to protect Kṛṣṇa just after He had drunk and drained the milk out of Pūtanā, even though He was still a little baby, is given by Śuka when he says : "Thus did the Gopīs, bound firmly to Him by love, protect Him" (*Bh. P.* X. 6. 30). For it is impossible that a love conditioned by passion would express itself on a little baby. Nor would it be possible for passionate women to do without (literally, "abandon") collyrium and the other cosmetics (cf. Chap. 29, Stanza 7). Rather, they would have decorated themselves with collyrium and everything else and come to him, just like Kaṁsa's hump-backed female slave, Trivakra (cf. *Bh. P.* X. 42. 1-12). For the love-making that occurred after that was no more or less than His gift of the Joy of His own Form (i.e., of Himself) after the manner of the mood of love, for His own Form has the moods as its very Essence, as holy scripture tells us in the words : "Mood indeed is He" (*Taitt. Upan.* II .7. 1). And from these words of the Blessed Lord : "The happiness that arises from the Self is *sāttvika*, that which arises from sensual objects *rājasa*, that which comes from delusion and wretchedness is *tāmasa*, and the happiness that has Me as its refuge is transcendent" (*Bh. P.* XI. 25. 29), we know that the happiness which is associated with the Blessed Lord most certainly transcends the worldly qualities (end of Viṭṭhala's interpolation).

Introduction to Stanza 17 : Having thus removed all King Parikṣit's doubts in this regard, Śuka resumed the narration by saying :

Stanza 17 : The Blessed Lord saw that the young women of Vraja had come into His presence, and He, the very best of speakers, spoke to them, confusing them with clever figures of speech.

Commentary : Those women who had been specifically invited by the Lord came, and He does not send them back. But some women came who were still affected by the qualities of material existence, and were married to another man. They had come simply because they had heard the sound of His flute, and so by the sound of His words He had to send them back. Since they were still subject to someone other than the Lord, they were not fit to worship the Lord through love. This game of the Lord's which was about to begin requires of its participants that complete surrender to the Lord which is characterized by Total Love of Him. And so the Lord made an effort to send these other women back. He saw that these women, the ones who "had been milking" and so forth, as noted earlier, were coming to Him, and He realized that they were coming for the sake of themselves alone. For the Blessed Lord knows everything and can do everything as well. But the maidens of Vraja, who were very sincere and belonged to Him alone, were also in this group, and the Lord saw that they were free of all impropriety, and was aware of this as He spoke. And so He said what He is about to say in order to remind them all of their obligations. Now it might be objected that, since these women had already been forbidden to go to Kṛṣṇa and yet had gone, they would not be turned back simply by this speech, and so the Lord's speaking would be wasted effort. To this Śuka replies ; "He, the very best of speakers." Of all those who speak, the Lord is the best. Therefore His speech must be understood in the heart. Therefore any women who go back because of this speech are precisely the ones who are not fit to participate in the action of this game. And besides, Śuka expresses the fact that the Lord has an extraordinary ability to send them back when he says ; "confusing them with clever figures of speech." "Clever figures of speech" are words joined in an especially charming way; with these He causes great confusion. Or perhaps the Lord spoke words of prohibition to confuse the women completely and to make their resolution to stay all the firmer : otherwise they would have gone. And so, while on the surface He orders them to go away, the deeper sense of His words is that He is not ordering them away at all.

Introduction to Stanza 18 : Śuka now narrates to us how the Blessed Lord, in the next ten stanzas, tells the ten different types of Gopī to go back to their homes :

Stanza 18 : The Blessed Lord said : "Welcome, O most fortunate of women ! Is there any favor I can do for you ? Is all well in Vraja ? Please tell me why you have come."

Verse : The women are described as having differences based on the three qualities, *tamas*, *rajas*, and *sattva*, and consequent differences in the final effects stemming from those qualities. The Lord therefore directs His words to them in exact accord with these ten differences.

Commentary : The Lord first sends back the *sāttvikatāmasa* Gopīs. Next He sends back those who are *rājasatāmasa*, and finally, the *tāmasatāmasa* Gopīs. These distinctions among the Gopīs He speaks to must be kept in mind in what follows. According to the wordly convention, the Lord first said "Welcome" to the Gopīs who had come. This is an inquiry after a person's welfare, as if the Lord were to say : "Did all of you get here safely and easily?" He also flatters them by saying : "O most fortunate of women !" You are ladies of great good fortune, and so your coming must have been safe and easy—and yet He inquires about it, since this is the way people ordinarily speak in such circumstances. Actually the women did come to the presence of the Blessed Lord unimpeded—free of obstacles. The Lord offers His services to the Gopīs who have come by saying : "Is there any favor I can do for you?" He was aware that they might have come to ask something of Him, and, if that was the case, they had only to say what it was. What is indicated by the word "favor" is that the Lord thought : "Actually they have not found me favorable naturally, but because they want something from me." The Gopīs' motive for asking a favor is of three kinds : to attain something they desire, to avert something undesired, or to acquire something they long for, but is impossible for them to get here and now. The Lord's words, too, reflect this threefold division, since He directs His words to the three possibilities involved. Since you have come running to me, has some disaster occurred in Vraja, which you come to tell me about ? And if you say you have not come for the first reason I have mentioned, then tell me for which of the others it was. If, first of all, you wanted no favor of me (i.e., an attainment of something desired), and secondly, nothing evil has happend in Vraja (i.e., for the prevention of something undesired), then thirdly : "Please tell me why you have come."

Introduction to Stanza 19 : When the Gopīs give Him no answer, the Lord tries another approach. Since He realizes that they may be thinking " Because You came out here, so did we," He says :

Stanza 19 : "Dreadful is this dark night, and dreadful the creatures that wander during it. Go back to Vraja. Women must not stay here, O lovely ones."

Commentary : This was the night, not the daytime. And the Lord's meaning is that, while it is quite all right to go to the forest to do something in the daytime, this is the moon that is shining now, not the sun. If one of them objects that, although it is night, we should still come, since there is plenty of light, the Lord answers her by saying : "Dreadful..." Indeed, even when the night has some light it is still "dreadful." i.e., frightening. Even a man who goes out on a bright night is afraid. Besides, "Dreadful are the creatures that wander during it." It is the dreadful and dangerous creatures that haunt the night, not the harmless ones. And so, when a harmless creature goes out during the night it is killed by the dreadful ones. Therefore, since you women know the nature of the night and the nature and habits of the creatures which are associated with it, go back. Then, since the Gopīs might say that, even though this is the case, we will stay close to you, because you are familiar to us, the Lord said. "Women must not stay here." For I am a man, and it is night, so women should not stay here with me. If you were to stay here something might happen that both of us would be sorry for. If you were old women or children, then you could stay. But you are "lovely", i.e., the very embodiments of the mood of love. Therefore, since the tendency to mistake the body for the real Self exists so strongly, you must go at all costs. The Lord speaks so cleverly here that the word "not" may be construed with the verb "stay" or with the verb "go back." And so His words might be taken to mean : "Do not go back to Vraja. Women must stay here !" Likewise in the two usages of "dreadful," so that the word "not" may be construed before each one. And so He would be saying : "This dark night is not dreadful; harmless also are the creatures that wander during it."[31]

Introduction to Stanza 20 : Then the Lord perceived that they might object with words like : "But we are your mistresses, and have come here only in order to meet you. Why are you sending us away"? And he answered them :

Stanza 20 : "Your mothers and fathers, your sons, brothers and husbands are all searching for you, since they cannot find you anywhere. Do not create such panic among your relatives !"

Commentary : Your mothers are the ones who have charge of you, but they have not come here. Therefore they will be searching for you. So do not create a situation of fear and panic for them. And if you say that they will not come looking for you at night because they are women, then certainly your fathers will. For your fathers will be worried about their family's good name being stained, and they will come here. But lest the women think that they should go back with their fathers when they arrive, Kṛṣṇa says : "they are all searching for you, since they cannot find you anywhere." For many other paths intervene between the ones leading out of Gokula and the one leading to the place where Kṛṣṇa is, and the Blessed Lord's power of Māyā situates herself on those paths, making sure that no one reaches the Blessed Lord's presence. And so, the fathers take some other path, and, still not seeing their daughters, they keep searching. By saying this the Lord also removes the Gopīs' suspicions that the place might be found. And He also says that there is "panic among

31. These ambiguities stem from the flexibility of Sanskrit euphony and word order. The phrase *rajanyeṣā ghorarūpā ghorasattvaniṣevitā* ("Dreadful is this dark night, and dreadful the creatures that wander during it") might be heard by the Gopīs as *rajanyeṣā aghorarūpā aghorasattvaniṣevitā* ("This dark night is not dreadful; harmless also are the creatures that wander during it"). And in the other example, the Gopīs might mistake the referent of the negative particle *na* in the phrase *pratiyāta vrajaṁ na-iha stheyam* by construing *na* with *pratiyāta* ("Do not go back to Vraja. Women must stay here !") rather than with *stheyam* ("Go back to Vraja ! Women must *not* stay here.").

your relatives." Then the Gopīs begin thinking that this is precisely why all the other Gopīs did not come here, and we shouldn't have come, either. And they begin to fear that their family's name will be disgraced. And, lest the Gopīs console themselves by thinking that their fathers know the way a woman thinks, and so they will not come, or they will realize that we have gone to see the Blessed Lord, Kṛṣṇa says : "your sons (will come)". For sons are all very protective of their mothers, and because of their love they are very ashamed when their mother is in any danger. And so they will certainly come here to make sure their mothers are safe. Then the Lord, realizing that the Gopīs would say that, after all, their sons are only children, says : "your brothers." For their brothers are old enough and quite able to make a thorough search, and they, too, possess a sense of shame. In fact, some of them may even die of shame when they see that you are nowhere to be found. Therefore you should go back because of the love of your brothers. Lest the Gopīs object that their brothers will not come searching for them out of fear of disgrace, for the brothers are young, and so are the Gopīs, Kṛṣṇa says: "your husbands." For husbands expect their sexual enjoyment, and this particular mood of love belongs to them alone, which is why people say that one person's wealth should not be given to another. Therefore the fulfilment of your sexual enjoyment should be with them alone. And so when they do not see you in the house or anywhere else, they will all certainly start searching. And after spending a long time without finding you, they will be afraid that you have died or been kidnapped. Lest the Gopīs say : "Why should we be concerned with them ?", Kṛṣṇa says: "panic among your relatives." For they are your relatives, and you should stay with them. And so, since your coming here has caused so much trouble, you should turn around and go back.

Introduction to Stanza 21 : After He has said this, the Lord notices that the Gopīs are looking around in every direction, and He says :

Stanza 21 : "You have seen this grove, in full flower, brightened by the rays of the full moon, and made even more lovely by the rustling of the leaves in the playful breeze that comes from the Yamunā."

Commentary : In this stanza the Lord addresses the *rājasa-rājasa* Gopīs; and in the next stanza He speaks to those who are *tāmasa-rājasa*. If you came out here to see the grove—well, now that you've seen it, you should go back. The Lord's deeper meaning is that now that the Gopīs have seen the grove in its entirety, they have also seen that there is nothing to fear in it, and therefore they should not go home. From His words the Gopīs can derive the message that they should go home only if they really need to. The Lord describes the grove as "in full flower" in order to arouse in the Gopīs a passionate attachment for others. His words also underline the fact that at this time only the flowers have bloomed—the fruits have not yet appeared. He means that the delight of love should take place in a forest that is in full flower. The Lord uses the very same words, inextricably bound together, both to confuse the Gopīs completely and to send them away from Him. In addition, the Lord says that the grove is "brightened" (literally "reddened") "by the rays of the full moon." These words arouse the mood of love. The grove is *tāmasa*, the flowers are *rājasa*, and the moon's rays are *sāttvika*. The word the Lord uses (*rākeśa*) indicates "the full moon". Where there is fulness, there must one stay. But anyone who is concerned with parts, phases and fractions should leave. The Lord then describes the wind in the grove when He says : "made even more lovely..." He means : "made lovely by the leaves which stir and tremble because of the playful breeze that comes from the Yamunā." This wind is said to have three qualities : a lovely fragrance, since it moves through the trees, playful movement, and coolness, since it comes from the water. Thus the wind is useful both for creating a beautiful description and for awakening the mood of love.

Introduction to Stanza 22 : After He has described the grove in this way and aroused in the Gopīs passionate attachment for others, the Lord tells them, in the present stanza, that they should go :

Stanza 22 : "So do not linger here, but go back to the cow-pens. And, faithful wives, be obedient to your husbands. Your children and the calves are bawling. Give the children your milk and milk the cows."

Commentary : Since you have fulfilled your purpose by seeing the forest, go back. But the suggested meaning is : "you have seen how beautiful this grove is. Do not go back." The words "do not linger here" mean that they should not stay any longer. But they may also be construed : "Linger—do not go for a while." For no one leaves the Blessed Lord and goes back to cowpens ! Besides, the Lord says "go back to the cowpens" because there lies the Gopīs' duty—to attend to the cows. Moreover, when the Lord says : "be obedient", He expresses the fact that those who go back to the cowpens will be fulfilling their duties. A woman's rule of life is to serve her husband, and in doing that you will indeed be "faithful wives." Or, the words "faithful wives" may be meant to modify the word "husbands." For in a previous life your husbands were your own faithful wives, and because they imagined themselves (at the time of death) as men they were reborn as men, whereas you were their husbands and have now become their wives. So you should consider the fact that this reversal can occur again in the future, and return to them. Your bounden duty is there, but the mood of love is here. By using the plural when He says "husbands", the Lord implies that the women should stay, for it would clearly be wrong for a woman to have "husbands" to go back to. Or, He implies, those of you who are "faithful wives" should go back. But, since none of you fit that description, you should not go back. For the faithful wives do not come here in the first place, since they are completely wrapped up in their worldly duties. Therefore the Blessed Lord's words, because they are full of the mood of love, indicate to the Gopīs an absence of concern on His part that they go back and fulfil their worldly duties.

Moreover, the calves are tied up, the children are hungry, and both are bawling. Therefore, to stop their crying you should feed the children with your own milk, and milk the cows. For you women live for the sake of others, not for yourself. But, the Lord implies, those who are seeking happiness should not go to a place where there is suffering.

Introduction to Stanza 23 : When the Gopīs' eyes became moist with tears of love at what He was telling them, the Lord responded to their tears by saying :

Stanza 23 : "Or, if you have come here because your hearts are compelled by intense love for me, that is only right. For all beings love me."

Commentary: I have invented all these arguments in vain, for you have really come for one purpose alone—to see me—because of your love. This idea, which is really the Lord's conviction, is presented sophistically, for the sake of continued argument. Because, if a person's hidden intention, whether good or bad, is spoken right out, the result is banal rather than artful. And so the Lord presents it as if it were a sophism. Those women who have intense love for me, and who make their love total and exclusive, so that their hearts are compelled by that Total Love—if you have come here because you are that kind of woman, then that is fitting and right. Lest the Gopīs object : "If this is so, then why are you delaying ?", the Lord says : "all beings love me." All beings are closely related to me, and they naturally, spontaneously love me. I need not do anything. For there is only love in me—not action. And so, now that you have understood this general, surface meaning of my words, go back to Vraja.

But it is also clear that the meaning of the Lord's words actually favors the Gopīs' staying. And so, in the stanza before this, the meaning "Linger—do not go for a while" proves to be the fruitful one, rather than the meaning "So do not linger here, but go back." For someone who has come out of love will not go back even if she is sent away. "Compelled" here means "controlled." When someone's heart is completely dependent on another, then no part of her is free from this dependence. And love must be exercised without deceit by both the Lord and the creature. This is the meaning.

Stanza 24 (no "Introduction" is given): "The highest rule of life for a woman is to serve her husband without any deceit, and, good women, to serve his relatives, and to nourish and maintain his children."

Commentary: Now that He has described the Gopīs in whom the quality of *rajas* is dominant, the Lord turns to those in whom *sattva* predominates. He first describes the Gopīs who combine *sattva* with *sattva* (i.e., the *sāttvika-sāttvika* Gopīs), and then those who combine *rajas* with *sattva*(i.e., the *rājasa-sāttvika*). In the words "The highest rule of life...", He teaches that the chief duty of women is to serve their husbands. By the very nature of things the Blessed Lord alone is the husband of all souls. And those souls who have become embodied as women must worship and serve the Blessed Lord alone in order to be free of infidelity. But the man who, according to the worldly convention, is considered one's husband because of marriage, he also must be worshipped and served. This alone is your highest rule of life. And in this there must be no deceit or trickery, for if there is deceit one's service will not be rewarded. Any other rule of life is inferior to this. "His relatives" refers to her father-in-law, etc. When the Lord addresses the Gopīs as "good women," He means that all these relatives of their husbands belong to them as well, and look to them for help. And "to nourish his children" means that a woman should give food and so forth to her husband's sons and daughters and give them her own milk to drink. Or, the Lord means that, just as your fathers and the other men of the house nourish and maintain you, so should you nourish and maintain the children.

Introduction to Stanza 25 : Even if one of them should say : "But my man is not fit to be a husband," the Lord answers :

Stanza 25 : "Even if a husband has some vice or has no luck at all, is old or stupid, has a serious disease or is poor, a woman who seeks to do well in this world and the next should not abandon him, as long as he is not guilty of a serious offense."

Commentary : The first kind of husband referred to is one who has a very bad habit—a vice such as gambling. The second, who has no luck at all, is poor. An old man is senile and loses the use of his senses. The stupid man is simply a fool. The next kind is an invalid who is in the grip of a serious disease. And lastly we have the poor man. But if the poor man is also lucky, his wife should not leave him, because there's always the chance... A wife should not abandon even a man who has all six of these faults, because she has no one else to go to. The contrast between the Blessed Lord, with His six great qualities, and the husband with these six faults is clearly intended here. But the man who is guilty of a serious offense (Skt. *pātaka*),[32] and he alone, should be abandoned. As has been said : "She should lovingly serve a husband who has not fallen." Moreover, this applies even to women who seek to do well in the world. If they desire fame and other rewards in this world and in the next, they should not abandon their husbands. Otherwise they will get a very bad name.

Introduction to Stanza 26 : But the Lord realizes that one of the Gopīs might object that, for a woman whose mind is set on the mood of love, her rule of life is no obstacle, since this mood arises only with respect to someone other than her husband. And He answers :

Stanza 26 : "Adultery keeps you from getting to heaven, and it brings dishonor. It is attained with difficulty, but turns out to be a mere trifle; and it causes fear rather than love. Adultery is completely reprehensible, O women of good family."

Commentary : O women of good family, adultery—intercourse with a lover—even when it produces the desired mood, is excluded from consideration by its many faults. The Lord has mentioned six faults involved in this act. "It keeps you from getting to heaven," i.e., it destroys one's chances in the next world. Even if Heaven had already been merited by faithful performance of one's duties, Heaven disappears when adultery is committed. And besides, in this world too adultery destroys a person's reputation. The word "and" in the text signifies that Hell (*naraka*) is another result of adultery. By saying "trifling" the Lord points out that in this act the experience of the desired mood and its delight will not be great. The pleasure one experiences is small and lasts no more than an instant. And though it is in essence a very intense form of pleasure, its duration is quite limited. And by saying "difficulty",

32. The lawgiver Manu enumerates the five "serious offences" as follows: "Killing a Brāhmaṇa, drinking (the spiritous liquor called) Surā, stealing (the gold of a Brāhmaṇa), adultery with a Guru's wife, and associating with such (offenders), they declare (to be) mortal sins (mahāpātaka)." Tr. Georg Bühler, *The Laws of Manu XI*, 55. *Sacred Books of the East*, vol. XXV, p. 441.

the Lord signifies that this kind of undertaking is troublesome, and to accomplish it successfully requires no small effort. Therefore adultery has a number of very undesirable consequences. Besides, even at the height of the experience it does not produce the desired mood, since adultery causes fear, and the mood of terror is completely contradictory to the mood of love. It is for precisely this reason that adultery is called "infidelity". From the very beginning of such an act the predominant and characteristic mood produced is the mood of fear, or terror. Moreover, He says "adultery is completely reprehensible," which means that in all places and at all times, and even if a good person were to do it, it would be condemned. Anyone who thinks that adultery is in accord with her rule of life is wrong. And so, since adultery is wrong for so many reasons, it is not fitting for an excellent woman of good family.

Introduction to Stanza 27 : Having thus instructed the Gopīs who were still affected by the three qualities of existence, the Lord now addresses Himself to those who have transcended these qualities :

Stanza 27 : "The kind of love for me that comes from hearing the scriptures, from seeing me, from meditation and from constantly singing my praises, does not come from this sort of intimate contact with me. Therefore go back to your homes."

Commentary : The Lord addresses these words to those Gopīs who might say : "Granted, these things are wrong from the worldly point of view, but they are not wrong on the Path of Devotion, or from the viewpoint of ultimate truth, for You are the Supreme Person." For there is no scriptural teaching to the effect that physical union should occur on the Path of Devotion. For Devotion consists of the nine steps of Hearing, etc.[33] There

33. These are the famous nine "parts" or "steps" (*aṅga*) of devotion (*bhakti*), enumerated in *Bhāgavata Purāṇa* VII. 5. 23. They are : "hearing (of the Lord's deeds)" (*śravaṇa*), "glorifying Him" (*kīrtana*), "constantly remembering Him" (*smaraṇa*), "attendance at His feet" (*pādasevana*), "worship" (*arcana*), "adoration" (*vandana*), "servitude" (*dāsya*), "friendship" (*sakhya*), and "the offering of oneself to Him" (*ātmanivedana*). In verses XVIb-XVIIa of his verse-treatise Bālabodha, Vallabha gives the following

is also the Devotion that takes the form simply of love (*prema*). And in this independent form of Devotion (which consists purely of love), there is that much less need of physical union. Rather, the love which has the Blessed Lord as its object transcends this world. This love is superior to all else. But worldly love, since it depends on passion and desire, is much lower. There are three causes of this transcendent love : "hearing, seeing and meditation." "Hearing," first of all, consists of reaching the firm conviction that both the denoted and intended meanings of the scriptural words and sentences which describe the Blessed Lord are in the Blessed Lord Himself. When this is so, external objects are excluded (from being intended or denoted by scriptural statements). If they were not, our love would be for some worldly object as well as for the Lord. After this comes "seeing", which consists of an experience of the meaning of the scriptures or of an actual vision of the Blessed Lord, due to His grace, for the sake of increasing the devotee's passionate desire for the Blessed Lord, as happened to Nārada and others. After this comes "meditation", which consists of thinking of the Lord by means of Yoga. By these alone, says the Lord, does love of me develop. And the love thus created is made permanent by "constantly singing my praises." And since this scriptural means is more effective, you should not cause your love for me to become worldly by constantly staying in my presence in this way. For worldly love, as we have already said, depends on passion and desire. Therefore go back to your homes. And so, even from the viewpoint of ultimate truth you should not stay. By the words "this sort of (intimate contact)" the Lord signifies that it is only love that is of this worldly kind that is forbidden, not love in its very nature, which is greatness itself. And since this Path of Devotion is prescribed for house-

teaching (which is relevant to the discussion above) on the relation between the nine "parts" of devotion and "love" (*prema*): "Souls are, by their very nature, defective. To free themselves forever of their defects, they should practice "Hearing" and so forth. For by the love which results from these practices, everything is accomplished that needs to be accomplished" (*jīvāḥ svabhāvato duṣṭā doṣābhāvāya sarvadā / śravaṇādi tataḥ premṇā sarvaṁ kāryaṁ hi sidhyati //*).

holders according to the scriptures, the Lord orders the Gopīs to go home.

Introduction to Stanza 28 : The Gopīs, then, have been told to go back home almost immediately after they had left, and the prospect of returning home seemed to them about as desirable as eating their own vomit. On the other hand, they thought, the Blessed Lord's word must not be disobeyed. With such contradictory alternatives, they concluded that the only course which would comply with both would be to abandon their bodies right there. But then they would not experience the joy of union with the Blessed Lord. Their resulting confusion as to what to do is expressed in the following stanza :

Stanza 28 : Śuka said : After hearing Govinda say exactly what they had hoped not to hear, the Gopīs, dejected, their dreams shattered, fell victim to a distress which they could not escape.

Commentary : The Gopīs heard the opposite of what they had wanted to hear, and this was unpleasant in two ways. For they could not figure out whether the Lord had spoken that way in order to test them, or whether He meant exactly what He said. They had listened to Him from start to finish, carefully determining the intention of His words, and they concluded that He was really telling them to go home. Even if the Lord did not intend His words to be taken in that way, the Gopīs would not have grasped His reason for speaking as He did, since they knew nothing about the clever juggling of words. They listened to His words without the least suspicion that they were false, since the word of the Lord Govinda is the word of God. And they listened without analyzing the words, since the Lord Himself was speaking. Consequently they became "dejected"—profound depression settled over their hearts. The reason for this is that "their dreams were shattered." And so they felt a great distress, and thought to themselves : "How can what we have been thinking and what the Blessed Lord has said be reconciled ?" Their distress pervaded the three worlds, and became inescapable, i.e., endless, because (they felt) they would not grasp the true meaning of the Lord's words even in hundreds of future lives.

Introduction to Stanza 29 : Next Śuka tells us what happened as a result of the Gopīs' distress :

Stanza 29 : The Gopīs cast their eyes downwards in grief; their lips, red as bimba-fruits, became parched from sobbing and sighing; and in their distraction they began writing in the dust with their feet. And, washing the saffron from their breasts with tears mixed with collyrium, they stood there, bearing their great weight of sorrow in silence.

Commentary : Their distress first made the Gopīs faint. After that, they turned their eyes downwards, as if to say : "Not one of us will show her face." Śuka says "in grief" because the Gopīs fully realized their grief, or because they felt united in grief. They felt grief also because of the sobbing that accompanies grief, and this sobbing, because of the heavy breathing it involves, dried out their lips which were as red as bimba-fruits. That was how the grief affected their faces, but they also started writing in the dust with their feet. That is how distracted their condition was. It was as if they were praying to Mother Earth to open and swallow them. Besides this, "washing the saffron from their breasts with tears mixed with collyrium, they stood there...in silence." The concealment of devotion is expressed by their eyes being downcast.[34] And their breath was stifled by the sobbing. The concealment of their hearts is expressed by their grief; the concealment of the mood of passionate desire by the dryness of their lips red as bimba-fruits. The concealment of their bodies is illustrated by their writing in the dust with their feet, the concealment of their senses by the tears, and the

34. "Concealment," in this and the following sentences, plays on one of the basic ideas of Vallabha's philosophy, which stresses "concealment", or "latency" (Skt. *tirobhāva*), and "manifestation" (*āvirbhāva*), as the opposite poles of existence· To put it briefly: everything is Kṛṣṇa/Brahman, but Kṛṣṇa Himself has the three absolutes, Being, Consciousness, and Joy (*saccidānanda*), fully *manifest*, while insentient beings (*jaḍa*) have only Being manifest, with Consciousness and Joy *concealed*. And souls (*jīva*) have Being and Consciousness manifest, but Joy concealed. The object of human life, then, is to bring the Joy that is within one from concealment to full manifestation. In the present passage, Vallabha stresses the concealment, for now, of the very qualities whose manifestation, in the union of love with Kṛṣṇa, will make the Gopīs' Joy fully manifest.

concealment of their loveliness by the absence of saffron. The concealment of their Joy is expressed by their heavy burden of sorrow, and the concealment of their consciousness by their standing in silence. They stood there, completely still, like pillars.

Introduction to Stanza 30: Śuka tells us in the next stanza how the Gopīs, standing there silently, noticed that the Blessed Lord, too, was standing there in silence, and so they asked something of Him:

Stanza 30 : The Gopīs had rejected all their other passions and desires for the sake of Kṛṣṇa, their greatest love, but He was speaking to them as if He were someone else, not their beloved. And so, wiping their eyes which had become swollen with weeping, the Gopīs, inflamed with love, excitedly stammered out these words.

Commentary : The phrase "He was speaking to them" may refer only to what the Lord had already said. Or it may indicate that the Lord said : "Why are you crying in this situation ? Be strong now, and go back to your homes." But he says this with a smiling face, so that the nectar of his words penetrates deep into their hearts, producing similar words in them. And then, awakened by the Blessed Lord's words, the Gopīs began to object to what He was saying. This is what the stanza describes.

The Lord alone is "their greatest love." And He has surrounded Himself here with all the trappings of love. But He is speaking in an entirely different vein. Yet Śuka is not saying here that the Blessed Lord was speaking to them as if He did not love them. For the Lord is never unloving. Rather He is their beloved, and He becomes someone indifferent, too, because He has the power of becoming anything. His love for them is not contradicted by His becoming like someone indifferent, not their beloved. For just as the Lord exists in the form of the world and in a form that is separate from the world, in the same way, Śuka says, "He was speaking to them as if He were someone else, not their beloved." He does not conceal His loving aspect—it is simply that He does not speak these words by means of that form of Himself, but by means of another form. With this type of Kṛṣṇa it is possible to argue.

The reward itself is never the means of attaining the reward. The reward can never say : "Choose me !" Instead it must be grasped, even by force, after all the obstacles have been cleared away. That is what Śuka is saying with the word "Kṛṣṇa," i.e., He who is eternal Joy (Joy is the reward. Therefore the Gopīs must grasp Him).

If the Gopīs were asked why they were persisting so stubbornly, they would say : "He alone is desirable." "But," the objector might say, "if the Great One is not ready to fulfil your desire, then you should desire lesser persons and things." To provide the Gopīs' answer to this, Śuka says : "The Gopīs had rejected all their other passions and desires for His sake". "For His sake," i.e., for the Blessed Lord's sake all passions and desires had been renounced entirely by the Gopīs. They had concluded that He alone was desirable, and they abandoned all their previous desires. As Scripture says : "And this person consists of desire" (*Bṛ. Ār. Upan.* IV. 4. 5). So, if even what has been abandoned may be taken up again, then how is it that the Gopīs do not take up (i.e., return to) their homes again, when the Blessed Lord Himself has commanded it ? Because He is the only desire that remains for them. The Gopīs concluded that, if this desire were not present, their very selves would disappear (i.e., their self is constituted entirely of this desire). And so, paying no attention to their final reward, they continued to strengthen their resolve. As Śuka says, "wiping their eyes which had become swollen with weeping," and putting all their clothes and so forth back in their proper places, with a good deal of eagerness and excitement they get ready to argue with Him. For the Blessed Lord opposes them by word only, and not with His whole Self. But the Gopīs know that those words can be refuted, and so they make this eager effort. A person who sets out on a journey does not turn back until the end has been reached. And so, the Gopīs start stammering words excitedly. But the words do not come out clearly, since anyone's speech would choke with fear at the task of refuting the words of God Himself. But the Gopīs had no fear because they were "inflamed with love." For love is the opposite of fear, and where there is even a little love, fear does not exist. Therefore they spoke out.

Verse : The Gopīs now refute, with ten stanzas, all that the Lord has said in His ten stanzas. And, by the measure of the additional prayer they make in an eleventh stanza, the Gopīs' words are victorious.

Introduction to Stanza 31 : The Gopīs realized that, in what the Blessed Lord had first said to them, namely "Welcome, o most fortunate of women" (Stanza 18), even though He praised them, His intention was to send them back home, not to welcome them into His presence. And, they thought, since that was so, no praise was involved there, but very cruel words instead, because the consequences of obeying His words were undesirable. And so, lest He say something like : "What am I to do in such an impossible situation?", they said this to Him :

Stanza 31 : The Gopīs said : "It is not at all fitting for You O Lord, to speak such cruel words to those who have renounced all things completely and have attained Your feet. Return our loving worship, o impossible one, do not abandon us !—just as that god, the Primeval Person, returns the worship of those who seek ultimate freedom."

Commentary : You have the power to do everything. And when someone who has such power speaks as if it were otherwise, that is harmful and cruel speech, and if he were compassionate he would not speak in that way. And that question which the Blessed Lord asked us, "Is all well in Vraja ?", should not have been addressed to us at all, since we "have renounced all things completely and have attained Your feet." For it is not right to take up again things which one has renounced. These words also make it clear that the Gopīs have not come there with the attitude that Kṛṣṇa is their illicit lover. For they have abandoned all the objects of the eleven sense-organs, too, along with all the lingering tendencies resulting from past actions and attachments of these senses (Skt. *savāsanāḥ*). They have abandoned all other alternatives and chosen this one, as they prove when they say : "(we) have attained Your feet." Otherwise they simply would not have attained the Lord's feet.

And in answer to the Lord's request to "please tell me why you have come" (Stanza 18), the Gopīs say : "Return our loving worship !" And in anticipation of the Lord's saying : "Something other than this must be done," the Gopīs have said : "O impossible one !" For it is an evil kind of obstinacy and stubbornness that says : "But I must not return your worship of love by love —something else must be done instead." It is like the stubbornness of people in general (literally, "of souls"; Skt. *jīvānām*). For they are eager to do anything and everything else, but they are not so eager to worship the Blessed Lord. And just as people's stubbornness is evil, so should Yours be considered in this case. For You Yourself have said : "In just the same way as they surrender themselves to Me, so do I love them in return" (*Bhag. Gītā* IV. 11). But that attitude is not evident here. If you really mean what You said there, then, "do not abandon us!" For You, and worship of You, have not been abandoned by us (Rather, all other things have). The Gopīs want to say that this worship through love[35] is not at all like loving any worldly object (Or : any "thing"; Skt. *viṣaya*, both in the stanza and here), but is of an entirely different nature. They are unable to express their meaning exactly, however, and so they use this example : "just as that god, the Primeval Person..." For a god returns the worship of all who worship him. Otherwise the scriptures would be meaningless. And all the more when "that god" is "the Primeval Person" (Skt. *ādipuruṣa*). And if worship is meaningful in the first part of the scriptures (which deals with ritual and sacrificial acts), it is much more meaningful in the second part (which deals with knowledge and loving devotion). But it is the Primeval Person who, above all others, must be served by worship. And He is the God. For the worship of a god can never produce the sin of infidelity. He is the first Husband of all, even when a woman worships another man (as husband).

35. The meaning of the very flexible Sanskrit verb-root *BHAJ* is the key to interpreting both this stanza and Vallabha's commentary on it. Its four meanings here are "to worship through love," "to worship," "to return someone's worship of love," and "to return someone's worship (of whatever kind)." These meanings, and others, of *BHAJ* will be explored thoroughly by Kṛṣṇa, the Gopīs and Vallabha in a forthcoming passage: Chapter 32, stanzas 16-22 (our Chapter IV).

The man she has married is not a worthy object of her worship. It is fitting for You not to accept us if we are guilty of having married another, but you cannot forbid us to worship You.[36] Consequently, just as a husband does not tolerate his wife's worshipping anyone but himself with her love, and, after first putting a stop to that he causes her to worship him with love, and he returns her loving worship, that is what You should do here. For this reason, the Gopīs are trying to point out, it is not right for even You to send us away. Besides, in this way the Blessed Lord[37] worships in return those who seek ultimate freedom. For He accepts them as belonging to His very own Self, and becomes manifest to them in the form of the Self, and He grants His own Joy to them. "For He alone causes Joy," as holy scripture says (*Taitt. Upan.* II. 7. 1). The Gopīs say : "He worships in return those who seek ultimate freedom" because the Blessed Lord makes Himself manifest for their sake, according to this law : "For Brahman has become manifest dependent on one of the following conditions (of the souls) : their merging into Him (in deep sleep) or their final fulfilment (ultimate liberation)" (*Brahma Sūtra* IV. 4. 16). Otherwise those who seek ultimate freedom would worship the Blessed Lord, but the Blessed Lord would not worship them in return. Therefore, He returns their worship by granting them their reward. And, just as You never make them return to their previous condition, but rather establish them permanently in Yourself, so, since You have made Yourself manifest for our sake, should You unite us with Your own Joy. This is what the Gopīs are saying He should do. (Here begins an interpolation by Viṭṭhala.) Thus in the terms of the Gopīs' prayer here, once the Lord has accepted them, His adopting the position of remaining in silence is refuted and proved invalid. Then, His

36. This is Viṭṭhala's "first interpretation" (*prathama pakṣa*), in his footnote (*ṭippaṇī*) on this difficult sentence of Vallabha's. His "second interpretaton" is : "We can reject our husbands (who are merely temporary), but we cannot reject worship of You (our Eternal Husband)."

37. Quite obviously, Vallabha here equates "the Blessed Lord" (*bhagavān*) with "the Primeval Person" (*ādipuruṣa*), and has intended this equation all along.

subsequent command that they go home (cf. Chapter V, stanza 39), and His letting them stay at home, and so forth, should be understood to be merely for the sake of strengthening the mood of love—not for the sake of their becoming bound to their home-life[38] (end of Viṭṭhala's interpolation).

Stanza 32 (no introduction is given): "You, O dear one, know the duties of all, and You have said that the duty proper to a woman is to attend to her husband, his children and his friends. Let it be so ! For You are God—the very basis of all teaching. You are, as all agree, the greatest love of all creatures; You are their kinsman, You are their very Self."

Commentary : The Gopīs say these words in order to answer the Blessed Lord's arguments that it is not right for women to abandon the duties that are proper to them, and therefore "Dreadful is this dark night...Women must not stay here" (Stanza 19). You know the duties of all, say the Gopīs, and You have said that the duty which is proper to a woman is to attend to these three : her husband, his children and his friends. This is because those who are expert in the treatises on duty have their minds on external things, and they teach the duties that relate to the body alone as the duties proper to a person. But they do not teach the duties relating to the Self, or to the Blessed Lord, because they do not know the Self. And so You, in speaking as an expert on duty, spoke without fully considering either us or Yourself (OR : "the Self"—*ātmānam*). We are only trying to make a thorough inquiry into the matter—not to refute You. To express this, they say : "Let it be so !" What you said about a woman having to do the duty that is proper to her, we grant that this is true. For the husband and the others are not the very essence of duty, nor are they even its basis. They are, rather, merely the instruments in our performing duty. And duty has two aspects : it must be performed and it must be learned. The children and others are the instruments in performing it, and the guru in learning it. Therefore this "attending to duty" which You speak of should come first of all with respect to the guru, otherwise one will

38. Vasu points out that this refers to the benefits that would arise from the Gopīs' separation from Kṛṣṇa by staying in their homes.

not even learn what duty is proper to her. The word of the Blessed Lord is primary (i.e., it is His word as our Guru)—it is not a mere repetition or explanation of what someone else has said. For before this we were ignorant of duty, otherwise that is what we would have been doing right now. And duty never becomes evident apart from worship of the guru. If it did, our duty would have become evident merely from our hearing Your words, and we would have gone home. Therefore make us worship You, so that what You have taught us may come to full accomplishment. For the doer of teaching (i.e., the guru) alone is "the very basis of teaching."

The Gopīs use an intimate form of address when they say "dear one" in order to emphasize that what they say is not contrary to the Lord's teaching. Besides, the duties proper to any one person are of many kinds. The objects of some duties are superior to oneself, of other duties, on the same level with oneself, and of still other duties, below oneself. The first kind of duty is superior to the second, and the second superior to the third. For instance, a woman's duty to serve her husband, sons and so forth is a duty with regard to those who are on her own level. Thus her duty to serve her ruler, the Lord, is more important—it is her primary duty. Otherwise, without His instigation, she would not engage herself in the service of her husband and her other duties at all. Therefore in the present context, too, You are the Lord, the Inner Ruler. But even in the form of the Inner Ruler You are not instigating us to serve our husbands and sons; rather You are inciting us to serve and worship You alone. Therefore, even in order to accomplish the duties You have spoken of, we must worship You first. Besides, duty has as its basis Him who has Duty or Righteousness as an eternal attribute—i.e, You, the Blessed Lord—and one's duty must be performed in a way that is not contradictory to that basis. And duty must be performed for the sake of its reward as well. If duty were not perfomed in accordance with its basis and for the sake of its reward, You would be impelling a person towards an undesired result, and would therefore be proved unreliable. Therefore the treatises on duty show a predilection for the body, and they teach the kind of duty which is in conformity with the body (as You seem to be doing).

Moreover, the law applies here that : "When a substance (to be ritually purified) and the purificatory rite itself (Skt. *saṁskāra*) are in opposition, the substance is the more important" (Here the substance refers to "the basis of duty," the Lord, and the rite itself to "duty"). Therefore, to one person it is his body that is dear, to another his Self, to another the Supreme Self and to another the sustainer of his body. But You embody all these Forms, therefore You are beyond measure "the greatest love"--pure Joy and the base of the highest love. You are also the "kinsman"— the sustainer of our bodies; and not only of us, but "of all creatures" who have bodies. (Here begins an interpolation by Viṭṭhala.) The sense of the scriptural passage : "For existence and destruction" (*Bh. P.* V. 1. 13) is here described as this : that the soul, having assumed the body which is given it by You alone, abides in that body in order to fulfil the purpose envisioned for it by you. Therefore this body belongs to the Blessed Lord—it has been established by the Blessed Lord alone. It should first be offered entirely to Him, and when—afterwards—it is no longer useful to Him, it may be given to another. For it is proper to a conscious being to be instigated by its Inner Ruler. Therefore what is indicated is that as long as such a being knows that the body is useful to the Blessed Lord, it will not give the body over to another (end of Viṭṭhala's interpolation). Therefore You alone are "the greatest love of all creatures"—all embodied beings. And one should give only a very dear possession to the most beloved. Besides, not only do You give all creatures their bodies, but You are their "kinsman" as well. He by whose effort the body is maintained is a kinsman. And "You are their very Self," since You are their Supporter. Therefore, by both laws, that of the superiority of the interior to the exterior and that of the superiority of the permanent to the impermanent, the service and worship of You, since You are the Blessed Lord, is the most important duty. And when our body is no longer of any use to You, if You instigate our minds so that we realize this, then shall we give our body to another, and in no other circumstance.

The consideration of Him who is the basis of duty is superior to the consideration of duty itself. And since all this that we have said would be contradictory (to what You have said) unless You accepted and agreed to it, we pray : "Let it be so !" Or perhaps by those words the Gopīs imply : "Since You exist in all forms (husband, son, etc.), You alone must be served." For if someone tried to serve everyone she is obliged to serve at once, her service would be at least partially obstructed, because she could not resolve the contradiction between her alternative obligations. Therefore that is not her duty which is obstructed by time and other factors, and is thus impossible. For scripture does not impose contradictory norms on us. Therefore even the treatises which teach us that it is our duty to serve our husbands, sons and so forth actually teach the service of You alone. What the Gopīs mean, then, is that from the viewpoint of both the stated teachings and the elaborative explanations of the treatises on duty, the service of You alone is proper.

Introduction to Stanza 33 : In the last stanza Śuka told us what was said by the Gopīs whose dominant characteristic is *rajas*. Now he recounts the words of those who are characterised by *sattva*:

Stanza 33 : "For the wise delight in love of You, who are their very Self. And what are husbands, sons, and all the others who are only sources of pain, by comparison with one's eternal love? Therefore have mercy on us, O Lord of bestowers of favor, and do not knowingly cut off the firm hope we have held so long in You, O lotus-eyes."

Commentary : Although the Lord has said : "Your mothers and fathers...are all searching for You" and "Do not create such panic among your relatives" (Stanza 20), there is the question of whether this course of action is being taken by us alone, for the very first time, or whether other people also act in this way. In this context another question arises, too : whether it is the inferior persons who obey their mothers and other relatives, or the best persons. And You must certainly consider whether the best persons are those who are incapable of serving and worshipping You, or those who are capable.

With this line of questioning in mind, the Gopīs quote as a normative example the conduct of the great ones. For those who are wise with respect to the Self, who desire what is best for the Self, and not for the body and the senses, they "delight in love of You" alone. For action proceeds from love. And the love which such a person directs toward the Blessed Lord, and that alone, makes the person himself lovable.[39] This point is proved in this context by the stanza : "This Lord of the Self, fully Self-satisfied, never chooses the respect of ignorant people; but, since He is compassionate, whatever respect a person has shown to the Blessed Lord is reflected in his Self, just as facial decorations are reflected in one's mirror image" (*Bh. P.* 7. 9. 11). And service and worship proceed out of love. Now if the service of one's sons and so forth were also one's true duty, then this service would result finally in some real gain for the Self. But when the Gopīs say "the wise," they indicate that the cleverness of these wise men consists in the fact that they see withdrawal—turning inward—as superior to active involvement in external duties and so forth. Only when one is incapable of controlling his senses must he act in relation to others, as is explained by the scriptural passage : "From whatever he may withdraw (from bondage to that is he freed"—based on the Hindi). When the senses are constrained away from the external world, they automatically go towards the Self.[40] But, in addition, the senses are directed to Self at one time only, and that is when, and if, they become useful to You. Therefore those who "delight in love of You" are "wise" by comparison with those who exercise mere sense-restraint and nothing more. This is the sense of the word "For" in the stanza.

The word "You" is used in the singular number here to connote, as it did before, the origin of all things and forms (such as husband, son, etc.) from one Person. And besides, You,

39. Emend the Sanskrit for this sentence from Telivala-Sankalia's *bhagavatkṛtameva jīvagāmi bhavatīti* to *bhagavatkṛta eva jīvagāmī bhavatīti*, on the witness of Viṭṭhala and the commentators Puruṣottama and Kākā Vallabhajī (the Lekhakāra).

40. Skt. *ātman* here means both "one's own Self" and "Kṛṣṇa the Inner Self," as is evident from the stanza.

"who are their very Self," have become their very essence, and this not according to some law of superimposition (of You upon what is not You), but in reality. Moreover, one must serve one's "love," and if one's "love" is not to be limited by time (if he is to be "one's eternal love," as the stanza says), then he must be You alone. Otherwise—if one's duty were not to serve the Eternal—then even the service (-worship; Skt. *sevā*) of an illicit lover would be one's duty, because just as one lifetime is a limiting factor with regard to one's husband, children, and so forth, so is a day (or however long the affair lasts) a limiting factor with regard to one's lover. Besides, one's husband, children and so forth cannot be causes of duty, since they are "sources of pain." For sources of suffering are never causes of duty, otherwise there would be no Saṁsāra.[41] Therefore "what are husbands, sons, and all the others?" One should have fear of them, or something else, but one should not consider them a motive for duty. This is what the Gopīs mean.

But there is one lone thing we must pray to You for, without which all the treatises and all reasoning would be fruitless. The Gopīs beseech Him in these words : "Therefore have mercy on us," that is, become gracious to us. For without Your grace all people wander in confusion and become involved with all the causes of suffering. And if You should say : "What means have you taken for attaining this grace?", we answer by addressing You as "Lord of bestowers of favor." For those who bestow favors are conscious of people's sufferings, since they are compassionate. Otherwise they would not bestow their favor even though someone had performed asceticism in hope of it. Of these bestowers of favor You are the Lord—the most compassionate of all. By means of this compassion and these favors You calm the sufferings of all people. Now we are the ones

41. Mr. Fatehchand Vasu (cf. Bibliography), in translating this passage into Hindi, explains that the "causes" or "occasions" of duty are so called because fulfilling one's duty with regard to them leads inevitably to joy—the lessening of Saṁsāra. And so, if serving one's husband or loving one's lover were "causes of duty", they would produce joy and destroy Saṁsāra. But they evidently do not, since they are "sources of pain" and since Saṁsāra still remains. Therefore they cannot be "causes of duty."

who are afflicted with suffering, and our affliction itself is a means, just as the self-affliction of asceticism is a means for others. We realize that this suffering must not be used as a means if it springs from a forbidden sentiment towards You (such as the sentiment of purely worldly love). But you might say : "Just as you have been serving your husbands for this much time, you should continue serving them, because you should finish that service. Even an action of secondary importance should be finished once it has been started. Therefore do not consider the matter any further—just serve your husbands." Our answer to that is : "do not knowingly cut off our firm hope." We have not served our husbands, or at least we have not continued serving them for its own sake, but rather in expectant hope of You. And we consented to serve them only to maintain ourselves and keep alive our hope in You in the meanwhile. And now if we who have come here do not attain what we desire, our hopes will be shattered. And when hope has gone our very life-breath, too, will go. That is why it has been said by one who knew well the heart of a woman (Kālidāsa) : "Only the chain of hope can tie down the heart." The basis of this statement will be found in the treatise on woman. Our hope in You alone has been firm and lasting, and if it is cut off we will surely fall, since we will have no basis to rest upon. The Gopīs' addressing the Lord with the expression "lotus-eyes" indicates that merely seeing His eyes fills them to overflowing with pleasure. (Here begins an interpolation by Viṭṭhala). The cause of their hope has also been expressed in this phrase, since Kṛṣṇa has looked at them with eyes that take away suffering in the same way lotuses cool something hot. These eyes take away their suffering because they express His feeling of love for them. The meaning is that their continuing to live until now is due entirely to the fact of His love for them (end of Viṭṭhala's interpolation).

Introduction to Stanza 34: The Lord had asked: "Have You come out to see this grove?" (not an exact quote, but the reference is to Stanza 21). And then He had described the grove to them. In response to this the Gopīs say :

Stanza 34 : "You have robbed us of our minds so easily,

which might be involved in the home, and, what's more, our hands, too, which might be doing the housework. Our feet as well, which cannot move a single step from Your feet. So how can we go to Vraja ? Or what would we do when we got there?"

Commentary : A desire to see the forest[42] could come at a time when the mind is in possession of itself. But you have robbed us of our minds, and that robbery did not even require any effort on your part. If the robbery of our minds had required any effort, you would not have been able to rob us of everything else as well. That is why the Gopīs say : "so easily." Or perhaps "You," as the embodiment of Joy, "have robbed us of our minds." For when absolute Joy is standing right in front of them, no one is going to focus on one of the substitute means of attainment (viz., the path of household duty, merit, and gradual attainment of reward) and follow it through religiously, step by step (since the Reward is already there, present to them). Much less does the idea of seeing the forest have any value. By saying : "which (our minds) might be involved in the home," the Gopīs indicate the robbery of their power of knowledge. But neither should You think, the Gopīs say, that we came to the forest in order to perform some action. This is why they indicate that their power of action, too, has been robbed from them, when they say : "and, what's more, our hands, too." Their hands "might be doing the housework," but the idea of performing any action in the forest is far-fetched because their strength had been robbed by passion. Our hands are enlivened by Your touch alone; if they do not have that, they are dead. Therefore the scriptural injunction to serve and worship You or anyone else becomes completely ineffectual when we have no hands. For no one can engage in an action without their hands. Besides, You have told us : "Now you have seen this grove" (Stanza 21), and Your intention was clearly : "Now you must turn around and go back to your homes." But this, too, is impossible, since "our feet cannot move even a single step from Your feet," i.e., from this place. So they certainly

42. Skt. *vana* means both "forest" and "grove". When it is used in a more intimate context, I prefer to translate it by "grove"; when in a more general context, by "forest."

cannot go to any other place. Your two feet have become the root, i.e., the basis or foundation,[43] of our feet, which are necessary for our movement. But if our feet have now gone to the very root, basis and foundation of their movement, how could they possibly go elsewhere ? That would be like saying that trees, which have also attained their root, could move. When the Gopīs say : "from Your feet," and mean by that "from this place," they also intend to say : "If You were to move, then we could go anywhere, but not apart from You." Therefore "how can we go to Vraja ?" And in case He suggests that they should be sent back on a cart or something like that, they say: "Or what would we do when we got there ?" It is true enough that a cart is a means that would get us home, but no one has found any substitute for hands in the performance of actions. There is no use going just for the sake of going. Rather we would go for the sake of serving our fathers, husbands, etc.; but if we could not do that (which we cannot without hands), it would be useless for us to go. This is why the Gopīs say : "Or what would we do when we got there ?" In saying this the Gopīs realize that action could be performed by a different procedure, independent of the hands, namely, by the Gopīs' being possessed by the feeling that they themselves are the Blessed Lord. But even in this case they could not breast-feed their children, since their milk would dry up because they no longer had hope.[44]

Introduction to Stanza 35 : The Blessed Lord had said to the Gopīs : "Go quickly !"[45] They give Him their answer in this stanza :

43. The Sanskrit word used for Kṛṣṇa's "feet"—*pādamūlam*—literally means, according to Shri Shyam Goswamy, "the root of the leg", hence the foot. This literal meaning gives Vallabha the opportunity to point out the deeper meaning.

44. The Gopīs' hope was for Kṛṣṇa's physical presence. Having lost that, they would have lost all hope.

45. The reference is to Stanza 22, though Vallabha does not quote the exact words. The words he uses here are *śīghraṁ gacchata*, while the words in the stanza are *tadyāta mā ciram*. I have translated these latter words, in stanza 22, as: "So do not linger here, but go back", because Kṛṣṇa is playing

Stanza 35 : "Dearest one, pour onto the fire of our love, kindled by Your soothing song and smiling glances, a flood of nectar from Your lips. If You do not, then we, our bodies consumed by the fire of separation from You, will travel by meditation the path Your holy feet tread, dear friend."

Commentary : We will go quickly indeed, if You do not do something to prevent it. By this the Gopīs mean that His silence is killing them. They don't even want to mention what might happen if they had to return home. "Dearest one, pour onto the fire of love that is in our hearts (literally : "The fire of the love-god, Kāma, who dwells in our hearts") a flood of nectar from Your lips," i.e., a torrent of the water of nectar from Your lips. And this fire has been started by You alone. They explain what has caused the fire when they say : "kindled by Your soothing song and smiling glances." First Your smile, then Your glance, then Your soothing song create in our hearts this passionate desire (literally : "produce Kāma, the god of passion"). And that ("he") is the fire. Your smile enkindles passionate desire, and Your glance inflames it. And Your song acts like the wind, especially Your soft, "soothing" song, which is like a wind that fans the flames from all sides at once. This fire has its source in the heart, and only the nectar from Your lips can penetrate to the heart. For only something which is full floods over, and by the Gopīs' mention of the fact that it is this "flood of nectar" which should be poured out, the greatness of the fire itself is suggested. Therefore to speak of pouring water over it is very apt. But since this is a supernatural fire, it can be calmed and brought under control only by supernatural means. Kāma, the god of passionate love, burns when he is dead. Only when he is alive does he abandon the form of fire, and at no other time. He lives by the nectar of immortality alone, but not the same nectar the gods drink to attain immortality, because then he would be given life by them alone. Rather, since he is the cause of creation, he never attains

on these words so that the opposite of the apparent meaning can be construed. Vallabha points this out in detail in his commentary on the stanza, as we have seen. But here Vallabha chooses to highlight the most apparent meaning of the phrase, which is indeed : "Therefore go quickly."

ultimate freedom.[46] Therefore he must be kept alive only by that secret, mysterious nectar which comes from Your lips (i.e., by Your kissing us). This is why the Gopīs speak merely of "pouring" nectar onto the fire. Otherwise they would pray that He extinguish the fire completely. For when Kāma is alive we, too, shall live, otherwise while he himself burns he will consume others as well. Then the Gopīs say : "If You do not..." If You do not, like a reciter of sacred spells, make Kāma live by pouring Your nectar upon Him, then "we, our bodies consumed by the fire that results from separation from You, will travel by meditation the path Your holy feet tread." Since we are ignorant of any other, independent path,[47] and You are our "dear friend," we will go by whatever path You take. (Here begins an interpolation by Viṭṭhala.) Just as You are causing us to suffer, so will we, when we have become this way (i.e., when we walk the path You tread), cause regret and other sufferings in You. This is the inner meaning of the Gopīs who speak these words (end of Viṭṭhala's interpolation).

If our body dies (viz., "consumed by the fire of separation"), then the Inner Ruler must go somewhere else. But no other body will be produced, because the seed of our past actions has been consumed by the fire of separation from You. Kāma, when he was burnt to a crisp by Hara (Śiva), did not rise up

46. It is common for Vallabha and his followers to stress that the work of the creator-gods—primarily Brahmā, but also Kāma, as pointed out here—is antagonistic to ultimate freedom (*mokṣa*). This is because the latter notion depends largely on introversion and withdrawal from the world, while, obviously enough, the former stresses activity and involvement in the world. On this cf. verse ten of Vallabha's verse-treatise *Bālabodhaḥ* and, especially, Puruṣottama's commentary on it (cf. Bibliography under "Sharma").

47. Or, Vallabha's reference here may be to a specific "Path of Independence" (*svatantramārga*). This would very likely be the "independent" path of "pure love" described briefly by Vallabha in his commentary on Stanza 27 above. And, almost certainly, the idea would also be present that, on this Path of Independence, it is the devotee who is independent, and the Lord depends on him, rather than the reverse, which is the normal case. This idea of the devotee's independence and the Lord's dependence is a very prominent one in Vallabha's "Path of Grace" (*puṣṭimārga*). This idea and interpretation is clearly reflected in the interpolation Viṭṭhala makes on this sentence.

again, but became the opposite of Hara, i.e., *Raha* (which means both "solitude" and "sexual intercourse"). If this Raha is especially intense, it is *viraha* ("separation" in the stanza), i.e., "complete solitude." Or alternatively, *vi-raha* can mean "having no solitude." Therefore it is our having no solitude with You that constitutes our "separation." Although the fire which was mentioned before (the fire of passionate love of Kāma) can burn, still it cannot reduce someone to ashes, unless it has entered all the limbs and even the smallest parts of the body and is awakened. It is the same as the case of ordinary fire, which cannot burn unless it is applied to dry wood. For, because of the complete destruction of that limiting factor (i.e., the seed which causes persons to be reborn), we will go to Your holy feet (i.e., we will die and attain liberation). Therefore, going back to our houses is out of the question. Rather, death has approached us instead. Remedy this for us quickly !

Introduction to Stanza 36 : Besides, You also said (in Stanza 23) : "Or, if you have come here out of intense love for Me." Now listen as we tell You the true nature of that love of ours which You praised :

Stanza 36 : "Since that moment, O lotus-eyes, when we touched Your footprints—that happy chance offered rarely even to Lakṣmī—since then, having attained—my God !—such supreme delight with You, who love the forest-people, we have never been able, even for an instant, to stay in the presence of others."

Commentary : O lotus-eyes, a mere glance from You destroys all suffering. At the very moment when we touched Your footprints, and ever since that time, we have been entirely incapable of staying in the presence of others even for an instant. That privilege is very difficult to attain—for You to make Yourself physically present and allow someone to touch Your feet. The place where the foot has left its impression, i.e., "the footprint", is what is meant here by the word Śuka uses (Skt. *pādatala*). Lakṣmī, too, lives by that alone. This was attested by the wives of the serpent Kālīya, when they said : "It was because She desired to gain eligibility to touch the dust of Your feet that Lakṣmī abandoned all her passions and performed penances"

(Bh. P. X. 16. 36). That privilege therefore represents the stage of the enjoyment of the reward. "That happy chance" which gives pleasure to Lakṣmī is "offered" by Your footprint alone, which is "rarely" impressed on her heart. All her pleasure is in that. But we touch that footprint here on the ground, unlike Lakṣmī, who receives it on her heart. And we have determined that if Lakṣmī attained this by ascetic practices which took away her fickleness, then we, too, by eliminating our fickleness, must stay here in total dependence on Your holy feet.

Besides "You love the forest-people." This, too, indicates we must totally renounce all attachments and stay here, in the forest. For the Blessed Lord is pleased only when there is complete absence of attachments (as among the renunciants who dwell in the forest). For the forest is characterized by the quality *sattva*, and it is *Vaiṣṇava*.[48] (Here begins an interpolation by Viṭṭhala.) Or these words of the Gopīs about the Lord's love for the forest-people may be meant to call to mind the women of the Pulinda tribe, who were dear to the Lord because they adorned their faces and breasts with the saffron from His feet, after some of it had remained in His footprints (cf. Bh. P. X. 21. 17). The Gopīs mean that by this example they, too, know in their deepest selves that his footprints themselves (i.e., as sacred objects in their own right), will bring about the highest reward for them, will be a means for them to attain love for the Lord, and will be very natural and familiar to them. But clearly they could not say all this, so they made the brief reference (end of Viṭṭhala's interpolation). Therefore for the sake of attaining You we are unable to stay in the presence of others. We are unable to stay in the presence of any one who has not surrendered himself entirely to you. This inability comes from the entry of the Blessed Lord's qualities into the Gopīs. For no one who has attained such a degree of love for the Lord can stay in the presence of someone who would destroy it. Just as someone

48. The Sanskrit word *vaiṣṇava* carries the connotation that the forest is an especially suitable and auspicious place for Viṣṇu and his followers, the Vaiṣṇavas—the name Vallabha uses to describe devotees of Viṣṇu generally, but especially of Kṛṣṇa. In addition, Viṣṇu is the presiding deity of the quality *sattva*.

who thinks his body is his Self runs away from the tige who would destroy his body, so the person who belongs otally to the Blessed Lord cannot stay in the presence of someone who lacks love for the Blessed Lord, for that person will destroy the devotee's constant state of love for the Lord. For one whose insight is sharp enough to realize this, the idea of going to some other god's place and considering him to be God is totally out of the question. Therefore Your praise of our "love" alone does not amount to much, since we, like Lakṣmī, exist for and love absolutely no one but You. Further, just as Lakṣmī took refuge in You by abandoning all else, and then attained the supreme delight of love with You, so have we. We constantly attain union with You in our dreams. Otherwise, we could not even remain alive. And so, since You have already enjoyed us, it is not right for You to send us to someone else.

Introduction to Stanza 37 : The Gopīs fear that the Lord might say :"But my union with Lakṣmī was in fulfilment of divine destiny, and it was her very first union. But your first act of union was with others, not me, and so there is a considerable difference." And so they address Him in this way :

Stanza 37 : " Even though Śrī had already attained her own place of repose on Your chest, yet, since many other gods were striving to be favored by a glance from Her, She earnestly desired the dust of Your lotus-feet, which belongs to Tulasī and is indeed worshipped by all Your servants. In the same way we, too, have taken refuge in the dust of Your feet.

Commentary: The Gopīs are saying that even Lakṣmi did not attain You "in fulfilment of divine destiny." Rather She undertook many strict ascetic practices in order to attain Your lotus-feet. She did not become Your very own because She is a woman, but because She is a devotee. Otherwise, when She attained her own, independent place of repose on Your chest, She would not have decided to enter into rivalry with Tulasī by desiring the dust of Your feet. The dust of Your feet belongs properly to Tulasī, for Lakṣmī, as a devotee, attained it (only) by her devotion. This (i.e., Lakṣmī's refuge in the dust of Hari's feet when She was being importuned by the other gods) has been described in the first book of this scripture (Bh. P. I. 18.

20; cf. also I, 16. 32). The Gopīs point out the sacredness of this dust when they say it is "worshipped by all Your servants." For Your servants' bodies have been created from that dust alone. The word "indeed" indicates the universally known fact that all your devotees have bodies which have been created from the dust of Your feet. Therefore Tulasī has been established there as the very embodiment of devotion. All those who attain this dust become servants of You alone. And so Lakṣmī, though She had already attained a place upon Your heart, was worried that another god might touch Her, and She desired the dust of Your feet. For once one has attained that, there is no longer so much as a doubt. But someone might ask : "Why would Lakṣmī be so afraid" ? And so the Gopīs say : "Because many other gods were striving to be favored by a glance from Her." All the other gods, Brahmā and the rest, were practising asceticism with one aim in mind: "May Lakṣmī (Fortune) look favorably on me." For if She did not, then none of their desired ends could be accomplished. And so, with the prayers of so many gods flooding in upon Her, She became afraid. After all, She thought, if someone of the gods were performing the most extreme and excessive penances, who knows what he might do ? But in desiring the dust of Hari's feet no such apprehension is involved. And once it is attained ther is no more room even for doubt. The Gopīs, having pointed out that Lakṣmī will never go to anyone else now that She has attained the dust of His feet, tell Kṛṣṇa that their situation is exactly the same when they say : "In the same way we, too..." Many men are asking for our favor, too. Precisely out of fear of that we first touched the dust of Your feet. Therefore, knowing that our bodies, too, have originated from the dust of Your feet, "we have taken refuge" totally—in every way possible—"in the dust of Your feet." The word "too" (used both in the sense of "likewise" and in the sense of "as well as others") refers to the Gopīs who did not come to the Lord at this time. Or it may refer to those women of the nobility (who were to enjoy Kṛṣṇa's love afterwards, in Mathurā and Dvārakā) whose bodies are similarly made up of the dust of His feet. And so (since we have surrendered totally to You) You have come here for our sake alone. Do not hide Yourself now.

You will not even remain hidden. The Gopīs' meaning is "Therefore You mustn't be so stubborn."

Introduction to Stanza 38 : Having thus proved that their bodies are meant to be enjoyed by the Blessed Lord alone, the Gopīs now make their prayer to Him :

Stanza 38 : "And so be gracious to us, Destroyer of sins, who have abandoned our homes and have reached Your holy feet, and whose hope consists entirely of worshipping You. Grant us, most splendid of men, the gift of being Your slaves, for our hearts are on fire with the searing passion kindled by Your lovely smiles and glances."

Commentary : In the first stanza of their response to the Lord (Stanza 31; cf. Stanza 32 as well), the Gopīs refuted Kṛṣṇa's teachings about their duty of obedience to their husbands. All the more did the idea that they should not abandon the service of their husbands stand refuted by those words. In this stanza, too, they pray that the Lord will accept their refutation of His teachings. When the Blessed Lord's Grace is absent, union should occur with the husband only, but Grace overrides all else, "and so" for that reason please "be gracious," please be merciful, for when You are gracious all will come to fulfilment. "But," You might say, "aren't you women asking for something that is opposed by your fate, and will therefore bring you suffering? How can that be called 'Grace'?" Our answer is : "Destroyer of sins." A 'sin' is an evil deed which causes suffering, but it is Your very nature to destroy the sins of all people who attain any sort of relationship with You at all. Then the Gopīs point out the cause for the Lord's Grace : "who (i.e., we) have reached Your holy feet." For whoever reaches Your holy feet attains Your Grace as well. The Gopīs now distinguish their level of eligibility from that of others by saying : "(We) who have abandoned our homes." They are saying, equivalently : "And do not grant this Grace of Yours in the form of an animal, or a son, or something else that other people might ask for." For the fact that they say they have left their "homes", in the plural, and not merely their "house', indicates that they have abandoned the Householder's stage of life as a whole. They give the reason why they also abandoned the service of their husbands and, in fact, all else when they say : "whose (i.e., our) hope consists entirely of worshipping You." With one hope alone—that of worshipping You—have we abandoned all that had existed previously in our lives. And now that we have come here, how can anything be said about resuming household duties ? And so they pray for a gift in the sentence that begins "Grant us...the gift" and ends with the words "kindled by Your lovely smiles and glances." "Your lovely smile," even though it deludes us, brings us joy—after all, it embodies absolute Joy simply because it is connected with You. And the "glances" which follow those smiles make our hearts burn with the searing fire of passion they enkindle. You who have the form of the "most splendid of men," a form lovelier than that of countless millions of Kāmas, grant us the gift of that slavery which accomplishes all the purposes of existence ! (Here begins an interpolation by Viṭṭhala.) Since the level of eligibility is different in different persons, there are many forms of servitude or slavery (Skt. *dāsya*) to the Lord. The particular form of slavery which the Lord should grant is made clear by the Gopīs' description of the fire that burns them. The proper form is the one which quenches the particular fire of suffering which the Gopīs have described themselves as victims of. Besides, slavery consists in this and in nothing else—offering to one's master something which he needs. Since this is so, just as the suffering we have described shows our tremendous need of You, so You should now make an effort to show Your need for us by enjoying us (in love). This is the final meaning of the Gopīs' prayer. Otherwise it would be out of place for them to speak of "the gift of slavery," since slavery is something that would be accomplished by the slaves' actions, not the master's. This is why they address Him as "most splendid of men" (literally, "ornament among men"; Skt. *puruṣabhūṣaṇa*), saying equivalently : "Having become a man, You have taken a form that is an ornament among men." For an ornament is on (i.e., has contact with) the throat and all the other limbs of the body. Acting just like an ornament, then, "grant us the gift of being Your slaves." Thus the Gopīs make two figurative references coalesce in the same sentence to bring across the meaning of their prayer. By the Gopīs' calling Kṛṣṇa an "ornament" they also express the fact that He, by Himself, brings to pass all the goals people desire (as an ornament is thought to do). And in addition, red lac is used when an ornament is inlaid with jewels, in order to render the ornament all the more brilliant. And even a man of high rank wears red lac, though it is lowly, to set off the ornament he is wearing. Likewise, contend the Gopīs, worldly passion (*kāma*) is useful in our present situation. But our choice of slavery to You was not taken out of limited, worldly passion. Rather our choice implies and expresses precisely the opposite[49] (end of Viṭṭhala's interpolation). And so here we are, eager to be Your slaves, but not desiring to marry You. Therefore, the Gopīs mean, there is no need for you to have had the sacrament of initiation, which according to the ordinary custom, would have to occur before marriage.

Introduction to Stanza 39 : Kṛṣṇa might say : "Why have all of you chosen to ask for gift of being my slaves, when the final reward of attaining my Heaven, and other, similar rewards exist ?" To this the Gopīs answer :

Stanza 39 : "We who have been gazing at Your face, framed by curls and graced by earrings, flowing with the nectar of the pool of your lips—set between your two broad cheeks—and glancing laughingly; and who have seen that brace of staff-like arms which remove all fear, and the chest which is Śrī's private pleasure-ground, let us be Your slaves."

Commentary : Here the Gopīs are answering the Lord's words in stanza 25 : "a woman who seeks to do well in this world and the next should not abandon her husband." For there are in this world three goals that people strive for. First, there is ultimate freedom, which is of four kinds. The second is the attainment of the Svarga-heaven by cultivating the power of Indra and other gods. And the third goal is the most abundant

49. Vasu, in his Hindi translation, explains Viṭṭhala's line of reasoning by saying that if the Gopīs had come out of simple passion, they would have asked Kṛṣṇa for the gift of love simply "on the basis that they were women" (Skt./Hindi *strītva*). Instead, they abandoned everything (including their consciousness of themselves as women) and came asking merely to be slaves, and this shows that they possessed "the purified passion that is love of God" (Skt./Hindi *śuddha snehātmaka kāma*).

prosperity (Skt. *paramā lakṣmīḥ*) here on earth. What the Gopīs prove in this stanza is that even these three goals are most perfectly attained by being a slave. First of all, the four kinds of ultimate freedom are : close resemblance to the Lord; attaining the Lord's Heaven; nearness to the Lord; and absorption, or merging, into Him (Skt. *sārūpya, sālokya, sāmīpya* and *sāyujya*). But these are useless before one becomes His slave. The superior quality of that vision of the Lord's lotus-face which is itself a form of Devotion by comparison with these four kinds of ultimate freedom is shown by the fact that when one sees Kṛṣṇa's lotus-face, all desires for those kinds of freedom disappear. The souls who seek 'close resemblance' become the Lord's curls, circling, like bees, around His lotus-face. These numerous curls frame His face, and remain there. But if there is still more devotion remaining in those who, like His curls, have attained close resemblance to the Lord, then why be satisfied with close resemblance? Moreover, Your face is "graced by earrings," which may mean either that the earrings grace Your face, or that Your face graces the earrings. 'Nearness' to the Lord means close proximity, but even when the most complete nearness is attained a person will not be closer to the Lord than these earrings are. If these two earrings are pictured as representing the Sāṃkhya and Yoga which depend on the Blessed Lord's teaching (e.g., in the Bhagavad Gītā and the Bhāgavata itself) and are likewise dependent on Him for their success or failure—then (the followers of) Sāṁkhya and Yoga gaze upon the Blessed Lord's face with the nearness of earrings. Why, then, be satisfied with nearness to the Lord ? And besides, as the Gopīs say : "Flowing with the nectar of the pool of your lips—set between your two broad cheeks." There must be a place where the nectar of the mood of love[50] can be drunk. And the nectar is on

50. "The nectar of the mood of love" translates the single Skt. word *rasa*, which is one of the most important words for Vallabha throughout his commentary, and particularly in this section. The meanings of *rasa* which Vallabha uses are: "fluid, sap" (in the present context, "nectar"); "(the sense of) taste", which, as in English, may mean ordinary taste or aesthetic taste; and "the proper or desired (aesthetic) mood." Vallabha uses the word *rasa* most frequently in the third sense—that of aesthetic "mood"—a usage he has already employed frequently in our text. But often he also plays on the possi-

your lips, between your cheeks. And so, by resting upon your cheek we can drink the nectar of your lips. For in 'attaining the Lord's Heaven' there is but limited joy, and the drinking of the nectar of the Akṣara Brahman.[51] But by comparison with the Akṣara, a place on the Lord's cheek, for kissing Him and other things, is much better. And, the Gopīs say, the nectar of the mood of love, which is on Your lips, is far superior to the nectar of the Akṣara Brahman. The phrase "graced by earrings" may be construed together with the phrase "your two broad cheeks" (to yield : "Your two broad cheeks, which are graced by earrings") in this sense, that the scriptural mood of Devotionw hich takes the form of mutual conversation about your great qualities is superior to the reward of 'nearness'. But (to return to our previous point) the superiority of the nectar of your lips to the Akṣara Brahman is obvious. Moreover, the Gopīs say "glancing laughingly." That is to say, on the Lord's Face there is first a laugh, then a glance. The sheer delight of Devotion is not present in those who have been absorbed into the joy of Brahman (i.e., those who have gained *sāyujya*—"absorption"—as their reward). For the Lord's laugh has the property of awakening all tastes and moods. And knowledge, too (represented by His glance), becomes manifest. But in the joy of Brahman these two, taste of the mood and knowledge, are not manifest to the person who is liberated, just as one who is submerged in water can neither

ble double or triple meanings of the word, as here. Thus he means the "fluid" of the "mood", which, in context, must mean the "nectar" of the "mood of love" (*śṛṅgārarasa*), which is, of course, the dominant mood of Kṛṣṇa's game with the Gopīs.

51. Vallabha interprets *sālokya*, "attaining the Lord's Heaven," as the reward which consists of merging into the Akṣara Brahman, which comes to those strivers on the Path of Knowledge who realize the identity of their Self (*ātman*) with Brahman. These persons actually do "attain the Lord's Heaven" in that they merge into the Akṣara Brahman, which is the "locus" or "environment" of Kṛṣṇa wherever He is, including His Heaven, since it is to Brahman that the scriptures attribute omnipresence. So, wherever Kṛṣṇa appears, the omnipresent Brahman is His "locus" (Skt. *adhiṣṭhāna*). But merging into Brahman is, of course, a lower reward than either merging into Kṛṣṇa/Parabrahman (*sāyujya*) or participation in Kṛṣṇa's eternal heavenly Game, which is the highest reward.

taste nor know the taste of the water he is drinking.[52] For the delightful taste of the experience (of the Lord) comes not when one has been absorbed into Him, but when one has a position somewhat separate from Him. And so, slavery alone is the desirable reward, and not ultimate liberation, because in the condition of slavery one sees the Blessed Lord's face, which is itself a form of Devotion.

By saying "and (we) who have seen that brace of staff-like arms," the Gopīs are teaching us that the attainment of Svarga, by becoming Indra or one of the other gods, is also of no use, because "(Your arms) remove all fear." In Svarga Indra has attained his very highest limit of accomplishment. But Indra and the other gods live in constant fear of the Daityas. And the only thing which removes their fear is the Blessed Lord's "brace of staff-like arms." And since that brace of arms is here right now, how could we even consider leaving those arms and becoming Indra ? The word "and", which introduces this phrase, suggests that the Lord not only grants the gods freedom from fear, but He also gives them, by means of His power of action which consists in sacrifices and so forth, the offerings from the sacrifices.[53] This was how Indra originally reached the fulfilment of his eligibility and was liberated. The word "staff" (= scepter) expresses the Lord's inviolable power of ruling. And the idea that the Lord's rule extends over both places, heaven and earth, is expressed by the word "brace". Because of this fact, the destruction of the Daityas occurs everywhere and entirely. Besides, the Gopīs say : "and (we have seen) the chest," too. All pleasure in all the worlds comes from Śrī (Fortune). But even Śrī finds pleasure there—on Your chest. The word "and" signifies that the Lord's chest is the

52. The "Joy of Brahman" (Skt. *brahmānanda*) is Joy of the Self alone, whereas the "Joy of worshipping Kṛṣṇa through love" (*bhajanānanda*; cf. Verse I of Chapter I above, and *passim*) is Joy with all the senses, body, Self, mind, and all faculties. Joy of the Self excludes even the knowledge that one is in Brahman, whereas the Joy of worship through love does not.

53. The definition of liberation (*mokṣa*) according to the Path of Sacrifice (*karmamārga*) is the absence of suffering (here given by Kṛṣṇa by the removal of Fear), and the presence of happiness (given in the form of the sacrificial offerings).

dwelling-place of Dharma as well.[54] Therefore, "let us be Your slaves," and nothing else. (Here begins an interpolation by Viṭṭhala.) The Gopīs' saying that their gazing at the Lord is the cause of their becoming His slaves shows that this type of gazing at the Lord does not occur in those people in whom this degree of love does not exist. What is meant by this passage is that, where the type of gazing is independent of scriptural law, it is right to consider non-applicable a scriptural law opposed to such gazing (i.e., the Gopīs had, by their love, passed beyond the scope of the positive and negative scriptural laws—such as serving their husbands and not worshipping Kṛṣṇa through love —which apply to persons who do not possess this love). Although the Blessed Lord has said, in stanza 26, "Adultery keeps you from getting to heaven...", pointing out six faults involved in their worshipping Him through love, yet those six faults are eliminated by the Lord's six great qualities. For certainly nothing that accomplishes the highest goals people strive for can be a sin. For it is only because of its result that a sin is reprehensible (end of Viṭṭhala's interpolation).

Introduction to Stanza 40 : But, the Gopīs think, the Lord might say : "The world despises women who meet secretly with illicit lovers. Therefore, for the sake of protecting the Path of the Good, what you have just said, even though you reasoned and interpreted scripture correctly, must not be done. Rather you should keep to the practices of hearing, seeing, etc." (as mentioned in stanza 27). In answer to this the Gopīs say :

Stanza 40 : "O dear one, what woman in the three worlds would not be dazed to distraction by the song of Your flute, with its nectar of soft sounds, so that she strays from the

54. Vallabha is here recognizing that in the traditional lists of Kṛṣṇa's "six great qualities" (Skt. *ṣaḍguṇa*) or "blessings" (*bhaga*) which make Him *bhagavān* ("the Blessed Lord"), the fourth quality, Śrī ("Splendor, Fortune") is sometimes replaced by Dharma ("eternal Right"). Thus Vallabha makes the point that Kṛṣṇa possesses both these qualities pre-eminently. The six great qualities are : Aiśvarya ("Power"), Vīrya ("Valor"), Yaśas or Kīrti (both meaning "Glory, Fame"), Śrī or Dharma, Jñāna ("Knowledge") and Vairāgya ("Detachment"). Naturally, both the Bhāgavata and Vallabha also mean the Goddess Lakṣmī when the word Śrī is used.

conduct of the Āryas ? After all, upon seeing this form of Yours—this greatest wealth of the three worlds—even the cows, the birds, the trees and the deer experienced such a thrill that their hair stood on end! "

Commentary : This rule of life which You have been teaching is for men, not for women, because it is impossible for women. And a rule of life that is impossible is not a valid rule of life at all. When one rule of life (i.e., that of our being faithful wives) thus perishes, Your own Form is the sole cause of its perishing, because you do astounding things. (Here begins an interpolation by Viṭṭhala.) Actually the Lord Himself protects the virtue (Skt. *dharma*) of the devotees who are closely related with Him. This He accomplishes by protecting them from all other inclinations and fostering their inclination to love Him. But the meaning is that there is also no inconsistency in saying that the Lord protects those who are related with His attributes (*dharma*; rather than related with Himself) by means of those very attributes.[55] Therefore, by His protecting certain devotees by Himself (rather than by His attributes), what is indicated is that they are His very dear ones (end of Viṭṭhala's interpolation). And the Gopīs' addressing the Lord as "dear one" indicates that they have no intention of deceiving Him.

Whoever is a woman, i.e., whatever person in this world is described by the word "woman", how could she fail, say the Gopīs, to stray from the conduct of the Āryas ? "In the three worlds" refers to the entire realm that is the effect of the three qualities, *sattva*, *rajas* and *tamas*. The *tāmasa* Gopīs, because of their delusion, had the impression that they were established

55. The key to Viṭṭhala's exegesis of Vallabha's meaning is that the Skt. word *dharma* is used in two (of its many) different senses here: first, as "rule of life, duty, performance of duty"; and second, as "attribute or quality" of a substance, here the Lord's "very own Form" (*svarūpa*). As we saw in the commentary on the previous stanza, Kṛṣṇa's Form has six "great qualities" or attributes (*guṇa* or *dharma*). Therefore, Viṭṭhala says, the *dharma* (duty) of the devotees who are united with the Lord's own Form is protected and assured by the very *dharma*-s (attributes) of that Form. The final meaning of Vallabha's sentence and Viṭṭhala's interpolation is that the Gopīs' original *dharma* has been replaced by Kṛṣṇa's *dharma*-s. The final sentence of Viṭṭhala's interpolation is meant to tell us this.

on the Path of conduct of the noble Āryas. But what they do is actually the reverse. The *rājasa* Gopīs were inclined, by their very nature, to do this sort of thing. And if anyone should think that the *sāttvika* Gopīs, precisely because *sattva* was their dominant quality, would have the right conception of their duty, that notion is disproved here. And the reason they abandon the Path of the Āryas is that they are "dazed to distraction by the song of Your flute, with its nectar of soft sounds." It is only because they are "dazed to distraction" that they stray from the conduct of the Āryas. This sort of delusion is caused by the factors which here take the place of the five factors of Ignorance,[56] since, because of the Gopīs' relation with the Blessed Lord, Ignorance does not obstruct them. Only other factors can obstruct them. And the strength of these other factors comes from the fact that they are "Your" factors, i.e., they belong to You. The soft, sweet, indistinct notes make manifest the nectar which is produced by the song of Your flute, and that song causes dazed fascination. A song causes fascination of the body. As Scripture says : "Women love a singer", and a woman is a woman in body only. A flute entrances the senses, because it is the very embodiment of the mood of love. Nectar entrances the life-breaths, and the notes entrance the heart (literally, "the inner mental faculties"; *antaḥ-karaṇa*). And the indistinct sounds entrance the Self, so that the entire person is completely enraptured. The Āryas are the persons who distinguish truth from falsehood and right from wrong on the basis of the valid means of knowledge (Skt. *pramāṇa*: also "Scripture"). If Scripture says, in the context of

56. The five "factors" (literally "knots"; Skt. *parvan*) of Ignorance (avidyā), which is a "power" (*śakti*) of the Lord, are, according to Vallabha in *Tattvārthadīpa-nibandha* I. 32: "mistaking the body for the Self" (*dehādhyāsa*), "mistaking the sense-faculties for the Self" (*indriyādhyāsa*), "mistaking the life-breath for the Self" (*prāṇādhyāsa*), "mistaking the inner mental faculties for the Self" (*antaḥkaraṇādhyāsa*), and "forgetting one's real nature" (*svarūpavismṛti*). Note that, though Vallabha goes on to say that these five factors cannot obstruct the Gopīs, he shows us that the stanza enumerates five factors created by Kṛṣṇa Himself: His song, His flute, its nectar, its notes, and its indistinct sounds, which "daze" them "to distraction."

one ritual (the Mahendrayāga) that Indra and Mahendra are different, they should be taken as such. This is because of the axiom : "Whatever name Scripture mentions separately should be taken to indicate a separate entity."[57] Otherwise Scripture would not prescribe the expiation, at the end of one year, to be performed by the man who had done the Indra-sacrifice, in the following words : "At the end of the year he should offer eight rice-cakes to Agni (Fire), the lord of vows" (probably *Taitt. Brāh.*). Therefore You Yourself, in whom there is no distinction of body, soul, senses and organs, do not correspond to the means of knowledge (*pramāṇa*) we have been provided with (i.e., your flute, your song, etc., which point to bodily love. Therefore we, Ārya women, are going astray precisely by following the means of knowledge). Actually, in the correct consideration of the matter, what is operative here is the strength of the Object of knowledge (Skt. *prameyabala*). If it were not, then the commands and prohibitions of Scripture (which are, exceptionally, not operative in the case of the Gopīs) would be useless. This (the commands and prohibitions regarding the path of Devotion) will be explained later, in the eleventh book of this scripture. Since what is contradictory to one Path is not necessarily contradictory to another, we cannot be accused of breaking any rule here. Śuka will treat this question more fully later on, just after he finishes his description of the Rāsa-dance, in the stanza which begins : "Violation of what is right...has been seen to mark the conduct of lords" (Bh. P. X. 33. 30). Therefore since we have already attained, here and now, the final reward of our Path, something which is viewed as disgraceful if it is used as a means while on the Path is not an obstacle for us. Besides, our breaking of the scriptural laws was not merely in terms of Sound, but in terms of Form as well. This is why the Gopīs refer to His Form as "this greatest wealth of the three worlds." From this Form come the welfare and prosperity of the three worlds. Just as the sun clothes the

57. Ritual deities consist of scriptural words, not necessarily of separate actual entities in every case, according to Pūrva Mīmāṁsā. Therefore, Indra and Mahendra are taken to be separate for ritual purposes, while in actuality they are the same entity.

day in beauty and the moon the night, the Blessed Lord's Form brings beauty to the three worlds. The word "this" emphasizes that the Lord's Form is immediately and entirely visible here. And the word *ca*[58] suggests the external activity of the Lord's Form—His glances and gestures. Having heard that Sound, and having seen this Form, what woman indeed would not stray from the conduct of the Āryas ? Let us stop this useless talk of means of knowledge. Someone can stray in another way too, since even the natural limitations of beings (i.e., objects of knowledge) disappear before the Blessed Lord's Form. And how, indeed, can such natural limitations be undone ? This is why the Gopīs say : "Even the cows, the birds, the trees and the deer..." For cows, unaware of any talk of means of knowledge, simply mate with their mothers. And birds eat everything and trees stand still. Trees can never feel anything that is outside themselves. Some people say they are entirely without sense-powers. And deer are afraid of everything. And yet if all these were embraced by the mood of love upon seeing the Blessed Lord's Form and hearing His song, so that their hair stood on end, and they thus manifested the qualities of a man of refined aesthetic taste, even though the Blessed Lord created them different from men, then it should be no surprise that we women have also shown some difference from our usual nature because of this sight.

Introduction to Stanza 41 : And so, in order to refute the teachings the Blessed Lord had just spoken to them, the Gopīs have explained the doctrines of the Path of Grace. But this Path is reached by means of the Blessed Lord's Grace alone, therefore the Gopīs pray to the Blessed Lord for this Grace in the following words :

Stanza 41 : "Clearly You have been born on earth to remove fear and suffering from Vraja, just as the divine

58. Skt. *ca* is normally translated by "and" or "also"; but in its context in this stanza I have translated it by "after all". This does not materially affect what Vallabha is saying, however, since he is using the commentator's occasional device of saying that a certain word, usually a particle like *ca* or *hi*, is being used to suggest, according to the rhetorical device of *dhvani*, an additional meaning.

Primeval Person (Nārāyaṇa) protects the heaven of the gods. Therefore, friend of the suffering, please lay Your lotus-hand on the breasts, aflame with suffering, and on the heads of Your maidservants."

Commentary : Neither what You have said nor what we have said has been either a help or a hindrance. And yet, You should consider Your reason for coming down to earth, and grant us Your Grace. Then the Gopīs tell the reason for His coming down : "You have been born on earth"—in manifest form—solely "to remove the fear and suffering of Vraja." Otherwise we do not see any reason why You, the Blessed Lord Himself, should have come down to earth. For a part of you, i.e., Saṅkarṣaṇa, comes down in order to remove the burden of evil from the earth. And Pradyumna comes to earth to be the object of the love of Your father Vasudeva and others (since He became incarnate as Kṛṣṇa's son—Vasudeva's grandson). And it is Aniruddha who comes to protect the sacred rules of life (*dharma*).[59] If not to remove fear and suffering from Vraja, then what object would be accomplished by another descent to earth ? "Clearly", then, "You are here to remove fear and suffering from Vraja." But we are suffering right now, not at some other time. And if we die of our suffering, then all of Vraja will suffer intensely, too. Therefore You must remove our suffering. The Gopīs fear Kṛṣṇa might say : "It would be right for Me to remove your suffering according to the scriptural laws, but not in a way that breaks those laws. Therefore I will gladly put out the fires of your passion or confer knowledge upon you." In answer to this the Gopīs say : "Just as the divine Primeval Person..." The Blessed Lord in the form of Brahman is impartial, i.e., He acts in the same way toward everyone. Yet He willingly shows partiality when He grants His Grace to Indra and the other gods by killing the Daityas. But He does

59. This is the first full reference in our section to the four "forms" or "manifestations" (Skt. *vyūha*) of the Supreme God (*puruṣottama*), a doctrine introduced and made famous by the Pañcarātra Vaiṣṇava scriptures. The four *vyūha*-s are: Vāsudeva, the Supreme God Kṛṣṇa Himself; Saṅkarṣaṇa, who has become incarnate in the context of our present story as Kṛṣṇa's elder brother Balarāma; Pradyumna; and Aniruddha.

not grant knowledge to the gods. If He can thus change His very own nature, then we must certainly say that He can change His words (i.e., the scriptural laws). Therefore, the Gopīs mean to say, just as the Primeval Person became a god and the protector of the heaven of the gods, so You, though You are the protector of the laws of personal and social duty, should become united with us. And so the Gopīs, in order to intensify the mood of love, invent a pretext and say : "Therefore, please lay Your hand on us." First put Your hand on our heads, for that will remove our fear. And then put Your lotus-hand, which flows with nectar and destroys all suffering, on our breasts, to put out the fire of suffering in our hearts. There would be nothing improper in this, for we are "Your maidservants." Or this statement of the Gopīs, these words that arouse the mood of love, may be viewed as a request to the Lord to feel the beauty of their breasts.

Introduction to Stanza 42 : Śuka now tells us what the Blessed Lord did in response to these prayers of the Gopīs :

Stanza 42 : Śuka said : "When He heard them speaking in such a flurry of despondence, the Lord of the masters of Yoga smiled compassionately. And though He delights in Himself, He began showing the delights of love to the Gopīs."

Verses : *Verse I* : By exercising lordship over His six great qualities, Hari by Himself delights in love in six ways. And the love that He makes by means of His very own Form as well is said to be of two kinds.[60]

Verse II : The ordinary sort of love-play is described first (in Stanza 42, above), and then, in terms of special love, the love that takes place in a group is first described (Stanza 43). After that, the love-game that involves external activity is described (Stanza 44), and then intimate, physical love (Stanza 45).

Verse III : Then many different types of love-play take place, which bring intense delight in many forms (Stanza 46). After this, the Gopīs' pride, aroused so that they may experience love

60. Vasu, in his Hindi translation, says that the two kinds here referred to are love in union and love in separation.

in separation, is described (Stanza 47). And, finally, the Lord disappears, for He is no worldly lover (Stanza 48).

Commentary : First Śuka describes the common, or ordinary (Skt. *sāmānya*), sort of love-game which Kṛṣṇa played in order to remove the suffering of the Gopīs. He says that "when the Lord heard" their words, spoken "in a flurry of despondence," i.e., in the depths of anxiety and depression, He "smiled...and began showing the delights of love to the Gopīs." To the question : "How can one who is without ordinary sense-faculties and motor-organs make love ?", Śuka answers by describing Kṛṣṇa as "the Lord of the masters of Yoga." For in Yoga and similar practices all things burst clearly into perception, even the supernormal powers like becoming small as an atom, etc. And so at that very moment the Lord made His own Form manifest by endowing it with sense-faculties and the rest. He did this not because He was filled with passion, for if that were the case, His passion would disappear when His seed was spent. Rather, since He saw that the Gopīs' love for Him would never leave them, "He smiled" broadly and beautifully, in order to save them, not in order to destroy them by regarding them as separated from Him after He had caused them to stray from the scriptural law. That is why Śuka says : "compassionately". He brought the delights of love to the Gopīs alone, but by His nature "He delights in Himself" alone. Or, the word "compassionately" may refer to the fact that the Lord was making the Gopīs the basis of His own experience of the mood of love.

Verses : *Verse I* : Every action which expresses it is present, but passion is nowhere to be found here. The complete fulfilment of the Gopīs' desire is accomplished by the passionless One. Consequently they, too, are free of passion.

Verse II : Clearly passion answered by passion would cause Saṁsāra to roll on and on. But by (the Lord's) absence of passion, there is no doubt that (the Gopīs') freedom from passion would be complete.

Verse III : Therefore no scriptural law was broken here, and moreover, this game of the Lord confers the reward of ultimate freedom. And so the person who hears the account of this game becomes totally free of passion.

Verse IV : Since this entire story of the Blessed Lord's games is described as free from passion, it will not arouse passion in the heart of one who hears it. This is the clear meaning of Śuka's words.

Further Commentary : The word "though" in the stanza is meant to distinguish the Lord's delight in Himself alone from the delight He confers by means of Himself. "He began showing the delights of love" means He began to make love in many ways. And he gradually made manifest an overwhelming abundance of the mood of love.

Introduction to Stanza 43 : Having thus described the ordinary love-game, Śuka narrates for us in the next three stanzas the special love-game the Lord played with the Gopīs :

Stanza 43 : With the Gopīs grouped around Him, their faces blossoming at the sight of the beloved, Acyuta, of noble conduct, His teeth gleaming white as jasmine-flowers in His great-hearted laugh, shone brilliantly, like the moon surrounded by stars.

Commentary : First of all the Lord mingled with the Gopīs, playing games which do not arouse passion. For first the Gopīs stayed a short distance away from Him, out of fear. Therefore His "conduct" was "noble". The nobility of conduct the Lord shows here has the mood of love as its object. And, as the mood of love began to manifest itself very intensely in the Gopīs, the Lord played all the love-games which are taught in the treatises on erotic love. From these games the Gopīs experienced inwardly the fulness of the mood of love. "Their faces blossomed" so that they could better see their "beloved", the Blessed Lord. Or, their faces blossomed at the sight of their beloved, just as flowers blossom because of the rays of the sun. In reality, the Gopīs did this for one reason only—to drink the nectar which was on Kṛṣṇa's lower lip, which represents greed (cf. Bh. P. II. 1. 32). And insofar as they do this, that nectar might disappear. To indicate that this would not happen, Śuka has said : "Acyuta", i.e., "non-flowing." And, to signify that the Gopīs did not fully attain that nectar, he says : "great-hearted." The "laugh" which is great-hearted causes the most intense passion, and the infatuation which the laugh has induced for the sake of passion alone, is in its turn the lone factor which has made the Gopīs' love grow to fulness. Then Śuka tells us that the Lord's brilliance shone from His teeth, which were exposed by His laugh. And His teeth were like jasmine-flowers, since, though they are normally reddish, they were made white by His laugh. His teeth are said to be as white as jasmine-flowers in order to make us realize that the love involved here also passed from the red of passion to the white of pure love. (Here begins an interpolation by Viṭṭhala.) At first, love pure and simple, without qualification, was present in the Gopīs. But now the Blessed Lord wishes to grant them, according to the method taught in the treatises on aesthetics, the Joy of Himself. And so He now produces in them a love which simultaneously is similar in kind to His Joy and qualified by passion. Therefore, to indicate the relation between the teeth and these two forms of love, Śuka uses the word *dvija*, "twice-born", hence "teeth" (because love, too, is twice-born here) (end of Viṭṭhala's interpolation). Since this is so, in order to erase the doubt that the brightness of the Lord's teeth might fade because He is eating fruit,[61] Śuka says: "(His teeth) gleaming white."

Although the Lord was enjoying the delights of love only because of the Gopīs' insistence and in order to remove the evils of the world, and not for His own pleasure, still He acted not like the One who has all His desires fulfilled, but like a worldly lover. And Śuka has pointed this out by an example, saying that "He shone brilliantly, like the moon surrounded by stars." In this stanza all those, and only those, love-games which involve external activity, and do not involve specific erotic positions, have been described.

Introduction to Stanza 44 : This first special love-game served to remove that passion which was an obstacle. Now in order to evoke the second special love-game, Śuka first describes all the trappings of that game :

61. Skt. *phala*, "fruit", also means "reward"; therefore this phrase also means: "because He is enjoying the reward." The objection seems to imply that the Lord's brightness in general could be expected to fade because He is enjoying, or after He has enjoyed, the reward.

Stanza 44 : As they were praising Him in song, the Lord, the shepherd of this flock of hundreds of lovely women, also began to sing. And, wearing His Vaijayantī-necklace, He wandered about, beautifying the forest.

Commentary : As He was being praised in song by the Gopīs who were gathered close to Him, He Himself began to sing. And after that He became the leader and protector, or "shepherd," of the many different groups among these hundreds of women, who are of different types. He makes a single group out of as many Gopīs as are ideal in number to arouse the mood of love when He mingles with them. In this way various kinds of groups were created. And He shepherded these flocks, even those who were at some distance, by comforting and encouraging them. Then Śuka describes Kṛṣṇa's appearance as He walks along and sings by saying : "Wearing His Vaijayantī-necklace." Wearing His Vaijayantī-necklace, which is studded with nine gems and is both part of and expressive of His very nature, which proclaims His Lordship and Power and is rich in His glorious Fame, and adorning and beautifying the entire forest, "He wandered about," pursuing the course of His game. For the course of this game consists in arousing the passion of the Gopīs. He is the one who brings their passion to its fulness. Or the phrase "He wandered about" may mean that He went from one forest or grove to another.

Introduction to Stanza 45 : Now that the Gopīs' passion has been awakened, Śuka tells us how the Lord made love with them, using all the erotic positions and so forth :

Stanza 45 : When the Lord had arrived, with the Gopīs, at the Yamunā's bank, with its snowy-white sands, He made love with them, as the wind carried the lovely fragrance of the water-lilies from the river's joyful waves.

Commentary : When He had arrived at the clear, soft sandy beach which forms the bank of the Yamunā, i.e., when He and all the Gopīs had arrived, He made the sand very soft and ideal for love-making by moving, arranging and piling it and so forth. And then "He made love with" the different kinds of Gopīs. The snowy coolness of the sands checked the inner heat of the lovers. And Śuka describes the outer coolness when he says : "the wind carried the lovely fragrance of the waterlilies from the river's joyful waves." The waves of the river flowed against the bank and communicated their joy to it. Or, the text may also be interpreted to say that it is the wind which is joyful. And this joy is communicated to the lovely fragrance of the water-lilies. And a lovely laziness is created by the joy which the fragrance produces. The coolness of the water-lilies comes from their relation with the water. And so we have the riverbank affected by this type of breeze. For in the erotic positions which are called "great" (Skt. *mahā-bandheṣu*), the wind is a necessary factor (e.g., for drying perspiration).

Introduction to Stanza 46 : By thus producing all the necessary sentiments and surroundings (OR : "by reason of their Total Love"; Skt. *sarvabhāvena*), the Lord produced in the Gopīs the type of love-play in which passion has the major role. Śuka tells us how, after this, the Lord pursued, starting with the eight kinds of embrace and so forth, the path of love's most intense delights, which includes all the movements which express passion :

Stanza 46 : By stretching out His arms and embracing them; by playfully caressing their hair; by pleasurably stroking their thighs, loosening their waist-cloths and fondling their breasts; by engaging in battles with fingernails; and by playful derision, glances, and smiles the Lord aroused the lovely women of Vraja to the peak of passion, and made love to them.

Commentary : He reached out His arm, either because the Gopī was some distance away, or to touch some part of her body. And then He pulled her roughly to Him and embraced her. Then He caressed her hands and hair, stroked her thighs, loosened her waist-cloth and fondled her breasts. He "caresses her hand" means He grasps it. Or this "caressing her hand" may be a veiled reference to the kind of intercourse in which the woman acts like a man. Thus He caresses her hair in order to lift it up and back. He strokes her thighs to achieve the arm-encirclement position. He loosens the knot of her waist-cloth so that, when the mood reaches its peak, she may get rid of it. And He fondles her breasts in order to arouse the mood of love still further. Thus He performs "the five touches" which are taught in the treatises on erotic love. "Playfully" refers to the joking words He utters to fix their passion fast, at its peak. Then the "battles with fingernails" describe the passionate wrestling and fighting in which the lovers hit, bite and scratch one another. And in whatever places Kāma is smouldering in his sleep of death, he is awakened there by these battles, just as happens to a beaten army when its king appears on the battlefield. And "playful derision" refers to the Lord's amorous chiding, and so forth, of the Gopīs, preceded by His "glances". And His "smiles" establish the mood of love fully. Thus the twelve kinds of passion (literally, "the twelve-fold Kāma"), latent in the twelve parts of the body, are awakened. That is why Śuka says : "He aroused the lovely women of Vraja." When lovers are together, passion (Kāma) takes the form of Rati's husband, the god of love, but when lovers are apart, passion takes the form of Agni—fire. After thus arousing in them the divine form of Kāma, the Lord "made love to" the Gopīs. The Lord made manifest only the pleasure of the Gopīs—He did not, by bringing passion to an end, produce the satedness that follows the climax.

Introduction to Stanza 47 : Śuka next describes how the Lord after causing the Gopīs to experience love in union with Him, prepares them to experience love in separation from Him by stirring up their pride :

Stanza 47 : After the great-souled Blessed Lord Kṛṣṇa had thus fulfilled all their desires, the Gopīs became proud, considering themselves far superior to all other women on earth.

Commentary : The Blessed Lord, who, in the manner described above, has the power of granting the fulness of every mood and sentiment; Kṛṣṇa, who is eternal Joy—the embodiment of the final reward—has "fulfilled all the desires" of the Gopīs. Consequently the Gopīs considered "themselves", i.e., their own Selves, to be fulfilled and complete, but they did not regard the Blessed Lord as full, nor did they regard their fulness as coming from Him. Someone might object : "But why did the Blessed

Lord act that way? Why didn't He keep these Gopīs lowly and humble?" So Śuka says: "the great-souled." For the Lord's soul, i.e., His Self, is great indeed. No one who enters deep water can escape being saturated, and a pot plunged into deep water cannot avoid being filled. Besides this, the Gopīs considered themselves superior among women, even superior to all the women on earth. And so, naturally, they "became proud." After all, they said to themselves, there are no other women like us. And so if He prays to us for it, we will grant Him the mood of love. Such thoughts made them proud. The qualities of the Blessed Lord Himself had taken possession of the Gopīs. Since this was the case, they thought: "Just as the Blessed Lord came under our control a little ago because we prayed to Him, so will we submit ourselves to His control if He prays to us." But this feeling of theirs was only for the sake of the mood of love, and did not constitute a fault on the Gopīs' part, because it was the Blessed Lord's own sentiment that now possessed them.

Introduction to Stanza 48: In this stanza Śuka tells us how the Blessed Lord, granting the gift of the mood of love in the form of identity with Him, disappeared externally:

Stanza 48: When He noticed that the Gopīs' good fortune had brought a certain conceit, and pride, upon them, Keśava, in order to bring this to an end and grant them His grace, disappeared on the spot.[62]

Commentary: The Gopīs' pride and sense of utter fulness did not constitute faults on their part, but this perception of themselves as superior to all other women on earth was certainly a fault. Śuka has repeated in different words his description of their state in order to show that the Lord disappeared precisely in order to remedy this fault. When the Lord noticed this well-known "conceit" of theirs at their great "good fortune,"

62. The verb form here, *antaradhīyata*, which definitely means "He disappeared," also means "He was absorbed into" or "He went within," i.e., He entered within the Gopīs and possessed them (this is what Vallabha means by "identity"—Skt. *aikyam*—in the introduction to this stanza). This second meaning is extremely important, as Vallabha will further point out, for understanding the Gopīs' behavior in the next chapter, which follows immediately upon this stanza.

which has been described above and was marked by their feeling of superiority to all other women, "He disappeared...in order to bring an end to this." Someone might raise the objection : "But didn't this feeling of the Gopīs result from their love-play with the Blessed Lord ? Since this was entirely His doing, then why did He disappear?" Śuka replies that "when Keśava noticed their pride, He disappeared on the spot in order to grant them His grace." This pride had to be removed. But pride is an interior emotion. Only someone who has no real capability will attempt to remove its external traces. The word "and" indicates that this pride was the Lord's own quality as well. Therefore He would grant His grace first to the Gopīs, and then to Himself.[63] "On the spot" means that right there, in the midst of the Gopīs, He "disappeared", or "went within," i.e., He became invisible. In case someone should object : "But these two things (removing the Gopīs' conceit and their pride) need not be done; why doesn't He simply overlook the faults?", Śuka's reply is simply : "Keśava." Just as the Lord Keśava (Kṛṣṇa) removed Brahmā's quality of *rajas* and granted Him ultimate freedom, and as He removed Śiva's quality of *tamas*, so He removed the conceit and pride of the Gopīs, in order to grant them ultimate freedom. And this disappearance of His was a bodily disappearance, because the Gopīs were at the elementary level of eligibility (the Gopīs are, at this point, *tāmasa* devotees).

63. According to Vasu's Hindi translation, the sense here is that Kṛṣṇa would first grace the Gopīs by removing their pride and putting them under His control; and then He would "grace Himself" by removing His own pride and putting Himself under their control (as, indeed, He had already done by answering their prayer that He make love to them). Thus the mutuality and equality between Kṛṣṇa and the devotee, a prime characteristic of Vallabha's Grace-Devotion (*puṣṭibhakti*) is what is stressed here.

CHAPTER II

(Bhāgavata Purāṇa Book X, Chapter 30)

Introductory Verses : Verses I-III : The Blessed Lord played this love-game in order to establish His own Joy in the Gopīs. This Joy has been produced externally. And now, so that it may enter within them and become full, the Blessed Lord Himself enters within them, taking His game along with Him. In this game there are four subjects to be described : The Gopīs' passionate attachment to the mood of love, Hari's actions, and the absence of pride.[1] These three are described here in the beginning, in their proper order, first by mentioning them briefly, then by defining them, and finally by pointing out their results.

Verse IV : In this twenty-seventh chapter Śuka describes how, upon the Lord's disappearance, the Gopīs, devoting themselves completely to Him by searching for Him and enacting His games, interiorized the mood of love.

Introduction to Stanza 1 : At the end of the last chapter the Blessed Lord's disappearance was described. Now Śuka describes how the first, immediate result of that event was an intense suffering that overwhelmed the Gopīs' hearts, which were so passionately attached to the mood of love ;

Stanza 1 : When the Blessed Lord went within, the women of Vraja immediately experienced great suffering because they

1. The fourth "subject to be described," according to Vasu's Hindi translation, is "singing the praises of the Blessed Lord's great qualities" (*bhagavadguṇagāna*). It is odd that Vallabha does not mention this here, but this is because it is not a subject of the present chapter. Vallabha mentions it immediately, however, in his first introductory Verse to the next chapter, as the subject of that chapter, which it quite clearly is.

could no longer see Him, just as female elephants suffer when they do not see the lord of the herd.

Commentary : When the Blessed Lord went within, along with His six qualities, lordly Power and the others, since the Gopīs did not look within themselves, they "immediately," and completely unexpectedly, experienced great suffering. The reason they did not reflect and search within themselves is that they are "the women of Vraja." And the reason for their suffering is "because they could no longer see Him." The fire of suffering, which is always present as the natural embodiment of passion (Kāma) when the beloved is separate, is put out by seeing him, touching him, and so forth. But when they no longer saw Him externally, as they had before, that suffering once more became natural and fitting. To point out that, for the Gopīs, touch was the chief source of satisfaction, Śuka cites this example : "Just as female elephants..." "The leader of the herd" is a bull elephant aroused to the peak of sexual excitement. As Vātsyāyana has said : "Only the bull elephant really knows sexual delight" (*Kāmasūtra*). And the commentator says: "In the rubbing and crushing that take place in the sex-act, the elephant (is the greatest)." Besides, there are lions about, and what's more, the females' time is ripe. Therefore the female elephants suffer greatly when they do not see the lord of the herd.

Introduction to Stanza 2 : Śuka now tells us how this fire of suffering wished to enter and possess the Gopīs, but since the Blessed Lord's game entered within them first, it drove the suffering away and caused itself alone to be manifest there :

Stanza 2 : The Gopīs, their minds utterly charmed and swelled by His movements, His love-stirrings, His glances and His smiles of deep affection, His heart-rejoicing words and the delights of His love-play, made their own all the actions and gestures of Lakṣmī's Lord, for He was, after all, their very Self.

Commentary : The Gopīs were so captivated by the Blessed Lord's body, speech and mind that they attained His own condition and sentiments—His very state of being—and they made their own each and every movement and action of the Blessed

Lord. Śuka first tells us about the bodily actions. "His movements," i.e., all His bodily actions, captivated them. Then they were captivated by the action of His mind together with His sense-faculties, as described in the words : "His love-stirrings, His glances and His smiles of deep affection." Deeply affectionate love is a quality of the mind. His smile proceeds from love, and its playful activity is meant to make the Gopīs abandon their religious attitude toward Him (? Skt. *svaniṣṭhatā*). If this were not so, then the result of the Lord's smiling at them would be an increase in knowledge. And so by His smile, by this unhurried, lingering smile, they were a bit dazed and bewildered, and were neither within themselves nor outside themselves, but the Blessed Lord became manifest in the very middle, and they came to partake of His qualities. Along with the smiles of deep affection went His "love-stirrings," such as His turning lazily to and fro, etc; and together with all this, "His glances," which were all sidelong glances. Śuka describes the bewilderment caused by His verbal actions, too, when He says : "His heart-rejoicing words." "Heart-rejoicing" (Skt. *manorama*) may mean that His words cause delight to the heart or that they find their delight in the heart. These heart-rejoicing words were the Blessed Lord's secret love-whisperings. For the Gopīs' minds would not be "utterly charmed" by mere ordinary words. For women to understand what is to be understood here there is no other way than the one the Lord used, in which the reward of their understanding is explained right at the beginning—namely, that the Blessed Lord's words are spoken for the sake of their happiness. Only then do His words produce that happiness. And Śuka indicates that some of the Lord's words had been spoken in order to indicate certain erotic positions and other details necessary to His love-games when he says : "His love-play." And these forms of love-play had differences of gradation and detail, for example : within the "outstretched" (OR : "upraised" *uttānaka*) position, there are several modes of intercourse, such as "the villagers' way" and so forth. And according to the threefold nature—*tāmasa, sāttvika* and *rājasa*—of the erotic positions the Lord used with the Gopīs, "their minds," which possessed the same threefold division, became "utterly charmed." Śuka means that for this reason (because their minds were utterly charmed) they did not experience suffering. When Śuka says "swelled" (here begins an interpolation by Viṭṭhala) the word "swelled" here indicates that the Gopīs' experience of an insanely abundant mood of love was the reason why they did not even investigate whether they were within themselves or outside themselves. Śuka intends to teach that the manifestation of the Lord's games in the Gopīs properly accompanies this mood (end of Viṭṭhala's interpolation)—Śuka means that their conceit was very intense—as is the nature of a woman—otherwise they would not have lost their attitude of being the Lord's slaves. At this time (i.e., in this mood of love) a game which the Blessed Lord plays only by Himself (such as herding the cows) would not be useful for the Gopīs, and so they did not experience such a game. This is what Śuka indicates when he says : "Lakṣmī's Lord," i.e., Lakṣmī's Husband. The Gopīs "made their own" His "actions and gestures," i.e., the love-play which Kṛṣṇa engages in with Lakṣmī. Since, though this is only one game, it contains many actions, Śuka has said : "all the actions and gestures." Someone might object : "But the manifestation of the Lord's own qualities in His slaves is forbidden." And Śuka replies to this : "He was, after all, their very Self." The Blessed Lord was in the Gopīs' very Selves, manifested just as He truly is. And so Śuka has mentioned briefly how the Gopīs averted suffering by making the Blessed Lord's games their very own. He will explain this in greater detail later. And we shall also explain the reason for the order of these games.

Introduction to Stanza 3 : After this, Śuka tells us, the Gopīs assumed the Blessed Lord's very own Form :

Stanza 3 : In moving, in smiling, in glancing, in speaking and in all else the beloved Gopīs assumed the outward forms of their Lover. And they, weak by nature but having Him as their very Self, proclaimed to each other "I am He" as they delighted in Kṛṣṇa's love-play.

Commentary : If someone else's qualities enter into a person, then it becomes contradictory for the two sets of qualities to exist in one person. Therefore the Gopīs superimposed their own qualities upon the Blessed Lord (since His qualities had taken possession of them). The four chief qualities are those of body, speech, mind and glance or gaze. The Gopīs assumed the outward forms of all these qualities. Their own external appearances were superimposed upon the qualities of the Blessed Lord. Otherwise, if this mutual assumption of the other's qualities were absent, this charming love-game would not be complete. Now to Śuka's description : "moving" is the bodily quality, and "smiling" the quality of the mind. "Glancing" involves the sense-powers, and "speaking" requires the vocal faculties. And all the other amorous gestures which Śuka calls "love-play", such as the erotic positions and so forth, are the very embodiments of sexual love. And "the beloved Gopīs," when they reached the stage of sexual enjoyment, became the opposite of their usual nature with regard to each and every quality connected with "their Lover," the Lord. As Vātsyāyana says : "In an excess of the mood of love, women become changed into men" (*Kāmasūtra*). Therefore, though the Gopīs were not by nature the lovers, but the objects of the Lord's love, they experienced such a change that their natures became the opposite and they "assumed all the outward forms of their Lover."

Then the Gopīs who had been some distance away from the Blessed Lord asked: "Where is the Blessed Lord ?" And the Gopīs who answer them, ignorant of the fact that the Lord had gone within (all of them), say : "He is Kṛṣṇa" or "I am Kṛṣṇa." Or perhaps one Gopī says : "I am He—I'm the one you're looking for," in order to convince the other Gopīs that she is indeed Kṛṣṇa. Unlike an actor, who dons a costume to create a false appearance, and is play-acting when he speaks his lines, the Gopīs were speaking from the depths of their Selves. To point this out, Śuka says the Gopīs are "weak by nature." Women are weak—they are incapable of acting out the part of the Blessed Lord. And the difference between a man and a woman is obvious. And so, aware that his words might be misleading, Śuka adds : "but having Him as their very Self." The Gopīs assumed not only the form of Him who has these qualities, but they assumed all His qualities as well. Their "love-play" was like that of Kṛṣṇa in that they used their bodies, their speech and their minds; and their "delights" included the various actions of love which He Himself had performed.

Introduction to Stanza 4 : Having thus mentioned and explained briefly the relationship which now existed in the Gopīs among these three factors—the suffering, the games of the Lord, and the Blessed Lord Himself—Śuka tells us how the Gopīs first of all searched for Him in order to relieve their suffering. These three factors act like the three qualities of material existence, in that each alternately tends to suppress the other two, and one of them becomes manifest by the Blessed Lord's will. So there is no sudden conflict among the acts, each associated with one of these three factors, but not mutually contradictory, which the Gopīs are now performing. Therefore whenever the Gopīs perceived the outer world, they asked about the Lord, as Śuka tells us in the next stanza. First of all they began singing, out of a tangled mixture of perceptions and emotions :

Stanza 4 : Singing in high-pitched voices of Him alone, and staying in a group, the Gopīs searched for Him like insane people, going from grove to grove of the forest. And they asked the large forest trees: "Where is that Person who, like (the element) Space, is both within and without all creatures ?"

Verses: *Verse I* : For sound is like smoke, which is a product of both internal and external conditions (as in the attempt to ignite a wet log; the fire of external separation from Kṛṣṇa burns the Gopīs, the logs, but the internal wetness that is the Gopīs' interior experience of Kṛṣṇa produces smoke when fire is applied). The sound of the Gopīs' singing billows forth profusely, like smoke. And like smoke, each log produces a different kind (i.e., it expresses the different feelings of each Gopī). Therefore in this context, because of the superiority of both the Lord and His qualities, the knowledge the Gopīs have is the highest knowledge.[2]

Verse II : Just as the Gopīs had come together, each by each, when they had heard the Blessed Lord's song, so it is clear that they were singing here so that the Blessed Lord might Himself come to them.

2. I am indebted to Shri Shyam Goswamy for the translation and interpretation of this extremely difficult verse. It also seems clear to me that this verse alludes to an earlier Hindu scriptural passage, *B. Ā. Upan.* II. 4. 10.

Verse III : But because that state of mind (that they themselves were Kṛṣṇa) was artificial, the Gopīs mingled together with one another. But as a result of that, on the basis of their special knowledge (that they were separate from Kṛṣṇa), it flashed into their perception all the more clearly that Kṛṣṇa had indeed disappeared.

Commentary: Then the Gopīs "searched" thoroughly, constantly asking : "Where is the Blessed Lord ?" It had not yet fully dawned on them that He had disappeared entirely, and they searched for Him randomly, without any set pattern. Śuka indicates this by telling us they searched "like insane people." An "insane person" may be one whose insanity is not clear to others, or one who is contemptible. As such a person cannot distinguish between himself and others, he also goes around without clothes or anything else. This was the condition the Gopīs had reached. They went from one grove to another in the forest. And besides, they were not only searching, but asking questions in the manner of insane people as well, as Śuka tells us in the sentence that begins : "And they asked..." For Śuka knows well the real nature of the Blessed Lord, and he sees clearly that Kṛṣṇa, whose hands, feet, face, stomach and all else are made up entirely of absolute Joy, exists everywhere. Another person can see this, too, if in addition to loving devotion, knowledge becomes manifest in him. Then all the Lord's hiding-places are destroyed ! But the Gopīs asked their questions on the assumption that the Lord was limited to one place. In order to point out their ignorance, Śuka has them say : "Who, like Space, is both within and without all creatures." For, as has been explained before, Space is the cause of the distinction between the inner and the outer. And He is like Space. For that reason alone is Space a mark of Brahman. Since they did not see Him existing, as He does, everywhere and in everything, and had given up the idea of searching within themselves, and did not ask any sentient beings where He was, they began asking the immobile objects. As Śuka says :"They asked the large forest trees." For trees are Vaiṣṇava.[3] And even a senseless Vaiṣṇava knows the movements of Viṣṇu, though the very cleverest non-Vaiṣṇava knows not.

3. For Kṛṣṇa's beautiful eulogy of trees as paradigms for human conduct, cf. Bh. P. X. 22. 30-36.

Introduction to Stanza 5 : Śuka tells us how the Gopīs first directed their questions to the three kinds of tree which have attained in this world the forms of Viṣṇu, Brahmā and Śiva, respectively, namely the pippal tree, the waved-leaf fig tree, and the banyan tree :

Stanza 5 : The Gopis said : "Have you seen, O pippal, O fig-tree, O banyan, that son of Nanda, who has stolen our hearts and minds with His love, His smiles and His glances, and run away ?"

Commentary : The Gopīs thought to themselves that since the pippal tree is the tree that belongs especially to Viṣṇu (Skt. *vaiṣṇava*), and, like Viṣṇu, it deserves homage in this world, it will probably know where He is. And yet, since it is senseless, and since it cultivates such a high opinion of itself—its name is the cause of this—it will not know (since the Lord does not make Himself known to the proud). For the pippal tree's name, *aśvattha*, means that a horse (*aśva*) stands next to it (*ttha*). Men take their place upon a horse, but the horse takes its place next to this tree. And Scripture tells us : "Because He (i.e., the Lord Prajāpati) took the form of a horse and took His place next to a pippal tree" (*Taitt. Brāh* I. 2. 1. 5). Thus the pippal tree's name. So the Gopīs thought : "Well, then, the pippal tree belongs to the Lord Prajāpati (Brahmā). So, instead of the pippal, we should ask Prajāpati's very own tree." And so they proceeded to ask the waved-leaf fig-tree by saying : "o fig-tree." But people say that this tree's ignorance is obvious from its very name (*plakṣa*). For this tree sprang up on earth because the gods caused the ritual purity and holiness to flow out of a sacrificial animal in order to make men ignorant. Therefore this tree is unholy and a cause of ignorance to all people. Therefore how would it tell us where He is ? For Scripture says : "The gods attained the Svarga-heaven by offering an animal, and they thought among themselves : 'But men will reach the same heights we have.' And so the gods cut off the animal's head and let its marrow flow out. And this marrow became the waved-leaf fig-tree."[4] Then

4. This etymological/mythical derivation of the fig-tree's name, *plakṣa* is based on the verb-root *pra-kṣar*, "to flow out." Since the *plakṣa* sprang

the Gopīs consider that since Śiva is entirely free of the bonds of action, and since He is a Guru of Viṣṇu's religion (Skt. *vaiṣṇa-vadharma*), they should ask Him. And so they ask the banyan tree, which is a form of Śiva. But this tree has a fault, too, which is reflected in its name. For on the banyan tree (*nyagro-dha*), all (*nitarām* = *ni*) the top branches (*agra*) grow downwards (*adhaḥ*). And the Gopīs thought that, since this tree finally sinks to such a low condition (and can therefore not attain know-ledge), there is good reason for our passing it by.

The word "you" in "have you seen?" (in the stanza) suggests the meaning : "Have you seen Him who is so closely related to you?" But, in case the trees should answer : "We have seen Him before," or "we always see Him, but why do you ask?", the Gopīs say : "He has stolen our hearts and minds...and run away." The trees might object : "But how can Viṣṇu Himself commit robbery?" The Gopīs answer simply : "The son of Nanda." If He has become the son of Nanda, then He must do the same things Nanda does. For cowherds steal curds, milk and other products. Therefore it is not all contradictory for us to say He has stolen our hearts. Or the Gopīs may simply be using the father's name to signify Him whom they consider their husband, since wives should not use the name of their hus-band. We didn't realize the king's son was a thief until He stole our hearts, but if He hadn't been stealing, then why would He have left his enjoyments and gone ? The trees might object again : "But the heart is within the body—how could someone grasp it to steal it ?" And the Gopīs answer that, as the heart is made up of the three qualities, He grasped it by three means : "by His love, His smiles, and His glances." His heart-stealing glances are preceded by love and accompani ed by smiles. And each of these means embodies one of the heart's three qualities—love embody-ing *sattva*, the smiles *rajas*, and the glances *tamas*. The Thief gained entrance by love, seized His treasure by His smiling and carried it off by His glances.

Introduction to Stanza 6 : Śuka describes how, when the Gopīs realized that these trees were not going to give them an

up from what the gods caused to flow out, the connection is established. There is quite a free variation between "l" and "r" in Sanskrit, so *plakṣa* and *prakṣa* could, without too much stretch of the imagination, be said to be the same.

answer, and that, though the trees were large, they bore little, and inferior, fruit, and were worshipped only by crows, they said to one another : "Let us ask the great, flower-bearing, fragrant trees." And so they asked the red amaranth and other trees :

Stanza 6 : "Red Amaranth, Aśoka, Nāga, Punnāga and Campaka ! Has Balarāma's younger brother, whose smile destroys the pride of conceited women, passed through nere ?"

Commentary : The Red Amaranth and Aśoka trees awaken passion, since Kāma uses the flowers of these trees as his arrows. The Nāga is the Nāgakesara tree, and its flowers, as well as those of the Punnāga and the Campaka, are beautifully fragrant. They distract even the person who is inflamed with passion. Therefore these five trees will know, think the Gopīs. They ask the trees : "Have you seen Balarāma's younger brother ?" And as before, the Gopīs give their reason for asking, saying this time : "Whose smile destroys the pride of conceited women." The Blessed Lord went away for no reason at all ! Since pride disappears merely at His smile, why did He have to go away, too? And certainly He couldn't have been afraid, since He is "Balarāma's younger brother," i.e., Balabhadra's brother—of course we must not use the name of our husband! But we have all remained proud. And so He went in order to defeat our pride. And these trees have probably not seen Him. For the *kurabaka* (Red Amaranth) derives its pleasure from an ugly-sounding howl (*KUtsita RAVA suKHA*), and is fond of such wailing. And the Aśoka destroys (*a*-)sorrow (*śoka*), but it does not confer happiness on anyone. And the Nāga, by its very name (*nāga* means "snake") causes terror. Or, if we take *nāga* to mean "elephant", it is still fearful, and Punnāga would mean "an elephant (*nāga*) among men (*puṁs*)." And the Campaka ends up being tasteless. And these trees are fruitless, too.

Introduction to Stanza 7 : The first group of trees had no flowers, and this second group had no fruits. The Gopīs thought that the ignorance of these trees might come from the fact that their flowers and fruits are used for purposes unrelated to the Lord. And they said to themselves : "But the Tulasī-plant has neither flowers nor fruit, nor is it used for other purposes." So Śuka now describes to us how they went to

Tulasī, famous because it is the Blessed Lord's own special plant and asked her where He was :

Stanza 7 : "O noble lady Tulasī, who love the feet of Govinda, have you seen your greatly-beloved Acyuta, who carries you constantly on His feet, along with your company of swarming bees?"

Commentary : The Gopīs address her directly by her name, "Tulasī", because they consider her their close friend. The Gopīs considered the fact that, if Tulasī, by remembering her original relationship with the Lord, should worship Him as if She were only a devotee, then her experience of the mood of love would not be complete. And so they think of her as the Blessed Lord's wife, and therefore call her "noble lady." Since this is also true (i.e., that She is His wife), her wealth of devotion is great indeed, and She is far superior to us or anyone else. This is why the Gopīs say : "who (i.e., Tulasī) love the feet of Govinda." Moreover, your sight is also a means for us. Because your counterpart (i.e., your sister—Tulasī) is on the Lord's feet. And if someone sees her counterpart on the same path, she will follow her.[5] That is why the Gopīs say : "Have you seen...Acyuta, who carries you constantly on His feet, along with your company of swarming bees?" Besides, the Blessed Lord is "your greatly-beloved," and if He had travelled on this path, you would certainly have seen Him.

Introduction to Stanza 8 : The Gopīs perceived that Tulasī, too, had no inclination to answer them, and they said to themselves : "How would she tell any other woman where He is, since she is interested, like any rival wife, only in proclaiming her own superiority?" And so thinking that the ordinary female plants would be their only helpers, the Gopīs ask four kinds of Jasmine in these words :

Stanza 8 : "Mālatī, Mallikā, Jātī and Yūthikā—have you seen Him? Has Mādhava passed by, stirring love in you by touching you with His hand?"

Commentary : "Mālatī, have you," in any one of your different forms, "seen Him?" Likewise "Mallikā, Jātī and

5. It is also possible that the bees, which constantly swarm after Tulasī, are what are referred to here as *sajātīya*, "counterpart (s)."

Yūthikā—have you seen Him?" These four kinds of creepers have very fragrant flowers, and the Blessed Lord loves them. Therefore did Mādhava stir your love by touching you with His hand as He picked your flowers with Lakṣmī? For Lakṣmī is with Him, thought the Gopīs, so He would have had to pick flowers to weave into Her hair.

Introduction to Stanza 9 : When the Gopīs realized that these plants, though they were female, were still fruitless, and small, and wrapped up in their own affairs, and favorable to the side of Lakṣmī, they said : "They will not tell us." And so they now ask the very greatest of trees, the mango-trees and others :

Stanza 9 : "O Cūta, Priyāla, Panasa, Aśana, Kovidāra, Jambu, Arka, Bilva, Bakula, Āmra, Kadamba and Nīpa—and you other trees who line the banks of the Yamunā and exist only for others—please tell us, who have been deprived of our very Self, which way Kṛṣṇa has gone."

Commentary : The Cūta and the Āmra are both mango-trees. But the Cūta's fruit is said to be sweet in nature, while the Āmra's is sour.[6] Or the difference in their names may come from the fact that they bear fruit at different times. The Priyāla, even when it is a seed, is very rich in sap (Skt. *rasa*). The Panasa (the bread-fruit tree) produces large fruit. These other trees, the Aśana and the rest, are abundant in both flowers and fruit. Why go into more detail? The phrase "you other trees" refers to the Madhūka and other trees of this kind. Those who are born only for the sake of others are said to "exist only for others" (cf. the eulogy of trees, Bh. P. X. 22. 30-36). And although all trees are born for the sake of others, these trees which "line the banks of the Yamunā" stand on the Yamunā's bank like ascetics in their postures of penance, and they would certainly see the Blessed Lord, awake from their trances, and tell us. Therefore "let them tell us which way He who is eternal Joy has gone," so that He may return to our

6. Here again, Vallabha is dabbling in pseudo-etymology. Cūta is similar to the verb-root CŪṢ, "to suck," hence the connection with sweetness. And Āmra resembles the adjective *amla/āmla*, which means "sour, bitter."

hearts. For the sake of arousing compassion the Gopīs say : "(we) who have been deprived of our very Self." Some people are deprived of a home, and some of money—some even of their bodies. But we are deprived of our very Selves. Therefore we are the most wretched and helpless of all. And so "please tell us," for our sake, "which way Kṛṣṇa has gone."

Introduction to Stanza 10 : Thus the Gopīs' wretchedness manifested itself in words of intense sorrow. But then they saw the prints of the Blessed Lord's lotus-feet on the ground, so they began praising the Earth:

Stanza 10 : "O Earth, we unfortunates ask what austerity you have performed that you look so beautiful, with your hair standing on end from the thrill of being touched by the feet of Keśava? Or might this burst of joy come from being touched by one of the strides of Urukrama, or from the embrace of the Lord when He took the form of a boar?"

Commentary : O Earth ! Have you performed some act of austerity? We, too, have been performing austerities, but we have not experienced any fruits. The desired results are never accomplished without merit, and this is much more so when the desired result consists of the Blessed Lord. Fearing the absence of merit in their own case, the Gopīs say, in their depression : "We unfortunates." But your relationship with Him does not involve His feet alone, for many other emotions of yours have been visibly affected. For "Keśava," the Giver of ultimate freedom to Brahmā and others, gave great joy to Earth when He touched her with His lotus-feet, after Brahmā had prayed that He descend to Earth. And it is evident that Earth perspired here, otherwise the footprints would not be clear. Another sign of joy is visible—and that is "your hair standing on end." Everywhere the Dūrvā-grass, normally bent, is standing up straight, and this thrilling of your hair makes you look especially beautiful. You look beautiful because of the joy of being touched by His feet. But, the Gopīs think, her hair is standing on end everywhere, whereas it would be doing that in only one place if she had been touched by Keśava's feet, just as her perspiration is in only one place. In trying to imagine the reason behind this, the Gopīs say : "Or might this burst of joy come from being touched by one of the strides of Urukrama?" The touch of Keśava's feet caused Earth to remember her previous contact with the foot of Urukrama (the Lord's incarnation as a dwarf). For Urukrama's stride encompassed Earth in her totality. Therefore this burst of joy came from her contact with His foot. Urukrama is the One who took three strides (Skt. *trivikrama*). The Gopīs cannot determine whether this joy could come from a stride, or simply from contact with His foot. For such joy as causes the hair to stand on end and embodies emotion that is *sāttvika* cannot come from mere contact with His foot, without any sexual enjoyment. Therefore the Gopīs venture another opinion: "or from the embrace of the Lord when He took the form of a boar?" With this the Gopīs show the identity of their situation with that of Earth.

Introduction to Stanza 11 : Now that they have asked all the immobile objects where the Lord is, the Gopīs begin asking the moving creatures as well :

Stanza 11 : "Wife of the black antelope, dear friend, has Acyuta passed by here with His beloved, striding with long legs and filling your eyes with joy? For in this spot the breeze bears the fragrance of the Lord of Gokula's jasmine-flower garland, which has been reddened by saffron from the breasts of His chosen love."

Commentary : O wife of the black antelope, has Acyuta passed by here, together with a woman, i.e., closely accompanied by a woman He loves—Lakṣmī or some other ? Have you seen Him who "fills your eyes with joy", going along this path, striding with His legs and all His lovely limbs ? We are sure He took this path because we have seen the prints of His lotus-feet. If you have seen Him, then we will be able to see Him, too. You, like us, are the wife of another, and you are our friend. This is why the Gopīs address her as "dear friend". She is their friend because she, like them, is in love with Kṛṣṇa, and her eyes and theirs are very much alike, and they both possess the same qualities—timidity and so forth. Otherwise (i.e., if you had not seen Him), your eyes would not be opened so wide. The antelope might ask : "But if He has already played His love-game with you, why do you want to see Him now?" The Gopīs answer : "Acyuta", which means "Imperishable" (i.e., His virility does not fail). And in case she asks : "how do you know He was accompanied by His beloved?", the Gopīs answer with the sentence : "For in this spot the breeze bears...of His chosen love." For in this spot the breeze bears the fragrance of the garland of white jasmine-flowers which the Lord of Gokula was wearing. This garland became reddened with the saffron from her breasts when He pressed against the body of His chosen love. For the fragrance is moist, reflecting the moistness of the saffron. And this moistness appears only when someone's emotional state is *sāttvika*. That is how we know He was in the company of His beloved.

Introduction to Stanza 12: After the Gopīs had asked the black antelope where Kṛṣṇa was, they reflected to themselves : "But she is right next to her husband, so she can't tell us anything." And so they ask the trees, whom the Blessed Lord had praised earlier :

Stanza 12 : "After putting one arm around His beloved's shoulder, and picking a lotus with the other, Balarāma's younger brother was followed by blind swarms of bees, drunk with the fragrance of Tulasī. O trees, did He acknowledge your respectful bowing here, casting glances of love as He passed by, or not?"

Commentary : After putting one arm around the shoulder of His beloved, and picking a lotus with His other hand, Balarāma's fearless younger brother was followed by the swarms of bees which are associated with Tulasī. O trees, the Blessed Lord earlier praised you as ideal devotees. Our question now is, did the Blessed Lord acknowledge the respectful bow which (as we can see) you just made to Him here, or not? That He put His arm around His beloved's shoulder is indicated by the evenness of their walking, for the path shows clear rows of both persons' footprints. And the occasional unevenness of the prints shows that they were trying to ward off the bees which were hindering their movements. And the trees are bowed down, to give Him their respectful greeting; and in order to make Him an offering of their fruit, they have touched their heads to the ground. Therefore we know that they did bow respectfully. But since they have not stood up again a doubt arises as to whether the Lord acknowledged their bowing or not. If He did not acknowledge it, the reason might be that this happened "as He passed by." For someone who is passing by pays no attention to his surroundings. Then the Gopīs reflect that the Lord passed very close to these trees, and if He had made any acknowledgment, surely it would have been heard. Then how can there be any doubt about it? Here, then, they say: "casting glances of love." He may have acknowledged their bowing with glances that proceeded from love, not with words. Therefore those who are standing nearby are the only ones who could know. No one else.[7]

Introduction to Stanza 13: The Gopīs say to themselves: "These trees are sages—their knowledge is complete—but for that reason they will not converse with women. So we should ask their wives." This they do in the following stanza.

Stanza 13: "Ask these creepers which entwine themselves around the arms of a large forest tree. Have you just been touched by the Lord's fingernails? Is that why all your leaves are outstretched with joy?"

Commentary: Ask these women (the creepers) who are embraced by the arms of a large forest tree, although there is really no opportunity to ask even them, since not only were they in the embrace of their husband's arms, but they were touched by the Blessed Lord's fingernails as well (when He was picking their flowers), so all their leaves are standing on end out of joy. For, when someone has just been immersed totally in one mood (here, the mood of love), there is no desire for any other mood. This is the reason for the saying: "The mood which is associated with the Blessed Lord destroys all else". And so, since they had received no answer from anyone at all, Gopīs fainted, as it were. This marks the end of the story of the Gopīs' questioning. It was the nine types of Gopī who were described here (i.e., in these last nine stanzas, after one

7. These last two brief sentences, especially coming in the place they do, at the end of the commentary on a stanza, are almost certainly meant as a terse aphorism, applicable to all devotees as well as to the trees. This is, of course, true of many of the sentences in Vallabha's commentary.

introductory stanza). The tenth type of Gopī was the one whom the Lord led away. Their searching for the Lord in this way established the mood of love permanently in these nine types of Gopī.

Introduction to Stanza 14 : Thus has Śuka narrated the Gopīs' efforts to remove the suffering caused by the Lord's disappearance. Now the Blessed Lord's games became manifest in them, in order to wipe out the suffering completely. Śuka therefore begins to describe the playful joy of these games, , but first he sums up what had happened before them :

Stanza 14 : Śuka said : "After thus speaking in the way madmen speak, the Gopīs were very discouraged in their search for Kṛṣṇa. And so they—having Him as their very Self—began to imitate each and every one of the Blessed Lord's games."

Commentary : The word "thus" is meant to express a manner or a way. In this manner, i.e., by asking questions to things which were not fit to be questioned because they could not answer, "the Gopīs spoke the way madmen do." In their search for Kṛṣṇa they had also become "very discouraged", in fact wretched. Their bodies and their powers of speech were exhausted. But in their minds those three factors—suffering, the Lord's games and the Lord Himself—were still operative, and upon the departure of the first the second became manifest, as Śuka points out when he says : "the Blessed Lord's games." "The Gopīs, who had the Lord as their very Selves, imitated each and every one of the Blessed Lord's games" that had been performed and described previously (i.e., in the earlier chapters of the Bhāgavata's Tenth Book). The word *unmatta-vacaḥ* ("speaking in the way madmen speak") has either been shortened in accordance with Vedic grammatical usage, or else we may say that the word "thus" signifies that the Gopīs' speaking in the way madmen do—which has been described over the last several stanzas -- extends this far and no farther.[8]

Therefore the Gopīs had become "very discouraged" in their search for Kṛṣṇa. Now the Blessed Lord's games are of six kinds, reflecting His own nature, and each of them is

8. I have tried to incorporate both these ideas in my translation of the stanza.

different from the others. This is the correct meaning of the phrase "each and every." When the Blessed Lord entered and dwelt in the Gopīs' hearts He brought His games along with Him. Whenever the Blessed Lord descends to the earth He always drinks and drains the milk from Pūtanā and performs all His other games, as is well known from the celebration of the feasts of the yearly cycle at Puri and other places (OR: "during the Puruṣottama-month"). Since Kṛṣṇa had manifested Himself in the Gopīs' minds, it was there that He had to play His games, since it was now impossible to perform them visibly and externally. Thus it was by the Gopis' meditative imagining (Skt. *bhāvanā*) alone that the Lord and His games became manifest to them. Then they merely imitated Him.

Verses : *Verse* I : The Gopīs who are completely beside themselves with loving devotion for Kṛṣṇa assume His role; whereas those whose frenzy is not quite so advanced and are envious of the woman He has led away assume, out of anger, the roles of those who hate Him.

Verses II-III : Due to the variation of moods produced by their differences in the qualities of *sattva* and the others, the Gopīs portray nine different games (in Stanzas 15-23). But none of the Gopīs' moods or roles is lower than that of other Gopīs, for they are all completely possessed by the games themselves, such as the cart-game and the others, and by whatever parts and sentiments the games involve.

Or once again, moved by their awareness of Hari in all things or by a longing to touch His feet, these same Gopīs assume the role of the wooden mortar in that game, or of the cart in that game, and so forth, in order to establish some relationship of contact with Him.

Stanza 15 : A Gopī who was portraying Kṛṣṇa drank milk from the breast of another, who assumed the role of Pūtanā. And another Gopī, who played the part of the baby Kṛṣṇa, bawled when she struck her foot against the Gopī who represented the cart.

Commentary : The first event of the Blessed Lord's life which the Gopīs portrayed was His drinking the milk and draining the life-breath from Pūtanā (cf. Bh. P. X. 6). One Gopī became Pūtanā, and another said : "I am Kṛṣṇa." Then the one, looking upon the other as the Blessed Lord, took her onto her lap. And the one portraying Kṛṣṇa drank milk from the breast of the one who represented Pūtanā. But the Gopī who played Pūtanā did not imaginatively establish in herself the thought of dying. And so she did not die. Nor did she imitate that part of the game. And the Gopī who represented Kṛṣṇa drank only the milk from Pūtanā's breast (and did not drain her life as well). She drank only the milk because she lacked the Lord's supernatural power. And in order to remove inauspiciousness two Gopīs portrayed the game in which Kṛṣṇa smashed the cart (cf. Bh. P. X. 7), as Śuka tells us in the sentence : "And another Gopī, who played the part of the baby Kṛṣṇa . . ." She acted like a baby, or she actually thought she was a baby, or she made herself like a baby. And "the Gopī who represented the cart" took a position in which she looked like a cart, and (the Gopī who was) Kṛṣṇa struck, i.e., kicked, her.

Introduction to Stanza 16 : Next Śuka describes Kṛṣṇa's game with Tṛṇāvarta (cf. Bh. P.X. 7) :

Stanza 16 : One Gopī, who played the part of a Daitya (Tṛṇāvarta), carried off another Gopī who meditatively assumed the role of the baby Kṛṣṇa. Still another Gopī crawled along the ground, dragging her feet behind her and panting noiselessly, as babies do.

Commentary : One Gopī made herself act like a Daitya, and another, by meditative imagination, attained the role of Kṛṣṇa when He was just past infancy. And the one who had made herself a Daitya carried off the one who was playing the part of the baby Kṛṣṇa. And "another Gopī, dragging her feet and panting noiselessly, crawled," i.e. moved along the ground. And just like the Blessed Lord in His "almost-toddler" stage, she went along like a baby, confused and afraid of everything, and with utterly charming little cooings and laughings. In the previous stanza we saw how four Gopīs portrayed two of the Lord's games. Those Gopīs were *tāmasa-tāmasa* in character. Here there are only three Gopīs, and they are *rājasa-tāmasa*. It has already been stated that there are differentiating characteristics in the games of the Lord's life, and we must note and investigate those characteristics here, too. So, alternatively, we may look at these stanzas in this way : three pairs of Gopīs have been described in these two stanzas, portraying three different games. But the one remaining Gopī has transcended the qualities of material existence. To put it still another way, many Gopīs attained one, single mood. By the Blessed Lord's will they attained a mood in which one quality of existence dominated, and thus by means of *rajas* they were excited and bewildered in many different ways, and so they assumed many different forms.

Introduction to Stanza 17 : In portraying the games of Vṛndāvana some Gopīs took the form of calves, and others represented their protectors, the cowherds. Śuka describes just how they did this :

Stanza 17 : Two Gopīs assumed the roles of Kṛṣṇa and Balarāma, and some other Gopīs portrayed the cowherds. And one Gopī (representing Balarāma) killed the Gopī who assumed the role of the Asura Vatsa, while another Gopī (who played Kṛṣṇa) killed the Gopī who had taken the part of the Asura Baka.

Commentary : "Two Gopīs assumed the roles of Kṛṣṇa and Balarāma," i.e., they became like Kṛṣṇa and Balarāma. And "Some other Gopīs portrayed the cowherds." The cowherds here were boys, not men—the word "cowherd" being a designation of caste. Still other Gopīs assumed the role of the calves the boys were protecting. This is signified by the first occurrence in the stanza of the word "and" (*ca*), which is used in the sense of the figure of speech called *samuccaya*.[9] Still another Gopī "assumed the role of Vatsa," i.e., she acted like the Asura Vatsa.[10] And the one portraying Balarāma became her killer.

9. *Apte's (large) Dictionary*, p. 1639, defines the figure of speech *samuccaya* as follows: "it consists in joining together two or more things, independent of each other, but connected in idea with reference to some common action." The figure fits the present context perfectly.

10. For the narration of the slayings of both Vatsa and Baka, cf. Bh. P. X. 11. According to the Bhāgavata account, Kṛṣṇa kills both these demons, though Balarāma helps in slaying Vatsa. But, as we shall soon see, Vallabha cites a quotation which raises a doubt as to whether Kṛṣṇa or Balarāma killed Vatsa. Vallabha tries to reconcile the conflicting traditions by contending that it was Balarāma who actually killed Vatsa, and Kṛṣṇa who threw Vatsa's body up into the trees.

And then—the second "and" indicates this—the Gopī who played Kṛṣṇa made the fruit fall from the trees (i.e., by tossing the body of Vatsa, who had assumed the form of a calf—Skt. *vatsa*—up into the trees). And "another Gopī," who was playing Kṛṣṇa, became the slayer of "the Gopī who took the part of the Asura Baka." It is well known in the world that it was Balarāma who killed Vatsa. As this very scripture later says: "The Daitya Pralamba and the Asuras Vatsaka (=Vatsa), Dhenuka and others were slain by Him (Balarāma)" (Bh. P. X. 43. 30). And so among the two, Kṛṣṇa and Balarāma, the Gopī portraying one killed the Gopī representing Baka, and the Gopī who played the other slew the Gopī who took the part of Vatsa.

Introduction to Stanza 18: Śuka describes how, after this last game, the Gopīs portrayed another Vṛndāvana-game, with Kṛṣṇa taking the form of a cowherd-boy :

Stanza 18 : Just as Kṛṣṇa used to call back the cows who had strayed far away by playing His flute, so the Gopī who imitated Kṛṣṇa made her imaginary flute play beautifully, (calling back the Gopīs who took the part of the cows,) while the Gopīs who were imitating the other cowherd-boys shouted : "Excellent ! Well done !"

Commentary : Some Gopīs took the form of the cows, while others portrayed the cowherd-boys. Then, "just as Kṛṣṇa used to call back the straying cows by playing on His flute," so the Gopī who imitated Kṛṣṇa in this game called back the Gopīs who were acting like the cows who wander away from the herd. She was playing on her imaginary flute, and playing such varied and lovely tunes that remaining Gopīs, who were imitating the cowherd-boys, shouted praises like : "Excellent! Well done!"

Introduction to Stanza 19 : Śuka now tells us how one Gopī participated in the play-acting by playing a game of the Lord's which has not been recorded in the Bhāgavata. But, since she perceived this game vividly in her imagination, she acted it out :

Stanza 19 : One Gopī put her arm around the shoulder of another Gopī and walked along, saying : "Am I not Kṛṣṇa ? Look at my sexy walk !" This Gopī possessed the Lord's own mind.

Commentary : In the previous two stanzas we saw, as we had before, three pairs of Gopīs. And the one Gopī in this stanza is the fourth. The Gopīs who played Kṛṣṇa and Balarāma and their opponents account for two pairs. And the Gopī who played the flute, along with the one who applauded her by saying "Well done," make up the third pair. But the Gopī in this stanza is beyond the three qualities of existence. This Gopī puts her arm around the shoulder of another Gopī, who has taken the form of a cowherd-boy, and they both walk along, while the first Gopī says : "O Gopīs, am I not Kṛṣṇa ? Look at my sexy walk !" In order to indicate that this involved no fault on the Gopī's part, Śuka says : "This Gopī possessed the Lord's own mind." At first she imitated only the Lord's bodily gestures. Then she imitated His speech as well.

Introduction to Stanza 20 : Śuka now illustrates in another way this fourfold nature of the Gopīs :

Stanza 20 : "Do not be afraid of this wind and rain, for I have determined to save you from it," said one Gopī as she stretched out the end of her garment with one hand and held it above the other Gopīs.

Commentary: The Gopī who plays Kṛṣṇa here has transcended the qualities of existence. And the other Gopīs assume the roles of the cows, the cowherds and their wives (thus illustrating the other three types of Gopī), and act as if they are terrified by the rainstorm. Then the first Gopī after saying : "Do not be afraid because of the wind and rain, for I have determined to save you from it," takes the end of her garment with one hand, holds it steady as if it were a mountain, and lifts it up. She holds it there as if it were Mount Govardhana (cf. Bh. P. X. 25), after "stretching it out" with some effort.

Introduction to Stanza 21 : Now Śuka describes the actions of a Gopī who is *sāttvika* in character.

Stanza 21 : One Gopī jumped up on another's back and pressed down her head with her foot, O king, while she said:

"Go, wicked serpent, for I have been born as the punisher of evil creatures like you !"

Commentary : One Gopī climbed atop another Gopī, and "pressed down her head with her foot," i.e. she struck her head hard with her foot. Śuka says "o king," addressing Parikṣit directly so that the king will believe him. This game is rough, and difficult to enact. Or perhaps the Gopī grabbed an overhanging tree-branch in order to do what she did. (Here begins an interpolation by Viṭṭhala.) But actually there is nothing improper in saying that the Gopī used no such support as a tree-branch, but re-enacted the game in precisely the same way in which the Lord had played it (end of Viṭṭhala's interpolation). The words "wicked serpent" refer to the serpent Kāliya (cf. Bh. P. X. 16). "Go" means "get out of this place," i.e., the Yamunā. "For I have been born as the punisher of evil creatures." The words "like you" are a form of direct address, and indicate Kṛṣṇa's intention not to kill Kāliya.

Stanza 22 (no Introduction is given) : Then one Gopī said : "Hey cowherds ! Look at this raging forest-fire. Quick ! Close your eyes, and I will provide for your safety immediately."

Commentary : A *rājasa* Gopī took the part of Kṛṣṇa in this game (cf. Bh. P. X. 17). And she said what Kṛṣṇa had said. Some of the other Gopīs took the part of the cows, and still others assumed the form of the cowherd-boys. And the one who had taken the part of Kṛṣṇa said : "Hey cowherds ! Look at this raging forest-fire." She saw this forest-fire because of the fire of separation from Kṛṣṇa that burned in her. Or, the fire appeared in her meditative fantasy. The entire game as well, which embodies the Blessed Lord, enters into this Gopī then and there, and so she sees the forest-fire and everything else. Because the other Gopīs have their own special characteristics, and have not entered into the role and mood of the Blessed Lord, as this one Gopī has, they do not pray to her for protection from the forest-fire. The same situation prevailed in the game where the wind and rain were beating down on them. The inner meaning here is that those games in which a Gopī assumes the role of Kṛṣṇa Himself enter only into those Gopīs who are beside themselves with love for the Blessed Lord. Those Gopīs see Him alone.

Introduction to Stanza 23 : Now Śuka describes the game of a *tāmasa* Gopī :

Stanza 23 : One Gopī tied a slender Gopī to a wooden mortar, using a flower-garland for a rope. And the fair-eyed Gopī who was tied covered her face out of fear and gave a perfect imitation of someone who is terrified.

Commentary : One Gopī tied another to a wooden mortar, using a garland of flowers as a rope, and a third Gopī stood still, playing the part of the mortar (cf. Bh. P. X. 9). The Gopī who did the tying was playing the part of Kṛṣṇa's mother Yaśodā. The Gopī who was playing the baby Kṛṣṇa had very beautiful eyes, and she became terrified and covered her entire face with her hand, giving a perfect imitation of fear.

In this ordering of the Lord's games, the three qualities of existence are the only motivating factors. Each and every Gopī made manifest the game corresponding to her own eligibility. And the game-playing ends with the present one, in which the Blessed Lord is brought under control. Otherwise the Gopīs would not have played the wooden-mortar game last. The games ceased when the Gopīs thought to themselves: "We mustn't play any more games after this one." Thus the end of the Lord's games is brought about when the Blessed Lord's mood is that of dependence. All His games disappeared in that game in which the Blessed Lord simulated fear. After this, asking questions, now as before, became uppermost in the Gopīs' minds. This is because perception of the outer world is necessary prior to asking questions. But the games took place because Kṛṣṇa went within them, and at that time they had no perception of the outer world. But for this reason Śuka did not sum up the questioning of the Gopīs (becaue it has not yet ended; the games had intervened).

Introduction to Stanza 24 : When Śuka said, earlier, "after thus speaking in the way madmen speak", he summed up the Gopīs' manner of speaking, but he did not sum up the Gopīs' questions themselves. And so now—after he has described the Lord's games right in the middle of his summation—now that the Lord's games have disappeared again, he resumes by telling us that the Gopīs were asking the trees and creepers of Vṛndāvana whether they had seen Kṛṣṇa:

Stanza 24 : Thus were the Gopīs asking the trees and creepers of Vṛndāvana about Kṛṣṇa. And they saw clearly, in a certain area of the forest, the footprints of the Supreme Spirit.

Commentary: The sense of the words "they saw clearly" is that, when the Gopīs again received no answer, the Blessed Lord entered within them, putting their confusion to flight and making them realize everything. The three means being used in the present situation—the Gopīs' searching for the Lord, their being possessed inwardly by His games, and the entry within them of the Blessed Lord Himself—have as their sole object the removal of their suffering. The Gopīs' questioning is an integral part of all these means, and so it is repeated everywhere. Therefore "the Gopīs were asking the trees and creepers of Vṛndāvana about Kṛṣṇa." Just after this they saw, "in a certain area of the forest," the Blessed Lord's footprints. Śuka says : "of the Supreme Spirit" (Skt. *paramātman*). This indicates that the Lord's feet bring about the attainment of the highest goals people strive for. For when the Blessed Lord enters within someone, that person becomes omniscient. The sole objective of such people is to see the Blessed Lord's feet, that is to say, the place where the Blessed Lord is. This is why Scripture says : "The sages see constantly that highest footstep, that supreme place of Viṣṇu" (*Ṛg Veda* I. 22. 20).[11]

Introduction to Stanza 25 : As mentioned before, these Gopīs are of ten kinds. Their forthcoming words, too, are of ten kinds. Here the Gopīs reflect that footprints are objects of ordinary sense-perception and can be seen by everyone. And so they set out to learn the real nature of these footprints. Therefore they first say :

Stanza 25 : "These footprints obviously belong to the great-souled son of Nanda. For they are marked with the

11. The fact that the Skt. word *pada* means "foot", "footprint," "footstep," and "place, abode," is the basis for the richness of interconnected meaning in the last two sentences. This exploiting of the meanings of *pada* is very widespread in Hindu devotional literature.

banner, the lotus, the discus, the hook, the grain of barley and His other signs."

Commentary: These footprints can be those of Nanda's son only—"obviously," i.e., truly, undoubtedly—for we perceive the special characteristics of His feet by means of these signs. And if someone objects: "but how is it that there are these signs?", the Gopīs prove their point by saying: "the great-souled," i.e., He who has a great Self (*mahātmā*). For He is the Self of the great ones; or He is Mahān, a form of Brahman (or Brahmā). These signs are on the Lord's feet so that He may accomplish various objectives. In the present context, too, they are very useful. This is why He made them clearly manifest. The Gopīs say that these signs "are marked" here in His footprints. Therefore it can be inferred that these were the Lord's feet, because of their unusual qualities. The fact that these marks exist is well known in the world, and everyone agrees to it. The sign of His banner is implanted there to assure His devotees that they will continually live without fear. The lotus is marked there to assure the devotees that they will worship Him in happiness. The discus stands there as a sign that the devotees will be protected, and the hook (Skt. *aṅkuśa*—a hook used chiefly as an elephant-goad) is placed there to signify the Lord's subjugation and control of the devotee's mind. The grain of barley signifies that the devotees will gain fame. And the words "His other signs" are meant to express the Lord's vajra-weapon and other characteristic marks, which stand for such things as the destruction of mountains of sins.

Introduction to Stanza 26: Śuka now tells us how, after they had determined that only the Lord's feet could have made these prints, because of the unusual marks in them, the Gopīs followed the Lord's path:

Stanza 26: The Gopīs became weary as they searched out each and every footprint, going farther and farther along the Lord's path. And when they saw a woman's footprints mixed closely with the Lord's, they became very dejected and began talking to one another.

Commentary: Knowledge results in action, and so Śuka describes the Gopīs' actions for us. The Gopīs became weary as they searched farther along the Lord's path. The meaning here is that they went along the path, searching for His footprints. Then Śuka points out how, in the midst of this activity, the Gopīs encountered an obstacle, when he says : "a woman's footprints." If the Gopīs had not been affected by the fault of jealousy, they would have gone straight to the Lord's presence. But since they fell under the sway of this fault, their minds were dulled. Śuka tells us that the Gopīs saw the Blessed Lord's footprints "mixed closely with" another row of footprints, which belonged to "a woman," i.e., to some Gopī. When the other Gopīs saw this, "they became very dejected," and then "they began talking to one another." They subordinated knowledge and action to speech, and took refuge in words. If they had not done this, they would have gone quickly along the path and found the Blessed Lord.

Introduction to Stanza 27 : Śuka next records for us the Gopīs' words of anger and jealousy :

Stanza 27 : "These footprints, too ! What woman do these belong to? What woman has gone away with the son of Nanda, who puts His arm on her shoulder just as the bull-elephant lays his trunk on the cow-elephant's shoulder?"

Commentary : It is impossible that another man would be here; neither can these footprints belong to a woman from another village; so they must belong to someone from our own group. This question of the Gopīs is meant to attain knowledge of the particular details by eliminating all the other possibilities. But there are no special marks on the foot that made this print. The word "too" in the text indicates that there are also signs on the ground which tell of the actions of the Blessed Lord and this woman. For she has surely gone away with the son of Nanda. Otherwise the Blessed Lord would not have gone. He was probably led away by her. The Gopīs speak of what great good fortune she has in comparison with them. The Lord "puts His arm on her shoulder"—literally, "He puts His forearm (Skt. *prakoṣṭha*) on her shoulder"—the forearm being that part of the Blessed Lord's arm which is below, but on the same side as, the palm of His hand. Some sort of contact between His hand and her body is indicated here, because the two sets of footprints are so close together. Moreover, it is because the Gopīs see that some manifestation of the mood of love has taken place between the two that they bring up this example: "just as the bull-elephant lays his trunk on the cow-elephant's shoulder." The bull-elephant stretches his trunk onto the cow-elephant's shoulder, and their feet get mixed up because their faces are turned toward each other, or because he is nuzzling her neck. And it looks as if these two have been doing something similar. The elephants have been used as an example here because the pleasure that comes through bodily contact is primary with them. Thus three types of Gopī have been described.[12]

Introduction to Stanza 28: The next two stanzas are spoken by a Gopī who has transcended the qualities of existence; in the first stanza she shows that the Gopī whom Kṛṣṇa led away is free of faults, and in the second she explains her positive qualities. The Blessed Lord did not enter within the *tāmasa-tāmasa* Gopī (therefore this type of Gopī does not speak in this section—Vasu).

Stanza 28: "The Blessed Lord Hari, the Powerful One, has just now been propitiated by her, and so Govinda has left us—the Beloved has led her away to a secret place."

Commentary: First of all the Gopīs point out, as reasons why Kṛṣṇa engaged in special love-play with this Gopī, her good fortune and her merit. This is what they mean when they say: "Hari has just now been propitiated by her." Although we, too, have propitiated Him, we have not propitiated Him "just now" —at this very moment. It does happen that even those who do not propitiate the Blessed Lord nonetheless achieve a relationship with Him, because there are examples of such people having achieved the final reward. But when the Blessed Lord has been propitiated, the final reward is in the control of the devotee who has propitiated Him. But there is gradation in this matter. And if someone objects: "But how can there be differences of gradation in the final rewards of persons whose actions are the same?" the Gopīs answer: "the Blessed Lord."

12. Namely: The Gopīs who ask and determine whom the other footprints must belong to; the Gopīs who remark what great good fortune she has compared to them: and the Gopīs who notice the contact between His arm and her body and bring up the example of the elephants.

Because of differences in means and materials for worship the actions of persons are different in every case. And He alone knows the differences of gradation in these actions. That is why He is the One who determines the rewards. An objection may arise in the Gopīs' own minds : "But shouldn't He have informed us of this, since it has served only to make us suffer?" But they quell their own doubt by saying : "Hari." For He who is the remover (Skt. *hartṛ*) of all suffering has made these present circumstances known to us precisely to inform us that there *is* difference. A Gopī might further object : "But our loving devotion is equal. Then why did the Lord not give a reward that was equal, in accordance with this devotion? And how is it that He has accepted her ritual action (of propitiation) if the reward being given to all of us alike is in terms of devotion alone?" To this the Gopīs answer : "the Powerful One." Sometimes He accepts loving devotion, sometimes ritual action, and sometimes He accepts only His own Will. For the Powerful One cannot be manipulated. "He places us firmly on the Path of loving devotion, not the Path of action," say the Gopīs. Therefore "Govinda," i.e., the Leader (Skt. *indra*) of all, "has left us, and the Beloved"—He loves her!—"has led her"—alone—"away to a secret place," i.e., to a lonely, hidden spot. For the mood of passionate love is aroused much more strongly in one woman alone than in a whole group of women. The Lord's reason for doing this was love, and the reason for His love was her devotion, or perhaps her action.

Introduction to Stanza 29 : After they had thus applauded the good luck of that Gopī, in order to prove that they spoke in that way because their jealousy had indeed hidden itself, the Gopīs praised their own good luck, too :

Stanza 29 : "How worthy, good friends, are those grains of dust that have touched the lotus-feet of Govinda. For Brahmā, Śiva, and Lakṣmī Devī have placed that dust on their heads, to drive away their sins."

Commentary : The word "how" is used in the sense of wonder or amazement; "good friends," i.e., female friends; "those grains of dust from His feet are worthy." This is said in order to prove the Gopīs are free from jealousy. Their meaning is : "Just as the grains of dust are worthy so is she (the Gopī who has gone with the Lord)." The Gopī who is speaking addresses her friends directly so that they will believe her, and to assure them that she is not deceiving them. The Gopīs say to themselves: "Because of the excellence of this dust, we should wear the dust on our heads in order to remove our fault." Previously this dust possessed no great eminence, when it was simply here on the ground; but when it touched the Lord's feet, it proved its worth. Its wealth (=worth) is Kṛṣṇa, just as Indra is the wealth of the gods. And just as one can obtain anything with wealth, one can obtain anything through the Lord. The Gopīs prove the worthiness of this dust in the sentence that begins : "For Brahmā ..." Brahmā, Śiva, and Lakṣmī Devī, i.e., Lakṣmī in the form of the Protector-Goddess Śakti...all these put on their heads the dust from the Lord's feet, in order to remove the faults that had arisen in reference to his or her own power. I have used the word "Goddess" (or "Deity" : Skt. *devatā*)—(and, by implication, the Gopīs have used the word "Devī" in the stanza)—in order to preclude the idea that this might be Lakṣmī in Her highest form, which consists purely of the Joy of Brahman. Because of all this, think the Gopīs, we, too, by placing this dust on our heads, will become free from fault and equal to that Gopī whom the Lord led away.

Introduction to Stanza 30 : And now some other Gopīs, whose natures are dominated by the quality *rajas*, speak :

Stanza 30 : "These footprints of hers upset us greatly, for they mean that the one of us Gopīs who has taken Him away is, in some hidden place, tasting the lips of Acyuta."

Commentary : We have spoken of the greatness of the dust of the Blessed Lord's lotus-feet, but "these footprints" of the greatest of the Gopīs, who is accompanying Kṛṣṇa so closely, "upset us." In fact, the Gopīs add, they upset us "greatly." Someone might object : "But if the Blessed Lord is going somewhere all alone, is it not proper, on the Path of Devotion, for Him to travel with a companion?" The Gopīs answer : "The lips of Acyuta are the lot of all the Gopīs alike, but this one Gopī has abandoned all of us, and is enjoying His kisses all by herself." And besides, she does this "in some hidden place," i.e., in a secret place, without the consent of the other Gopīs.

Someone might also ask: "But won't the Blessed Lord be indifferent now, after having relations with so many women? And if so, how would He really experience enjoyment with her?" To this the Gopīs answer simply : "Acyuta", i.e., the Imperishable, the Unfailing. For He is the One whose desire, whose passion, is full (Skt. *pūrṇakāma*). And so it never fails Him.

Introduction to Stanza 31 : Next we hear how still other Gopīs became depressed even after this—for a new reason :

Stanza 31 : "There are no more of her footprints here. At this point her lovely feet hurt from being scratched and scraped by the clumps of grass, and the Lover lifted up His beloved."

Commentary: "Look here ! What are we to make of this ?", thought the Gopīs. "She was just drinking the nectar of Kṛṣṇa's lips, and her foot-steps were still going along very close to His, but starting here we see no more of her footprints. This cannot be explained as a normal result of what preceded it." And so the Gopīs come to this conclusion : "(her) feet hurt from being scratched and scraped by the clumps of grass." Then, since she was in that condition, the Lord "lifted her up," i.e., He picked her up, and He carried her on His hip, or His shoulders. "He actually must have picked her up with His hands," they think, and for this reason they become even more depressed. To someone who might ask : "but how is it that the Lord would do such a thing?", the Gopīs answer simply : "His beloved." She is very much loved by Him, just as He is by her. That is how we know that she did not climb up on His shoulders—He just lifted her up.

Introduction to Stanza 32 : But the two of them could not have gone far in that way. And so the Gopīs now tell us how Kṛṣṇa and His beloved stopped to rest for a while, and the Lord picked some flowers for her :

Stanza 32 : "Here the Lover gathered flowers for His beloved. See ? There are the partial footprints where He stood on tip-toe."[13]

13. Vallabha evidently follows the Vṛndāvana manuscript for his text of the Bhāgavata, since R. V. Joshi, in his *Śrīrāsapañcādhyāyī-Sāṁskṛtika-Adhyayana* (cf. Bibliography), notes that every manuscript but the Vṛndāvana

Commentary : Kṛṣṇa gathered the flowers by picking them from a tree. But no one should suspect that the Lord would do this for His own sake. For she is tired, therefore He does this "for His beloved" alone. For she is unable to do it. And so the Gopīs say : " the Lover gathered flowers." For she is practically a midget compared to the Blessed Lord, and besides, She is unable to stand on her tip-toes. Therefore it was "the Lover" who did this. "He stood on tip-toe" in order to pick the flowers. That is why His footprints are only "partial", and His heels do not appear in them. The Gopīs say : "See?" in order to remove the doubts of the other Gopīs by pointing out the footprints.

Introduction to Stanza 33 : Śuka tells us how other Gopīs noticed something more :

Stanza 33 : "But here the Passionate One fashioned a chaplet—a topknot for the hair of the one who returns His passion. Surely He sat down here, next to His beloved, to weave the flowers into her hair."

Commentary : He decorated her hair by using His fingernails to weave it into a braid or to crown her with a crest of flowers. The word "but" is intended to eliminate any other opinion. For it is hardly likely that He is giving her a lecture about divine knowledge here ! And so the Gopīs say : "the

manuscript records the following 1 1/2 ślokas as preceding the present stanza : *imānyadhikamagnāni padāni vahato vadhūm/gopyaḥ paśyata kṛṣṇasya bhārākrāntasya kāminaḥ//atrāvaropitā kāntā puṣpahetor mahātmanaḥ/*. Joshi therefore reads the above matter, which describes how Kṛṣṇa's footprints became deeper because He was carrying His chosen one, and how Kṛṣṇa set her down again in order to pick flowers for her, as Stanzas 32 and 33a, in his text--the addition of the present stanza making Joshi's Stanza 33 an oversized śloka of six *pāda*-s. Thus Joshi ends up with 45 stanzas in this chapter, compared with Vallabha's 44. The Gītā Press edition of the Bhāgavata agrees with Joshi. But the Nirnayasagar Press edition (for these two Bhāgavata editions, cf. Bibliography under "Bhāgavata") comes closer to agreeing with Vallabha, since it parenthesizes the first four *pāda*-s of the disputed 1 1/2 ślokas, and begins its stanza 32 with the line *atrāvaropitā...*, thus making its stanza 32 an oversized śloka, unlike Vallabha and the Vṛndāvana manuscript, but agreeing with them on the total number of stanzas for the chapter: 44. All the texts and manuscripts, of course, read the stanza which Vallabha is presently commenting on.

Passionate One fashioned a chaplet... for...the one who returns His passion." He could do this (i.e., make the chaplet), while He was standing, too. But He could not weave the flowers into her topknot while standing. First He would have to put the flowers in His lap, and then weave them in one by one. Therefore : "He sat down here..to weave the flowers into her hair." "Next to His beloved" means right at her side, or facing her. For only in that way could He see the shape her topknot was taking.

Introduction to Stanza 34 : Thus have the Gopīs described to us how the Lord led her away, produced all the surroundings, and decorated her, all for the sake of sharing the mood of love. Now they describe the culmination toward which all this activity had been directed :

Stanza 34 : "He delighted in Himself and enjoyed the pleasures of love with her as well, and His delight in Himself remained undiminished. Thus He showed the bankruptcy of worldly lovers, as well as the hard-heartedness of women."

Commentary : Because of the fulness of His passion "He delighted in Himself and enjoyed the pleasures of love with her as well." The words "as well" mean "as well as with Lakṣmī," or "as well as with those Gopīs who had merged into Him" (cf. Chapter I, stanzas 9-11). Or it may mean : "She, too, enjoyed the pleasures of love." "His delight in Himself" means that He delights in Himself alone. And by these actions He, who is free of passion, made her passion as full as she desired. Even in this condition He still delighted in Himself alone, for He established Himself in her so that she could be the basis of His experience of the mood of love. His chief delight is in Himself alone, and His pleasures and love-games are in Himself alone. Therefore His delight in Himself "remained undiminished" by either the senses, the heart and mind or external objects.[14] If His own Joy goes to another person or thing, then He will experience love for that person or thing.

14. This is because His delight is in *ātman*, literally "the Self", but in context "Himself"; and the *ātman* is, of course, more interior than the senses, the heart and mind, and external objects. So Kṛṣṇa's delight is unimpeded. He establishes Himself in this Gopī and therefore delights in Himself. This interpretation of Vallabha's seems particularly ingenious and profound.

Someone might ask : "How is it that the Lord made love in such an improper place, and with such great effort ?" And so the Gopīs give His reason : "Thus He showed the bankruptcy of worldly lovers." For worldly lovers are pitiable lot. (As Kālidāsa says): "For those who are afflicted by passion lose their discrimination." It is these people that the Lord imitates here. If He did not, these people would never be able to achieve constraint in Him. There is a second reason why the Lord acts in this way, as the Gopīs point out : "as well as the hard-heartedness of women." That is to say, His actions also demonstrate the meanness of women. For there is no helplessness in women, nor is there tenderness—instead, once they have a man in their control, they show only wickedness. As Scripture says : "These women have the hearts of wolves (cf. Ṛgveda x.95.15)". Therefore the Lord delighted in love in this way in order to instruct both these groups.

Introduction to Stanza 35a : After thus describing for us how all these things became vividly clear, in their innermost reality, to the Gopīs, because the Lord had entered within them, Śuka now sums up :

Stanza 35a : Śuka said : Thus these Gopīs, not quite in their right minds, went on their way, pointing out things as they had happend.

Commentary : In this fashion "the Gopīs went on their way," i.e., they walked along, pointing out and explaining the different games the Blessed Lord had played. Śuka explains the reason why there were so many types of Gopī simply by saying "Gopīs", in the plural. For they had not become the Blessed Lord's very own by means of the scriptures, but by their very nature. And since people's natures are of many different types, Śuka's speaking of the Gopīs in the plural is quite fitting. Besides, the Gopīs speak not out of any knowledge that they have attained—rather they are speaking while they are "not quite in their right minds." Or one might interpret the stanza to say that the Gopīs became unsettled in mind as they were pointing out the games Kṛṣṇa had played. This unsettled condition may be because the three ways (their searching for Kṛṣṇa, their possession by His games, and His entry within them) have now been completed, too. Therefore they went no farther and they spoke no more.

Introduction to Stanzas 35b-38 : Thus Śuka has described for us the essential nature of these Gopīs. In the following three and one-half stanzas he describes the essential nature of that Gopī whom Kṛṣṇa chose especially :

Stanzas 35b *and* 36 : Then that Gopī whom Kṛṣṇa had led away, after leaving the other women in the forest, also began thinking of herself as the most excellent of all women. "My Lover has left the Gopīs who desired Him so passionately, and is returning my love fully,", she thought.

Stanza 37 : After they had gone from the place where they had made love to another part of the forest this Gopī, now very vain, said to Keśava : "I simply cannot go any farther. You'll have to take me where You want to go."

Stanza 38 : When He had been spoken to in that way, the Lord said to His beloved : "Climb up on your own shoulders !" And then Kṛṣṇa went within—He disappeared—and that maiden was burnt by the pain of remorse.

Verse : In order to see clearly the fault she committed, four things must be considered : first, the fault of conceit itself, and then the arrogant words she spoke; next, the Lord's answer to her words, and finally, His disappearance—just as He had dissappeared before, from the sight of the other Gopīs.

Commentary on Stanza 35b : Since Kṛṣṇa is eternal Joy, He led away that Gopī who, unlike the other Gopīs, had not committed the fault of conceitedness, in order to make His Joy present in her. The other Gopīs became mere women. But she had remained an entranced, innocent Gopī. And so Kṛṣṇa left the other women in the forest, and led her away with Him. He left them there so they might gain the powers of discrimination that come from forest-dwelling.

Verse : But since she did not act in a befitting manner, the ruling sentiments of her womanly nature, the idea that she was in demand, and so forth, destroyed her innocence, and she, too, became like the others.

Commentary on Stanza 36: Śuka tells us : "Then that Gopī ...also began thinking of herself as the most excellent of all women." The word *ca* (which normally means "and") is used here in the sense of "also" to indicate the connection between this Gopī's present actions and the other Gopīs' previous actions.

Śuka says "then", which indicates that this Gopī had not shown this attitude previously, when the other Gopīs had. This teaches us that the Blessed Lord does not abandon a person because of the faults committed by a group that person is in, but only because of a fault committed by that individual. Śuka likewise recounts for us the thoughts of this Gopī, which were the cause of her fault : "My Lover has left the Gopīs..." She thought : "He has left" all these "Gopīs" even though they "desired Him so passionately, and He is returning my love fully." And she thinks of Him as "my Lover," since He is doing all those things which I love to have done to me, and nothing which I dislike. Therefore I am "the most excellent of all women." This must be true, because there is no other way to explain all these things.

Commentary on Stanza 37 : This Gopī's excellence—her superiority to the other Gopīs—consisted in the fact that she was free from fault, and not in any other quality or virtue of hers. And so Śuka describes for us the error of this Gopī, the words she spoke after she had gone astray through conceit, in the stanza which begins : "After they had gone from the place where they had made love..." They went some distance "from the place where they had made love", and came "to another" especially lovely "part of the forest." This Gopī, "now very vain," thought : "He is going somewhere for His own sake, not for my sake. So why should I wear myself out for somebody else's sake ?" Then she, since she was not eligible for such great Favor from the Blessed Lord, and was unable to cope with or assimilate the Grace she had received,[15] addressed herself to Him who gave ultimate freedom to Brahmā and the others, who is entirely free of the limitations of body, senses, etc., and who is the full embodiment of Supreme Joy—Keśava. Śuka tells us her words in the sentence that begins : "I simply cannot..." I simply cannot walk any farther. And in case Kṛṣṇa should say "But we have to get to the place where we want to go," she

15. This is the literal meaning of Vallabha's words. Viṭṭhala, in a footnote (*not* an interpolation), interprets the key phrases as: "She was not eligible for the kind of Favor the other Gopīs had received, and she was already satiated by the Grace the Lord had bestowed upon her."

adds : "You'll have to take me where You want to go," i.e., wherever You have a mind to go, You, and You, alone take me.

Commentary on Stanza 38 : Then the Blessed Lord, who is extremely clever, answered this Gopī's words in the stanza which begins : "When He had been spoken to in that way..." Since He had made her "His beloved," He spoke to her in reply. And His answer was : "Climb up on your own shoulders!"[16] For she wished to do some acting—she wanted to act out the mood of love that had entered into her.[17] But if she places her feet on the ground in acting out this drama, the mood of love would be degraded, because the necessary height of dramatic sentiment would not be present. And so the Lord said : "Climb up on your own shoulders!" It is a superb young actor indeed who can dance around and act out his part after he has climbed up on his own shoulders! For the Lord is advising the impossible. "But," He might say, "that is precisely what she prayed for." For the Blessed Lord has in mind the acting out of the transcendent mood of love, and this is not

16. Actually the Sanskrit is more vague than my translation. The words *skandham āruhyatām* mean, literally, "climb up on the shoulder." And so in context they might mean: "climb up on my shoulder (s)." But since the imperative verb form is in the middle voice, which normally is reflexive and refers to the subject performing some action upon himself or for his or her own benefit, the most probable meaning (in the present dramatic situation, too) is: "climb up on your own shoulders!" This is the meaning Vallabha opts for, but he exploits fully the other meaning, too.

17. Vallabha sees an extra meaning in the exchange of words between this Gopī and Kṛṣṇa. The Gopī's actual words (at the end of the last stanza) had been: *naya māṁ yatra te manaḥ*, which, in context, meant "You'll have to take (or lead) me where You want to go." But because of the similarity of the words *naya* (from *NĪ* "to lead or take") and *abhinaya* (from *abhi-NĪ*, "to act out a part dramatically"), it is possible for Kṛṣṇa to have construed her words as a prayer that He "let me act out whatever (or "let me act in whatever part") You wish." And so Vallabha has Kṛṣṇa interpret her words in this way, and answer by saying: "Climb up on your own shoulders." For He had in mind, as Vallabha will tell us, the acting out of the transcendent mood of love. And if she were going to do this, she could not remain on the ground. The apparent—and much more probable—meaning of the Bhāgavata's words is, of course, quite different. Vallabha seems to want to say that both meanings are intended.

possible if she keeps her feet on the ground. The Lord might say : "But if she were unable to do this, then why would she say she wanted to (act out whatever I had in mind)? That is why my mind is on this alone. And if she will do this, then I will take (or lead) her away with me. For no one who is ineligible is fit to be led away." But this Gopī thought : "The Blessed Lord would not speak in a misleading way, and so it is impossible that He is telling me to climb up on my own shoulders rather than on His." But it was because she was under the control of delusion that she understood His words in this way. And when Kṛṣṇa saw that this was the case, and what she desired to do under the control of delusion, He "went within—He disappeared." For He is "Kṛṣṇa," who is eternal Joy. And so she became just like the other Gopīs before her, as Śuka tells us : "that maiden was burnt by the pain of remorse." The word "maiden" indicates that this Gopī was a virgin who was observing the vow (to Kātyāyanī cf. Bh. P. X. 22). In this, too (OR : in reference to the other Gopīs, too), she transcended the qualities of existence. Therefore, "she was burnt by the pain of remorse," i.e., she was full of repentance.

Introduction to Stanza 39 : This Gopī not only experienced inner remorse; she expressed herself externally as well, with the words of profound grief that spring from inner remorse, as Śuka now tells us:

Stanza 39 : "Ah Master! Lover! Dearest Love! Where are You ? Where are You, strong-armed One? Please let me, Your miserable slave, see You, dear friend, present here, right next to me."

Commentary : The word "ah!" is uttered in the sense of deep remorse. The Gopī says to herself : "I have committed a wrong. Yet You, Master, You alone are my Lord. Therefore You should drive my fault far away, but You should not abandon me." The Lord might say : "Even while I am far away I will protect you." To this the Gopī answers : "Lover!" By this she means : "You alone are the enjoyer who increases our love, and we are at present the object of Your enjoyment. So You should stay right here, in our presence." The Lord might answer : "Solely to oblige you I will protect you, because I do not desire to enjoy you. For the enjoyer does not initiate enjoyment simply because the object of enjoyment wishes to." In response to this the Gopī says : "Dearest Love!" "For there is no other object of my love by whom I shall live." And then she speaks the words of a woman who is in the deepest distress : "Where are You? Where are You ?" She had become blind because delusion held sway over her and she had fallen down. Therefore she addresses the Lord as "strong-armed One" so that He will lift her up. For His power of action is great indeed. Therefore my fault alone should be driven far away—I should not be driven away. For I am a "slave," and what's more I am "Your" slave—the slave of You alone. And by my very nature I am "miserable". I bother you with ill-considered begging, so please don't treat my words as anything but that. In response to this prayer of hers Kṛṣṇa, who is supremely merciful, lifted her up and brought her back to normal by means of His invisible form. Then she spoke to Him again : "Dear friend," please clothe Yourself with Your other bodily qualities as You touch me, and "let me see You", i.e., show Yourself to me visibly. You are present here, but please make Your presence visible. Saying this, and no more, she remained standing there. And the Blessed Lord, too, remained right there.

Introduction to Stanza 40 : Now Śuka narrates what happened after this :

Stanza 40 : The other Gopīs were not far away, as they were still searching for the path of the Blessed Lord. And they saw their friend, still dumbstruck by the embraces of her Lover, and suffering.[18]

18. Even though my Bhāgavata text with Subodhinī reads *gopyo vicetasaḥ* ("The other Gopīs, still distracted") in this stanza, I feel we must read *gopyo 'vidūrataḥ* ("The other Gopīs were not far away"), because that is the only reading Vallabha himself cites and explains in his Subodhinī on the stanza. How this escaped our editor's notice I don't know. Of the printed Bhāgavata texts I have at hand, Joshi's text and the Gita Press text both read *'vidūrataḥ*, and the Nirnayasagara Press text reads *vidūrataḥ*. At any rate, *vicetasaḥ* is wrong on all counts relevant to the present undertaking.

Commentary : "The other Gopīs", mentioned before, were searching for the Blessed Lord's path and since "they were not very far away" from her, "they saw her." Śuka mentions the reason why their former anger at her disappeared when he says : "suffering." For no one can be angry at a woman who is suffering. Śuka refutes the notion that there could be any other cause for her suffering when he says : "dumbstruck by the embraces of her Lover." She had been completely stunned, to the extent that she fainted, by the Blessed Lord's embraces. And she is also "their friend." And so, many of the Gopīs showed their true friendship by bringing her out of her stupor, and consoled her by quoting the proverb : "Sorrow cannot stay where there are five people."

Introduction to Stanza 41 : The Gopīs had at first told each other that the Blessed Lord had left them merely out of curiosity (OR : to go to some festive occasion: Skt. *kautukārtham*), and not because of any fault on their part. Otherwise they would have directed their efforts entirely to remedying their fault. Kṛṣṇa led that one Gopī away so the other Gopīs might come to know that their realization of their fault was due entirely to the Blessed Lord's Grace, and not to themselves. And He later abandoned that Gopī so that she could tell the other Gopīs the truth. And so, merely because such was the Wish of the Blessed Lord, she told them everything. This was the logic behind what is narrated now, as Śuka tells us :

Stanza 41 : The other Gopīs listened intently as she told them that they had appropriated pride from Mādhava, but the contempt they showed came from their own wickedness. And the Gopīs were totally amazed.

Commentary: "They had appropriated pride from Mādhava, but the contempt they showed came from their own wickedness." And though "she told them" much, and they listened much, what they concluded from it all was the following : that the great respect they had received from Kṛṣṇa was not due to their own qualities, but to the qualities of Lakṣmī's Husband alone, since these Gopīs are parts of Lakṣmī. But "the contempt they showed" was a result of "their own wickedness"—their hardness of heart—and this quality belonged to them alone. The word "but" implies also the other results of their fault, such as their depression, their wandering, both physical and mental, and so forth. As a result of this, the Gopīs realized the great supernatural power of the Blessed Lord, and they "were totally amazed." As a result of her words, they came to an accurate understanding of things, and they realized that the Blessed Lord cannot be found by searching and so forth.

Introduction to Stanza 42 : After this the Gopīs thought : "What is the cause of the Blessed Lord's Grace?" And they concluded that their only means for attaining His Grace was to abandon everything completely, even to the extent of abandoning their bodies. Śuka tells us how they acted in accordance with their conclusion :

Stanza 42 : Then the Gopīs entered the forest as far as the moonlight had penetrated. And when they saw that darkness had enveloped the rest of the forest, they came back out, (away) from Hari (OR : Hari's Gopīs came back out).

Commentary : "Then they entered the forest." They entered the forest to turn away from their delusion. Someone might object : "If those who had also gone to the forest (i.e., the Gopīs' fathers, husbands, etc.) became deluded, then why should the Gopīs enter the forest ?" But they went only "as far as the moonlight had penetrated." They did not enter the very dense part of the forest. When the moonbeams themselves did not penetrate the thicknesses of the forest, then "they saw that darkness had enveloped the rest," and "they came back out", i.e., they became turned away.[19] A doubt might arise as to why, after making such an initial effort to go into the forest, and failing to accomplish this, they came back out (i.e., they became turned away; *nivṛtta*). In answer to this Śuka says : "from Hari." This may mean either "away from the presence of Hari" or "the Gopīs, who were closely related to

19. At the beginning of his commentary on this stanza, Vallabha told us that the Gopīs entered the forest "to turn away from--i.e., to remove--their delusion" (Skt. *mohanivṛttyartham*). Now he tells us that because "they came back out" (*nivavṛtuḥ*), they "became turned away (viz., from delusion)" —Skt. *nivṛttā jātā*. The whole process is a clever play on the verb root *ni-VṚT*, "to turn back, turn away, remove, dispel," and its derivative forms.

Hari," i.e., "of Hari." Therefore they came back out--they turned away—from the darkness. For those who are the Blessed Lord's very own do not enter into darkness. The Blessed Lord Himself turned them away.

Introduction to Stanza 43 : Someone might object : "But if they have come back out of the forest, then they will certainly go to their homes." Śuka answers this in the following stanza:

Stanza 43 : With their minds on Him, their conversation about Him, their movements imitating His movements, and with Him as their very Self, the Gopīs sang the praises of His great qualities, and completely forgot themselves and their homes.

Commentary : "The Gopīs...completely forgot themselves and their homes." "Themselves," i.e., their bodies, and "their homes," i.e., their dwelling-places. But if they have completely forgotten everything connected with themselves and their homes then why are they going toward their homes ? Śuka tells us the reasons for their forgetting. Five reasons are described by the phrase "with their minds on Him" and the other four phrases. Memory is born in the mind, but their minds were directed to the Blessed Lord exclusively, and so "with their minds on Him... they forgot," i.e., they had no memory. Śuka describes another faculty which contributed to their forgetting everything when he says : "Their conversation about Him." When other women are passing on some news about someone else, then, in connection with their story of that person, they might remember her house and so forth. But all these Gopīs are talking only about the Blessed Lord, and consequently they do not remember anyone or anything else. "Granted," someone might say, "but surely the bodily actions by which we relieve our hunger and quench our thirst are necessary, and in doing these things we will remember our body and other faculties." Śuka's answer to this is : "their movements imitating His movements." For, just as before, the movements and actions of the Blessed Lord Himself had entered within the Gopīs. "But still," the objector continues, "in every act of knowledge part of the Self springs to our awareness, in terms of the 'I' when we say: 'I know this pot' or 'I know that cloth'. So how is it that they are not aware of their Selves?" Śuka replies : "with Him as their very Self." He alone is their Self. This thought was very natural to their minds, because at all times they thought of and imagined Kṛṣṇa as their very Self. Therefore only the Blessed Lord springs to their awareness when anything reminds them of their "Self", and they have no awareness of their body or other faculties. The objector persists: "But Nyāya doctrine says: 'Similar objects (i.e., those that give rise to mental associations), and the Unseen (i.e., the impressions left by past actions—*Karma*), and anxiety and other, similar things awaken the seed of memory', so how is it that they forget even under the force of the Unseen?" Śuka answers: "The Gopīs sang the praises of His great qualities." If they had remained silent, they would have had their faculty of memory. But since they were so passionately attached to another person, they were intent on doing other deeds (i.e., deeds that had reference to Him). Therefore they "sang the praises of the great qualities" of this person—the Blessed Lord. For actions with reference to the Lord's great qualities destroy even very bad karmic impressions. And so their memory is not awakened even by karmic impressions.

Introduction to Stanza 44: When King Parikṣit indicates a desire to know what happened next, Śuka narrates the following stanza:

Stanza 44: The Gopīs came once again, as they were meditatively imagining Kṛṣṇa, to the bank of the Yamunā. And, coming together in a group, they sang the praises of Kṛṣṇa, for they longed for Him to come there.

Commentary: The Gopīs returned to where they had been previously on the riverbank. Someone might object: "But how did they get there if they were without their powers of discrimination?" Śuka answers simply: "as they were meditatively imagining Kṛṣṇa." Because the Blessed Lord desired this and the Blessed Lord instigated them to decide this way, the Gopīs decided: "In that place alone will the Blessed Lord make love." And besides: "That place is very beneficial for us." And so they went there. They thought to themselves: "It may well be the destiny of someone of us that He will come here, or He may come out of love or out of His merciful Grace." Because of these uncertainties, they "came together in a group." Then, since they did not have any other means of attainment, "they sang the praises of Kṛṣṇa," who is eternal Joy. For singing the praises of Hari's great qualities is the only means for attaining the removal of faults. So "they sang...for they longed for Him to come there," and they thought : "Once our fault has been removed, He will surely come here of His own accord."

Verses : *Verse* I : Lord Kṛṣṇa's Gopīs were of two kinds : the married women and the virgins; and in each of these two kinds there were nine types of Gopī, differentiated according to the qualities of existence which predominated in each. Whether they are considered as a collection of groups or individually, their pride had now disappeared, but they were without means of attaining the Lord.

Verse II : Since they held the singing of Hari's praises very dear, these lovers of Hari did that simply in order to live. Because they were uncertain, they came together in a group. But they sang the praises of Hari's great qualities in accordance with their own particular personality-types (as detailed in the opening Verses of Chapter 31).

CHAPTER III

(Bhāgavata Purāṇa Book X, Chapter 31)

Opening Verses : *Verse* I : In this twenty-eighth chapter Śuka tells us how the Gopīs, since they had expressed contempt, now praised Hari by singing of His great qualities, both because it was their nature to praise Him constantly, and because of the fault they had committed.

Verse II : There were nineteen different kinds of Gopī, according to their different levels of eligibility. Therefore they sang a nineteen-fold song of praise (represented by the nineteen stanzas of the chapter) which pleased Hari greatly.

Verse III : The married Gopīs are said to be of four kinds : the *rājasa*, the *tāmasa*, the *sāttvika*, and those who are beyond the three qualities of existence (*nirguṇa*). (The first four stanzas, then, are sung by *rājasa-sāttvika*, *tāmasa-sāttvika*, *sāttvika-sāttvika*, and *nirguṇa* married Gopīs, respectively).

Verse IV : Likewise the virgin Gopīs, who make the most excellent prayer to Kṛṣṇa, are divided according to those who have transcended the three qualities, the *sāttvika*, the *tāmasa*, and the *rājasa* (Stanzas 5-8, then, are sung by *nirguṇa*, *sāttvika-sāttvika*, *tāmasa-sāttvika*, and *rājasa-sāttvika* virgin Gopīs, respectively).

Verse V : Śuka speaks in a special way of those Gopīs who had become expert at meditatively imagining Kṛṣṇa. These were all virgins, and they joyfully sang three stanzas of praise.

Verse VI : The *sāttvika-rājasa*, *tāmasa-rājasa* and *rājasa-rājasa* virgin Gopīs have thus become very famous (as the singers of these three stanzas : 9-11). After this, the *tāmasa-rājasa*, *rājasa-rājasa* and *sāttvika-rājasa* married Gopīs sing three stanzas (Stanzas 12-14).

Verse VII : Then again three types of married Gopī sing Hari's praises in the next three stanzas, the first of which begins with the words : "When You roam.." (Stanza 15). The singers of these stanzas are the *sāttvika-tāmasa*, the *tāmasa-tāmasa*, and the *rājasa-tāmasa* married Gopīs, respectively.[1]

Verse VIII : And two types of virgin Gopī, the *sāttvika-tāmasa* and the *rājasa-tāmasa*, praise Kṛṣṇa in the next two stanzas (18 & 19). And this completes the nineteen stanzas, because there are none among the virgin Gopīs who are *tāmasa-tāmasa*.

Verse IX : Or, the number of stanzas may be interpreted in this way : after the virgin Gopīs pray to Lord Kṛṣṇa in seven stanzas (I-3; 5-8), they add two stanzas later (13&14), making nine (the married Gopīs also sing nine stanzas : 9-12; 15-19). And the chapter's fourth stanza is sung by all the Gopīs together. And that makes a total of nineteen stanzas.

Verse X : The particular love-attitude (Skt. *bhāva*) toward Kṛṣṇa of each Gopī is expressed in the particular words which each one uses. Otherwise the variety which is present in their hymn of praise would not bear any relationship with the very modes of that variety.[2]

1. My translation of the second sentence of this verse is not what Vallabha's Sanskrit actually says, because what Vallabha says in this verse contradicts what he says in his Introduction (*ābhāsa*) to Stanza 15. Vallabha's words in the present verse are: *rājasī tāmasī caiva sāttvikīti vibhedataḥ*, which would be translated as: "The singers of these stanzas are the *rājasa-tāmasa* , the *tāmasa-tāmasa* and the *sāttvika-tāmasa* married Gopīs, respectively." But Vallabha clearly gives precisely the opposite order in his Introduction to Stanza 15, which is the weightier text, since in it he gives his reasons for positing that order for Stanzas 15-17. So, following the lead of Vasu in his Hindi translation and the other commentators whom Vasu quotes, I have given here the order Vallabha enunciates in his Introduction to Stanza 15. Thus I as well as others gloss over Vallabha's apparent mistake, but at least preserve consistency, which it seems to me is the most crucial factor in this confusing matter of which type of Gopī is singing which stanza. In the next verse, too (Verse VIII), Vallabha lists the opposite of the order he indicates in his Introduction to Stanza 19. Once again, I have followed the order indicated in Stanza 19's Introduction, as has Vasu, for the sake of consistency.

2. In other words, variety and its modes would both exist, but without the unifying connection which is provided by the particular love, and the particular expression of that love, of each Gopī.

Introduction to Stanza 1 : Some Gopīs who combine *rajas* with *sattva* (and are therefore *rājasa-sāttvika*) begin this song of praise :

Stanza 1 : The Gopīs said : "Complete is Vraja's victory over all other places, now that You have taken birth here. For now Indirā (Lakṣmī) takes refuge here forever. O merciful One! Look upon us, Your very own, who search for You, with bated breath, in every direction."

Commentary : The word "victory" is used here to assure an auspicious beginning, i.e., to remove all obstacles, so that this hymn of praise may gain the desired fruit. Otherwise the word "victory" would not be placed at the beginning of the stanza.[3] "Vraja" as a whole has attained the object of its desire because it is here that You have descended to earth. But it is we alone who have not attained the object of our desire. The Gopīs say that Vraja has become superior to all other places because He has descended to earth there in order to express to Kṛṣṇa the idea that He should make every possible effort to insure that they attain the object of their desire. Their words are : "Complete is Vraja's victory over all other places, now that You have taken birth here." "Victory" is the status of being superior to all else. And "complete victory" means that Vraja is superior even to Vaikuṇṭha. For the Blessed Lord does not play this kind of game (i.e., the *avatāra-līlā*—being born on earth) even in Vaikuṇṭha.

3. I have taken a few—I believe legitimate—liberties here with the stanza's first few words and Vallabha's explanation of them, for the sake of conciseness and impact in my English rendering. The stanza's words *jayati ..adhikam........ vrajaḥ* mean, literally: "Vraja conquers or is victorious pre-eminently." Therefore, the Skt. word from which I have derived the translation "victory" is actually a verb-form (*jayati*). Some form of the verb-root *JI*, "to conquer or be victorious," is very often used at the beginning of a composition to assure, as Vallabha says, an auspicious beginning and successful conclusion for the undertaking. And what Vallabha says in the present sentence is that the placing of the verb-form *jayati* at the very beginning of the stanza proves that this meaning is intended here, since "otherwise one would not put the verb-form at the very beginning" (*anyathā kriyāmādau na prayuñjyāt.*) This exceptional syntactic usage clinches Vallabha's interpretation of the meaning.

Although the Lord was actually born in Mathurā, Mathurā did not attain, by His birth there, the status of superiority to all other places. Only Vraja attained this. Someone may object : "But the Blessed Lord's being born here is not recognized in the world as a reason for Vraja's superiority to all other places, because He had to be born in one place to the exclusion of all others. Therefore you must put forth another reason which is readily admitted in the world." To this the Gopīs say : "For now Indirā takes refuge here forever." It is to this place, Vraja, that Lakṣmī resorts always. She takes refuge with the attitude of someone who is abandoned and destitute. In Vaikuṇṭha, say the Gopīs, Lakṣmī is the permanently ordained wife of the Lord, and so She never has to take refuge. But here in Vraja we, too, are His wives, and so He has many wives. In this situation Lakṣmī becomes much more insecure. She says to herself: "When, when will my chance come?", and She worships Him constantly. For that reason—because of Lakṣmī's abiding presence here—the world considers Vraja superior to all other places. Then again, this same Lakṣmī has taken refuge in Gokula as well. The word "for" in the stanza has the sense of "this is the proper reason" (for the preceding assertion). For She is a faithful wife. And when the Husband, of His own accord, stays in a certain place because of His dependence on others, to proclaim His merciful grace to His devotees, as has been explained in our commentary on the wooden-mortar game (cf. *Subodhinī* on Bh. P. X. 9), then why should anyone be astonished that His Wife feels all the more compelled to seek refuge in that same place ? This superiority of Vraja to all other places, because You took birth here, is known to everyone (OR : "belongs to all its people as well"; Skt. *sarvajanīna*). Therefore there is nothing low or improper about Your making love here, nor does any sorrow cloud the mind of Lakṣmī concerning this. For because You have accepted Vraja, so has She.

For this reason—since You have come here for this—You should "look upon" this Gokula, i.e., You should simply see it one time. Or, the meaning of this part of the stanza may be that the verb "look upon" refers, not back to Gokula, but forward, to its object, viz. "us, Your very own." On this interpretation the stanza would run : "Look upon us, Your very own, who search for You, with bated breath, in every direction." The Gopīs are contending that the Lord's conduct is improper in this matter, and they point out the impropriety in the following way : "Brahmā and the others who dwell in the heavenly worlds, having determined that You have come down to earth and are in Vraja, are assembling here. But we and the others who actually live in Vraja are searching every which way for You. Now this is very improper!" But Kṛṣṇa might argue : "There is no loving devotion to Me among the inhabitants of Vraja. If there were, they would die when they are separated from Me. Therefore it is quite fitting that those who are not devoted to Me do not see Me." And the Gopīs reply : "for You, with bated breath." For Your sake alone we hold our breaths—our very life ! The Gopīs mean that at the moment they come to know that they are no longer of any use to Kṛṣṇa, they will abandon their lives. The only reason they "are searching for You" is so that You may revivify them and make them breathe again. If You delay even for a moment, our life-breath will leave us.[4] Otherwise they would go back to Vraja, saying : "Morning will come soon" (OR : "He will come back only in the morning"), and to search for Him now would be useless. Instead they say, in utter helplessness : "Your very own are searching in every direction for You—and You are here somewhere!" And so this prayer is uttered : "Please look upon Your very own just once." Thus one of the Gopīs prayed that Kṛṣṇa would look upon her. And the Gopīs' addressing the Lord as "merciful One" points out that it is not right for the very life of women to depend entirely on whether or not their husband looks at them. "But even if the Blessed Lord should look upon us, no gain would follow from that. Nevertheless, our prayer is that, once He has seen our helplessness and misery, He will show Himself to us."

4. It is rare for Vallabha to switch so abruptly from speaking in the third person to speaking in the first person (portraying the Gopīs' words) and back again. But this passage's Sanskrit indicates these switches quite clearly, with the result that here, even more than in the many other passages in which he does this, Vallabha's, and the reader's, intimacy with what is happening is established.

Introduction to Stanza 2 : The fact that the Gopī who sang the last stanza possessed *rajas* together with *sattva* was demonstrated by her description of the injustice of her miserable state. Now, a Gopī who combines *tamas* with *sattva* describes how the Lord's not looking upon the Gopīs is a means of murdering them, and she prays that He not murder them ·

Stanza 2 : "O Lord of love! With those eyes of Yours, which steal away the splendor (OR : Śrī = Lakṣmī) that is within a lovely lotus in bloom on an autumn lake, You, O Bestower of favors, are killing us, Your despised, hired slave-girls! Isn't this murder ?"

Commentary : In the autumn season a lake abounds in lotuses, which are born in the water and bloom to their full loveliness at that time. And a certain person has the kind of eyes, O Bestower of favors, that steal away the very splendor that is within a lotus. And with these same eyes He also kills, and so is He not a murderer? For no matter what the means are by which another person's life-breath leaves him, the one who produced these means and brought about this end is a murderer, and is guilty. By this reasoning the Gopī explains how the Blessed Lord's eyes are murdering all of them. As the famous saying tells us : "With His eyes He stole away health (OR: "life"; Skt. *āyus*), minds and strength". In just the same way You usually look upon us with cruel eyes. Otherwise why would our very life-breath be choking and stifling? We know that Your form is made up of pure Joy, and a mere glance from that form would make us live. Therefore, since that is clearly absent, You are doing nothing but murdering us. Moreover, we do not deserve to be murdered, for we are Your "slave-girls," and "despised" slave-girls at that. For women and uninvolved bystanders are never killed. What's more, we are Your "hired" slave-girls, and You are "the Lord of love." When we call upon You to accomplish for us any of the objects of human endeavor, all of which You control, the different names by which we address You are determined by the particular area of Your authority which we are referring to. Thus when we are on the Path of observance of the rules of life (Skt. *dharma-mārga*), we call upon You as "Protector of the Rules of Life," or "Brahmaṇya" (untranslatable, but approximately "Religious One"), or "Lord of the Sacrifice," and so forth. And when we call upon You in order to acquire material objects (*artha*)—the second goal of human endeavor—we say "Lord of Lakṣmī (Fortune)," or "Giver of every kind of success," and so forth. Likewise when we seek ultimate freedom (the fourth goal), we say "Mukunda", or "Lord of Yoga" or "Seat of Knowledge," and so forth. This is how people address You when they are seeking observance of the rules of life, or material objects, or ultimate freedom. That is precisely why we address You now as "Lord of Love." For wherever there is love, in the form of sexual union, in this world, You are its Lord. And without Your command sexual love does not go forth into this world. Therefore we have been given to You, by Brahmā or Kāma (the gods of creation), as "hired slave-girls", in order for You to introduce sexual love into the world. Our "fee" is a kind of toll that provides for maintenance of the Path and clears all obstacles from it. If sexual love should remain constrained and locked up in the Blessed Lord alone, then the mood of love would not exist in the world. We have come here so that You may make this love spread from Yourself over the entire world through us. But bringing that to pass must be the farthest thing from Your mind, because instead of that you are killing us! If this is so, then all the treatises on passionate love (Skt. *kāmaśāstra*) would be worthless, and the third of the four objects of human endeavor (i.e., *kāma*) does not even exist ! Therefore You must by all means do what You have invited us here to do. Or instead, that deed must be performed at some time or other, but right now You must restore us to life by appearing before us in the flesh.

The Gopīs prove the murderous nature of Kṛṣṇa's eyes when they say: "(those eyes of Yours) which steal away the splendor." For the person who is a thief is murderer as well. And his murderousness is in exact proportion to his skill as a thief. That is why the Gopīs say : "which steal away the splendor that is within." The thieves who do their work in narrow passes and fortresses have to be extremely skillful. And all the more so if the fortress is surrounded by water. Now a "lotus," as we know by its name—*sarasija*—is born in water. And what's more, lotuses always stay in their natural fortress, the water.

Besides, lotuses are "lovely," i.e., well-born and powerful. And in addition to all this, the daylight hours are free of such dangers as the cold and so forth. And so this kind of theft is impossible from all viewpoints : place, time, the nature of the victim, and so forth. Thus, when He steals the wealth that is within, or in the possession of, such a strong man,[5] why should anyone be surprised that He will steal away the life-breath that is within ordinary Gopīs and other weaklings ? For a very strong man resorts to theft in order to avoid disgrace (i.e., the disgrace of an openly violent act). But Kṛṣṇa will not get away with that here, for, as these Gopīs say : "Isn't this murder ?"

Or, if we interpret the stanza's words to read "by not looking (at us)" rather than "with those eyes of Yours,"[6] then these Gopīs are saying : "You are killing us by not looking at us ! Isn't this murder?" We have come here for the sake of love, but love has gone far away, and death has arrived in its stead. If this is so—since love has not become manifest here —then You would not be "love's Lord." For a Yogī, even if he has the ability to create a horse, is not called "Lord of horses." But if he actually does make a horse manifest, then is he given that name. Besides, why should anyone be surprised if we are killed, since even Lakṣmī would not survive if You did not look upon Her ? That is why these Gopīs have said : "Which steal away the splendor, i.e., Śrī—Lakṣmī." For if Śrī, who rests continually on Your bosom,[7] were taken away from it, She would surely die for lack of nourishment, just like an embryo that is taken out of the womb. And though many different times, places, substances and things combine to make up

5. Vallabha is personifying the lotus here.

6. This is easier than it looks (!). By reading *adṛśā*—"by not looking"—rather than *dṛśā*—"with (those) eyes (of Yours)," we have the meaning Vallahba is now treating as his preferred alternative. In the stanza the Sanskrit reads—*śrīmuṣādṛśā*, which may equally well be (and, according to Vallabha, have been) taken as *śrīmuṣā dṛśā* or *śrīmuṣā adṛśā*.

7. Vallabha discovers the author's further clever double meaning, which matches the double meaning of "splendor/Śrī". Just as it is the "splendor that is within" (udara-śrī) the lotus which is stolen away, so is it Śrī, who rests on Your "bosom" (udara), whose life is stolen away when You do not look at Her.

Her life, yet if You do not look upon Her, She does not live. And it is exactly the same with us.

Morever, You are the "Bestower of favors" to all people —how incredible it is, then, that You are killing us ! For someone who bestows favors is seen visibly. Or (to explain another alternative reading)[8], we are "Your slave-girls, not hired, but for free"—to bé Your slave-girls is our rule of life ! So we should not be killed. By thus meditatively imagining many different facets of His cruelty, certain Gopīs reproach the Blessed Lord.

Verse: The Gopīs' interior experience of the mood of love is rich and strong, but this mood can never be perfectly full until it has expressed itself externally. And so their mood finds its outlet through speech.

Introduction to Stanza 3 : Still other Gopīs say, in effect, in the next stanza : "You have protected all of us tender, defenseless creatures many times and in many ways in the past. Protect us now, too."

Stanza 3: "From death that resulted from drinking poisoned water; from serpent and Rākṣasa; from wind and rain, lightning and fire; from Maya's son Vṛṣa; from danger on every side, You Bull, You have constantly protected and saved us."

Commentary : The poisoned water was the water of the lake in which the serpent Kāliya stayed. When they drank that water, all the children and cows died. But You restored them to life. The serpents were Kāliya, Sudarśana and others, and the Rākṣasas consisted of Tṛṇāvarta and the rest. The Gopīs use the singular number to refer to all the serpents and all the Rākṣasas as an aggregate. You also protected us from the wind and the rains that Indra sent down upon us. In the midst of this there were bolts of lightning and "fire," i.e., forest-fire. Again the Gopīs use the singular to refer to many different phenomena as if they were one. You protected us also from

8. The text Vallabha follows (presumably, as before, the Vṛndāvana manuscript) reads *śulkadāsikā*—"hired slave-girls." But he is aware of another reading, which both the Gita Press and the Nirnayasagara Press edition follow: *aśulkadāsikā*—"slave-girls for free." Once again, the Sanskrit text is sufficiently ambiguous to give equal credence to either reading : *te śulkadāsikā* or *te'śulkadāsikā*.

"Vṛṣa, the son of Maya," i.e., the Asura Vyoma (cf. Bh. P. X. 37. 29-34). The Gopīs' knowledge of things both past and future[9] is not a matter of importunity or stubbornness on their part, for they are omniscient. And, thinking to themselves that there is no sense simply multiplying words, they say: "from danger on every side." And they tell us the reason for His protecting them when they say : "You Bull!" For the husband is the one who protects.[10] What the Gopīs mean is : "Since You are always our protector, protect us now, too." These murderers we have mentioned were outside of us, but this present danger of death is right inside us. So we must be protected in every way.

Introduction to Stanza 4 : Still other Gopīs—these are fully aware of the Blessed Lord's greatness and power—praise in song His real nature. Therefore, while they think to themselves "Just as He grants ultimate freedom to those sages who have reached true knowledge, so will He grant us the kind of ultimate freedom that befits us," they sing the following stanza in His praise :

Stanza 4 : "Surely You are not the son of a Gopī, You who see the innermost Self of every creature. Asked by Vikhanas (Brahmā) to protect all beings, o Friend, You took birth in the line of the Sāttvatas."

Commentary : If the Blessed Lord is really the son of Nanda, then all the reproaches the Gopīs have made against Him are justified. "But that is not so," say these Gopīs, and so each and every one of these reproaches is unjust. The word "surely" is used here in the sense of certainty (not merely in the sense of emphasis). In other words, the fact in this matter is not in some way hidden from us—the fact, namely, that He is not "the son of a Gopī," i.e., of Yaśodā. If He were Yaśodā's son, then just as He was made dependent on her, or known by her, so would He be dependent on or known by us

9. The killing of Vyoma is a future event, since it does not occur until Chapter 37 of the present account. It is true that the stanza's words here are "Vṛṣa, the son of Maya." But Vyoma is introduced, in his brief and tumultuous appearance, as the son of Maya (Bh. P. X. 37. 29).

10. Vallabha takes the word *ṛṣabha*—primarily "bull," but by extension "the male" of any species of animal, to mean "husband" (*bhartṛ*) here.

Gopīs, too, since He would in fact be the son of the lord of Gokula (Nanda). For only in equality (of knower, knowledge, and object of knowledge) is there a relation between knowledge and its source (the knower). Besides, not only are You the Lord of Vaikuṇṭha and the Supreme Person, but "You see the innermost Self," i.e., the heart, "of every creature," i.e., of us and everyone else. And if You were to see the degree of suffering that is in our hearts, then You would certainly become gracious to us. Therefore, nothing more need be said on this topic.

But besides this, You have come here for no other reason than to foster and protect us and others like us. And if You were to realise that we are perishing, You would certainly foster and protect us. The Gopīs express the fact that the Lord was specially besought to act as Protector, and did not come to earth because it was His own wish, when they say : "Asked by Vikhanas." Vikhanas is Brahmā, because it is said that Brahmā, who continually investigates the meaning of all the Vedas, "digs up or pierces through to (*KHANati*) the meaning in a special way (*VIśeṣeṇa*)." Therefore the Vaikhānasa doctrine which was created by Brahmā and teaches the worship of the Blessed Lord, is the only Path whose ritual worship the Blessed Lord accepts. This is the type of ritual worship (*pūjā*) performed at Veṅkaṭa and other sacred places. And so, in order that He might also receive the ritual worship of all, He was besought in prayer by Brahmā to protect all. This was His main reason for coming to earth. And in the same way, since You (not only "see", but also) are "the innermost Self of all living souls", You are their "Friend." Since You are of such a nature, in order to make friendship manifest in the world "You took birth," i.e., manifested Yourself, "in the line of the Sāttvatas," i.e., of the Yādavas, or the Vaiṣṇavas.[11] And so You clearly came for this purpose (also). First of all You, as our "Friend" (i.e., as Inner Controller), move and inspire us according to Your will, but the special nature of this second, new coming of Yours must be explained. And this coming embodies the total offering of Yourself to us (OR : "em-

11. Vallabha is apparently saying here that the name Śāttvata refers ethnically to the Yādavas, but spiritually to all Vaiṣṇavas.

bodies the total offering of one's Self", presumably "to You"; Skt. *sa cātmanivedanarūpo bhavati*). And so what are we to pray for ? We mean that only what is right should be done.

Introduction to Stanza 5 : Still other Gopīs, who are *sāttvika-sāttvika*, and thus distinguished by greater excellence from the Gopīs whose dominant quality is *rajas*, think to themselves: "The Blessed Lord will not grant something He is not asked for." And so they pray, in this next stanza, that the Blessed Lord will grant them this relationship with Him : that He put His hand on their heads.

Stanza 5 : "Greatest of the Vṛṣṇi clan, place on our heads —we who have come to You for refuge, driven by fear of Saṁsāra—that lotus hand of Yours, O Lover, which instils fearlessness, grants desires (AND/OR : "stirs passion"; *kāmada*), and has taken the hand of Śrī in marriage."

Commentary : O Lord, our hearts are bursting ! Therefore "place Your lotus hand on our heads," so that cooling refreshment may spread over every limb of our bodies. For a lotus is cool and cooling (by nature). And in addition, it is born in water, i.e., in a lake or pool (Skt. *sarasija*). Besides, Your hand alone is the ground of both the lake and the lotus.[12] Therefore this lotus does not acquire, by being plucked and so forth, the heat which other plants possess. The Gopīs address the Lord as "Lover," i.e., "Desired One" (*kānta*). This indicates, first of all, that the Lord would make the Gopīs dependent on Him by placing His hand on their heads. Besides, Your hand not only removes suffering entirely, but "grants desires" as well. It grants a "desire" (OR : "a passion"; kāma), i.e., what the Gopīs have longed for. "But", someone might say, "how can the Blessed Lord, the Supreme Person, the object of meditation of the Yogīs, touch women ?" And the Gopīs

12. This is Vallabha's poetic interpretation of the compound word used for Kṛṣṇa's "lotus hand"—Skt. *karasaroruha*—which may be interpreted: "that (lotus) which grows in the lake of Your hand." The compound word certainly means "lotus hand", simply, and Vallabha recognizes this, but he takes advantage of the flexibility possible in resolving Sanskrit compounds to make the point that Kṛṣṇa's hand is both lake and lotus, and thus doubly cool and doubly fit—unlike a lotus that has already been plucked out of the water—for quenching the fires of suffering.

answer : "(that lotus hand of Yours which) has taken the hand of Śrī in marriage." For Lakṣmī's hand has been taken, i.e., grasped, in marriage by the Lord. Consequently the Blessed Lord is a householder (since marriage constitutes entry into the householder's stage of life; also, a householder can touch women). The Gopīs mean here that, since the Lord grasps the hand of Lakṣmī, what is wrong with His touching our heads with His hand? "The Lord has indeed married Lakṣmī," continues the objector, "but He grasped her hand merely because this is a necessary part of the marriage rite. But what reason is there for His touching you women ?" The Gopīs' answer here is : "we who have come to You for refuge, driven by fear of Saṁsāra—that lotus hand of Yours...which instills fearlessness." Just as there are laws concerning the marriage rite, so there are laws about protecting those who have come for refuge. And, say the Gopīs, the laws about protecting those who take refuge have greater weight than those that concern the marriage rite. For the latter apply to everyone, whereas the former apply to a lord. The objector might say : "But isn't this way of acting forbidden ? Then how is it 'protection' ?" The Gopīs reply : "Greatest of the Vṛṣṇi clan." For Vṛṣṇi was the progenitor of the line of the Yadus. He had many wives, and was thus the origin of many different lineages. And even in his long line of progeny You are the "greatest"—the best. It is relevant in this context that it is women who have come to You "driven by the fear of Saṁsāra." For Saṁsāra is not evil by its very nature, but because it is the cause of unbearable suffering. And we, too, are experiencing great suffering from sources we see and from the Unseen. And You are the one who removes our suffering. The "fearlessness" that the Gopīs have expressed is because of this alone. And so when the Gopīs call the Lord "Lover" they mean : "You alone are our husband. Therefore You should be mindful of the vow we women have observed (OR : "of the husband's vowed duty to protect His women"; Skt. *strīṇāṁ vratamanusmaran*), and do what we so strongly desire."

Introduction to Stanza 6 : And now a Gopī who combines *tamas* with *sattva* prays that the Lord bring about the same end, but with a boldness that makes her prayer quite different from that of the previous Gopīs :

Stanza 6 : "Destroyer of the sufferings of Vraja's people! Hero of women, whose smile destroys the pride of Your people! Return our loving worship, O Friend ! Who doesn't know that we are Your servants ? Show us Your beloved lotus face !"

Commentary : O Blessed Lord, these other women don't know how to speak. But I have considered this matter fully, and I am telling You the conclusion I have come to. And I address You as "Friend" to assure You that I am not trying to deceive You. My friendly counsel to You is : "Return our loving worship." But the Lord might object : "How dare you speak with such audacity—asking Me to do something forbidden?" The Gopīs answer simply : "Your servants." For You have made this promise : "In just the same way as they surrender themselves to Me, so do I love them in return" (Bhagavadgītā IV. 11). Therefore just as we, Your maidservants, serve and worship You with love, so should You worship us with love. To signify that both our service of You and Your promise are well known, we have said: "Who doesn't know...?" But this one promise of Yours is not the only reason why You should return our worship of love—there are other reasons, too. First of all, Your reason for coming down to earth is to be the "Destroyer of the sufferings of Vraja's people." And so You should eliminate the pain of those who live in Vraja. There is no suffering that is greater than this suffering of ours. This is the general reason for Your descent to earth. The Gopīs point out the particular reason when they say : "Hero of women." Kṛṣṇa is the Blessed Lord. For strong men such as Kāma and the like, when they take possession of people, are driven out only by heroes. Among these strong men Kāma is the chief, and he has many forms. But even though he fulfil someone's desires entirely, with every object internal and external, he must be driven out because he provides no place of refuge for those who depend on him. It is for this reason (because they fulfil people's desires for what they need) that the generous givers gain even more fame in the world than heroes. Therefore You are the supreme Hero. For You fulfil, by giving the Joy that is within You, the desires of the completely destitute, which even Brahmā is powerless to fulfil.[13] And this fact concerning You is universally known. And so we call You "Hero of women." No one else in the world but Kṛṣṇa deserves this name, because there is no other whose desires (kāma) are completely fulfilled (OR : "whose passion is full"). And so, in view of both the general and the particular reason for Your coming down to earth, "Return our loving worship."

But the Lord might say : "This is true, yet I am not returning your love precisely in order to remove the fault of pride." To this the Gopīs respond; "whose (i.e., Your) smile destroys the pride of Your people." "Your people," i.e., Your worshipping servants; their "pride," i.e., their arrogance! Your "smile" has as its purpose the destruction of that pride. To abandon Your people is no way to remove their pride; to accomplish that You should, rather, smile. For Your "smile" is a slow, soft laugh. "And His laugh is a *māyā* ("magic trick") which drives people mad" (Bh. P. II. 1.31; cf. also *Subodh.* on X. 35. 4-5), as scripture says. The slowing and dulling of this māyā (i.e., this laugh, from the laugh which has caused their pride to the slow smile which destroys it) will cause pride to be inactive in Your devotees. For without the delusion caused by Māyā no one would become proud. Because of this, the only workable means is for You to contract Your laugh (to a smile). True, an attribute of "Your very own people" is faulty, but not their Substance (Skt. *dharmī*). If it were, they would not be (OR : "would no longer be") "Your very own people." This, then, is the supernatural means. According to worldly standards, too, these women, because of Your laughter, consider themselves Your equal. But when You reduce Your laugh to a smile, then their pride disappears. Besides, pride is clearly a fault. But this fault remains only as long as the proud person does not see Your smiling face. For no woman can look upon such a face

13. Vasu makes good sense out of this passage by saying there are two types of "hero" (*vīra*), the *dānavīra*—"the hero through generous giving", and the *yuddhavīra* "the fighting hero." Kṛṣṇa is the "Supreme Hero" (*mahāvīra*) because He gives more than any worldly benefactor, and of course His martial supremacy is also universally recognized.

and still keep her pride. The Lord might object : "But how could you know this, since this means (for removing pride) is not well known in the world ?" The Gopīs answer : "Show us Your beloved lotus face." The lotus grows in water, and a face that is like a lotus flows with the nectar of immortality. And the Gopīs' argument is that no one's fault can remain after she has drunk the nectar of immortality. And the Gopīs argue further that, if the Lord has any doubt that this means will be effective, He should merely show His face one time and see for Himself. Besides, pride is an attribute of the mind, but "Your beloved face" steals away the mind. And an attribute cannot remain when its ground has been stolen away. And the loving worship of a friend by a friend is only right.

Introduction to Stanza 7 : But a Gopī who combines *rajas* with *sattva*, and who is therefore higher than the Gopī who sang the previous stanza, now prays to the Lord, in still another way, for the very same thing :

Stanza 7 : "Your lotus foot destroys the sins of people who bow in complete humility before it. It follows the cows as they graze, and it is Śrī's dwelling-place as well. You placed it on the hood of the serpent Kāliya—now place this lotus foot on our breasts, and drive out Kāma, who lies heavy on our hearts."

Commentary : This Gopī says, literally : "Make Your lotus-foot on our breasts." She has shortened the imperative verb-form, from the normal *kṛṇuṣva* to *kṛṇu*, according to the Vedic rules for elision. She actually means : "place" Your foot on our breasts. She states her reason for making this prayer when she says : "drive out Kāma, who lies heavy on our hearts"—Kāma lies hidden in our hearts like a thief. She uses the word "breasts," in the plural, to refer to all the Gopīs collectively. Or perhaps the Gopīs think that their breasts have been cut off by their separation from Kṛṣṇa. The Gopīs' prayer that the Lord lay His hand on their heads would have brought Him very near to them. Then the prayer that He worship them with love would have resulted in His sexual union with them. But this present prayer has a mood that is quite the opposite, or else it speaks of a special erotic position, other than the horizontal position. For the word "foot" is used in the singular, not the plural. For by the Lord's placing His foot on the Gopīs' breasts, Kāma, who now dwells in their hearts, will leave. Or, perhaps the Lord would playfully lie down while the Gopīs group around Him, and place His foot on the breasts of each as they stand in a circle. But the Lord might say: "How do you expect Me to put my soft foot on your rough breasts?" And the Gopīs answer: "You placed it on the hood of the serpent Kāliya." For our breasts are certainly not as rough as Kāliya's hood! And just as You drove out entirely the fault that was within him by placing Your foot on Him, so You must do the same thing here.

Your foot is like a lotus, which is born in water. And so it will immediately quench the fire that is within us. But in case the Lord should say: "It is hardly right for Me to place my foot on women's breasts," the Gopīs say: "It is Śrī's dwelling-place." Lakṣmī, they say, is worthy to touch Your foot, so why should there be any doubt about other women? If the Lord should say: "But you have become deluded—how can there be any way of helping you?", the Gopīs' answer is: "it (Your foot) follows the cows as they graze." The cows graze in the grass, and Your foot follows them, i.e., You go behind them to be of help to them. Even if You, the Blessed Lord Himself, were to pray that they do so, would they reject the grass and eat the nectar of immortality instead? No! For cows, grass is the nectar of immortality. Likewise Kāma is our nectar of immortality. So how can You, who are supremely merciful, lose anything by doing this? Kṛṣṇa might object: "But you have sinned by not keeping your sense-faculties in control, and in other ways. After your sin has been removed I will place my foot on your breasts." To this the Gopīs answer: "Your lotus foot destroys the sins of people who bow in complete humility before it." We have bowed before You in total humility—our sins cannot be removed in any other way. But simply because of the Grace of Your feet, the sins of the humble have disappeared. And we, too, are "people." i.e., embodied souls like they. By speaking of this "complete" humbling of themselves before the Lord, the Gopīs indicate that they have abandoned the Path of obedience to the prescribed rules of life (Skt. *dharma-mārga*), and all other paths as well. And since they regard their body as their true Self, they lack Knowledge, too (i.e., they have no connection with the Path of Knowledge). But those who have humbled themselves completely surely cannot fall any lower! Therefore Your foot alone destroys their sins, whether it is thought of, or seen, or touched, or embraced.

Introduction to Stanza 8 : A Gopī who is still more advanced than the last who spoke, prays to the Lord for the same object in yet another way :

Stanza 8 : "O lotus-eyes, with the nectar of Your lips—Your sweet words and lovely phrases, which delight the minds of the wise—O Hero, fill these dazed and bewildered women who carry out Your commands—fill us full!"

Verse I : In the last three stanzas the Gopīs asked for the Lord's help in the form of His hand, His whole body, and His foot. Now they pray in song that He should help them with His face, too.

Verse II : Insofar as everything Kṛṣṇa has said up until now was not spoken clearly and openly, to that extent the Gopīs never experienced the fulness of the mood of love. For it is an invariable rule that this will not happen until He speaks openly.

Commentary : O Lord, "fill to fulness with Your sweet words, these Gopīs who are dazed and bewildered." For this dazed delusion is the condition that immediately precedes death. The Gopīs state the reason why the Lord should fill them full when they say : "(we) who carry out Your commands." This means either that the Gopīs do everything He orders them to do, or that they perform worship of Him (according to His commands). The Gopīs deny that the Lord could possibly lack the ability to do what they want when they say: "O Hero." For heroism exists for the purpose of removing the sufferings of the afflicted. And by specially pointing themselves out as "these...women," the Gopīs indicate that they will die if He delays even for an instant. In case the Lord should say : "But how can delusion be dispelled by mere words ?", the Gopīs answer : "with Your sweet.." For delusion is a form of Māyā, and it can be dispelled only by You in Your highest form—the form that is absolute Being, Consciousness and Joy. By saying : "with Your sweet..", the Gopīs are telling the Lord that His words are the very embodiment of Joy. Honey has an extraordinary taste. And whatever is associated with honey, as are Your words, is "sweet."[14] And "Your phrases are lovely," i.e., they steal away one's heart. This theft of the heart by your sayings is successful because they teach what is true as well as what is pleasing. Therefore the Gopīs have described the Lord's words as the very embodiment of Being (*sat*, "Being"—to be construed with *satya*, "what is true"). And Your words and phrases "delight the minds of the wise," i.e., they bring joy to the sage. By saying this the Gopīs describe the Lord's speech as the very embodiment of Knowledge (*jñāna*, "knowledge," is the proper action of *cit*, "Consciousness"). For the wise are delighted by Knowledge alone.

The eyes are part of the face, and they, too, should be put to use when You speak. This is why the Gopīs say : "O lotus-eyes." For Your eyes, like lotuses, are cooling, and so they put out the fire of the suffering of others.

Besides that, "fill us full" with the sweet liquor, and the nectar, of Your lips. You must speak to us, and look upon us, and make us drink. For in order to revive people who have fainted, powerful spells are recited and cooling substances like lotuses are applied. And when no other remedy works, they are given the nectar of immortality to drink. Or they drink secret potions (OR : "secret moods;" *atirahasyān rasān*). But since this faint of the Gopīs cannot be remedied by any simple ordinary device, they address the Lord as "Hero," thus showing that their condition has reached the final stage of desperation. For now they remember all the things which they have not prayed to the Lord for, and this causes their stupor and faintness to be all the greater.

Introduction to Stanza 9 : After they had thus prayed so fervently to Him for these four things, the Gopīs began to think that they themselves were the reason for His not granting their prayers, and they refute this notion by singing the following stanza :

14. Vallabha plays here upon the direct etymological connection between *madhu* "honey," and *madhura* "sweet," the word used in the stanza.

Stanza 9 : "The nectar of Your story restores life to those who have been burnt out, is praised by poets, and destroys sin; it is good fortune to those who hear it, it is endowed with splendor (*śrī*), and it has spread all over the world. Those who recite it are the great benefactors of mankind" (OR : "the great benefactors, who are not mere men"; OR : "the great benefactors, who are free of birth and death"; cf. Commentary).

Commentary : The Lord might make this objection thought the Gopīs : "Everything you have prayed for would be given to true devotees, but not to those who are not devoted to Me. And your lack of devotion is proved conclusively by the fact that you are separated from Me, yet you are still alive. But the Blessed Lord does not depend on anyone, and so there is no need of your being alive for Him to accomplish what He wants. For He has millions of slave-girls who are like Lakṣmī. Hence, for you to say : 'we search for You, with bated breath (X. 31, 1),' is also inconsistent (with everything I have just said). Therefore it is useless for you to pray to Me." The Gopīs answer by saying : "The fact that we have remained alive is none of our doing. It is only the story of Your deeds that has prevented our life-breath from escaping because of our separation fromYou. For Your story has the same sort of power You Yourself have. Like Yourself, Your story possesses the six great qualities, grants ultimate freedom, and embodies absolute Joy." For "Your story is like the nectar of immortality." The nectar of immortality consists of the mood and essence (Skt. *rasa*) of the Blessed Lord Himself. For whatever has the effect of preventing the death, rebirth, and so forth of all people is called "the nectar of immortality." Therefore (by its identity with nectar) the ability of Your story to grant ultimate freedom and the fact that it embodies absolute Joy have also been proved.

Now the Gopīs describe the six great qualities of the Lord's story by means of the six phrases which begin with "(it) restores life to those who have been burnt out." For Your story restores to life those who have been burnt in the fires of Saṁsāra. For it is well known that the nectar of immortality removes suffering. And the utter Detachment (Skt. *vairāgya*) of the Blessed Lord, or His Knowledge (*jñāna*), extinguish all the fires of suffering. The suffering which is inherently associated with sacred actions (Skt. *saṁskāra*) is destroyed by Knowledge, and the suffering which does not suitably accompany sacred actions is destroyed by complete renunciation (i.e., Detachment). That is why total renunciation alone is taught by the Smārtas (i.e., those who follow the scriptures) who are unable to perform sacred actions.[15] Therefore Knowledge and Detachment put out the fires of suffering. The Lord might say : "But water and other things immediately extinguish fires, too." This is why the Gopīs have said : "(it) is praised by poets." For Knowledge or Detachment have been praised by all the poets, who are enlightened sages and have a taste for the meaning of words. The Lord might follow that by saying : "But women have the same ability to quench immediately the fires of a man's suffering." In order to refute this the Gopīs say : "(it) destroys sin." The famous verse which enumerates the Blessed Lord's six great qualities reads, in certain manuscripts : "Of total Power and Right," instead of the more usual : "Of total Power and heroic

15. I am indebted, for my interpretation of these last two difficult sentences, to the independent note (*lekha*) written by Goswāmī Vallabhalālajī on these sentences, and translated into Hindi by Vasu on page 191 of his work. Vallabhalālajī explains that the "suffering which is inherently associated with sacred actions" is that suffering which afflicts the devotee when he perceives the sacred actions (prescribed ritual actions, association with holy men, etc., says Vallabhalālajī) as *other than* the Blessed Lord Himself. This suffering is destroyed by the Knowledge, due to Kṛṣṇa's grace, that these sacred actions are identical with the Lord Himself. The devotee then perceives these actions as being Kṛṣṇa alone, and this knowledge destroys the suffering caused by his former split perception. And Vallabhalālajī explains that "the suffering which does not suitably accompany sacred actions" is the suffering that comes from association with, say, a woman, an outcaste, or someone or something of the sort (who are not allowed to take part in sacred actions). Such association, he says, destroys even Knowledge, and so the suffering it brings can be removed only by renunciation—Detachment. Vallabhalālajī's note extends no further than this. But I assume that at least one of the meanings Vallabha intends in his not entirely clear sentence about the Smārtas is that the Smārtas go straight to the avoidance of all suffering associated with sacred actions by renouncing them completely, and having utter Detachment destroy all the suffering.

Strength."[16] The heroic Strength which accomplishes the supernatural is identical with the Lord's great quality of "Right" (*dharma*). And whatever relates to what is Right removes sin. The Lord's great quality of Right is also characterized by the previously mentioned attribute, i.e., "it accomplishes the supernatural" (OR : "the nectar of immortality is also characterized by the quality of Right which we have been describing"). And the fact that the Lord's story possesses this great quality (*dharma/vīrya*) and its effects is universally known. Kṛṣṇa might raise a new objection by saying : "But the same ability to remove sin immediately is possessed by rites of expiation and other means." In answer to this the Gopīs say : "it is good fortune to those who hear it." Expiation-rites involve things which are inauspicious by their very nature, like smearing oneself with cowdung and fasting. It is bad luck even to hear about such things—they are so horrible. But it has been proved by experience that simply to hear this noblest of stories brings Joy. That is why we say it is "good fortune to those who hear it." By this expression the Gopīs attribute the quality of "Fame" (*kīrti*=*yaśas*) to the Lord's story. Someone might suspect that the good fortune the Lord's story involves for those who hear it is of the same quality as the good fortune that comes from hearing about the birth of a son and so forth. To refute this notion the Gopīs say : "It is endowed with splendor (Śrī)." For hearing of the birth of a son is an occasion when one loses wealth rather than gains it. But the nectar of the Lord's story is "endowed with Śrī," and therefore associated with gaining wealth because Lakṣmī, Dame Fortune herself (Lakṣmī = Śrī, "Splendor," which is also the fourth of the Lord's great qualities), seeks and depends upon this nectar.[17] Because of this both the teller and the hearer of this story acquire Śrī, i.e., both Fortune and Splendor. "But," Kṛṣṇa might object, "that happens also when one hears that he has become the king." And the Gopīs' refutation for this is : "It has spread all over the world." But a kingdom and what is associated with it are

16. The śloka reads thus : *aiśvaryasya samagrasya dharmasya* (*OR* : *vīryasya*) *yaśasaḥ śriyaḥ*//*jñānavairāgyayoścaiva ṣaṇṇā bhaga itīranā*//

17. Vasu suggests that Lakṣmī is dependent on the Lord's story for her own fame.

limited. The Blessed Lord's Power (Skt. *aiśvarya*) however, is not. It pervades everyone and everything everywhere, inside and out, say the Gopīs. In the same way the nectar of His story has pervaded all places, and it produces the effects of its Power everywhere. Therefore, say the Gopīs, in its nature and in its qualities Your story is just like You, and it is that story which has kept us alive—not our own efforts (OR : "not Your efforts"—Vasu seems to say this). Thus the Gopīs express what amounts to an actual superiority of the Lord's story. For, they say : "Sometimes You are actually making people die, and it is at that very moment that the nectar of Your story restores them to life." The Blessed Lord is independent, and the nectar that is His story is dependent on others. To that extent the two are different. Besides this, You come down to the earth in response to the earnest prayer of Brahmā and the others—and now that You have come to earth, You disappear! But Your story has come along with You, and it does not disappear. That is why "those who recite" such an immortal story here on earth are truly "the great benefactors," i.e., givers of great wealth. And they—Vyāsa and the others—have become very famous. They are "great benefactors" and they are also "not mere men," i.e., not human persons. They are nothing but embodiments of the Blessed Lord.[18] Or, the word *ajana* may mean that they are "free from" the faults of "birth and death."

But the nectar that is Your story is fluid rather than solid—only when death is imminent can it prevent that death. It cannot coalesce all at once, at a single time and place, and thus arouse a definite mood (as You can). The difference, then,

18. Here Vallabha is reading the Skt. text of the stanza as *bhūridā ajanāḥ*, instead of *bhūridā janāḥ*, which all three texts in my possession, including the text printed with the *Subodhinī*, read. Vallabha evidently takes *bhūridā janāḥ*, as the correct reading, and he gives here two alternative interpretations of the word *ajanāḥ:* either "not men" or "men free from birth (and death)." In my translation of the stanza, I have followed the vast majority reading of *bhūridā janāḥ* and have given Vallabha's two interpretations of *ajanāḥ* in parentheses. This ambiguity once again results, of course, from the fact that a manuscript would simply read *bhūridājanāḥ*, without separating out the words.

between You and Your story is like the difference that exists between a solid mass and liquid. Otherwise our efforts would be directed towards Your story alone, and not towards You. But since it is useful for averting death in times when we are separated from You, we praise Your story in our song as having the Blessed Lord's own qualities. And the reason we say that the tellers of the Blessed Lord's story have given much is because it is by dint of them and the story they tell that we have continued to live. This stanza has been sung by a Gopī who combines *sattva* with *rajas*.

Introduction to Stanza 10 : A Gopī who combines *tamas* with *rajas* sings the following stanza.

Stanza 10 : "O Lover! Your stinging laughter and Your looks of love, Your captivating movements and perfect auspiciousness for meditation, the words and promises which go straight to our hearts as You whisper them to us in secret—You trickster!—for all these things disturb our minds greatly!"

Commentary : Perhaps we would be able to go on living on the basis of Your story, if Your personal qualities did not disturb us so greatly. For just as there are six great qualities in the Blessed Lord, so there are six bewildering, baffling qualities too. Otherwise we could have attained what we desired on the basis of Your story alone. The Gopīs think that for this very reason[19] the Blessed Lord, in addition to His other games, is playing a trickster's game on them with the help of Māyā. It is because of the fault that is in their own nature that they perceive the Blessed Lord in this way, just as someone who has a fever perceives in the food he is eating a bitterness that is not there. That is why this Gopī has said : "Your stinging laughter, etc.... all these things disturb our minds greatly." The Lord laughs loudly and derisively. As, when He leaves one Gopī—who has become exhausted since she is, after all, merely human—and goes to be with another, if after that He comes back to the first Gopī, His laughter rings out, and she becomes all the more disturbed. By addressing Kṛṣṇa as

19. "For this very reason" (Skt. *tadartham*), i.e., either to keep what the Gopīs desire from being fulfilled, or to reveal and exercise His six "baffling" qualities, or both.

"Lover" this Gopī is saying that the memory of her union with You has become a very disturbing one. On the other hand, those women who have not enjoyed union with You are not disturbed. Besides this, "Your look of love" also disturbs us greatly when we recall it. When it either is directed toward another or is a form of subtle trickery because it arouses a false confidence in us, it is a source of great disturbance. If it were not meant to be that, then there would not be such a contradiction between Your look of love and its effect. Or perhaps Your look is meant to elevate (OR : "to weigh or test"; Skt. *uttolaka*) our minds. It also gives birth to hope. And hope, in its turn, causes exertion (and hence disturbance : Vasu).

But "Your captivating movements," too, are a source of disturbance to us, i.e., Your movement which is accompanied by the playing of the flute and so forth. The Blessed Lord's own mood is made present externally because of His Form (Skt. *ākāra*), which is pure Joy. And the three graceful curves of His body, along with the other movements of His Form, are especially captivating. But even before that we had meditated on You, and even mere meditation, because it is directed towards You, is "auspicious" and yields a happy result. But that, too, is now a source of disturbance to us, for You have disappeared.[20] The word "Your" (expressed only once in the Sanskrit) is to be taken as relating to all the subject-phrases of the sentence. But its chief application is to this last phrase : "Your perfect auspiciousness for meditation." "For," the Gopīs think, "He accomplishes these other things—His laughter, His looks of love, and His captivating movements—by Māyā." Thus we have seen four sources of disturbance that are connected with the "form" (the body and all that is external) aspect of the Lord. Now the Gopīs point out two more which are connected with the "name" (interior, mental and verbal) aspect, namely : "the words...You whisper...to us in secret" and "the promises which go straight

20. Or: "for it (meditation) has disappeared." Vallabha says merely *tirohitatvāt*. But the two meanings may come to the same, since it was Kṛṣṇa's Form as above described which the Gopīs meditated upon, and the complete disappearance of that Form would imply that they could no longer even meditate upon it.

to our hearts." The words which the Blessed Lord communicates to the Gopīs in secret, in a place apart, embody true Knowledge. Or perhaps He is merely communicating knowledge derived from the treatises on erotic love—this knowledge consists of reminding the Gopīs of the erotic positions and so forth. The words He says in this context penetrate straight to the Gopīs' hearts. Or the Gopīs may mean that the words He speaks about erotic positions are suited to us, the mistresses, and not merely to Him, the lover. (Thus they "go straight to", or "touch", our hearts). Therefore these words are truly sources of happiness to us, but if You deceive us, they will cause only disturbance. The word "for" in the stanza indicates that this conclusion of the Gopīs has been proved by all their experience with the Lord.

Introduction to Stanza 11 : The next stanza is sung by a *rājasa-rājasa* Gopī:

Stanza 11 : "When, O Master, You go out of Vraja, driving the herd before You, we think of Your feet, lovely as lotuses, and how they are walking on pebbles, blades of grass and sharp stubble. And then, Darling, our minds become clouded with grief for You."

Commentary : Under the force of our love for You, our minds become distressed whenever anything bad is happening to You. But even when we are in real torment, You do not become distressed for our sake. This looks to us like a contradiction of justice. "When You go out of Vraja, driving the herd before You"—say the Gopīs—then, as You walk along, "Your feet," which are more delicate and beautiful even than lotuses,[21] "O Master, come upon the pebbles, blades of grass, and sharp stubble" which are in Your path. The pebbles or stones, the blades of grass, and sharp stubble of Kuśa-grass and the like, are *tāmasa, sāttvika* and *rājasa,* respectively. Or, when this Gopī says "pebbles", she may mean grass that is very much like pebbles, i.e., very rough grass. And when the Lord sets His foot on these clumps of stiff, sharp grass, think the Gopīs, He certainly must find it painful. In fact the Lord

21. Keep in mind that Kṛṣṇa is still a boy here, not yet a hardened warrior.

does not experience pain, and yet, "Darling," i.e., dear Husband, "our minds still become clouded with grief for You."

The fact that Kṛṣṇa "goes out of Vraja" at daybreak indicates that He would be tired to start with. And His walking would also tire Him out. That is why this Gopī mentions these things first. Actually Your feet never leave their dwelling-place within us. Yet it is You alone who make them move, to drive the cattle. Besides, You lead the cows of Vraja into the wilderness, and they wander and graze where there are no paths. Therefore You, too, must walk where there is no path. And You wear no sandals, so that the earth and all that lies on it may be graced by the touch of Your feet. Besides, You would not wear the hide of the very animals You are protecting. And so, "Your feet, lovely as lotuses, are walking on pebbles, blades of grass and sharp stubble." Your feet, since they are like lotuses, should rightfully stand only in water, or in some place that is filled with water. And if they are still more beautiful than lotuses, they should have their rightful dwelling-place in Lakṣmī or in us. By addressing Him as "Master," the Gopīs point out that though many boys are assigned to this task, yet You are the only one who goes.

There are three kinds of terrain in the forest : the hilly areas, the wilderness, and the border areas (OR : "marshes"; Skt. *kaccha*). You may encounter pebbles, blades of grass and sharp stubble, one in each of these areas, or You may find all three in every place. You become exhausted and unable to go any farther, and You stay in one place. That is when we begin to worry, and think to ourselves : "I must go there myself and rest His feet on my heart." The stanza's words may also be interpreted to say "Darling of our minds." In other words, He alone makes our minds stable, so now (in His absence) they are unstable.

Introduction to Stanza 12 : Thus we have heard, in the last seven stanzas, seven different types of virgin Gopī. And the four stanzas preceding those were sung by four types of married Gopī. From here on we have a succession of six types of married Gopī, and it is these we now hear, beginning with the following stanza, which is sung by a married Gopī who combines the qualities of *tamas* and *rajas*. For these married Gopīs are unable to go out to see Kṛṣṇa during the day. Therefore, when the Blessed Lord comes at twilight, then they see the Blessed Lord, and passion arises in their minds. In the stanza following this, the Gopī, since she combines *rajas* with *rajas*, will pray that He assume a particular erotic position (i.e., placing His foot on their breasts; Stanza 13). And then (in Stanza 14), a Gopī who combines *sattva* with *rajas* will pray for the nectar of His lips. But the passion of the virgin Gopīs is constant.[22] The stanza reads as follows :

Stanza 12 : "As the day dissolves You return, bearing a face that is like a forest-lotus, covered with locks of black hair and soiled with the dust of the herd. And as You glance at us, showing us that face again and again, O Hero, You grant our minds the gift of passion."

Commentary : "As the day dissolves" means "at twilight." The use of the word "dissolves" indicates the Gopīs' hatred of the day. For now is the time of *rajas* and the time of passion (*kāma*). The "locks of black hair," surrounding His face as bees surround a lotus, awaken the mood of love. For those locks, which drink the nectar of the beauty of His lotus-face, become the very things which awaken the mood in the Gopīs.[23] Therefore "bearing a face which is like a lotus, covered with such locks... O Hero, You grant our minds the gift of passion." (Here begins an interpolation by Viṭṭhala) Because it is twilight and because Kṛṣṇa's face is surrounded by the black-colored locks, its normal lustre is shadowed over. By the use of these words and the word "forest-lotus," the similarity of the Lord's face to a blue lotus is indicated. Likewise the fuller and fuller flowering of the blue lotus, until it opens completely when it sees the face of its beloved, the moon (also means : "the moon-face of its beloved"), as well as its not flowering before that time, are indicated here. By this our Lover's passionate attachment to all of us is expressed. This is why this

22. Since the virgin Gopīs can see and be with Kṛṣṇa during the day, too: Vasu.

23. Keeping in mind the connection between *rasa*, "mood" OR "fluid," and *amṛta* "nectar", we can more easily follow the comparison of the bees and the locks of hair, both drinking the "nectar" of Kṛṣṇa's face and simultaneously arousing the "mood" of love.

Gopī has not used the more usual epithet, "that which grows in water," for "lotus," but says instead, "that which grows in the forest" (*vanaruha*). What she is suggesting by these words is the conditions and environment of the forest, and so He is showing us a face which bears only those qualities (end of Viṭṭhala's interpolation). His face is "soiled with the dust of the herd" of Vraja's cows. And "showing us that face again and again" means that Kṛṣṇa walks down the middle of the road and looks, in turn, at each of the Gopīs, who are standing on either side. Therefore He shows His face repeatedly. Or perhaps, after He has passed them He turns around repeatedly and looks at them. By looking at them in this way He indicates His desire and need for them, and this arouses their passion. If He had looked at them continuously, the Gopīs would have tasted the delight of the mood of love then and there, and this would not have been an occasion in which passion was aroused. This is why He shows His face again and again—to inflame, as it were, the fire of passion. Having acted in this way, Kṛṣṇa now has an unavoidable battle on His hands, whether He decides to fulfil the Gopīs' passion, or to reject it. The Gopīs indicate this when they address Him as "Hero."

The words "soiled with the dust of the herd" indicate the hard work the Lord had done that day. "And," the Gopīs think, "He will find relief from His toil and exertion with us alone." And the Gopīs say "lotus," i.e., that which grows in the forest. In the forest alone can this lotus (Kṛṣṇa's face) be enjoyed in every way. And so that is where we should meet with Him. With this the Gopīs refute in advance any statement of Kṛṣṇa that He will grant them the gift of His love in their homes. The word "bearing" indicates that the Lord brings about this condition deliberately, with real effort. If He washed His face first, and then came to the Gopīs, His looking at them with His bright, calm, grace-giving face might make them experience Knowledge. But this dust (pun here—*rajas* means "dust" as well as the second quality of material existence) that is connected with the herd is passion alone, without anger. Just as, when one holds out a pot, the food in it is given to be eaten and enjoyed, so when He holds out, i.e., "bears", this face, the nectar of love that is there, the essence of which is passion, is made present in their minds. That is why Kṛṣṇa is "bearing" this face. And so, since He has given us this face for our enjoyment, we should waste no time in enjoying it. This passion is an unexpected gift of Yours, and it can be fulfilled by no one but You.

Introduction to Stanza 13: Some Gopīs who are more gifted than the one who sang the last stanza now pray that Kṛṣṇa will place His foot on their breasts, just as the virgin Gopīs had done :

Stanza 13: "Please place on our breasts, O Lover, that lotus-foot of Yours, which grants the desires of those who bow low before it, is worshipped by the lotus-born (Brahmā), embellishes the earth, should be meditated on in adversity, and is, O Destroyer of anxiety, the essence of peace."

Commentary : It is true that this stanza is repetitive (of stanza 7 above), but here the sacredness of the Lord's feet is exalted even more than in the previous stanza. Here His feet are described as bestowing His great qualities, whereas previously their capacity for removing faults was emphasized. "O Lover," i.e., You who are the maker of love, "please place Your lotus-foot on our breasts." The Gopīs explain the reason for their prayer when they say : "O Destroyer of anxiety" (Skt. *ādhihan*), or, as some texts read : "O Destroyer of suffering" (*ārtihan*). Both the fire of suffering that consumes their hearts and their anxiety must be removed. That fire will go out only with Your plainly visible help. We have placed Your feet firmly in our hearts, and they do not go outside. You Yourself, then, must appear and place them on us externally.

Now this Gopī enumerates the six great qualities of Kṛṣṇa's lotus-feet, which are just like the six great qualities of the Blessed Lord Himself. The first of these is His Lordly Power, which she refers to when she says : "(that lotus-foot of Yours) which grants the desires of those who bow low before it." For those who bow before it with special humility, and who take refuge in no one and nothing else, the Lord's foot "grants their desires"—it gives them everything they long for. Only a powerful Lord could act in such a way. The Gopīs say "those who bow low before it" because the desire, and the granting of desires, which are present in the Lord's feet, simply cannot be grasped or received by proud, unbending people.

Next, the Gopī sings : "(which) is worshipped by the lotus-born." She demonstrates here that the Lord's feet are the embodiment of what is Right. For they have come here simply because of the prayer of Brahmā. The Gopī tells us that the Lord's feet are an embodiment of His quality of Fame when they say : "(which) embellishes the earth." Or, as an embellishment which adorns the earth, they may be thought of as an embodiment of Splendor. Then again, the Lord's foot as an object which "should be meditated upon in adversity" is seen as an embodiment either of Fame or of Splendor. The superior nature of these feet in themselves is expressed by saying they are exactly like lotuses. And that the Lord's feet are "the essence of peace" refers to the fact that they are incomparably blessed. Because of this they are an embodiment of Knowledge. Your feet have been described as "lotus-feet" and You have been addressed as "Destroyer of suffering." Since this Gopī has thus ascertained the relation between these two facts (the cool lotus destroys the heat of suffering), she has shown that Your feet possess Your quality of Detachment, too (since detachment destroys suffering).

The Gopīs address the Lord as "Lover" because a lover causes the beloved to attain what she desires. Conversely, they address Him as "Destroyer of suffering" because He removes what is not desired. Or, alternatively, the Gopīs are praying that Your feet, which help the world in five ways (now to be explained), may help us in one way. "Your feet grant desire," i.e., passion (*kāma*), to the women "who bow low before them," as has already been stated when the Gopīs said : "O Hero, You grant our minds the gift of passion (stanza 12)". Or, the meaning may be that the Lord cuts out, i.e. destroys, passion in those whose humility is great.[24] And the Lord's feet are wor-

24. Vallabha is here suggesting that the epithet applied to Kṛṣṇa's foot in this stanza, *kāmada*, which usually would be interpreted as "granting desires", may also be interpreted as "destroying desire (s)." This is quite valid bacause the suffix *-da*, which more often comes from the Skt. verb *DĀ*, *dadāti*, "to give" would most frequently mean "giving." But the

shipped by either him who is born from the lotus, i.e., Brahmā, or by Her who is born from the lotus, i.e., Lakṣmī. Those who are born from the lotus worship the Lord's feet to acquire either lordly power (Brahmā) or passion (Lakṣmī). Or, what are equal to, matched with, or born from His lotus-feet (i.e., His toenails ?). Otherwise, how would these (toenails) have achieved birth from His lotus-feet ?[25]

And "Earth," too, when she is an unadorned woman, is not enjoyed, and so Kṛṣṇa places His foot on her. Even by comparison with the Blessed Lord Himself, His feet are powerful. By simply "meditating on them in adversity," all misfortune is driven far away. And the Gopīs' prayer is that, just as the Lord's feet give every kind of help to these five others we have mentioned, so let them help us. By these words all the positions of sexual union have also been hinted at.[26]

Introduction to Stanza 14 : Immediately after this, some Gopīs who are still more advanced make the following prayer :

Stanza 14 : "Bestow on us, O Hero, the nectar of Your lips, which increases the sheer thrill of love, destroys our sor-

lexicographers also recongize as valid and fairly frequent the use of the same suffix to convey the meaning of the different verb *DĀ* (or *DO*), *dyati*, "to cut, cut out, destroy." Thus the epithet might mean "destroying passion."

25. Vallabha's absolutely impenetrable Sanksrit for these last two sentences is : *tattulyaṁ vā. anyathā tāni caraṇapaṅkajajanma katham prāpnuyuḥ.* Here we must remember that the word Vallabha is exploring the possible meanings of is the stanza's word *padmaja*, "lotus-born," i.e., Brahmā, Lakṣmī, or, as seems here to be the thrust, "what is born from His lotus feet." Vasu interprets this as referring to Kṛṣṇa's "toenails." And this seems to account better than any other possible explanation for the neuter plural subject (tāni) of the second sentence. Kṛṣṇa's toenails are "equal to" His lotus feet in that they, as well as His feet, are composed of pure Being, Consciousness and Joy, as is the whole of Kṛṣṇa's form. And equal gives birth to equal. This is the best I can do with Vallabha's Sanskrit, Vasu's Hindi, and my own resources. I eagerly await further suggestions.

26. If this sentence means that all the words of the stanza have a double meaning, and refer also each to a particular position of sexual union, the task of figuring them out is beyond me. I might add that it was also beyond Vasu. Perhaps an expert on *kāmaśāstra* ? I don't think the words need be interpreted in this way, however. Probably Vallabha is speaking in a looser, generally allusive sense: a prayer for this erotic position conjures up the images of all the other erotic positions, too.

row, is kissed, with fitting grace, by Your melodious flute, and makes people forget their love for anyone or anything else."

Commentary : "Bestow on us...the nectar of Your lips." Here, too, the nectar of Kṛṣṇa's lips bestows (when He kisses) His great qualities. Here the Gopīs intend to express the fact that this nectar possesses only four of the six great qualities, because the qualities of Knowledge and Detachment are neither necessary nor desirable here. The Gopīs indicate the lordly Power of this nectar when they say : "which increases the sheer thrill of love." The Gopīs' limited passion becomes painful to them when it unites with the Lord's unlimited passion. Just as different liquids (*rasāḥ*) serve to awaken one's hunger, so this nectar of the mood of love (*rasa*) awakens passion. Besides, not only does this nectar of love strengthen passion—it removes all faults of the mind and heart as well. Therefore the fact that this nectar "destroys sorrow" proves that it embodies the qualities of Knowledge and Detachment, too, besides embodying lordly Power and Right. The Gopīs next tell us how this nectar embodies the quality of Fame : "The nectar of Your lips...is kissed, with fitting grace, by the flute with its clear, melodious sound." For the Fame of Your flute-playing is spread far and wide by those who appreciate music. And the flute is Your greatest devotee, and so it is the flute that kisses the nectar of Your lips. But the flute only kisses the nectar—it does not drink it. That this nectar embodies the quality of Splendor is shown in the words : "(it) makes people forget their love for anyone or anything else." For she (Splendor = Śrī) causes a person to forget everything. Because this quality of making people forget all else accomplishes in itself the ends of human striving, the Gopīs have described it as having the force of the Object of knowledge (Skt. *prameya*).[27] The previous phrase,

27. The word *prameya* is a technical term in Vallabha's system, meaning Kṛṣṇa Himself, the supreme object of Knowledge. But it nearly always occurs as second in the ordered series of four: *pramāṇa, prameya* , *sādhana* and *phala*, which we are about to see here. In this passage Vallabha is construing this set of four together with the "ends of human striving" (*puruṣārtha*), usually given as four : *dharma, artha, kāma* and *mokṣa.* But the correlation here seems to be loose—with Vallabha intending to express that the nectar of Kṛṣṇa's lips bestows each and every object of human endeavor.

concerning the flute, expressed the force of this nectar as means of knowledge (*pramāṇa*). The quality of destroying sorrow expresses its force as final reward (*phala*). And lastly, this nectar's quality of strengthening love establishes it firmly as a means of attainment (*sādhana*). Thus the nectar of Your lips both embodies in itself and bestows upon us all the objects of human existence. By the word "people" the Gopīs mean either "us, who have the proper level of eligibility," or "those objects of human striving which are very difficult to attain."[28] By the word "bestow" the Gopīs mean that, even if this nectar should not be given, yet, since bestowing generously is another of Your great qualities, it can be given to us. For, by addressing Him as "Hero" the Gopīs remind the Lord that heroism cannot possibly be present in one who does not give generously.

Introduction to Stanza 15 : We have heard three different types of Gopī in the last three stanzas. Now we hear from three more types, whose dominant quality is *tamas*. The first type, who berate the gods, are *sāttvika-tāmasa*. The second type criticize the Blessed Lord, and they are *tāmasa-tāmasa*. And the third type blame themselves—they are *rājasa-tāmasa* :

Stanza 15 : "When You roam about the forest during the day, an instant (OR : the time it takes to blink an eye) becomes a million years for us, since we do not see You. But when You return, and we gaze at Your beautiful face and curly locks of hair—that god is a fool who created lids over our eyes !"

Commentary : When You are roaming around in the forest during the day, in those daylight hours an instant becomes a million years ! The Gopīs state the reason for this when they say : "since we do not see You." But when we see You again, and "gaze at Your beautiful face and curly locks of hair, then that god who created eyelids in us"—that Brahmā—"is a fool!" Just as he did not create eyelids in the gods—which we know because they have supernatural vision—so it was unjust of him to

28. How the word I have translated by "people" (Skt. *nṛṇām*) might refer equally to actual people (i.e., "us," the Gopīs) or to "objects of human striving" (*puruṣārthānām*) I don't know. But I see no other way of interpreting Vallabha's Sanskrit, which says: *nṛṇām asmākamadhikāriṇāṁ durlabha-puruṣārthānāṁ vā*.

create eyelids in us, who are seeing something even more supernatural than the gods see. And so, since he has done something that is not right, he is a fool. And the gods live for a long time, but so do we, since "an instant becomes a million years for us." The word "instant" is not in the usual feminine gender here.[29]

If there were any purpose in Your going out to the forest, then we wouldn't be upset. But You merely wander around there during the day, and a person cannot accomplish anything worthwhile in the forest. Besides, it is impossible for us to go out. Thus the gods were created by the Blessed Lord, and that stupid god Brahmā created eyelids in poor women like us.

Introduction to Stanza 16 : A group of Gopīs, less gifted than the last, now sings :

Stanza 16: "Defying the commands of our husbands and sons and their families, our brothers and our relatives, we have come here, Acyuta, to be near You. And now we are entranced by the song of Your flute, You who know the comings and goings of all—You deceiver!—for who else would abandon women in the night?"

Commentary : "Acyuta," i.e., unfailing One—You, unlike us, are free of the fear that Your passion will ever be exhausted. Our husbands and our sons and their families, i.e., those in their lineage, as well as our brothers and relatives—the authority of all these should never be transgressed. Yet we have defied even them and come to You. "You who know the comings and goings of all" means that it is You alone who give (make possible) whatever movement is made by each and every creature. Or this phrase (Skt. *gatividaḥ*) may mean that we, the Gopīs, "know the situation, or scope," that is to say, we know the proper proportion and distinction between worshipping our husbands and families and worshipping the Blessed

29. Vasu interprets this by saying that Skt. *truṭi*, "instant," when not in the feminine—and presumably in the masculine—gender, means "the time it takes to blink an eye." If this is an accurate interpretation of Vallabha's meaning, it provides a lovely figurative addition to the stanza's meaning. The present phrase would then mean: "the time it takes to blink an eye becomes a million years for us." This doubles the Gopīs' reason for cursing Brahmā for creating eyelids in them!

Lord. Besides, "we are entranced by the song of Your flute." Therefore, having deluded us and brought all of us here, "what kind of person would abandon women in the forest at night," so thatwe will fail in both our obligations—to worship our husbands and to worship the Blessed Lord? For women should never be abandoned at any time—even less so in the forest—especially at night! The reason the Gopīs call the Lord a "deceiver" is that He has not given them the very thing He summoned them there to give. We are relatives (by marriage) of deceivers.[30] Therefore we do not go to them as if they were our husbands (?).

Introduction to Stanza 17 : In the next stanza a group of Gopīs, more advanced than the last, blame themselves alone :

Stanza 17 : "The words You spoke to us in secret, which aroused passion in our hearts; Your face, laughing heartily as it looked at us with love; the broad chest we gazed at—the dwelling-place of Śrī; our minds, which so passionately crave all these, are now constantly dazed and deluded."

Commentary : "Our minds, which passionately crave, are now dazed and deluded," say the Gopīs. There are three causes for this, and three qualities associated with these causes. The Lord's words, His laughter and His chest; and passion, Joy and persons with the proper level of eligibility.[31] The first three are the causes, and the next three the qualities.

"The words which You spoke to us in secret," i.e., in a separate place, or, perhaps, the knowledge You communicated

30 This may be a reference to Stanza 5 of Chapter 30 (our Chapter II), where Vallabha describes the cowherds, the Gopīs' husbands, as people who "steal curds, milk, etc." Vasu interprets this and the following sentence as saying that the Gopīs are the cowherds' wives in name only, while their real Husband is Kṛṣṇa alone. This does seem to offer the best explanation for the second, difficult sentence: *ato 'smākaṁ teṣu na praveśaḥ*. I am not entirely convinced that this is what Vallabha means. But other great female *bhakta-s* besides the Gopīs, such as Mahādeviyakka and Mīrābāi, seem often to have found their husband an obstacle to their real Husband.

31. This statement of the three causes and three qualities is put into two *pāda-s* in the *anuṣṭubh* meter by Vallabha, as follows: *vākyaṁ hāsyam uraścaiva kāmānandādhikāriṇaḥ*. In Vallabha's next paragraph, the connection between words (cause) and passion (quality) is evident ; the next connection is between Kṛṣṇa's laughter and His love (=Joy); and lastly there is the connection between His chest and Śrī, whose level of eligibility is the highest.

to us, "aroused passion in our hearts," just as before. And "Your face laughed heartily as Your gaze told us of Your love." And "Your broad chest is the dwelling-place of Śrī."

Or perhaps the Gopīs are expressing here the fact that the Blessed Lord's body possesses His six great qualities. For from Your body, when we used to gaze at You bodily, came the words spoken to us in secret. And the arousing of passion in our hearts came from Your body, too. Likewise its face laughed loudly, and its look betokened love. And "we gazed at" its broad chest, and that chest was the dwelling-place of Śrī.[32]

The Gopīs also explain here that the four functions of means of knowledge (Kṛṣṇa's words), object of knowledge (the passion they arouse), means of attainment (His laughing face) and final reward (His looks of love) are present concretely in the Blessed Lord's form (body). And they have described the Fame and Splendor (Śrī) of His chest in order to gain for themselves a dwelling-place on it. The Gopīs' previous attitude of pride is absent now, simply because they have seen the Lord's face, whose hearty laugh destroys pride. Consequently their passion is aroused, and it becomes strong and permanent when He looks at them with love. And from this comes their eligibility to dwell on His chest. Thus their own skill in sexual enjoyment is what their first phrase—"the words You spoke to us in secret"—refers to (since He would not speak to them "in secret" if they were not skilled). And when their passionate craving ran away with them and they began thinking that everything would happen this way (just as they desired), their

32. It is not easy to discover the correlations between Kṛṣṇa's six great qualities and the six things mentioned here. But I think we can pin down at least four of them with some assurance. The "words spoken in secret" obviously betoken Knowledge, as mentioned above in this stanza's commentary. The "arousing of passion" would embody Power, as in the commentary on Stanza 14 above. Kṛṣṇa's "broad chest" is said by Vallabha, a few sentences from now, to embody Fame; and its being "Śrī's dwelling-place" explicitly links it with Splendor. As for the "hearty—and derisive (cf. Stanza 10)—laughter" (*prahasita*), this may signify Detachment. And lastly, His "looks of love" must link up with His second great quality, Strength/Right (*vīrya/dharma*), but I have no idea how.

minds became dazed and reaped only confusion. "Since we did not get what we wanted," they thought, "a constant state of stupor has come over us." In this state they could not tell whether they were alive or dead, and they thought: "Cursed be this life!" This is what the Gopīs' words mean.

Introduction to Stanza 18: Then one more virgin Gopī, who had been intent on her desire through all this time, makes this prayer to the Lord:

Stanza 18: "Dear one, Your bodily presence here destroys the sins of those who dwell in Vraja's groves, and it is a great blessing to all. Relent a little, and grant a small dose of (the medicine of) Your bodily form, which drives out the diseases which afflict the hearts of Your people, to us, too—for our hearts are sick with passionate craving for You."

Commentary: "This bodily presence—this manifestation—of Yours destroys the sins of the people who dwell in Vraja's groves." And it is an unparalleled "blessing to all the world" as well. And by the special shape You have here given it, it removes our faults in particular. Your form bestows Your great qualities on all people. "Relent a little," then, "and grant (to us) a small dose of (the medicine of) Your form." The reason why it is necessary for You to relent and grant us Your help is that "our hearts are sick with passionate craving for You." Our hearts, i.e., our innermost selves passionately desire You alone. In case Kṛṣṇa says: "What should I relent and give you?", the Gopīs continue: "(the medicine of) Your bodily form, which drives out the diseases which afflict the hearts of Your people," i.e., of Your Gopīs. It defeats these diseases and destroys them entirely. Your form destroys the sins of some, and grants the final reward of others. Please let it, in our case, become the destroyer of our disease.

Introduction to Stanza 19: And lastly, a Gopī who combines *rajas* with *tamas* sings wearily:

Stanza 19: "That beautiful lotus-foot of Yours, O Lover, which we, trembling with fear, place slowly and softly on our rough breasts, and on which You now roam about the forest—is it not hurt, perhaps, by the pebbles and other sharp objects? At least our thoughts, wandering after You in confusion, so tell us, whose very life You are."

Commentary: We tremble with fear as we place, slowly and softly, Your beautiful lotus-foot on our breasts. The reason we place it there slowly and softly is that our breasts are "rough." The Gopīs address the Lord as "Lover" because they are placing His foot on their breasts out of love for Him. And they call His foot "beautiful" because it is large, perfectly formed, cooling and fragrant, and it quenches the fires of suffering. That is why they put it on their breasts. They place it there boldly because He is their Lover. On this same delicate foot You walked away and left us, and because of our fault of pride "You are now roaming about the forest." If someone could cause pain to another without himself suffering pain, he would do it; but not if he experienced the pain, too. That is why the question occurs to us : "is it (Your foot) hurt or not ?" The Gopīs add the word "perhaps" to indicate that they are guessing. "Is it not hurt ?" therefore means that it probably is hurt. The Lord might say to them : "On what basis are you guessing that my foot is hurt?" The Gopīs reply : "Our thoughts, wandering after You in confusion, so tell us." Our power of thinking is just wandering around. But if it knew for certain that Your foot was hurt, our intellect would come to rest peacefully once more. This uncertainty makes them uncertain about when He will come out of the forest again, too. They express the reason for their concern about this when they say : "...us, whose very life You are." The Gopīs' lives are lived for the sake of the Blessed Lord's games alone. We explained before how our minds were exhausted with suffering. Now we are telling You that our fainting and stupor have brought us right to death's door. You must become aware that the state of all of us has culminated in this stupor. For re-entering Your games (as in the last chapter), we used speech; but in order to stand once again in the presence of Your very Form, we sing. Thus we have heard described the sufferings the Gopīs endured with regard to their means of attaining the Lord's presence and His testing of them.

CHAPTER IV

(Bhāgavata Purāṇa Book X, Chapter 32)

Verse I: In this twenty-ninth chapter we are told that the Gopīs gained the Blessed Lord's Grace by their lamentation, with the result that they became happy and learned the reasons behind what had happened to them.

Verse II: For Hari does not become pleased with some one because the person is rich in means of attainment. No—in fact complete helplessness on the part of the devotee is the lone means of gaining Hari's good graces.

Verse III: And when He is pleased, He destroys the sufferings of all people everywhere. And then He uttered the sentences of explanation to the Gopīs, with a view toward their (His and the Gopīs') worship of one another through love.

Introduction to Stanza 1: After thus narrating for us, in the last chapter, the Gopīs' hymn of praise, and, in the chapter before that, their incoherent talking, Śuka sums up both these for us in the following stanza. And, he adds, when they found that neither of these was a means for attaining the Lord's Grace, they took to lamentation:

Stanza 1: Thus the Gopīs, after praising the Lord in song and talking incoherently in different ways, O King, began crying loudly but appealingly, out of intense desire to see Kṛṣṇa.

Commentary: In the manner described above, all the Gopīs "praised the Lord in song and talked incoherently." We have described their singing and talking as if it were all of the same kind, while in fact both these were accompanied by many kinds of wailing and crying. When neither their song nor their talking gained the Lord's favor, they all came together and began a great lamentation. Śuka tells us the reason they lamented when he says: "out of intense desire to see Kṛṣṇa." The

Gopis surely did not do this in order to protect their own bodies.

Introduction to Stanza 2 : And then the Blessed Lord, after He had become Brahmā, Viṣṇu and Rudra, became Kṛṣṇa once again,[1] as Śuka tells us :

Stanza 2 : Then the Hero, the Grandson of Śūra, became present in their midst, His lotus-face smiling. He wore a yellow garment, and a garland hung round His neck—the love god of Kāma himself, right there in front of them!

Commentary : The Blessed Lord became present right in the midst of the Gopīs. The Blessed Lord parted the curtain of Māyā and appeared clearly. Therefore Śuka calls Him Śauri (literally, "descendant of Śūra") here because He is the grandson of Śūra, but in addition, His heroism (Skt. *śaurya*) is to be manifested here. For He has come down and taken birth in the line of the Yadus in order to remove the sufferings of all. And "His lotus-face is smiling" in order to remove the Gopīs' fault of pride. There is a trace of laughter on His face. The Gopīs' total bewilderment has pleased Him, and so He smiles. Or, perhaps two smiles cross His lotus-face, indicating first that the devotees' fault has left them (because He has smiled at them), and secondly that He comes in response to their devotion.

Śuka next describes the form in which the Lord had now come : "He wore a yellow garment." He held the edge of the yellow garment in His hand in order to cover His laughter. Or, He appeared in the form He assumes in His highest heaven, Vyāpi-Vaikuṇṭha, where He had been making love with Lakṣmī during this time. "And a garland hung round His neck" means that He was wearing a garland of forest-flowers. And, on His way to the Gopīs, He had accepted the worship of Brahmā and the other gods, or perhaps of Lakṣmī (OR :

1. Shri Shyam Goswamy's very original insight for explaining this passage is that Kṛṣṇa had become Brahmā the Creator by arousing the Gopis' passion; then Viṣṇu the Preserver by fostering and strengthening it; and then Rudra by destroying their passion. Now He once again becomes Kṛṣṇa—pure Joy. This rings truer than Vasu's convoluted and less convincing explanation.

"perhaps the garland was Lakṣmī's" : Vasu). This is why some sort of delay on His part has been indicated. This is explained by what we were told in the first stanza of the preceding chapter : "For now Indirā (Lakṣmī) takes refuge here." He has appeared here only now because it was not fitting that He neglect Lakṣmī. This is why the Lord's coming here was spoken of before. (Here begins an interpolation by Viṭṭhala) Or, alternatively, we may say that Śuka states the reason for the Lord's present behavior by means of the two qualifying phrases (the first regarding His yellow garment, the second His garland). If the Lord did not appear now, there would be no mood of love in the Gopīs, nor would there be Fame in Him.[2] But He wears the yellow garment as a means of bringing about the mood of love by covering Himself. And He wears the garland which is full of His Fame. This is what Vallabhācārya means when he says (in the second sentence of this commentary): "(the Blessed Lord) appeared clearly." Vallabhācārya's words mean that, if things were otherwise, and Kṛṣṇa hid His Form from the devotees, then quite obviously these two objects, the yellow garment and the garland, would not have been mentioned (end of Viṭṭhala's interpolation).

Someone might ask : "How is it that the Lord has not been subdued by Kāma, since Kāma's own army (the women) has been exhausted ?" Śuka's reply to this is : "the love god of" even "Kāma himself." On the earthly level, Kāma is the god of love. On the level of the Self, however, "Kāma himself" is actually present in the hearts of all. But the god of love of even this Kāma, the god of love on the divine level, is Kṛṣṇa, because He is the totality of everything and everyone. Therefore even Kāma, the love god, is entranced (by Him). So Kṛṣṇa cannot be deluded even by Kāma. And the Lord takes the form of Kāma here. Therefore when the Gopīs' utter helplessness became evident, Kṛṣṇa made Himself present in the form of Kāma to remove their helplessness. In this

2. Vasu explains this by saying that the mood of love would be absent from the Gopīs *a fortiori*, because they would have died from their even more prolonged separation from Him, and their death would have been a disgrace (*apakīrti*) to Him—the opposite of Fame (*kīrti*).

way He made them rich in Kāma, i.e., in passion, as He had before.

Introduction to Stanza 3 : Śuka describes what happened next in the following words :

Stanza 3 : When the hapless Gopīs saw that He, their most dearly Beloved, had come, their eyes flowered (like lotuses), out of love, and they all arose at once, as if the breath of life had returned to their bodies (also : "and all the parts of their bodies arose at once, as if the breath of life had returned to them" cf. Comm.).

Commentary : "When they saw that He had come...they all arose at once." Having already described Kṛṣṇa's manifestation of Himself, the "coming" which Śuka now describes is meant to explain the attitude and reaction of the Svāminīs (the Gopīs; cf. Commentary on Chapter Five, Stanza 35) upon seeing Him. Or perhaps Śuka's words signify that the Lord first became manifest within the Gopīs, but now He came before them externally.

Someone may object: "Why should anyone be surprised that the Gopīs stood up when the Blessed Lord came?" The answer to this is that there was no life (also: "no soul", *Skt. jīva*) left in the Gopīs—they were lifeless— this is the point of the example Śuka uses.[3] "The parts of their bodies" means their hands, their feet, and all their other members. It was "as if the breath of life had returned to them." When we make an effort to do something, we generally employ only one limb of our body, but in breathing all the parts of the body cooperate. That is why Śuka uses the plural number—to indicate that every Gopī's entire body arose at the same time. We must think here in terms of five things; the body, the sense-faculties, the life-breath, the interior faculties (Skt. *antaḥkaraṇa*), and the soul. Elsewhere the arising of the soul is dependent on the arising of others—the body and

3. Vallabha interprets in two ways the sentence that begins in my translation of the stanza with "and". I have parenthesized the second interpretation in my translation. It is evident that Vallabha intends to explain the first interpretation when he quotes and explains the relevant words at the beginning of his commentary on this stanza, but it is the second interpretation which he begins to elucidate now, and which the reader should refer back to.

the faculties. But here it is when the soul (Skt. *jīva*) has come that all the others arise. For the soul had entered within the Blessed Lord, and therefore it came along in the company of the Blessed Lord, and only upon the Blessed Lord's arising did it arise. But the interior faculties—those of the heart—have also arisen. Śuka points out the cause of this when he says: "their most dearly Beloved." The Blessed Lord is absolutely and pre-eminently Beloved. And so when the interior faculties saw Him, they arose. The Gopīs' love for the Blessed Lord made "their eyes flower." This expression tells us that the Gopīs' sense-faculties arose "out of love" for Him. (Here begins an interpolation by Viṭṭhala) The Lord came for one lone reason—so the Gopīs might see Him, and their seeing Him was accomplished right at the start—merely by His coming. But the flowering of their eyes was separate from that. By thus referring to that attribute of a flower (its blooming or flowering), the similarity of the Gopīs' eyes to lotuses is expressed. By Śuka's saying that the Gopīs' love for Kṛṣṇa is the cause of the flowering of their eyes, he indicates that this effect of their love had been absent until this time, and appears only now, just as lotuses do not flower until the sun appears. Since everything had remained hidden during His separation from them, this effect, too, had remained hidden. This is why Śuka calls the Gopīs "hapless", because he wants to express their incapability, in Kṛṣṇa's absence, of producing even one of the effects of His presence. And the Blessed Lord is the life-breath of all life-breaths. And Śuka says "He" to indicate that it was the Lord's bodily appearance, which was the very thing the Gopīs had desired in the prayers they had been making, that caused the Gopīs' bodies to arise (end of Viṭṭhala's interpolation).

Introduction to Stanzas 4-8: Śuka tells us, in the following five stanzas, what the Gopīs did after they had arisen and were standing there with the Blessed Lord:

Stanza 4: One Gopī joyfully took Śauri's lotus-hand between her own as she made the añjali-gesture. Another placed His arm, smeared with sandal-paste, on her shoulder.

Stanza 5: A delicate Gopī received in her hands, open in añjali, the betel-mix He had chewed. And one Gopī, consumed by fire, placed His lotus-foot on her breasts.

Stanza 6: Another Gopī, trembling with the anger that comes from love, knit her brows in a frown. And, biting her lips, she glared at Him, as if to kill Him with the sidelong glances she cast.

Stanza 7: Another Gopī, her eyes never blinking, stared in rapture at His lotus-face. And though she drank in the sight, she was never filled, like the holy ones when they gaze at His feet.

Stanza 8: And a particular Gopī took Him into her heart through the narrow passageway of her eye, and then shut her eye. And there she remained, embracing Him, as all the hair of her body thrilled—immersed, like a Yogī, in the sea of Joy.

Commentary : Previously there were many types of Gopī, but now that the Blessed Lord has appeared the Gopīs show only seven differences of type. The One Blessed Lord has made Himself manifest for the sake of all these. The Gopīs who stand in front, and are therefore nearest the Lord, are described first. The seven kinds of Gopī enumerated are: those who are characterized purely and completely by the quality *sattva*; those who are likewise characterized only by *rajas*; those who combine *rajas* with *sattva*; those who transcend the three qualities; and the rest.[4] "One Gopī joyfully took Śauri's (Kṛṣṇa's) lotus-hand between her own as she made the gesture called *añjali*." The Blessed Lord held out only one of His hands, for, as we recall from the second stanza, He was holding the edge of His yellow garment with His other hand, to hide His laughter. To take someone's hand between one's own in *añjali* is a gesture of great respect. Śuka uses the name Śauri to indicate Kṛṣṇa's heroism. And Śuka says "joyfully" to indicate the disappearance of the suffering described above.

"Another Gopī," thinking to herself: 'I will get still closer to Him than she', "placed His arm on her shoulder." Thus, or at least to that extent, she is embraced by Him. Later on in this narration the way the Lord employs this Gopī in His game (OR: "her separation from Him"; Skt. *viniyoga*) will be described in her own words: "When shall He place His arm, fragrant with the scent of aloes, on my head?" (Bh. P. X. 47. 21).

4. Vallabha will characterize "the rest" when he describes them in particular.

Therefore Śuka has used the words "smeared with sandal-paste" here to indicate that this same natural attribute of fragrance which the Lord's arm possesses will bring about this Gopī's constraint in Him. The Lord's arm is "smeared," i.e., anointed, with sandal-paste. The reason the sandal-paste is there, as has already been mentioned, is either that the Lord received it as part of an act of worship of Him by the gods, or that it was smeared on His arm while He was embracing Lakṣmī. And as for the betel-mix He was chewing, He may have acquired that, too, from either of these same sources. And so the Lord reflects, in the accoutrements of His appearance, the actions of both Lakṣmī (OR: Lakṣmī and the Gopīs) and the highest gods. Lakṣmī and the Gopīs desire to rise up (over or upon Him),but the highest gods (bow down to) worship Him.

And so, another of the Gopīs "received in her hands, open in añjali, the betel-mix He had chewed." Śuka points out her suitability for receiving this betel-mix by describing her as "delicate," which means that her limbs are soft and lovely. And "one Gopī," who either was some distance away from the Lord, and thus could not see Him or be seen clearly, or could not arise when He came, somehow managed to sit near Him and "placed His lotus-foot on her breasts." Śuka tells us the reason why she could not stand up and why she placed His foot on her breasts when he says: "consumed by fire." For she had been suffering the most intense anguish because of her separation from Him. This is why Śuka has described her as "one Gopī."

"Another Gopī," who was also some distance away from the Lord, had *tamas* as her dominant quality. And under the influence of *tamas* she "knit her brows in a frown" and "glared at Him, as if to kill Him with the sidelong glances she cast." In the Sanskrit words of this passage we see an example of the rule whereby one omits a consonant when the very same consonant occurs in the next syllable. The passage in its full form would read *kaṭākṣakṣepaiḥ* ("with the sidelong glances she cast"). Instead, because of the rule, we see *kaṭākṣepaiḥ*. She is described as "trembling with the anger that comes from," i. e., along with, "love." And, "biting hard on her lips," she stood there distressed and trembling. The knitting of her brow reflects the crookedness of her mind. And the anger that accompanies her love shows the confused state of her senses. And the disturbance of her body is evident from her biting her lips. The words "as if to kill Him" show that her very life-breaths are pulsating violently, so that her means of attaining knowledge has also deteriorated. "Sidelong glances" mean that she looks at Kṛṣṇa out of the corner of her eye. This signifies that her dominant emotion is that of reproach. Just as threatening is the vocal form of reproach, the sidelong glance, when repeated over and over, is a facial expression of reproach. And she bends her brows so as to knit them either to make her emotion of reproach as full as possible, or to control the influences of Time (Skt. *kāla*). By her anger she intends to control her very nature (*svabhāva*), and she bites her lips in order to destroy her greed (cf. Bh. P. II. 1. 32.). And she distorts her knowledge so that she may not reach ultimate freedom (i.e., mere *mokṣa*). And the object of her intention of "killing" Him is to refute and defeat all the means of right knowledge (*pramāṇa*; probably the ordinary scriptural means of knowledge are here referred to). By all these means her worldly devotion becomes strong, and full, and graced.[5] It was to point this out that Śuka described this Gopī.

After thus describing that abundantly graced Gopī (Skt. *atipuṣṭām*), Śuka describes the very highest type of Gopī[6] in the stanza that begins: "Another Gopī stared..." This Gopī's fault of pride was removed by the sight of the Blessed Lord. Therefore she desired to establish the Blessed Lord in her heart by meditation. And so she brought Him in through her eyes, and established the Blessed Lord in her heart. Here she would drink the nectar of His beauty, as Śuka tells us by using the words "His lotus-face." She drinks, with "her eyes never blinking." Drinking consists of the ingestion of a fluid substance. If she had blinked as her eyes were drinking in this sight, the flow of this nectar of delight (also: "this mood"; Skt. *rasa*) would have been interrupted. That is why she drank with unblinking eyes. Because of the rarity of this nectar of beauty, her eyes open to receive it like a pair of hands in añjali. The worship that pro-

5. Skt. *yato laukikī bhaktiḥ puṣṭā bhavati.*

6. Vasu says that this is a *nirguṇā* Gopī, and Vallabha quite clearly implies just that.

ceeds from love, and no other, is what Śuka intends to convey here. And even though the Lord entered within her in His entirety, with every one of his qualities, was totally engrossed in her and became dependent on her, so that whenever she wished, she looked into her heart and saw Him, still "she was never filled" —she never had enough of this sight—bacause of the extreme beauty of the object of her vision. Nor was any absence of motive on her part an obstacle to her, as Śuka points out by using the following example: "like the holy ones when they gaze at His feet." For the holy ones have done all there is to do—all their objectives have been accomplished—yet they spontaneously delight in the Lord's feet—this mood has become their very nature—even though nothing at all will be gained or avoided by it.

And still another Gopī, who was on an equal level with the last, and was standing at some distance from the Blessed Lord, grasped Him by using the methods of Yoga, as Śuka tells us in the stanza which begins: "And a particular Gopī took Him into her heart.." The Gopī of stanza six was an example of worldly devotion and the Gopī of the last stanza followed the Path of Devotion. But this Gopī was an adherent of Yoga. Therefore she saw every part of the Lord's body (i.e., not just His face). But she makes her two eyes one; otherwise her vision would be split. For the Gopī in the last stanza, seeing Kṛṣṇa was her only motive. But this Gopī is a rare one, as Śuka tells us when he says: "a particular Gopī." And the word "Him" signifies here that this is He, whom this very same Gopī described earlier with the words: "Surely You are not the son of a Gopī" (Chapter 31, Stanza 4). Śuka uses the singular when he says "through the narrow passageway of her eye" to signify that she caused the Lord's form to enter through this narrow passageway, and then "she took Him into her heart" (Skt. *hṛdi kṛtya* or *hṛdikṛtya*). Even in a non-compounded verb form, the indeclinable participle may end in *-ya* as *kṛtya* does here. Or, the form *hṛdikṛtya* is a compound of the *aluk*-type. And then this Gopī "shut her eye," thinking to herself: 'Since I do this, may the One who is inside me never go out.' For to her mind the Blessed Lord no longer remains present outside. Or Śuka means to convey that she has taken possession of her very own Portion. The second "and" in the stanza indicates that she has turned all her senses away from external things. And so, since her inner Joy was complete, "all the hair of her body thrilled." Someone might object that this thrilling of the hair of her body out of purely individual joy will not make her a true Gopī. To answer this Śuka adds the phrase: "there she remained, embracing Him." It was when she was in a *sāttvika* emotional state that this thrilling of the hair pervaded her (cf. Footnote 11 of Chapter Six). Therefore "she remained, embracing Him" inwardly. And she held onto this state of things, to the exclusion of all other conditions. Someone might object: "But isn't there something she must do after this? Doesn't she have to have intercourse with the Blessed Lord, converse with Him, and go home? How has she established this state permanently?" Śuka's reply to this is: "like a Yogī." For a Yogī, by means of his transcendent condition alone, accomplishes everything which he must do after he has entered the trance. In just the same way, this Gopī will accomplish everything by means of the very condition she is in. And so, "there she remained." Besides, she is "immersed in the sea of Joy." She has plunged, over her head, in Joy. And she has no perception of what is outside her. And it is only when one perceives the outside world that he can examine and plan to do things. But when one's Joy is complete, there is no desire at all.

Introduction to Stanza 9: After thus describing the proper actions of particular kinds of Gopīs individually, Śuka tells us what happened with regard to the goal of the Gopīs as a group:

Stanza 9: All the Gopīs were utterly beside themselves with joy at the sight of Keśava, and they left far behind them the suffering that arose out of separation from Him, just as people do when they reach the presence of the Wise one.

Commentary: Śuka uses the Lord's name, "Keśava," in order to ask us this rhetorical question: "What great effort would it take for Him who effected the final reward for even those who were dominated by the qualities of *rajas* and *tamas* in their strongest forms,[7] to save these Gopīs, who are agitated by comparatively small degrees of the three qualities?" And the "sight" of Him refers either to their seeing Him or to His brilliant lustre, both internal and external. Because of this they "were utterly beside

7. Such as Brahmā, Śiva, Śiśupāla and many others.

themselves with joy." Just as worldly people are overjoyed when they become the ruler of a kingdom, or when a son is born to them, so "all the Gopīs" were overjoyed at this sight. Thus Śuka conveys to us that what they desired has come to pass. He further tells us that they were freed from what they did not desire when he says: "They left far behind them the suffering that arose out of separation from Him." Someone might object that, if this were so, the Gopīs would have attained ultimate freedom. For when the circle of Saṁsāra is broken and the greatest happiness is experienced because the Blessed Lord appears before one's very eyes, certainly no goal of human striving can remain. Śuka answers this objection by saying: "when they reach the presence of the Wise one." "The Wise one" is the witness connected with deep sleep (Skt. *suṣupti*). The manifestation of the Blessed Lord in deep sleep (Skt. *svāpyaya*) is what Śuka has referred to here.[8] And souls, along with the impressions of their past action, enter into Him. And, Śuka intends to tell us, just as "people," i.e., persons with the proper level of eligibility, "reach His presence," enter into Him, and then return again to waking life, so the Gopīs in this situation will return to ordinary life, rather than reach ultimate freedom. And so they become "people," as the stanza says, once more. But this does not happen to persons of the highest level of eligibility. Śuka uses the example merely to communicate the partial analogy of the Gopīs to people who reach the Wise one in deep sleep. But the Blessed Lord has made Himself physically present to the Gopīs.

Introduction to Stanza 10: Having thus described for us the Gopīs' actions with regard to Him, Śuka now narrates the Blessed Lord's actions regarding them:

Stanza 10: Surrounded by those women who had been freed from all their sorrows, the Blessed Lord Acyuta glowed brilliantly, revered father, like a man in possession of all his powers (also: "like the Person"—Skt. *puruṣa*—"Surrounded by all His Powers"—Skt. *śakti*).

Commentary : Śuka refutes here the objection that the Blessed Lord, in having intercourse with these ordinary women,

8. Cf. *Brahma-sūtra* I. 1. 8, in which *svāpyaya* is mentioned, and is explained as here by Vallabha in his *Aṇubhāṣya*.

would become something other than His full, real Self. For if that were so, contends Śuka, then the Blessed Lord's disappearance would have been something He did for His own sake, and not for the Gopīs' sake. For holy scripture tells us: "He never became indifferent and stopped (His lovemaking); therefore He does not make love by Himself, alone" (Variant of *B. Ā. Up.* I. 4. 3.). Even the world at large (OR: an ordinary person), when it sees the Blessed Lord simply by Himself, does not experience joy. But it experiences great joy when it sees Him in His highest form, "surrounded by all His Powers." This is also supported by the saying: "When a man and a woman are making love, one cannot be happy while the other is sad." And if, as before this, the Gopīs are sad, then they will not be at their very best. So Śuka says here: "(surrounded) by those women who had been freed from all their sorrows." "Those women" are, of course, the Gopīs who have just been spoken of, and whose qualities have just been described. They had surrendered themselves entirely to Him. And right in the middle of things, sorrow had come upon them. Now that this sorrow has been removed, they are as before. And the Blessed Lord is endowed with His six great qualities—lordly Power and the others. Yet if He, like an ordinary man, had merely limited passion, He would not "glow brilliantly," i.e., in a way so different from others. But Śuka shows that the Blessed Lord's desire is full and limitless by calling Him "Acyuta," i.e., the Unfailing One. Therefore, "surrounded by those women...He glowed brilliantly"—even more brilliantly than He normally does.

The hearer, by showing that he believes what the speaker has said, nourishes the speaker, as it were, like the father who nourishes the son for his own sake. This is why, as he proceeds further, the speaker in turn delights the hearer by telling him the most secret things. Otherwise, concluding that the hearer is ineligible for listening to such matters, he would not tell him supernatural things. During the present narration, Śuka sees that King Parikṣit puts his trust in what he has said, and so, because of his great happiness and love and filial sentiment, Śuka calls the king "revered father."

Since someone might object that, if things were as Śuka described them, the Blessed Lord would not be present here in

His natural state, because of the graded degrees and differences of His beauty, Śuka says: "like a man in possession of all his powers." Just as an ordinary man appears in the eyes of the world not to shine when all his abilities are lying hidden, but if he makes manifest his powers of action, knowledge and the rest, he shines brilliantly, so the Blessed Lord, who at first merely glowed, now "glowed brilliantly" in the eyes of all and in the hearts of those who have a taste for the beautiful when "His Powers," i.e., the Gopīs, became manifest. He achieved a transcendent degree of beauty. And so the Blessed Lord, and He alone, possesses Supreme Joy, as holy scripture says: "For He alone grants Joy" (*Taitt. Upan.* II. 7. 1.).

Introduction to Stanza 11: In this stanza Śuka tells us what the Lord did in order to produce Joy in the Gopīs:

Stanza 11: The Pervasive One took the Gopīs along with Him, and they all sat on the bank of the Kālindī (Yamunā). And on the bank, the flowers of the jasmine and coral trees were bursting into bloom, and the breeze bore their lovely fragrance, as the bees buzzed.

Commentary : Taking the Gopīs along with Him, and sitting down with them on the smooth, level riverbank, Kṛṣṇa became "the Pervasive One' (Skt. *vibhu*), i.e., He became pervasively present among them. Kālindī—the Yamunā—is the virgin daughter of Mount Kalinda. And Kalinda's name means "he destroys (*dyati*) the Age of Strife (*kali*)." So by using this word Śuka indicates to us that on Kālindī's banks there will be no strife either among the Gopīs themselves or between the Gopīs and the Blessed Lord. Śuka uses the second half of the stanza to show us how suitable the riverbank is for the Lord's games. It is suitable on all four sides as well as above and below. He first describes how auspicious its location is from all sides, i.e., in every direction. "The flowers of the jasmine and coral trees are blooming, and the breeze carries their lovely fragrance, " while "the six-legged ones," the bees, hover around. The three qualities of the wind—its softness, coolness and fragrance—are clearly implied here. And the flowers practically overflow with honey. The bees are drunk with the honey, and their lazy buzzing makes a useful background for music and song. The flowers bloom for the sake of the breeze alone. The fragrance of the jasmine flowers is calming, while that of the coral tree's flowers is strengthening. The point of this is to say that these two fragrances awaken, respectively, hidden and visible passion.

(Here begins an interpolation by Viṭṭhala) Śuka uses the present participial form, i.e., "bursting into bloom" (Skt. *vikasat*) and deliberately avoids using the completed past form, i.e., "had burst into bloom" (*vikasita*), to indicate that the flowers began blooming just as the Lord stepped onto the bank, and had not bloomed before that. Since this is so, Śuka is telling us that everything which exists and happens in this situation does so entirely on the basis of its usefulness for the Lord's game, and for no other reason. And so at the very moment any object is needed, just then, and only then, is it, and only it, effected. If this were not so, a much, much longer night would have had to pass while this game which has been described over the last three and one-half chapters was being played. And since there would be no other reason but the game for these flowers to bloom at this moment, they would not have bloomed, and Śuka would not have described them as "bursting into bloom." Since this is so it is evident that Śuka intends to convey to us that the breeze and the other effects, since they are spoken of in connection with the now-blooming jasmine flowers and so forth, were brought into play only now, and not before this (end of Viṭṭhala's interpolation). "Breeze" and "fragrance" are described by two separate words here in order that we may perceive the fragrance independently. Thus we see described here water all around, fragrance on every side, flowers everywhere, a breeze blowing all about, and sound from every direction.

Introduction to Stanza 12: Śuka now tells us how perfect a location the Yamunā's bank is with regard to the things that are "above" it:

Stanza 12: The bank was peaceful and blessed, for the abundant beams of the autumn moon had driven away the darkness of the night. And soft sands had been piled on the bank by the waves, the hands of the black river Kṛṣṇā (Yamunā).

Commentary : The darkness of night had been destroyed by the great multitude of beams of the autumn season's moon. This made the bank a very peaceful, auspicious and beautiful place. Its blessedness is especially evident in this, that if the ghosts and goblins of the night swarmed onto the riverbank, then, since the darkness had disappeared, they would find the place completely unsuitable to them. And Śuka intends also to convey to us that all the things the Gopīs had previously desired could be brought to pass here, without the interference of any obstacle. So there were no ugly or contemptible things anywhere around the bank, or above it or below it.

Śuka describes the virtues of what is below the bank in the sentence that begins: "And soft sands..." This river which bears the Blessed Lord's name sacramentally purified the earth for the sake of His lovemaking. "The black river Kṛṣṇā," using "the waves which formed her hands, piled soft sands on the bank." If her waves were not like hands, the sands would not be spread evenly. And, in addition to its level smoothness, the coolness as well as the softness of the sand is expressed by this idea of the waves piling it up. And so this was the sort of bank that the Lord reached, or which, having reached, He stood upon. His sitting down will be described later. For He sits down simply when He feels like sitting down (OR:only in the proper emotional atmosphere).[9]

Introduction to Stanza 13: Śuka describes for us the Gopīs' actions in the following stanza:

Stanza 13: The afflictions which had tortured the Gopīs' hearts were driven out now by the joy of seeing Him, and they proceeded, even as the holy scriptures do, to the very end of their desires. Spreading on the sand their upper garments, which were marked with the sandal-paste from their breasts, they prepared a place for the Self's dear Friend to sit.

Commentary : Though their sorrow had gone, the fire which is passion still remained, because they had not enjoyed union with the Lord. When He had gone once more to this same place to accomplish precisely that, "the joy of seeing Him"—of seeing

9. This seems to contradict Vallabha's interpretation of the preceding stanza, where he clearly says that *nirviśya* (literally: "having reached or entered upon") means *upaviśya*, "having sat down." In the present three sentences he is also commenting on the meaning of *nirviśya*. In both passages the Sanskrit is absolutely clear. I don't know how this is to be reconciled.

that He came in an attitude of love—"drove out the afflictions which had tortured their hearts," for now they were sure of what would happen. Śuka next tells us what happened now that the Gopīs' fault had thus been removed: "they proceeded ... to the very end of their desires." What the Gopīs desired was union with Him in some form or other. But the union that occurred was accompanied by material surroundings and qualities that were more endless and boundless than what they desired. Therefore the Gopīs reached what was "the very end of their desires," i.e., even of their wildest dreams. In case someone might object: "But how could they attain what they didn't desire?," Śuka says: "even as the holy scriptures do." For the constant preoccupation of the holy scriptures (Skt. *śruti*) is to describe the great qualities of the Blessed Lord. And by keeping strictly to this, their duty, the holy scriptures attain what words, as well as that which precedes words—mind—cannot attain, namely, the very Essence of the Blessed Lord. In the words of holy scripture itself: "from Whom words turn away after failing, together with the mind, to reach Him" (*Taitt. Upan.* II. 4.1)—that Joy of the Blessed Lord is "the very end of desire." The holy scriptures exist to instruct and teach us about Him. For all men agree on that point. The scriptures tell us: "It is that Person described in the Upaniṣads whom I am asking you about" (*B. Ā. Up.* III. 9. 26); "Therefore I am well known in the world and in the Vedas as the Supreme Person" (*Bh. Gītā. XV.* 18); "The very word which all the Vedas speak" (*Kaṭha Upan.* I. 2. 15). By these and other quotations it is proven conclusively that the holy scriptures are the means of knowing Brahman. We have also the aphorism: "That (Brahman) is the central idea (OR: "ground, basis": Skt. *pratyaya*) of all the Upaniṣads (Brahma Sūtra III.3.1).[10] The meaning of the Vedas transcends this world—so also do their words. And in the world there is no hint or sign.[11] And yet people, convinced that these holy scriptures tell us constantly

10. Vasu says this axiom: *sarvavedāntapratyayam*, means: "There is knowledge of Brahman alone from all the Upaniṣads." My reason for disagreeing is the neuter gender of *pratyaya*, a word of masculine gender. This implies, it seems to me, that the statement is predicate to an understood *tad* (*brahma*).

11. Presumably of both the words of the Vedas and their meaning.

about the Blessed Lord's objective and His action, attain purity of heart by hearing these scriptures, and come to think that they themselves have power with reference to the transcendent. By the Blessed Lord's Will, the holy scriptures also teach (OR: "give"; OR: "effect"; Skt. *pratipādikā*) precisely that. And in this matter holy scripture does not have any need of worldly means or rational argumentation. In the same way the Gopīs, too, attained "the very end of their desires."

The thought occurred to the Gopīs that if the Blessed Lord, the Giver of the highest objects of human striving, should decide to go somewhere else, or to someone else, then because of the relationship of attributes with their ground or substance, we will not attain the object of our striving. Thus, in order to worship Him ritually and offer themselves entirely to Him, they prepare the ground for Him to sit upon, as Śuka tells us in the sentence which begins: "Spreading on the sand their upper garments..." The women of this region wear three pieces of clothing: an under-garment, a breast-piece, and an upper garment. Now all the Gopīs gave their upper garments to make a seat for Him. There are two kinds of upper garment; the type that is worn at all times, and the type that is worn when one makes love. These latter are delicate and fine. Śuka intends to convey that it was this second kind of upper garment the Gopīs gave to the Blessed Lord, since he says: "which were marked with the sandal-paste from their breasts." The sandal-paste was originally dry, but it had become moist during the earlier love-play, and so the upper garments were smeared with it. With these, then, "they prepared a place." Someone might be doubtful as to why the Gopīs put their upper garments down, on the ground. So Śuka says: "for the Self's dear Friend." He alone is the Friend of the Self, He protects the Self, and our body and Self are for Him alone. And so they thought: "What covers our upper parts is also for Him." And so they acted correctly in their preparation of a seat for Him.

Introduction to Stanza 14: In order to get across to us the fact that, after this, the Blessed Lord became seated everywhere among the Gopīs, Śuka describes how the Lord sat down on the seat they had given to Him:

Stanza 14: Then this Blessed Lord, this Mighty One, whom masters of Yoga contemplate as seated in the depths of their hearts, sat right there, and glowed brilliantly in the midst of the circle of Gopīs as they honored Him. And He assumed the form that is Lakṣmī's sole heaven in the three worlds.

Commentary : Kṛṣṇa is called "Blessed Lord" (Skt. *bhagavān*) here because He brings to pass the effects of these six "blessings" (*bhaga* = *guṇa*—His "great qualities").[12] Someone might object: "But isn't removing one's upper garment in public an improper manifestation of a mood?[13] In the light of this, how is it that the Lord sat down?" Śuka answers: "this Mighty One." "This," that is to say, "He"—the One whom the Gopīs had previously prayed to. And "Mighty One" tells us that He is omnipotent—He can do anything and everything. By this Śuka informs us that Kṛṣṇa created divine garments for the Gopīs—garments which will not get wet even when the Gopīs play in the water. Therefore the Omnipotent One, "this" One whom the Gopīs had prayed to, "sat right there." (Here begins an interpolation by Viṭṭhala) Or, we may answer the objection in this way. When Śuka uses the pronoun "this" (Mighty One), he intends to tell us that, since there was no improper manifestation of a mood at the time when the Gopīs had no clothes at all, when the Lord stole their clothes at the same time He was granting the favor they were praying for (cf. Bh. P. X. 22), how could there be such an improper manifestation in the present situation, when only their upper garments are missing? If the person stretches his objection and says: "Well, isn't that previous example you refer to also an improper manifestation of a mood?", then Śuka's answer is: "Mighty One." For this Mighty One has the power to act, i.e., to do things. So, if a certain act were an improper manifestation of a mood, then He would not

12. OR: "because He accomplishes the objectives of the Gopīs"—Vasu. The Sanskrit runs: *bhagavāniti teṣāṁ kāryasādhakatvam*. The reason I disagree with Vasu is that the pronoun would be *tāsām*, not *teṣām*, if it referred to the Gopīs.

13. OR: "pseudo-mood." Skt. *rasābhāsa* has both these meanings. The context is the norms for what is tasteful according to the treatises on aesthetics.

perform that act. But since He also has the power not to act, it is impossible for Him to leave the seat the Gopīs have specially given to Him, even for the reason that there is an improper manifestation of a mood involved. But since He has the further power to act in another way, He can produce a mood even by means of an improper manifestation of a mood. Therefore, Śuka's meaning is that there is nothing improper in the conduct described here (end of Viṭṭhala's interpolation).

Someone else may object: "How could the Blessed Lord use as a seat things which had been defiled by stains that came from the various acts of sexual enjoyment?" Śuka answers: "Whom the masters of Yoga contemplate as seated in the depths of their hearts." The heart of a master of Yoga is pure. And so naturally, the depths of his heart are pure as well. Also, the seat of the Blessed Lord is merely "contemplated" as being there—the Lord's seat is not actually prepared there. A mental form of the Lord sits in the heart of the Yogī—the Lord Himself does not actually sit there. Śuka's intention in using this example is to point out that this seat which the Gopīs have prepared is the chief seat of the Lord.[14] Therefore "He glowed brilliantly"—His radiance was unequalled.

As before, He went into "the midst of the group of Gopīs." Śuka means here that the Gopīs sat all around Him. The Blessed Lord is the head of the assembly, and consequently the Gopīs "honored Him." Then the Blessed Lord "assumed," for the sake of the Gopīs, such "a form" that as many heavens of Indra

14. Actually I am more inclined to translate the stanza's words: *yogeśvarāntarhṛdi kalpitāsanaḥ*—which Vallabha here clearly indicates should be translated as "whom masters of Yoga contemplate as seated in the depths of their hearts"—as "for whom a seat is prepared in the depths of the hearts of the masters of Yoga." My reason is that I think the participial form *kalpita* is intended to connect directly with the last stanza's verb-form—from the same root—*aciklpan* (a causative form just as the participle used in this stanza is causative), "they (the Gopīs) prepared a place for Him to sit." But Vallabha clearly interprets differently, taking the verb-form of the last stanza to refer to preparation of an actual seat, and the participial form of this stanza to refer to a mentally prepared, or imagined, i. e., a "contemplated" seat. At any rate, Vallabha's answer to the objector seems to be that this actual, "chief" seat of the Lord is *a fortiori* more pure than the "contemplated" seat (which everyone recognizes to be pure) in the hearts of Yogīs.

and the other gods as possess the form of Lakṣmī, "in all the three worlds," became this "sole heaven" of theirs (OR:of them—the Gopīs—and all the forms of Lakṣmī)—so that the enjoyers of each and every form of Laksmī taste delights that are merely a small part of this heaven. And all the excellent and valuable things which are needed for this purpose but are normally kept separate by place, time and other factors, the Lord made manifest then and there, by assuming this form of Himself.

Introduction to Stanza 15: The Gopīs had thought that the Blessed Lord's previous ingratitude to them (i.e., His leaving them without fully returning their worship of love) had been directed toward removing a fault from His own heart. But now that they see that He has become propitious toward them, they want to give Him an opportunity to refute their notion. And so they prepare to ask Him some questions, in order to determine whether in the opinion of people in general, the Blessed Lord is guilty of the fault of ingratitude or not. Śuka describes these circumstances in the following stanza :

Stanza 15 : After greeting with a song of homage the One who enkindles their passion with the teasing movements of His eyebrows and the playful glances that are preceded by laughs, the Gopīs took His feet into their laps and fondled them with their hands as they began to speak to Him words of praise tinged with anger.

Commentary : The Gopīs first "greeted Him with a song of homage," so that they could ask Him some questions afterwards. Someone may object: "But why are they thinking this way at this time? Since their final Reward has come to them, they should simply enjoy it (Him)." Śuka's answer to this is: "Who enkindles their passion." The Lord inflames the Gopīs' passion constantly. And the words Śuka uses suggest a second sense: that the Lord renders them bodiless.[15] Therefore the effect the

15. This is a pun on Śuka's word *anaṅga*, "he who has no limbs, or body" i.e., Kāma or "passion", whose body Śiva burnt to a crisp. Vallabha is saying here that the words "the one who enkindles their passion" (Skt. *tam anaṅgadīpanam*) also carry the suggestion "the One who renders them bodiless," or, in Vallabha's paraphrase, "produces in them an absence of limbs" (Vallabha's Skt.: *aṅgābhāvaṁ sampādayati*).

Gopīs desire will not be produced by a single act of enjoyment. Besides, even before such an act of sexual intercourse, their exhaustion would be too great. Śuka means that if this exhaustion comes through their own fault, then the fault must be removed. But if it results from an attribute of the Blessed Lord, then the Gopīs must stubbornly speak out their objection to the Lord, or pray to Him, and then experience the final Reward.

Śuka describes the means by which the Lord enkindles the Gopīs' passion when he says: "with the teasing movements of His eyebrows..." Or, Śuka's enumeration of the means may be meant to convey that the Gopīs should pray to Him not to use these means. "The teasing movements of His eyebrows," along with "the playful glances preceded by His laughing," inflame the passion of the Gopīs. The Lord uses five means here: His laughing, His play, His glances, His teasing and His eyebrows. And if five causes are at work, the effect is unimpeded. Māyā, who is associated with the Lord's laugh (cf. Bh. P. II. 1. 31), is the great bewilderer, who makes the Gopīs forget their own nature. And the Lord's "play"(Skt. *līlā*—"game") causes them to be passionately attached to Him. His "glance" produces knowledge with regard to His game. If it did not, His game and their passionate attachment to it would be destroyed by the knowledge the Gopīs would have that there was something other than it. His "teasing movements" nourish this knowledge and attachment. And His "brow" acts as Yama, who is Time—the Controller. Or, these actions of the Lord may equally embody His role as Giver of Grace.

And so, in order to ask Him some questions, the Gopīs first pay Him respectful homage, as Śuka tells us in the sentence beginning: "the Gopīs took His feet into their laps.." Śuka means that the Gopīs took the Blessed Lord's feet with their hands, and put them in their laps, where they fondled and caressed them. And as they fondled His feet they spoke "words of praise" in order to gain His attention and favor. And because they perceive this fault in the Blessed Lord: "So He abandons even those who have surrendered themselves to Him with Total Love!" their words were "tinged with anger." Even if a fault is lessened by using certain means, it is never removed entirely until the Blessed Lord Himself uproots it. And so the Gopīs "began to speak to Him" in the manner of people who are entering into a dispute.

Introduction to Stanza 16: Now Śuka tells us what the Gopīs asked:

Stanza 16: The Gopīs said: "Some people return the worship of those who worship them. Others do precisely the opposite—they lovingly worship those who do not return their loving worship. Still others do not worship either of these. Will You please give us a straight explanation of this ?"

Commentary : Three different positions people adopt are brought into question here, and the questions regard both the reward and the nature of these attitudes or positions, in accordance with whether the people worship or do not. Among these three, "some people return the worship," in precisely the same way, "of those who worship them." Then again, "other people lovingly worship" even "those who do not return their loving worship." But "still other people do not worship either of these." The reward of these three positions and of their two counterparts as well (i.e., those in the first group who initiate the worship, and those in the second group who do not return people's loving worship) must be explained here.

"Are those who worship in accordance with the worship they have received (i.e., the first group mentioned in the stanza)ungrateful, or are they cunning deceivers, or are they perfectly right," ask the Gopīs. If someone washes another person's feet, and the other in turn washes his feet, then what of that? The reward must be given to him who does what is required for the reward. And if he stipulates that the one to whom he does this must do it in return, and then performs the act, then it must indeed be done in return. A doubt arises only when someone does something without expecting any return.

There may (considering the second group, or position, now) sometimes be a fault involved in lovingly worshipping a person who does not return one's worship of love, as, for example, when a passionate woman comes to a man who is free of passion. Sometimes assistance may be given, if some object is desired, at other times love, at other times the performance of one's duty, say the Gopīs. A single, definite reward of this group must be expressed by the Lord.

Or what is the reward of the one who does not worship in the first place? Or what is the reward of those who do not worship both the types mentioned above (those who worship expecting a return and those who worship expecting no return), or of the members of both these types? Or where is there any usefulness in the means they have employed? "Please explain all this to us, exactly as it is." The Gopīs say "You," addressing the Lord directly, to make Him attentive. The first group mentioned in the stanza worships in accordance with the worship others have paid them. Others worship only on the premise that their worship will not be returned. Both these groups, then, perform worship. But the others are entirely without worship.[16]

Introduction to Stanza 17: The Blessed Lord now explains, in the next three stanzas, the differences among these groups and the specific reward of each:

Stanza 17: The Blessed Lord said: "Since, dear friends, those who worship one another in turn are striving merely for their own personal gain, there is no friendship or performance of duty involved in that worship. For it is done for the sake of their own profit, and for no other reason."

Commentary : Here The Lord gives the Gopīs His definitive teaching with regard to the first group mentioned in the previous stanza. "People who worship one another in turn are striving merely for their own personal gain." "Their own, exclusive personal gain"—this is the one end and the one reward of their striving. For it is only after knowing one another that these people worship one another. And they make their worship revolve around considerations of more or less, and higher or lower. Consequently they cannot deceive one another. And so their whole

16. We seem to come, finally, to three "positions" or "attitudes" towards worship (Skt. *bhajana*), which have five agents: three worshipping and two non-worshipping. In the first "position" stated, both subject and object (="counterpart" above) are agents of worship. In the second "position," the subject is an agent of loving worship, making a total of three agents of worship; while the object of the second "position", the man who does not worship in return, is a non-agent of worship. In the third "position," the subject worships no one, and so he is our second non-worshipper. And the two kinds of people whom he does not worship, viz., those who worship him expecting a return, and those who worship him expecting no return, have already been classified above.

endeavor is "for their own gain"—and mere worldly gain at that. Someone might express the doubt: "But aren't both the parties involved in this mutual worship brahmans? If so, then the performance of duty, or love, is involved in their worshipping one another. How can it be merely for their own personal gain?" Kṛṣṇa's answer is: "there is no friendship or performance of duty involved in that worship." For the one brahman instantly bursts into anger when he finds out that the other has not worshipped him in return. So no friendship is involved here. Neither is performance of duty. As Āpastamba says (*Āp. Dh. Sū.* II. 7. 17. 8): "That alms offered to demons which goes by the name of 'banquet' goes neither to the fathers nor to the gods. Instead it wanders about the earth, bereft of merit, like a cow who has lost her calf, until it finds another shelter." Even in worshipping one's guru no performance of duty is involved, if both guru and disciple have in view merely their own profit. But if the worship of the guru is done in accordance with the scriptures, that guru and disciple do not come under this category of "those who worship one another." Rather, knowledge constitutes the reward of that worship. The Lord addresses the Gopīs as "dear friends" to assure them that He is not deceiving them.

The words "those who" imply a comparison with merchants, who, as is well known, engage in business affairs solely for their own profit. And though the performance of duty and other actions are also merely for the sake of personal gain, these things are not accomplished by mutual worship. Neither is friendship accomplished, if something other than friendship is sought. The Lord explains what use this worship has as a means of attainment when He says: "for the sake of their own profit." Even when it is perceived to be something done for others, it is actually done for one's own sake. The same is true even when one donates his personal service or gives other things. The reward for such acts of giving is the removal of one's suffering. Any person at all could be our source of knowledge for this certainty—which is why the Lord uses the word "For" here. When He says: "and for no other reason," the Lord means that this worship is not performed in order to help others. Because such an act of worship arouses anxiety in the heart of the other person, as to how he will repay it. So the fruit of such worship is the accomplishment of one's personal interests, purely on a worldly level. These acts of worship are fulfilments of duty in name only, not in fact.

Introduction to Stanza 18 : Kṛṣṇa now tells us that the people who lovingly worship[17] those who do not worship them in return are of two types:

Stanza 18: "People, such as compassionate persons and parents, who lovingly worship those who do not worship them in return—this is blameless performance of duty, O lovely ones, and this is friendship."

Commentary : There are two possible reasons why people lovingly worship those who do not return their worship, but remain silent (OR: "remain covetous")[18]—a worldly reason or a reason based on the Vedas. The first is love, the second is the commandment. And friendship and accomplishment of duty are the respective rewards of this worship. The person who lovingly worships for the first reason must, in the context of his friendship, provide help to his friend at the proper moment. Were he not to do this, he would be ungrateful. If the help rendered to someone who does not worship in return is done as a part of a worshipper's duty, then the one who does not worship in return should perform an expiation. Because the worshipper's virtue

17. I have translated the derivatives of the root *BHAJ*, in the context of these particular worshippers, as "loving worshippers", "lovingly worship," etc., bringing out the love-connotation of *BHAJ* as well as the primary meaning of "worship" given to it here. This is the only "position" to which the words "loving worship" apply. All the others merely "worship" or "do not worship." The reader probably noticed that I have made this distinction from the time when this "position" was first described, in Stanza 16 and Commentary.

18. The issue in this phrase is whether the correct Skt. reading is *tṛṣṇīṁsthitān*— "(those who) remain covetous"—which Telivala-Sankalia, and Vasu, following them, read; or *tūṣṇīṁsthitān*— "(those who) remain silent." The former usage is not recognized in either dictionary —Apte or Monier-Williams—available to me, while the latter is recognized by both as a valid, even frequent usage. Besides, Vasu translates the phrase as if it were definitely *tūṣṇīṁsthitān*—his Hindi is *cup rahane vāloṅ*—without bothering to emend the Sanskrit. I therefore propose to emend Telivala-Sankalia's (and consequently Vasu's) reading of *tṛṣṇīṁsthitān* to *tūṣṇīṁsthitān*, but I have translated the former as a parenthetical alternative to the latter, on the off chance that the former might exist somewhere in Sanskrit literature. But, as should be evident, neither does the idea of "covetousness" accord very well with the context.

or sin goes, along with his help, to those who receive that help. Concerning the performance of duty where obligatory action, or a deity, is the chief element—the Lord does not intend to say anything about these two here, because in these two cases no question arises concerning repayment, by the being who is worshipped, of the worship received. Likewise the question raised here does not apply to a situation in which there is inequality between the worshipper and the one he worships, as, for example, when a man pulls a cow out of the mud. But where it is possible for one who has received help to repay it, and he does so, and the person he helps does not return his worship, then the first person's worship is "blameless fulfilment of duty," and "friendship" is its reward.[19]

By saying "compassionate persons and parents," the Lord indicates a difference in level of eligibility among the persons involved, for He refers in one case to compassionate people and in the other to a blood-relationship. The Lord says "such as" in order to extend the application of this statement of His by indicating that this same attribute is seen in other people, too. Even cruel people who are fixed firmly in Saṁsāra will occasionally perform an act of loving worship for the destitute, and thus become like loving friends. The Lord says "such as" in order to include all such people. And indeed all these people are of one type, since the people compared and the persons to whom they are compared are not different, considering that they have all been blood-relatives in one or another of their previous existences.

The Lord says "blameless" because blame comes to the worshipper through the return of his help by the one he has worshipped. But because of the absence of that, their performance of duty is "blameless." The Lord says "this", meaning "here" or "in such a case." He thus indicates that when it is impossible for the one worshipped to return the favor, in that case, too, there has been "performance of duty." This is why some worshippers do not accept the return of their wor-

19. For a good scriptural contextualization of this doctrine, cf. the Bhagavad-Gītā's description of *sāttvika*, *rājasa* and *tāmasa dāna* ("giving") in Chapter XVII, verses 20-22. Vallabha's description here has its equivalent in the "*sāttvika* giving" of verse 20.

ship even when it is being done. The word "and" in this context indicates that there is performance of duty in friendship, too. Kṛṣṇa addresses the Gopīs as "lovely ones" to persuade them to believe what He has said. And He associates their beauty with their excellent performance of duty.[20]

Introduction to Stanza 19: Then again, there are those who do not worship at all; they worship neither those who worship in order to be worshipped in return, nor those who worship out of friendship. But there is no difficulty with regard to those who worship in order to perform duty. Certain non-worshippers, then, do not worship the two types of worshippers just mentioned. Neither do non-worshippers worship those who do not worship in return, whether the destitute or those who are eligible in the performance of duty. The Lord explains to us the nature of these non-worshippers in the following stanza:

Stanza 19: "It is true that certain people do not worship even those who worship them. How, then, would they worship the people who do not return their worship? For those who do not worship either delight in the Self, or they have attained all their desires, or are ignorant of what has been done for them, or do injury to their guru."

Commentary : "Some" great men "do not worship even those who worship them. How, then, will they worship those who do not return their worship?" These non-worshippers are of four types, according to the rule explained above (in the stanza's third sentence). Among these four types two are correct in what they do, and two are not. For those who do not worship those who are eligible in the performance of duty are the lowest,

20. This last sentence is a pun on the word Kṛṣṇa has used to address and describe the Gopīs. Skt. *sumadhyamāḥ*, "lovely ones," means literally, "you whose middle parts are beautiful." Then in the present sentence Vallabha says, literally: "their excellent middleness comes through their performance of duty alone" (Skt. *dharmeṇaiva uttamamadhyamatā*). Or, as Vasu interprets it: "Because it is by performance of duty alone that they possess excellence and middleness." I presume he means the "excellence" of the highest devotees and the "middleness" of the middle range of devotees, who in Vallabha's system are also quite advanced. I have translated the way I have because *sumadhyama* definitely means "lovely, beautiful," and I feel this meaning is intended to pervade Vallabha's pun as well, though Vasu's meaning is also probably intended.

while those who do not worship those who have worldly reasons, (such as friendship) are the highest.[21] The Lord enumerates these four types separately, in order to prevent confusion. He mentions first those who "delight in the Self," i.e., those who delight in and love the Self alone. For them there is no need to have their body and so forth worshipped by another, and so they do not consider this to be worship, or pay attention to it. And they do not consider even their own body, etc., to be a means for worshipping the people who are worshipping them.

Likewise others within this group "have fulfilled all their desires," i. e., they have fully attained what they want. If someone says, to a person who has just eaten, "eat," or "do not eat," then in the first case the person will not do it, and in the second the one who speaks is repeating the obvious, because he is referring to an accomplishment that is already complete. So in both cases his words (and, in the analogy: his attempts to worship) are useless. In such circumstances the performance of duty of the worshipper who is proceeding on the basis of duty will be accomplished. Or, the ignorance of the putative worshipper will become apparent.

Now the Lord points out the other two types of person,the lowest, in this group. First of all, those who "are ignorant of what has been done for them,"[22] i.e., of the help given them by worshippers, do not worship either kind of helper (the one who worships expecting a return or the friend), even when they are capable of returning the favor. Their ignorance is the only reason why they do not worship. But the persons

21. Emend the Telivala-Sankalia-Vasu reading of *laukikanimittās te uttamāḥ* (all nominative) to *laukikanimittāṃs te uttamāḥ* (accusative plus two nominatives), or else the sentence cannot make contextual sense. This assumes merely the omission of the *anusvara* dot in the printed text. Vasu, as before, translates as though the emendation were made, but does not bother to make it.

22. The Skt. compound here translated, *akṛtajña,* also means "ungrateful." But Vallabha's interpretation rules out that connotation for this group and reserves it for the next. So, instead of interpreting *akṛtajña* as "ungrateful," he interprets it perfectly literally.

who know they have received help, and still do not worship in return, are said to "do injury to their guru." For anyone who brings about the ends which people strive for is a guru, and he should be worshipped. And when it is within the power of the person who has received favors to help his guru in adversity, and he neglects him, then he has done injury to him, and thus becomes an "injurer of his guru." Thus has the Lord explained the virtues and faults of all four types of persons who are in this group.

Introduction to Stanza 20: The desire to know which group among all these the Blessed Lord belongs to arises in the Gopīs' hearts. Since He does not worship even though He is capable of worshipping, He cannot be included in either of the first two relationships—those who worship each other in turn and those who worship people who do not worship in return. Someone might bring up the following objection: "Let us say that the Gopīs worshipped Kṛṣṇa out of love, and consequently worship in the terms of the second relationship. Then the Blessed Lord (*bhagavān*) is not included in terms of membership in that relation (since the second member of that relationship is known not to worship). And the Lord (*īśvara*) is not included as a member in any of these three relationships. Therefore what are we considering, and how?" This thinking is incorrect. For everyone agrees that the Gopīs are objects of enjoyment. And the very fact that they offered themselves completely to be enjoyed exhausts any possibility of further thought on or investigation of them (since they offered away their very selves). Therefore it is the nature of the Blessed Lord alone which must be investigated. If the Lord, too, is to be worshipped for the sake of a reward, His nature need not be investigated (cf. Commentary for the reason why). If a visible reward in an everyday matter is sought, then what we must investigate is whether the Blessed Lord accepts what is being given or not. Since He accepted this worship (of the Gopīs) previously, He does not fit into the category (within the third relationship) of those who delight in the Self or those who have fulfilled all their desires. Since He first engaged in the process (by accepting their worship), the complete abandonment of the Gopīs, even when He has been satisfied, is not right.[23] Therefore He must belong to the third category—those who are ignorant of what has been done for them; but that is not right either, since He is omniscient. So Kṛṣṇa now removes the Gopīs' doubt about whether this is the way lords who grant rewards sometimes act:

Stanza 20: "But I, dear friends, do not worship even those creatures of mine who worship Me, in order to change their attitude of mind, so they will become like a poor man who got rich and then lost all his wealth, so that now his anxiety over the wealth he lost lets him know no concern for anything else."

Commentary : By the word "But" Kṛṣṇa excludes Himself from the group He described in the last stanza. And by addressing the Gopīs as "dear friends" He means that neither should they suspect that they might be members of the group which worships Him as Lord (*īśvara*). They are, rather, His dear friends, who are His peers in the mood of love. And they are intensely devoted to a single goal. When Kṛṣṇa says "I", He is emphasizing the fact that He is the Blessed Lord, and not a human soul. For that reason He cannot be considered a member of the four types described in the last stanza, which consist of those who delight in the Self, etc. He says, in effect: "I am delight pure and simple—not delight in the Self. This is indisputable, because there is nothing in Me, like a body, which is separate from the Self. And since desire does not exist in Me, the designation of 'a person who has attained all His desires' does not apply to Me, either. Therefore My nature and condition are different—they are not the same as those of a soul." Therefore Kṛṣṇa has expressed this condition of His exactly in the words: "But I, dear friends....not"!

The Blessed Lord's next words in the Stanza are: "I....do not worship even those creatures of mine who worship Me." And here He adds a further reason: "in order to change their attitude of mind." "Their" attitude means "the souls'" attitude. And the word "creatures" refers to living beings (=souls) only. The Blessed Lord has no need of anyone. But the Blessed Lord as the embodiment of the Reward is needed by all without excep-

23. This apparently eliminates the possibility of the Blessed Lord's being included in the fourth category of the third relationship—those who "injure their guru." Besides, the notion of the Blessed Lord being able to "injure His guru," whether literal or figurative, is absurd to start with.

tion. Since this is so, everyone desires to worship Him or desires some means of attaining Him. "But," Kṛṣṇa would argue, "if I come among them in the form of a means of attainment, then I destroy their worship, because I create an obstacle for their future worship and render their past worship useless."[24] For the Blessed Lord is needed in four ways: as the object of enjoyment in two ways, and as the Enjoyer in two ways. As object of enjoyment He is needed in His role as fulfiller of people's desires, or after the manner of independence.[25] And He is also needed as Enjoyer because He alone accepts the objects offered with loving devotion by His devotees, or because every existing thing is an object for Him to enjoy. In the first of these four roles the worship would be destroyed, because He would grant only a small reward, since, despite the greatness that comes from His being what He is, time is a limiting factor in this first role (i.e., people would stop worshipping when their desires were fulfilled). But in the second role the same thing would happen (i.e., Kṛṣṇa would become the object of enjoyment: Vasu), but by means of excessive worship, so that Kṛṣṇa would say: "That is not the worship of the Gopīs," and He would not worship those people in return in order to bring about in them the condition of the Gopīs. And in the fourth role, Kṛṣṇa would say: "I am not an enjoyer according to the pattern of the objects of My enjoyment because I have no need of anything." Rather, the sum and substance of His teachings here is that His non-worship is precisely for the sake of loving devotion. And the Blessed Lord tells the Gopīs how His attitude and practice of non-worship will succeed by the example which begins: "like a poor man.." When a man is poor to start with, and later becomes rich—if he then loses

24. It is not entirely clear whether Vallabha intends Kṛṣṇa to stop speaking directly here, or whether he intends to speak in the voice of Kṛṣṇa right up to and including the sentence that begins: "Rather, the sum and substance of His teachings here...." It doesn't make much difference, since this is meant to be totally authoritative doctrine, as if directly from Kṛṣṇa, if not directly from Kṛṣṇa.

25. Lālūbhaṭṭa's *Yojanā* (sub-commentary) on this sentence, as translated by Vasu, says Vallabha refers here to those who worship Kṛṣṇa day and night, in union and in separation, in order to become independent themselves and have Kṛṣṇa dependent on them.

his wealth, he is consumed with anxiety about it, and is so intent on and immersed in that anxiety alone that he knows nothing else. This situation is well known in the world. In this way the Gopīs, too, might first be bereft of the Blessed Lord. And if they attained Him, and He then disappears, from that time their minds become fixed on and immersed in Him alone, so that they will forget the outside world completely. The reason the Gopīs had their minds fixed on Him has been explained above (when Vallabha said: "And they are intensely devoted to a single goal.")

Introduction to Stanza 21: After thus explaining to the Gopīs the reason why He does not worship them, Kṛṣṇa tells them that in the present situation He is indeed worshipping them:

Stanza 21: "For after you abandoned, as you did, for my sake, the world, the Vedas, your very Selves and all that was yours, O helpless ones, in order to follow me, I worshipped you, though my worship was not visible, when I disappeared. And so you, my loved ones, should not be angry with me, your Lover."

Commentary : It is in reference to the question the Gopīs asked previously—"how can You justify abandoning women in the forest at night?"[26] —that Kṛṣṇa speaks as He does in this stanza. Two things are to be done here: non-worship—so the Gopīs will keep worshipping Him continually; and worship—in order to protect the Gopīs in the night. And when Kṛṣṇa says "I worshipped you, though My worship was not visible, when I disappeared," He indicates that both these things are accomplished when He worships them invisibly. He points out His reason for worshipping them in the sentence that begins: "For after you abandoned, for my sake.." For My sake alone these Gopīs left the world, the Vedas, and everyone and everything that was theirs. To refute the ideas that the Gopīs abandoned all these things in vain or in order to gain ultimate freedom, Kṛṣṇa has said: "you abandoned ..for my sake." For in the first instance their abandonment of all would cause undesired consequences, and in the second this abandonment would not put the burden

26. As has not been unusual, Vallabha does not quote the stanza's words exactly as they stand, but nearly so and with the same meaning. The stanza's words were: *yoṣitaḥ kas tyajen niśi* (Chapter III, stanza 16), while Vallabha's words here are *araṇye striyo rātrau kathaṁ tyaktavyāḥ.*

on Me. Three things are to be abandoned. It is difficult to renounce the world. And the Vedas constitute the Path of the Āryas. And persons in the world could come to know that such (i.e., abandoning the Vedas) is the method only if they had learned it from Me. And it is difficult to leave one's husband, children, relatives and so forth, especially when one has not actually attained Me, but leaves them for My sake, with only the burning desire of attaining Me. Then that person becomes most desired of Me, and beloved. My sentiment in response to such acts was expressed when I said: "Abandoning all duties entirely, come to Me alone as Your refuge! From all sins will I free you—do not be sorrowful" (*Bh. Gītā* XVIII. 66). And so when someone abandons these three things entirely, I worship that person. (Here begins an interpolation by Viṭṭhala) But in truth the word *sva* in the stanza (which Vallabha interprets as "all—everyone and everything—that was yours") means "their very Selves." Otherwise, since the abandonment of one's husband, children and so forth is already included in the abandonment of the world and the Vedas, the word *sva* would be meaningless. Likewise one abandons one's Self only when one cannot consider the object of love to be one's own Self. The meaning is that, since the Blessed Lord is the object of the Gopīs' love because He is their be-all and end-all, they have abandoned their Selves and all else (end of Viṭṭhala's interpolation).

The word "For" has the sense of: "And this meaning is correct." For those who are devoted to no one else must be protected. And the words: "in order to follow me" indicate that the Gopīs are seeking one single Reward. Kṛṣṇa addresses the Gopīs as "helpless ones" to indicate that His worship of them is not fulfilled visibly, as is His worship of the holy ones. The words "I worshipped you, though my worship was not visible, when I disappeared," may be read alternatively to mean "I worshipped you, though my worship was not visible, and I did not disappear (from the scene entirely)."[27] Or, "worship" may mean "sexual

27. As we have had occasion to note before, the flexibility of Sanskrit sometimes provides the occasion for two opposite meanings, both possible. Here the accepted reading, for Vallabha as well as all the printed texts at my disposal, is: *mayā parokṣam bhajatā tirohitam mā* ("I worshipped you,

enjoyment" here, and this would yield the meaning: "I, the enjoyer, remained hidden while I enjoyed"—meaning: "I was not seen by you." By saying these things Kṛṣṇa excludes Himself from the group of non-worshippers. Since this is so, the Gopīs' anger may by aroused. So Kṛṣṇa says: "And so you should not be angry with me," i.e., do not falsely attribute to Me the faults of ignorance of what has been done for Me and so forth. For I am your "Lover." When one's lover is evil, it is necessary for the loved one to be just the same, for it is impossible to abandon one's lover. And besides, you are "my loved ones." For the attributes of knowledge of what has been done for one and so on cannot apply in the matter of love—they are applicable, rather, on a level of relationship where indifference prevails.

Introduction to Stanza 22: Having thus cleansed their minds with these words, Kṛṣṇa praises the Gopīs in the next stanza, in order to remove the contradiction (of His own conduct) to the Path of Devotion:

Stanza 22: "I am unable, even within the span of an Age of the Wise One, to repay you, who are completely blameless, and who have worshipped Me after breaking the unmoldering chains of the home. May that in itself repay you perfectly."

Commentary : The words "who are completely blameless" here mean "whose worship is free of faults." The phrase "to repay you" refers to an act of repayment of the Gopīs' worship by the Lord. And the words "within the span of an Age of the Wise One" mean "within an Age of Brahmā." Or perhaps they mean "within the time spanned by an Age of Manu," or "within the unending age of those who are especially wise, i.e., the sages who have attained final knowledge." "I am unable," says the Lord, because of the dissimilarity between worship and its repayment. Your (i.e., the Gopīs') worship is free from deceit, whereas Ours

though my worship was not visible, when I disappeared"). But the Skt. may also be interpreted to read: *mayā parokṣam bhajatā atirohitam mā* ("I worshipped you, though my worship was not visible, and I did not disappear"). In my opinion, one reason Vallabha notes this alternate possiblility is to remind us that He did not disappear entirely—i. e., He did not become completely latent, as opposed to manifest, in the Vallabhite opposition of the technical metaphysical terms *tirohita/āvirbhūta*. Rather, as we have already seen, He "went within" the Gopīs and disappeared merely from their sight.

would be deceitful. For a mirage, even one which contains a great deal of water, is not equal to even a small amount of real water. True worship is impossible even for Brahman, because it is an attribute that can belong only to souls. Kṛṣṇa specifies this further in the clause which begins: "who have worshipped me.." For the "chains of the home" are "unmoldering" since, even though they age, they do not wear away. "Breaking" the chains refers to cutting them away; and the word "who" refers to "you famous Gopīs." Those chains by which you originally remained bound for your own sake—you have offered completely the content of those chains (i.e., all the things involved in those chains) as well as your very Selves to Me alone. It is possible to break or get out of external, real chains. But not those chains which are the home—when one is covered and bound tight on all sides. Thus this worship of yours is the same as the worship of those who perform supernatural things. Then Kṛṣṇa says: "perfectly." This is a specification rich in feeling. "May that..repay..perfectly" means "may there be full return." For the perfect ones, when they do a great deed, are fully pleased with the deed itself, and they neither expect nor desire repayment. Therefore worship does not exist in Me, since worship is an attribute of souls alone. The Lord means here that for this reason, if in the future you Gopīs find great pleasure in worship, simply of itself, then worship! But if not, you should do as you please. "For," He means to say, "no one can do the impossible."

CHAPTER V

(Bhāgavata Purāṇa Book X, Chapter 33)

Five and a half Verses: *Verse* 1: In this thirtieth chapter we hear described how Hari, pleased and beloved, set in motion, for the sake of His own Joy, the game which is also played by Kāma, and which is very rarely achieved by Indra and the other gods.

Verse 2: The reward of one who listens to the account of this game is also expressed, for the benefit of all, in this chapter. Even for one whose viewpoint is worldly, what is described here is authoritative teaching.

Verse 3: But the passion which has the mood of love as its essence is very secret indeed. It was to describe this that Bharata composed his third treatise.[1]

Verse 4: Therefore the Blessed Lord danced here, and made the Gopīs dance likewise, so that the passion which was lying dormant in every part of their bodies might make itself clearly manifest.

Verse 5: Water and wind become the materials for relief from exertion and chill. He makes the highest divine level of reality appear on earth in this place alone.

Verse 5-1/2: This surpassing happiness called passionate love Kṛṣṇa enjoys—no one else.

1. Here, according to Vasu, the "third treatise" of Bharata Muni, the traditional sage of love and all the other moods, refers to the *kāmaśāstra*—"the treatise, or tradition of treatises, on passion or erotics." That Bharata's "third" treatise would be on *kāma* makes sense in that *kāma* is the third of four goals of human existence. It may be, however, that Vallabha is referring to the *Nāṭya Śāstra*, the *locus classicus* for the description of moods (*rasa*), for Bharata is much more famous for his composition of this work. But if that is the case, I don't know how to explain the word "third".

Introduction to Stanza 1: Kṛṣṇa drove away the Gopīs' suffering by reason of their Total Love as well as by the force of proper means of knowledge and Object of knowledge. If this suffering is due to ignorance, only then is it, and can it be, driven away. Otherwise, this suffering would have been given to them by the Blessed Lord alone. But since the Blessed Lord did not really leave the Gopīs when He appeared to abandon them, then the Blessed Lord is not the cause of their suffering. Rather, ignorance alone is the cause. And so when this ignorance of theirs disappeared as a result of the Blessed Lord's words, the suffering that was rooted in ignorance also disappeared, as Śuka tells us in the following stanza.

Stanza 1: The eminent Śuka said: "When the Gopīs had heard these charming, well-phrased words of the Blessed Lord, they left behind them the suffering which had resulted from separation, and their desires were both strengthened and satisfied by touching the limbs of His body."

Commentary : "When they heard the Blessed Lord's words, the Gopīs left behind them the suffering which had resulted from separation from Him." They thought to themselves: "This separation came about only through an error on our part." Someone might raise this objection: "How can ignorance be removed merely by words?" Śuka replies simply: "(the words) of the Blessed Lord." And Śuka says, explicitly, "the Gopīs," in order to forestall any supposition to the contrary.[2] In case someone further objects: "But how can these words of Kṛṣṇa fail to raise doubt in the Gopīs' minds?", Śuka says: "charming, well-phrased." His words are so delightful they steal the mind away. And it is only when the mind is uncertain that doubt can arise. But because of the very nature of the word of the Blessed Lord, no doubt arises in the mind. And so they got rid of the suffering that had resulted from separation and came to realize: "We were never really separated from Him." It was just like when someone awakens from a dream—he pays no attention to the suffering that was part of his dream. And, Śuka says: "their desires were both strengthened and satisfied by touching the limbs of the Blessed Lord's

2. The supposition that someone other than the Gopīs, i.e., someone perhaps unworthy, had heard the Blessed Lord's words: Vasu.

body." In other words, all their desires were fulfilled, apart from any action on the Blessed Lord's part, simply by the limbs of the Blessed Lord's body.

Introduction to Stanza 2: When He had thus removed, by His body and His words, what was standing in the way of the Gopīs' freedom from sorrow and their happiness, Kṛṣṇa began to do what He had to do, as Śuka tells us in this stanza:

Stanza 2: Then and there Govinda, surrounded by those jewels of women—so devoted to Him and so joyful—started the Rāsa-game, as the Gopīs linked their arms together.

Commentary : Śuka uses the name "Govinda" to signify that Kṛṣṇa became Indra—the Leader—for the sake of this game alone. The name Govinda also tells us that, like Indra, He requires not common, but extraordinary enjoyment. "Surrounded by those jewels of women so devoted to Him...He started the Rāsa-game." The Rāsa is a special dance in which many women participate, and it is called Rāsa because it results in an outward expression of the mood of love (*rasa*). For the only purpose of dance is the visible manifestation of a mood. In this Rāsa dance there is "playing", or "a game" (*krīḍā*)—it is Kṛṣṇa's own Game (*līlā*). In the playing of the game the mood of love arises in the mind, and in the dance this mood is aroused in the body. But Kāma resides in the enjoyer in this game, and the enjoyer's role is therefore the dominant one. And the mood is produced by the group as a whole—this is why the word "Rāsa-game" is expressed in the singular. For then the mood of passionate love is produced in the same way as the sweet taste (*rasa*) of sugar or the intense delight (*rasa*) of devotion.[3] Śuka points out the suitability of the Gopīs for this mood when he mentions that they are "so devoted to Him." In other words, it is incumbent on the Lord to produce this mood in those who were so devoted in carrying out their vow concerning Him (cf. Bh. P. X. 22). And the Gopīs' lone intention is to do what the Blessed Lord intends.

3. The following approximation of Vasu's translation, which says a bit more than the Sanskrit, brings across Vallabha's meaning quite well: "In the same way, i.e., collectively, as the sweet taste of sugar comes from a lump composed of many grains, or the intense delight of devotion comes from the love of a large group of devotees."

Someone may object that this particular mood is transcendent, and cannot be produced in worldly people—so the Lord's undertaking is useless, for no one can produce oil from a pile of sand.[4] Śuka's answer to this is: "those jewels of women." For by nature women are of three types, in accordance with the differences among the three worlds (i.e., presumably: divine, human and demonic).[5] And among human women there are four different categories: the Padminī (the lotus-like), the Citriṇī (the multi-talented), the Śaṅkhinī (the conch-like), and the Hastinī (the elephant-like). And according to the differences in the dispositions resulting from the actions of their past lives, there are fourteen further divisions of women: those who thave the characteristics of a horse, and so on. But among all women these Gopīs are "jewels." By their own extraordinary qualities they reflect and illumine the Lord's great qualities. Therefore by their Total Love of Him they are suitable women for Him to produce the mood of love in. As Śuka says, He is "surrounded" by them. Kṛṣṇa Himself is the central jewel of the necklace (also: "the jewel of heroes in drama or dance"; Skt. *nāyakamaṇi* means at least these). Therefore these jewels among women are suitable for Him. And they all act as a group in order to experience one and the same mood. This passage establishes what we have said earlier (cf. Chapter III, Stanza 2 and Commentary)—that the Gopīs were given to the Blessed Lord by Kāma or Brahmā as "hired slave-girls", so that the mood of love may be made visibly manifest here on earth.

If someone objects that these Gopīs are human souls, while the Blessed Lord consists of pure Joy, and that consequently the desired mood cannot be produced because of this dissimilarity, Śuka's answer is: "so joyful." The Gopīs became like the Blessed

4. Lest contemporary concerns give us the wrong impression here, the word I have translated as "oil" (Skt. *tailam*), is "sesamum oil," or that type of oil generally—not crude.

5. OR: "For according to the differences of nature which we see in the world, women are of three types": Vasu. The Sanskrit reads: *svabhāvataḥ striyastrividhāḥ, lokabhedena.* The reason I disagree with Vasu is that I don't think he takes suffcient account either of the position or of the case-cum-compound relationship of the word *lokabhedena.* Besides, Vallabha tells us about the women in this world in the next sentence.

Lord. Their Joy was complete. Śuka describes the way the Gopīs decided to group together for the dance when he says: "the Gopīs linked their arms together." Each Gopī linked arms with a Gopī on either side of her so that they formed a circle. But they did not link arms with the Blessed Lord.

Introduction to Stanzas 3 & 4: Though the Blessed Lord was united with them even while He stood outside the Gopīs' circle of joined hands, Śuka now tells us how He made His entry into this circle:

Stanzas 3-4: The joyous festivity of the Rāsa-dance, embellished by the circle of Gopīs, was fully set in motion by Kṛṣṇa, the Lord of Yoga, who entered the circle between the two members of each pair of Gopīs, and put one arm around the neck of each Gopī, so that all these women would think that He was in her presence alone. Meanwhile the sky all around was crowded with a hundred heavenly chariots, containing the sky-dwellers (i.e., gods) and their wives, both of whose very Selves had been carried away by ardent desire.

Commentary : It was "the joyous festivity of the Rāsa-dance" alone that was "fully set in motion" here, because it is the mood of love that is predominant in this dance, and all the other things are merely secondary. The words "joyous festivity" mean the joy that makes the mind forget everything. Śuka points out the special characteristic, "embellished by the circle of Gopīs," in order to produce many moods of the same kind, so that festive joy may be caused. Śuka's meaning is: "embellished by many different kinds of circles of Gopīs." A festival, too, is adorned by many different groups, or circles, of brahmans and so forth. Here, too, women of like nature have been united for the sake of the mood, and have formed a number of different circles. The festive joy is "embellished" by these circles. And therefore (successively) strengthening moods have been produced here, so that each preceding mood is strengthened by each successive circle. It would be improper for this particular mood to take place in any other festivity. The full setting-in-motion referred to in the stanza is the permanent Manifestation of the joyous festivity of the Rāsa-dance.

"But," someone may object, "since differences in time as well as differences of action and individual nature will all present obstacles, how can a mood which originates in many persons and places become one?" Śuka's answer to this is: "the Lord of Yoga." For He is fully cognizant of every means. Yoga alone unveils the existence of the Blessed Lord's Power and the other great qualities in all things, and so Yoga holds the first place among means of attainment. And it is an established fact that, in His Power, which is here His Yoga, mood can be made to be the root or basis in everyone and everything. Besides, He is "Kṛṣṇa"—He, and He alone, is Eternal Joy. A fire that is already blazing can kindle the fire that is latent in everything.

Śuka tells us how this Blessed Lord made His entry among these Gopīs when He says: "between the two members of each pair of Gopīs." The Gopīs must be pictured here as forming a circle, but matched separately in pairs, two by two. It is inaccurate to picture this in terms of a pair of Gopīs dancing in one place, as a pair (rather there is a circle, or actually, many circles, of pairs of Gopīs). And so in the middle of each pair of Gopīs, at the point where their two hands joined, just where His waist would be, the Blessed Lord arose and became present. Śuka next describes how, once the Blessed Lord had become present in this way, He related Himself to the Gopī who stood on either side of Him: "Kṛṣṇa. .entered the circle between the two members of each pair . .and put one arm around the neck of each Gopī." As each Gopī put a hand on his back, the Lord put one hand around each one's neck. Thus there were eight Kṛṣṇas for sixteen Gopīs. Otherwise this would have been an improper manifestation of mood (OR: a pseudo-mood—a false appearance of mood; Skt. *rasābhāsa*), because each Gopī would see two Kṛṣṇas. This is what Śuka means when he says: "so that all these women would think that He was in her presence alone." It was the Blessed Lord's wish that each Gopī fail to perceive that the Blessed Lord was facing each one of the Gopīs and embracing each one of them by the neck. Rather, each Gopī thought He was in her presence alone, and not in the presence of all the other Gopīs. The Lord multiplied His forms precisely for this reason. Therefore one must not look for an equal number of forms of Kṛṣṇa and the Gopīs, since His intention was to number half as many as they. It is in a forthcoming stanza—the one which says: "as many forms of Him as there were cowherd-women." (Stanza 20 of this chapter)—

that Śuka will tell us that the number of forms of the Blessed Lord and the number of Gopīs becomes equal. And in that reading which is accepted by some people, and says: "Mādhava was at the side of each lovely Gopī"(*aṅganāmaṅganāmantare mādhave*), the word "Mādhava" should actually be in the nominative case, so that the meaning is:"Mādhava was in between every two lovely Gopīs" (i.e., the proper reading is: *aṅganāmaṅganāmantare mādhavaḥ*). And in that reading the plural number (*aṅganām*) is used in the sense of the dual (i.e., "every two lovely Gopīs"). Or, the quotation about Mādhava is meant to refer to an entirely different circle—not the one described in the Bhāgavata—because that quotation goes on to describe Kṛṣṇa playing the flute in the middle of the circle, whereas here He dances for the purpose of manifesting the mood of love. Even if there is desire for song here, that "ardent desire" is attained by the gods alone (OR: exists on the part of the gods alone), as the stanza's words suggest. What Śuka describes in stanza seven of this chapter when he says: "like an emerald set in the midst of gold ornaments" is said merely to express the fact that Kṛṣṇa could be seen. In that way alone (by shining like an emerald) could the Lord be seen by both the Gopīs and the gods. Thus, there is nothing unsuitable in the way we have explained the present stanzas.

All the gods and so forth, who possess transcendent knowledge, became fully aware that, since all the surroundings which contribute to the mood of love have been said to exist here, that mood will surely become manifest to all. Therefore they come in order to see Kṛṣṇa and these circles, as Śuka tells us in the sentence that begins: "Meanwhile the sky all around.." "The sky all around" became crowded with a hundred heavenly chariots. For a dance that takes place underneath a canopy gives rise to the mood of love. Otherwise there would not be variety and attractiveness above (the dancers). For this reason "the sky was crowded with a hundred heavenly chariots." In just the same way men and women unite with one another in order to produce the mood of love, they assume different erotic positions, and are so pictured in a painting. For this reason the Blessed Lord has placed and ordered the gods and so forth here, in a way which resembles a painting. This is why Śuka goes on to say: "whose very Selves had been carried away by ardent desire." The Lord incited everyone and everything to act in this way, for the sake of His Game. Therefore, even in the context of the "ardent desire" of the gods, nothing happened except exactly what He wished. The gods' wives had come in order to partake of the mood of love, but the Blessed Lord's Wish was that they form part of the picture—the painting. Śuka describes how the gods in their heavenly chariots became part of the picture when he says: "containing the sky-dwellers. ." The dwelling-place of these gods is the Svarga-heaven. Śuka adds "and their wives" in order to exclude the notion that the gods possessed any emotion other than the desire to see Kṛṣṇa and His Game. The women are subordinated here to indicate that their emotion—the desire to partake of the mood of love—is secondary. For those who dwell in Svarga are fully acquainted with the mood of love, and are well-suited to it. "But," someone may object, "the Lord's Game should not be seen; then how is it that the gods are taking all these steps to see it?" Śuka's reply to this is: "whose very Selves had been carried away by ardent desire." Their intelligence or their very essence, their Self, had been carried away by their mind, which was overwhelmed by the Lord's Game and deprived of its power of reasoning. Therefore they acted purely on the basis of their own *dharma*, and they did not even think about the Blessed Lord's *dharma*.[6]

Introduction to Stanza 5: In the next stanza, Śuka tells us how, after what has just been described, the dance began exactly as it should have begun:

Stanza 5: Then the booming of the kettle-drums began, and flowers rained down, as the Gandharva husbands, accompanied by their wives, sang in praise of the untainted Fame of Kṛṣṇa.

6. The word *dharma* here absolutely defies translation. The closest I can come, with only the vaguest feeling of accuracy, is "sense of what is right." The gods acted out of a practically instinctive "sense of what was right" for them. And they did not, nor could they, consider what was right from the Blessed Lord's point of view, since their intelligence (*buddhi*) had been stolen away. Vasu rightly picks up on Vallabha's earlier expressed correlation (between the gods' having their very Selves stolen away and the Blessed Lord's inciting them to do precisely what He wanted) by saying that this was how the gods ended up doing what Kṛṣṇa wanted them to.

Commentary : First came the playing of the kettle-drums. For, as holy scripture says: "Or the most perfect sound is that which is made by the kettle-drum." Then there was a shower of flowers right at the outset, to assure a blessed beginning for this undertaking. This well known gesture of respect with flowers has come at this point to show that either the mood of love or its presiding Lord and Master is being paid homage. And the fact that the plural number is used in the phrase" flowers rained down" shows that there were separate showers of different kinds of flowers. Then the group, or choral, singing was begun, as Śuka tells us when he says: "the Gandharva husbands (AND/OR: "the lords of the Gandharvas")..sang in praise." Only the best singers sang here, because they knew it was the Blessed Lord who would hear them. The "Gandharva husbands" means Viśvāvasu and the other Gandharvas. Since they were eligible for this, they commit no fault by seeing what they are seeing, no more than a dancer commits a fault by watching his female students dance.[7] If it were otherwise, then Indra and the other gods would commit a fault when they see Lakṣmī in the arms of the Blessed Lord. There is no fault on the part of the Gandharvas here because of the law that says: "When an intended object (the Game) and a thing which is a mere means for carrying it out (like the Gandharvas) conflict, the intended object is the weightier of the two." "Yet it might well be possible that the Gandharvas' mentality would be quite the contrary," someone may speculate. Śuka answers this with the qualifying phrase: "accompanied by their wives." And to further exclude the possibility of the Gandharvas' committing the fault of sensuality, Śuka says: "the untainted Fame of Kṛṣṇa." For that Fame erases every taint. Therefore no emotion was produced in either the Gandharvas or their wives except those feelings and objects which were useful and suitable at that particular time.

Introduction to Stanza 6: After thus describing the singing, the playing of musical instruments, and so forth, which were

7. I follow Vasu's Hindi for these last two clauses, for which Vallabha's Sanskrit says nothing more than: *naṭānām iva teṣāṁ darśanaṁ na doṣāya.* Vallabha's reference may be simply to dance-students generally, male and/or female.

going on outside the Rāsa-circle, Śuka describes the instruments which, in the midst of the dance itself, were useful to the mood of love:

Stanza 6: A noisy confusion of sound came from the bracelets, anklets and tiny bells of these women as they danced with their Lover in the Rāsa-circle.

Commentary : We normally expect musical instruments to be in three places: in some lower place, such as on or near the ground; some place in the middle; and somewhere above. Thus alone are different rhythms created. And so here, too, we hear the sound of "the bracelets" above, and of the "anklets" below. And in the middle are the "tiny bells." Since everyone's arms are joined together here in a circle, wherever two hands meet the bracelets strike against each other and produce a sound. Or, Śuka will describe later, in the eighth stanza of this chapter, another way of producing sound, when he says: "with the movements of their feet." Śuka says: "with their Lover," i.e., they danced together with Kṛṣṇa The reason all of them started to dance was so that they could all achieve union with the Blessed Lord. The word "and" in the stanza is meant to indicate that the Gopīs also made other, humming sounds with their voices. And as they all joined together in one group, there was such a "confusion of noises" that someone standing at a distance would not be able to distinguish what was making one sound from what was making another. In order to explain what might be responsible for such a situation, Śuka says: "In the Rāsa-circle," that is to say, in the circle of the whole multitude of moods (*rasa*). Just as, if a śūdra were to hear and study the Vedas, the power of both the scriptural words he recites and of the student himself would be laughed to scorn because a śūdra does not have the eligibility for this, and besides, the śūdra would be committing a sin, so, if anyone except a true devotee of this were to listen to this account, then because of that listener's lack of eligibility and because this mood transcends this world, the mood would depart from everyone in the circle of listeners. When people are going to hear this account, then, let them first investigate thoroughly whether there is such a listener, for that would bring about undesirable results for all concerned, and would thus constitute a real evil.

Introduction to Stanza 7: Someone may raise this doubt: "Now that the Blessed Lord has entered into the midst of the dance, His presence may, at times, not shine forth clearly, because He will be secondary to the dance as a whole." But Śuka describes, in the following stanza, how the Blessed Lord's radiance even then became and remained evident to all:

Stanza 7: In that dance the Blessed Lord, Devakī's son, shone with surpassing brilliance together with the Gopīs, like an emerald set in the midst of gold ornaments.

Commentary : By His very Nature Kṛṣṇa's radiance is brilliant, but here He "shone with surpassing brilliance." As has been said: "He attains unparalleled brilliance when He is together with His Powers (literally, "His Śaktis," i.e., here, the Gopīs)" (cf. Chapter IV, Stanza 10 and Commentary). Someone may object that the Lord sometimes shows forth the brilliance that comes from Himself alone. But it is to refute this that Śuka has said: "together with the Gopīs." And if someone objects: "How can He be even more radiant with the Gopīs when He is brilliant by His very nature?", Śuka answers simply: "the Blessed Lord." It is just the same as when the Blessed Lord appears with all His great qualities (i.e., His "blessings") manifest. If someone argues that the Blessed Lord's great qualities are superior to all else, whereas these women are not, Śuka's answer to that is: "Devakī's son." For just as He became the son of Devakī because of her devotion, so has He become manifest for the purpose of helping women alone. And so, by communicating His very own power to the Gopīs as well, He has attained this intensity of brilliance. If the objector's doubt persists, and he says that the brilliance of something natural will not shine forth when it is surrounded by fabricated things, Śuka answers by giving the example: "like an emerald set in the midst of gold ornaments." The emerald—the gem which came forth from Garuḍa's mouth—is natural. But ornaments made of gold are fabrications. Yet when these gold ornaments are set around it, they make the natural gem shine all the more brilliantly.

Introduction to Stanza 8: After thus describing the first segment of the dance, Śuka portrays for us in the following stanza the main portion—the dance proper:

Stanza 8: With the movements of their feet and the waving of their arms, the coquettish arching of their eyebrows accompanied by smiles, and the bending of their waists, the shake and bouncing of their breast-cloths, and with the swaying of their earrings against their own and His cheeks, these brides of Kṛṣṇa, their faces perspiring and the knots of their braids and girdles come loose, now sang in praise of Him as they flashed brilliantly, like bolts of lightning in a circle of black clouds.

Commentary : The words "the movements of their feet" indicate all the dance-steps—those which take the form of the *cārī* step, in which the dancer turns on one foot, and those of the *karaṇa* step, where the dancer whirls on both feet. And "the waving of their arms" indicates all the different hand-movements. Śuka wants to indicate to us that, as one of the Gopīs' body-parts made a movement or step all other limbs joined in perfect unison with that movement. Śuka has also described the different movements of their eyebrows and all the side-long glances, enhanced by slow, sweet smiles, which the Gopīs cast. Each of these movements came about as each mood and thrill of joy penetrated the Gopīs' hearts. And the "bending" tells us that the Gopīs' waists bent this way and that according to the movements to and fro or the whirling round and round of the upper parts of their bodies. And by the frenzied movement of all the limbs of these women who had been engulfed by the mood of love, the mood becomes one. Or, it was by their movements to and fro and their whirling that their "breast-cloths" were "bouncing" because of their bouncing breasts. Thus Śuka highlights the shaking and bouncing that affected all their limbs in this dance. And when Śuka says: "with the swaying of their earrings against their own and His cheeks," he describes in a phrase all the different movements of their heads. Among all the head-movements Śuka chooses to describe the swaying of the Gopīs' earrings to point out that these created brilliant flashes, like those of lightning-bolts. By the words: "with the swaying..against the cheeks," Śuka means to tell us that all beauty (OR: "brightness, lustre"; *kānti*) has been exhausted there. For on His cheek is the lone mood and nectar of love. The nectar of love is to be drunk, and it is drunk from His cheek alone. And the lightning-flash of their earrings is meant to illuminate His (black) cheeks alone.

And then, in order to express the fact that the mood of love (also: "fluid"; *rasa*) which was within the Gopīs had become absolutely full and burst forth, Śuka says: "their faces perspiring." In addition, "the knots in their braids and girdles came loose." Since the mood and its fluid that was present in every part of their bodies had become one, their bodies acquired a certain fineness or subtlety. And as a result of this, the knots in their long, thick braids and in their girdle-string, too became loose.

In case someone objects: "How is it that such exertion is evident here?", Śuka says: "these brides of Kṛṣṇa." For these women are enjoyers of the Reward who is Eternal Joy. And so in their actions of enjoyment some exertion is involved. And such women, out of their own inner happiness, also "sang in praise of Him." And so, by reason of the very strainings of their bodies and so forth, "they flashed brilliantly," i.e., they shone with special brilliance. Someone may object: "But whether or not there is brilliance depends on whether or not it is seen by people in general. How were these Gopīs seen at that time by all?" Śuka answers this by saying: "they..like bolts of lightning." For a lightning-bolt can never be seen for a long time. But it produces real brilliance when it flashes in a circle of clouds. And in that mass of cloud-black Kṛṣṇas, the Gopīs were overshadowed by the Blessed Lord. But from either side of Him a Gopī occasionally sprang into view and was at least partially visible. Therefore their brilliance did not bring about a fault on their part, but became a special brilliance peculiar to them alone.

Introduction to Stanza 9: After thus describing for us the close-knit, intense dance, Śuka now describes the middle portion of the dance:

Stanza 9: The sweet-voiced Gopīs, in love with love, sang out in high-pitched voices as they danced. And, as they were delighted by the touches of Kṛṣṇa, this world was pervaded by their song (OR: what they sought by their song was fulfilled; cf. Comm.).

Commentary : "As they danced" may mean that, while the Gopīs were dancing, they began to sing in high-pitched voices. Or it may mean that they first "sang in high-pitched voices," and then started to dance. In either case, Śuka gives the reason for their behavior when he says: "The sweet-voiced Gopīs, in love with love." "Sweet-voiced" means that the Gopīs' voices had the kind of sound which excites love. And "in love with love" means that only the union of love was pleasing to them. It is well known that both the Gopīs' singing and their dancing cause infatuation. Someone may object: "Since the Gopīs so strained and exerted themselves in the previous dancing, how can they continue to go on like this?" Śuka's answer is: "they were delighted by the touches of Kṛṣṇa." Since the Blessed Lord was touching them everywhere, with different kinds of touches such as rubbing and so forth, the Gopīs "were delighted" by this—their inner Joy became full. Śuka describes the excellence of the Gopīs' song, which was meant to make the Lord forget everyone and everything else, in the words: "this world was pervaded by their song." In this interpretation we construe the words to mean: "by whose song this, i.e., the world, was pervaded." Or, alternatively, the words may be interpreted to mean that the reward which the Gopīs sought for their dancing, singing and so forth, was granted. In that case we would translate the phrase "what they sought by their song was fulfilled," or, to put it literally, "by singing for the sake of that, that was fulfilled."[8] Śuka intends to point out here that this world is pervaded by the mood of love by reason of the songs which people compose and perform, which illumine that mood (OR: which enlighten the world).

Introduction to Stanza 10: All this was done for the sole purpose of making the mood of love manifest in the world. The Blessed Lord also added His own sound to the singing, in order to make the sound which was being produced full of the nectar of immortality. And this sound had to be made sweetly. By it the world was to be filled. Someone may object: "But isn't this impossible?" To answer this Śuka narrates the following stanza:

Stanza 10: One Gopī intoned, together with Mukunda, the pure, unmixed types of note, and she was honored by Him, as He showed His love for her by saying: "Well done! Well done!"

8. The stanza's Sanskrit for this phrase reads: *yadgītenedamāvṛtam*. Vallabha states his first interpretaion in the words: *yāsām gītenedaṁ jagad vyāptam*; and his alternative interpretation is as follows: *yadarthametannṛtyādikaṁ, tat saphalaṁ jātam*.

Another Gopī raised her voice to the very same note—the fixed note of the song—and the Lord honored her as well.

Commentary : Together with Mukunda a certain Gopī intoned the unmixed types of note. This "one Gopī" had achieved perfect love of the Blessed Lord. Śuka gives us the reason for the Blessed Lord's joining His own sound with the singing when he says: "Mukunda." It was entirely for the sake of granting ultimate freedom (*mukuṁ = muktim + da = Mukunda*: "Kṛṣṇa the Giver of Freedom") that He gave full utterance to His own sound in the Upaniṣads.[9] Here, too, there is oneness of both, and equality of sound. And there are two effects involved in ultimate freedom: one's release from his previous body, with all its concomitants, and the attainment of Brahman. The usefulness of the Upaniṣads consists in their removing all other things for the sake of securing these two effects.

The primary notes of music are *ṣaḍja* and the six others. There are differences of type in these seven notes, as when the peacock sings *ṣaḍja* and when other birds, or men, or other creatures sing *ṣaḍja*. Likewise there are sub-classifications of type among the notes. If these notes are joined together in their proper order, as in the manifestation of mood and delight, which is the intention for which they were produced at the creation, then the different types of note are "pure and unmixed." The Blessed Lord alone can do this—no one else. If the Gopīs have intoned these notes properly, then the Lord's happiness is fully justified. That is when Śuka says: "She was honored by Him," i.e., by the Blessed Lord. There is no reason to be surprised at the Lord's singing in this way, for He is Brahman, and the proper order of music has proceeded in a regular, logical fashion from His own thought. "But," the Lord thinks, "other people do not know the real nature of music, so how in the world are they doing this?" And so the Gopī who was able to do this "was honored by Him." And besides, this Gopī's intoning brought on the additional effect of the

9. AND/OR: "It was entirely for the sake of granting ultimate freedom that He made His sound full in reference to (the Gopīs who embody) the Upaniṣads": Vasu. This rings true since Vallabha considers the Gopīs to be the embodiments of holy scripture (*śruti*), which includes the Upaniṣads, as Vallabha will confirm later, in his Introduction to Stanzas 14-15 of Chapter 35 (our Chapter Six), where he refers to the Gopīs of that chapter's stanzas 16-17 as *śruti-s*.

Lord's saying: "Well done! Well done!" The Blessed Lord Himself thus "shows His love For her." Kṛṣṇa's saying "well done!" twice expresses the goodness of the Gopī's accomplishment both in itself and with respect to its reward. And His love is because of the equality, i.e., the complete similarity of what she did (to what He does).

Another Gopī, since she saw that the intoned note had been taken up by the Blessed Lord, raised her voice to the same intonation, as Śuka tells us in the sentence that begins: "Another Gopī". As "the very same"—intoned—"note " was fixed and unchanging, she, too, "raised her voice" to it. In other words, she joined this sound of hers to the fixed sound. The fixed sound is the sound which causes all others—it is the basic, stable sound of the composition. For the musical rule reads: "The sound with which the Rāga begins is called the stable, fixed sound." Or, Śuka may mean that she joined her sound to the Blessed Lord's sound alone (OR: "that the Blessed Lord's sound alone is the fixed tone"; Vasu). For the Gopī would say to herself: "This is the note that the Blessed Lord has sung." Certain people argue that this Gopī joined her sound in terms of clapping her hands to set the rhythm, and so forth. But this opinion does not stand up under investigation. Since she thus joined her singing to the fixed tone, the Blessed Lord "honored her greatly." And the words "as well" signify that He also honored, i.e., granted, what she most desired. Śuka's meaning is that, since the Gopīs acquired this sort of inner competency, what must we say of their outward ability? The word "greatly" shows us that the Lord honored her above all the other Gopīs. The two Gopīs described in this stanza embody the Blessed Lord's Power and His heroic Strength, respectively. Four other Gopīs will later be explained, in their proper order, as embodiments of the Blessed Lord's four other great qualities.

Introduction to Stanza 11 & 12: Fame rests on the Blessed Lord alone as its support. It is in this context that Śuka has described the bodily movements of two Gopīs in the two stanzas which follow:

Stanza 11: One Gopī, exhausted from the Rāsa-dance, hung on, with her arm, to the shoulder of the Club-Wielder (Kṛṣṇa), who was beside her, as the jasmine-flowers braided, bracelet-like, into her hair shook loose (OR: "as her bracelets and jasmine-flowers shook loose").

Commentary : Worn out completely by the Rāsa-dance, one Gopī held on, with her arm, to Him who was standing on one side of her. Śuka calls Kṛṣṇa "the Club-Wielder" to emphasize the Blessed Lord's steadiness. If He had acted otherwise, and exerted Himself too much, the Rāsa-circle would be broken. This Gopī's exhaustion comes from an excess of the delight of the mood of love. Otherwise she would not have continued to direct her activity toward this mood. It is possible that, if she were leaving the circle, the Blessed Lord, too, would grasp her hand in order to keep the circle intact. Therefore, "beside her," on one side, was the Blessed Lord alone. And by putting her arm around the neck of the Blessed Lord who was at her side, she embraced Him as the climbing vine embraces the tree. Someone may object that, since the Blessed Lord had first put His arm around her neck, and she in turn put her arm around Him, the relationship described here might merely be that of two friends. In order to refute this Śuka has said :"as the jasmine-flowers braided, bracelet-like, into her hair, shook loose," i.e., the jasmine-flowers she was wearing in the shape of a bracelet became loose. A garland of jasmine-flowers was tied into her braided hair, in the form of bracelet-like rings. That this shook loose demonstrates this Gopī's weakness from excitement and exhaustion. And it likewise demonstrates her faithfulness and her aptness.[10]

Stanza 12: Then another Gopī, when she smelled the fragrance of the blue lotus of Kṛṣṇa's arm, which was smeared with sandal-paste, as it lay on one of her shoulders, her hair stood on end for joy, and, ah!, she kissed it.

Commentary : Yet another Gopī smelled Kṛṣṇa's arm, which was smeared with sandal-paste and possessed a fragrance even greater than that of the blue lotus, as it lay on one of her shoulders. And she was so suffused with joy, so full of absolute Joy, that all her hair stood on end and she kissed His arm. First of all His form

10. Or, as Lālūbhaṭṭa interprets in his *Yojanā* on this last sentence: this demonstrates Kṛṣṇa's faithfulness and trustworthiness.

and His touch became present to her. Then she experienced His fragrance and the taste (*rasa*) of Him, too. The word "ah!" is said in the sense of astonishment. The word translated as "then" (*tatra*) may have either of two meanings: at that very moment; or, in Him, i.e., the Blessed Lord, alone. Thus Śuka has described, in these last two stanzas, the way Kṛṣṇa made use, in such circumstances, of two different Gopīs who were standing on either side of Him. Or, the words "as it lay on one of her shoulders" (*ekāṁsa-gatam*) may mean: "One Gopī (different from the one of the last stanza) smelled Kṛṣṇa's arm as it lay on her shoulder" (i.e., *ekā aṁsagatam bāhum..āghrāya*). Hence the commentators who say that the Gopī of the last stanza is the one who has acted in this stanza are wrong. But, since the Lord is Eternal Joy, He communicates the same mood and delight to all the Gopīs.[11]

The blue lotus blooms only at night. And women find it charming and beautiful. It is not merely the fragrance that comes from sandal-paste that causes this Gopī's act of smelling, but a fragrance entirely different from that, a fragrance unknown to ordinary people, but known to those whose emotion transcends this world entirely. This transcendent fragrance is known to these people by the fact that it comes together here with the fragrance of the sandal-paste, and is comparable to it. This special characteristic (viz., that the Lord's arm has the fragrance of the blue lotus) is meant also to point out the Lord's natural fragrance. And His smearing His arms with sandal-paste is meant to break down the Gopīs' sense of discrimination and their firmness. The entering within her (of Him, or His fragrance, or both)

11. OR: "Since the Lord is Eternal Joy, He possesses the same nectar of delight on every part of His form as He does on His lips": Vasu. This is in response to an objection, which Vasu says Vallabha is responding to but Vallabha gives no indication he is responding to, that this Gopī should not kiss Kṛṣṇa's arm, since the nectar of delight (*rasa*) is on His lips (*adhara*). Vallabha's Sanskrit says simply: *sadānandatvāt sarvatraiva samarasatā*. Vasu's translation reflects a true enough doctrine of Vallabha(in fact, I suspect Vasu must have got the idea from one of Vallabha's sub-commentators on this passage), but I think the evidence is scant that this is the doctrine Vallabha is referring to here. I am not sure my translation is the correct one, either, but I believe it fits in better with the context. This is another example, if we needed another, of Vallabha's terse, cryptic style, which begat such an abundant brood of sub-commentators.

by means of her smelling is this Gopī's special characteristic. She embodies the Blessed Lord's great quality of Splendor.

Introduction to Stanza 13: Śuka now tells us how the betel-leaf, which had been taken by the Blessed Lord, was now taken, as if it were the gift of Knowledge, by one of the Gopīs:

Stanza 13 : The Lord gave the betel-leaf He had chewed to one Gopī who put her cheek, which was made beautiful by the flashing of her earring as it was shaken this way and that by the dancing, up against His own cheek.

Commentary : In the words: "(one Gopī) who put her own cheek up against the Blessed Lord's cheek," Śuka indicates this Gopī's need of and desire for the Lord, and her dexterity as well. Even though He was not facing her directly, He gave generously to her merely because of her dexterity. Śuka intends to tell us, by the words he uses, that the Blessed Lord gave to her His own great quality of Knowledge. By reason of this, this Gopī will become the teacher of all the other Gopīs when the Blessed Lord is not present. In order to point out this Gopī's aptitude for Knowledge, Śuka indicates that she possesses the powers of worldly knowledge and effective action when he says: "(her cheek) which was made beautiful by the flashing of her earring as it was shaken this way and that by the dancing." Her cheek was adorned with the brightness of the earring which was tossed about by her dancing. Her power of action was based on the dance, while her power of knowledge was based on the earring. The shaking of her earring by reason of her power of action is equivalent to the excessive repetition and memorization involved in learning. Or, the shaking of the coil (*kuṇḍala*) which is the earring, since it is the very essence of Yoga, represents the various means of attainment.[12] The lovely gleam of this earring represents her experience here. And devotion is beautified by it. And her devotion (represented by her cheek) is united with the love of the Blessed Lord for her. Just as she has passionately loved the Blessed Lord, so has the Blessed Lord passionately loved her as well. The idea that the Lord's cheek

12. Vallabha here plays on the connection between the word *kuṇḍala*, "coil, earring," and Kuṇḍalinī Yoga, in which the coil of the serpent Śakti is shaken loose by various Yogic means.

is equivalent to the devotion that embodies the goal which is to be attained is also expressed here. This Gopī wanders around the root or basis (of Knowledge; i.e., Kṛṣṇa's cheek) in the same way Lakṣmī Herself does. She turns round and round, and studies Him who has Lakṣmī, and thus the equivalence of the betel-leaf and Knowledge is established (when the Lord gives her the betel-leaf). And the words "(the betel-leaf) He had chewed" show that the Blessed Lord gave her the gift of fully-attained Knowledge, without her having to work her way through all the means of attaining Knowledge.

Introduction to Stanza 14 : Śuka now tells us how still another Gopī placed on her heart the Blessed Lord's hand, which is flawless and constant, the embodiment of action, and the very self of Detachment, so that she might be a companion for (the Gopī who embodies) Knowledge :

Stanza 14 : Another Gopī was dancing and singing, her ankle-bells and waist-bells jingling. And exhausted, she placed the blessed lotus-hand of Acyuta, who was beside her, on her breasts.

Commentary : This Gopī steadily continued her dancing and singing. And just as, in a dramatic performance, either another's hand or one's own hand is used or placed somewhere for support, so she placed the Blessed Lord's hand on herself. Śuka tells us of her singing and dancing in order to indicate to us that this Gopī possessed the knowledge that relates to sound and the action performed in relation with that knowledge. And her anklets and the girdle round her waist, both decorated with bells, were "jingling." The upper part of her body was engaged in performing the singing. And the dance was acted out by her feet. From the dancing alone came the sound of her anklets and waist-bells. And Śuka's intention is to indicate that this sound intensified the emotion in her, and by this sound her previously established, complete power of action came to total fruition. She was "exhausted," and so she placed the lotus-hand of the Blessed Lord, who was on one side of her, on her breasts, in order to put out the fire of exhaustion she was suffering from. Everyone knows that the lotus has the property of cooling things that are hot. This Gopī's strain and exhaustion are indicative of her joy. And Śuka has said that the Blessed Lord was standing on one side of her, and she remained standing at His side, indicating by this that her abandonment of her previous actions (of singing and dancing) was merely external. In order to remind us of the indefatigable nature of the Blessed Lord's Power of Action, Śuka calls Him by the name "Acyuta." And since the union of love, too, will later take place between Kṛṣṇa and this Gopī, the action described here is performed to make sure there is no obstacle to that. And since someone may raise the doubt that the Lord's hand will not extinguish the fire that is in this Gopī, since it will only fan the flames of passion and all that accompanies it, Śuka has said that the Lord's hand is "blessed." That which is "blessed"—the Lord's hand—alone embodies good fortune, since the Blessed Lord is the embodiment of absolute Joy.

Introduction to Stanza 15 : After thus revealing to us the essence of those six Gopīs (viz., that they embodied the six great qualities of the Blessed Lord), Śuka goes on to describe, in terms of its essence, the general game in which all the Gopīs participated:

Stanza 15 : The Gopīs, having gained for themselves the Lover who never fails or tires, Acyuta, who is the one and only Beloved of Śrī, sang His praises as He put His arms round their necks, and they played.

Commentary : The "Lover" who is "Acyuta" ("Unfailing," or "Imperishable") can be none other than the Blessed Lord. He is the one who grants Eternal Joy, both inwardly and outwardly. It is because of this alone that He is "the one and only Beloved," i.e., the supreme Love, "of Śrī," who is the archetype of all women (Skt. *sarvastrīṇām mūlabhūtā*). "Having gained" such a one "for themselves," they "sang in praise of Him" alone and "they played." Someone may object that, since the Gopīs have attained Supreme Joy, it is only fitting that their action now cease, and that there be no further action. Therefore how is it that they continue to act by "playing?" Śuka has answered this by saying: "as He put His arms round their necks." The Gopīs were pervaded by the Blessed Lord's action alone— no action of theirs was involved here. Their singing and other action becomes possible because the Lord has placed His own Power of Action on their necks. This Action has the form of a Power (*śakti*)—and this explains the independence (of action) of the Gopīs.

Introduction to Stanza 16 : After this, Śuka describes the dance of the Lord and the Gopīs, which resembles the dance of Rādhā (the Gopī Kṛṣṇa loved most)[13] and Dāmodara (Kṛṣṇa):

Stanza 16 : The Gopīs, their faces glowing radiantly with perspiration, and their cheeks adorned by the tips of the curls that looped round the blue-lotus blossoms in their ears, and with the ringing of their bracelets and anklets providing the instrumental music, danced together with the Blessed Lord, their garlands having fallen from their hair, in the partnership of the Rāsa-dance, while the bees filled the role of singers.

Commentary : This, too, is for the sake of the Rāsa alone, but here the mood of love (*rasa*) is produced in the Gopīs one by one. This is why Śuka has used the word "partnership," and no other—because the Lord and the Gopīs were engaged in a very close sort of dance. "Bees" are the "singers" for this dance, but the musical instruments remain the same as before, as Śuka tells us when he says: "with the ringing of their bracelets and anklets providing the instrumental music." When Śuka says there was a "ringing" sound of their bracelets and anklets, he means that the sounds of bells were the only sounds of musical instruments to be heard. And Śuka says "their garlands having fallen from their hair" in order to point out the Gopīs' intense involvement in the dance. (Here begins an interpolation by Viṭṭhala) Or, alternatively: the bees have been described as the singers here. And bees are constantly seeking the juice that is present only in flowers. Since these flowers were separated from the bees and they were deprived of their juice, the Gopīs gave their garlands to the bees, for the Gopīs were completely delighted at the way the bees sang in perfect tune with their dancing. Otherwise the Gopīs would not have overlooked the fact that they should keep these garlands in their hair, since they were the cause of their hair's glow of beauty, which is directed toward the mood of love. In this passage, then, both the bees' skill in singing and the awareness of that skill on the part of the Lord's beloved ones are suggested (end of Viṭṭhala's interpolation).

13. This is the sole reference by name to Rādhā in the *Subodhinī* on the love games.

Śuka describes how radiant the Gopīs looked at the beginning of this dance in the sentence that begins: "The Gopīs, their faces glowing.." If they were not still radiant, then it would not be fitting for them to begin a second dance after they had been exhausted by the dance described previously. Or, it would not enhance the mood of the entire occasion. Śuka tells us that the Gopīs placed blue-lotus flowers in their ears, and these did not fall out, in order to indicate their dexterity. And the curls that looped round these lotuses were like bees, drinking the nectar of the mood of love. And the tips of their curls remained there in the form of ornaments. That is how the Gopīs' cheeks looked. And the perspiration that was there, the water that seeps out from within the body during exertion, resulted from the Gopīs' intense involvement in the dance. Because of this a certain transcendent "radiance" (śrī) was produced on "their faces." It was as if both cheeks of each Gopī were adorned with pearls. By this, the strain of exertion on their faces has been removed. And, along with the Gopīs, "the Blessed Lord," too, expressed the external manifestations of the mood prevalent in the dance. Or perhaps what is indicated here is that He did not, of His own accord, stop this game. Śuka says: "the Gopīs," indicating that it was because of the Blessed Lord alone that the Gopīs had come to this point, not because of themselves. That is why Śuka says: "together with the Blessed Lord," meaning that just as the Blessed Lord danced, so too, did the Gopīs dance.

Introduction to Stanza 17 : Now that the mood of love has thus been made manifest, Śuka tells us how, in order to arouse this mood to its highest pitch, the Lord enacted visibly the gestures described in the treatises on erotics:

Stanza 17 : Thus, with embraces and with touches of His hands, with loving glances, unrestrained love-play and with laughter, the Lord of Ramā enjoyed the delights of love with the beautiful women of Vraja, just as a little boy plays delightedly with his own mirrored image.

Commentary : "Embraces" and so forth have been described in the treatises on erotics. "Thus" only, i.e., in order to arouse the mood of the occasion, does the Lord embrace the Gopīs. Then there are the "touches of His hands"—the Blessed Lord touches many different parts of the Gopīs' bodies with His hands. Then there are His "loving glances," which project outwardly His deep inner emotion. And after that, the "laughter" of desires fulfilled. Thus He performs these embraces and other actions, ending in laughter, with all the Gopīs. Someone may object: "But how is it that He has pursued the delights of love with ordinary women?" Śuka's answer is: "the Lord of Ramā (Lakṣmī)", i.e., the Lord of Her who is Delight itself. And this Delight (i.e., Ramā/Lakṣmī), too, has entered, by the Blessed Lord's command, into all the Gopīs.[14] Śuka tells us that the Gopīs, too, are suitable for the Lord to rest upon, or dwell in, when he calls them: "the beautiful women of Vraja." "But," the objector might continue, "how is it that the One who delights in Himself delights in love with these women? Lakṣmī is the very Joy of Brahman, and so it is quite proper for the Lord to make love to Her. But it is wrong for Him to have sexual intercourse with these women, since they have not become Brahman (or, simply: "they are not Brahman")." Śuka answers this objection by saying: "just as a little boy." For when a little boy puts a mirror or some water in front of himself, and he sees himself right there in it, he delights in it. In the same way, the Blessed Lord has put here His own power, or Himself, and, having made both Brahman and Brahman's Joy manifest here, "He enjoyed the delights of love." If the objector insists: "This, too, is improper. What about that?", Śuka's answer is still: "just as a little boy." By this Śuka means that, just as the Lord played His childhood game, so He played this game, too. (Here begins an interpolation by Viṭṭhala) Or, to explain this in another way: even if, at some time, the Lord's manner of action were precisely the same, the experience of this particular mood of love could not happen to Lakṣmī, but only to these Gopīs. This is what Śuka indicates by using the two phrases "the Lord of Ramā" and "with the beautiful women of Vraja." For He is the Lord, Master and Husband of Ramā. But these "beautiful women" are connected with "Vraja," i.e., related to other people, but they are not married.[15] So, when the Lord is making love to Ramā,

14. Here Vallabha, like the author of the stanza he is commenting on, plays on the etymological connection of Ramā, the name used here for Lakṣmī, with the verb form used in the stanza, *reme*. Both words come directly from the root *RAM*, "to make love, to pursue the delights of love."

15. The virgin Gopīs are, of course, "not married" at all (except, in their minds, to Kṛṣṇa). And the married Gopīs are "not married" to Kṛṣṇa.

the particular mood described here cannot be experienced either by the Lord or by Ramā, because of the very nature of the particular essence of this mood. This is what Śuka means. And if someone objects that it is improper for the Lord (OR: "a lord"; *īśvara*) to be doing this, Śuka's answer is: "like a little boy." For He is also described as acting in ways other than the Lord would act in the charmingly confused games of His childhood, which are narrated in passages such as: "As He was stealing the fresh butter, He saw his own reflection rise up in the nearby crystal pillar" (compare Bh. P. X.9. 6ff). For He acted in this way, even though He has the Fulness of Knowledge, because such was the nature of the mood of His childhood games. This is precisely the case here, too, for it is entirely valid to say that what is expressed in the words of holy scripture: "Mood indeed is He" (*Taitt. Upan.* II. 7. 1), is that all this is of the very essence of His Nature, since it falls within the purview of mood. Śuka means to tell us that there is no reason for even a doubt to arise here (end of Viṭṭhala's interpolation).

By the words of the comparison: "just as a little boy plays delightedly with his own mirrored image," Śuka has indicated that just as the Lord, or His inner emotion, was, so also were the Gopīs and their inner emotion. For that is precisely the nature of a mirror-image. Here the Lord makes love with many of the Gopīs at one time, and then again with two of them at once. The conclusion—His making love with each of them individually—will be described only later.

Introduction to Stanza 18 : Now that the Blessed Lord's attributes have thus entered within the Gopīs by reason of their Total Love, Śuka describes their complete absorption in the great mood (*mahārasa*), which is preceded by their forgetting their own bodies and all else:

Stanza 18 : Their senses overwhelmed by the ecstasy of touching His body, the women of Vraja were not able to arrange or rearrange quickly their hair, their woven-silk dresses, or their breast-cloths, or, O best of the Kuru race, their garlands and ornaments, which slipped off.

Commentary: The excessive joy which was produced by their touching the Blessed Lord's body was a profound emotion which made them forget their own bodies and all else. The Gopīs' "senses" were "overwhelmed" by this ecstasy. All the Gopīs were at a loss as to what they should do. And so they were unable to hold against themselves, or support by themselves quickly or entirely, their long, flowing hair, or the woven-silk dresses which were wound round them, or their breast-cloths. Śuka tells us the reason why the Gopīs were affected so deeply by such a small stimulus when he calls them "the women of Vraja." They were exerting themselves mightily, too, as Śuka points out when he says: "their garlands and ornaments..slipped off." Since their senses had been overwhelmed, the Gopīs could not think in the ordinary, worldly way. And since they were simple Gopīs, they could not think on the level of the highest truth. And because of their exertion they could not think even of their bodies. Therefore, Śuka means to tell us, the hair or garments that were covering their upper, middle and lower parts were held in place by the Blessed Lord alone, not by themselves. Although it may have appeared to someone else as if the Gopīs were holding up their own garments, in fact they were not holding them up by themselves. Śuka addresses King Parikṣit directly, saying "O best of the Kuru race," to insure that there be no error on the part of both speaker and listener here, and for the sake of mutual trust.

Introduction to Stanza 19 : After thus describing the collective game, Śuka describes for us, in the next stanza, the amazement of the gods' wives and of the moon, in order to indicate to us that no one at all achieved thorough understanding of this game:

Stanza 19 : When they saw this special game played by Kṛṣṇa, the wives of the gods were dazed, wounded by passion, and the hare-marked moon, with his host of stars, was awestruck.

Commentary : No woman's husband is Supreme Joy. For Joy cannot be given by one who is without Joy. "For," as holy scripture tells us, "He alone gives Joy" (*Taitt. Upan.* II. 7. 1). And the word "alone" in this scriptural passage is used in the sense of the negation of all others. In addition, this is a "game" with a "special" characteristic, and a soul certainly does not know this "special game." By saying "the wives of the gods," Śuka has indicated to us that the Blessed Lord has granted the gods' wives the special favor of seeing all these things. And the fact that women saw this does not constitute a fault. For it produces nothing but a "daze," or delusion, in them, and not complete understanding, nor the mood of the game. The ordinary (i.e., not the transcendent or divine) moon, too, saw all this. This is because the Gopīs' bodies have Soma as their essence. As holy scripture says: "Soma (i.e., the moon) is the First" (*RV*. X. 85. 40).[16] The women, too, are ordinary.[17] And yet the moon's seeing is not helpful even to the moon—this is what Śuka indicates to us when he says: "the hare-marked." For the moon bears a stain. And there is also the (stainless, divine) moon—Full of Joy (cf. Commentary on Chapter I, stanza 2). "With his host of stars" means "together with all the constellations (his wives)." This tells us that even if the moon is passionately aroused by his wives, his mind cannot be attracted to enjoying them. Thus the word "and" in the stanza signifies that the moon, too, "was dazed." Again—just as the passion of these wives of the gods became aroused as they looked at Him again and again immediately after they had become dazed, and thought to themselves: "We, too, must go there and take part in this game by embodying passion," and then became "wounded by passion," so the moon also made an effort to enter into the Blessed Lord. Thus the moon, too, became "wounded by passion." By this fact that the moon (which "represents Kṛṣṇa's *semen*," as we saw in Subodhinī on Chapter I, stanza 2) has become wounded by passion a supporting argument has been expressed for the view that, in the sexual act, satisfaction is reached upon ejaculation (the contrary view is that the continual action of coition provides the satisfaction). This is because the parts of this moon alone will be ejaculated by the Lord. Otherwise the aphorism "Satisfaction comes from simultaneous ejaculation" would be contradicted.[18] Because, if the moon had not entered into the

16. This refers to the general conception that it is only the moon which has enjoyed virgins (Shri Shyam Goswamy).

17. "The women" here seems to refer to the Gopīs.

18. Emend Telivala-Sankalia's *sahasradarśanānmuktir* to *sahasravaṇānmuktir* ("Satisfaction comes from simultaneous ejaculation"), on the basis

Lord, there would not be simultaneous ejaculation (Note: Perhaps because, as said above, Soma is already the essence of the Gopīs' bodies. Also, cf. Stanza 26 below). Besides, it is "with his host of stars," i.e., together with his wives, that the moon became "awestruck." This indicates that the mood of awe, or wonder, is the only one that has been produced here; no other mood has been produced.

Introduction to Stanza 20 : After thus explaining to us the intense involvement in the mood produced by the Blessed Lord of the gods' wives and the moon according to their ordinary, or elemental, level of reality, as well as of the moon according to its divine level of reality,[19] Śuka tells us in the next stanza that Kṛṣṇa made love with each Gopī individually. For each Gopī had performed her vow with this prayer: "O goddess, make the cowherd Nanda's son my husband" (Bh. P. X. 22. 4).

Stanza 20 : After multiplying Himself so that there were as many forms of Him as there were cowherd-women, this Blessed Lord made love with these Gopīs, even though His delight is in Himself, playfully—as a game.

Commentary : Having made as many forms of Himself as there were women of the cowherd caste, by revealing His Power of Māyā in many places, He thus becomes clearly manifest in these different places.[20] This is the great sexual delight, and He has

of Vallabha's negation immediately thereafter, in the words *sahasravaṇābhāvāt*, and because of the context of *nisarga*, "ejaculation," and because Viṭṭhala explains *sahasravaṇān-* in his *Tippaṇī*.

19. Here Vallabha seems to confirm (I say "seems" because his word is merely *ādhidaivikasya*, not *ādhidaivikasya candrasya*, though the reference does seem to be to the moon), that he was speaking, in his commentary on the last stanza, about two levels of the moon's reality. Thus, presumably, the moon which was "Full of Joy" is the moon on its divine level and perhaps the moon which entered into the Lord is, too (although Viṭṭhala says that this moon was the moon "on the level of the Self"—*ādhyātmika*). All the other statements are presumably about the "ordinary" moon. The trouble is that Vallabha has made no distinction perceptible in the Sanskrit between, or among, the different levels.

20. Or, it is quite possible, and it would also be in accord with Vallabha's doctrines, to translate his words: *tatra tatra māyodghāṭanena tathā tathā prakaṭo bhavati*, in this way: "by lifting the veil of Māyā in many places, He thus becomes clearly manifest in these different places." This is how Vasu

the power to act in this way because, as Śuka says, "this" is the "Blessed Lord." The word "this" signifies that He has come down to earth for the sake of this alone. Here "He made love with these Gopīs" in order to reward their vow. But His delight in Himself is not the same as it had been before. Śuka is trying to tell us just this when he says: "even though His delight is in Himself." But not in mere delight in Himself—because the moon has entered into Him—is lovemaking possible here. Yet even in this condition it amounts only to delight in Himself. For, as the rule says: "An excess has subsequently entered there—not a lessening of this." Moreover, Śuka has pointed out the predominance of delight in Himself alone in the words: "playfully—as a game." Just as a great man, such as a king, also does, for the sake of the game, something which is unsuitable to his high status, such as going on foot, like an ordinary soldier, when he is hunting; and just as the Lord plays other games during His descent to the earth, so has He performed this game. This is what Śuka means.

Introduction to Stanza 21 : Śuka next tells us how, after this, the Gopīs' lovemaking came to an end:

Stanza 21 : The Gopīs were exhausted by this excess of love-play, and He, compassionate, wiped their faces lovingly, good sir, with His most blessed hand.

Commentary : The Gopīs became completely exhausted by this very intense love-play, with its many different erotic positions. And so, for the sake of the next game, He wiped their faces with His hand. Because "He" is Kṛṣṇa—and He had come down to earth for this very purpose. Śuka uses the plural number in referring to the Gopīs in order to signify that all of them had become exhausted, and the Lord did this to all of them. And the reason Kṛṣṇa acted as He did is that He is "compassionate."

takes the passage, and it is consonant with Vallabha's teaching that Kṛṣṇa is everything everywhere but in some places He is "clearly manifest" (*āvirbhūta* or *prakaṭa*) as such, while in other places He is only "latent" (*tirobhūta*). It is by His Power of Māyā that He makes Himself latent. The key to interpreting this passage, then, is the meaning of *udghāṭanena*, which can mean "by revealing or lifting" in the sense of "lifting forward" or "using" His Māyā, or "by lifting" (the veil of) Māyā and revealing things as they really are. I think the former interpretation is more likely, while Vasu prefers the latter, but both are likely, and perhaps the ambiguity is intentional.

The Lord was affected by compassion, and to show that this compassion is not remote and indifferent, Śuka says: "lovingly." And to indicate that, when the Lord wiped the Gopīs' faces, their suffering was surely removed, Śuka describes the Lord's hand as "most blessed." Śuka addresses Parikṣit with the words "good sir" to assure the king that he is not deceiving him. Thus, after first removing the Gopīs' sufferings, the Lord established His Supreme Joy in them.

Introduction to Stanza 22 : Śuka next tells us what the overjoyed Gopīs did after that:

Stanza 22 : The Gopīs—with their flashing gold earrings, their lustrous hair, and the radiance of their cheeks, and with His laughing glance, like the nectar of the gods—honoring their virile Lover, sang in praise of the sacred works He had done, filled with joy by the touch of His fingernails.

Commentary : The Gopīs, honoring Him, sang in praise of the deeds He had done. The reason they sang is that they were immersed completely in the *rajas* quality. Śuka has cited a pair of causes for this immersion: the first concerns the Gopīs' own nature and the second results from something done by the Blessed Lord. He describes first the cause which concerns the Gopīs' own nature. The gold which was "flashing" had been removed from the fire after being made brilliant by it, and these two gold earrings, along with their hair, which was lustrous in its beauty, brought radiance to the Gopīs' cheeks. The radiance on the Gopīs' cheeks was either flame-colored or yellow, while the lustre on Kṛṣṇa's cheeks was a gleaming black. Thus this triad of brilliant loveliness in the Gopīs embodied the effect of the *rajas* quality which was its basis. This description makes clear that the Gopīs were suitable for all that is excellent.

And that "glance" which is preceded by a "laugh" has fully attained, as it were, "the nectar of the gods." Here, too, an interrelated triad has been described: the interior passion, the glance and the laugh. This causal triad belongs to the Blessed Lord. Therefore, "honoring," i.e., either paying reverence or showing pride, by means of these two triads, the Gopīs "sang in praise of the things the Lord had done" to remove the fault which arose from their having a mind opposed to what was being done by their hearts. Śuka tells us that these deeds of the Lord not only removed sins, but embodied religious merit as well, when he says "the sacred works He had done." The works the Blessed Lord performed removed sin and caused religious merit as well. Therefore the Gopīs were free from fault. And their accumulation of religious merit is described in the next game. Śuka has said that the Lord manifested His Joy to make the Gopīs forget their previous troubles. The "fingernails" he refers to are those of the Blessed Lord—the pain caused "by the touch of His fingernails" reminds the Gopīs of their enjoyments of sexual union with Him, and they are "filled with joy." And the position at the end of the stanza of the words "filled with joy" indicates that their interior Joy was made full by their singing as well.

Introduction to Stanza 23 : After this, as Śuka tells us in the following stanza, together with the Gopīs who were now His equals (because they possessed full Joy), the Blessed Lord played a water-game:

Stanza 23 : Accompanied by the Gopīs, and pursued by bees, the protector-Gandharvas of His garland, which was now colored with saffron-paste from the Gopīs' breasts and crushed by the contact with their bodies, the Lord, exhausted, entered the river's waters to remove the fatigue of all, just as a weary bull-elephant plunges into the water with his female-elephants, after breaking the dam.

Commentary: "Accompanied by the Gopīs" means the Lord was joined by all the Gopīs. He entered the Yamunā at midnight in order to play in her waters. Śuka points out the reason for this when he says: "to remove the fatigue." He removes the fatigue from every part of the Gopīs' bodies by this water-game alone. Śuka describes the splendor which the Blessed Lord possessed as He went with the Gopīs when he says: "pursued by bees, the protector-Gandharvas of His garland." Or perhaps he is here describing the characteristics of Yamunā.[21] "The protector-Gandharvas" means the protectors of the Gandharvas, that is

21. This presumably refers to the fact that the word "pursued" may be read, in the stanza's Sanskrit, either as *anudruta* (*ḥ*), "He, pursued," or as *anudrutā*, "She (Yamunā), pursued." Yamunā would presumably be pursued by bees for the "garland" of flowers She wears on her banks and in her waters. The probability of this meaning is very remote, and Vallabha

to say, the best Gandharvas. The Lord was pursued, then, by these bees who are the most excellent Gandharvas. In company with this retinue, the Lord moved quickly and "entered the water." He did this in order to ward off the fragrance, too. For the lotus-fragrance of the Gopīs, who are Padminī ("lotus-like", the highest of the four kinds of women), was present in the perspiration that resulted from the sexual union. And the act of "pursuit," or "running after," is the swift movement of feet by reason of the disturbance, and the obstacle (to returning home), caused by that fragrance. And Śuka has stated that these bees belong completely to the Blessed Lord. And these bees are attached to that "garland which is crushed by the contact" of two bodies. Or, Śuka's words may mean: "on whom (i.e., Yamunā) there is such a garland." In other words, "She has been colored by the saffron-paste of their breasts." The garland is the Blessed Lord's alone. But the Yamunā, too, is colored by the saffron-paste from the Gopīs' breasts. In this garland are the fragrance of His body, of the flowers and of the saffron from their breasts. And there is an extraordinariness to this garland because it is His very own. Śuka characterizes the bees with the epithet "the protector-Gandharvas" because these bees—as enjoyers of this fragrance—are not on the ordinary, but on the divine level.

Śuka gives the reason why the Lord acted without consideration when he says: "just as a weary bull-elephant." Śuka notes this characteristic— "weary" or "exhausted"—for the sake of the Lord's going along with the game. For the Blessed Lord was described as having quite a different emotion up to and including His sexual union with each of the Gopīs individually. But because of the passing of that game and its emotion, His game of weariness or fatigue has become manifest. And by saying "with his female elephants," Śuka tells us that the exhaustion of the others has been removed.

Dams are built to hold back water. But these are all broken by such an elephant. And in this situation the Blessed Lord, too, has

most likely points it out to enrich the stanza with greater power of suggestion (*dhvani*). Besides, this foreshadows Vallabha's seeing, later in the commentary here, the possibility of Yamunā's being intended in other words of the stanza as well.

broken all the laws and limitations which apply to Himself as Brahman, i.e., the limitation of His delight to Himself alone, and in the process He has broken the limitations which apply to human souls as well, because of His touching the Gopīs, which embodied human sexual passion, and because of His sexual enjoyment of other mens' wives. All that had happened previously was that the Gopīs had touched the Blessed Lord—but the Gopīs had surely not been touched by the Blessed Lord. Because He was free from passion. The limitations of place and time have also been broken. Therefore just as the greatest of bull-elephants drives the guardian deity of the water far away, in order to sport about in the water, so the Lord wilfully entered the water here. This is Śuka's meaning.

Introduction to Stanza 24 : And there the Lord played His water-game, as Śuka tells us :

Stanza 24 : He and they were now fully in the water as these girls splashed Him, and they looked at Him with love as their loud laughter flowed in on Him from all sides, O dear one. He was praised by the gods, who rained down flowers from their heavenly chariots, and He made love in whatever way He wished—since His love here is the game of the bull-elephant.

Commentary : "He" is, of course, the One mentioned before—accompanied by the Gopīs. And, all of them being "fully in the water, these girls began to splash Him." And then "they looked at Him with love." As He was being splashed from all sides by these girls who were laughing loudly, completely absorbed in the frolicking, He went to the Gopī who was immediately opposite Him and made love to her. And He made love in the same way with all the Gopīs.

Just as Śuka speaks after already possessing knowledge of the Lord's greatness, and with the most intense love of Him—a love (OR: "an inner emotion") perfectly free of fault[22]—so is he aware that king Parikṣit is listening in precisely the same spirit. And so,

22. Vallabha here describes Śuka as perfectly fulfilling the definition of Devotion (*bhakti*) which Vallabha has adopted from the *Nārada Pañcarātra*: "Devotion is unshakable, all-surpassing love for Kṛṣṇa, preceded by knowledge of His greatness" (*māhātmyajñānapūrvastu sudṛḍhaḥ sarvato'dhikaḥ sneho bhaktiriti proktaḥ....*).

to indicate that the king falls into the same category as Śuka himself does as regards love of the Lord, Śuka addresses him as "dear one." By this Śuka means: "It is only because all this is so that I am narrating this game to thee."

In case someone asks how it happened that the gods did not prevent all this, Śuka says: "He was praised by the gods, who rained down flowers from their heavenly chariots." All the gods showed only joyous approval, not prohibition, of this. Otherwise the mood of passionate love would never become manifest in the world.

The word "girls" is used to express the unreflected nature of their conduct. And "they looked at Him with love" alone, as if to say: "Don't let this splashing bring out Your warrior's mood!" By the words "in whatever way He wished," Śuka tells us that the Lord made love even forcibly, by violence. They also imply that, even then, His delight of love was in Himself alone. But He made fully His own the game of the bull-elephant.[23] The example of the elephant tells us that to the exact extent there was splashing with water, there was happiness, and great sexual pleasure as well.

Introduction to Stanza 25 : Śuka now tells us how, after this, Kṛṣṇa played the flower-gathering game:

Stanza 25 : After this, the Lord, surrounded by the swarms of love-crazed Gopīs and bees—just like a tusker, his rut-fluid streaming, with his female elephants—went into the little grove on the black Yamunā, a grove swept pleasantly in all its shady reaches by the breeze which bore the fragrance of the blossoms of land and water.

Commentary : Immediately after the water-game, the Lord went once again into the little grove, on the black (Kṛṣṇā) Yamunā, whose reaches in every direction were swept pleasantly by the wind which carried the fragrances of the blossoms of land and water. And He was "surrounded by the swarms of love-crazed Gopīs and bees." Once again Śuka has given us an example to account for the movement of the bees: "just like a tusker, his rut-fluid

23. These last three sentences explain the range of meanings Vallabha sees in Śuka's use of the word *svayam*, to cover most of which meanings I have translated by "in whatever way He wished," since the game of the bull-elephant forms the context for this usage.

streaming"—i.e., his temple-juice flowing over his cheeks and elsewhere. The "tusker," i.e., the elephant, is accompanied by his cow-elephants, and by bees as well. The pursuit of the bees shows us that the fluid which normally remains inside the elephant has come out. And by the words "went into" Śuka has told us that the Lord played a number of different games everywhere in this grove. In one place He ripped up the creepers, and in another He tore branches off trees. In the same way, He broke the laws of both the Path of Limitations and worldly conduct by acting contrary to them. This threefold game is (therefore) entirely transcendent and extraordinary. And after this, He made love indiscriminately (OR:"Therefore He made love without thinking (of such laws)").

Introduction to Stanza 26 : After thus describing the game, Śuka now sums up:

Stanza 26 : And so the Lord, accompanied by this flock of women so fond of Him and so truthful and fulfilled in their desires, and confining His seed firmly within Himself, passed joyfully all these brightened-by-moonbeam nights, whose tales are told in the poetry of autumn and which are the refuge of the mood of the season.

Commnetary : The Lord thus enjoyed the delights of love of "these nights," which were "brightened by moonbeams"—the ordinary rays of the moon (cf. Stanza 19 and Commentary above). And during all these times the form of His game was the same as the form described above. This is contradicted by no one and nothing at all. If someone asks what was the reason for such love-making, Śuka answers : "accompanied by (this flock of women) so truthful and fulfilled in their desires." Those women whose desire is true are "truthful and fulfilled in their desires." And since the Lord was together with them, Śuka says He was "accompanied by (this flock of women) so truthful and fulfilled in their desires." Or, the word *sa* ("accompanied by") may alternatively be interpreted to mean: "He", "whose desires are true and fulfilled," had been prayed to by them for this favor.[24] So,

24. The text Vallabha follows, and the printed version I have of it (i.e., the text in Telivala-Sankalia's edition of *Subodhinī*), reads *sasatyakāmo* for the stanza-phrase under discussion. The Gita Press and Nirnayasagara Press editions of the Bhāgavata, however, read *sa satyakāmo*, thus definitely

too, in the game, His desire (*kāma* = desire, lust, semen) remained entirely true, and was not meager or cheap, nor did it come to have the untrue and evil as its object. As Śuka says: "this flock of women, so fond of Him." There is no doubt about the propriety of the Lord's desire for the virgin Gopīs, who loved Him in every way (and whose love was legitimate since they had no husbands), or for those who were eternally bound to Him (like the Gopīs who stayed at home, or Lakṣmī), or for those women (in Dvārakā) who were later married to Him. And as far as the married Gopīs are concerned, they had surrendered to Him in Total Love. And the breaking of the laws which later occurs is done in order to strengthen the mood of love. As has been said: "The scope of the treatises extends only to the point where people are slowly approaching the mood. But once the circle of love has been set in motion there is no place for treatises nor for order" (probably *Kāmasūtra*). And so it is only the desire (*kāma* = semen) that is true that the Lord has established in the Gopīs. This is the *kāma* that culminates in ultimate freedom. This *kāma* will surely attain the Blessed Lord. And so, "He passed these nights joyfully." Immediately after this, "He kept His seed confined within Himself alone." But He did not establish (the seed of) His love in them, for had He done so, they would have children by Him. Thus were all these nights passed, and the autumn, too, was passed. And the "stories told in poetry", too, came to pass. For He made love in the way described in poetry, and after the fashion narrated in the *Gītagovinda*, too. Śuka tells us the reason for this when he says that these nights "are the refuge of the mood of the season." The mood of passionate love, as is well known, belongs pre-eminently to these autumn nights. Insofar as a person does not subordinate himself to the dominant mood, to that extent he lacks aesthetic taste. Or perhaps Śuka's words mean that these nights find their refuge in the mood of the tales which appear in poetry which is describing autumn. These nights are not well known to the world; rather they are described only in poetry. For in poetry there is an absence of restrictions and obligations and the like—there is a singleness of delight, and no dependence on anything else; and

favoring the alternative explanation Vallabha gives here. I, too, am inclined to favor the latter reading.

other, like qualities as well. Just like this, Śuka means to tell us, were these nights of the Blessed Lord's Games.

Introduction to Stanza 27 : After hearing this game described in these terms, a doubt arose in king Parikṣit's mind. He anxiously expresses his doubt, in order to have it removed, in the following three stanzas:

Stanza 27 : The King said: "But surely it was to establish firmly what is right, and to destroy what is opposed to it, that the Blessed Lord, the Lord of the universe, descended to earth along with a part of Himself."

Commentary : What Kṛṣṇa has done is in direct contradiction to His descent to earth, to the laws of the world and the Vedas, and to Himself as Lord. The cause for such action must certainly be explained. For He could have, and has, accomplished His Game fully even in the absence of this game. King Parikṣit first explains the contradiction between Kṛṣṇa's conduct and His descent to earth. The Blessed Lord has come down to earth in order to establish firmly what is right. This we know from His own words in the *Bhagavadgītā*: "and for the firm establishment of what is right" (IV. 8), as well as the removal of what is evil. The Blessed Lord's descent to earth was for these two purposes alone. His killing of demons and so forth, and His relieving Earth of her burden, were both for the purpose of removing evil. When the king uses the words: "But surely," he means that Kṛṣṇa's descent to earth was for this purpose alone, and for no other. "The Blessed Lord" (one of whose six great "blessings"—*bhaga*—is "Right"—*dharma*) is the means for accomplishing this. Otherwise how could it possibly be that He whose desires are completely fulfilled would ever descend to earth? And help comes to the world by means of these two purposes of His descent alone.

"Along with a part of Himself" means along with Balabhadra (Kṛṣṇa's brother Balarāma). Having come to earth, His reason for so doing (i.e., for bringing Balabhadra) is that He is "the Lord of the universe." For He (Balabhadra) is the Protector of all. And so Kṛṣṇa acted in this way in order to protect the world.

Introduction to Stanza 28 : Parikṣit continues in the next stanza, as if he were asking : "What of all this, then, if things were the way I have described them?"

Stanza 28 : "Why has He who is the Builder, Commander and Watchman of the dams of righteousness gone against the current, O brahman, by violating other mens' wives?"[25]

Commentary : He is the Builder of what protects the laws of right conduct. And He Himself is the "Commander" or "Teacher" (Skt. *vaktṛ*). And He is the "Watchman," the "Protector" of them against damage. Yet, being all this, He has gone "against the current"—He has acted contrary to them. What is right has been destroyed, and what is evil has been established. Evil has been done, spoken and protected. Therefore this going against the current is wrong. The king addresses Śuka by the name "brahman" to indicate that Śuka must explain the reason for this. The king points out in a single phrase the essence of the five things he has mentioned (i.e., the destruction of right, the establishment of evil, and the doing of, speaking, and protection of evil) when he says: "by violating other mens' wives."

Introduction to Stanza 29 : And to forestall the objection that the Lord might have acted out of passionate desire, Parikṣit says:

Stanza 29 : "Even though His desires are completely fulfilled, the Lord of the Yadus did this reprehensible deed. To what end? Cut away this doubt of ours, O strict observer of vows!"

Commentary : He is the One by whom all desires are attained from within Himself alone. And since He is "Lord of the Yadus," even if there were such a desire He could have many women. Yet even though this was His situation He did "this reprehensible deed," the kind people condemn. What was His purpose in doing this? It is impossible to conceive these two things—His status and His deed—together, because the two facts are mutually contradictory. And there is no unity of contradictory things. And even though the Lord is the ground of all contradictory attributes (cf. Footnote 27 on Chapter VI, stanzas 22-23), His purpose here must be explained. This action did no good to the world at large,

25. I have chosen to try to reproduce the sustained metaphor which this Bhāgavata stanza is. Others, like Vasu, have chosen to substitute the things represented for the figures themselves, in which case the translation comes out something like: "Why has He who is the Creator, Teacher and Protector of the laws of what is right gone against them, O brahman, by violating other mens' wives?"

nor to Himself. For He is perfectly complete in Himself; and the law alone does good to the world, and thus to the Gopīs as well. And for the Lord who is the Inner Ruler, there is nothing that is not easy to accomplish. Therefore, since all this is true, "to what end" did He do this? What was His purpose? "Cut away this doubt of ours," i.e., of all of us. Besides, "O strict observer of vows," you observe vows whose very nature is right conduct. If this act were, as it were, improper, you would not have narrated it. Or if it were wrong, you would have simply no taste, or relish, for it. And it appears to be wrong, therefore you must explain it and its reasons fully. This is Parikṣit's meaning.

Introduction to Stanza 30 : Śuka answers first the first objection Parikṣit has made—that the Lord acted in a way contradictory to His descent to earth:

Stanza 30 : Śuka said: Violation of what is right as well as recklessness have been seen to mark the conduct of lords. But for the more brilliant no fault is involved in this, just as fire, though it consume everything, is not at fault.

Commentary : Śuka is, in effect, saying to the king: "Are you asking whether this conduct is not the conduct of lords (*īśvara*), or whether someone who has come in order to do one thing does another?" For it is not the case that a person who has come to effect something does not destroy something. Nor does someone who has come even to effect something else abandon his own rule of life. A lamp, for example, which is placed somewhere in order to give light, will still burn—cause a fire—if brought into contact with some part of the house. Therefore this is the rule of life of a lord. If it were not, he simply would not be a lord. For the law of a lord in all his actions is not like the law of businessmen. Śuka enumerates these rules of life, or ways of acting, of lords when he says: "violation of what is right as well as recklessness," and so forth. "Violation of what is right" is a transgression of an existing law, and "recklessness" is doing something about which no laws exist. And both these features have been seen in the conduct of the Lord. "For there is certainly nothing dubious in what has been seen," as the axiom says. The words "as well as" in the stanza indicate that these ways of acting have been seen in those who worship and serve the Lord as well, or in persons who possess heroic strength and so forth.

Or, this conduct may be called "recklessness" because the deed has been done rashly—without consideration. "But," someone questions, "if this is so, why would there not be a result of such a deed?" To this Śuka answers: "But for the more brilliant..." For the very brilliant such conduct does not produce evil (and its consequences), since the words of commandment and prohibition apply to those who need to be commanded. As this is true in the world, so is it true in the Veda as well. To illustrate the truth that this conduct does not produce fault in the very brilliant, who are able to burn up the evil consequences of all their acts, Śuka gives the following example: "Just as fire, though it consume everything, is not at fault." For even were it to consume all people, fire would not be guilty of murder. It eats up everything, or it eats what should not be eaten. Likewise, drinking up everything, penetrating everywhere, and becoming connected with everything, it does first one such thing and then another. When planted in the ground that is the Self and sprinkled with the water of false knowledge, the seed of actions begins to sprout good and evil conduct. But this is not so in salty ground whose water has been dried up by the fiery heat of true Knowledge!

Introduction to Stanza 31 : If the king wonders how this particular deed can be done, basing his objection on the saying: "For even among the brilliant this deed is not praiseworthy," and on the contradiction between such conduct and the saying: "By imitating the deeds of whom (i.e., the brilliant) the ordinary people attain prosperity,"[26] Śuka's answer is as follows:

Stanza 31 : For one who is not a lord should never perform such a deed even in his mind. One who does such a thing out of stupidity is destroyed, just as anyone but Rudra would have been destroyed by drinking the poison churned up from the milky ocean.

Commentary : What has been done by the Lord here should not be done by one who is not a lord. As long, and only so long, as it rests on the support of lordly power, this deed will not result in anything undesirable. Therefore, "never", i.e., at no time, should someone act this way, even out of intense longing. In fact—

26. Both the sayings quoted here come from Bh. P. III. 12. 31, the context of which stanza is very apposite to the topic treated here.

why waste words?—he should not act this way "even in his mind." But for lords, this deed is equal to (i.e., it falls within the scope of) their lordly power. Just as, for someone who is not a lord, even to desire lordly power merits death, and for someone who is ineligible for a great kingdom to desire such a kingdom merits death, so a person should not perform such a deed even in his mind. Śuka points out the annulling factor inherent in wrong conduct when he says: "one who does such a thing. . is destroyed." A person who "out of stupidity" does not realize the necessary concomitance of this deed with lordly power and does just this one deed, is destroyed by that single deed. Someone may object: "But how can one and the same deed be non-destructive relative to one person's inner attribute (i.e., lordly power) and conduct, and destructive relative to another's ?" Śuka answers this in the clause that begins: "just as anyone but Rudra. ."[27] Someone different from Rudra, i.e., someone who does not possess strength and valor equal to Rudra's, but nonetheless consumes entirely the Kālakūṭa poison which came from the ocean of milk, is destroyed. This reprehensible deed, too, is just as destructive as the Kālakūṭa poison. Such an act confers splendor on no one but a lord, for by this act Rudra became Nīlakaṇṭha, the Blue-throated One. In precisely the same way here, Kṛṣṇa became Gopījanavallabha, the Beloved of the Gopīs!

Introduction to Stanza 32 : Śuka now answers the objection king Parikṣit had raised along the lines of the quotation: "by imitating the deeds of whom the ordinary people attain prosperity":

Stanza 32: The speech of lords is true; their conduct is likewise true—sometimes. An intelligent man will model his conduct after what the lords themselves say, which is true and right.

Commentary : Only the speech of lords is true—not their conduct. Sometimes their conduct also is true—when it corresponds to what they say. There are many different rules of life for

27. Vallabha here reads, in his commentary, *yathā arudro*, "just as anyone but Rudra," while all three of my printed texts of the Bhāgavata—even the one printed with Vallabha's Subodhinī!—read *yathā rudro*. It is the equal-chance option we have seen so many times before—that of splitting the Sanskrit into *yathā arudro* or *yathā rudro*. But since, here, either reading has to mean what Vallabha says, Vallabha's reading makes more sense.

lords. Just as they may conduct themselves in accordance with their lordly power, so they may be the very Self of what is right, or they may base their conduct on compassion. In this context, what a lord does by means of lordly power, knowledge and detachment, that is called spontaneous or free conduct. "The intelligent man" should not imitate that kind of conduct. Surely lords do not preach something other than what is right. For when they speak, it is for the sake of others, and they speak according to the other's level of eligibility. Therefore they do not preach anything contradictory to the right behavior of those who listen to them.

Introduction to Stanza 33 : To the objection: "As they do not preach such conduct to others, why do they not refrain from practising it themselves?", Śuka answers in the following stanza :

Stanza 33 : For those who are free of the notion of "I", O lord, there is no profit to be gained by right conduct in this world, nor does any loss result from wrong conduct.

Commentary : For these lords, there is no "profit," i.e., no purpose or motive, for "right conduct," because all one obtains from such conduct are the endless results of one's actions. "Neither does any loss result" from its opposite—"wrong conduct." And to point out to us that it is not only lords who are free from the undesirable results of forbidden acts, but the sages as well, since knowledge and detachment share the same nature as lordly power, Śuka says: "For those who are free of the notion of 'I'." For them, nothing at all is done by anyone, for they are free of the proud, false notion that they are agents. And Śuka addresses Parikṣit as "lord" to indicate that the king, as a lord, is different from ordinary people.

Introduction to Stanza 34 : In order to explain that when an action done with knowledge alone causes no undesirable results, what must be said of an action that is done with Lordly Power?, Śuka gives the following stanza:

Stanza 34 : How much less, then, can there be any connection of the Lord of all beings—animal, human and divine as well—with the good and evil results of the deeds of those whom He rules over?

Commentary : No one can doubt a lord's right to beat a servant or to act otherwise toward his servants (e.g., by changing them to other places: Vasu). And as it is in this world, so is it in the higher world. Doubt arises only concerning the ruler and the extent of his realm. But there is no other Ruler except the Blessed Lord, as Śuka points out when he says: "of all beings," i.e., of all things which have a soul. Kṛṣṇa is the Lord and Ruler of all beings—"animal, human and divine as well"—of all living as well as insentient things which are effects of the three constituent qualities of worldly existence and of all beings who are not made of these three qualities. The words "as well" refer to the fact that Kṛṣṇa is Lord of the Self, too. And the Lord, precisely as Lord, is related with servants—"those whom He rules over." "How can there be any connection" of Him "with the good and evil results" caused by the virtuous and evil acts which they perform? For no wrong deed is possible, in this world or in the next, to the Lord whom no one rules over, in His relation with His maidservants, who have become His very Self. That this is realized only by the devotees who have penetrated the inner depths does not detract from the praiseworthiness of the Lord's conduct.

Introduction to Stanza 35 : Nor should a fault be suspected in the Lord's conduct here even by one who is convinced of the preponderant importance of actions, according to the thinking of the Path of Action. Such a person might argue that just as excellence stems from right knowledge and actions, as in scriptural passages such as "this sacrifice belonged to Parameṣṭhī (Brahmā) in the beginning," and "in the beginning this universe was surely Brahman" (*B.Ā. Up.* I.4.10 and 11), and "he understood the Self indeed" (variant of *B.Ā. Up.* I.4.10), so too can decline stem from wrong knowledge and actions. Śuka now answers this objection:

Stanza 35 : Those who delight in worshipping the dust of His lotus-feet; those who have the bonds of all their actions burst asunder by the superhuman powers of Yoga; and the sages as well; they all move as they wish and none of them are bound by their actions. How, then, will a mere form that He has assumed by His own Wish be bound by its actions?

Commentary : Not all persons who perform the same action obtain the same result. For if this were so, it would follow that the treatises on these matters are useless. A person who is originally engaged in excellent actions does not fall because of an occasional wrong action. In this context there are three paths, and a person following one of these three paths does not suffer a fall, according to Śuka's words here. The first of these is the person who has set out on the Path of Devotion, and is strong and thriving (Skt. *puṣṭa*) in the practice of devotion. According to Śuka, this person does not suffer a fall by reason of any action. These are the people who "delight in worshipping" those outstanding devotees of the Lord who are "the dust of His," i.e., the Blessed Lord's, "lotus feet." Merely by remembering the Blessed Lord's great qualities in the company of the Blessed Lord's devotees, these persons forget completely the little specks of apparent happiness they had formerly seen and heard, and "they move as they wish." For them the goodness or evil of an action is neither a help nor a hindrance.

Śuka tells us that the same is true on the Path of Action when he says: "those who have all the bonds of their actions broken by the superhuman power of Yoga." For Yoga is a great and powerful mode of conduct (*dharma*), as scripture tells us when it says: "For this is the highest mode of conduct." Its "superhuman powers" are the perfection of the lordly power of becoming as small as an atom and so forth. These include the perfection of knowledge and so forth as well. By these powers "the bonds of all their actions," including the bonds resulting from their previous actions, are "burst asunder." And these persons, too, "move as they wish."

Śuka refers to the Path of Knowledge, too, by saying, "and the wise as well...move as they wish." And "none of them" at all "are bound." These persons are free from the bonds of their actions—indeed from all associations— everywhere and in everything. Śuka then poses to himself the question: "Since this condition prevails on the Paths which the Blessed Lord founded, then what must we say of the Blessed Lord Himself?" And he answers it by saying: "How, then, will a mere form that He has assumed by His own Wish be bound by its actions?" By His own Wish, for the sake of enjoyment, the Lord had assumed as many forms "as there were cowherd-women" (Stanza 20 above). How, indeed, could any bond of action affect such a form? For once He had produced their effect, He who assumed these forms once again concealed them. So what action of His could result in a bond?

For it is an established fact that each action is particular to its own agent. If there were a question here of particular, individual souls, then a bond would indeed result from each action. For, like space itself, the forms of the Blessed Lord are different and particular to each place in which they occur. Just as the body functions as a single unit despite the different foods which go to make it up, so the Blessed Lord, limiting Himself in accordance with His own Wish, becomes manifest in one place despite the differences of place involved in His having hands, feet, and so forth, on all sides (i.e., in short, His all-pervasiveness). Or, this may refer to the forms of the Svāminīs (Gopīs).[28] And so, in no way is a bond resulting from action possible here, neither by thinking in terms of the means of knowledge (*pramāṇa*; scripture) nor by considering the Object of knowledge (*prameya*; Kṛṣṇa).

Introduction to Stanza 36 : "Nevertheless," says an objector, "a bond would result from this action simply because the law of worldly conduct has been broken, if we think in terms of the intended thrust of Kṛṣṇa's words in the maxim: 'Whatever the best of men does...the world at large imitates' (*Bh. Gītā* III. 21). For the three types of persons mentioned in the last stanza are perfected souls who have renounced the world entirely, not rulers of the daily affairs of this world. So your example compares dissimilar things." To this Śuka replies:

Stanza 36 : The One who moves within the Gopīs and their husbands and all embodied souls, He is the Ruler who assumes a body here in sport—to play His game.

Commentary : Surely it is nowhere forbidden for a person to touch what belongs to him. And neither of the interpretations, "this woman is another (different from Me)" or "this woman belongs to another (man)" is applicable to the Blessed Lord.[29]

28. Svāminī, "lady" in the sense of wife of a lord, or "lord-ess" in her own right, a term used to refer to the Gopīs only occasionally by Vallabha but very frequently by Viṭṭhala and the subsequent authors, seems to be used here precisely to emphasize the lordliness, and, probably, the divinity of the Gopīs, and the fact that they too, have descended to earth with Kṛṣṇa. Consequently, of course, their forms are not bound by action and its results.

29. Vallabha is explaining, in this sentence, the two possible ways of breaking the Skt. compound *parastrī*, which almost certainly is meant to refer back to the compound *paradārā*, "other mens' wives," used by Parikṣit in

For the Blessed Lord is the Self of both "the Gopīs and their husbands." Someone might object that the Gopīs' relatives and all worldly people would not think this way. So Śuka has added that the Lord is the Self of "all embodied souls" as well. The Blessed Lord is "the One who moves within." Or, "the one who moves within" may refer to the soul in the form of the mouth's life-breath (*āsanyo jīvaḥ*; cf. *Bṛ. Āraṇ. Upan.* I. 3. 7). To sum up the doctrines of all the philosophers, Śuka expresses himself in the general phrase: "The One who moves within." He alone—this Blessed Lord who is "the Ruler"—made Himself visibly present "in sport—to play His game," and, like an actor, "He assumes a body" of a man. In reality He is neither a man, nor a woman, nor anything else. For, as holy scripture says: "He is neither a woman nor a eunuch nor a man." Therefore according to no line of thinking at all is fault possible for Him.

Introduction to Stanza 37 : The objector (Parikṣit) may continue: "Well even so, what was His purpose in acting this way?" Śuka replies:

Stanza 37 : To give Grace to His devotees, Kṛṣṇa has resorted to a human body, and He takes part in these kinds of games. Having heard these games a person becomes completely intent on Him.

Commentary : Solely for the sake of giving Grace to His devotees, Kṛṣṇa assumed a body which had the same form as those of His devotees. Had His been different from theirs, He would not have gained their trust. And so, just as He manifested Himself in a human body to give Grace to humans, so, to give Grace to the Gopīs as well, "He takes part in these kinds of games," to confer His very own Joy on Gokula. For without the entry of each and every one of His attributes into His devotees, each and every one of their faults would not have been removed. Or, alternatively: He assumed a human body and played these games because respect and trust toward the human bodies of His devotees

Stanza 28, in voicing his doubts about Kṛṣṇa's conduct. Vallabha says that, no matter how you break the compound, it cannot apply to the Blessed Lord, for the reasons which he, following Śuka, will now explain.

had arisen in Him.[30] In addition, the Great One whose desires are totally fulfilled is able to give everything—but not thus to give His very Self in a manner forbidden. Therefore, whoever hears this game, which embodies the giving of what is not to be given and must be preceded by constraint in Him, that person becomes "completely intent"—in every way—on the Blessed Lord. That is why the Blessed Lord conducted Himself in this way. Śuka has expressed this in the words: "Having heard these games a person becomes completely intent on Him."

Introduction to Stanza 38 : But someone may raise the question that, since according to the laws of the world women are dependent on others, the Lord's act of taking to Himself unmarried girls and women not given to Him in marriage would arouse great distress in the minds of the cowherds of Vraja and result in their condemning the Lord's actions. Śuka removes this doubt in the following stanza.

Stanza 38 : It is certain that the men of Vraja did not envy or condemn Kṛṣṇa—dazed and deluded by His Māyā, each and every one of them thought that his wife was staying right at his side.

Commentary : These men did not envy the Blessed Lord, i.e., they did not look upon Him with jealousy. Even though they knew, at the beginning, what was happening, yet when they were "deluded by the Blessed Lord's Māyā, they did not condemn Him." On the contrary, later "they thought their wives had remained right at their sides," for they were "men of Vraja," who do not investigate what happens before and what after. Or, the phrase "men of Vraja" may mean that they fully accepted these actions of Kṛṣṇa. Śuka's meaning in any case is that it is impossible for such men to impute fault to the Lord. Śuka says: "it is certain" because this matter is known to all. Also in the Blessed Lord's presence, along with the Gopīs, was "His Māyā," for the sake of causing delusion. It was merely a perception of the men of Vraja that constituted their misapprehension. Everything

30. If this alternative explanation were accepted, the stanza would translate roughly as follows: "Having placed His trust in the human body of His devotees, for the sake of granting them Grace, Kṛṣṇa takes part in these kinds of games, having heard which a person becomes completely intent on Him."

else of theirs belonged to the Blessed Lord alone. By (their) mere thinking alone there is exclusion of all faults (here). And by the same process the imputation of fault to the Gopīs, too, is prevented.

Introduction to Stanza 39 : After thus clearing away all the doubts and questions which arose in connection with the game he had described, Śuka sums up by describing the game's ending :

Stanza 39 : When the early moments of dawn came, and Vāsudeva gave them leave—for they did not want to—the Gopīs went to their homes, loving the Blessed Lord and loved by Him.

Commentary : "The early moments of dawn" refers to the rising of the dawn's light. And Śuka says "when (these moments) came," meaning "when they had fully arrived." The Blessed Lord then entered within the Gopīs in His aspect of Inner Controller and produced in them the desire to return to their homes. Then they were allowed to depart by the Blessed Lord. The Blessed Lord does this because He is the Giver of ultimate freedom. "Vāsudeva gave the Gopīs leave to go home" because He considered the fact that, if the Gopīs practice interior recollection of Him until twilight, then they will become eligible for ultimate freedom. Although no desire to go home is present in them, since they have just worshipped the Blessed Lord through love by completely abandoning all things, and might say "What have I to do with a home, or with people?", still they are "the Gopīs"—their minds are neither contrary nor stubborn. Nonetheless, they did not love their homes, but "loved the Blessed Lord" alone. Nor did they fear Saṁsāra, because they were "loved by the Blessed Lord."

Introduction to Stanza 40: In the next stanza, Śuka describes the reward for hearing the acount of this episode, in order to indicate that this conduct of Kṛṣṇa's had as its purpose ultimate freedom:

Stanza 40 : The person who, endowed with faith, hears repeatedly and then recounts this special game of Viṣṇu with the brides of Vraja, first attains supreme Devotion to the Blessed Lord, then swiftly throws off passion—that disease of the heart—and becomes, in no long time, a person of constancy.

Commentary : Śuka is referring to a person who, having become "endowed with faith," would listen to a well-told narration of "this special game of the Blessed Lord with the brides of Vraja." Or he would "recount" the story to others. For Śuka's words, "and then", refer to the first two steps of devoton: "hearing" the story of the Lord, and its immediate consequence, "glorifying" Him by telling the story to others. And Śuka's words, "the person who," mean that there is no restriction according to class, etc. (e.g., caste, sex, stage of life), in this matter—anyone at all can do this. Thus the Blessed Lord grants ultimate freedom because a person has heard the Greatness of the Blessed Lord described. And from hearing every aspect of the deeds and knowledge of the devotees, too, he "attains supreme Devotion to the Blessed Lord." After this, by means of the Devotion that has grown strong within him, "he very quickly throws off passion," which had constituted a "disease of the heart." The passion which is situated as an obstacle in the heart in the first place, very quickly creates an obstacle to devotion, too, but the devotee quickly drives it far away merely by hearing the story of the Lord. After this, even if the person is beset by a recurrence of his previous tendencies, he "becomes, in no long time, a person of constancy." Therefore this episode, together with its purpose, must be listened to resolutely. And, since the reward constitutes the subject-matter here (in this chapter especially), the reward has been explained.

CHAPTER VI

(Bhāgavata Purāṇa Book X, Chapter 35)

Four Verses : *Verse* I : In this thirty-second chapter we hear described how the Blessed Lord Hari filled the Gopīs, interiorly, with His own Joy. Because of this alone is He called "the One whose Joy is Full" (i.e., because He filled the Gopīs full with His own Joy).[1]

Verse II : The Blessed Lord had entered within the Gopīs. And now, after they have drawn Him out again through their mouths, He enters within them oncc more, fully and perfectly, through their ears. Then is He firmly, forever established in them.

Verse III : Both word and meaning have dominant importance in this chapter; this is why the stanzas come here in mutually related pairs which together form a single sentence. And what Kṛṣṇa does through all the months of the year is the matter that is expressed here.

Verse IV : And so, there is one pair of stanzas for each month here (making 24 stanzas), plus an introductory stanza, and a final one concerning the reward. And—taking the first and last stanzas as an additional pair—we come up with a total of thirteen pairs in the chapter.

Introduction to Stanza 1 : Having thus described the game the Gopīs played with the Blessed Lord at night, Śuka eliminates

1. The major point of this Verse is that Hari, in this chapter, fills the Gopīs *interiorly* with His Joy—having already filled them exteriorly in the preceding chapters. But the reason behind my translation and parenthesized clarification of the second sentence—both done at Shri Shyam Goswamy's instigation—is that it is not the Gopīs' very own Joy-aspect (*ānandāṁśa*) which becomes full here. This occurs only later, after the Gopīs have gone through all the required means. What happens here, rather is that Kṛṣṇa fills them full with *His own* Joy, thus giving them a thorough foretaste of the Reward which they will experience permanently later.

the suspicion that they will merely set the wheel of Saṁsāra turning again during the day by telling us that they became totally preoccupied in these days with describing the Blessed Lord's great qualities. And, describing for us how sorrow, at the beginning, was the factor necessitating their singing of His great qualities, Śuka also explains how, at the end, joy had become the factor. Now at the beginning, and when they first set these songs in motion, the worst sort of sorrow and suffering pervaded the Gopīs' days. This is what Śuka describes for us in the first stanza :

Stanza 1 : Śuka said : When Kṛṣṇa had gone off to the forest, the Gopīs' minds and hearts ran off after Him. By singing very intimately, then, of Kṛṣṇa's Games, they passed their days in sorrow.

Commentary : The fact that only "the Gopīs" are mentioned here means we should understand that no other women are intended here but the ones who took part in Kṛṣṇa's love-games.[2] When He who is Eternal Joy "had gone off to the forest... their minds ran off after Him" alone. Their minds could not bear the idea of grasping anything else. The word "ran off", or "flowed", expresses their dissolution or absorption in Him. Because of that, their minds, having attained a very subtle form of existence, flowed forth, or spread around from all sides, and thus grasped the Game of Him who is Eternal Joy. Therefore they began "singing very intimately of Kṛṣṇa's Games." Just as Kṛṣṇa's Form embodies Eternal Joy, so do His Games. And it is in order to indicate that these Games have Eternal Joy as their very Self that Śuka uses Kṛṣṇa's name a second time in the stanza. Otherwise he would merely have used the word "His." And had he done that, Kṛṣṇa's Games would achieve no more than association with Him, rather than being an embodiment of Eternal Joy. And it was necessary that this be said, because in a person's separation from Kṛṣṇa Himself there is nothing apart from Him that can cause a person to go on living, because everything else is totally inferior to Him. Because to

2. I am indebted to Vasu for the key insight in interpreting this passage. Vallabha's Sanskrit reads: *kevalapadāt pūrvoktā grāhyāḥ*. This would normally be an explanation of an occurrence of the word *kevala* ("merely, only"), which doesn't occur anywhere near this context!

this, with great mental agony "they" somehow or other "passed their days." But when once more the Gopīs' minds are absorbed in accounts of many various deeds of the Blessed Lord, and thus achieve a real oneness, then will their desires be fulfilled. "Now every object connected with Him is shattered and scattered about," say the Gopīs, as they pass their days "in sorrow." And when Śuka uses the word "days'" we should note that the Gopīs are holding their breath, somehow, for the sake of the night.

Verse 1 : Hari's most excellent Game is the one which is preceded by His playing the flute. In all these following pairs of stanzas, the cause which gives rise to the meaning which is to be expressed is described in the first stanza.

Verses 2-3 : The wives of the gods, and the cows as well; the rivers, the trees and the creepers; the winged creatures, and the clouds, too; Brahmā and his kind, and the Gopīs as well; the does of the forest, the gods and the Gandharvas; and the Blessed Lord Hari Himself (i.e., in the last two pairs of stanzas in the chapter), are described in the second of the pairs' stanzas as true connoisseurs of the beauty of His flute-playing.

Verse 4 : But the Blessed Lord alone is the real connoisseur. Hari Himself is the only one who truly appreciates. Therefore at the end (i.e., in the last two pairs of stanzas) the Blessed Lord has been twice described as preoccupied with those who are preoccupied with nothing but Him.

Verses 5-6½ : The brilliant power of His flute's sound is first described as it affects three types of feminine creatures (i.e., the gods' wives in the stanza-pair 2-3; the cows in 4-5; and the rivers in 6-7); and next, as it affects types of male (the trees in 8-9; the birds in 10-11; and the clouds in 12-13). Likewise Brahmā and his peers (14-15), the Gopīs (16-17), and the does (18-19). These three groups have been described as threefold (on the basis of the three qualities). But all the gods who appear, scattered throughout these stanzas (e.g., 20-21 as well as 2-3 and others), are not to be classified in these threefold three groups. For all, even those who cannot recognize the beauty of His playing, are united by the majestic power of the thing. Thus in this chapter the flute has been described as conferring its reward in twelve ways.

Introduction to Stanzas 2-3 : The women predominate at first among the connoisseurs to be described in this chapter, and chief among them are the gods' wives. And so, in order to express the powerful effect of Kṛṣṇa's flute-playing upon them, the Gopīs describe the way in which the song of His flute arises.

Stanzas 2-3 : The Gopīs said : "When. O Gopīs, Mukunda (Kṛṣṇa), resting His left cheek on His left shoulder, sets His flute upon His lower lip, His eyebrows dancing, and makes it burst into sound, His delicate fingers lazily fol owing or resting on the path of its holes, then the women who course the sky in their heavenly chariots along with the Siddhas, awestruck upon hearing His playing, became a bit ashamed; their minds became dedicated entirely to seeking Kāma, and they fainted, totally oblivious of their waistcloth's knot's undoing" (OR : "become", "become", and "faint": perfect verb-forms in present sense).

Commentary : The connection between the two stanzas is as follows : "When Mukunda...sets His flute upon His lower lip...and makes it burst into sound...then"—at that moment—" the women who course the sky in their heavenly chariots... fainted." The sound of Kṛṣṇa's flute is of five kinds, depending on whether He holds His face to one or the other side, or straight, or pointed upwards or down. The first of these—when He turns His face away to the left—awakens passion (*kāma*) in women. And when He holds it to the right, this awakens passion in both men and women. When upwards—the gods; when downwards, the beasts and birds; and when straight, all the insentient beings as well. In this context His turning His face to the left awakens passion in the women who are the wives of the gods. And thus is it described in the stanzas. A doubt may well be expressed that, since existence as a god is greater than existence as a human being, these wives of the gods will not be stunned and distracted by a merely human sound. But we have the saying : "The bend of His brow is the seat of Brahmā" (Bh. P. II. 1. 30). And He has here joined the graceful play of His eyebrows with the song of His flute, as the Gopīs have told us. "Resting His left cheek on His left shoulder...His eyebrows dancing." The eyebrow involved here is the right eyebrow, for that is precisely the way this is done in the theatre. "Dancing" means He was raising His eyebrows. The "lower lip" has been described earlier as something which has greed as its essence (cf. Bh. P. II. 1. 32). If the flute is set to rest completely on that lip (i.e,, on greed), it does not confer Supreme Joy; rather it awakens mere passion. Therefore, upon hearing its song these women would attain only the pain that comes from separation, and not Supreme Joy. But if the Blessed Lord's Power of Action were to become strong even when resting on greed, then the Reward could be attained even from a greedy flute. But this, too, is not the case here, say the Gopīs. For "His delicate fingers (are) lazily following or resting upon the path of its (the flute's) holes." Because it is proper that the flute should be played within the notes of the low scale at the beginning. The flute's "paths" are its holes. When the holes are stopped tightly by the fingers, a high note results; when the pressure is medium, a note in the central scale; and when "delicate" or soft, a low note results.

The form of direct address : "O Gopīs", is used to convey that this flute-playing is an experience witnessed by all of them. The Gopīs have expressed the purpose here by calling Him "Mukunda." For Mukunda says to Himself : "If the world is purified by the sound of My flute, I will grant it ultimate freedom." Since He thus played the flute for the good of the world, those persons who were not eligible for ultimate liberation experienced only passion, as the Gopīs tell us when they say : "then the women who course the sky..." "Heavenly chariots" are the flying vehicles in which all who are born in the race of gods ride; and the gods' wives are called "the women who course the sky in their heavenly chariots." Because they are eligible by reason of their womanhood and their fitness to be enjoyed, they are ineligible for ultimate freedom. And they are moving "along with the Siddhas." These women have the powers to grant everything except the Blessed Lord. And they themselves are great virtuosos at singing. When they first heard the sound of His flute, they were "awestruck." After that, when they perceived it was He who was playing the flute, they "became a bit ashamed" at the slight overflow of passion they felt, saying to themselves : "Our husbands will come to know." And after that, in order to protect themselves against the raging flood of passion they felt, and fearing they would die of passion, "their minds became dedicated entirely to seeking Kāma." They acted in the same way as those timid creatures who offer themselves to their slayer even before the *coup de grâce*. And just after that, tormented by passion, "they fainted." The Gopīs tell us that this faint made them forget everything completely. Thus they were "totally oblivious of their waistcloth's knot's undoing." And, the Gopīs want to point out, if the sound of Mukunda's flute awakened such an overwhelming passion in these divine women, why should anyone be surprised if it makes us faint immediately ?

Introduction to Stanzas 4-5 : The Gopīs now describe the rising sound of Kṛṣṇa's flute in another way, in order to tell us that the same thing happened to the cows, too, in reaction to the sound of His flute :

Stanzas 4-5 : "Alas, O helpless ones, listen to this wonder ! When Nanda's boy—with His smile like a pearl-necklace, and a stationary lightning-bolt on His chest—when this Giver of happiness to the afflicted ones makes His flute coo like a bird, the bulls of Braja, the beasts and cows by the herd, their minds stolen, even from far away, by His flute's playing, after just biting off clumps of grass, picking up their ears, they stood stock still, entranced as if asleep—as if painted in a picture" (OR : "they stand" : perfect form in present sense).

Commentary: "O helpless ones, listen to this wonder!" The connection between the stanzas is as follows : "when Nanda's boy makes His flute coo like a bird," then "the bulls and the cows...after just biting off clumps of grass...stood stock still, entranced as if asleep." Passion, among animals, is directed to one's own kind, not to something higher, nor something lower. But the mule has another condition entirely ! Also, the association, for the sake of lovemaking, of someone great with low persons is a pseudo-mood. Therefore, dismissing passion which is characterized by intercourse, Kṛṣṇa constrains the eating which is so completely vital to the animals. His previously described "resting of His left cheek on His left shoulder," and His other gestures, are continued here. But in that very context, the due specification of differences in gesture should be understood (i.e., as noted above, Kṛṣṇa turns His face downwards when playing the flute to the animals). The Gopīs say

"Alas!" in dejection. For here is "the wonder" : that for which even cows stop all activity, at that our activity does not cease ! These cows are more excellent even than the gods' wives. For the gods' wives, only naturally, were filled with passion for the the Supreme Person. But this behavior of the cows is amazing !

The Gopīs address each other as "helpless ones" in the light of their inability to go there and see Him. "Listen" to what I have to tell you. Here the Gopīs are of nine types. And further, there are three different kinds of transcendent Gopī, in accordance with Action, Knowledge, and Devotion. This categorization refers to the condition of only the speakers of each pair of stanzas. The first three pairs of stanzas are sung by *rājasa* Gopīs. (The first pair was sung by *sāttvika-rājasa* Gopīs). This pair is sung by *rājasa-rājasa* Gopīs. And every clarification that is needed anywhere in these stanzas follows from the clarifications made at the beginning. First of all, say the Gopīs, listen as I describe the Blessed Lord's Form. She describes Him in four ways. "His smile is like a pearl-necklace." "A stationary lightning-bolt is on His chest." He is "Nanda's boy." And He is "the Giver of happiness to all the afflicted." The cause for these things is to be found in the stanza's word "this" (in "this Giver of happiness"). Otherwise—if He were not "this" boy of Nanda's and "this" Giver of happiness—He would not become clearly present before us. Or perhaps the Gopī has said this after she saw Him going out to the forest in the second *muhūrta*.[3] In that case there are as many stanza-pairs in this chapter as there are *muhūrta-s* in the day. For we are told, in the treatise which reasons out the nature of the production of Soma, that there are twelve muhūrta-s between dawn and dusk. The smile or laughter of others shows teeth that are lined up as straight as a rope, and are a funny, mixed, off-color white. But the Blessed Lord's smile, or laugh (Skt. *hāsa*), is decorated, at intervals, by the beauty of His teeth, like a necklace of pearls. And these pearls are set in a row alternately with rubies. By this description the fact that His laugh is a cause of delusion in the Saṁsāra of the world is firmly established.[4] The basis everywhere in elucidating

3. A *muhūrta* is a period of forty-eight minutes.

4. Skt. *hāsa* may mean "laugh, laughter, or smile." In the present sentence the first basic idea is that Kṛṣṇa's "laugh" is a Māyā which drives

meaning (about God) is the clear implication of what is heard in the scriptures. And the clear implication of this passage and the earlier stanza (II.1. 31) is that: Māyā (His laugh) is divided at intervals by the parts of His love (His front teeth). Just as there is no doubt about something which has been seen, and we order everything simply in accordance with what has been seen, because we have the axiom : "There is certainly nothing dubious in what has been seen, for that would be contradictory," this is the way we ordinarily think in the world. We say that under no circumstances can something that is contradictory to what has been seen be accepted. In the same way, hearing is the rule of thumb for those who follow the Vedas. Insofar as a matter which is to be understood becomes clear through it, to that extent what is in accordance with what has been heard in scripture about any matter may validly be said.[5] Not only does His "smile/laugh" make firm one's passionate attachment to his children, his wife, and so forth in Saṁsāra, but it also strengthens his attachment to wealth. The stanza's words : "a stationary lightning-bolt on His chest" mean : "upon Whom Lakṣmī (Fortune, Wealth) is stationary." Thus the Gopī has said that the Lord, having done two things (i.e.. strengthened attachment to children, etc., and secondly, to wealth) in order to overcome the strength of the valid means of knowledge (*pramāṇa*, i.e., the scriptures), now has accomplished two others in order to overcome the strength of the Object of knowledge (*prameya*, i.e., the Blessed Lord). For "this one" (i.e., the Blessed Lord Himself) alone has become "Nanda's boy." And having come of His

people mad, i.e., deludes them; and the second idea is that Kṛṣṇa "laughs at" the deluded. These ideas are based on the Bh. P. stanza II. 1. 31, which says: "His molars (grinders) are Yama (the god of death), His front teeth are the parts of His love, and His laugh is a Māyā that drives people mad...." (*daṁṣṭrā yamaḥ snehakalā dvijāni, hāso janonmādakarī ca māyā*). In addition, the idea expressed in the succeeding sentences of the Commentary —that the Lord's "twice-born teeth," i.e., His front teeth, are "the parts of His love," is also obviously based on the same Bhāgavata-stanza. The assignment of different functions to different parts of the Lord's body does not always, according to Shri Shyam Goswamy, bear a clear logical relationship.

5. In other words, we can reason by implication from what we have heard in the scriptures.

own accord, He "gives happiness to the afflicted ones." And the proof of this is that this is exactly what we are seeing! For the high and mighty do not act in this way. And so this a "wonder". He "makes His flute coo like a bird" in order to communicate this idea alone.

Or, to explain it in another way: the flute is played with His face playfully pointed downwards, relative to His face's previous position. And then "His chest reflects the smile that is like a pearl-necklace."[6] That His smile is stationary on His chest, and that even the gaps in the smile are preserved there is another wonder. Kṛṣṇa's Śrīvatsa is also most excellent; and so its stability is described here in order to show His splendor. One's love grows stronger when such a one is Nanda's boy. Besides this, He helps us. "Making it coo" is a special way of playing the flute. This playing attracts to itself the inner functions and attributes of the life-breath of all. When this playing steals away the functions and attributes of the life-breath and so forth (i.e., mind, etc.) of even the beasts, what must we say about its effect on others? This is the question the Gopī raises as she describes the stealing of these things from the animals. For when such a thing happens to only one being, some other cause may be proved responsible. Therefore this Gopī has said : "by the herd," i.e., collectively. She means that wherever the sound of His flute penetrates, this happens to all who hear it. The "bulls of Braja (=Vraja)" are big-humped and full of wild frenzy. And even the bullocks who draw carts in Braja are as vigorous as the freeroaming bulls. And when she says that these bulls are in the vicinity of Braja alone, the word "Braja" signifies that she means to include all the other village animals, too. The "beasts" and "cows" mix together in herds in the forest. And so, when she uses the word "beasts," this is to signify that the forest animals are included as well as the village animals. But why multiply words ? Every single animal "has its mind stolen away" by the playing of His flute ! Nor are they even able to go near the place where the Blessed Lord is playing. Rather,

6. I.e., rather than taking the stanza's word *hārahāsa* (*urasi*) as nominative, it may be taken as locative modifying *urasi*, while still retaining its exact present form.

their minds are stolen "even from far away." This shows that this attribute is entirely natural to the sound of Kṛṣṇa's flute, and it is not brought about merely in the Blessed Lord's immediate vicinity.

And the "clumps of grass" have been "just bitten off"—the cows are able neither to throw them away, nor to chew them. And when this Gopī says that even the simple effort it takes to chew has been prevented, she shows that all other actions have been made all the more impossible. And the word "clumps" expresses the real necessity of what they were doing previously. And she says the animals "pick up their ears" lest they faint, as the gods' wives did. Having abandoned all other means, they "picked up their ears" as the only means to prevent their fainting.[7] She says : "entranced as if asleep" to show that they then turned away from the outside world completely. And then, they were pervaded completely by the sound. And after that again, they became like cows and so forth "painted in a picture." They became even stiller than the most immobile objects. And the use of the word *citra* ("painting") here for the second time in this stanza-pair (*citra* meant "wonder" above) shows that its present meaning, as "painting", surpasses its previously expressed meaning.

Introduction to Stanzas 6-7 : The Gopīs describe the sound of Kṛṣṇa's flute once again, in order to tell us how the sound of His flute caused an intense longing to arise even in the rivers, which are completely insentient :

Stanzas 6-7: "When Mukunda—occasionally, and in the company of Balarāma—decked out with clusters of peacock feathers and imitating the outfit of a wrestler—with Palāśa leaves tied round Him and painted with mineral dye—invites (with His flute) all the cows together with the cowherd boys, dear girlfriend, then even the rivers, the flow of their waters interrupted, long intensely for the dust of His lotus feet, wafted on

7. Vallabha's Sanskrit for the above sentence is: *anyat sarvam parityajya karṇameva sādhanaṁ dhṛtavantaḥ*. The above translation is Shri Shyam Goswamy's interpretation. My own is as follows: "Having abandoned everything else completely, they 'pick up,' i.e., they take up, the ear as their only means of attainment."

the wind; but they, like we, of little merit, the waves that are their arms trembling with love, stay still, their waters numbed."

Commentary : The introduction of Kṛṣṇa's flute-playing and its possession of the hearts of the Gopīs, as well as the external appearance of the God, have been described in the first two stanza-pairs.[8] And now the entry of His Games is described. For the action of rivers is incessant. But the cessation of action of sentient beings can be, and indeed has been, seen in their sleeping, fainting and so forth. But rivers simply never stop flowing. All the more in the case of great rivers (such as Yamunā). They cannot even be dammed up. But, even they have ceased to flow at the sound of Kṛṣṇa's flute. His "mineral dye" is, for instance, red chalk, or something of the sort. And Kṛṣṇa wore "leaves." Or, He painted His body with mineral dyes in the shape of leaves. And lotus-leaves are also tied round His head to provide the proper shape. And having done all this, the result was the "outfit," decoration, and outward appearance of a wrestler. So He, by tying on Himself these clusters and so forth which make up the outfit of a wrestler, was "imitating the outfit of a wrestler." Or rather, He tied on an imitation. For what is unnatural is nothing but a ridiculous imitation, like someone who is merely play-acting at wrestling. By this we know that this particular sound of His flute has been suggested by this Gopī to be useful only for His dancing with them (the Gopīs). Thus has His Power of Action been described as going forth from Him and dwelling in the sound of His flute, and this is the reason why the rivers are drawn to Him. When the word "occasionally" is used, it refers to the times when Kṛṣṇa has enthusiasm for using His Power of Action. That is why the Gopī then says : *sabala*, which means both "powerful" and "in the company of Balarāma."

When this Gopī addresses another Gopī as "dear girlfriend," she is saying that this following meaning is suggested as a secret, and she wants to assure her she is not deceiving her. For

8. Or, Vallabha's Sanskrit: *āveśo devaveśaśca pūrvaṁ nirūpitau* may with equal likelihood be interpreted: "The possession (of the cows, etc., by the sound of His flute), and the garments of the gods' wives have been described in the first two stanza-pairs."

the Gopī who is speaking probably went to see Kṛṣṇa at that time, under the pretext of bathing or something of the sort. When He has thus donned this outfit, He—who is either our Enjoyer by His very Nature, or has become our Enjoyer—is "together with the cowherd boys." By this she signifies that the Game of Vaikuṇṭha itself is being played here. Besides, Lakṣmī is present (with Him) together with us at night, and is present (with Him) together with the cowherd boys during the day. This is why this Gopī's words of direct address indicate a secret.

Then, "He invites the cows" with the sound of His flute, since the sound of His flute is the subject-matter of this entire chapter (although not specifically mentioned in the stanzas). Or, alternatively, He does not take up the flute, in order to call them with a sound that is equivalent to that of His flute. And the Gopī tells us the reason why He invites the cows when she says : "Mukunda." Having called them forth, He Himself bestows liberation on them because of their absence of means, saying : "For ultimate freedom should be given to these cows."[9] Or, to establish His own Joy in them (as an alternative to liberation). In the calling of the cows the idea has been expressed that once His Power of Action has gone forth, it performs a great work. And when the Gopī says "then," she means that the rivers, too, knowing the etymological meaning of the word *gāḥ* ("cows", but deriving from the root *GAM*, "to go"), and saying to themselves : "We go perpetually," stopped when they heard His invitation. At that very instant, "the flow of their waters (was) interrupted." For no one at all can transgress the Blessed Lord's command. And the word she uses for "rivers" (*saritaḥ*, from the root *SṚ* "to go, move") has captured perfectly the single reality of their nature—to flow. And their sole desire is to become Vaiṣṇava. For the ocean is their lord. But, as the Gopī says, they "long intensely for the dust of His lotus feet," so that the Blessed Lord may become their Husband. And the Gopīs, in saying "wafted on the wind," indicates the means by which they may be united with that dust.

9. The name Mukunda is given its etymological derivation here. The traditional etymology of the name is: *mukuṁ* (=*muktim*) *dadāti iti mukundaḥ* ("Mukunda means 'He who grants ultimate freedom'").

The wind has brought this dust for their sake. Thus are they related with this wind. And the wind needs water. But since only those who belong completely to the Blessed Lord attain union with the Blessed Lord, this longing for the dust of His feet has deep implications. But here the goal of these rivers is passion alone, since they are goddesses.[10] This is the reason why, later, Yamunā will become so (i.e., a wife of Kṛṣṇa; cf. Bh. P. X. 58. 22). But in their present state their luck does not extend so far, as the Gopī says in the words : "they ...of little merit." Their merit is not great, so they will not simultaneously attain the form of both cows (as they try become by obeying the Lord's invitation), and protectors of cows by day (which rivers are since they furnish water, grass, etc.), and women by night (since they desire the Lord as their Husband). For desired objects are not attained without merits. And the Gopī tells us how she came to know that this is the rivers' desire when she says : "like we." "They, like we, are of little merit." Otherwise we would become cows or cowherd boys during the day. Therefore they come to know by their own example that the rivers may long as intensely as they want, but their purpose is not fulfilled. Besides, this Gopī has described how, because of the rivers' *sāttvika* expressions as well, the constant emotion that is in their heart is indicated, when she says : "the waves that are their arms trembling with love."[11] Their waves are trembling out of love—not because of the wind. Therefore they seem to be suffering from the painful fires of separation. And besides, they show the stillness of pillars, too, as the Gopīs say in the words : "their waters numbed." Thus have the three

10. Here is the reasoning: these rivers desire *rajas*, "the dust (of the Lord's feet)" but as they are goddesses, and thus female, Vallabha's "deep implication" is that they desire *rajas*, which also means "semen," from Kṛṣṇa, and Kāma is the one who will fulfil that need.

11. Apte's dictionary quotes for us the eight "*sāttvika* expressions" (*sāttvika bhāva-s*) in poetry or drama. *stambhaḥ svedo 'tha romāñcaḥ svarabhaṅgą 'tha vepathuḥ| vaivarṇyam aśrupralaya ityaṣṭau sāttvikāḥ smṛtāḥ||*. Thus the eight expressions are: "standing still as a pillar; perspiring; thrilling of the hair; stuttering or cracking of the voice; trembling; going pale; weeping; and loss of consciousness." Of these the fifth, "trembling," is exemplified here. And in a few sentences the first will also be exemplified.

types of *rājasa* Gopī been described (the present stanza-pair having been spoken by *tāmasa-rājasa* Gopīs).

Introduction to Stanza 8-9 : In order to describe the different kinds of *sattva*, the Gopīs describe the Blessed Lord, too, in this way, in the next three stanza-pairs. The creepers, the birds and the clouds are all *sāttvika*. These become filled with Devotion by the sound of His flute. First among these three we hear about the Vṛndāvana forest's creepers and trees, which are Vaiṣṇava. The sap (and mood : *rasa*) of love rise in them by reason of the sound of His flute. In order to describe this the Gopīs have spoken of His flute's sound in a different manner. And for the sake of that, the Blessed Lord, too, must be described in a different manner. And He must be described in accordance with Devotion, and in accordance with the world and the Vedas. Among these the first is according to Devotion :

Stanzas 8-9 : "For when He, His heroic Strength recounted skillfully by His companions and followers, His wealth and grandeur immovable, like that of the Primeval Person, moves about the forest, calling the cows with His flute as they graze on the cliffs of the mountains, the forest's creepers and trees, as if fully to reveal Viṣṇu in themselves, show forth their riches of flowers and fruits, bowing low their branches with their burden, and they shoot forth flowing streams of honey as all their limbs thrill with love."

Commentary : Like "the Primeval Person" and like the Supreme Person, whose heroic deeds of Strength, such as creating the world and so forth, are "recounted" as unparalleled in their excellence by the Vedas who are their followers, so is "His heroic Strength", by His "companions, followers," and worshippers, the cowherd boys. And this Gopī has described His greatness as superior to all others' according to worldly standards, too, when she says : "His wealth and grandeur immovable, like that of the Primeval Person." His wealth, of course, refers to Lakṣmī. And this praise has been re-echoed by all His followers—the gods and everyone else. And worldly people, because they deal with Him on an everyday level, say there is no one comparable with Him but Puruṣottama (who, of course, He is). Therefore there is no simile here (because there are no two different Beings compared). And the Gopī has given us the reason why the description is made in terms of difference (between the Primeval Person and Kṛṣṇa) when she says : "He...moves about the forest." He who moves about the Vṛndāvana forest has adopted the *sāttvika* expressions, because He is established on the soil of *sattva.* As "the cows graze on the cliffs of the mountains," He goes there Himself, and to help the animals to level ground from the jagged edges He "calls" them. And to show that He is not an ordinary cowherd boy, He "calls them with His flute" alone. We come to know through His future conduct that He has penetrated the forest by means of His flute. Otherwise the trees would not react in such a way. When "He" is playing in different parts of the forest, whenever He "calls out" with His flute, then "the forest's trees ...shoot forth flowing streams of honey." This is how the stanzas connect. The word "For" is used in the sense of : "And this meaning is correct." If it were otherwise, they would not recognize the sound of His flute, nor would He call them by their names. Therefore by means of His flute the Blessed Lord penetrated all the trees. Likewise later on the same principles will apply.

"The forest's creepers," realizing that the Blessed Lord was "moving about" very near them, and that He was "calling," i.e., inviting, His very own, revealed fully the Joy that was within themselves, in order to bring to fulfillment His enjoyment of them (i.e., His very own). And the "trees" did precisely the same. Just as women and men who belong to the Blessed Lord become filled with Joy when the Blessed Lord and those who belong to Him have come together, and they give what is their very own for the sake of His enjoyment, so did these creepers and trees also give. In case someone objects : "But this attribute belongs to creatures that can move—not to immobile things," the Gopī speaking here has said : "fully to reveal Viṣṇu in themselves, (they) show forth.." In sentient beings alone are both the Power of Action and the Power of Knowledge of the Blessed Lord manifest. And their possession of Being, Consciousness and Joy becomes manifest gradually. All this comes about when the Blessed Lord has entered and dwelt within them. And, reasons the Gopī, if He has entered and dwelt within these trees and creepers, too, and now becomes revealed, then all this is only fitting. These trees and so forth are endowed with five attributes,[12] and so they, "as if fully to reveal Viṣṇu in themselves, show forth..." The Gopī tells us that the first revelation came about in them by the power of action when she says : "(show forth) their riches of flowers and fruits." For where the Blessed Lord enters and dwells, there secondary fruit (*phalam*; also "reward") and the highest fruit come to be. Because of this action of His, the creepers and trees come to "show forth, as if fully to reveal..." Their flowers constitute their secondary fruits, but their fruits are their highest fruit. And they showed forth "their riches" of all these. And the Gopī points out that they show an excess of Being for the sake of the Blessed Lord when she says : "bowing low their branches with their burden." To refute the objection that it is possible that the branches are bowing because of their burden, too, she has mentioned their "bowing low" first, and their "burden" only afterwards. And she has described that excellence of Consciousness which embodies knowledge when she says : "all their limbs thrill with love." For loving devotees alone experience the thrilling of all the hairs of their body out of love. (Here begins an interpolation by Viṭṭhala) Even the creepers and trees which had not previously been green then became green; and each of their limbs displayed a stoutness which made them bulkier than before. And the special characteristic of their bright freshness here is the thrilling of all their limbs with love. And besides, the Gopīs are the ones who possess the sweetness of the nectar that is in His flute's sound, and so it is they alone who can search out its nature. So it is most fitting that their words do not bear investigation by another. Therefore we must not write too much here! (end of Viṭṭhala's interpolation). And in the "flowing streams of honey" the trees and creepers make evident externally, for the Blessed Lord's sake, the Joy that is present within them. Their awareness of all this is surely their power of knowledge.

12. The reference is almost certainly to Bh.P. X. 22. 32, where Kṛṣṇa, in His eulogy of the trees, first points out the general altruism of trees, and then five specific manifestations of it. He says: "Look at these highly blessed trees, which live exclusively for the sake of others. While they themselves bear patiently wind, rain, heat and frost, they ward off all these from us."

Introduciion to Stanzas 10-11 : The sound of Kṛṣṇa's flute had its effect on the birds as well, and the Gopīs describe in this next stanza-pair how the sound of His flute took a form that was useful to the birds. Although the birds become silent sages when He is playing the flute (cf. Bh. P. X. 21. 14), and their love for the Blessed Lord results not from His song and so forth, but from their very nature; still, in the view of the world they may be looked upon simply as birds (OR : still, if sages sometimes view things in a worldly manner, they may see the Lord simply as a boy). Therefore these stanzas describe how the worship of love is accomplished in the birds through His external form and the sound of His flute :

Stanzas 10-11 : "When the Handsomest of the handsome, surrounded by swarms of bees drunk with arrogance from the wine of the Tulasī, with its divine fragrance, which is in His garland of forest-flowers, makes His flute coo, honoring the loud, droning sound so dear to them (OR : honoring them just as they liked, and honoring their loud, droning sound; cf. Comm.), then the cranes and swans in the lake, and the birds the of the air, all fly close to Him, their minds stolen away by the beautiful song, and they worship Hari, their minds held in firm restraint, ah!, their eyes closed tight and their silence kept total."

Commentary : The birds' main characteristic is their form and color, and they can distinguish differences of form and color.[13] The sound of Kṛṣṇa's flute does good to those who belong to Him, and does not mind even an offense on the part of one who belongs to Him. As the bees were buzzing, so He, imitating that sound, made His flute sound just like a buzzing bee. By comparison with birds, bees are lowly and despised. And the "swarms" of bees, too, are of many different species. And their song is not in the least unloud. And the Lord "honors" even this. Even so, the bees were "drunk with arrogance." And this arrogance is improper on the part of the bees. For Tulasī, unlike other flowers, is not a cause of arrogance. And even more so "with its divine fragrance." And still more when it is "in

13. In this last phrase: *rūpabhedavidaḥ*, Vallabha is quoting the words of Bh. P. III. 29. 30, and thus puts the birds in their proper place in the hierarchy of beings.

the garland" worn by the Blessed Lord. But if He honors even them, then those "cranes" in the lakes and so forth, who are true connoisseurs, able to distinguish between water and milk—how could He fail to honor them?

The bees are "drunk" with the juice of "Tulasī, with its divine fragrance, which is" also "in His garland of forest-flowers." He also "honors" the bees "just as they like," i.e., He does not drive them away as they buzz around the forest-garland He is wearing. But, insofar as He does not panic them, to that extent He "honors" them. And so, when He "makes His flute coo", "honoring" the bees, then the water-birds "in the lake"—"the cranes," who are associated even by their name (*sārasa*) with the devotees who possess the mood of devotion (*sarasa*), "the swans," who can distinguish between water and milk, and "the birds of the air," who move in the heights, "all fly close to Him." And these birds are, by comparison with men, eligible to worship the Blessed Lord through love. And now the Gopī gives their characteristics : "their minds (are) stolen away by the beautiful song." "Beautiful" means that the Blessed Lord's song brings about freedom from passion. And this form of worship of theirs is according to the Path of Devotion. But their worship was not the worship of those who stay in their own respective places and worship their own Inner Controller, nor of those who worship their own Self on the Path of Knowledge. This is why she has said : "(they) all fly close to Him... and worship Hari," i.e., they worship Him from very nearby. For they have been called silent sages by the Blessed Lord. And the Gopī states the difference between them and the bees in respect to worship when she says : "their minds held in firm restraint." By firm restraint of the mind is loving worship of the Blessed Lord given full importance, not by a mind which is distracted by anything and everything. And besides, this Gopī says : "ah !" out of joy. She means that this blessedness belongs to them alone. They are the most perfect in loving worship who are devoid of external activity. In external activities while worshipping the eyes and voice should be strictly controlled. The one who keeps these two under strict control speaks of no one but Him and sees nothing but Him, as the Gopī says in the words : "their eyes closed tight and their silence kept total." The birds observed a vow of silence. Now they are completely intent on His sound. Therefore they close their eyes lest their mind go somewhere else. Thus these Gopīs, because of their *sāttvika* nature, have described the blessedness of these birds.

(Here is added a long interpolation by Viṭṭhala) Or, alternatively, there is this to be said concerning this pair of stanzas. These silent sages possessed a superb taste for devotion, but thinking themselves useless for this Game because they were men, they became birds, and aroused, with their varied cooing and twittering songs, the mood of love in the Blessed Lord and His devotees. And, thinking that they have achieved their goal, they consider sound alone as excessively dear to themselves. This is why mention is made here of the usefulness of the qualities of Kṛṣṇa's "garland of forest-flowers," which embodies the Fame which has sound as its chief element. As holy scripture says : "Just as the fragrance of a tree in full flower is borne from afar, so is the fragrance of a virtuous man" (*Mahānār. Up.* VIII. 2). In this passage fragrance and fame are described in exactly the same terms. Now because Kṛṣṇa's forest-garland embodies His Fame, the songs which fully describe this Fame are necessary. And these songs are not possible without the tasting of that mood of love. And so "Tulasī" has the fragrance that embodies the transcendent devotion which will be described (in the stanza-pair 18-19). And Tulasī's "nectar" (*madhu* in the stanza) is an essence of the most transcendent devotion, which makes one forget everything else. Therefore the bees, intoxicated so that they have no awareness of their bodies and so forth, and do not even care about the attributes of the Lord, come right up next to Him and buzz loudly. But actually, this alone is the most perfect worship of the Lord—this worship that is done by the bees. That is why their song alone is "totally desired by" (*abhīṣṭam*—"so dear to (the bees)"—in the stanza) the Lord.

Besides, since the Gopīs avoid words like "beautiful" (*cāru*) to describe the fragrance, and have used the word which has the suffix which means 'being in',[14] and since the fragrance that is in the Blessed Lord's garland of forest-flowers here has not

14. This refers to the sense of the suffix-*ya* in the stanza's word *divya*, "heavenly" or "divine."

actually been borne from heaven, and since it will soon be said (cf. the next stanza-pair) that the Gopīs are the goddesses of Vraja, and since the root *DIV* has as its primary meaning "to play," therefore this fragrance comes from the Lord's play with the Gopīs. This we conclude from the fact that the two words *divya* and *gandha* ("fragrance") are used together in the stanza. By this it is suggested that, just as an object that is in heaven (*divya*) cannot be understood by a person who is in the other world (i.e., on earth), so this fact is intelligible only to the devotee who is in the world of the Lord's most private Game. Therefore, to indicate that the Lord's mood, too, was excited by this fragrance, the word "coo" has been used. Besides, except for Kṛṣṇa Himself, no one can know the nature of the juice, fragrance, and so forth, of Tulasī. As the Gopīs themselves say : "of Tulasī whose fragrance He loves" (cf. Stanza 18-19 below), and again : "After putting one arm around His beloved's shoulder, and picking a lotus with the other, Balarāma's younger brother was followed by blind swarms of bees, drunk with the fragrance of Tulasī" (cf. Chapter II, stanza 12). That is why in these passages they speak of the fragrance and juice of Tulasī alone instead of the fragrance and juice of the flowers of the forest-garland. And the Gopīs have used the word "families of bees" (*kula* as "families" rather than "swarms") precisely to indicate that these bees, who are enjoying the juice and fragrance of Tulasī, are not ordinary but extraordinary—different from and superior to all other bees. This is why they used the word *ali* for "bee". For the word *alam* ("enough") is expressive of fulness. In the same way, the bees here possess that fulness, and that is why this word is used. And besides, he whose delight is never exhausted, and who never destroys his delight, he is called *ali* (based on *a*-, "not", plus *lī*, "be destroyed, absorbed, exhausted"). Although in the latter case, *ali* should have a long -*ī* (*alī*), still, according to the axiom of holy scripture : "The real noun is *daśahūta*. And in spite of its being *daśahūta* they call it *daśahotā* for the sake of secrecy. For the gods, as it were, love secrecy" (cf. *B. Ā. Up*. 4. 4. 2. and *Ait. Up*. 1. 3. 14). And from the Blessed Lord's own saying : "The hidden is very dear to Me" (Bh. P. XI. 21. 35), we know that the Lord loves to keep secret whatever He loves. And in the present context the fact that the bees strengthen the Lord's private mood is to be kept secret, and so the Lord made this word have a short final syllable for his own secret reasons. And thus these bees alone are *ali*, while other bees are called *bhramara*. And so we should understand that when these *ali-s* are also called by other names, this is done with a special purpose in view.

Since the Gopīs have not spoken here of high notes, nor of much singing, we should understand that the song which they have described in terms of loudness alone has a burden of joy which cannot be carried by anyone but the Lord. And to connote that there is no limit to the greatness of the bees' song, the Gopīs have used the word *alaghu* ("not soft or light, but loud and abundant"). Since this is the case, how could He possibly refrain from "honoring" them? By the word "when" in the stanza, we should understand that He, overwhelmed by His drinking of the nectar of their song, stands silent for a long time, and only occasionally "makes His flute coo" as He overflows with this joy. He makes His flute coo in this way in order to awaken the love of those He loves by means of the love awakened in Him by the bees' song. This is why the word "song" is used later in the stanza by the Gopīs, not now. This signifies that it was after this, when His own mood of love had become full, that He began to sing. And it is suggested in the stanza's opening words, by the Gopīs' use of the word *tilaka* to describe Him as the "Handsomest of the handsome," that just as the *tilaka* stands on the forehead, which is the place of luck, likewise this Form stands in the presence of the women who are the luckiest of all. So these opening words should be understood as a *karmadhāraya* compound (i.e., *darśanīyatilako* should be translated "He who is both handsome and superior"). For in the hearts of the Gopīs nothing is handsome except the Beloved.

Although in this chapter Kṛṣṇa's Form and His Sound are equally important, yet in this stanza-pair special importance is attached to Sound. Otherwise the birds would not be described as "having their eyes closed tight." Here is the reason for this. His flute's song was heard by the birds only when they were "in the lake." And that song has one single aspect to its nature —that it "steals away their minds by its beauty." Therefore, completely dependent on His Sound, they come together very "close to Him." But the Gopīs intend to convey, by describing in the very beginning the handsomeness of His Form as the cause of the Sound, that the birds experience the taste of His Form, too, in their experience of the taste of His Sound. And this, too, is amazing : that by means of a song which is an imitation of the song of intoxicated bees, the birds "held their minds in firm restraint" and constrained the movements of all their senses. Since this is the condition of the birds—this drinking of the nectar of His song—therefore He must have assumed such a form. Because the consequent coming of such sound is caused only by such a form. And the condition of the "families of bees," too, since they drink the wine of the fragrance of Tulasī, is fully equal to that of the birds. And we should understand that, afterwards, by force of their nature, the condition in which they are described—as "intoxicated"—took precedence. But because the birds are silent sages, even afterwards they will remain immersed continuously, and in an interior manner, in the nectar of His song. Thus they are not described as "intoxicated." Or, alternatively, because of the nature of the Lord's Joy, their intoxication is proved without any need of explicit mention, and therefore it has not been described. At that point, the condition of the birds, too, will be that of the bees. But in fact, the "loud, droning" song of the families of bees intoxicated by the nectar of the Lord's form as described here, because it is so desired by the Lord, is experienced by Him with perfectly concentrated restraint of mind. And the Lord then both sings it and makes His flute coo with it. And upon hearing this, it is most fitting that the birds, too, become intoxicated by it. In fact, there is no way they can avoid it. We think this is the right explanation. Yet, since they have expressed the beauty of His Form at the beginning, and because they were overwhelmed with the desire to see that Form, a certain depression settled over the Gopīs when they recalled the birds' obstacle to seeing Him (i.e , their closing their eyes) even though they had attained the necessary condition (of nearness). And that is why they have said : "alas!"[15] (end of Viṭṭhala's interpolation).

15. Thus Viṭṭhala has taken the stanza's word *hanta* in the sense of a particle of dejection—which it definitely often is—where Vallabha has

Introduction to Stanzas 12-13: A cloud does good to everyone and everything. Therefore a Gopī now describes, as before i.e., in a pair of stanzas), how the sound of Kṛṣṇa's flute gave rise to love in a cloud, too :

Stanzas 12-13 : "When, together with Balarāma, He sports playfully—tying on a garland as an ear-decoration on the peaks of an earth-upholder, O goddesses of Vraja, and, already Joyful, fills with joy all else as He makes everything resound with the roar of His flute, a cloud, its heart fearing a great transgression, is thundering deep and low in imitation, and has rained down on its Friend showers of its flowers, making its shadow an umbrella for Him."

Commentary: "O goddesses of Vraja," i.e., the Gopīs, who embody the protective goddesses of Vraja. One Gopī has described the others in this way, thinking that thus she will gain their confidence. "When...He makes everything resound," i.e., fills everything, "with the roar of His flute," then a cloud, "its heart fearing a great transgression...rained down on its Friend," i.e., the Blessed Lord. And, with the "shadow" of its own body, it provided an "umbrella" for Him. Or, it provided the umbrella first, and then rained Flowers. This sound of His flute is endowed with great strength. Having driven away all the qualities which belong to "everything," it becomes full and fills (all else) by itself alone. "A cloud" also embodies the appearance of the Lord (since it is black, Skt. *kṛṣṇa*), being made up of a mass of smoke, light, water and wind. Since everything has been led to its fulfillment by the Blessed Lord alone, this cloud, being now itself of secondary importance, "rained down" on the Blessed Lord alone, in order to make its own birth meaningful.

In this context, the Gopī describes with four qualifying adjectives the type of agent—the Blessed Lord—by whose type of flute-sound all this comes to pass. Otherwise—if the Blessed Lord did not have the qualities necessary to make His flute have these effects—then the Gopīs' speaking of His making everything

specifically said, just above: "This Gopī says: 'ah!'—*hanta*—out of joy," another frequent meaning of *hanta*. Viṭṭhala rarely expresses such open disagreement with Vallabha as in this interpolation.

resound would be a mere assertion. In order to tell us, in this regard, that Kṛṣṇa's Power of Action was at its fullest, the Gopīs have said : "together with Balarāma." They also wish to indicate by saying this that this action of His is even greater than His action of creating the world (which was effortless—accomplished merely by thought). And when they tell us that He "sports playfully" while wearing an "ear-decoration," i.e., an ear-ornament, in the form of a "garland," they have described His Game. For a garland is rich in Fame. His ear is the ten directions (cf. Bh. P. II. 1. 29). And the Game by which His Fame has become full in all ten directions is surely the most excellent Game of all. Or perhaps the Gopīs are referring to the Bhāgavata and the other scriptures which propound the Blessed Lord's Fame and constitute an ornament with respect to all the Vedas. In these scriptures His Fame is linked with His Game-playing, and propounds and explains it. Thus has the greatness of His Power of Action, with regard to its essence (Balarāma) and its qualities (Fame), been described by the Gopīs.

And they have also described the greatness of His Will, which cooperates with His Power of Action, when they said : "already (Himself) Joyful, (He) fills with joy all else."[16] After thus describing the excellence of His Power of Action, which was the cause of His flute's sound, a Gopī describes His excellence with regard to place as well as when she says : "on the peaks of an earth-upholder." They who uphold even the earth, which is the basis of all, on the high places of those mountains is this sound produced. And so how could it fail to fill "everything"? His flute's "roar", i.e., its deep and powerful echo, "makes resound," i.e., fills with sound. Thus the action of this sound has been described as greater than even a cloud's. It was then that a "cloud" which was passing over the great Vāsudeva, "its heart fearing a great transgression" in passing over the Blessed Lord, stood still just above Him. Even when it tried to go onwards, it realized that the Blessed Lord, the life of everything, who is as blue-black as the darkest cloud,

16. "Will," "wish," or "Desire" (Skt. *icchā*) is defined by Vallabha as an attribute of pleasure (which leads to joy), since every desire is a desire for pleasure.

was its Friend; and so "it rained down on its Friend showers of its flowers," that is to say, the raindrops which are its flowers. In other words, the cloud paid Him homage with flowers. And it did not merely pay Him homage, but bestowed kingship on Him as well, as the Gopī points out when she says : "making... an umbrella for Him." And it did not stop at bestowing mere kingship, either, but made a total offering of itself, too, as the Gopī tells us in the words : "its shadow." When the sun has gone down, the cloud's standing above Him does not provide a shadow. This is why its shadow has been pointed out separately.

Introduction to Stanzas 14-15 : In order to tell us of three most excellent types of being, and that the sound of Kṛṣṇa's flute had some effect on them, too, the Gopīs describe the sound of His flute, and the Blessed Lord as well, in the next three stanza-pairs. Doubt, delusion, and the renunciation of all things were brought about by the sound of His flute in the sages, the holy scriptures (i.e., the Gopīs who embody the holy scriptures), and the forest-dwellers, respectively. In the present stanza-pair the Gopī describes the sound the Blessed Lord had His flute make for the sake of creating a doubt in even those who, among the three just mentioned, are the Gurus of all, i.e., Brahmā and the others :

Stanzas 14-15 : "When He who knows well the various comings and goings of the cowherd boys, when Your Son, O faithful Yaśodā, setting His flute 'neath His lower lip—red as a bimba-fruit (OR : "the enlightening sun of His lower lip"; cf. Comm.)—led forth the scales and kinds of sound learned purely by Himself in His manifold playing of the flute, then the lords of gods, led by Indra, Śiva and Brahmā, upon hearing the sound from each of their libations, these poet-sages, their necks and their minds bowed in appreciative homage, fell into a worried depression, no longer sure they knew all the elements of music."

Commentary : What is of a type that transcends the world, and yet is born in the world, creates a doubt. In response to the possible objection that a form which is not heard of in the Vedas does not exist in Īśvara, and Brahmā is well aware of the fonts and places of all knowledge (i.e., the Vedas), so how could any doubt arise in him—the Gopī speaking here has said : "learned purely by Himself in His manifold playing of the flute." The flute is one of the group of wind-instruments with holes. The different kinds of flute, too, have been described in the treatises. And these are known by Brahmā. But these modes of Kṛṣṇa's playing are "manifold". And these modes have been "learned purely by Himself" ; He alone learned the ways of producing these sounds clearly. By this the Gopī has told us that the Sound-Brahman is eternal (i.e., uncreated; therefore prior to the Vedas). The power of action is the means for attaining that Sound-Brahman, and if that power is of this world, then how will this sound become transcendent ? The Gopī dispels this doubt by pointing out the transcendence of this power of action, too, in the words : "He who knows well the various comings and goings," i.e., the different characteristics of the wanderings, "of the cowherd boys." The wanderings of the cowherd-boys are not spoken of in the Vedas. Rather, they are worldly. But they may exist in a universe other than this one. They are not well known anywhere else in the world, nor even in the Vedas. But the Blessed Lord "knows well" everything everywhere. And so a mode which even Brahmā does not know is the very mode He has produced. "But," it may be objected, "how can He who has become manifest in Brahmā's creation do something which is unknown even to Brahmā ?" To this the Gopī replies : "your Son." They are speaking to Yaśodā, who has joined the group of women. Hence there is no talk here of passionate love and other such topics; rather, unforbidden excellence alone has been described. Just as, though He is your son, He does things which are impossible for you to account for, even in your mind, the same has happened in this universe of Brahmā, too. They address her as "faithful" in order to gain her trust in what they say.

And the Gopīs have stated the cause for the ignorance when they say: "setting His flute 'neath His lower lip red as a bimba-fruit" (OR : "the enlightening sun of His lower lip"). As has already been stated,[17] His lower lip has greed as its essence. And so it is not well known in the world; that is to say, the

17. Cf. Bh. P. II. 1. 32 and *Subodhinī* on stanzas 2-3 of this chapter.

nectar or taste of that lip is not granted by the Blessed Lord. Moreover, having the appearance of a *bimba*, it is enlightening like the sun.[18] For those who are to be enlightened do not know the real nature of the enlightener.[19] And on that lip this flute has been placed, for the sake of proclaiming its excellence because of that fact, too. The words "all the scales and kinds of sound" refer to the different classes of sound—*ṣaḍja* and all the other notes. "When He led forth," i.e., created anew, then, in their effort to understand this thoroughly, these gods, even though their main concern is to preside over the three qualities of worldly existence, also came together in terms of the three times. But to indicate that this time (of Kṛṣṇa's Game), too, is on the divine level, the Gopīs have used the word : "libation." They "heard the sound" of His flute "from each of their libations."[20] "Indra" is *sāttvika*, "Siva" *tāmasa*, and "Brahmā" *rājasa;* and they "led" these gods. Indeed, all the gods are composed of the three qualities of worldly existence. And they were "poet-sages"—thus they were also skilled in sound. For Indra, the lord of the three worlds, is at all time intent on sound. But Śiva is the creator of the treatises on sound. And Brahmā is the guru of them both. Hence the Gopīs use the name Parameṣṭhī ("standing at the head, highest, chief") for Brahmā. To express the absence of distraction from their minds, the Gopī has said : "their necks and their minds bowed in appreciative homage." Their necks were bent very low in order to portray externally the bowing of their minds. The mind is what grasps. And the bowing here is complete—from all sides. And they also became "no longer sure they knew all the elements of music." It mustn't be thought, either, that, out of indifference, after considering these sounds for some time they remained

18. Here I cannot determine which way Vallabha is interpreting the stanza's word *bimba*, which means both "the disk of the sun" and "the bimba-fruit," which when ripe is red and is conventionally used in comparisons involving red lips—usually of women, it is true, but it could certainly be applied to a boy. Likely as not, he is playing with both meanings.

19. Cf. *B. Ā. Upaniṣad* II. 4. 14.: "How would one know Him through whom one knows all this? How, indeed, would one know the knower?"

20. The libations are three: morning, noon, and afternoon; and so coming "from each of their libations" is how these gods "came together in terms of the three times," as Vallabha has said.

silent in ignorance. For we have been told that "they fell into a worried depression"—they became faint with anxiety. Or, they were deluded by His flute's sound. For this very reason, the view that this was a pseudo-sound (i.e., an uncultured expression of the notes), is also refuted. Because this sound produces transcendent joy, and the transcendent mood of love.

Introduction to Stanzas 16-17: "But leave aside this talk of what happened to others," say the Gopīs, "for the sound of Kṛṣṇa's flute causes an overturning of even our natures, too !" The Gopīs then describe this in a pair of stanzas, as they had for the others who preceded them :

Stanzas 16-17 : "Relieving the pain the cattle's hooves had inflicted on Vraja's earth with the leaves and soft petals of His lotus feet, marked with such varied shapes as the banner, the Vajra-weapon and the lotus, His gait like that of the mightiest of bulls and His flute singing high, He roams; and by this we, with shock-waves of passion granted to us by His glances brimful of the delights of love, are stymied into the stillness of trees, and lose all consciousness, by fainting, of our clothing and braids."

Commentary : When "He roams...His flute singing high," then "by this" sound "we" Gopīs "are stymied into the stillness of trees," and all of us, "by fainting, lose all consciousness of our clothing and braids," i.e., our masses of hair. Thus the stanzas connect. "This sound of His flute is made for our sake alone," think the Gopīs, knowing this by its move and manner (Skt. *ceṣṭayā*), and because of their experience. By its move and manner here, the flute's sound is produced for the sake only of those who dwell in Gokula. How could the Lord, pervaded by such a move and manner (i.e., by such a desire and endeavor; Vasu) possibly do any other action, or produce any other effect ? And so, the Gopīs have described first of all the Blessed Lord's doing good for Gokula.

"With the leaves and soft petals of His lotus feet," i.e., with its ten toes or with the different portions of the soles of His feet. "Relieving the pain the cattle's hooves had inflicted on Vraja's earth," i.e., the torment caused by the continual plodding of the cattle and other beasts over the ground of

Vraja—indeed, their violation of that ground—the Blessed Lord's walking over that earth has been described as soft—soft and playful. The injured portion of Vraja's earth has been healed by the touch of His feet, with their playful movement. But the aspect relating to the Self, and the aspect relating to the divine, of that portion of earth, have been relieved of suffering by the marks His feet bear—the banner, the Vajra, and so forth. Specifically, the *tāmasa* aspect of the earth, which relates to the elemental, is healed by "the banner"; the *rājasa* aspect, relating to the Self, by the "Vajra-weapon"; and the *sāttvika* aspect, relating to the divine, by "the shape," i.e., the mark, of "the lotus." These "varied" and beautiful shapes are "marked" on His feet. By this, according to both the worldly and the transcendent manner has the pain inflicted on Vraja's earth been relieved.

Three things are of paramount importance in Vraja; its earth, the cows, and the Gopīs. Among these the Gopīs have already described His relieving the earth's pain by walking on it. Now they tell us how, by His walking and His action, He removes the suffering of the cows. Their words are : "His gait like that of the mightiest of bulls." "The mightiest of bulls" is a huge bull with a massive hump. And just as such a bull lopes lazily, and has fun doing it, so Kṛṣṇa, by loping in that way, has been said to be like a remover of the suffering of the cows, too. "And His flute singing high, He roams." Then is Kāma born in us Gopīs by the sound of His flute, and we become stiller than the immobile creatures. This is what the Gopīs have expressed in the words : "by this." Kāma is born by His flute's sound—because of its very nature. And besides, "shock-waves of passion are granted to us by His glances brimful of the delights of love." And so, rendered stock still by these shock-waves, we "are stymied into the stillness of trees." Someone may say that their interior knowledge remains intact, but with regard to that the Gopīs say : "we lose all consciousness..." If the objector retorts by saying that in deep sleep, too, they do not know, the Gopīs have said, specifically to refute that objection : "by fainting." Attentive concern and knowledge of their clothing and hair is extremely necessary to women. That this happened to them right at the beginning of the sound of Kṛṣṇa's flute tells us what happened here with regard to their walking, their sight and all other things as well.

Introduction to Stanzas 18-19 : The Gopīs next describe, in two stanzas, as before, the sound of Kṛṣṇa's flute according to the way in which it affected the does of the forest :

Stanzas 18-19 : "When, on occasion, the Jewel-Wearer, counting up on the garland of Tulasī (OR : "counting up on His jewels"; cf. Comm.), whose fragrance He loves, the cows on every side, and whenever, casually laying an arm on the shoulder of a loving cowherd companion, He has sung, the wives of the black antelopes, deprived of their minds by the soft, warbling sounds of His flute, sit down near Kṛṣṇa; and following after Him whose great qualities are as numerous as the drops of the ocean, these does, like Gopīs, are liberated totally from their hopes and desires for home-life."

Commentary : The "jewels" are the forms, on the divine level, of the cows. Therefore the "Jewel-Wearer" is He who wears these jewels on Himself. Or, the jewels are meant to be tokens of remembrance—that is to say, the jewels are reminders of His beloved ones. And so with these He, "on occasion, counts up the cows on every side."[21] By telling us in this way that the cows and their attributes are established on the Blessed Lord alone—with Him as their foundation—the Gopīs point out that the cows are free of Saṁsāra. For the same reasons, the Gopīs are, too (i.e., as His beloved ones). And again, for

21. As must be evident from my translation of the stanzas, I have an apparent disagreement with Vallabha concerning the first stanza's first line. The line reads thus in the Sanskrit: *maṇidharaḥ kvacidāgaṇayan gā mālayā dayitagandhatulasyāḥ.* I think the most likely meaning of this line, based on probabilities of word-meanings and actualities of case relationships, is this: "When, on occasion, the Jewel-Wearer (i.e. , Kṛṣṇa, who constantly wears the famous Kaustubha-jewel on His chest), counting up on (i.e., by means of) the garland of Tulasī, whose fragrance He loves, the cows on every side...." But Vallabha quite clearly interprets the passage to mean that Kṛṣṇa is wearing a garland of jewels with which He counts the cows. And he explains the meaning, or meanings, of these jewels in his commentary There is a way, however, and not an unlikely one, of reconciling our two different interpretations: that Kṛṣṇa is wearing a garland of jewels (useful for counting) interwoven with Tulasī.

the same reason, "these does" are also free from Saṁsāra. Since there is no basic difference because of the fact that they are all animals, then if Kṛṣṇa is the Savior from Saṁsāra of the village animals, He will be the Savior just as particularly of the beasts of the forest. And so, that these beasts manifest a complete preoccupation with Kṛṣṇa is only right.

Kṛṣṇa is marked unmistakably here by means of the "garland of Tulasī, whose fragrance He loves"—and this phrase also implies many other things Kṛṣṇa loves. Just as the Blessed Lord loves the deep blue-black form (i.e., color; *rūpa*), and loves the touch of women, the sound of the flute and the taste of fresh butter, so does He love "the fragrance of Tulasī." And the excellence that is in that Tulasī and its fragrance has been realized experientially by a few *sāttvika* persons. Such is Tulasī. And therefore Kṛṣṇa wears a garland of Her. And the wives of the black antelopes acted on the basis that, for this reason, when we also shall become His beloved ones, He will wear us, too, or at least our attributes, on Himself. The black, or spotted, antelope, has been enjoined, in the Vedas, for use.[22] Thus the action of these wives of the black antelopes is directed towards the use of them in loving Devotion.

Moreover, the Gopīs say : "When," i.e., whenever, or on occasion, "laying an arm on the shoulder of a loving", i.e., exceedingly loving, "cowherd companion." Or in accordance with Pāṇini's rule : "And in the expression of strong desire, the past or present tense may be used to convey a future idea" (*Aṣṭādhyāyī* 3.3. 132), the Gopīs' words "whenever He has sung", may refer to a situation where, in the middle of things, someone expresses a desire to hear Kṛṣṇa sing. And just as Kṛṣṇa will fulfil the desire of that cowherd-boy by singing, so will He fulfil desires where the attributes of love and worshipful service truly exist. And so, to bring about that state of fulfilment of desires, these does, "like Gopīs," worship Kṛṣṇa with love. And, since these does have lost all awareness of their bodies,

22. In the Vedas, only the lands where the black antelope was native were considered holy—fit for the performance of rituals. Also, its skin is worn during the period of celibate study, and is recommended as a seat for meditation. (Shri Shyam Goswamy).

there is no absence of passion by reason of a difference in species between them and Kṛṣṇa. It is then that there is "soft warbling...of His flute." An unexpected, special, mind-stealing quality of sound is the essence of "soft warbling." If this soft warbling has gone forth from His flute, then other sounds as well, because of their relation with that warbling, deprive the does of their minds. Thus the Gopīs use the word : "sounds." It is well known that animals are brought under control by sound. So the deprivation, or cheating of their minds comes from the dawning upon them of the idea that Kṛṣṇa will use them only now. And so, "deprived of their minds by the.. sounds, (they) sit down near Kṛṣṇa." Just as someone sits down and awaits death by fasting, so do they "sit down near Kṛṣṇa." In case someone objects : "How is it that wives of others, who are of the houses of others, sat down near someone else?", the Gopīs have said : "the wives of the black antelopes" (Skt. *kṛṣṇa* means both "black antelope," and, of course, "Kṛṣṇa"). By their use of the word kṛṣṇa the Gopīs tell us that these does became His wives. Or, the deprivation of the does' minds may mean that they forgot about color and became totally and exclusively preoccupied with sound. Or perhaps, by reason of the sound of His flute, which has such brilliant power, the does, with the thought that Kṛṣṇa is in the kṛṣṇa-antelope, too, "sit down near Kṛṣṇa." "But," someone may say, "if the black antelope can be mistaken for Kṛṣṇa.. then its sound, too, can be mistaken for Kṛṣṇa's sound. And so why would they abandon their mates and come to Kṛṣṇa ?" This is why the Gopī has said : "whose great qualities are as numerous as the drops of the ocean." There are one, or perhaps two, qualities in the kṛṣṇa-antelope. And so, wherever the Blessed Lord goes, there "following after Him," all "these does are liberated totally from their desires and hopes for home life." They have abandoned even the wish to go home.

(Here Viṭṭhala adds an interpolation) Only by nearness to Him is the delightful nectar of the mood of the Blessed Lord drunk. And so the does, having attained this very sweet love of Him, "like the Gopīs," became totally intent on Him. And since Kṛṣṇa sees the similarity, and the very same gaze, in the eyes of His beloved ones and the eyes of these does, then the emotion with which He looks upon the Gopīs is the very same as the love with which these does also look upon Him, and a love for Him of precisely the same kind as the love of the Gopīs is produced in these does as well. And it is precisely the same with the "soft warbling of His flute" (i.e., presumably, it has the same effect on the does as it has on the Gopīs). This is the sole reason why the word *rava* ("sound"), which has as its essence the seed of fire (in the syllable *ra* : Vasu) and the seed of the nectar of immortality (in the syllable *va* : Vasu), has been used here by the Gopīs.[23] Because upon hearing those sounds both scorching, searing pain and the quenching of the fire of that pain come about (in both the Gopīs and the does). Therefore the Gopīs' speaking of themselves as the example here is entirely fitting (end of Viṭṭhala's interpolation).

Introduction to Stanzas 20-21 : Having thus described in nine different manners the sound of His flute, the Gopīs now describe in three ways, according to the manner of (and in the words of) those who have transcended the worldly qualities, how the Blessed Lord brought the entire world under His control with His flute's sound :

Stanzas 20-21 : "Donning festive garb by wearing a garland of white jasmine or oleander, and surrounded by the cowherd-boys and the herds, Nanda's son, O blameless one, your darling boy, who bestows happiness on those who love Him, has played merrily in Yamunā's waters; a lazy breeze blows, agreeably, along the bank, paying Him reverence with the touch of sandalwood-scent it bears, and those crowds of minor deities who are bards have encircled Him with their offerings of song and instrumental music."

Commentary : When the Blessed Lord "has played merrily in Yamunā's waters"—here too, the sound of His flute, since it is required and referred to in both the foregoing and the future stages of His game, is understood, because it is the subject-matter of this chapter; but since there is no special, particular

23. According to Shri Shyam Goswamy, the *Ekākṣarakośa*, which both Vallabha and Viṭṭhala use frequently, is the source for such correspondences as *ra=agni* and *va=amṛta*.

mode of flute-playing here, it has not been mentioned separately—then "the crowds of minor deities...have encircled Him." This is how the stanzas connect. And when the Gopīs say "in the Yamunā's waters," they use the locative case in the sense of 'nearness to'. Or, the locative is used in the sense of actual *locus* (i.e., they are literally "in" the Yamunā). It is possible that the cows and cowherd-boys are standing in the water because they are hot. And there Kṛṣṇa "plays merrily" with the cowherd-boys, and thus this is a water-game. And they also wash down the cows, and so forth. The flute's sound is His helper for calming distress and anxiety everywhere.

In case someone doubts whether Kṛṣṇa was decorated at this time, the Gopīs have described His decoration in the words: "Donning festive garb by wearing a garland of white jasmine or oleander." They mention the flower-garland alone because the doubter may think that Kṛṣṇa would certainly be decorated with ornaments on His clothing and so forth, but He would not be decorated with flowers. Garlands are of many kinds. His "garb" is decked out in such a way with these as to make it simply stunning. But here He has decked Himself out in a fashion meant to produce the mood of humor (*hāsyarasa*). But since someone may raise the question as to how it happened that the Blessed Lord played such an ordinary game, the Gopīs have said : "Nanda's son...your darling boy." By the game by which He becomes the son of Nanda, by (and by virtue of) that very game He brings about an ordinary game, too. And the Gopīs address Yaśodā as "blameless one" to make sure she doesn't get angry and to secure her trust. And He has become "your darling boy." By this they are saying that you—Yaśodā—are the cow, and He is your calf.[24] And by this word the Gopīs have also pointed out Yaśodā's unawareness of all Kṛṣṇa's hidden moods and delights. Otherwise He would not have played the game in which He allowed Yaśodā to tie Him to the mortar (cf. Bh. P. X. Chap. 9). And since the Gopīs have placed the words of direct address, "O blameless one," in the middle, between "Nanda's" and "your," they

24. Here the Gopīs have called Kṛṣṇa Yaśodā's *vatsa*, which means "calf" and "dear offspring" in general.

have indicated the blamelessness of both Nanda and Yaśodā. And since He is the "darling boy" of such a woman, the blamelessness refers to the Blessed Lord as well. The fact that Kṛṣṇa is marked by a fulness of great qualities—indeed by an excess of them—is expressed by the Gopīs' subsequent characterization of Him. That is to say : in addition, "He bestows happiness on those who love Him." This means that whatever persons possess love for Him—then just as they have loved Him, in exactly the same way does He play His game with them. By these words has the cause for every one of His games been expressed ! And where there is play by reason of attachment to His games, that is "playing merrily." This "playing merrily" should be understood here as including His water-game, His dancing-game, and His flute-playing game. Otherwise there would be no need of or use for the "instrumental music" of the minor deities, and so forth.

For it is beings who possess knowledge who are to be brought under control here. And in this the "breeze", or wind, is producer of knowledge. And the gods are the basis of that. Among the gods, moreover, the "crowds of minor deities" and "bards" are intent on manifesting external knowledge. And so the distinguishing characteristic which they possess, by comparison with the others, has been expressed by the Gopīs. But first of all the Gopīs describe the breeze, which is the cause. As "a lazy breeze" is "agreeable," that is how this one "blows along." And as the word "agreeably" (*anukūlam*) also means "along the bank" (*anukūlam*=*kūlasamīpe*; emended from Telivala-Sankalia's *kulasamīpe*), the good the breeze does is further indicated, since this describes the breeze's coolness. And the words "with the touch of sandalwood-scent" point out its fragrance. And these words also tell us that the breeze comes from the south.[25] Or, the breeze's coolness and agreeableness are increased by its contact with the sandalwood-paste which

25. This is because the word *malayaja*, "a sandal-tree or sandal-wood," means, literally, "born in the Malaya mountain range" of Kerala in South India, a range which abounds in sandal-trees, according to Apte, who also notes that: "poets usually represent the breeze from the Malaya mountain as wafting the odour of sandal trees . . . which peculiarly affects persons who are smit with love."

the Blessed Lord has applied to His own body. The breeze "bears the touch of sandalwood-scent," or perhaps its touch is "as if of sandalwood-scent." Since this breeze is of such a nature, it will produce love of the Blessed Lord in all who are there, without exception. The Gopīs describe the breeze as "paying Him reverence." As the breeze may indeed pay him reverence with its own three qualities (laziness, coolness and fragrance), so, for precisely that purpose, it blows, thus showing its extreme suitability for subjection to His control. And the "crowds of minor deities" as well as the "bards"—the Gandharvas and so forth—have become proclaimers of His Fame. And they are singers as well. The Gopī's word "who" means those who belong to the Blessed Lord. With their "instrumental music," which is a *tāmasa* means of attainment, their "songs", which are *rājasa* means, and their worship, i.e., "their offerings," which are *sāttvika* means, they "have encircled Him." They have done what was desired in everything.

Introduction to Stanzas 22-23 : Having thus described the variety that exists in the type of beings which transcends the worldly qualities, the Gopīs now describe, in these two final stanza-pairs, the deeds of the Blessed Lord alone:

Stanzas 22-23 : "Since the Mountain-Holder who loves Vraja's cows, and whose feet are hymned with worshipful homage on the path by the elders, has gathered the great wealth of cows together with songful flute at day's end, His fame praised in song by His followers, then, causing joy to well up in the eyes of the Gopīs even with the gleam of His toil, His garland coated with the dust of the herd's hooves, He comes, eager to bestow His blessings on His friends, this Moon who came forth from the womb of Devakī."

Commentary : The herd of cows which the Blessed Lord is now leading to the cowpens, He leads by His Grace. Otherwise, even if they had been involved in only one game (cf. Stanza 4-5), they would already be liberated. The same is true for the Gopīs. But, by His Grace alone, He acts as He does in order that both these may experience the Joy of worshipping Him through love. The Gopīs tell us the cause for this when they say : "Since," i.e., because of which. He is "the Mountain-Holder." If He were not granting the Joy of worshipping Him through love, then He would not hold Mount Govardhana aloft.[26] It is in order to tell us that this particular Greatness of the Blessed Lord is known to all people that Gopīs have said : "whose feet are hymned with worshipful homage on the path by the elders." "The elders" are well informed in every way. It is only by those who know much that the Blessed Lord can be worshipped. And so "He has gathered the" entire "great wealth of cows together," having separated them from the forest (OR : separating them again, afterwards, to their own individual cowherd-boys). Or perhaps "gathered together" means He brought all of them together very near to Himself, or restored them to their own proper place—near Himself. "At the day's end," say the Gopīs, since it would be bad for the cows to stay in the forest after that. And the other reason is that Kṛṣṇa wants to play His other game (with the Gopīs, at night). His "flute" became "songful." This was in order to remove strain and exhaustion, and also to inform the inhabitants of Vraja that He is coming. The effect of the flute's sound is to be expressed later. And Kṛṣṇa makes not only the Gopīs successful and happy in attaining what they desire, but the Gopas (cowherd-boys) as well. It is to tell us this that the Gopīs have described the hymn of praise the Gopas sang : "His Fame praised in song by His followers." "His followers" means His worshipful servants. By this we are told that the Gopas, too, sing of Him at night, just as the Gopīs do during the day. Otherwise the constraint of all would not come to pass. Precisely to tell us that Kṛṣṇa alone knows the effect of such activity and constraint,

26. The idea here is that Kṛṣṇa showed special mercy to the devotees of Vraja by telling them to worship no one but Him. He delights in Himself and has all His desires fulfilled, and so needs no one's worship, but by His special Grace here He makes the people of Vraja worship the one God, Himself, and no other. The consequence, of course, was that Indra, enraged at not being worshipped, sent a deluge of rain on Vraja (Cf. Bh. P. X. 24.ff.). So Kṛṣṇa lifted Mount Govardhana over Vraja to protect it from Indra's wrath. This notion is reflected in Vallabha's teachings by his forbidding his followers to worship a god other than Kṛṣṇa or to use anything that has not first been offered to Kṛṣṇa.

and He alone produces it, the Gopīs have used the word "joy" !

"With the gleam of His toil..causing joy to well up in the eyes" of those who are in Vraja, "He comes, eager to bestow His blessings." This is how the Gopīs' words connect. In the opinion of those who hold that toil is absent from, or alien to, the Blessed Lord, its presence here is intended merely as a show. But our considered principle is that there is toil. For, as holy scripture tells us : "Being a Supporter (Skt. *bhartā*), being supported He supports ; the one God has entered within in many ways; when He becomes fatigued with the burden, after appointing someone else to bear the burden He disappears again" (*Taittirīya Āraṇyaka* III 14. 1). Also (this is our considered principle) because He is the ground of all attributes. But since He is the ground of all contradictory attributes, He is also not-fatigued-from-toil. But He is not merely "not-fatigued-from-toil", without also being its contradictory opposite.[27] Others say that His toil brings happiness. Thus the "gleam" that is associated with it is "the gleam of His toil" here. That gleam of toil, when it is present on a husband or lover,[28] does no good for ordinary women. Yet it has become a great benefactor for us alone, say the Gopīs, when they use the words : "causing joy to well up in (our) eyes." "Eye" here is used in the sense of "our looking, our seeing." If the Blessed Lord were

27. The point is that, philosophically speaking, God can never be fatigued. But for the sake of devotional worship, Kṛṣṇa is fatigued, hungry, in need of clothing, etc., so that those who love Him can refresh Him, feed Him, clothe Him, etc. Here Vallahbha's devotion goes in a direction which philosophy is too logical to allow. In general, too, Vallabha's important teaching of Kṛṣṇa/Brahman's being "the ground of contradictory attributes" (Skt. *viruddhadharmāśrayatā*) forms his cardinal exegetical principle. By this principle, Vallabha can assert that even the apparently contradictory attributes which scripture posits in Kṛṣṇa/Brahman should not arbitrarily or subjectively be subordinated, one set to the other (as with the so-called *saguṇa* and *nirguṇa* attributes). Rather, they should all be accepted without prejudice, as having scriptural authority, and therefore being true of Kṛṣṇa/Brahman.

28. OR: "on a dramatic hero"; this last is possible but not likely. But Skt. *nāyaka*, the word used here, has all these meanings and more; however I think Vallabha must mean one or the other of the two I have translated above.

not weary from His toil, then He would move quickly. Then there would not be a prolonged, continuous presence of Supreme Joy in our looking at Him. And by the words "causing to well up"—literally "leading upwards"—the Gopīs mean that Kṛṣṇa has made their Joy much greater than the amount of joy that affects them when they see Him in a crowd. And, explaining this manner of the Blessed Lord's Fame, which is directed towards His giving all the objects of human striving, a Gopī gives the supporting argument which proves His toil when she says : "His garland (s) coated with the dust of the herd's hooves." Grains of dust that are kicked up by the wind do not adhere firmly, nor do they settle in permanently. But the dust that comes from the cattle's hooves does precisely that. Because it is the cows who have hooves and it is they who are the subject-matter here, the word "cow" is not actually mentioned in this phrase. For the reasoned conclusion here is the same as that in the saying : "Or cows which are whole-hoofed (i.e., not cloven-hoofed)." By this the hoof has been described as *dharma,* the dust (*rajas*) as *artha* and the "coating", or penetration, of His garland with it is described as *kāma.*[29]

But then the Gopīs have described the effect He intends by His coming in the words : "on His friends," i.e., on everyone, without exception, who is associated with Him, every single one of "His blessings" are to be "bestowed." What has been expressed through the Gopīs here is the entry of His Joy into all. And the Gopīs have used the word "this", pointing out Kṛṣṇa specifically, from which the fact that the game is in Himself has been indicated.

And the Gopīs have described the specific attribute present in the Blessed Lord for the purpose of destroying the suffering of all in general with the words :"(this) Moon who came forth from the womb of Devakī." Since holy scripture tells us : "Aditi is Devakī, Aditi is the sky, Aditi is the intermediate space between heaven and earth" (*RV* I, 89. 10: *TĀ* I. 13. 2), then because this Aditi has come down to earth in the form of Devakī, she (Devakī) embodies the sky. In her the moon

29. This makes sense in the context of these being three of the four "objects of human striving" mentioned above.

must necessarily and certainly arise. And since She has taken a special form, the moon, too, must produce a special effect. Ordinary suffering is threefold, and so is the suffering caused by separation from the Blessed Lord. This "Moon" (Kṛṣṇa) destroys the threefold suffering, too—it has already been proved that, as explained above, He is the Giver of Joy. He "comes to be in the womb of Devakī."[30] He alone is the "king of stars" (*uḍurāja*, i.e., the moon). And just as the moon is born in the eastern mountain from which he arises, but he is the husband of the constellations alone, so was He born in Devakī, but He gives Joy to us alone !

(Here begins a long interpolation of Viṭṭhala) Or, to explain this in another way: these Gopīs are afflicted by separation from the Blessed Lord, so they had no "joy" because they had no contact with His body in the manner they desired. Thus they remained afflicted. But, for their eyes, seeing is the main thing, and by that alone does "joy well up in" them. And thus we should understand the compound *ārtadṛśīnām* as meaning "in the eyes of us who are afflicted."[31] And the final *-a* in *ārta* is short (not long, which would indicate the desired feminine gender) in accordance with Vedic usage. For it is not the affliction of the eyes alone which is to be described here. For the Gopīs have tasted the sweetness of His Form in the other ways as well. And so it is possible for affliction to arise in all the other sense-faculties, too. Then only (i.e., when Kṛṣṇa removes the affliction of all the sense-faculties) will there be "joy" everywhere, because there will be no desire that He "bestow His blessings" again. And their saying, just after the present passage, that He is "eager to bestow" them would also be inappropriate. "Joy" of the eyes is external alone. But the *locus* of interior joy is the mind. And because the mind is not satis-

30. My translation in the stanza and Vallabha's interpretation here differ slightly but not significantly.

31. Viṭṭhala here reads *śramarucārtadṛśīnām*, i.e., "causing, with the gleam of His toil, joy to well up in the eyes of us who are afflicted." Vallabha, on the other hand, has read: *śramarucāpi dṛśīnām*, i.e., "(causing joy to well up) in the eyes of the Gopīs even with the gleam of His toil." All three printed editions of the Bhāgavata which are available to me agree with Vallabha's reading.

fied, that joy is not present now. But this joy will later be present, when they see Him at the time of love-making. It is to indicate this that the Gopīs have said "up" (in the sense of "ahead, in the future") in the stanza. Just as the Gopīs, in the passage : "they came forward and bunched together, their eyes eager to see" (Bh. P. X.) felt their eyes afflicted with the same eagerness to see Him even after they had seen Him, so should we presume this to be the case here. That is why they have said "in the eyes" here. Even the case of the phrase "in the eyes" (literally : "of the eyes"; *dṛśīnām*) is genitive, thus showing the definite connection of "joy" here with "the eyes." And besides, by their saying that the Blessed Lord is the agent in this "welling up" of joy, it is indicated that their joy is external, and brought about by their Beloved, and thus comes from the nature of the act of seeing Him, not from themselves. For this reason the bringing of joy even by one who has "the gleam of toil" is fitting. Otherwise when they in their day-long eagerness see the exhaustion from toil of their most Beloved as He comes home, no joy would be theirs, because they would fear this obstacle to their upcoming delights of love. Instead they would become even more depressed than they had been. But besides, the Gopīs would say : "Outside of us there is no one by whom our Lover could get rid of His exhaustion. And so, after this, we will do just that." So in this context, the fact that Kṛṣṇa has "a gleam of toil" or exhaustion, is perfectly fitting. Also when they describe the "gleam" of this exhaustion they suggest that it is a gleam in the sense that it presents no obstacle to the fulfilment of their desires. If someone objects : "But what if this exhaustion comes from His just having made love with another woman ? How will there be joy in your eyes then?", the Gopīs deny that this could be so in the words : "His garland coated with the dust of the herd's hooves." For if this exhaustion came from His loving another woman, then her make-up, or collyrium, or what have you, would be smeared on His garland—not the dust kicked up by the cows' hooves! If it is said that the dust is associated merely with the time it took Him to come, we grant that this is possible. But, precisely to indicate that the dust had been there for a long time, the Gopīs have used the word "coated." For it is impossible to build up that amount of dirt in a short time. Besides, if what you say were true, there would not even be a garland, because it would have got in the way of the love-play. And so it should be understood that: "He comes, eager to bestow His blessings on His friends," i.e., on us.

When the Gopīs say : "He comes," it should be understood that, since they have mentioned no object of His action of coming, His object is exactly what they have said. The meaning is as follows. Pāṇini tells us : "That which is most desired by the 'agent' is the 'object' of his action" (*Aṣṭādhyāyī* I. 4. 49). By this we know that, since the Blessed Lord is the agent here, we alone, and no one else, are the ones He most desires. Otherwise the stanza's words would have been "He comes to Vraja." Although the Blessed Lord desires to bring about the constraint of all, and so Vraja, too, is most desired by Him, still the superlative degree defined by the word "most desired" applies to us alone. That is why they have spoken as they have. The Gopīs have said "this" (in "this Moon") merely to point Him out directly. Otherwise, if we were not the most desired by Him, why would He show Himself to us in this way ? In order to point out the absence of duplicity in His interior feeling of Himself as faithful Lover (OR : the absence in the Lord of the duplicity in his interior feeling of himself which a clever Casanova would have), the Gopīs have said : "who came forth from the womb of Devakī." For Devakī is flawless in every way. And, the Gopīs mean, He who became manifest in her womb is exactly the same. To answer the question : "What is the special relation of such a Person with you ?", the Gopīs have said : "Moon." Just as the moon removes the suffering of all, even from afar, but by being the husband of the constellations he removes the suffering in his immediate vicinity, so Kṛṣṇa also removes the suffering of all from afar, but by being our Husband He does so from nearby. Thus our relation is very special indeed. And as the moon, standing in the circle of constellations, appears more beautiful by reason of them and removes the suffering of all of them, so Kṛṣṇa, when He stands in our circle, appears more beautiful because of us and likewise removes our suffering. This is implied by the word the Gopīs use for "moon"—*uḍurāja*,—"king of stars" (end of Viṭṭhala's interpolation). This entire effect is to be brought about by the sound of His flute, which we know because that is the subject-matter of this chapter.

Introduction to Stanzas 24-25 : Having just described the general game directed to all, a Gopī now describes the game created by the flute in the Gopīs alone, caused and brought to pass by the Blessed Lord alone :

Stanzas 24-25 : "His eyes rolling with rapture, bestowing a trace of pride upon His friends, He with His garland of forest-flowers, His face as pale white as the jujube fruit, adorning His delicate cheek with the rich Splendor of gold earrings, the Lord of the Yadus, whose love-play is like that of the greatest bull-elephant, at day's end This One, like the lord of the night, His face beaming with joy, approaches and comes near, liberating Vraja's cows' day's suffering's endless heat entirely."

Commentary : "The Lord of the Yadus, His face beaming with joy, approaches." The sounds of His flute which have been described before should be understood here. Thinking : "We have described ten games above, and all these were for the sake of us alone," the Gopīs enumerate the characteristics of the Blessed Lord in ten ways. One and the same Blessed Lord is described in both the preceding and the present stanza-pairs, according to the Gopīs, so even though this is a separate stanza-pair, there is no hard and fast distinction between the two. In the sound of His flute everywhere the *rajas* quality is uppermost, think the Gopīs, and this sound has come to fruition for our sake. And so they have said : "His eyes rolling with rapture." The word "rapture" here means full knowledge by reason of the presence of His Joy. To cause all sensual objects to turn away – in order to make it clear that this rapture occurs only on the Path of Knowledge—His eyes have been described as "rolling." This attribute has been described as being present in, or relating to, the Blessed Lord.

In order that His Form may remain and abide (in the Gopīs), such a One also "bestows a trace of honor (Skt. *māna*)", i.e., He grants them His respect—He pays them homage. By this it becomes known to the Gopīs that "He is accessible to us." Or, the Gopīs' word *māna* may mean "pride," because the *rajas* quality is the one clearly manifest here. Thus the Gopīs' words would mean : "bestowing a trace of pride." Or again, their words may mean that He "cuts off" or "destroys" their "pride", because Knowledge is clearly manifest there.[32] Also, among these three possible meanings, one or another effect, whichever is produced, has been described as merely "a trace." To someone who may ask : "But what is the reason why He who is perfectly Full should act in this way towards you good women ?", the Gopīs have answered : "upon His friends." There is specificity here because of the word "His". By the use of this word these Gopīs are the friends "of Him" alone. Even a great person has to pay attention to the needs of his friends. A Gopī has told us the need Kṛṣṇa fulfils for people in general in the words : "He with His garland of forest-flowers." Thus, Kṛṣṇa is making manifest (to all) the garland of forest-flowers which is full of His Fame. Next, the Gopīs say : "His face as pale-white as the jujube-fruit." Here the word *badara* (which may mean either the jujube tree or its fruit) is expressive of the fruit (*phalam*; also "reward") For this fruit, because of heat, produces at various times a different radiance. Thus when it is half-ripe, it has a "pale-white" color. But later it becomes red. In the same way He is now half-impassioned, but later He will be extremely passionate, according to the Gopīs. This is their special character resulting from His "bestowing a trace of pride" upon them. And the means of attainment is His Fame, which is why they put that distinguishing characteristic in the middle, between the two characteristics of His bestowing pride on them and His pale-white face. Or, alternatively : by the word "pale white" (*pāṇḍu*) here, the reddish quality alone is expressed. Then, in that case, it has been indicated that the two words used for "face" (*vadana* and *vaktra*, both of which can mean "face" or "mouth") mean "mouth", and indicate the drinking of the nectar of His lips. Or, the meaning here may be that

32. Here the issue is not whether the word *māna* means "honor" or "pride" but whether the verbal suffix *-da* which is added onto *māna* (thus *mānada*) is to be taken in the sense of *dadāti*, "He gives, bestows" or *dyati*, "He cuts off, destroys." Both are quite possible, although the former is more frequent.

this drinking of the nectar of His lips is to be enjoyed by forest-dwellers alone (since the jujube-fruit is a wild fruit). Therefore we should go to the forest and enjoy it there. With these words these particular Gopīs cause all the Gopīs to know this.

Next, the Gopīs have also pointed out this characteristic : "adorning His delicate cheek with the rich Splendor of gold earrings." Because of the absence of a growth of beard there, and because His cheek is the dwelling-place, or storehouse, of Joy, the fact that it is "delicate," for purposes of sexual enjoyment, is proved. For on the cheek alone is the nectar of the mood of love fully attained. The word "gold" is used to indicate yet another color. By this especially excellent Supreme Joy also, the mood of passionate love, and no other, is caused to be aroused in Him for our sake, think the Gopīs, and thus they conclude for certain that "the Blessed Lord's coming is for our sake alone, in every way ! Otherwise He would not make all these different movements, decorations and signs with and on His head here, right before our eyes."

In case a question arises to the effect that, though He is Great, still He is a child—He is, after all, "Nanda's boy"—and so how will He play this extraordinary game. the Gopīs remove this doubt with the words : "the Lord of the Yadus." He is the Lord of the Yādavas. For they are polygamous. And, in the context of the breaking of laws which Kṛṣṇa will do in this game, the Gopīs have added the further distinguishing characteristic : "whose love-play is like that of the greatest bull-elephant." In His tremendous sexual prowess and delights He is as great as a king of elephants! Without Him (OR : without that), there would not be fulfilment, think the Gopīs. But with reference to that sexual delight, too, He will first of all remove all our previous suffering completely. The Gopīs have expressed this in the words : "like the lord of the night." He is the Lord of the night in all her fulness. Therefore He will bring joy in a special way to those who have betaken themselves to the night! If someone should raise the question that Kṛṣṇa is the Lord of the day, too, so how is it that you are saying He is "like the lord of the night," the Gopīs have said simply : "This One." He stands there, the Ornament of everything. But now He is exhausted from toil, as it were. "At day's end This One, like the Lord of the night," i.e., like the moon, destroys suffering, even from a great distance, immediately. But later, too, He is like the lord of the night. This last is precisely the meaning intended to be implied in the next distinguishing characteristic the Gopīs describe in Kṛṣṇa, because, "His face beaming with joy," i.e., His face having become bright and full of grace, "He approaches," i.e., "comes near." This emotion does good and is helpful to the Gopīs alone. Kṛṣṇa's performance of good to all generally has been described previously. But the Gopīs sum up this helpfulness to all once again when they say : "liberating Vraja's cow's day's suffering's endless heat entirely." As much suffering as there has been, throughout the entire day, "of Vraja" and "of the cows,"[33] He causes all that suffering to be removed entirely, say the Gopīs.

Introduction to Stanza 26 : Having thus described the constraint of the women, Śuka sums it up, and in the process of doing so he sums up the constraint of all those who are present in this treatise-section (of the Bhāgavata) :

Stanza 26 : Śuka said : Thus the women of Vraja, O King, rehearsing in song the Games of Kṛṣṇa, one after another, delighted their days in love, their minds on Him, their hearts in Him alone—these blessed women!

Commentary : Śuka addresses Parikṣit directly with the words "O King" in order to gain his confidence. Even when these "women" were in "Vraja," the following is the method by which they "delighted their days in love" even in these circumstances in which they were bereft of union with the Blessed Lord. They "rehearsed in song the Games of Kṛṣṇa" alone, "one after another," in the Games' due order, in order to conform themselves to the long time of their separation and of the performance of Kṛṣṇa's daytime Games; and the Gopīs also sang "one after another," in due order. And to signify that

33. Vallabha and I differ slightly here on the interpretation of the stanza's compound word *vrajagavām*. Vallabha takes it as a *dvandva*-compound: "(the suffering) of Vraja and the cows," while I interpret it as a *tatpuruṣa*-compound: "(the suffering) of Vraja's cows." Perhaps the two are equally likely. And Vallabha's commentatorial contextualization of his interpretation is certainly beautiful.

Kṛṣṇa's Fame, which in and of itself embodies His Joy, became present to the Gopīs, and that both their power of action and their power of knowledge were fixed upon, and in, the Blessed Lord alone, Śuka has said : "their hearts in Him...their minds on Him." For the intellect is uppermost in knowledge, and the will is uppermost in actions. Thus both the Gopīs' passionate attachment to the Blessed Lord and their forgetting the world totally—in every way—have been described. Someone may ask : "But how has the Gopīs' constraint come to complete fruition in this way?" Śuka's proof for this has been stated in his words : "these blessed women !" Great indeed is their success, and overwhelming the abundance of their good fortune. And thus all is well.

APPENDIX : THE SANSKRIT TEXT

श्रीकृष्णाय नमः ।

श्रीगोपीजनवल्लभाय नमः ।

श्रीमदाचार्यचरणकमलेभ्यो नमः ।

श्रीसुबोधिनी

(दशमतामसफलप्रकरणम् ।)

श्रीमद्वल्लभाचार्यप्रकटिता ।

षड्विंशोऽध्यायः*

ब्रह्मानन्दात्समुद्धृत्य भजनानन्दयोजने ।
लीला या युज्यते सम्यक् सा तुर्ये विनिरूप्यते ॥१॥

लौकिकस्त्रीषु संसिद्धस्तद्द्वारा पुरुषे भवेत् ।
स्वानन्दानुभवार्थं हि योग्यतापि निरूपिता ॥२॥

ततो हि भजनानन्दः स्त्रीषु सम्यग् विधार्यते ।
तद्द्वारा पुरुषाणां च भविष्यति न चान्यथा ॥३॥

स्त्रिय एव हि तं पातुं शक्तास्तासु ततः पुमान् ।
अतो हि भगवान् कृष्णः स्त्रीषु रेमे ह्यहर्निशम् ॥४॥

बाह्याभ्यन्तरभेदेन आन्तरं तु परं फलम् ।
ततः शब्दात्मिका लीला निर्दुष्टा सा निरूप्यते ॥५॥

ततो रूपप्रपञ्चस्य पञ्चधा रमणं मतम् ।
आत्मना प्रथमा लीला मनसा तु ततः परा ॥६॥

वाक्प्राणैस्तु तृतीया स्यादिन्द्रियैस्तु ततः परा ।
शारीरी पञ्चमी वाच्या ततो रूपं प्रतिष्ठितम् ॥७॥

षड्विंशे तु हरिः पूर्वं जीवानानन्दयत्स्वयम् ।
ते चेत् समर्पितात्मानस्तत्रोपायश्च रूप्यते ॥८॥

*NOTE : The difference between Vallabha's numbering of the chapters of the Bhāgavata Purāṇa's Tenth Book (which is used in the following Sanskrit text) and the traditional numbering of the same chapters is explained in Footnote 1 on Chapter One, on page 48 above.

आत्मा यावत् प्रपन्नोऽभूत्तावद्वै रमते हरिः ।
सोऽन्तःकरणसम्बन्धी तिरोधत्ते हरिश्च सः ॥६॥

प्रथमं भजनानन्दं निरूपयितुं स्त्रीषु स्वानन्दः स्थापनीय इति तासु रत्यर्थमिच्छां कृतवानित्याह भगवानपीति ।

श्रीशुक उवाच—**भगवानपि ता रात्रीः शरदोत्फुल्लमल्लिकाः ।**
वीक्ष्य रन्तुं मनश्चक्रे योगमायामुपाश्रितः ॥१॥

'मयेमा रंस्यथ क्षपा' इति या रात्रयो वरत्वेन दत्ताः, स्त्रीणां रमणार्थाः, ता रात्रीर्भगवान् परिगृह्य, सर्वास्वेव रात्रिषु ता आधिदैविकीरारोप्य, पूर्णत्वात्तासां पूर्णिमारूपाः कृत्वा, ऋतुमपि शरदमेव कृत्वा, तस्यापि कार्यं पुष्पाण्येव कृत्वा, रसोद्दीपकत्वेन सर्वां सामग्रीं विधाय, पश्चाद्रमणार्थं स्वानन्दप्रकाशकं कामपितामहं मन उत्पादितवान् । तत्र सर्वासु संकल्पः स्वस्मिन्नपि बोधनीयः । तत्र वेणुरपि सहायतां प्राप्स्यति । ततः कामवर्णनम् । अतः प्रथमं तादृशं मनः कृतवान् । यद्यपि एतत्प्रणालिकाव्यतिरेकेणापि स्वानन्दं तत्र स्थापयितुं शक्तः, तथापि मर्यादा तिष्ठत्विति भगवानपि मनश्चक्रे । नन्वेवं सति स्वानन्दः स्थानत्यागात् अन्यथा भवेत्, ततः स्वरूपादपि प्रच्युतः स्यादित्याशंक्याह योगमायामुपाश्रित इति । योगमाया हि यथास्थितमेवान्यत्र स्थापयति, यथा सङ्कर्षणम् । लीलार्थं सापि पूर्वं परिगृहीतेति नापूर्वं किञ्चित् । यथा प्रमाणे रक्षायां च बलभद्रोपयोगः, एवं कार्ये योगमायायाः । तत्राप्यन्तरङ्गा योगमाया, अन्यत्र स्थितं प्रमाणमन्यत्रापि योजयति, अन्यत्र स्थितं चानन्दमन्यत्र । अतः प्रमाणातिरिक्तमार्गो भक्तिमार्गश्चाग्रे विततौ भविष्यतः । याश्च रात्रयो रमणार्थमेव निर्मिताः, ता एव परिगृहीताः, अन्यथा साधारणीपरिग्रहे सर्वत्रैवानन्दः स्यात् । शरदि ऋतावुत्फुल्ला मल्लिका यासु । ता दृष्ट्वा रमणार्थं मनः कृतवान् । योगमायां च समीप एवाश्रित्य स्थितः ॥१॥

नूतने तस्मिन् मनसि देवता नास्तीति, अनधिष्ठितं च कार्यं न साधयिष्यतीति तदधिष्ठातृदेवं चन्द्रं च ससृज इत्याह तदोडुराज इति ।

तदोडुराजः ककुभः करैर्मुखं प्राच्या विलिम्पन्नरुणेन शन्तमैः ।
स चर्षणीनामुदगाच्छुचो हरन् प्रियः प्रियाया इव दीर्घदर्शनः ॥२॥

यदैव मनः कृतवान्, तदैव तस्याधिदैवतमुडुराज उदगात्, उदितो जातः। यद्यप्येकदा रात्रयो दृष्टाः, तथापि क्रमेणैव तासां स्थितिः । भगवन्मनश्चन्द्रस्याधिदैविकत्वात् पूर्ण एव सः, निष्कलङ्कश्च । मनस्येवाविर्भूते तस्याविर्भावः, क्रीडायामुपरतायामुपरतिः, मध्याकाशपर्यन्तमेव गमनम्, नास्तमयः कदाचिदपि । सोऽपि चन्द्रः स्त्रीणां

मनांसि उडुस्थानानीति तेषामपि रक्षकः। इदं प्रथमतया जात इति पूर्वस्यामेव दिशि तस्योदय उच्यते। 'सा दिग्देवाना'मिति। तस्या दिश इन्द्रो देवता अधिपतिश्च। इदानीं भगवानेवेन्द्र इति तस्य रेतोरूपः तस्यामुद्गतः। अतः प्राच्याः ककुभः मुखं मध्यभागं स्वकरैः स्वकिरणैः विलिम्पन् उदगात्। तस्या मुखे न रागः स्थितः, प्रतिस्पर्धिन्यां सूर्यसम्बन्धेन रागसंभवात्, अतः अस्या अपि मुखं कुङ्कुमसदृशैः करैरारक्तं क्रियते। यदि चन्द्रः स्वदिशो मुखं न रञ्जयेत्, तदा भगवन्मनोऽपि स्त्रीणां हृदयं न रञ्जयेत्। कराः शन्तमाः, शीतलत्वात् तापहारकाः। किञ्च, अरुणेन गुणेन कृत्वा अत्यन्तं कल्याणरूपाः। अरुणो हि रागप्रधानः। पुरुषोऽपि यद्यनुरागेण स्पृशति, तदा सुखं भवति। ननु अस्य चन्द्रस्य यदि अधिष्ठातृत्वमात्रम्, तदा मनस्येव उदयो भवेत्, यद्यन्धकारनिवृत्तिः प्रयोजनम्, तदा भगवतैव अन्धकारो निवर्तेत, यदि वा उद्दीपकत्वम्, तदापि भगवतैव तत्संभवः, अतोऽस्यासाधारणं कार्यं वक्तव्यमिति चेत्, अत आह स चर्षणीनां शुचो हरन्निति। चर्षण्यः सर्वत्र परिभ्रमणशक्तयः। ता सर्वत्र परिभ्रान्ता अपि न क्वापि परमानन्दसम्बन्धिन्यो जाताः। यदि वा कश्चिन् मुच्येत, तथापि ता न प्रवेशं लभन्ते। ततः पूर्वमेव ता निवृत्ता भवन्ति। अतस्तासां शोकस्तिष्ठत्येव। चर्षणीसहितानां जीवानां वा। तासां शोकः इदानीमेव निवृत्तः। शक्तिसहितानामेव परमानन्दानुभवस्य वक्तव्यत्वात्। प्रायेण तदानीन्तना जीवाः तादृशशक्तियुक्ताः। तस्मिन्नुदिते परमानन्दानुभवोऽवश्यंभावीति। तथा सति प्रयोजनत्रयम्, दिग्देवताया मुखसम्मार्जनं, चर्षणीनां शोकदूरीकरणं, अन्धकारनिवृत्त्यादिश्च। कण्ठोक्तं द्वयमपि तदेकसाध्यमिति वक्तुं दृष्टान्तमाह प्रियः प्रियाया इति। दीर्घकाले दर्शनं यस्य। महता कालेनागतो भर्ता प्रियः प्रियायाः पतिव्रतायाः शोकं दूरीकृत्य मुखसम्मार्जनं च करोति। न चैतत्कार्यमन्यथा सिध्यति ॥२॥

एवं मनस उत्पत्तिमुक्त्वा तद्देवतायाश्च ततः सङ्कल्पोत्पत्त्यर्थं तच्छब्दयोनित्वं निरूपयन् तद्दर्शनेन वेणुनाद उत्पन्न इत्याह दृष्ट्वेति।

दृष्ट्वा कुमुद्वन्तमखण्डमण्डलं रमाननाभं नवकुङ्कुमारुणम्।
वनं च तत्कोमलगोभिरञ्जितं जगौ कलं वामदृशां मनोहरम् ॥३॥

कुमुद्वांश्चन्द्रः, पृथिव्यां सर्वत्रैव मुदं कृतवानिति। तथाकरणे सामर्थ्यं अखण्डमण्डलमिति। न खण्डं मण्डलं यस्य। एतस्य रसोत्पादने विभावत्वमप्यस्तीति ज्ञापयितुं रमाननाभमित्युक्तम्। लक्ष्म्या अयं भ्राता भवतीति, रमाया आननवत् आभा यस्य, तथोक्तः। किञ्च, नवकुङ्कुमवदरुणवर्णमपि। तेन विवाहसमये यथा लक्ष्मीमुखम्, तथायं वर्तते। अतो नूतनकामजनकः। किञ्च, वनमपि रसपोषकम्। तस्य कोमलगोभिरल्पकिरणैः अभितो रञ्जितमारक्तयुक्तम्। (किरणानां रसदोग्धृत्वम्। वन एव पाल्यमानत्वं च ज्ञापयितुं गोपदम्। रमाननाभत्वेन पूर्वं निरू-

***This figure indicates the traditional number of the chapter.**

पणाद्यथा तन्नूतनकटाक्षा भावोदयहेतवः । तथैतेऽपीति ज्ञापनाय च गोपदमिन्द्रिय-स्यापि वाचकमिति तथा । अधुना भावोत्पत्तिरेव तत्पोषस्तु स्वामिन्यागमनादिनाग्रे भावीति ज्ञापयितुं कोमलपदम् । यत्र तेन वनमपि रज्यते, तत्र यदर्थमागतः तद्रागं कथं न कुर्यात् ।) ततः सङ्कल्पद्वारा कामजनने सर्वं कार्यं भविष्यतीति कलं यथा भवति तथा जगौ, गानं कृतवान् । तच्च गानं वामदृशां सुन्दरदृष्टीनां स्त्रीणां मनोहरमिति । 'तस्माद्गायन्तं स्त्रियः कामयन्त' इति श्रुतेः । अर्थाद्गीतेन सर्वाः समाहृता इति । यदि व्यक्तमधुरं गीतं कुर्यात् तदा गीतमेव शृण्वन्त्यः तत्रैव स्थिता भवेयुः । यासां पुनर्दृष्टिर्नोत्तमा, तास्तु नाकारिता एव ॥३॥

ततः सर्वाः स्त्रियः समागता इत्याह निशम्येति ।

निशम्य गीतं तदनङ्गवर्धनं व्रजस्त्रियः कृष्णगृहीतमानसाः ।
आजग्मुरन्योन्यमलक्षितोद्यमाः स यत्र कान्तो जवलोलकुण्डलाः ॥४॥

यद्यपि भगवता कुमारिका एवाहूताः, तथापि आह्वानं सदृशमिति, निरोधोऽपि कर्तव्य इति सर्वा एव समागताः । किञ्च, यद्भगवता गीतं तदनङ्गमेव वर्धयति, अङ्गं तु नाशयत्येव । अतो नूतन उत्पन्नः कामः ता आनीतवान् । किञ्च, व्रजस्य स्त्रियः पूर्वमपि भगवदीयाः, अतः कृष्णेनैव गृहीतं मनो यासाम् । अतः शीघ्रमेव यत्र कान्तस्तत्रागताः । अनेन आकारिता एव प्रथमागता इत्युक्तम् । तासां मुख्यः कान्त इति । अत एवान्योन्यमलक्षित उद्यमो यासाम् । ता हि प्रत्येकमेव भगवन्तं पतित्वेन स्वीकृतवत्यः । स पूर्वमुपात्तो यः कान्तः । तासां शरीरविचारेऽपि दृष्टिर्न जातेति वक्तुं जवेन लोले कुण्डले यासामिति कर्णपीडाननुसन्धानं प्रदर्शितम् । ताः स्त्रियो गौडदेशस्थाः । तत एव कुमारिकाः समागता इति । पूर्वं मथुरादेशस्थितानामपि अनागरीणां कुण्डले एव । ताटङ्कयोरेव वा कुण्डलत्वम् ॥४॥

प्रसङ्गादन्यासामप्यागमनमाह दुहन्त्य इति ।

दुहन्त्योऽभिययुः काश्चित् दोहं हित्वा समुत्सुकाः ।
पयोऽधिश्रित्य संयावमनुद्वास्यापरा ययुः ॥५॥

तासां वा क्रियापराणाम् । तत्र काश्चन षोडशसहस्रव्यतिरिक्ताः नवविधाः समागताः, दशविधा वा । गुणानां त्रैविध्यान्नवविधत्वम् । निर्गुणाश्चैकविधाः । जातिकुललोकधर्मपराः तिस्रस्तिस्र उदीरिताः । तत्र गोपजातीयाः दुग्धपराः । तत्र दुग्धस्योत्पत्तिस्थितिप्रलयान् कुर्वन्ति तास्तिस्रः प्रथममुदीरिताः । एवंविधा अपि गणश इति वक्तुं सर्वत्र बहुवचनम् । काश्चिद्दुहन्त्य एव दोहं दोहनलक्षणं कर्म मध्ये त्यक्त्वा भगवदाभिमुख्येन ययुः । गौर्वत्सश्च बद्धौ, दोहनपात्रं च अर्धदुग्धम्, यः

समयः सर्वथा त्यक्तुमशक्यः, तस्मिन् समये समागताः । तथा समागमने हेतुः समुत्सुका इति । सम्यगुत्सुकाः, को वेद क्षणान्तरे भगवान् क्व गमिष्यतीति । अन्याः पुनः पयः अधिश्रित्य तथैव ययुः । भोजनार्थं पयसि पच्यमानाः गोधूमकणाः संयावशब्देनोच्यन्ते । तेषां दाहे सर्वनाश इति । पक्वदशैव संयावशब्देनोच्यते । अतस्तदप्यनुद्वास्य काश्चन अभिययुः । अपरा इति सर्वत्र गुणैर्भिन्नस्वभावत्वम् । एवं तिस्रो राजस्यः ॥५॥

सात्त्विकीराह परिवेषयन्त्य इति ।

परिवेषयन्त्यस्तद्धित्वा पाययन्त्यः शिशूनथ ।
शुश्रूषन्त्यः पतीन् काश्चिदश्नन्त्योऽपास्य भोजनम् ॥६॥

भर्तुरपत्यस्यापि सेवा स्त्रीधर्मः । तत्र भर्तुर्भोजने शयने च सेवा स्वधर्म : । अतिबालकानां पुत्राणां स्तनदानं च । परिवेषणं च सृष्टिरिव, रेतस उत्पादकत्वात् । स्तनदानं पालनम् । शिष्टमन्यत् । सर्वत्र तत्तद्धित्वेति ज्ञेयम् । अन्या इत्यपि । तामसीराह अश्नन्त्योऽपास्य भोजनमित्यादि ॥६॥

लिम्पन्त्यः प्रमृजन्त्योऽन्या अञ्जन्त्यः काश्च लोचने ।
व्यत्यस्तवस्त्राभरणाः काश्चित्कृष्णान्तिकं ययुः ॥७॥

लिम्पन्त्यः शरीरानुलेपनं कुर्वन्त्यः, प्रमृजन्त्य उद्वर्तनादिकं कुर्वन्त्यः, गृहं वा लिम्पन्त्यः, प्रमृजन्त्यः आभरणानि, भाण्डानि वा प्रमृजन्त्यः । अत्रापि पूर्ववदेव क्रमः । शरीरसेवातः गोसेवा मुख्या, ततः पतिसेवेति । 'अञ्जन्त्यः काश्च लोचने' इति गुणातीताः । अतः 'काश्च लोचने' इति दुर्लभाधिकारः सूचितः । ज्ञानमार्गशोधिका इति निर्गुणत्वम् । तासामागमने दैहिकविचारोऽपि न जातः, किम्पुनस्तद्धर्माणामिति वक्तुं वस्त्राभरणयोर्व्यत्यासमाह व्यत्यस्तेति । व्यत्यस्तानि विपरीतानि वस्त्राण्याभरणानि च यासाम् । एवमुद्यमः सर्वासामेव साधारणो निरूपितः । 'व्यत्यासो मार्गगता' विति केचित् । तन्मध्येऽपि काश्चित्कृष्णान्तिकं ययुः, काश्चिन्न । याः पुनः शब्दपरा जाताः, ता उद्युक्ता अपि नागताः, याः पुनः शब्दापेक्षां त्यक्तवत्यः, ताः सर्वतो निरपेक्षाः विपरीतावश्यकदेहधर्माः भगवदन्तिकमागताः ॥७॥

सर्वासामनागमने हेतुमाह ता वार्यमाणा इति ।

ता वार्यमाणाः पतिभिः पितृभिः पुत्रबन्धुभिः ।
गोविन्दापहृतात्मानो न न्यवर्तन्त मोहिताः ॥८॥

'रक्षेत्कन्यां पिता विन्नां पतिः पुत्रस्तु वार्धके । अभावे ज्ञातयस्तेषां न स्वातन्त्र्यं

क्वचित्स्त्रिया' इति चत्वारो रक्षकाः । अतो यथायथं पतिभिर्वार्यमाणा जाताः, काश्चन पितृभिः, तथैव पुत्रैर्बन्धुभिश्च । ते हि निरुद्धा अपि फलरसानभिज्ञाः, साधनप्रवणाः । स्वद्वारैव स्त्रीणां भजनं भजनं मन्यन्ते, न तु स्वातन्त्र्येण । तथापि गोविन्देनापहृतः आत्मा अन्तःकरणं यासाम् । निवारणं हि श्रौत्रम् । प्रवर्तकश्च भगवान् । अन्तःकरणारूढाश्च पुरुषाः । न हि नौका प्रवाहवेगाद्गच्छन्ती तिष्ठ तिष्ठेत्युक्ता तिष्ठति । भयं स्वधर्मो वा तासां नास्तीत्याह मोहिता इति । यदि ताः कृष्णान्तिकं न गच्छेयुः, तदा मूर्च्छिता इव प्राणाँस्त्यजेयुः । (सर्वात्मभावज्ञापनायैवाधुना व्रजस्थानामेतदागमनज्ञानं कारितवानिति ज्ञेयम् । अन्यथाग्रे 'मन्यमानाः स्वपार्श्वस्था'निति वाक्याद्यथा वनस्थित्यज्ञानं सम्पादितवान्, एवं पूर्वमेवागमनाज्ञानमेव कथं न सम्पादयेत् । 'प्रक्षालनाद्धि पङ्कस्ये'ति न्यायेन तज्ज्ञानं सम्पाद्य तत्सम्भावितदोषाभावसम्पादनात्तदसम्पादनस्यैव वरीयस्त्वादिति) ॥८॥

एवं दशविधानां भगवत्समीपगतिमुक्त्वा, यासां कालः प्रतिबन्धकः । पूर्वमेव भक्तियुक्ताः, ता भजनानन्दमननुभूयैव, प्रतिबद्धा एव, भगवत्सायुज्यं प्राप्तवत्य इत्याह अन्तर्गृहगता इति त्रिभिः ।

अन्तर्गृहगताः काश्चिद् गोप्योऽलब्धविनिर्गमाः ।
कृष्णं तद्भावनायुक्ता दध्युर्मीलितलोचनाः ॥९॥

दुःसहप्रेष्ठविरहतीव्रतापधुताशुभाः ।
ध्यानप्राप्ताच्युताश्लेषनिर्वृत्या क्षीणमङ्गलाः ॥१०॥

तमेव परमात्मानं जारबुद्ध्यापि सङ्गताः ।
जहुर्गुणमयं देहं सद्यः प्रक्षीणबन्धनाः ॥११॥

दैवगत्या काश्चिद्गृहमध्ये स्थिताः, गोपभार्याः चातुर्यानभिज्ञाः, अप्रौढाः पतिसहिताः, पतिभिरेव संरक्षिताः, अलब्धविनिर्गमा जाताः । ततः प्रतिबन्धनिवृत्त्यर्थं कृष्णमेव ध्यातवत्यः, परं तद्भावनायुक्ताः, **भगवान्** जारः स्वयमभिसारिका इति । अन्यथा प्रतिबन्धो न स्यात् । तादृश्योऽपि मीलितलोचनाः सत्यो भगवन्तं दध्युः ध्यातवत्यः, ततो मुक्ता जाताः । ननु तत्र ज्ञानाभावात् विहितभक्त्यभावात् भगवतोऽपि सान्निध्याभावात् कथं मुक्ता इत्याशंक्य, कर्मक्षयात् मुक्ता इति वक्तुं कर्मक्षयप्रकारमाह दुःसहेति । दुःसहो यः प्रेष्ठविरहः स एव महानग्निः तस्य यस्तीव्रस्तापः, तेन धुतानि निर्धूतानि ज्वालितानि भस्मसात्कृतानि अशुभानि यासाम् । फलभोगे कर्म क्षीयत इत्यविवादम् । कोटिब्रह्मकल्पेषु कुम्भीपाकादिनरकेषु यावत् दुःखं भवेत्, तावत् दुःखं भगवद्विरहे क्षणमात्रेण जातम् । ततः सर्वपापफलभोगः समाप्तः । पुण्यक्षयप्रकारमाह ध्यानप्राप्तेति । सर्वपापक्षये भगवान् ध्याने प्राप्तः ।

अच्युतः परमात्मा। न तु समागतोऽपि जारत्वेन, अन्यथा ततोऽपि कर्मशेषः स्यात्। तस्य योऽयमाश्लेषः, तेन या निर्वृतिः, तया क्षीणं मङ्गलं पुण्यं यासाम्। कोटि-ब्रह्मकल्पेषु स्वर्गादिलोकेषु यावत्सुखमनुभूयते, तावत् भगवदाश्लेषे क्षणमात्रेणैवानुभूतम्। अतः पुण्यक्षयोऽपि जातः। ततो मुक्ता जाता इत्याह तमेव परमात्मानमिति। सुखभोगार्थमेव भगवान् पूर्वमाश्लिष्टः, भोगे जातेऽपि वियोजकपापाभावात् न वियुक्ताः, अतः संगता एव स्थिताः। शरीरं तु प्रारब्धकर्मनिर्वाणमपतत्। यद्याश्लिष्टो भगवान् न भवेत्, तदा तत्र प्रविष्टाः तद्गतं धर्माधर्मफलं बुभुजुः, भगवति प्रविष्टत्वात् मुक्ता एव जाताः। तदाह तमेव परमात्मानमिति। पूर्वं सम्बन्धसमये यद्यपि जारबुद्ध्यापि संगता एव, ततः कर्मबन्धस्य प्रक्षीणत्वात् गुणमयं देहं जहुः। तदा अज्ञानमन्यथा ज्ञानं वा त्रिक्षणावस्थायीति न तयोः प्रतिबन्धकत्वम्, वियोजकाभावात् शरीरान्तरोत्पादकाभावाच्च। अविद्या परं तिष्ठति, सा भगवच्छक्तिः, भगवत्संगतं न व्यामोहयतीति सापि निवृत्ता। ततः मुक्ता जाता इत्यर्थः॥११॥

अत्र राजा श्रुतिविरोधमाशङ्कते कृष्णमिति।

राजोवाच — **कृष्णं विदुः परं कान्तं न तु ब्रह्मतया मुने।**
गुणप्रवाहोपरमस्तासां गुणधियां कथम्॥१२॥

'तमेव विदित्वातिमृत्युमेति नान्यः पन्था विद्यतेऽयनाये'ति श्रुतौ ज्ञानमेव साधनत्वेनोक्तम्। तत्रैव पुनः 'भक्त्यैव तुष्टिमभ्येति विष्णुर्नान्येन केनचित्। स एव मुक्तिदाता च भक्तिस्तत्रैव कारणम्'। उभयोश्च निर्णयः, 'ज्ञानयोगश्च मन्निष्ठो नैर्गुण्यो भक्तिलक्षणः। द्वयोरप्येक एवार्थो भगवच्छब्दलक्षण' इति। 'भक्त्या मामभिजानाती' त्यपि भगवतोक्तम्। ततो मर्यादायां ज्ञानेनैव मुक्तिः, पुष्टौ भक्त्या ज्ञानेन वा। एतासां तु न द्वयम्। भक्तिरपि सगुणा, ज्ञानमपि सगुणम्, उभयं च तामसम्। अतः कथं मुक्तिरिति। तदाह ताः कृष्णं कान्तं परं विदुः। कान्तः पतिर्जारो वा, न तु ब्रह्मतया विदुः। मुन इति सम्बोधनमत्र निर्णयपरिज्ञानार्थम्। विरोधस्तु स्पष्टः। तासां भगवति स्वस्मिंश्च गुणबुद्धिरेव। गुणबुद्धिश्च गुणप्रवाहस्य मूलम्, अन्यथा गुणबुद्धिनिवारकाणि सर्वाण्येव शास्त्राणि व्यर्थानि भवेयुः। वैदिकपक्षस्त्वसंभावित एव। अतो गुणधियां गुणबुद्धियुक्तानां गुणप्रवाहोपरमः कथम्॥१२॥

तत्रोत्तरमाह उक्तमिति चतुर्भिः।

श्रीशुक उवाच—**उक्तं पुरस्तादेतत्ते चैद्यः सिद्धिं यथा गतः।**
द्विषन्नपि हृषीकेशं किमुताधोक्षजप्रियाः॥१३॥

नृणां निःश्रेयसार्थाय व्यक्तिर्भगवतो नृप।
अव्ययस्याप्रमेयस्य निर्गुणस्य गुणात्मनः॥१४॥

**कामं क्रोधं भयं स्नेहमैक्यं सौहृदमेव वा ।
नित्यं हरौ विदधतो यान्ति तन्मयतां हि ते ॥१५॥**

**न चैवं विस्मयः कार्यो भवता भगवत्यजे ।
योगेश्वरेश्वरे कृष्णे यत एतद्विमुच्यते ॥१६॥**

एतत्सप्तमस्कन्ध एवोक्तं शिशुपालमुक्तौ । यथा शास्त्रद्वयं भक्तिज्ञानप्रतिपादकं साधनम्, तथा भगवत्स्वरूपमपि । भगवान् हि मुक्तिदानार्थमेवावतीर्णः । सच्चिदानन्दरूपेण प्रकटः । अतो यः कश्चन येनकेनाप्युपायेन भगवति सम्बन्धं प्राप्नोति, स एव मुच्यते । ज्ञानभक्त्योस्तु आविर्भावार्थमुपयोग : । आविर्भावश्चे द-न्यथा सिद्धः, तदा न ज्ञानभक्त्योरुपयोगः । अत्र तु भगवान् स्वत एवाविर्भूतः, मुक्तिदानार्थं सर्वसाधारण्येन, ईश्वरेच्छाया अनियम्यत्वात् । अत आविर्भावः स्वेच्छया, भक्त्या ज्ञानेन वा । भगवदवतारातिरिक्तकाले द्वयमेव हेतुः । अवतारदशायां तु न तयोः प्रयोजकत्वम् । वर्षाकाले जलं सर्वत्र सुलभिमिति न कूपनदीनामनुपयोगः शङ्कनीयः । तदाह पुरस्तात् सप्तमस्कन्धे यथा चैद्यः शिशुपालः सिद्धिं भगवत्सायुज्यं गतः । द्विषन्नपि द्वेषं कुर्वन्नपि । यद्यपि द्वेषकृतो दोषः प्रतिबन्धको भवति, तथापि स्मरणेन तदघं हृत्वा तत्र सायुज्यं प्राप्तः । किञ्च, नापि तस्य दोषोऽस्ति कश्चन । द्वेषादयोऽपि भगवतैवोत्पादिताः । तदाह हृषीकेशमिति । इन्द्रियप्रेरकोऽयं यथासुखं भावानुत्पादयति । यत्र द्वेषस्यापि मोक्षसाधकत्वम्, तत्र अधोक्षजप्रियाः किमु वक्तव्या मुक्तिं गच्छन्तीति ॥१३॥

अत्र मुख्यामुपपत्तिमाह नृणां निःश्रेयसार्थायेति । प्राणिमात्रस्य मोक्षदानार्थमेव भगवान् अभिव्यक्तः, अतः इयमभिव्यक्तिः निःश्रेयसार्थैव । अन्यथा न भवेत् । असाधारणप्रयोजनाभावात् । भूभारहरणादिकं च अन्यथापि भवति । अतो निःश्रेयसार्थमेव भगवतोऽभिव्यक्तिः प्राकट्यम् । नृपेति सम्बोधनं कदाचिद्राजा कथञ्चिद्गच्छति तद्वतिदिति ज्ञापयितुम् । प्रकारान्तरेण तादृशस्य नाभिव्यक्तिः सम्भवतीति वक्तुं भगवन्तं विशिनष्टि । आदौ भगवान् सर्वैश्वर्यसम्पन्नः अपराधीनः कालकर्मस्वभावानां नियामकः सर्वनिरपेक्षः किमर्थमागच्छेत् । किञ्च, स्वार्थं गमनाभावेऽपि परार्थं वा स्यात्, तदपि नास्तीत्याह अव्ययस्येत्यादिचतुर्भिः पदैः । अन्येषां कृतिसाध्यं ज्ञानसाध्यं वा यद्भवति तदुपयुज्यते । भगवाँस्तु अव्ययत्वात् अवि-कृतत्वात् न कृतिसाध्यः । अप्रमेयत्वात् ज्ञानसाध्योऽपि न । देहादिभजनद्वारा भजनीयो भविष्यतीत्यपि न, यतो निर्गुणः, निर्गता गुणा यस्मात् । गुणेषु विद्यमानेष्वेवान्यस्य प्रतिपत्तिस्तत्र भवति, यथा क्षुधि सत्यामन्नदानम्, कामे सति स्त्र्युपयोगः, इन्द्रियेषु सत्सु तद्विषयाणाम् । अतो भगवतः सेवकपूरणीयांशः कोऽपि नास्तीति भजनीयोऽपि न भवति । किञ्च, लीलार्थं यद्यपेक्षेतापि, तथापि सर्वं तस्यैव, यतः सर्वगुणानां स

एवात्मा । अतः साधनप्रकारेण नान्यस्याप्युपयोगः । अतः स्वपरप्रयोजनाभावात् यदि साधननिरपेक्षां मुक्तिं न प्रयच्छेत्, तदा व्यक्तिः प्रयोजनरहितैव स्यात् ॥१४॥

एवं सति येन केनाप्युपायेन य एव सम्बध्यते, तस्यैव मुक्तिर्भवतीत्याह काममिति । कामादयः षट् साधनानि भगवत्सम्बन्धे । तत्र कामः स्त्रीणामेव, क्रोधः शत्रूणामेव, भयं वध्यानामेव , स्नेहः सम्बन्धिनामेव, ऐक्यं ज्ञानिनामेव, सौहृदं भक्तानामेव । सख्यं तेष्वेव सिध्यतीति । पूर्वसिद्धज्ञानभक्त्योः नात्रोपयोगः । तेषां मर्यादया स्वतन्त्राविर्भावस्य नियतत्वात् । एकस्य तूभयत्वे संयोगपृथक्त्वन्यायेन निर्णयः । वेत्यनादरे । अन्यो वा कश्चनोपायो भवेत्, परं सर्वदा कर्तव्यः, अन्यथा 'अन्ते या मतिः सा गति'रिति अन्यशेषतामापद्येत । कर्मवशाच्च नान्ते भगवतः स्मरणम्, अन्यस्येव, प्रपञ्चविरोधित्वाद्भगवतः । अतो नित्यं ये विदधते, ते तन्मयतामेव प्राप्नुवन्ति । ननु कामादिषु क्रियमाणेषु दुःखान्तराभिभवे कथं नित्यं करणं सम्भवति, तत्राह हराविति । स हि सर्वदुःखहर्ता, नित्यं तद्भावनायां जगदेव तदात्मकं स्फुरति । दृष्टिः कामेनानुरक्तेति किम्पुनः स्वात्मा । अतस्तदात्मका एव भवन्ति । सर्वत्र भगवदावेशात् ।

जीवेऽन्तःकरणे चैव प्राणेष्विन्द्रियदेहयोः ॥
विषयेषु गृहेऽर्थे च पुत्रादिषु हरिर्यतः ॥१॥

तादृशीं भावनां कुर्यात् कामक्रोधादिभिर्यथा ।
पूर्वप्रपञ्चविलयो यथा ज्ञाने तथा यतः ॥२॥

किञ्च, आदावेव गोप्यो मुक्ताः, किमाश्चर्यम्, बहव एवाग्रे मुक्ता भविष्यन्तीति । तदाह न चैवमिति । एवं असंभावनारूपो विस्मयो न कार्यः । असंभावितबुद्धीनां अन्यथा स्फुरणनियमात् । यतो भगवान् । यत्किञ्चिन्मोक्षे ज्ञानादिकमुपयुज्यते, एतत्सर्वं भगवत्येवास्ति । यदि ज्ञानव्यतिरेकेण मोक्षो न भवेदिति ज्ञास्यति, तदा सिद्धत्वात् ज्ञानस्य, तदपि दास्यति । किञ्च, अन्यः सन्देहं कुर्यादपि, भगवतो माहात्म्यं न दृष्टमिति, भवता तु न कार्यः, गर्भ एव माहात्म्यदर्शनात् । किञ्च, निर्दुष्टे सर्वं संभवति । तत्र दोषाणां मूलं जन्म, तदभावे दोषाभाव इति । तेन अजत्वात् निर्दुष्टः । अन्ये सर्वे हि जायन्ते, न तैस्तेषां मुक्तिः सम्भवति, तुल्यत्वात् । किञ्च, यो हि साधनपरः, स मुच्यते । तत्र साधनं मनः सर्वतो निवृत्तम् , तथा योगेन भवति, तस्य योगस्य च नियामको भगवानेव । यद्यन्यस्यापि मोक्षो भवेत्, भगवदिच्छयैव भवेत् । योगादिसाधनानां तन्नियम्यत्वात् । किञ्च, सदानन्दो भगवान् फलात्मा । यः कश्चिन्मुच्यते, स एतमेव प्राप्स्यति । अतः साधनैरप्ययमेव प्राप्यः । सोऽत्र स्वयमेव सम्बध्यत इति न किञ्चिदनुपपन्नम् । किञ्च, एतत्परिदृश्यमानं सर्वमेव जगत् यतो

विर्मुक्तिं यास्यति। भावनया गोकुले स्थित आह, ज्ञानदृष्ट्या वा। साक्षात्परम्परया वा सर्वानेव मोचयिष्यतीति तदग्रे वक्ष्यति 'स्वमूर्त्ये'ति श्लोकद्वयेन।

(यद्वा, अत्र राजानुपपत्तिं शङ्कते कृष्णमिति। एताः कृष्णं कान्तं परं विदुः, न तु ब्रह्मतया, अतो गुणप्रवाहोपरमः कथं संगच्छत इति। अत्रायं भावः। ब्रह्मत्वेन विज्ञानं हि शास्त्रीयम्, तच्च सात्त्विकं भवितुमर्हति। 'सत्त्वात्सञ्जायते ज्ञान'मिति वाक्यात्। एतास्तु गुणातीतस्यानन्दमात्रकरपादमुखोदरादेः प्रकटस्यानन्तगुणपूर्णस्य सौन्दर्यादिगुणेषु परिनिष्ठितधियः। अतो निर्गुणत्वाद्गुणप्रवाहोपरमः कथं संगच्छते। उपरमस्याभावरूपत्वेन प्रतियोगिसापेक्षत्वादत्र च प्रतियोगिन एवाभावादिति। मुन इति सम्बोधनं शुद्धसत्त्वाविर्भावे ज्ञानोदयस्यानुभवसिद्धत्वेन सम्वादार्थम्। अत्रोत्तरमाह उक्तमिति। पुरस्तात्सप्तमस्कन्धे 'गोप्यः कामा'दित्यादिना। अत्रायमर्थः। यथा भगवति गुणातीत एव परिनिष्ठितबुद्धित्वेऽपि द्वेषस्य तत्र प्रयोजकत्वात् चैद्यादीनां तामसत्वम्, तथैतासामपि निर्गुण एव परिनिष्ठितबुद्धित्वेऽपि जारत्वबुद्धेस्तत्र प्रयोजकत्वात् सगुणत्वमेवेति लक्ष्यते। अयं च रसः सर्वभावप्रपत्त्येकलभ्यः। न हि जारत्वबुद्धौ सर्वभावप्रपत्तिः। कामपूरकत्वेनैव तत्संभवनियमात्। अत्र च सगुणत्वस्य प्रतिबन्धकत्वाद्यथा चैद्यादीनां स्वाधिकारानुसारेण तादृशशरीरनाशे तत्पदप्राप्तिः स्वाधिकारानुसारेण, तथैतासामपि स्वाधिकारानुसारेण तथात्वे सगुणत्वोपरमेण सर्वभावप्रपत्त्यैव ततो निजपतिभजनमिति सर्वमवदातम्। अन्यथा 'ये यथा मां प्रपद्यन्त' इति मर्यादा भज्येत। एतदेव मनसि कृत्वाह उक्तं पुरस्तादेतत्त इति। ननु तथापि तादृशप्रपत्तेरेव मूलत्वात्कथं सर्वभावप्रपत्तिसाध्यं फलं भविष्यतीत्यत आह द्विषन्नपीति। अयमर्थः। मोक्षसुखानभीप्सुस्तद्विरुद्धद्वेषकर्ता च चैद्यः। तस्मै यथा ज्ञानिनामपि दुर्लभां मुक्तिं दत्तवान्, एवं तादृक्प्रपत्तिमूलानामप्येतासां तादृशं फलं दत्तवानिति। एतेन यथा द्वेषमुक्त्योस्तारतम्यम्, तथान्यशेषभजनैतद्रसयोरपीति सूचितम्। ननु गोकुलस्य भगवत्क्रीडोपयोगित्वेन सर्वथाङ्गीकृतस्य सर्वस्यैव निर्गुणत्वे कथमेतासां सगुणत्वमुच्यते। किञ्च, अग्रेऽपि यदि सर्वभावप्रपत्तिलभ्यमेव फलं दित्सितं भगवतः, तदा पूर्वमेव स एव भावः किमिति नोत्पादित इति चेत्। अत्र वदामः। यासां साक्षाद्भगवत्सम्बन्धस्तासां सर्वासामेव रासमण्डलमण्डनानां शरीरमपि गुणातीतमेवेति ज्ञापयितुं भगवानेव कतिपयगोपीः सगुणदेहाः स्थापयित्वा, पूर्वोक्तानां भावोऽपि निर्गुण इति ज्ञापयितुमासां सगुणं भावमुत्पाद्य, एतन्निवर्तकोऽपि स्वयमेव, नान्य इत्यपि ज्ञापयितुं तन्निवृत्तिं विधाय, अग्रे भाविस्वविरहजदुःखस्वसङ्गमजसुखयोः कर्माजन्यत्वमपि ज्ञापयितुं कर्मक्षयप्रकारेण स्वप्राप्तिं विधाय, मत्स्वाम्येव सर्वमिदं कृतवानिति निगर्वः। अत्र पुष्टिमार्गाङ्गीकारान्मर्यादामार्गीयानुपपत्तयोऽनवसरपराहता इति सर्वमनवद्यम्। अत एव श्रीशुकोऽपि 'जहुर्गुणमयं देह'मिति सगुणदेहत्यागमेवोक्तवान्, अग्रे गुणातीत-

तत्प्राप्त्यभिप्रायेण, गोप्यत्वात्स्पष्टं नोक्तवान । अन्यथा गुणमयपदवैयर्थ्यं स्यात् । ननु पूर्वोक्तज्ञापनायैवेद कृतवानिति कथं ज्ञेयम्, उपपत्त्यभावादित्याशंक्योपपत्तिमाह नृणानिति । अयमाशयः । लीलायां तत्स्थितभक्तेषु च सुतरां रासस्थासु, या साधारणत्वबुद्धिः, सा सदोषत्वारोपापरपर्याया । तासामगुणत्वात्तस्य दोषरूपत्वाद्भगवत्स्वरूपे लीलायां च सगुणत्वप्रसञ्जकत्वाच्च । एवं सत्येतल्लीलाया मुक्तिप्रतिबन्धकत्वमेव स्यात्, न तु तद्धेतुत्वम् । तथा सत्यवतारप्रयोजनं विरुध्येतेत्यन्यथानुपपत्त्यैव तथोच्यत इति । ज्ञापनप्रयोजनमपीदमेवेति ज्ञेयम् । व्याख्यानं पूर्ववत् । नन्वियदवधि सगुणास्वेतासु कृताया लीलायाः पूर्वोक्तदोषप्रसञ्जकत्वं दुर्वारमित्याशंक्य पूर्वलीलाकृतितात्पर्यमाह काममिति । इदं हि साधारण्येनोच्यते । य एवं नित्यं विदधते, ते तन्मयतां यान्तीति, नत्वेतदगोपभार्याविषयकमेव । अत एव क्रोधाद्युक्तिरपि । अन्यथाऽप्रस्तावेनात्र तन्निरूपणमयुक्तं स्यात् । तथा च सगुणेनापि भावेन भजते भगवान् स्वानुरूपमेव फलं ददातीति ज्ञापनाय पूर्वलीलेत्यर्थः । अन्यथा मुख्याधिकारिणामेव भगवत्प्राप्तिरिति ज्ञानेऽन्येषामप्रवृत्त्या मुक्त्युच्छेदः स्यात् । एवं शास्त्रमप्रयोजनकं च स्यात् । मुख्याधिकारिणां स्वत एव प्रवृत्तेः । स्वरूपलीलयोस्तु न कदाचित्सगुणत्वम्, लीलाविषयाणां सगुणानामपि निर्गुणत्वापादकत्वात् । नहि दोषनिवर्तकमौषधं रोगिसम्बद्धं सत् तद्वद्भवति । तथा सति तदनिवर्तकत्वापत्तेः । लीलाया विषयसाजात्यनियमे सगुणनिर्गुणभक्तयोरेकया वेणुवादनादिलीलया निरोधो नोपपद्येत । क्रोधादिवत्कामोपाधिकभावस्यापि जघन्यत्वज्ञापनायापि क्रोधादिनिरूपणं ज्ञेयम् । तन्मयतां निर्गुणतामित्यर्थः । ननु साक्षादङ्गसङ्गित्वेपि सगुणत्वस्थितिं वस्तुशक्तिः कथं सहते । वह्निसम्बन्ध इव तूलस्थितिमित्येको विस्मयः । लौकिकरीत्या कामभाववतीष्वलौकिकस्य रमणं द्वितीयः । क्रोधादिभाववतां तत्फलमननुभूयैव भगवत्प्राप्तिश्चापरः । स्नेहवत् समानफलत्वं च । यशोदानन्दने हि ता भाववत्यः, तस्य च वनस्थितस्यैतद्ध्यानप्राप्तिश्चान्यः । एतासां तदैव निर्गुणदेहप्राप्तिर्विनैव तत्साधनमिति चेतरः । सर्वात्मभाववत्स्वेव करिष्यमाणलीलाया अनुभवः । अन्यस्यास्तु तद्रहितानामपीत्यनेकविस्मयाविष्टं राजानं ज्ञात्वा तन्निवारकं क्रमेण वदन् पूर्वश्लोकोक्तभावयतां भगवत्प्राप्तौ हेतूनप्याह न चैवमिति । आद्यविस्मयाभावार्थमाह भवतेति । अत्रायं भावः । पूर्वमनिवर्त्यब्रह्मास्त्रतोऽपि गर्भेऽपि रक्षितवान् भवन्तम्, प्रयोजनमस्तीति । अधुना तु तदभावाद्बालवाक्यादपि न रक्षतीति भवतैवानुभूयते । न हि एवावता वस्तुशक्तौ काचिन्न्यूनता । इच्छाशक्त्यधीनत्वात्सर्वासां शक्तीनाम् । तस्याः सर्वतोऽधिकत्वात् । न हि मन्त्रप्रतिबन्धदशायामग्नेरदाहकत्वमिति तच्छक्त्यपगम एवेति वक्तुं युक्तम् । प्रकृतेऽपि यासां साक्षादित्यादिनोक्तप्रयोजनार्थं भगवता तथा कृतमिति ज्ञात्वा भवता तु विस्मयो न कार्यः । अनुभावाननुभवेनान्यः कुर्यादपीति । द्वितीयतृतीयादिकं परिहरति

भगवतीति । तत्रेश्वरो हि सर्वरसभोक्ता भवति । 'सर्वरस'इति श्रुतेः । कामरसो हि तादृशभाववतीषु विशिष्टोऽनुभूतो भवति । कामशास्त्रे तथैव निरूपणात् । तथा चैश्वर्यवत्ययं विस्मयो न कार्यः । तथा भगवद्वीर्यस्येतरसाधनासाध्यसाधकत्वेनात्युग्रत्वात् क्रोधादिदोषमन्यानिवर्त्यमपि स्ववीर्येण हरिर्निवारयितुं समर्थ इति तादृशे स विस्मयो न कार्यः । यशो ह्यसाधारणम्, असाधारणे कर्मणि सति भवति । यदि स्नेहवत्स्वेव मुक्तिं दद्यात् न द्विट्सु, तदान्यसाधारण्येनासाधारणं यशो न स्यात् । भयद्वेषादिमत्स्वपि स्नेहादिमत्समानफलदाने ह्यसाधारणत्वेनासाधारणं यशः स्यात् । तथा च तादृशयशसः सहजत्वेन तद्ज्ञापकधर्मा अपि हरौ सहजा एवेति नायं विस्मयः कार्यः । श्रीर्लक्ष्मीः । सा चैतादृशस्नेहवती यद्वक्षसि स्थितिं प्राप्यापि चरणरजः कामयते, प्रत्यवतारं चावतरति । सदा तद्वत्त्वेन हरिः स्नेहरसाभिज्ञ इति तद्वत्सु स्वरूपदानं युक्तम् । ऐक्यं हि ज्ञानमार्गे । हरेश्च ज्ञानवत्त्वेन तेषु तथा युक्तम् । सौहार्दं हि सख्ये सति भवति । तच्च समानशीलव्यसनेष्वेव । 'नाहमात्मानमाशासे मद्भक्तैः साधुभिर्विना । श्रियं चात्यन्तिकीं ब्रह्मन् येषां गतिरहं परा । साधवो हृदयं मह्यं साधूनां हृदयं त्वहम् । मदन्यत्ते न जानन्ति नाहं तेभ्यो मनागपि' इत्यादिवाक्यैर्यथा भगवतो भक्तातिरिक्ते रागाभावो, भक्तेष्वेव च राग इति वैराग्यवत्त्वम्, तथा भक्तानामपि भगवतीति सौहार्दयोग्येषु सौहार्दं ददातीति पूर्वोक्तवैराग्यवत्त्वात् तेषु तथा करणं युक्तमिति भावः । यशोदानन्दन इत्यादिनोक्तविस्मयाभावार्थमाह अज इति । यदि भगवतो जीववत् कुत्रापि जन्म स्यात्, तदान्यत्र बहिःस्थितोऽत्रान्तर्हृदि कथमागतः, तत्र सन्नेवेति शङ्का स्यात् । तदभावात् । स्वेच्छया यथा मायाजवनिकां दूरीकृत्य यशोदागृहे प्रकटः, तथा वने, तथैवान्तर्हृद्यपीत्यजे नायं विस्मयः कार्यः । अग्रिमोक्ततदभावार्थमाह योगेश्वरेति । योगिनो हि योगबलेन भोगार्थमनेकानि शरीराणि युगपत्क्षणमात्रेण सृजन्ति । तेषां च योग आगन्तुको धर्मः । भगवाँश्च तादृग्धर्मसम्पादकः फलदाता चेति तेषामपीश्वर इति सहजानन्तशक्तिमानिति तास्वलौकिकदेहसम्पादनमात्रं न विस्मयहेतुर्भवितुमर्हति । अग्रिमतदभावायाह कृष्ण इति । 'कृषिर्भूवाचक' इति वाक्यात् सदानन्दस्वरूपो भगवान्, निर्दोषपूर्णगुण इति यावत् । तेन कृष्णातिरिक्तस्य वस्तुमात्रस्यैव सदोषत्वात्तत्रापि स्वास्थ्यहेतुत्वं जानतः सदोषत्वमेवेति निश्चयः । इयं च लीला स्वरूपानन्दरूपा तादृश्येवेति सर्वात्मभावरहितेष्वेतदनुभवायोग्यत्वान्नायं विस्मयः कार्य इत्यर्थः । किञ्च, एतासां तु स्नेहः पूर्वोक्तः साधनत्वेनासीत्, 'गोकुलं त्वह्न्यपापृतं निशि शयान'मिति वाक्यात् सर्वसाधनविमुखं सदपि प्रतिक्षणं स्वरूपे लीयते, अग्रिमाग्रिमलीलारसानुभवार्थम्, भगवान् परं पुनः पुनः पृथक्कृत्य तामनुभावयतीत्यचिन्त्यानन्तशक्तिमति न किञ्चिदाश्चर्यमित्याशयेनाह यत एतदिति । शुकस्त्वधुना लीलेतराननुसंधानाद्भावनया तत्रैव स्थित इत्येतदित्युक्तवान्, वर्तमानप्रयोगं च कृतवान्, तामेव लीलामनुभवतीति

सर्वमनवद्यम् । नन्वेतद्वैपरीत्यमपि सुवचम् । तथाहि । एता अपि पूर्वोक्तमध्यपातिन्य एव । अत एव पूर्वश्लोके तासामनिवृत्तिमुक्त्वा तादृशी सा लोकेऽत्यसम्भावितेति सा कथमुपपद्यत इत्याशङ्कानिरासायाह अन्तर्गृहेत्यादि । अत्रायं भावः । पूर्वं हि वचनेन निवर्तनम् । तथा सति निवृत्तिर्हि विपरीतस्वक्रियया भवति । सा चातिदूरे, यतस्तत्सजातीयाः काश्चिद्भर्त्रादिकृते क्रियया प्रतिबन्धे तत्प्रतिबध्यं देहमपि त्यक्त्वा भगवत्सङ्गता जाताः । तथा चैतादृश्यः पूर्वोक्ताः सर्वा इति युक्तैवानिवृत्तिः । किञ्च, तद्भावनायुक्ता इति पदे तच्छब्दस्य पूर्वपरामर्शित्वेन पूर्वं च पूर्वोक्तानामेव भावस्योक्तत्वादेतद्भावसजातीयभाववत्त्वं पूर्वोक्तानामपीति गम्यते । तेनैतन्निष्ठाशेषधर्मवत्त्वं तत्रापि सिध्यति । एतासां मुक्तिर्दत्तेति तन्निवृत्तिं विना न सेति तथोक्तम् । तासां न तथेति न तथोक्तमिति चेत् । अहो शङ्काढ्यमानिनो मौढ्यदार्ढ्यं तव । यस्मादालोचनलोचनराहित्येन बाहिर्मौख्यासत्सङ्गाख्यगिरिगर्ताघातपातविवशाशयः परोक्तमपि नानुसंधत्से। तथा हि । यच्छङ्कानिरासायैतत्कथावतारिता, तद्भावश्च त्वया वर्णितः, तत्र त्वां पृच्छामः, तदर्थमियं कथा कल्पिता, उत सिद्धैवानूदिता । अन्त्य एव संमतश्चेत्, तत्रापि त्वां पृच्छामः, एतासां प्रतिबन्धे को हेतुरिति । स्वप्रियास्वपि सगुणत्वं ख्यापयितुमेतासां प्रतिबन्धो हरिणैव कृत इति चेद्ब्रवीषि, हन्त एवं विचारकस्य तव शतधा हृदयं नास्फुटत् कुतस्तन्न जानीमः । यतो मर्यादाभक्तिमार्गीयसेवाविषयकश्रद्धाया अपि निर्गुणत्वम्, तत्र साक्षादङ्गसङ्गिनीषु सगुणत्वं ब्रवीषि । किञ्च, 'ता मन्मनस्का मत्प्राणा मदर्थे त्यक्तदैहिका' इत्यादिना प्रभुणैव, 'एताः परं तनुभृत'इत्यादिनोद्धवेन, 'नोद्धवोऽण्वपि मन्न्यून'इत्यादिना भगवता स्तुतेनापि चरणरेणुप्रार्थनापूर्वकं स्तुता इति क्व तद्गन्धशङ्कापि । ननु कामोपाधिस्नेहवत्त्वेन तथोच्यत इति चेत् । न । तथा स्नेहे भगवतोऽपि विषयान्तरतुल्यत्वेन 'संत्यज्य सर्वविषया'निति कथनानुपपत्तेः । विषयार्थमेवागमनात् । न च भगवतो विषयत्वेऽपि तदतिरिक्तविषयाणां त्यागोऽनूद्यत इति वाच्यम् । 'तव पादमूलं प्राप्ता' 'इत्युक्तिविरोधात् । न हि कामिन्य एवं वदन्ति, किन्तु भक्ता एव । किञ्च, अतितोके पूतनासुपयः पानान्तरं रक्षाकरणे श्रीशुकेन हेतुरुक्त 'इति प्रणयबद्धाभिर्गोपीभि'रिति । न हि तादृशे कामोपाधिकः स संभवति । न वा तादृशीनामञ्जनादित्यागः संभवति, प्रत्युत तदादिसर्वं प्रसाध्यागमनम्, कुब्जावत् । तदनन्तरं यद्रमणम्, तत्तु 'रसो वै स'इति श्रुतेः स्वरूपस्य रसात्मकत्वाद्रसरीत्या स्वरूपानन्ददानमेव । 'सात्त्विकं सुखमात्मोत्थं विषयोत्थं तु राजसं । तामसं मोहदैन्योत्थं निर्गुणं मदपाश्रय'मिति भगवद्वाक्यात् भगवत्सम्बन्धिसुखस्यापि गुणातीतत्वमेव) ॥१६॥

एवं प्रासङ्गिकं परिहृत्य प्रस्तुतमाह ता दृष्ट्वेति ।

ता दृष्ट्वान्तिकमायाता भगवान् व्रजयोषितः ।
अवदद्वदतां श्रेष्ठो वाचःपेशैर्विमोहयन् ॥१७॥

यास्तु समाहूताः समागताः, ता न निवार्यन्ते, याः पुनः सगुणाः समागताः अन्य-सम्बन्धिन्यः, ताः शब्दश्रवणात् समागता इति शब्देन निवारणीयाः। अन्यशेषतया भजनमयुक्तमिति। करिष्यमाणलीला तु सर्वभावप्रपत्तिसाध्या, अतो निवारणार्थं यत्नमाह। ता 'दुहन्त्य' इत्याद्याः अन्तिकमायाता दृष्ट्वा, स्वार्थमेवागता इति निश्चित्य, भगवान् सर्वज्ञः सर्वसमर्थोपि, ता अपि ब्रजयोषितः अपावृताः स्वकीयाश्च। अतः सर्वानुपपत्तिरहिता अपि दृष्ट्वा अवदत्। धर्मप्रबोधनार्थं वक्ष्यमाणमुक्तवान्। ननु ताः पूर्वं निवार्यमाणाः समागताः, कथमेतद्वाक्येन निवृत्ता भविष्यन्ति, अतो व्यर्थो वाक्प्रयास इति चेत्, तत्राह वदतां श्रेष्ठ इति। ये केचिद्वदन्ति, तेषां मध्ये श्रेष्ठः। अतो हृदयगाम्यस्य वचनं भवति। अतो यावद्वचनेन निवृत्ता भवन्ति, तावन्न कृतौ योजनीयाः। किञ्च, अलौकिकमप्यस्य निवर्तने सामर्थ्यमस्ति, तदाह वाचः-पेशैर्विमोहयन्निति। वाचःपेशाः वाक्सौन्दर्ययुक्ताः शब्दाः, तैर्विशेषेण मोहयन्। अथवा। ता दृढीकर्तुमेव सम्यक् मोहनार्थं निषेधवाक्यान्युक्तवान्, अन्यथा गच्छेयुरेव। अतः अर्थतो निवारयन् अपि पर्यवसानतो न निवारयति ॥१७॥

भगवद्वाक्यान्याह स्वागतमित्यादिदशभिः। दशविधानां निवारकाणि।

श्रीभगवानुवाच—**स्वागतं वो महाभागाः प्रियं किं करवाणि वः।**
व्रजस्यानामयं कच्चित् ब्रूतागमनकारणम् ॥१८॥

तमोरजःसत्त्वभेदाः स्वान्तपर्यवसानतः।
निरूप्यन्ते स्त्रियस्तासु वाक्यान्यपि यथायथम् ॥१॥

प्रथमतस्तामससात्त्विक्यो निवार्यन्ते, ततस्तामसराजस्यः, ततस्तामसतामस्यः, एवमग्रेऽपि विभाज्याः। प्रथमं समागतानां लौकिकन्यायेनाह स्वागतमिति। कुशल-प्रश्नोऽयम्। वो युष्माकमागमनं स्वागतं किमिति। स्तुतिमाह महाभागा इति। भवतीनां महद्भाग्यम्, अतः स्वागमनमेव, तथापि पृच्छयत इति लोकोक्तिः। वस्तुतस्तु निष्प्रत्यूहं भगवन्सामीप्यमागता इति। समागतानामुपचारमाह प्रियं किं करवाणि व इति। किञ्चित्प्रार्थयितुमागता इति लक्ष्यन्ते, तथा सति तद्वक्तव्यम्। अर्थात् नाहं स्वभावतः प्रियः, किन्तु कामतः प्रिय इति ज्ञापितम्। तत्प्रयोजनं त्रिविधं भवति। इष्टरूपमनिष्टनिवृत्तिरूपं देशकालव्यवहितं कामितं च। तत्रापि त्रैविध्यमस्तीति वाक्यत्रयं वा। यद्भवत्यो धावन्त्यः समागताः, तत्र किं व्रजे कश्चन उपद्रवो जातः यद्ज्ञापयितुं तेषां समागमनम्, पूर्वपूर्वानङ्गीकारे उत्तरोत्तरवाक्यम्। यदि प्रियमपि न किञ्चित्कर्तव्यम्, व्रजे च न काप्यनुपपत्तिः, तदा आगमनकारणं ब्रूत ॥१८॥

तत्राप्यनुत्तरे स्वयमेव पक्षान्तरं कल्पयति। यथा भवन्तः समागताः, तथा वयमपीत्याशङ्क्याह रजनीति।

रजन्येषा घोररूपा घोरसत्त्वनिषेविता ।
प्रतियात व्रजं नेह स्थेयं स्त्रीभिः सुमध्यमाः ॥१९॥

एषा रजनी, न तु दिनम् । दिवस एव ह्यरण्ये कार्यार्थं गम्यते, अयं तु चन्द्रः, न तु सूर्य इति भावः । नन्वस्तु रजनी, तथापि प्रकाशस्य विद्यमानत्वात् आगन्तव्यमेवेति चेत्, तत्राह घोररूपेति । प्रकाशयुक्ताप्येषा वस्तुतो घोररूपा भयजनिका । प्रकाशयुक्तायामपि रात्रौ गच्छन् पुरुषो बिभेतीति । किञ्च, घोरसत्त्वनिषेविता । घोराण्येव सत्त्वानि रात्रिं निषेवन्ते, नत्वघोराणि । अतो रात्रौ अघोरो निर्गतो घोरैरुपहन्यते । अतः स्वभावधर्मसंसर्गिणां स्वरूपं ज्ञात्वा व्रजं प्रतियात । नन्वेवं सति तवैव स्थाने स्थास्यामः, परिचितो भवानिति चेत्, तत्राह नेह स्थेयं स्त्रीभिरिति । वयं हि पुरुषाः, रात्रिश्चेयम् । अतोऽत्र स्त्रीभिर्न स्थातव्यम् । तथा सत्युभयोरपि विक्रिया स्यात् । किञ्च, भवत्यो यदि वृद्धा बाला वा भवेयुः, तदा स्थीयेतापि । भवत्यस्तु सुमध्यमाः रसात्मिकाः । अतो देहाध्यासे विद्यमाने सर्वथैव गन्तव्यम् । स्थितिपक्षे नञ्प्रश्लेषो घोरपदयोर्ज्ञेयः, न प्रतियातेति च ॥१९॥

अथ वयमभिसारिका एव त्वामुद्दिश्य समागताः, किमिति प्रेष्यन्त इत्याशङ्क्याह मातर इति ।

मातरः पितरः पुत्रा भ्रातरः पतयश्च वः ।
विचिन्वन्ति ह्यपश्यन्तो मा कृढ्वं बन्धुसाध्वसम् ॥२०॥

भवतीनां मातरो नियामिकाः, तास्तु नागताः, अतो भवतीनामन्वेषणमपि करिष्यन्ति । अतस्तासां साध्वसं भयं मा कृढ्वम्, मा कुरुत । न च वक्तव्यं ता अपि तथा स्त्रीत्वाद्वा नागमिष्यन्तीति, तत्राह पितर इति । तेषां कुले कलङ्कशङ्कया ते समागमिष्यन्त्येव । तर्हि तैः सह गन्तव्यमिति चेत्, तत्राह विचिन्वन्ति ह्यपश्यन्त इति । गोकुलान्निर्गतानां कृष्णस्थानागमने मध्ये बहवो मार्गाः स्फुटिताः सन्ति, तत्र भगवन्माया तिष्ठति यथा न कोऽपि भगवत्समीपं गच्छति, अतो मार्गान्तरेणैव गताः अपश्यन्तः सन्तः विचिन्वन्त्येव । अनेन स्थितौ शङ्काभावोप्युक्तः । बन्धुभ्यः साध्वसमिति च । तस्मात् सर्वा नागता इति नागन्तव्यम् । कुले च कलङ्को भविष्यतीति च । न च तेऽपि स्त्रीस्वभावं जानन्तीति नागमिष्यन्तीति चेत, भगवदर्थं वा समागता इति, तत्राह पुत्रा इति । पुत्राणां सर्वथा रक्षकत्वं महती लज्जेति तेषु दयया भयाभावार्थं गन्तव्यम् । ननु ते बालका इति चेत्, तत्राह भ्रातरा इति । ते हि समर्था अन्वेषणे लज्जावन्तश्च, अतो लज्जया अदृष्ट्वा कदाचित् शरीरमपि त्यजेयुः । अतो भ्रातृस्नेहाद्गन्तव्यम् । ननु ते अपकीर्तिभयादन्वेषणे न गमिष्यन्ति, तरुणास्ते, तरुण्यो वयमिति चेत्, तत्राह वः पतय इति । तेषां भोगापेक्षाप्यस्ति, तेषामेव चायं

रसः, अतः परस्वं नान्यस्मै देयम् । भोगस्य ततोऽपि सिद्धिः । सर्व एवापश्यन्तः गृहे अदृष्ट्वा अवश्यं विचिन्वन्ति । ततो बहुकालमदृष्ट्वा नाशशङ्कया अपहारशङ्कया च भयं प्राप्स्यन्ति । न च वक्तव्यं किमस्माकं तैः, तत्राह बन्धुसाध्वसमिति । ते हि बान्धवाः, तैः सहैव स्थातव्यम् । अतो बलवद्बाधकस्य विद्यमानत्वात् व्याघुट्य गन्तव्यमिति ॥२०॥

एवमुक्ते परितो विलोकयन्तीराह दृष्टं वनमिति ।

दृष्टं वनं कुसुमितं राकेशकररञ्जितम् ।
यमुनानिललीलैजत्तरुपल्लवमण्डितम् ॥२१॥

एषा हि राजसराजसी, अग्रिमा राजसतामसी । यदि वनदर्शनार्थमागतम्, तदा दृष्टमेव वनम्, अतः प्रतियातेति । अर्थात् सर्वदा दृष्टमेवैतद्वनम्, नात्र भयमिति ज्ञापितम् । गृहे च न गन्तव्यमिति । यदि गृहगमनापेक्षा, तदैव गन्तव्यमिति वचनात् । तच्च वनं कुसुमितमिति वर्णयति, यथा तासामन्यासक्तिर्भवति । इदानीं पुष्पाण्येव जातानि, न फलानीति वा । कुसुमिते वने रतिः कर्तव्येति भावः । सर्वत्र मोहः प्रेषणं चानुस्यूतम् । किञ्च, राकेशस्य चन्द्रमसः करैः रञ्जितम् । उद्दीपका एते । वनं तामसम्, पुष्पाणि राजसानि, चन्द्रकिरणाः सात्त्विका इति । अयं राकेश इति पूर्णचन्द्रः । अतः पूर्णत्त्वे स्थातव्यम् । पर्वादिबुद्धौ तु गन्तव्यमिति । वायुमपि तत्रत्यं वर्णयति यमुनेति । यमुनासम्बन्धिनानिलेन लीलया ये एजन्तः कम्पमानास्तरुपल्लवास्तैर्मण्डितमिति । जलसम्बन्धात् लीलया चलनात् तरूणां सुगन्धानां सम्बन्धात् त्रिगुणो वायुरुक्तः । वर्णनायां रसोद्बोधके चोपयुज्यते ॥२१॥

एवं वनं वर्णयित्वा अन्यासक्तिमुत्पाद्य ततो गन्तव्यमित्याह तद्यातेति ।

तद्यात मा चिरं गोष्ठं शुश्रूषध्वं पतीन् सतीः ।
क्रन्दन्ति वत्सा बालाश्च तान्पाययत दुह्यत ॥२२॥

तत्तस्माद्वनं दृष्टमिति कार्यस्य सिद्धत्वाद्यात । एतादृशं वनमिति मा यातेत्यपि ध्वनिः । चिरं मा विलम्बो न कर्तव्यः, चिरं मा यातेति च । न हि कश्चिद्भगवन्तं विहाय गोष्ठं गच्छति । किञ्च, गोष्ठं यात । तत्र गवां शुश्रूषणमपि भवति । किञ्च, तत्र गतानां धर्मः सिध्यतीत्याह शुश्रूषध्वमिति । पतिसेवा स्त्रीणां धर्म, तत्रापि भवत्यः सतीः सत्यः । पतिविशेषणं वा । पूर्वजन्मनि ताः पतिव्रताः स्त्रियः स्थिताः, पुरुषभावनया पुरुषा जाताः, भवन्तश्च पुरुषाः विपरीता जाता इति, अग्रेऽपि वैपरीत्यं भविष्यतीति विचार्य गन्तव्यमिति भावः । धर्मस्तत्र, रसस्त्वत्रैवेति । पतीनिति बहुबचनात् धर्माभावश्च । या भवतीनां मध्ये पतिव्रताः ता वा गच्छन्त्विति । सर्वासामेवातथात्वे न गन्तव्यमेवेति । न हि पतिव्रताः समायान्ति,

लौकिकधर्मपरायणाः। अतो भगवद्वाक्यं रसालत्वात् तदभावमेव सूचयति। किञ्च, वत्सास्तथैव बद्धाः, बालाश्च क्षुधिताः, ते क्रन्दन्ति। अतस्तेषां रोदननिवृत्त्यर्थं तान् पाययत स्तनम् दुह्यत च गाः। परार्थं च भवतीनां जीवनम्, न स्वार्थम्। अतो दुःखितानां स्थाने सुखाकाङ्क्षिभिर्न गतव्यमिति ॥ २२॥

एवमुक्ते याः स्निग्धदृष्ट्यो जाताः, ताः प्रत्याह अथवेति।

अथवा मदभिस्नेहाद्भवत्यो यन्त्रिताशयाः।
आगता ह्युपपन्नं तत् प्रीयन्ते मम जन्तवः ॥२३॥

मया वृथैवैते पक्षाः कल्पिताः, वस्तुतस्तु मां द्रष्टुमेवागताः। स्नेहात् सिद्धान्तोऽयं पूर्वपक्षार्थमनूद्यते। निरुक्तो भावो गुणात्मको दोषात्मको वा न फलं प्रयच्छति, लौकिको भवति, अतः अनूद्यते। मयि योऽयमभितः स्नेहः सर्वभावेन तेन कृत्वा यन्त्रितः आशयो यासाम्, तादृश्यश्चेद्भवत्यः इहागताः, तदुपपन्नमेव। तर्हि को विलम्ब इति चेत्, तत्राह प्रीयन्ते मम जन्तव इति। मम सम्बन्धिनः सर्व एव जन्तवः स्वयमेव प्रीता भवन्ति। न तु मया किञ्चित्कर्तव्यम्। स्नेह एव मयि, न तु कृतिरिति। ततः साधारणमिममर्थं ज्ञात्वा प्रतियात। स्थितिपक्षे तु स्पष्ट एवार्थः। तद्यात मेति फलिष्यति। न हि स्नेहादागतः प्रेर्यमाणोऽपि गच्छति। यन्त्रितो वशीकृतः। अन्तःकरणे अन्याधीने जाते न किञ्चिदवशिष्यते। निष्कपटा च प्रीतिः कर्तव्येत्युभयत्र भावः ॥२३॥

भर्तुः शुश्रूषणं स्त्रीणां परो धर्मो ह्यमायया।
तद्बन्धूनां च कल्याण्यः प्रजानां चानुपोषणम् ॥२४॥

एवं राजसीः निरूप्य सात्त्विकीर्निरूपयति। सत्त्वयुक्ताः निरूप्यन्ते। ततो रजोयुक्ताः। स्त्रीणां मुख्यो धर्मः भर्तृशुश्रूषणमित्याह भर्तुरिति। स्वभावतो जीवानां भगवानेव भर्ता, तत्रापि स्त्रीणां स्त्रीशरीरं प्राप्तानां व्यभिचाराभावाय भगवानेव सेव्यः। लौकिके तु परिग्रहात् भर्तृत्वेनाभिमतः सेव्यः। स एव परो धर्मः। तत्राप्यमायया। कापट्ये तु न सेवायां फलम्। अन्ये सर्वे धर्मा अवराः। तद्बन्धूनां श्वशुरादीनाम्। कल्याण्य इति सम्बोधनात् भवतीनां सर्वेऽपि सन्तीति ज्ञापितम्। प्रजानां पुत्रादीनामनुपोषणं अन्नादिदानेन स्तनादिदानेन च। पित्रादिभिः पोष्यमाणानां स्वतोऽपि पोषणं वा ॥२४॥

तथापि स पतिः समीचीनो न भवतीति चेत्, तत्राह दुःशील इति।

दुःशीलो दुर्भगो वृद्धो जडो रोग्यधनोऽपि वा।.
पतिः स्त्रीभिर्न हातव्यो लोकेप्सुभिरपातकी ॥२५॥

दुष्टं शीलं यस्य। द्यूतादिदुर्व्यसनवान्। दुर्भगो दरिद्रः। वृद्धः इन्द्रियविकलः। जडो मूर्खः। रोगी महारोगग्रस्तः। अधनो वा। अधनोऽपि भाग्यवांश्चेत्, तदा संभावनया स्त्रीभिर्न त्यज्यते। एवं षड्दोषयुक्तोऽपि स्त्रीभिरनन्यगतिकाभिः पतिर्न हातव्य:। स्पष्ट एव विरोधः। षड्गुणो भगवान्, षड्दोषः स इति। पातकी तु हातव्य एव। 'भजेदपतितं पति'मिति वाक्यात्। किञ्च, तत्रापि लोकेप्सुभिः। येषामिह लोके परलोके च कीर्त्याद्यपेक्षा, तैर्न हातव्य एव, अन्यथा अपकीर्तिर्भवेत् ॥२५॥

ननु कामरसे निविष्टमनसां न धर्मो बाधकः, परस्मिन्नेव रसोत्पत्तिरिति तत्राह अस्वर्ग्यमिति।

अस्वर्ग्यमयशस्यं च फल्गु कृच्छ्रं भयावहम्।
जुगुप्सितं च सर्वत्र ह्यौपपत्यं कुलस्त्रियः ॥२६॥

हे कुलस्त्रियः, औपपत्यं जारसम्बन्धः तद्रसालमपि बहुदोषग्रस्तम्। तत्रत्यान् षड् दोषानाह। अस्वर्ग्यं परलोकनाशकम्। पूर्वं धर्मेण सिद्धोऽपि स्वर्गः तस्मिन् अपगच्छति। किञ्च, इह लोकेऽपि यशो दूरीकरोति। चकारात् नरकोऽपि। नापि तत्र रसभोगो महानित्याह फल्गिवति। अल्पमेव तत्सुखं क्षणमात्रसाध्यम्, स्वरूपतो महदपि कालतःपरिच्छिन्नमपि। कृच्छ्रमिति। कष्टसाध्यम्, नाल्पेन प्रयासेन सिध्यति। अतो बलवदनिष्टानुबन्धि। किञ्च, अनुभवकालेऽपि न रसमुत्पादयति। यतो भयजनकम्। शृङ्गारविरोधी भयानकरसः। अत एव व्यभिचारशब्दवाच्यः। मुख्यतया भयानकरसमुत्पादयेत् विशेषतः प्रथमतः। किञ्च, सर्वत्रैव जुगुप्सितम्। सर्वदेशेषु सर्वकालेषु तत्कृत्वा यदि सत्कर्मापि कुर्यात्, ततोऽपि जुगुप्सितो भवेत्। धर्मबुद्धिस्तत्र विचिकित्सैव भवति। अतो बहुदोषग्रस्तत्वात् उत्तमाया नैतद्युक्तम् ॥२६॥

एवं सगुणाः प्रबोध्य गुणातीताः प्रबोधयति श्रवणादिति।

श्रवणाद्दर्शनाद्ध्यानान्मयि भावोऽनुकीर्तनात्।
न तथा सन्निकर्षेण प्रतियात ततो गृहान् ॥२७॥

ननु लौकिकदृष्टावेते दोषाः, न तु भक्तिमार्गे, परमार्थदृष्टौ वा, भवांस्तु पुरुषोत्तम इति चेत्, तत्राह श्रवणादिति। न हि भक्तिमार्गे सम्बन्ध एव कर्तव्य इति शास्त्रमस्ति। भक्तिर्हि नवविधा श्रवणादिरूपा। प्रेमरूपा च। स्वतन्त्रपक्षे तु सुतरामेव नापेक्षा। स्नेहस्तु भगवद्विषयकः अलौकिकः। स एव सर्वाधिको भवति। लौकिकस्तु कामशेषतां प्राप्तः हीन एव भवति। तस्यालौकिकस्य कारणानि त्रीणि। श्रवणं दर्शनं ध्यानमिति। आदौ श्रवणं, भगवद्वाचकानां पदवाक्यानां भगवति शक्तितात्पर्यावधारणम्। तथा सति विषयो व्यावर्तितो भवति, अन्यथा अन्यत्रापि

स्नेहः स्यात् । तदनु दर्शनं, तदर्थस्यानुभवः । कृपया भगवत्साक्षात्कारो वा भगवत्कामार्थः नारदादेरिव । ततो ध्यानं, योगेन चिन्तनम् । एतैरेव मयि भावो भवति । स चोत्पन्नो भावः अनुकीर्तनात् स्थिरो भवति । यथायमुपायः शास्त्रीयः साधीयान्, न तथा निरन्तरसान्निध्येन जातो लौकिकः । स हि कामशेष इत्यवोचाम । अतो गृहान् प्रतियात । अतः परमार्थविचारेऽपि न स्थातव्यमिति । तथेत्यत्र प्रकार एव निषिद्धः, न स्वरूपतो महत्त्वं निषिद्धम् । गृहस्थितानां च विहितं भवतीति गृहगमनमाज्ञापितम् ।।२७।।

एवं तासां गृहगमने बोधिते तत्परित्यागानन्तरं पुनर्ग्रहणं वांताशनमिव मन्यमानाः, भगवद्वाक्यं चानुल्लंघ्यमिति विचार्य, अतिविरोधे उभयानुरोधिशरीरपरित्यागः कर्तव्य इति निश्चित्य, तत्रापि भगवत्सम्बन्धानन्दाभावादितिकर्तव्यतामूढा जाता इत्याह इति विप्रियमिति ।

श्रीशुक उवाच—**इति विप्रियमाकर्ण्य गोप्यो गोविन्दभाषितम् ।**
विषण्णा भग्नसङ्कल्पाश्चिन्तामापुर्दुरत्ययाम् ।।२८।।

विगतं प्रियं यस्मादिति, उभयथापि प्रियाभावः । किं परीक्षार्थमाह, आहोस्विदभिप्रेत एवायमर्थ इति । आ समन्तात् श्रुत्वा, वाक्यतात्पर्यं निर्धार्य, सत्यं गमनमेव वदतीति निश्चत्य, अनभिप्रेतत्वेऽपि तत्प्रसवहेतुमलभमानाः, गोप्यो नैपुण्यरहिताः, गोविन्दस्य स्वामिनः देवभाषितत्वेन अनृतशङ्कारहितमीश्वरवाक्याच्च निर्धाररहितमाकर्ण्य, विषण्णा जाताः, मनसि परमं विषादं प्राप्ताः । तत्र हेतुर्भग्नसङ्कल्पा इति । तदा परां चिन्तां प्रापुः । कथमस्मद्विचारितं भगवद्वाक्यं चैकमुखं भवतीति । सा चिन्ता त्रैलोक्यं व्याप्य चेदं जन्मजन्मान्तराणि च निर्द्धारमलभमाना दुरत्यया पर्यवसानरहिता जाता ।।२८।।

ततः चिन्तया यज्जातं तदाह कृत्वेति ।

कृत्वा मुखान्यवशुचः श्वसनेन शुष्यद्-
बिम्बाधराणि चरणेन भुवं लिखन्त्यः ।
अस्त्रैरुपात्तमषिभिः कुचकुङ्कुमानि
तस्थुर्मृजन्त्य उरुदुःखभराः स्म तूष्णीम् ।।२९।।

चिन्तया प्रथमं मूर्च्छिता जाताः । ततः मुखान्यव अवाङ्मुखानि कृत्वा, कमपि स्वमुखं न प्रदर्शयिष्यामि इति अवाङ्मुखानि कृतवत्यः । अवगताः शुचः याभिस्ताः, शोकसम्बन्धिन्यो वा जाताः । शुचः श्वसनेन शोकसम्बन्धिना श्वासवायुना शुष्यन्ति बिम्बवदधराणि येषाम् । तादृशानि मुखानि कृत्वा, चरणेन च लिखन्त्यः, तथैवा-

वस्था भवतीति। भूमिविवरमिव प्रार्थयन्त्यः, उपात्तमषिभिः अस्त्रैः कुचकुङ्कुमानि मृजन्त्यः, तूष्णीं तस्थुः। मुखस्य अवाक्त्वेन भक्तितिरोभावः। श्वसनेन प्राणपीडा, शोकेनान्तःकरणस्य, बिम्बाधरशोषेण कामरसस्य, पदा भूमिलेखनेन शरीरस्य, अस्त्रैरिन्द्रियाणाम्, कुङ्कुमाभावेन कान्तेः, दुःखभरेण आनन्दस्य , तूष्णीं स्थित्या चैतन्यस्य तिरोभावो निरूपितः। केवलं स्थाणुवत् स्थिताः ॥२९॥

एवमपि स्थितौ तूष्णीं स्थितं भगवन्तमालक्ष्य कश्चिद्विज्ञापयामासुरित्याह प्रेष्ठमिति।

प्रेष्ठं प्रियेतरमिव प्रतिभाषमाणं
कृष्णं तदर्थविनिर्वर्तितसर्वकामाः।
नेत्रे विमृज्य रुदितोपहते स्म किञ्चित्
संरम्भगद्गदगिरोऽब्रुवतानुरक्ताः ॥३०॥

भाषणं पूर्वोक्तमेव। अथवा। तस्यामप्यवस्थायां किमिति रोदनं क्रियते, स्वस्था भवत, गृहे गच्छतेत्येव वदति, परं हसन्मुखः, तदा तासां हृदये वाक्यामृतानि प्रविष्टानि सजातीयानि वाक्यान्युत्पादितवन्ति, तदा भगवदुद्बोधिता एव ताः भगवद्वाक्यानि पूर्वपक्षयितुमारेभिर इत्याह प्रेष्ठमिति। प्रेष्ठो भवत्येव। स्वसामग्र्या तथा सम्पादितत्वात्, परं वदत्यन्यथा, तथाप्यप्रियमिव प्रतिभाषमाणमिति नोक्तम्। न हि कदाचिदपि भगवानप्रियवद्भवति, किन्तु प्रियो भवति, इतरोऽपि भवति, सर्वभवनसामर्थ्यात्। इतरत्वे न प्रियत्वं बाध्यते। यथा जगज्जगदतिरिक्तरूपश्च। तदाह प्रियेतरमिव प्रतिभाषमाणमिति। यः प्रियोंऽशः, तं न तिरोधारयति। किन्तु वाक्यं न तेन रूपेण वदति, किन्तु रूपान्तरेण, तदा तेन सह वादः कर्तुं शक्य इति। न हि फलं क्वचित्साधनं भवति, मां वृणुतेति वा वदति, परं बलादपि प्रतिबन्ध-निराकरणं कृत्वा स ग्राह्य एव। तदाहं कृष्णं सदानन्दमिति। ननु कोऽयं निर्बन्धः, स एव काम्य इति, महाँश्चेन्न मन्यते, तदा अल्पतरा अपि काम्या इति, तत्राह तदर्थविनिर्वर्तितसर्वकामा इति। तदर्थं भगवदर्थं विशेषेण निर्वर्तिताः सर्वे कामा याभिः। अयमेव काम्य इति निश्चित्य पूर्वमेव सर्वे कामास्त्यक्ताः। 'काममयश्चायं पुरुषः'। यदि त्यक्तोऽपि गृह्येत, तदा भगवदुक्तमेव गृहं कथं न गृह्येत। तस्मादय-मेव कामः अवशिष्यते। स चेन्न भवेत्, स्वरूपहानिरेवेति निश्चित्य, फले मानमकृत्वा दृढीभूय, रुदितोपहते नेत्रे विमृज्य, यथास्थानं सर्वं प्रापयित्वा, किञ्चित्संरम्भेण, वादार्थमुद्यमः संरम्भः। भगवान् हि वाक्येन निराकरोति, न तु स्वरूपतः। वाक्यं तु निराकार्यमिति तदर्थं संरम्भः। सर्वोऽप्यन्तं गत्वा परावर्तते, परं संरम्भेण गद्गदा गीर्यासाम्। वर्णानां न स्फुटनिर्गमनम्, ईश्वरवाक्यनिराकरणे यतो वाणी बिभेति। एतासां तु न भयम्। यतः अनुरक्ताः। रागो हि भयप्रतिपक्षः। यत्र रागः स्वल्पोऽपि, न तत्र भयम्। अतः अब्रुवत उक्तवत्यः ॥३०॥

वाक्यानां बाधवाक्यानि तावन्ति प्रार्थनाधिका ।
एकादशविधास्तेन तासां वाचो जयन्ति हि ॥१॥

यद्भगवता प्रथममुक्तं 'स्वागतं वो महाभागा' इति, यद्यपि भगवता वयं स्तुताः, तथापि प्रेषणाभिप्रायेण, न तु स्वस्मिन्नागता इति । तथा सति नेयं स्तुतिः, किन्त्वतिक्रूरं वचनम्, अनिष्टपर्यवसानात् । नन्वशक्ये किं कर्तव्यम्, तत्राह मैवं विभो इति ।

श्रीगोप्य ऊचुः—**मैवं विभोऽर्हति भवान् गदितुं नृशंसं**
संत्यज्य सर्वविषयांस्तव पादमूलम् ।
प्राप्ता भजस्व दुरवग्रह मा त्यजास्मान्
देवो यथादिपुरुषो भजते मुमुक्षून् ॥३१॥

भवान् सर्वमेव कर्तुं समर्थः । समर्थश्चेदन्यथा वदेत्, नृशंसमेव भवति, दयायां विद्यमानायां न वदेदिति । यच्च भगवतोक्तं 'व्रजस्यानामय'मिति, तदस्माकं नोद्देश्यम्, यतः सर्वविषयानेव संत्यज्य तव पादमूलं प्राप्ताः । अनेन त्यक्तार्थपरिग्रहः अनुचितः । नापि जारत्वेन समागतमिति निरूपितम् । एकादशेन्द्रियाणामपि विषयास्त्यक्ताः सवासनाः । तत्र विनिगमकं तव पादमूलं प्राप्ता इति । अन्यथा पादमूलप्राप्तिरेव न स्यात् । यदुक्तं "ब्रूतागमनकारण'मिति, तत्राहुः भजस्वेति । अन्यत् कर्तव्यमिति चेत्, तत्राहुः हे दुरवग्रहेति । दुष्टोऽयमवग्रहः, आग्रहः यद्भजनं न कर्तव्यम्, अन्यत्कर्तव्यमिति । यथा जीवानाम् । ते हि सर्वं कर्तुं वाञ्छन्ति, न भगवद्भजनम् । यथायमाग्रहो जीवानां दुष्टः, तथात्रापि भवितुमर्हति । 'ये यथा मां प्रपद्यन्ते' इति तु नास्ति । यदि तदभिप्रायेणैव तथा, तदा मा त्यजास्मान् । अस्माभिर्न त्यज्यत इति । एतच्च भजनं न विषयवत्, किन्तु प्रकारान्तरेणेति विशेषतो वक्तुमशक्ताः दृष्टान्तेनाहुः देवो यथेति । देवो हि सर्वानेव भजते, अन्यथा शास्त्रं व्यर्थं स्यात् । तत्राप्यादिपुरुषो देवः । पूर्वकाण्डेऽपि भजनं सार्थकम् , सुतरां उत्तरकाण्डे । आदिपुरुषस्तु सेव्य एव भवति, देवश्च । न हि देवभजनं व्यभिचारजनकं भवति । पुरुषान्तरभजनेऽपि प्रथमभर्ता। विवाहितःअभजनीयो भवति। अनङ्गीकारस्तूचितः, नत्वभजनम् । एतेन स यथा स्वातिरिक्तभजनं न सहते, तन्निवृत्तिपूर्वकमेव स्वभजनं संपाद्य स्वयं भजते, तथा त्वयापि कार्यम् । अतस्तत्र प्रेषणं तत्राप्यनुचितमिति ज्ञाप्यते । किञ्च, यथा मुमुक्षून् भजते भगवान् । आत्मीयत्वेन परिगृह्णाति, आत्मतया स्फुरति, स्वानन्दं तेभ्यः प्रयच्छति । 'एष ह्येवानन्दयाती'ति श्रुतेः । 'स्वाप्ययसम्पत्त्योरन्यतरापेक्षमाविष्कृतं ही'ति न्यायेन भगवान् तदर्थमात्मानं प्रकटीकरोतीति मुमुक्षून् भजत इत्युक्तम् । अन्यथा मुमुक्षव एव भगवन्तं भजन्ते, न तु भगवान्, अतः फलद्वारा भजनम् । यथा तेषां पुनः पूर्वावस्थां न सम्पादयसि, सततं स्वस्मिन्नेव स्थापयसि, तथा अस्मदर्थमाविर्भूय स्वानन्देन वयं योजनीया इति एतत्कर्तव्यमित्यर्थः । (एतेन

प्रार्थनया सकृदङ्गीकृत्य तूष्णींभावपक्षो निरस्तः । अग्रे गृहगमनाज्ञापनगृहस्थितिसम्पादनादिकं तु रसपोषायैव, न तु गृहार्थमिति ज्ञेयम्) ॥३१॥

यत्पत्यपत्यसुहृदामनुवृत्तिरङ्ग
स्त्रीणां स्वधर्म इति धर्मविदा त्वयोक्तम् ।
अस्त्वेवमेतदुपदेशपदे त्वयीशे
प्रेष्ठो भवाँस्तनुभृतां किल बन्धुरात्मा ॥३२॥

यदपि भगवतोक्तं 'स्त्रीणां स्वधर्मपरित्यागोऽनुचित' इति, अतः 'एषा रजनी घोररूपा, नेह स्त्रीभिः स्थेय'मिति । तत्राप्याहुः यत्पत्यपत्येति । पतिरपत्यानि सुहृदश्च । एषामनुवृत्तिः स्त्रीणां स्वधर्म इत धर्मविदा त्वया उक्तम् । बहिर्मुखा हि धर्मशास्त्रज्ञाः, शारीरमेव धर्मं स्वधर्ममाहुः । नत्वात्मधर्मं भगवद्धर्मं वा । यतस्ते अनात्मविदः । तथा धर्मविदैव त्वया, नत्वस्मान् विचार्य, आत्मानं वा, त्वयोक्तम् । तस्याप्यस्माभिर्विषयनिर्धारः क्रियते, न दूष्यते । तदाहुः अस्त्वेवमेतदिति । स्त्रीभिः स्वधर्मः कर्तव्य इति यदुक्तम्, तदेवमेवास्तु । नहि पत्यादयः धर्मस्वरूपम्, नाप्याधारः, किन्तु निमित्तम्, । स च धर्मः अनुष्ठीयमानः प्रमीयमाणश्च भवति । अनुष्ठीयमाने पुत्रादयो निमित्तम् । प्रमीयमाणे गुरुः । अतः सा अनुवृत्तिः प्रथमतो गुरावस्तु, अन्यथा स्वधर्मो ज्ञात एव न स्यात् । न च भगवद्वाक्यमनुवादकम् । पूर्वमस्माकं धर्मज्ञानाभावात् । अन्यथा तदेव क्रियेत । नापि सेवाव्यतिरेकेणायं धर्मः स्फुरति । अन्यथा वचनमात्रेणैव गतं स्यात् । अत उपदिष्टस्य सिद्ध्यर्थं सेवां कारय । उपदेशस्य पदमाश्रयः कर्तैव भवति । अङ्गेति कोमलसम्बोधनात् नास्माभिः प्रतिकूलतया निरूप्यते । किञ्च, स्वधर्मा अनेकविधाः, स्वापेक्षयोत्कृष्टविषयाः, समानविषयाः, हीनविषयाश्च । तत्र पूर्वपूर्वधर्मप्राबल्यम् । यथा स्त्रीणां पतिपुत्रादीनां स्वसमानानां सेवा धर्मः । एवं स्वनियामकस्येश्वरस्यापि अनुवृत्तिर्मुख्यो धर्मः । अन्यथा तत्प्रेरणाभावे पतिसेवादौ न प्रवर्तेत । अतः प्रकृतेऽपि भवानीश्वरः अन्तर्यामी तादृशोऽपि भूत्वा पतिपुत्राद्यर्थं न प्रवर्तयसे, किन्तु स्वसेवार्थमेव प्रेरयसि, अतो वाक्योक्त धर्मसिद्ध्यर्थमपि भवानादौ सेव्यः । किञ्च, धर्मी धर्ममूलः, तदविरोधेन कर्तव्यः, फलार्थं च कर्तव्यः, अन्यथा चेत् अनिष्टेऽपि पुरुषं प्रवर्तयन् अनाप्तः स्यात् । अत एव धर्मशास्त्रे प्रियत्वात् शरीरस्य तदनुरोध उक्तः । 'द्रव्यसंस्कारविरोधे द्रव्यं बलीय' इति न्यायाच्च । तत्कस्यचित् प्रियो देहः, कस्यचिद्दात्मा, कस्यचित् परमात्मा, कस्यचिन्निर्वाहकः । भवाँस्तु सर्वरूपो भवति, यतः अत्यन्तं प्रेष्ठः परमप्रेमास्पदमानन्दः । बन्धुदेहनिर्वाहकश्च । किञ्च, न केवलमस्माकम्, किन्तु तनुभृतां सर्वेषामेव देहधारिणाम् । ('भवाय नाशाये' त्यत्र त्वया दत्तमेव शरीरं त्वद्विचारितप्रयोजनार्थं जीवो गृहीत्वा तिष्ठतीति निरूपितम् । अतः स देहः

भगवदीयः भगवतैव स्थापितः, तस्मै निवेद्य, तदनुपयोगे जाते, पश्चादन्यस्मै देयः। चेतनो हि प्रेर्यः। अतः यावद्भगवदुपयोगं ज्ञास्यति, तावन्नान्यस्मै दास्यति, बोधितोऽपि।) यतस्तनुभृतां त्वमेव प्रेष्ठ। प्रेष्ठाय च देयं प्रियं वस्तु। अत्रार्थे किलेति प्रसिद्धिरेव प्रमाणम्। किञ्च, न केवलं देहदाता, किन्तु बन्धुरपि, येन प्रयत्नेन शरीरं बिभर्ति स बन्धुः, आत्मा धारकश्च। अतः अन्तरङ्गबहिरङ्गन्यायेन नित्यानित्यन्यायेन वा भ(ग)वत्सेवैव मुख्या। यदा पुनस्त्वदनुपयोगः, तत्रापि चेत्तथा प्रेरणम्, तदान्यस्मै दास्यामो, नन्यथेति। धर्मिविचारो धर्मादप्यधिकः। एतच्च त्वदनङ्गीकृतं सर्वमेव विरुद्धं भवतीति प्रार्थ्यते अस्त्विवति। सर्वरूपत्वात् त्वमेव सेव्य इति वा। अन्यत्र एकदा सर्वसेवा प्राप्ता, अंशतो बाधिता स्यात्, विनिगमनाभावाच्च। अनेन स धर्मोऽपि न भवति, यः कालादिना बाध्यते, अशक्यश्च भवति। न हि प्रमाणं विरुद्धं विधत्ते। अतः पत्यादिसेवाविधायकं च शास्त्रं त्वत्सेवामेव विधत्ते। अतः अनुवादपक्षे स्वतन्त्रविधानपक्षे वा भवत्सेवैवोचितेति भावः ॥३२॥

एवं राजसीनां निरूप्य सात्त्विकीनां निरूपयति कुर्वन्ति हीति।

कुर्वन्ति हि त्वयि रतिं कुशलाः स्व आत्मन्
नित्यप्रिये पतिसुतादिभिरार्तिदैः किम्।
तन्नः प्रसीद वरदेश्वर मा स्म छिन्द्या
आशां धृतां त्वयि चिरादरविन्दनेत्र ॥३३॥

यद्यप्युक्तं 'मातरः पितर' इति, 'मा कृढ्वं बन्धुसाध्वस'मिति, तत्किमिदं प्रथमतयास्माभिरेव क्रियते, आहोस्विदन्येऽपि कुर्वन्ति। तत्रापि किमधमाः मात्राद्यनुवृत्तिं कुर्वन्ति, आहोरिवदुत्तमाः। उत्तमा अपि त्वत्सेवायामशक्ताः, आहोस्वित् शक्ता इति विचारणीयम्। अस्मिन्नर्थे निर्णायकं महतां चरित्रमाहुः। ये त्वात्मनि कुशलाः आत्महितार्थिनः, न तु देहेन्द्रियाणाम्, ते त्वय्येव रतिं कुर्वन्ति। स्नेहेन हि क्रिया भवति। भगवत्कृतमेव जीवगामि भवतीति। तदुपपादितम्, 'तच्चात्मने प्रतिमुखस्ये'त्यत्र। प्रीत्या च सेवा भवति। यदि पुत्रादिसेवापि धर्मः स्यात्, तदा पुरुषार्थत्वेनात्मपर्यवसायिनी स्यात्। 'कुशला' इत्यनेन तेषां कौशलमेतत्, प्रवृत्त्यपेक्षया निवृत्तिरुत्तमा। इन्द्रियदमनसामर्थ्याभाव एव अन्यगामि कर्तव्यम्, यतो निवर्तते'त्यत्र निरूपितम्। निरुद्धानीन्द्रियाण्यात्मगामीनि भवन्ति। तत्राप्यात्मगामीनि तदैव भवन्ति, यदि त्वदर्थमुपयुक्तानि भवन्ति। अतः केवलनिग्रहकर्त्रपेक्षया ये त्वयि रतिं कुर्वन्ति, ते कुशला इति हिशब्दार्थः। त्वयीत्येकवचनेन च पूर्ववदेकत्र सर्वसंभवो निरूपितः। किञ्च, भवान् स्वात्मा स्वरूपभूतः, नत्वध्यासन्यायेन तथा जातः। किञ्च, प्रियस्य हि सेवा कर्तव्या, स चेत्प्रियः कालपरिच्छेद्यो न भवति, स भवानेव, अन्यथा जारसेवापि धर्मः स्यात्, जन्मवत् दिनस्यापि परिच्छेदकत्वात्।

किञ्च, पतिसुतादयश्च न धर्महेतवो भवितुमर्हन्ति । यतः आर्तिदाः । न हि धर्मनिमित्तानि कदाचित् दुःखदानि भवन्ति । अन्यथा संसारो न स्यात् । अतस्तैः किम् । तेषां भयमस्तु, अन्यद्वा, न तैः किञ्चित्प्रयोजनमित्यर्थः । परमेकमेव प्रार्थनीयम्, यदभावे सर्वं शास्त्रं युक्तिश्च व्यर्था स्यात् । तदाहुः, तत्तस्मात् प्रसीद्, त्वं प्रसन्नो भव । त्वदप्रसादादेव लोका भ्रान्ताः दुःखहेतुष्वपि प्रवर्तन्ते । ननु किं साधनं प्रसादे भवतीनामिति चेत्, तत्राहुः वरदेश्वरेति । ये हि वरान् प्रयच्छन्ति, ते लोकानां क्लेशं ज्ञात्वा, यतो दयालवः, अन्यथा तपसि क्रियमाणे वरं न प्रयच्छेयुः । तेषामपि त्वमीश्वरोऽतिदयालुः । तद्द्वारापि सर्वेषां दुःखशमनं करोषि । अतो वयं क्लिष्टाः । क्लेश एव साधनम्, तपोवत् । निषिद्धप्रकारस्तु यद्यत्र कश्चन भविष्यति, स न कर्तव्यः । ननु यथैतावन्तं कालं पतिसेवा कृता, एवमेवाग्रेऽपि कर्तव्या, प्राप्तत्वात् । गौणमपि कर्म समारब्धं समापयेदिति, तस्मादविचार्यैव पतिसेवां कुरुतेति चेत्, तत्राहुः मास्म छिन्द्या आशां धृतामिति । नास्माभिः पतिसेवा कृता, तदर्थं वा स्थितम्, त्वदाशया स्थितम् मध्ये स्थितिनिर्वाहार्थमेव तदङ्गीकारः । इदानीं चेत् समागतानामभिलषितार्थो न सिध्येत्, तदा आशा भग्ना भविष्यति । तस्यां गतायां प्राणा एव गमिष्यन्तीति । अत एव केनचित् स्त्रीहृदयज्ञेन निरूपितम्, 'आशाबन्धो हृदयं रुणद्धी'ति । एतस्य मूलमपि स्त्रीशास्त्रे भविष्यति । चिरात् त्वय्येव धृताम्, तस्यां छिन्नायां अवलम्बनाभावात् अधः पतिष्याम इति । स्मेत्ययमर्थः प्रसिद्धः । अरविन्दनेत्रेति सम्बोधनं दृष्ट्यैवाप्यायकत्वं निरूपयति । (आशाहेतुरप्यनेनोक्तः, तापहारकदृष्ट्या दर्शनात् । भावोद्गारिण्या एव तथात्वात् । इयदवधि जीवनमप्यत एवेति भावः ।) ॥३३॥

यदुक्तं 'वनदर्शनार्थं किमागता'इति, ततश्च वनवर्णना कृता, तत्राहुः चित्तं सुखेनेति ।

चित्तं सुखेन भवतापहृतं गृहेपि
यन्निर्विशत्युत करावपि गृह्यकृत्ये ।
पादौ पदं न चलतस्तव पादमूला-
द्यामः कथं व्रजमधो करवाम किं वा ॥३४॥

वनदर्शनेच्छा तदा भवति, यदा चित्तं स्वस्मिन् तिष्ठेत् । तत्तु त्वयैवापहृतम्, तत्रापहारे न तव प्रयासः, तथा सति सर्वं नापहृतं स्यात्, तदाह सुखेनेति । भवता वा आनन्दरूपेणापहृतम् । न हि साक्षात् परमानन्दे सति कश्चित् परम्परया पाक्षिकं साधनं गृह्णाति । वनदर्शनं दूरे, गृहेऽपि यच्चित्तं निर्विशति । अनेन ज्ञानशक्तेरपहार उक्तः । नापि मन्तव्यं वनं किञ्चित् कार्यार्थमागता इति । तदर्थं क्रियाशक्तेरप्यपहारमाह उत करावपीति । यौ गृह्यकृत्ये निर्विशतः, दूरेणापास्तं

वनकृत्यम्, कामेन बलस्य हृतत्वात् । त्वत्स्पर्शेनैव करौ सजीवौ भवतः । नो चेन्मृतौ । अतः सेवाविधिरपि हस्ताभावात् कुण्ठितः । न हि कररहितं कर्मणि कश्चिन्नियुंक्ते । किञ्च, यत् व्याघुट्य गन्तव्यमित्यभिप्रायेण वनदर्शनं जातमित्युक्तम्, तदप्यसम्भावितम् । यतोऽस्माकं पादौ द्वावपि तव पादमूलादस्मात् स्थानात् एकमपि पदं न चलतः, नान्यत्र गच्छतः । पादानां गतियुक्तानां मूलभूतौ त्वत्पादौ, तस्यापि चेन्मूलं गताः, तदा कथमन्यत्र गच्छेयुः, अन्यथा वृक्षाणामपि गतिः स्यात्, मूलं गतानाम् । 'अस्मात् स्थाना'दिति वक्तव्ये, यत् 'तव पादमूला' दित्युक्तम्, तत् त्वद्गमने सर्वत्र गन्तुं शक्यते, न तु त्वद्व्यतिरेकेणेति ज्ञापितम् । अतः कथं यामः । शकटादिना प्रेषणीया इति चेत्, तत्राहुः । अथो अथ तत्र गत्वा किं वा करवाम । यथा शकटादिकं गृहे यातनार्थं साधनमस्ति, न चैवं हस्तयोः कार्यकरणे किञ्चित् लोकसिद्धम् । न केवलं गमनेन प्रयोजनम्, किन्तु पित्रादिसेवार्थं गमनम्, तदभावाद् व्यर्थमेव गमनमिति भावः । तदाहुः । अथो अथ किं वा करवामेति । हस्तनिरपेक्षा कृतिः भिन्नप्रक्रमेण भगवद्भावेन भवतीति तथोक्तम् । अनेन स्तनपानमप्यशक्यं निरूपितम् । आशाऽभावे सर्वत्रैव शोषात् ।।३४।।

यद्भगवता शीघ्रं गच्छतेत्युक्तम्, तत्राहुः सिञ्चाङ्गेति ।

सिञ्चाङ्ग नस्त्वदधरामृतपूरकेण
हासावलोककलगीतजहृच्छयाग्निम् ।
नो चेद्वयं विरहजाग्न्युपभुक्तदेहा
ध्यानेन याम पदयोः पदवीं सखे ते ।।३५।।

वयं शीघ्रमेव गमिष्यामः, यदि त्वं प्रतिबन्धं न करिष्यसि । अनेन तूष्णींभावेऽपि मरणम्, परावृत्तौ तु न किञ्चिद्वक्तव्यम् । हे अङ्ग । त्वदधरामृतपूरकेण त्वदधरागृत-प्रवाहजलेन नो हृच्छयाग्निं सिञ्च । स चाग्निः त्वयैवोत्पादित इति । तत्कारणमाहुः हासावलोककलगीतजेति । तव योऽयं हासपूर्वकः अवलोकः कलगीतं च, ताभ्यां जातो यो हृच्छयः कामः, स एवाग्निः । हासः कामजनकः, अवलोकः सन्धुक्षण-कर्ता । गीतं वायुरिव, तत्रापि कलगीतं सर्वतो वायुः । सोऽपि जातो हृदये । हृदय-गामि च त्वदधरामृतमेव । पूरो हि वस्तु प्रवाहयति, तस्यात्र सिञ्चनकरणत्वे-नोक्त्याऽग्नेरतिमहत्त्वं ध्वन्यते । अतो युक्ता सिञ्चनोक्तिः । अलौकिकश्चाग्निः अलौकिकेनैव शाम्यति । कन्दर्पो हि मृतो ज्वलति, स हि जीवन् अग्न्यवस्थां त्यजति, नान्यथा, अमृतेनैव च जीवति, तत्रापि न देवभोग्येन, अन्यथा तैरेव जीवितः स्यात्, सृष्टिकारणत्वात् नास्य मोक्षः । अतोऽतिगुप्तेनैवाधरामृतेन तस्य जीवनम् । अतः सिञ्चनमेवोक्तम् । अन्यथा निर्वापणमेव प्रार्थयेयुः । कामे जीवति जीविष्यामः, अन्यथा स स्वयं ज्वलन् अन्यानपि ज्वालयिष्यति । तदाहुः नो चेदिति । सिञ्चनेन

यदि मन्त्रवादीव न जीवयिष्यसि, तदा विरहेण जनितो योऽग्निः, तेनोपभुक्तदेहाः ध्यानेन ते पदयोः पदवीं यामः। स्वयं स्वतन्त्रमार्गाज्ञानात्, त्वं च सखा येन मार्गेण गमिष्यसि, तेनैव वयमपि यास्यामः। (यथा त्वमधुनास्मभ्यमार्तिप्रदः, तथा वयमपि तथाभूतास्तुभ्यं पश्चात्तापादिहेतवो भविष्याम इति गूढाभिसन्धिः 'ते पदयोः पदवीं यामे'ति वक्त्रीणामिति ज्ञेयम्।) देहे गते त्वन्तर्यामिणा क्वचिद्-गन्तव्यम्, देहान्तरस्य तु नोत्पत्तिः, बीजस्य दग्धत्वात्। हरेणैव दग्धो न कामः प्ररोहति, स विपरीतो रहो भवति। तत्रापि विशिष्टो विरहः एकान्ताभावरूपो वा। अनेन त्वया सह एकान्ताभावे विरहत्वम्। यद्यपि पूर्वोक्ताग्निनैव दाहः सम्भवति, तथापि भस्मसात् करणे न तस्य सामर्थ्यम्, यावत् सर्वाङ्गेषु सूक्ष्मावयवेष्वप्यग्निः प्रविश्य नोद्बुद्धो भवति। यथा वह्निसम्बन्धेन शुष्कं काष्ठं ज्वलति। तत उपाधेर-त्यन्तं गतत्वात् ते पदयोर्गमनम्। अतो गमनं दूरापास्तम्, प्रत्युत मरणमुप-स्थितमिति शीघ्रं प्रतिकारं कुरु ॥३५॥

किञ्च, यदप्युक्तं 'अथवा मदभिस्नेहात् आगता'इति, यदस्माकं स्नेहः स्तुतः तत्र याथार्थ्यं शृण्वित्याहुः यर्हीति।

यर्ह्यम्बुजाक्ष तव पादतलं रमाया
दत्तक्षणं क्वचिदरण्यजनप्रियस्य।
अस्प्राक्ष्म तत् प्रभृति नान्यसमक्षमञ्जः
स्थातुं त्वयाभिरमिता बत पारमयामः ॥३६॥

हे अम्बुजाक्ष, दृष्ट्यैव तापनाशक, यर्हि यस्मिन् क्षणे तव पादतलं अस्प्राक्ष्म, तत्प्रभृति नान्यसमक्षं अञ्जः सामस्त्येनापि स्थातुं पारयामः। साक्षात् चरणस्पर्शो दुर्लभः। यत्र पुनः पादः प्रतिफलितः, तत्पादतलमुच्यते। रमापि तेनैव जीवति। तदुक्तं नागपत्नीभिः। 'तवांघ्रिरेणुस्पर्शाधिकारः यद्वाञ्छये'ति। अतस्तत् फल-स्थानीयम्। रमायाः क्षणं सुखं तेनैव दत्तम्, क्वचिद् हृदये समागतम्, सुखं तत्रैव भवतीति तत्र स्पर्श एवास्माकं भूमिष्ठस्य, न तु लक्ष्मीवत् हृदये तत्तलमायाति। अस्माभिर्विचारितम्, लक्ष्म्या चेदेतत्प्राप्तम्, तपसा चाञ्चल्यपरिहारेण, तदा-स्माभिरपि चाञ्चल्यपरिहारेण तन्निष्ठतया स्थातव्यम्। किञ्च, अरण्यजनाः प्रिया यस्य। तेनापि सर्वसङ्गपरित्यागेन स्थातव्यं। सङ्गाभाव एव भगवत्तो-षहेतुरिति। अरण्यं हि सात्त्विकं वैष्णवं च।(एतेन पुलिन्दीस्मारणं वा। पादतल-सम्बन्धिकुङ्कुमसम्बन्धेनैव ता अपि प्रिया आसन्निति। तेन पादतलस्य फल-पर्यवसायित्वं प्रभुप्रीतिसाधकत्वं च सहजमिति वयमप्यात्मनि तथैव जानीम इति भावः। स्फुटमिदं न वक्तुं शक्यमित्येवमुक्तम्।) अतः त्वत्प्राप्त्यर्थं नान्य-समक्षं स्थातुं शक्नुमः। सर्वथा त्वां यो न प्रपन्नः, शक्त्यभावः तद्धर्मप्रवेशात्,

यो हि यस्य घातकः तद्भावापत्तौ तस्याग्रे स्थातुं न शक्तो भवति । यथा व्याघ्राग्रे देहाभिमानी, तथा भगवदीयः, भगवद्व्यतिरिक्तो हि तद्भावं नाशयिष्यतीति । यत्रैवं सूक्ष्मेक्षिका, तत्रान्यस्य स्थाने गमनं, तस्य च देवतात्वेन भावनं दूरापास्तम् । अतः प्रीतिमात्रस्तुतिर्या सा अल्पीयसी । अनन्यभावा एव वयं लक्ष्मीवत् । किञ्च, यथा सर्वपरित्यागेन लक्ष्मीः चेत् त्वां शरणं गता, तदा त्वया अभिरमिता जाता, तथा वयमपि जाताः । सर्वदैव स्वप्ने त्वत्सम्बन्धं प्राप्नुमः । अन्यथा जीवनमेव न स्यात् । एवं भुक्तपूर्वा वयं नान्यत्र प्रेषयितुमुचिता इति ॥३६॥

ननु तस्या दैवगत्या सम्बन्ध आसीत्, स च प्राथमिकः, भवतीनां तु प्रथमतोऽन्यत्रैव सम्बन्धः, अतो वैषम्यमिति चेत्, तत्राहुः श्रीरिति ।

श्रीर्यत्पदाम्बुजरजश्चकमे तुलस्या
लब्ध्वापि वक्षसि पदं किल भृत्यजुष्टम् ।
यस्याः स्ववीक्षणकृतेऽन्यसुरप्रयास-
स्तद्वद्वयं च तव पादरजः प्रपन्नाः ॥३७॥

लक्ष्मीरपि न दैवगत्या भवन्तं प्राप्तवती, किन्तु त्वच्चरणारविन्दार्थं महत्तपः कृतवती । सा न स्त्रीत्वेन त्वदीया, किन्तु भक्तत्वेन, अन्यथा वक्षसि स्थलं प्राप्य स्वतन्त्रम्, तुलस्या सह सापत्न्यमप्यङ्गीकृत्य, चरणरजो न कामयेत् । चरणरजस्तुलस्या भवति, भक्ता हि भक्तेः । तदुपपादितं प्रथमस्कन्धे । तस्य रजसः माहात्म्यमाह भृत्यजुष्टमिति । तद्रजसैव भृत्यानां शरीरोत्पत्तेः । किलेति प्रसिद्धिः । सर्व एव भक्ताः त्वच्चरणरजसैव सम्पादितदेहवन्तः । अतस्तुलसी तत्र भक्तिरूपा प्रतिष्ठिता । तद्रजःप्राप्तिर्येषाम्, ते त्वत्सेवका एव भवन्ति । अतो लक्ष्मीः, अन्तःकरणे स्थानं प्राप्यापि, अन्यः स्प्रक्ष्यतीति चिन्तया, रजश्चकमे । तस्मिन् प्राप्ते तु न शङ्कापि । ननु किमेतावद्भयं लक्ष्म्याः, तत्राहुः । यस्याः स्ववीक्षणकृते अन्यसुरप्रयासः । अन्ये सर्व एव ब्रह्मादयो देवाः तपः कुर्वन्ति, 'लक्ष्मीरस्मान् पश्य'त्विति । अन्यथा तेषां कोऽपि पुरुषार्थो न सिध्येदिति । अतो बहुभिः प्रार्थ्यमाना भीता जाता । कश्चिदत्यन्तमपि तपः कुर्यात्, रा, को वेद, किं कुर्यादिति । रजःकामनायां तु नेयं शङ्का । प्राप्तौ तु सन्देह एव न भवति । एवं चरणरजसः प्राप्तौ अनन्यगामित्वं निरूप्य स्वस्य तथात्वमाहुः तद्वद्वयं चेति । अस्मानपि बहवः प्रार्थयन्ति, तद्भयादेव पूर्वं चरणरजः स्पृष्टम्, ततो देहोऽपि तच्चरणरजसा समुद्भूत इति सर्वथा तव पादरजःप्रपन्नाः । चकारात् या अपि साम्प्रतं नागताः । या वा महिष्यः, ता एतादृशशरीरयुक्ता एव । अतोऽस्मदर्थ एव समागतो भवान् । नात्मानं गोपय । नापि गुप्तः स्थास्यसि । तस्मान्नाग्रहः कर्तव्य इति भावः ॥३७॥

एवं स्वस्य भगवदेकभोग्यशरीरत्वमुपपाद्य प्रार्थयन्ति तन्न इति ।

तन्नः प्रसीद वृजिनार्दन तेंऽघ्रिमूलं
प्राप्ता विसृज्य वसतीस्त्वदुपासनाशाः ।
त्वत्सुन्दरस्मितनिरीक्षणतीव्रकाम-
तप्तात्मनां पुरुषभूषण देहि दास्यम् ॥३८॥

पूर्वश्लोकेनैव भर्तृशुश्रूषणविधिर्निराकृतः । तदपरित्यागः सुतरामेव तेनैव निराकृतो भवति । अनेनापि निराकरणं प्रार्थयन्ति । भगवत्कृपाभावे तादृशेनैव सम्बन्धो भवेदिति, कृपा हि सर्वतोऽधिका, तत्तस्मात्कारणात् प्रसीद, प्रसन्नो भव, त्वयि प्रसन्ने सर्वं सेत्स्यतीति । ननु भवतीनां प्रतिकूलमदृष्टं दुःखप्रापकमस्ति, अतः कथं प्रसाद इति चेत्, तत्राहुः वृजिनार्दनेति । वृजिनं दुःखजनकं पापम्, स्वभावत एव सर्वेषां येन केनापि सम्बन्धेन तदर्दयसि । प्रसादे हेतुमाहुः तेंऽघ्रिमूलं प्राप्ता इति । यस्तु चरणतलं प्राप्नोति, स प्रसादमपि । स च प्रसादः पशुपुत्रादिरूपो मा भवत्विति स्वाधिकारमन्येभ्यो व्यावर्तयन्ति विसृज्य वसतीरिति । गृहस्थाश्रमस्त्यक्तः, न तु गृहमात्रमिति वसतीरिति बहुवचनम् । परित्यागेऽपि हेतुमाहुः त्वदुपासनाशा इति । त्वत्सेवां करिष्याम इति आशामात्रेणैव पूर्वसिद्धं त्यक्तम् । तत्र समागतानां पुनर्गृहसम्बन्धे किं वक्तव्यमिति । अतो देयं प्रार्थयन्ति त्वत्सुन्दरेति । तव सुन्दरं यत्स्मितं मोहकमप्यानन्दजनकं त्वत्सम्बन्धात् परमानन्दरूपं तादृशस्मितपूर्वकं यन्निरीक्षणं, तेन जातः तीव्रो यः कामः, तेन तप्तान्तःकरणानां अस्माकं, पुरुषाणां भूषणरूप, अनन्तकोटिकन्दर्पलावण्यरूप, स्वतः पुरुषार्थरूपमेव दास्यं देहि । (अधिकारिभेदेन दास्यस्यानेकविधत्वादीयं रूपं स्वतापोक्त्या व्यज्यते । उक्ततापविशिष्टानां यदेतत्तापनिवर्तकं तदिति । किञ्च, प्रभोरपेक्षितवस्तुसमर्पणे हि दास्यं भवति, न त्वन्यथा । एवं सति यथास्माकमुक्ततापेन प्रचुरा त्वदपेक्षा, तथा तवास्मदपेक्षायां स्वयमुद्यम्यास्मदुपभोगः कार्य इत्यर्थः पर्यवस्यति । अन्यथा दास्यस्य कृतिसाध्यत्वेन दानोक्तिरनुपपन्ना स्यात् । अत एव तथा सम्बोधनं पुरुषो भूत्वा भूषणरूपेति । तद्धि कण्ठादिषु सर्वेष्वङ्गेषु भवति । त्वमपि तथा भूत्वा दास्यं देहीति वाक्यैकवाक्यतया प्राप्यते । भूषणत्वोक्त्यैव स्वतन्त्रपुरुषार्थताप्युक्ता । मणिखचितं तद्विभूषणत्वसम्पत्त्यर्थं मध्ये लाक्षावदपि भवति । तेन महानपि तद्धारणार्थं लाक्षामपि धारयति, तुच्छामपि, तथा मध्ये कामोपयोग इति न तदुपाधिकृतं दास्यवरणम्, अपि तु तद्विपरीतमिति भावः ।) अतो दास्यार्थिन्य एव वयम्, न तु विवाहार्थिन्यः। अत उपनयनाद्यपेक्षापि न लोकव्यवहारेण कर्तव्येति भावः ॥३८॥

ननु भवतीनां सर्वासामेव दास्यवरणे को हेतुः, सालोक्यादेरपि फलस्य विद्यमानत्वात्, तत्राहुः वीक्ष्यालकावृतमिति ।

वीक्ष्यालकावृतमुखं तव कुण्डलश्रि
गण्डस्थलाधरसुधं हसितावलोकम् ।
दत्ताभयं च भुजदण्डयुगं विलोक्य
वक्षः श्रियैकरमणं च भवाम दास्यः ॥३९॥

अनेन लोकेप्सायां पतिर्न त्यक्तव्य इत्यत्रोत्तरमुक्तम् । लोके हि पुरुषार्थत्रयम् । चतुर्विधो मोक्षः । इन्द्राद्यैश्वर्यभावेन स्वर्गप्राप्तिः । इहलोके परमा लक्ष्मीः । तदत्र त्रयमपि दास्ये सर्वोत्कृष्टमस्तीति तदुपपादयन्ति । प्रथमं सारूप्यं सालोक्यं सामीप्यं सायुज्यमिति मोक्षभेदाः ते दास्याग्रे अप्रयोजकाः । यतो मुखारविन्ददर्शनेन ते कामा निवर्तन्ते इति भक्तिरूपमुखारविन्दस्य तदपेक्षयोत्कृष्टधर्मवत्त्वं निरूप्यते। अलकाः सारूप्यमिव प्राप्ता भ्रमराः । ते बहव एवात्र आवृत्य मुखं तिष्ठन्ति । अतः सारूप्यं गतानामपि यदि भक्तिशेषत्वम् , तदा किं सारूप्येण । किञ्च, मुखं कुण्डलश्रि, कुण्डलाभ्यां श्रीर्यस्य, कुण्डलयोर्वा श्रीर्यस्मात् । सामीप्ये हि नैकट्यं भवति। अत्यन्तसामीप्यं जायमानमपि कुण्डलादप्यधिकं न भविष्यति । ते चेत्सांख्ययोगरूपे भगवत्प्रमाणावलम्बिनी भगवदधीनगतिमती पुनर्भगवन्मुखनिरीक्षके, तदा किं सामीप्येन । किञ्च, गण्डस्थलाधरसुधमिति । गण्डौ स्थलरूपौ विशालौ । स्थले हि रसः पातुं शक्यत इति । अधरे च सुधा यस्मिन् । गण्डस्थले स्थित्वा अधरसुधा पातुमत्र शक्येति । सालोक्ये हि आनन्दमात्रमक्षरामृतपानं च । अक्षरापेक्षयापि गण्डस्थले स्थितिः चुम्बनाद्यर्थमुत्तमा । अधररसश्च अक्षररसादुत्तम इत्युक्तम् । कुण्डलश्रीयुक्तं गण्डस्थलमित्यस्मिन् पक्षेऽपि सामीप्यात् भक्तौ शास्त्रीयो रसः अधिको निरूपितः, परस्परं त्वद्गुणवादरूपः । अक्षरादाधिक्यं तु अधररसे स्पष्टमेव। किञ्च, हसितावलोकमिति । हसितपूर्वकमवलोको यस्मिन् । ब्रह्मानन्दे प्रविष्टानां न भक्तिविलासः । हासो हि सर्वरसोद्बोधरूपः । ज्ञानं चाविर्भूतम् । ब्रह्मानन्दे तु द्वयमप्यव्यक्तम्, जले निमग्नस्य जलपानवत् । अनुभवरसो हि भिन्नतया स्थितौ भवति । अतो भक्तिरूपमुखस्य दृष्टत्वात् दास्यमेव फलम्, न मोक्षः । भुजदण्डयुगं च विलोक्य इन्द्रादिभावेनापि स्वर्गो न प्रयोजक इति निरूपयन्ति दत्ताभयमिति । स्वर्गे इन्द्रः परमकाष्ठां प्राप्तः । तेऽपि दैत्येभ्यो निरन्तरं भीताः इन्द्रादयः । तेषामप्यभयदातृभगवतो भुजदण्डयुगलम् । तच्चेदत्रैवास्ति, तत्परित्यज्य किमिन्द्रत्वेन । चकारात् न केवलमभयमात्रं प्रयच्छति, किन्तु क्रियाशक्त्या यज्ञादिना हविरपि प्रयच्छति । यथाग्रे इन्द्रः स्वाधिकारसमाप्तौ मुक्तो भवति । दण्डपदेनानुल्लंघ्यशासनत्वमुक्तम् । उभयत्र च दण्डो युगपदेन निरूपितः । ततो हि सर्वथा दैत्यनाशो भवति । किञ्च, वक्षोऽपि विलोक्य । लोकानां श्रिया रमणं भवति । श्रीरपि तत्र रमते । चकाराद्धर्मस्यापि । अतो दास्य एव भवामः । (अत्र वीक्षणस्य दासीभवनहेतुत्वोक्त्या यत्रायं भावो नास्ति, तेषां नैतद्वीक्षणमस्ति, विधिप्रयुक्तत्वा-

भावेन तद्विपरीतविध्यनङ्गीकारश्च युक्त इति ज्ञाप्यते । यदप्युक्तं भगवता 'अस्वर्ग्य'मित्यादि स्वभजने दोषषट्कम्, तदपि षड्भिर्गुणैर्निवारितम् । न हि परमपुरुषार्थसाधकं पापं भवति । फलत एव पापस्य निन्द्यमानत्वात्) ।।३९।।

ननु तथापि लोकविद्विष्टं स्त्रीणामभिसरणम्, अतः सन्मार्गरक्षणार्थं प्रमाणसिद्ध-मप्येतन्न कर्तव्यम् । अतः श्रवणदर्शनादिकमेव कर्तव्यमिति चेत्, तत्राहुः का स्त्रीति ।

का स्त्र्यंग ते कलपदामृतवेणुगीत-
सम्मोहितार्यचरितान्न चलेत्त्रिलोक्याम् ।
त्रैलोक्यसौभगमिदं च निरीक्ष्य रूपं
यद्गोद्विजद्रुममृगाः पुलकान्यबिभ्रन् ।।४०।।

अयं धर्मः पुरुषाणां वक्तव्यः, न तु स्त्रीणाम्, असंभावितत्वात् । नह्यसंभावितो धर्मो भवति । एवं धर्मनाशे धर्मस्थापकं स्वरूपमेव हेतुः, अद्भुतकर्मत्वात् । (वस्तुतस्तु स्वरूपसम्बन्धिनां भक्तानां धर्मं स्वरूपेणैव रक्षति । तच्चान्यभावेभ्यो रक्षणमेतद्भावपोषणं च । ये स्वरूपधर्मसम्बन्धिनस्तांस्तैरेवेति न किञ्चिदनुप-पन्नमिति भावः । अत एवैवं स्वरक्षणेन स्वान्तरङ्गत्वज्ञापनाय) अङ्गेति सम्बो-धनम्, अप्रतारणाय च । या स्त्री लोके स्त्रीशब्दवाच्या सा कथमार्यचरितान्न चलेत् । त्रिलोक्यां सत्त्वरजस्तमःकार्यरूपायाम् । तामसीनां मौढ्यात् आर्यचरिते स्थितिं मत्वा तन्निराकरणम् । राजसीनां स्वभाव एव । सात्त्विकीनां सत्त्वाद्धर्मबुद्धिमाशंक्य तन्निराकरणम् । आर्यमार्गपरित्यागे हेतुः ते कलपदामृतवेणुगीतसम्मोहितेति । सम्मोहिता आर्यचरिताच्चलत्येव । सम्मोहः पञ्चपर्वाविद्यास्थानीयैः । भगवत्स-म्बन्धात् अविद्या तु न बाधते, परमन्य एव बाधकाः । तेषां बलं ते इति, त्वदीया इति । कलान्यव्यक्तमधुराणि यानि पदानि तत्राविर्भूतं यदमृतं तदेव वेणुद्वारा गीतं तेन संमोहः । गीतं देहमोहजनकम्, 'गायन्तं स्त्रियः कामयन्त' इति । स्त्री तु देह एव । इन्द्रियाणां व्यामोहको वेणुः, रसात्मकत्वात् । अमृतं प्राणानाम् । पदान्यन्तःकरणस्य । अव्यक्तता आत्मन इति सम्यग्विमोहिताः । आर्याः प्रमाण-बलविवेकिनः । प्रमाणे हि इन्द्रमहेन्द्रयोरपि भेदस्वीकारः । पृथगुपस्थिताः सर्व एव भिन्ना इति । अन्यथा इन्द्रयाजिनोऽग्रे सम्वत्सरान्ते प्रायश्चित्तश्रवणं न स्यात्, 'सम्वत्सरस्य परस्तादग्नये व्रतपतये पुरोडाशमष्टाकपालं निर्वपे'दिति । अतो देहव्यतिरिक्तः स्वरूपेणोपस्थितोऽपि प्रमाणबले विरुध्यते । वस्तुविचारस्तु प्रमेयबलमाश्रित्य, अन्यथा विधिनिषेधविधयो व्यर्थाः स्युः । तदुत्तरत्र वक्ष्यति एकादशे । अतो मार्गान्तरविरोधो मार्गान्तरे नोपयुज्यत इति मर्यादाभङ्गोऽत्र न दूषणम् । एतस्योत्तरमग्रे शुकश्च वक्ष्यति, रासानन्तरम्, 'धर्मव्यतिकरो दृष्ट' इति । तस्मादत्र फलस्य सिद्धत्वात् साधनदृष्ट्या अपकीर्तिः नास्मत्प्रतिबन्धिका । किञ्च,

न केवलं नाम्ना मर्यादाभङ्गः, किन्तु स्वरूपेणापि, तदाहुः त्रैलोक्यसौभगमिति । त्रैलोक्यस्यापि सुभगत्वं यस्मात् । यथा सूर्येण दिनम्, चन्द्रमसा रात्रिः, तथा त्रैलोक्यमेव भगवद्रूपेण सुन्दरतां याति । इदमिति प्रत्यक्षसिद्धम् । चकारादनुभावाँश्च । तच्छ्रुत्वा एतद् दृष्ट्वा का वा आर्यचरितान्न चलेत् । अस्त्वियं प्रमाणवार्ता दुर्बला, प्रकारान्तरेणापि चलति, भगवतो रूपेण प्रमेयमर्यादाप्यपगच्छति । या कथमपि नान्यथा भवति । तदाह यद्गोद्विजद्रुममृगा इति । गावो हि प्रमाणवार्तानभिज्ञाः, मातरमपि गच्छन्ति, द्विजाः पक्षिणः सर्वभक्षाः, द्रुमाः स्थावराः, कदाचिदपि बहिः सम्वेदनरहिताः, निरिन्द्रिया एवेति केचित् । मृगाः सर्वतोभयाः । तेऽपि चेद्भगवद्रूपेण गीतेन वा आश्लिष्टरसाः पुलकानि धारयन्ति, रसिकमनुष्यधर्मानाविष्कुर्वन्ति । ये भगवता अन्यथैव सृष्टाः । स्त्रियस्तु स्वभावतोऽप्यन्यथाभवन्तीति नाश्चर्यं किञ्चिदत्र ॥४०॥

एवं भगवदुक्तानां वाक्यानां निवारणार्थं पुष्टिसिद्धान्तं निरूप्य एतद्भगवत्कृपैकसाध्यमिति भगवत्कृपां प्रार्थयन्ति व्यक्तमिति ।

व्यक्तं भवान् व्रजभयार्तिहरोऽभिजातो
देवो यथादिपुरुषः सुरलोकगोप्ता ।
तन्नो निधेहि करपङ्कजमार्तबन्धो
तप्तस्तनेषु च शिरस्सु च किङ्करीणाम् ॥४१॥

नापि त्वदुक्तमस्मदुक्तं वा किञ्चित्साधकं बाधकं वा, तथापि स्वावतारप्रयोजनं विचार्य अस्मासु कृपा कर्तव्या । तत्प्रयोजनमाहुः । भवान् व्रजभयार्तिहर एव व्यक्तमभिजातः । व्रजस्य आर्तिः पीडा भयं च त्वया दूरीकर्तव्यम् । अन्यथा साक्षाद्भगवतोऽवतारे प्रयोजनं न पश्यामः । भूभारहरणं तु सङ्कर्षणांशेन । वसुदेवादिप्रियं प्रद्युम्नेन । धर्मरक्षा त्वनिरुद्धेन । यदि व्रजभयार्तिनिराकरणं न क्रियेत, तदा किमवतारान्तरकार्यं स्यात् । अतो व्यक्तं भवान् व्रजभयार्तिहरः । इदानीं यथातिरस्माकम्, तथा न कदापि । अस्मदपगमे तु सर्वस्यापि व्रजस्य महती आर्तिः । अत आर्तिनिवृत्तिः कर्तव्या । ननु मर्यादयैव निवृत्तिकरणमुचितम्, न तु अमर्यादया, तथा सति भवतीनां कामशान्तिः, ज्ञानं वा, भवत्विति चेत्, तत्राहुः देवो यथादिपुरुष इति । भगवान् ब्रह्मरूपः सर्वसमः, तथापि इन्द्रादिषु कृपां कुर्वन् दैत्यान् मारयन् विषमतामङ्गीकरोति । न तु देवेभ्यो ज्ञानं प्रयच्छति । यत्र स्वरूपमेवान्यथाकरोति, तत्र वाचमन्यथाकरोतीति किं वक्तव्यम् । अतो यथादिपुरुषोऽपि देवो भूत्वा सुरलोकगोप्ता जातः तथा भवानपि धर्ममर्यादारक्षकः, अस्मत्सम्बन्धं करोत्विति भावः । तदेव रसपोषणार्थं व्याजेनाहुः तन्नो निधेहीति । आदावस्माकं शिरसि हस्तं स्थापय । यथा अस्माकमभयं भवति । ततोऽस्माकं हृदयतापनिवृत्त्यर्थं स्तनेषु च करपङ्कजममृतस्रावि तापनाशकं निधेहि । अनौचिती तु नास्ति । यतो वयं किङ्कर्यः । परीक्षार्थं वा एतत् द्रष्टव्यमिति रसोक्तिः ॥४१॥

एवं प्रार्थनायां भगवान् यत्कृतवान् तदाह इतीति ।

श्रीशुक उवाच—**इति विक्लवितं तासां श्रुत्वा योगेश्वरेश्वरः ।**
प्रहस्य सदयं गोपीरात्मारामोप्यरीरमत् ॥४२॥

षड्गुणैश्वर्यभावेन षोढा रेमे हरिः स्वयम् ।
स्वरूपेणापि शृंगारो द्विविधोऽपि निरूपितः ॥१॥

सामान्यरमणं पूर्वं विशेषे मेलनं पुरा ।
बाह्येन रमणं पश्चात् आन्तरं च ततः परम् ॥२॥

ततो नानाविलासेन जातकेलिविभेदतः ।
विप्रलंभस्य सिद्ध्यर्थं तासां मानमुदीर्यते ॥३॥

तिरोभावस्ततश्चापि नायं लौकिककामुकः ॥

प्रथमं तासां तापापनोदनार्थं सामान्यलीलामाह । इति तासां विक्लवितं परमवैक्लव्यभाषितं श्रुत्वा प्रहस्य अरीरमत् । ननु निरिन्द्रियः कथं रेमे, तत्राह, योगेश्वराणामपीश्वर इति। योगादिषु सर्वे पदार्थाः स्फुरन्ति, अणिमादयोऽपि, तथा तदैव स्वरूपमेवेन्द्रियादिभावेन प्रकटीकृतवान् । न तु स्वस्य कामेन । तथा सति बीजनिवृत्तौ कामो निवर्तेत। तासां यथा न कदाचिदपि स भावो गच्छति, तदर्थं प्रहस्य प्रकर्षेण हास्यं कृत्वा, तासामुद्धरणार्थं, न तु भिन्नगणनया मर्यादायां पातयित्वा नाशनार्थमिति। तदाह सदयमिति। गोपीरेवारमयत्, स्वयं त्वात्माराम एव। तासां रसाधारत्वाय वा सदयम्।

क्रिया सर्वापि सैवात्र परं कामो न विद्यते ।
तासां कामस्य सम्पूर्तिर्निष्कामेनेति तास्तथा ॥१॥

कामेन पूरितः कामः संसारं जनयेत् स्फुटः ।
कामाभावेन पूर्णस्तु निष्कामः स्यात् न संशयः ॥२॥

अतो न कापि मर्यादा भग्ना मोक्षफलापि च ।
अत एतच्छ्रुतौ लोको निष्कामः सर्वथा भवेत् ॥३॥

भगवच्चरितं सर्वं यतो निष्काममीर्यते ।
अतः कामस्य नोद्बोधः ततः शुकवचः स्फुटम् ॥४॥

आत्मारामस्य आत्मनैव रमणं व्यावर्तयितुमपिशब्दः । अरीरमत् बहुधा रेमे।। उत्तरोत्तरं रसाधिक्यं च प्रकटितवान् ॥४२॥

एवं सामान्यलीलामुक्त्वा विशेषलीलामाह ताभिरिति त्रिभिः ।

ताभिः समेताभिरुदारचेष्टितः प्रियेक्षणोत्फुल्लमुखीभिरच्युतः ।
उदारहासद्विजकुन्ददीधितिर्व्यरोचतैणाङ्क इवोडुभिर्वृतः ॥४३॥

अजातस्मरकेलिभिः प्रथमतः ताभिः समेतो जातः मिलितः । पूर्वं भयात् पृथक् स्थिताः । तत उदाराणि चेष्टितानि यस्य । अत्र औदार्यं रसविषयकम् । यथा तासां महानेव रस आविर्भवति, तथा कामशास्त्रसिद्धलीलाः सर्वा एव कृतवान् । ततस्ता अन्तःपूर्णरसाः । प्रियस्य भगवत ईक्षणार्थमुत्फुल्लानि मुखानि यासां तादृश्यो जाताः । प्रियेक्षणेन वा सूर्यकिरणैरिव उत्फुल्लानि मुखानि । वस्तुतो लोभस्थितरसार्थमेव तथाकरणम् । एतावति कृते रसो निवर्तते, तदभावायाह अच्युत इति । तासामपि रससमाप्त्यभावाय उदारेति । उदारो यो हासः पूर्णकामप्रदः, कामार्थमेव यो मोहः तेनैव स्नेहः सम्वर्धितः । तदाह । हाससहिता ये द्विजाः त एव कुन्दपुष्पाणि, आरक्तान्यपि हासेन शुभ्राणि, तेषु दीधितिर्यस्य । कुन्दत्वं स्नेहस्यैतन्मात्रपर्यवसानार्थम् । (पूर्वे निरुपधिरेव स्नेहः स्थितः, भगवता परं रसशास्त्रोक्तरीत्या स्वरूपानन्दं दातुं तत्सजातीयः कामोपाधिकः स्नेहोऽधुना जनित इति ज्ञापनाय स्नेहरूपरदानां द्विजपदेन कथनम् ।) तथा सति फलभोगात् कान्त्यभावमाशंक्य तत्र दीधितिरुक्ता । यद्यपि भगवान् तन्निर्बन्धेन रेमे, जगद्दोषनिराकरणार्थं च, न तु स्वयम्, तथापि न पूर्णमनोरथ इव, किन्तु यथा लौकिकः, तदाह दृष्टान्तेन । एणाङ्कः उडुभिः नक्षत्रैः सह यथा व्यरोचतेति । बन्धातिरिक्ताः सर्वा बाह्या एव लीला उक्ताः ॥४३॥

एषा विशेषतः प्रथमलीला बाधककामनिवारिका। द्वितीयलीलाया उद्बोधार्थं पूर्वसामग्रीमाह उपगीयमान इति ।

उपगीयमान उद्गायन् वनिताशतयूथपः ।
मालां बिभ्रद्वैजयन्तीं व्यचरन्मण्डयन् वनम् ॥४४॥

ताभिरुपगीयमानः निकटे गीयमानः स्वयमप्युद्गायन् जातः । ततः वनिताशतानामनेकविधस्त्रीणामनेकविधानेव यूथान् पातीति तथा जातः । यावतीभिर्मिलितो रसहेतुर्भवति, तावतीनामेकं यूथम् । एवमनेकरूपाणि कृतानि । तेषामत्र रक्षणं दूरादेवाश्वासनेन च । तदा गायतो गच्छतः रूपमाह मालामिति । वैजयन्तीं नवरत्नखचितां स्वाभाविकीमैश्वर्यप्रबोधिकां कीर्तिमयीं मालां बिभ्रत् , वनमेव सर्वं मण्डयन् अलंकुर्वन्, व्यचरत् लीलागतिं कृतवान् । एषा हि गतिः तासां कामोद्बोधिका । स तासां कामपूरकः । एकस्मात् वनात् वनान्तरं वा गत इति ॥४४॥

एवमुद्बुद्धे कामे ताभिः सह बन्धादिभिः रेम इत्याह नद्या इति ।

नद्याः पुलिनमाविश्य गोपीभिर्हिमवालुकम् ।
रेमे तत्तरलानन्दिकुमुदामोदवायुना ॥४५॥

नद्याः पुलिनमच्छं कोमलमाविश्य, आसमन्तात् प्रविश्य, रमणे बन्धादिभिरतिकोमलं कृत्वा, गोपीभिरनेकविधाभिः रेमे । हिमाः शीतलाः वालुका यत्रेति अन्तरूष्मा निवारितः। बहिः शैत्यं चाह तत्तरलानन्दीति । तस्या नद्यास्तरलास्तरङ्गाः ताभिः कृत्वा आनन्दयुक्तं **पुलिनमेव** । आनन्दयुक्तो वायुर्वा । कुमुदानां चानन्दयुक्तसुगन्धः । तस्यानन्दजनकत्वेनैव मान्द्यं निरूपितम् । शैत्यं च कुमुदानां जलसम्बन्धात् । तादृशवायुना सहितं पुलिनम् । महाबन्धेषु वायोरप्यपेक्षा ।४५।।

एवं सर्वभावेन तासां जातस्मरकेलित्वं सम्पादितम् । अतः परं अष्टविधालिङ्गनादिपूर्वकं चेष्टितकामादियुक्तं रसविलासचरित्रमाह बाहुप्रसारेति ।

बाहुप्रसारपरिरम्भकरालकोरुनीवीस्तनालभननर्मनखाग्रपातैः ।
क्ष्वेल्यावलोकहसितैर्व्रजसुन्दरीणामुत्तम्भयन् रतिपतिं रमयांचकार ।।४६।।

दूरे स्थितामवयवं वा स्प्रष्टुं बाहुप्रसारणम् । ततो बलादपि परिरम्भः । ततः करालकोरुनीवीस्तनानामालभनानि । करालभनं हस्ते ग्रहणम् । पुरुषायितलीलासमबन्धे वा । एवं कचोन्नमनार्थं अलकानां स्पर्शः । ऊरुस्पर्शो बाहुबन्धार्थः । नीवीस्पर्शः पुष्टे रसे मोचनार्थः । स्तनयोस्तु रसोद्गमनार्थः । एवं पञ्चस्पर्शा विहिताः । नर्म परिहासवचनानि कामस्तम्भनार्थम् । ततो नखाग्रपाताः नखक्षतदन्तक्षतताडनादयः कामयुद्धनिरूपकाः । तत्तत्स्थाने स्थितः कामः तैरुद्बोध्यते, यथा सेनावधे राजा समायाति । क्ष्वेलिः क्ष्वेलिका प्रस्तोभनादिः, तत्पूर्वकान्येवावलोकनानि । हसितानि रसस्थापकानि । एवं द्वादशविधोऽपि कामः द्वादशाङ्गेषु स्थितः प्रबुद्धो भवति, तदाह व्रजसुन्दरीणामुत्तम्भयन्निति । संयुक्तः कामो रतिपतिः, वियुक्तस्त्वग्निरूपः । एवमाधिदैविकं काममुद्बोधयन् रमयांचकार गोपीनां सुखमेव प्रकटितवान्, न तु कामान्तेन विरतिमुत्पादितवान् ।।४६।।

एवं संयोगशृङ्गारमुपपाद्य विप्रयोगमुपपादयितुं तासां मानमाह एवमिति ।

एवं भगवतः कृष्णाल्लब्धकामा महात्मनः ।
आत्मानं मेनिरे स्त्रीणां मानिन्योऽभ्यधिकं भुवि ।।४७।।

पूर्वोक्तप्रकारेण भगवतः सर्वरसदानसमर्थात्, कृष्णात् सदानन्दात् फलरूपात् लब्धकामाः प्राप्तमनोरथाः सत्यः आत्मानमेव पूर्णं मेनिरे, न तु भगवन्तं पूर्णम्, तेन वा स्वपूर्णताम् । ननु भगवानेवं कथं कृतवान्, न्यूना एव कथं न संरक्षिताः, तत्राह महात्मन इति । भगवान् महानेवात्मा । न ह्यगाधे जले प्रविष्टः अमग्नो भवति, घटो वा अपूर्णो भवति । किञ्च, आत्मानं स्त्रीणां मध्ये अभ्यधिकं मेनिरे, भुवि चाभ्यधिकम्, भुवि स्त्रीणां मध्ये वा । अत एव मानिन्योऽपि जाताः । न ह्यस्मत्सदृशोऽन्याः सन्ति । अतोऽस्मान् यदि प्रार्थयिष्यति, तदा रसं दास्याम इति मानयुक्ता जाताः ।

भगवद्धर्मास्तासु समागताः । तथा सति यथा प्रार्थनया पूर्वं भगवान् वशे जातः, एवं वयमपि भविष्याम इति । रसार्थमेवैवं भावः, न तु दोषरूपः, भगवद्भावात् ॥४७॥

भगवांस्तु ऐक्येनैव रसं प्रयच्छन् बहिस्तिरोहितो जात इत्याह तासामिति ।

तासां तत्सौभगमदं वीक्ष्य मानं च केशवः ।
प्रशमाय प्रसादाय तत्रैवान्तरधीयत ॥४८॥

इति श्रीमद्भागवते महापुराणे दशमस्कन्धे षड्विंशोऽध्यायः ॥२६॥

मानः पूर्णता च न दोषाय । स्त्रीषु भूमौ च यदाधिक्यज्ञानं स दोषो भवति । तदनूद्य परिहारार्थं तिरोहित इत्याह । तासां तत्प्रसिद्धं पूर्वोक्तं सर्वोत्तमत्वलक्षणं सौभाग्यमदं तस्य, तस्य मदस्य प्रशमाय अन्तरधीयत । ननु भगवद्रमणेन हि तासामेवं भावः, अतः कृत एवेति कथं तिरोधानं कृतवानित्याशङ्क्याह । वीक्ष्य मानं च प्रसादाय तत्रैवान्तरधीयतेति । मानापनोदनं कर्तव्यम् । मानस्त्वान्तरः । अशक्तो हि बहिरपनोदनार्थं यत्नं करोति । चकारात् स्वधर्मं च । अतः प्रसादाय, प्रथमतस्तासाम्, पश्चात् स्वस्य च । तत्रैव गोपिकासु यूथमध्ये वा अन्तर्धानं प्राप्तवान् । नन्वेतत् द्वयमपि न कर्तव्यम्, उपेक्षिताः कुतो नेति चेत्, तत्राह केशव इति । यथा रजोगुणं ब्रह्मणो निवार्य, तस्मै मुक्तिं दत्तवान्, यथा वा शिवस्य तमोगुणं निवार्य, एवमेतासामपि मदं मानं च निवार्य, मुक्तिं दातुं तथा कृतवानित्यर्थः । कायिकतिरोभावोऽयम्, प्रथमाधिकारित्वाद्गोपीनाम् ॥४८॥

इति श्रीभागवतसुबोधिन्यां श्रीमल्लक्ष्मणभट्टात्मजश्रीवल्लभदीक्षितविरचितायां दशमस्कन्धविवरणे षड्विंशाध्यायविवरणम् ॥२६॥

श्रीकृष्णाय नमः

सप्तविंशोऽध्यायः ।

स्वानन्दस्थापनार्थाय लीला भगवता कृता ।
स बाह्यो जनितः पुष्टो यथान्तर्निविशेत्पुनः ।।१।।

तदर्थं भगवांस्तासु लीलया सहितोऽविशत् ।
चत्वारोऽत्र निरूप्यार्थाः रसासक्तिर्हरेः क्रियाः ।।२।।

गर्वाभावश्च तत्रादौ निरूप्यन्ते क्रमान्त्रयः ।
उद्देशतो लक्षणतः फलतश्च यथायथम् ।।३।।

सप्तविंशे तिरोधानाल्लीलान्वेषणतत्पराः ।
रसमन्तर्गतं चक्रुर्गोपिका इति रूप्यते ।।४।।

पूर्वाध्यायान्ते भगवतस्तिरोभाव उक्तः, ततस्तदनन्तरं प्रथमतः तासां रसासक्तचित्तानामापाततो महांस्तापो जात इत्याह अन्तर्हिते भगवतीति ।

श्रीशुक उवाच—**अन्तर्हिते भगवति सहसैव व्रजाङ्गनाः ।**
अतप्यंस्तमचक्षाणाः करिण्य इव यूथपम् ।।१।।

भगवति अन्तःप्रविष्टे षड्गुणैश्वर्यसहिते यावदन्तरनुसंधानं न कृतवत्यः, तावत् सहसैव अकस्मादतप्यन् । अन्तर्विचाराभावे हेतुः व्रजाङ्गना इति । तापे हेतुः तमचक्षाणा इति । तापः सहज एव स्थितः कामात्मा तद्दर्शनस्पर्शादिभिः शान्तो भवति । यदा पुनः पूर्वसिद्धं बहिर्दर्शनं न जातम्, तदा तत्ताप उचित एव । तासां स्पर्श एव मुख्य इति ज्ञापयितुं दृष्टान्तमाह करिण्य इवेति । यूथपो महामत्तगजः । 'रतिं गज एव जानाती'ति वात्स्यायनः । 'रत्यां विमर्दे गज' इति विवृतश्च । सन्ति च सिंहाः, तथात्र कालः । अतः करिणीनां यूथपादर्शने महानेव क्लेशः ।।१।।

यदा पुनः स तापः अन्तःप्रवेष्टुमैच्छत्, तावता भगवल्लीला अन्तःप्रविष्टा तापं दूरीकृत्य स्वयमेवाविर्भूतेत्याह गत्येति ।

गत्यानुरागस्मितविभ्रमेक्षितैर्मनोरमालापविहारविभ्रमैः ।
आक्षिप्तचित्ताः प्रमदा रमापतेस्तास्ता विचेष्टा जगृहुस्तदात्मिकाः ।।२।।

ता भगवदीयैः कायवाङ्मनोभिः वशीकृताः तद्भावमापन्नाः तास्ता एव भगवच्चेष्टा जगृहुः । प्रथमतः कायिकीमाह । गत्या कायचेष्टया वशीकृताः । तत इन्द्रियसहितमनश्चेष्टया वशीकृता जाता इत्याह अनुरागेति । अनुरागः स्नेहो

मानसः, तत्पूर्वकं स्मितम्, तस्य विलासः स्वनिष्ठतात्याजनार्थः । अन्यथैवं सति ज्ञानमेवोदयं प्राप्नुयात् । अतः स्मितेन मन्दहासेन ईषद्विमोहिताः, न बहिर्गताः, नान्तःस्थिताः, किन्तु भगवति मध्ये स्फुरिते तद्धर्मेषु च समागताः । अनुरागस्मितेन सहितो यो विभ्रमो विलासः अलसवलितादिः तत्सहितानीक्षितानि, सर्व एव कटाक्षाः । वाचिकैरपि विमोहमाह मनोरमालापेति । मनो रमयतीति, मनसि रमते इति वा, मनोरमः, योऽयमालापः, भगवतो गुह्यभाषणानि, केवल-वाक्यस्य चित्ताक्षेपकत्वं न भविष्यतीति प्रामाण्यावधारणं स्त्रीणां प्रकारान्तरेण न भवतीति फलमेवादौ निरूपितम् । सुखार्थं हि भगवद्वाक्यानि तदानीमेव च सुखमुत्पादयन्ति । ते चालापाः क्वचिद्बन्धादिबोधका लीलोपयोगिन इत्याह विहार इति । तत्रापि विलासाः अवान्तरभेदाः, यथोत्तानके ग्राम्यादयः । तैः पूर्व-कृतैः तमःसत्त्वरजोरूपैः त्रिविधमपि चित्तमाक्षिप्तमिति आक्षिप्तचित्ता जाताः । अतस्तापं न प्राप्तवत्य इति भावः । प्रमदा इति । ('बाह्याभ्यन्तराननुसन्धाने हेतु-भूतोत्युत्कटरसभावोऽत्र मदपदेनोच्यते। तेन प्रभुलीलाविष्करणं युक्तमिति भावः । किञ्च,) प्रमदाः प्रकृष्टो मदो यासां स्वभावत एव, अन्यथा दास्यभावान्न प्रच्युताः स्युः । तदा केवलभगवतः लीला स्वानुपयोगिनी साम्प्रतं च नानुभूतेति रमापते-र्लक्ष्मीपतेः, लक्ष्म्या सह विलासरूपां चेष्टां जगृहुः । एकस्या अपि बह्वयश्चेष्टा इति तास्ता उक्ताः । नन्वीश्वरधर्माविष्करणं दासीनां निषिद्धमिति चेत्, तत्राह तदात्मिका इति । भगवानेवात्मनि यासाम्, तथात्वेन स्फुरितः । अतो भगवल्लीला-ग्रहणं तापनिवारकत्वेनोद्देशत उक्तम् । विस्तरमग्रे वक्ष्यति । क्रमहेतुत्वं च वक्ष्यामः ॥२॥

ततो भगवतः स्वरूपपरिग्रहो जात इत्याह गतिस्मितेति ।

गतिस्मितप्रेक्षणभाषणादिषु प्रियाः प्रियस्य प्रतिरूढमूर्तयः ।
असावहं त्वित्यबलास्तदात्मिकाः न्यवेदिषुः कृष्णविहारविभ्रमाः ॥३॥

धर्माश्चेत् स्वस्मिन् समागताः, तदैकत्रोभयधर्मा विरुद्धा इति भगवति स्व-धर्मानारोपितवत्यः । कायवाङ्मनसां दृष्टेश्च चत्वारः प्रधानधर्माः । तेषां सर्वेष्वेव प्रतिरूढा मूर्तिर्यासाम् । भगवद्धर्मेषु स्वमूर्तिरारोपिता । अन्यथा अन्योऽन्यधर्मा-भिनिवेशाभावे सम्यक् विलासो न स्यात्, तदाह । गतिः कायिकी, स्मितं मानसम्, प्रेक्षणमैन्द्रियकम्, भाषणं वाचिकम्, तदादयो यावन्तो विभ्रमाः बन्धादयः रति-रूपा एव । तेषु सर्वेष्वेव प्रियस्य सम्बन्धिषु स्वयं प्रियाः भोगावस्थामेव प्राप्ताः विपरीता जाताः । 'रसाधिक्ये स्त्रियः पुरुषत्वमापद्यन्त' इति वात्स्यायनः । अत एव स्वयं प्रियायोग्याः प्रतिरूढा विपरीततया आरूढा मूर्तयः स्वरूपाणि यासामिति । तत्र यासां भगवानल्पव्यवहितः पूर्वमासीत्, ताभिर्भगवत्प्रश्ने कृते, अन्तर्हिताज्ञानात्

तन्नोत्तरवक्त्यो भवन्ति । 'असौ कृष्णः' 'अहं कृष्ण' इति । अथवा । योऽन्विष्यते, सोसावहमिति । अन्यासां प्रतीत्यर्थं नटः कपटवेषं कृत्वापि वदंति क्रीडायाम्, तथा न, किन्तु स्वत एवेत्याह अबला इति । अबलाः स्त्रियः भगवद्रूपाविष्कारे च बलरहिताः । स्पष्टवैलक्षण्यं च स्त्रीपुरुषयोः तथा कथने प्रतारकत्वमालक्ष्याह तदात्मिका इति । न केवलं धर्म्यापत्तिः, किन्तु तद्धर्माणामपीत्याह । कृष्णवत् विहारः कायवाङ्मनोव्यापारः, विभ्रमाः तत्रत्या विलासाः यासाम् ॥३॥

एवं तापलीलाभगवतामुद्देशतस्तासु सम्बन्धमुक्त्वा प्रथमं तापनिवृत्त्यर्थं अन्वेषणं कृतवत्य इत्याह । गुणानामिव त्रयाणामेषामन्योन्योपमर्दनेन भगवदिच्छयाविर्भाव इति न परस्परकार्यप्रतिबन्धकता आपाततः । अतो यदा प्रपञ्चसम्वेदनम्, तदा पृष्टवत्य इत्याह गायन्त्य इति । प्रथमतो मिश्रभावात् गायन्त्यो जाताः ।

गायन्त्य उच्चैरमुमेव संहता विचिक्युरुन्मत्तकवद्वनाद्वनम् ।
पप्रच्छुराकाशवदन्तरं बहिर्भूतेषु सन्तं पुरुषं वनस्पतीन् ॥४॥

शब्दो हि धूमवल्लोके बाह्याभ्यन्तरयोगतः ।
विराजते विनिर्गच्छन् तारतम्यं च गच्छति ।
अतोऽत्र धर्मिधर्माणामाधिक्याज्ज्ञानमुत्तमम् ॥१॥

यथा भगवतो गानात् स्वयमागत्य संगताः ।
एवं स्वयं भगवत आगत्यर्थं जगुः स्फुटम् ॥२॥

कृत्रिमत्वात्तु भावस्य मिलिताश्च स्वतोऽन्यतः ।
ततो विशेषविज्ञानात् तिरोभावोऽस्फुरत् स्फुटः ॥३॥

तदा विचिक्युः क्व भगवानस्तीत्यन्वेषणं कृतवत्यः । तत्रापि न सर्वात्मना तिरोभावः स्फुरित इति अन्वेषणेऽपि अनियतवृत्तयो जाता इत्याह उन्मत्तकवदिति । अज्ञात उन्मत्त उन्मत्तकः, कुत्सितो वा । स यथा स्वपरिविवेकं न जानाति, वस्त्रादिरहितश्च भवति । एवमवस्थां प्राप्ताः । एकस्माद्वनात् वनान्तरं गताः । किञ्च, न केवलमन्वेषणमात्रम्, किन्तु उन्मत्तकवत् पृच्छन्ति स्मेत्याह पप्रच्छुरिति । शुको हि भगवत्स्वरूपाभिज्ञः आनन्दमात्रकरपादमुखोदरादिं कृष्णं सर्वत्रैव विद्यमानं पश्यति । यदि भक्तिसहितं ज्ञानमाविर्भवति, तदा अन्योऽपि पश्यति। सर्वत्रैव तिरोधाननाशात् । तादृशमेताः परिच्छिन्नं मत्वा पृच्छन्तीति तासामज्ञानकथनार्थमाह आकाशवदन्तरं बहिर्भूतेषु सन्तमिति । बाह्याभ्यन्तरविवेकहेतुराकाश इति पूर्वं निरूपितम् । तद्वदेवायमपि । अत एवाकाशस्य ब्रह्मलिङ्गत्वं । एतादृशं सर्वत्रैव विद्यमानमदृष्ट्वा, आत्मनि विचारं त्यक्त्वा, चेतनांश्चापृष्ट्वा, स्थावरान्

पृच्छन्ति। वनस्पतीन् पप्रच्छुरिति। ते हि वैष्णवा इति। मूढा अपि वैष्णवा एव हि विष्णुगतिं जानन्ति, नत्वत्यन्तं निपुणा अप्यवैष्णवाः ॥४॥

तत्रापि प्रथमं विष्णुब्रह्मशिवतां लोके प्राप्ताः अश्वत्थप्लक्षवटास्तान् पृच्छन्ति दृष्ट इति।

दृष्टो वः कच्चिदश्वत्थ प्लक्ष न्यग्रोध नो मनः।
नन्दसूनुर्गतो हृत्वा प्रेमहासावलोकनैः ॥५॥

अश्वत्थो हि वैष्णवो वृक्षः, विष्णुवत् लोके सन्मानमर्हतीति प्रायेणायं ज्ञास्यति, तथाप्ययं स्तब्धः स्वोत्तमभावनया न ज्ञास्यतीति तदर्थे हेतुभूतं नामाह। अश्वस्तिष्ठत्यस्मिन्निति अश्वत्थः। लोकास्त्वश्वे तिष्ठन्ति, अस्मिंस्त्वश्वस्तिष्ठतीति। 'अश्वो रूपं कृत्वा यदश्वत्थेऽतिष्ठत्' इति श्रुतेः। तर्हि प्राजापत्योऽश्वत्थ इति तदपेक्षया प्रजापत्यो वृक्षः प्रष्टव्य इति प्लक्षं पृच्छन्ति प्लक्षेति। तत्रापि तस्याज्ञानं नाम्ना वदन्ति। अयं हि मनुष्याणामज्ञानार्थं पावित्र्यक्षारणादुत्पन्नः अपवित्रः लोकानामज्ञानहेतुरेव। अतः कथं वक्ष्यतीति। 'पशुना वै देवाः स्वर्गं लोकमायन्, तेऽमन्यन्त मनुष्या नो त्वा भविष्यन्तीति, तस्य शिरश्छित्त्वा मेधं प्राक्षारयन्, स प्लक्षोऽभव' दिति श्रुतेः। तर्हि कर्मसम्बन्धरहितः वैष्णवधर्मोपदेष्टा शिवः प्रष्टव्य इति तद्रूपं न्यग्रोधं पृच्छन्ति न्यग्रोधेति। तस्यापि दूषणम्। नितरामग्राण्यधो यस्येति। अतोऽन्ते हीनभावं गच्छतीति अग्रे गमने हेतुर्भविष्यति। वः युष्माकं सम्बन्धी भवद्भिः किं दृष्टः। प्रश्नसम्भावनायां कच्चिदिति। दृष्टोऽस्माभिः पूर्वम्, सर्वदैव वा, ततः किं भवतीनामिति चेत्, नो मनः हृत्वा गत इति। ननु स विष्णुः कथं चौर्यं करिष्यतीति, तत्राहुः नन्दसूनुरिति। नन्दस्य चेत् पुत्रो जातः, तदा तत्कार्यं कर्तव्यम्। ते हि दधिदुग्धादिचौर्यं कुर्वन्ति। अतो मनश्चौर्यमपि नात्यन्तं विरोधि। भर्तृनामाग्रहणं वा। अत एव हरणपर्यन्तं प्रभुपुत्र इति न ज्ञातः। अन्यथा भोगं परित्यज्य कथं गच्छेत्। नन्वन्तःस्थितं मनः कथं गृहीतमित्याशंक्य, त्रिविधं मनः त्रिभिरपि धर्मैर्गृहीतवानित्याह प्रेमहासावलोकनैरिति। प्रेमपूर्वकहास्यसहितान्यवलोकनानि मनोहराणि। तमोरजःसत्त्वभावा उक्ताः। प्रेम्णा अन्तःप्रवेशः, हास्येन ग्रहणम्, अवलोकनेन हरणमिति ॥५॥

तेषामनुत्तरं मत्वा, एते अमुख्यफला महान्तोऽपि काकसेव्या एवेति, ये महान्तः पुष्पवन्तः सुगन्धाः, तान् पृच्छाम इति कुरबकादीन् पृच्छन्ति कच्चिदिति।

कच्चित् कुरबकाशोकनागपुन्नागचम्पकाः।
रामानुजो मानिनीनां गतो दर्पहरस्मितः ॥६॥

कुरबकाशोकौ कामोद्दीपकौ। एते कामबाणपुष्पाः। नागो नागकेसरः, पुन्नागश्चम्पकश्च

अतिसुगन्धपुष्पाः । ते हि कामिनं व्यावर्तयन्ति । अतः पश्चाप्येते ज्ञास्यन्तीति । रामानुजः कच्चिद्भवद्भिर्दृष्ट इति पृच्छन्ति । पूर्ववदेव प्रयोजनकथनम् । मानिनीनां दर्पहरं स्मितं यस्य । व्यर्थमेव गतो भगवान्, स्मितमात्रेणैव दर्पो गच्छति, किं गमनेन । भयं तु नास्त्येव, यतो रामानुजः बलभद्रभ्राता, भर्तृ नाम न ग्राह्यमिति । वयं सर्वा एव मानिन्यः स्थिताः । अतोऽस्मद्दर्पदमनार्थं गतः । प्रायेणैतैर्न दृष्टः । कुत्सितरवात् कं सुखं यस्य । रोदनप्रियोऽयम् । अशोकश्च शोकनाशक एव, न तु कस्यचित् सुखं प्रयच्छति । नागोऽयं नाम्नैव भयानकः । गजपक्षेऽपि पुंसामपि नागः । चम्पकोऽपि परिणामविरसः । अफलाश्चैते ॥६॥

पूर्वोक्तास्त्वपुष्पाः, एते अफलाः । फलपुष्पाभ्यां नानाविधविनियोगसंभवादज्ञानं मत्वा, तुलस्यास्तदुभयं नास्तीति भगवदीयत्वेन प्रसिद्धां पृच्छन्ति कच्चिदिति ।

कच्चित्तुलसि कल्याणि गोविन्दचरणप्रिये ।
सह त्वाऽलिकुलैर्बिभ्रत् दृष्टस्तेऽतिप्रियोऽच्युतः ॥७॥

तुलसीति सम्बोधनं सखीमिव मत्वा । सा चेत् पूर्वसम्बन्धस्मरणेन भक्तेव भगवन्तं भजेत्, तदा रसो न पुष्ट इति तां भगवत्पत्नीं मन्यमाना आहुः कल्याणीति । एवमपि सति भक्तिप्रधानेत्यस्मदाद्यपेक्षया उत्कृष्टेत्याहुः गोविन्दचरणप्रिय इति । किञ्च, तव दर्शने उपायोप्यस्ति । त्वत्सजातीयस्य तत्र विद्यमानत्वात् । सजातीयो हि सजातीयं मार्गस्थं दृष्ट्वा गच्छति । तदाहुः । अलिकुलैः सह त्वा बिभ्रत् दृष्ट इति । किञ्च, ते भगवानत्यन्तं प्रियः, यद्यनेन मार्गेण गतः स्यात्, अवश्यं त्वया दृष्टः स्यादिति ॥७॥

तत्राप्यरुचिं मत्वा, इयं सपत्नीवत् स्वोत्कर्षं ख्यापयन्ती कथमन्याभ्यो वक्ष्यतीति, साधारण्यः स्त्रिय एवास्माकमुपकारिण्य इति, ताः पृच्छन्ति मालतीति ।

मालत्यदर्शि वः कच्चित् मल्लिके जाति यूथिके
प्रीतिं वो जनयन् यातः करस्पर्शेन माधवः ॥८॥

हे मालति, वः युष्माभिः प्रत्येकं नानारूपाभिः दृष्टः कच्चित् । तथैव मल्लिके, हे जाति, हे यूथिके । एताश्चतस्रो लताः अतिसुगन्धपुष्पाः भगवत्प्रियाः । अतः वः युष्माकं करस्पर्शेन प्रीतिं जनयन् पुष्पावचयं कुर्वन् माधवो लक्ष्मीसहितः । लक्ष्म्या सह तिष्ठति, अतस्तस्याः चूडाबन्धनार्थं पुष्पावचय आवश्यक इति ॥८॥

ननु यद्यप्येताः स्त्रियः तथाप्यफला इति, अल्पा इति, स्वार्थपरा इति, लक्ष्मीपक्षपातिन्य इति न वदिष्यन्तीति ज्ञात्वा आम्रादीनत्युत्तमान् वृक्षान् पृच्छन्ति चूतेति ।

चूतप्रियालपनसाशनकोविदारजम्ब्वर्कबिल्वबकुलाम्रकदम्बनीपाः ।
येऽन्ये परार्थभवका यमुनोपकूलाः शंसन्तु कृष्णपदवीं रहितात्मनां नः ॥९॥

चूताम्रौ मधुराम्लप्रकृतिकौ । कालभिन्नफलौ वा । प्रियालस्तु बीजेप्यधिकरसयुक्तः । पनसो महाफलः । अन्ये चाशनादयो वृक्षाः पुष्पफलप्रधानाः । किं बहुना । अन्येऽपि ये मधूकादयः । परार्थमेव जन्म येषां ते परार्थभवकाः । किञ्च, यद्यपि सर्व एव वृक्षाः परार्थजन्मानः, तत्रापि ये यमुनोपकूलाः, यमुनाया उपकूले तपस्विन इव तिष्ठन्ति, ते ह्यवश्यं भगवन्तं पश्यन्ति बोधयन्ति च । अतः सदानन्दस्य पदवीं शंसन्तु । यथास्मद्धृदये समायाति । दयार्थमाहुः रहितात्मनामिति । केचित् गृहरहिताः धनरहिताः देहरहिता वा । वयं त्वात्मरहिता एव । अतः सर्वापेक्षया वयं दीनाः । अतः कृष्णपदवीमस्मदर्थे शंसन्तु ॥९॥

एवमतिविलापे दीनतायामाविष्कृतायां भूमौ भगवच्चरणारविन्दानि दृष्टानि, तदा भूमिं स्तुवन्ति किं ते कृतमिति ।

किं ते कृतं क्षिति तपो बत केशवांघ्रिस्पर्शोत्सवोत्पुलकिताङ्गरुहैर्विभासि ।
अप्यंघ्रिसंभव उरुक्रमविक्रमाद्वा आहो वराहवपुषः परिरम्भणेन ॥१०॥

हे क्षिति । ते त्वया किं वा तपः कृतम् । अस्माभिरपि तपः कृतमेव, परं नैवं फलमनुभूतम् । सर्वथा पुण्यव्यतिरेकेण नेष्टसिद्धिः । सुतरां भगवल्लक्षणा । स्वस्य तदभावमाशङ्क्य बतेति रोदे । न केवलं तव पादसम्बन्धमात्रम्, किन्त्वन्येऽपि भावा दृश्यन्त इत्याहुः । केशवस्य ब्रह्मादेरपि मुक्तिदातुः ब्रह्मप्रार्थितचरणारविन्दस्य अंघ्रिस्पर्शेन उत्सवो यस्याः । स्वेदो दृश्यत एव, अन्यथा पदानि स्पष्टानि न भवेयुः । अन्योप्युत्सवो दृश्यते, उत्पुलकिता च । सर्वत्र दूर्वाङ्कुरा उत्थिता इति अङ्गरुहैः रोमाञ्चैः कृत्वा विशेषेण भासि । उत्पुलकिताङ्गरुहैर्वा । अंघ्रिस्पर्शोत्सवा विभासि । ननु सर्वत्रैव पुलको दृश्यते, यदि केशवांघ्रिस्पर्शेन स्यात्, तत्रैकदेशे स्यात्, स्वेदवदित्याशङ्क्य हेत्वन्तरमुत्प्रेक्षन्ते अप्यंघ्रिसंभव उरुक्रमविक्रमाद्वेति । अपीति संभावनायाम् । अनेन चरणस्पर्शेन पूर्वस्थितचरणस्पर्शः स्मृतः । स तु सर्वत्र भूमौ व्याप्तः । अतस्तेन अंघ्रिणा संभवो यस्य उत्सवस्य । उरुक्रमः त्रिविक्रमः । तस्य विक्रमात् पदन्यासाद्वेति तत्राप्यनिर्धारः । न हि चरणसंबन्धमात्रेण संभोगरहितेन सात्त्विकभावरूपः उत्सवो रोमाञ्चो भवितुमर्हति । तदर्थं पक्षान्तरमाशङ्कते आहो वराहवपुषः परिरम्भणेनेति । अनेन स्वसमानता च वर्णिता ॥१०॥

एवं स्थावरान् पृष्ट्वा जङ्गमान् पृच्छन्ति अपीति ।

अप्येणपत्न्युपगतः प्रिययेह गात्रैस्तन्वन् दृशां सखि सुनिर्वृतिमच्युतो वः ।
कान्ताङ्गसङ्गकुचकुङ्कुमरञ्जितायाः कुन्दस्रजः कुलपतेरिह वाति गन्धः ॥११॥

हे एणपत्नि, कृष्णसारपत्नि, प्रियया कयाचित् लक्ष्म्या अन्यया वा उपगतः मिलितः स्त्रीसहितः, अनेन मार्गेण गच्छन्, स्वगात्रैः स्वावयवैः, भवतीनां दृशां सुनिर्वृतिं तन्वन् दृष्टः कच्चित् । अनेनैव मार्गेण गत इति चरणारविन्ददर्शनात् निश्चीयते । यदि दृष्टो भवेत्, तदा अस्माभिरपि द्रष्टुं शक्यत इति । त्वं त्वःयस्य पत्नी अस्माकं च सखी भवसि । अत आहुः हे सखीति । सखित्वं कृष्णानुरक्त्या, नेत्रतुल्यत्वेन भीरुत्वादिधर्मैः । अन्यथा भवतीनां विकसितनयनानि न भवन्तीति । ननु कृतलीलः किमिति प्रार्थ्यते, तत्राहुः अच्युत इति । ननु कथं ज्ञायते प्रियया उपगत इति, तत्राहुः कान्तेति । कान्ताया अङ्गसङ्गे यत्कुचयोः कुङकुमं तेन रञ्जितायाः कुन्दस्रजः कुन्दपुष्पमालायाः गोकुलपतेः सम्बन्धिन्या इह गन्धो वाति । आर्द्रश्च गन्धः आर्द्रं कुङकुमं ज्ञापयति । सात्त्विकभावादेवार्द्रता । अतो ज्ञायते प्रियया सङ्गत इति ॥११॥

एवं हरिणपत्नीं पृष्ट्वा इयं भर्तृसमीपे वक्तुमशक्तेति पूर्वं भगवत्स्तुतान् वृक्षान् पृच्छन्ति बाहुमिति ।

बाहुं प्रियांस उपधाय गृहीतपद्मो रामानुजस्तुलसिकालिकुलैर्मदान्धैः ।
अन्वीयमान इह वस्तरवः प्रणाम किं वाभिनन्दति चरन् प्रणयावलोकैः ॥१२॥

प्रियाया अंसे बाहुमुपधाय द्वितीयेन हस्तेन गृहीतपद्मः रामानुजो निर्भयः तुलसिकायाः सम्बन्धिनो येऽलयः तेषां कुलैः कृत्वा अन्वीयमानः पश्चाद् गम्यमानः । हे तरवः । पूर्वं भगवता भक्तत्वेन स्तुताः, अतो भवद्भिः कृतं प्रणाममिहैव किमभिनन्दति, न वेति प्रश्नः । प्रियांसे बाहुमुपधायेति समतया गमनेन लक्ष्यते । उभयोः पदानां पङ्क्त्याकारेण गमनात् । कदाचित्पादानां चाञ्चल्येन भ्रमरोपरुद्धगत्या तन्निवारणार्थं यत्नो लक्ष्यते । तरवश्च नम्राः, नमस्कारार्थमेव फलोपहारं कृत्वा भूमिसम्बद्धशिरसो जाताः । अतो ज्ञायते प्रणामः कृत इति । अनुत्थानात्संदेहः अभिनन्दति न वेति । अनभिनन्दने हेतुः चरन्निति । यो हि गच्छति, सः अनवहितोऽपि भवति । ननु निकट एव स गच्छति । यद्यभिनन्दनं कृतं स्यात्, तदैव श्रूयेत, कथं संदेह इति चेत्, तत्राहुः प्रणयावलोकैरिति । प्रणयपूर्वकमवलोकैः, न तु वाचा । अतो ये निकटस्थाः, त एव जानन्ति, नान्ये ॥१२॥

ते ज्ञानिनो वृक्षा स्त्रीभिः सह सम्भाषणं न करिष्यन्तीति तत्पत्न्य एव प्रष्टव्या इत्याहुः पृच्छतेमा लता इति ।

पृच्छतेमा लता बाहूनप्याश्लिष्टा वनस्पतेः ।
नूनं तत्करजस्पृष्टा बिभ्रत्युत्पुलकान्यहो ॥१३॥

वनस्पतेर्बाहुनाश्लिष्टा अप्येताः पृच्छत । यद्यपि तासामप्यनवसरः, ताश्च पुनर्भर्तृभुजालिङ्गिता अपि भगवत्करजैरेव नखैः स्पृष्टाः सत्यः उत्पुलकानि बिभ्रति । न हि रसान्तराविष्टानां रसान्तरार्थं स्पृहा भवति । अत एव ज्ञायते 'सर्वोपमर्दी भगवत्सम्बन्धी रस' इति । एवं सर्वेषामेवावचने मूर्छिता इव जाता इति । एतदन्ता प्रश्नकथा । नवविधा एता गोप्यो निरूपिताः । दशमी तु भगवता नीयते । एवमन्वेषणेन रसस्थैर्यं निरूपितम् ।।१३।।

एवं तिरोधानेन जाततापनिवारणार्थं यत्नो निरूपितः । एतदुपमर्दिका भगवल्लीला प्रादुर्भूता । तस्या विलासं वक्तुं पूर्वोपसंहारपूर्वकमुपक्रमते इतीति ।

श्रीशुक उवाच—**इत्युन्मत्तवचो गोप्यः कृष्णान्वेषणकातराः ।**
लीला भगवतस्तास्ता ह्यनुचक्रुस्तदात्मिकाः ।।१४।।

इतिशब्दः प्रकारवाची । एवंप्रकारेण प्रश्नायोग्येऽपि प्रश्नकरणादुन्मत्तवाचो गोप्यो जाताः । कृष्णस्यान्वेषणे कातरा अपि, दीना अपि, जाताः । तनुर्वाक् श्रान्ता । मनसि तु त्रयो वर्तन्त इति प्रथमस्यापगमे द्वितीय आविर्भूत इत्याह लीला इति । भगवतस्तास्ताः पूर्वमुक्ताः कृताश्च तदात्मिकाः सत्यः अनुचक्रुः । उन्मत्तवच इति छान्दसो ह्रस्वः । अथवा । इति पूर्वोक्तमुन्मत्तवचः एतावदिति । ततो गोप्यः कृष्णान्वेषणार्थं कातरा जाता इति । भगवतो लीलाः षड्विधाः स्वाभाविक्यस्तासामपि भेदाः तास्ताः । युक्तश्चायमर्थः । भगवति हृदि समाविष्टे लीलाभिः सहिते । यदा यदा भगवानवतरति, तदा तदा पूतनासुपयःपानादिकं करोति, तथैव संवत्सरलीलायां पुरुषोत्तमादिषु प्रसिद्धिः । एतासामपि मनसि आविर्भूतेन कर्तव्यं तत्साक्षात्कर्तुमशक्यमिति भावनयैवाविर्भूत इति अनुकरणमात्रं कृतवत्यः ।।१४।।

भक्त्यातिमत्तास्तद्भावमीयुन्मत्तास्तु रोषतः ।
द्वेषभावं समाश्रित्य क्रीडन्त्यो जातमत्सराः ।।१।।

तस्याविगुणभावेन नवलीलाः प्रपेदिरे ।
अतो न न्यूनभावोऽत्र ह्याविष्टाः शकटादिभिः ।।२।।

सर्वत्र हरिबुद्ध्या वा पादस्पर्शेच्छया पुनः ।
उलूखलादिभावोऽपि तत्सम्बन्धप्रसिद्धये ।।३।।

कस्याश्चित्पूतनायन्त्याः कृष्णायन्त्यपिबत्स्तनम् ।
तोकायित्वा रुदत्यन्या पदाहन् शकटायतीम् ।।१५।।

प्रथमतो भगवच्चरित्रं पूतनासुपयःपानमिति, काचित्पूतना भूता जाता, अन्या

'अहं कृष्ण' इत्युक्तवती, तदा तामङ्के भगवद्बुद्ध्या अगृह्णात्। ततस्तस्याः पूतनायन्त्याः कृष्णायन्ती स्तनमपिबत्। तस्यास्तु मरणभावना न स्थितेति, सा न मृता। नाप्यनुकरणं कृतवती। कृष्णायन्ती च स्तनमात्रमेव पिबति। अलौकिकसामर्थ्याभावात् इति स्तनपानमात्रमुक्तम्। अमङ्गलतानिवृत्तये च शकटभङ्गलीलामाह तोकायित्वेति, तोकवदाचरति, आत्मानं तोकं मन्यते वा, तोकवदात्मानं कृत्वा वा। शकटायतीं शकटवत् स्थितां, अहन् ताडितवती ॥१५॥

तृणावर्तलीलामाह दैत्यायित्वेति ।

दैत्यायित्वा जहारान्यामेका कृष्णार्भभावनाम् ।
रिङ्गयामास काप्यंघ्री कर्षन्ती घोषनिःस्वनैः ॥१६॥

दैत्यवदात्मानं कृत्वा कृष्णस्यार्भं बाल्यं भावयन्ती, कृष्णार्भभावनां तामेका आत्मानं दैत्यायित्वा जहार। काऽपि अंघ्री कर्षन्ती घोषनिःस्वनैः रिङ्गयामास चलितवती। यथा बाल्ये मुग्धप्रभीतवत् घोषप्रघोषरुचिरं भगवान् गच्छति। पूर्वश्लोके चतस्र उक्ताः लीलाद्वयेन, तास्तामसतामस्यः। अत्र तिस्र एव राजसतामस्य इति। चरित्रलीलायामुक्ता विशेषा अत्राप्यनुसंधेयाः। अथवा। युगलास्तिस्रो निरूपिताः। गुणातीता त्वेका। पुनः प्रकारान्तरेण बह्व्यः एकभावमापन्नाः भगवदिच्छया प्रधानगुणभावं प्राप्य रजसा अनेकधा विक्षिप्ताः बहुरूपा जाताः। ।१६॥

वृन्दावनक्रीडायां वत्सपालकरूपा जाताः। तत्र प्रकारमाह कृष्णेति ।

कृष्णरामायिते द्वे तु गोपायन्त्यश्च काश्चन ।
वत्सायतीं हन्ति चान्या तत्रैका तु बकायतीम् ॥१७॥

द्वे कृष्णरामायिते, कृष्णरामवत् जाते। काश्चन गोपायन्त्यः। गोपा अत्र बालकाः। जातिशब्दोऽयम्। वत्सरूपाश्च काश्चन जाताः। चकारेण समुच्चिताः। अन्या पुनर्वत्सायिता, वत्सासुरवदाचरति। तां घ्नती च जाता। कृष्णायिता अर्थात् चकारात् फलानि पातयन्ती च। अन्या पुनः बकायन्तीं घ्नती जाता। वत्सवधो लोके बलभद्रकृत इत्यपि प्रसिद्धः।। 'प्रलम्बो निहतोऽनेन वत्सको धेनुकादयः'। अत उभयोर्मध्ये एका बकायतीम्, अन्या वत्सायतीम् ॥१७॥

ततः परं गोपरूपेण वृन्दावनलीलामाह आहूयेति ।

आहूय दूरगा यद्वत् कृष्णस्तमनुकुर्वतीम् ।
वेणुं क्वणन्तीं क्रीडन्तीमन्याः शंसन्ति साध्विति ॥१८॥

गोरूपाः काश्चन जाताः, गेपालरूपाः काश्चन । तत्र यद्वत् कृष्णः दूरगाः गाः आहूय वेणुक्वणनं करोति, एवं दूरगा गोपीराहूय तं कृष्णमनुकुर्वती काचित् जाता ताम्। वेणुं क्वणन्तीम्, ततो नानाविधक्रीडां कुर्वतीं अन्याः गोपायिताः साधुसाध्विति शंसन्ति ॥१८॥

एका पुनः क्रीडायां कृतापि लीला भागवते अनुक्ता तां भावयित्वा तादृशीं लीलां कृतवती, तदाह कस्याश्चिदिति ।

कस्याश्चित् स्वभुजं न्यस्य चलन्त्याहापरा ननु ।
कृष्णोऽहं पश्यत गतिं ललितामिति तन्मनाः ॥१९॥

अत्रापि पूर्ववत् युगलास्तिस्त्रः । चतुर्थ्येषा । कृष्णरामायिते द्वे युगले । साध्वाशंसनसहिता वेणुनादनपरा च तृतीया । एषा तु निर्गुणा । कस्यांचित् गोपरूपायां स्वभुजं स्थापयित्वा चलन्ता, अपरा गोपरूपा, अतोऽन्या । ननु हे गोप्यः अहं कृष्णः, मे ललितां गतिं पश्यतेति । दोषाभावार्थमाह तन्मना इति । पूर्वे कायिकीं चेष्टां केवलां कृतवती । इदानीं वाचा सहिताम् ॥१९॥

पुनः प्रकारान्तरेण चातुर्विध्यमाह मा भैष्टेति ।

मा भैष्ट वातवर्षाभ्यां तत्त्राणं विहितं मया ।
इत्युक्त्वैकेन हस्तेन यतन्त्युन्निदधेऽम्बरम् ॥२०॥

एषैव निर्गुणा । काश्चन गोगोपगोपीरूपा जाता वृष्टिभीता इव । तदा वातवर्षाभ्यां हेतुभूताभ्यां मा भैष्ट, मया तत्त्राणं विहितं इत्युक्त्वा एकेन हस्तेन अम्बरं नयन्ती, पर्वतवत् स्थापयन्ती, ऊर्ध्वं निदधे । गोवर्धनवत् धारितवती, यतन्ती प्रयत्नं कुर्वन्ती वा ॥२०॥

सात्त्विक्याश्चेष्टामाह आरुह्येति ।

आरुह्यैकां पदाक्रम्य शिरस्याहापरां नृप ।
दुष्टाहे गच्छ जातोऽहं खलानां ननु दण्डधृक् ॥२१॥

एकामारुह्य, पदा च आक्रम्य, शिरसि पादाघातं कृत्वा । नृपेति सम्बोधनं विश्वासाय । एषा लीला कठिना । उपरि वृक्षशाखामवलम्ब्य वा तथा कृतवती । (वस्तुतस्तु या लीला यथा प्रभुणा कृता, सा तथैवात्राविर्भवति इति निरालम्बनत्वेऽपि नानुपपत्तिः।) हे दुष्टाहे कालिय । इतो गच्छ । यतोऽहं खलानां दण्डधृक् जातः । ननु इति सम्बोधनं अमारणार्थम् ॥२१॥

तत्रैकोवाचेति ।

तत्रैकोवाच हे गोपा दावाग्निं पश्यतोल्बणम् ।
चक्षूंष्याश्वपिदध्वं वो विधास्ये क्षेममञ्जसा ॥२२॥

राजसी पुनस्तत्रैका जाता । उवाच च वक्ष्यमाणम् । गोरूपाः काश्चन । गोरूपास्तथापराः । एका तु कृष्णरूपा आह । हे गोपा उल्बणं दावाग्निं पश्यतेति । विरहेण दावाग्निं दृष्टवती, भावनया वा तथा भानम् । सर्वापि क्रीडा भगवद्रूपा तत्र तत्राविशतीति दावाग्नेरपि दर्शनम् । अन्यासां विशेषाकारेण तस्यां भगवद्भावाभावात् न तत्प्रार्थना । एवमेव वातवर्षस्थलेऽपि । अतिमत्तानामेव भगवद्भावेन तल्लीलावेशात् तस्य एव दर्शनमिति निष्कर्षः ॥२२॥

तामसीमाह बद्धेति ।

बद्धान्यया स्रजा काचित् तन्वी तत्र ह्युलूखले ।
भीता सुदृक् पिधायास्यं भेजे भीतिविडम्बनम् ॥२३॥

उलूखले कयाचिद्बद्धा स्रजा मालया, उलूखलस्थानीयापि काचित् । अन्या तु यशोदारूपा । तदा भीता सती सुदृक् उत्तमदृष्टियुक्ता आस्यं पिधाय, हस्तेन सम्पूर्णं मुखमाच्छाद्य, भीत्यनुकरणं भेजे । अत्र क्रमे गुणा एव प्रयोजकाः । तत्तदधिकारानुसारेण तत्तल्लीलाः प्रादुर्भवन्ति । भगवद्वशीकरणान्ता च लीला । अन्यथान्ते उलूखललीला न कृता स्यात् । नातः परं कर्तव्यमस्तीति लीलाया विरतिः । एवं लीलाभावमुपपाद्य भगवद्भावे वक्तव्ये भगवतो भीतिविडम्बनलीलायां सर्वा लीलास्तिरोहिता : । ततः पूर्ववत् पुनः प्रश्न एव स्थितः । तस्य संवेदनपूर्वकत्वात् । एतत्त्वावेशेन जातमिति संवेदनराहित्यम् । अतस्त्वस्य नोपसंहारः ॥२३॥

पूर्वं तु 'इत्युन्मत्तवच'इति वचनमेवोपसंहृतम्, न तु प्रश्न उपसंहृतः । अत इदानीं मध्ये लीलामुक्त्वा तस्यास्तिरोधाने पुनरेव वृन्दावनलतास्तरून् कृष्णं पृच्छमाना जाता इत्याह एवमिति ।

एवं कृष्णं पृच्छमाना वृन्दावनलतास्तरून् ।
व्यचक्षत वनोद्देशे पदानि परमात्मनः ॥२४॥

तदा पुनरनुत्तरे प्राप्ते भगवानाविशन् मोहं दूरीकृत्य सर्वं ज्ञापितवानित्याह व्यचक्षतेति । तापापनोदार्थं एव त्रयम्, अन्वेषणं लीलावेशो भगवदावेशश्चेति । तत्र प्रश्नोऽन्तरङ्ग इति स एव सर्वत्रानूद्यते । वृन्दावनलताः तरून् कृष्णं पृच्छमाना जाता इति । ततो वनोद्देशे वनभूमौ भगवतः पदानि दृष्टवत्यः । परमात्मन इति । पदानां परमपुरुषार्थता सूचिता । भगवदावेशे हि सर्वज्ञता भवति । तेषां च कार्यं **भगवत्पददर्शनम्** । 'तद्विष्णोः परमं पदं सदा पश्यन्ति सूरय' इति श्रुतेः ॥२४॥

एता अपि पूर्ववत् दशविधाः । तथैव तासां वचनानि । पदानि प्रत्यक्षयोग्यानि सर्वैरेव दृश्यन्त इति तेषां याथात्म्यज्ञानं साध्यम् । अतः प्रथमं आहुः पदानि व्यक्तमेतानीति ।

पदानि व्यक्तमेतानि नन्दसूनोर्महात्मनः ।
लक्ष्यन्ते हि ध्वजांभोजचक्रांकुशयवादिभिः ॥२५॥

एतानि पदानि नन्दसूनोरेव । व्यक्तं सत्यम्, नात्र संदेहः । चिह्नैः पदानां विशेषज्ञानम् । चिह्नान्येव कथं भवन्तीत्याशङ्क्य, तत्रोपपत्तिमाहुः महात्मन इति । महतामप्यात्मा महान् वा ब्रह्मरूपः । तस्य तत्तत्कार्यार्थं पदे चिह्नानि भवन्ति, प्रकृतेऽपि तेषामुपयोग इति तदभिव्यक्तिः क्रियते । तानि चिह्नान्याह लक्ष्यन्त इति । अनुमीयन्ते पदानि । असाधारणधर्मैः । लोकेऽप्येतादृशोऽर्थः प्रसिद्ध इति सम्मतिः । ध्वजस्य स्थापनं भक्तानां निर्भयवासार्थम् । अम्भोजस्थापनं सुखसेव्यत्वाय । चक्रस्थापनं रक्षायै । मनोनिग्रहार्थं अङ्कुशस्थापनम् । कीर्तिसिद्ध्यर्थं यवः । वज्रादयोप्यादिशब्देनोच्यन्ते, पापपर्वतादिनिराकरणार्थाः ॥२५॥

एवमसाधारणधर्मैः पदानि निश्चित्य, तन्मार्गेण गता इत्याह तैस्तैरिति ।

तैस्तैः पदैस्तत्पदवीमन्विच्छन्त्योऽग्रतोऽबलाः ।
वध्वाः पदैः सुपृक्तानि विलोक्यार्ताः समब्रुवन् ॥२६॥

ज्ञानं क्रियापर्यवसायीति क्रिया निरूप्यते । तत्पदवीमन्विच्छन्त्योग्रतोऽबलाः जाताः, पदान्यन्विष्य तत्पदवीं गता इत्यर्थः । मध्ये तासां प्रतिबन्धमाह वध्वा इति । यदि तासां मत्सरदोषो न स्यात्, गच्छेयुरेवान्तिकम् । दोषवशाच्च परं कुण्ठिता भवन्ति । तदाह । वध्वाः कस्याश्चिद्गोपिकायाः पदैः सुपृक्तानि पंक्त्याकारेण गतानि भगवत्पदानि दृष्ट्वा तानि विलोक्य च आर्ता जाताः । तदा अन्योऽन्यमेवाब्रुवन् । ज्ञानक्रिययोरुपसर्जनं कृत्वा वाचि प्रतिष्ठिता जाताः । अन्यथा शीघ्रगमने भगवान् प्राप्तः स्यात् ॥२६॥

तासामसूयावाक्यान्याह कस्याः पदानीति ।

कस्याः पदानि चैतानि यातायाः नन्दसूनुना ।
अंसन्यस्तप्रकोष्ठायाः करेणोः करिणा यथा ॥ २७ ॥

पुरुषोऽत्र न संभाव्यते, नापि ग्रामान्तरस्त्रियः, अतोऽस्मन्मध्य एव कस्याश्चिद्भविष्यन्तीति । अयं प्रश्न इतरपरिच्छेदेन विशेषज्ञानार्थः । न त्वत्र पदे लक्षणानि सन्ति । चकाराद्भवगतः तस्याश्च चेष्टाज्ञापकानि चिह्नान्यप्युच्यन्ते । सा हि नन्द-

सूनुना सहैव याता । अन्यथा भगवान् न गच्छेत् । तयैव प्रायेण नीतः । स्वापेक्षया तस्या महद्भाग्यमाहुः । अंसे न्यस्तः प्रकोष्ठभागो यस्याम् । प्रकोष्ठभागो भगवदीयः करतलादर्वाचीनभागः । तावता करेण क्वचित्सम्बन्धः सूचितः । तावदेव नैकट्यं पदयोरिति । किञ्च, मध्ये तयोः रसाविर्भावोऽपि जायत इति दृष्टान्तेनाहुः करेणोः करिणा यथेति । करेणोरंसे करिणा यथा हस्तः प्रसार्यत इति । करेणुः स्त्री, तस्या अंसे यथा करी हस्तं प्रसारयति, तदा पदानि मिलन्ति, संमुखश्च भवति, उद्धृष्टकण्ठा वा भवति । स्पर्शसुखमेव प्रधानमिति गजो दृष्टान्तीकृतः । एवं त्रिविधा गोपिका उक्ताः ॥२७॥

गुणातीताया वाक्यद्वयमाह । दोषाभावप्रतिपादकं गुणप्रतिपादकं च । तामसतामसी भगवदाविष्टा न भवतीति । अनयाराधित इति द्वाभ्याम् ।

अनयाराधितो नूनं भगवान् हरिरीश्वरः ।
यन्नो विहाय गोविन्दः प्रीतो यामनयद्रहः ॥२८॥

तत्र प्रथमं तया सह विशेषरमणे तस्या भाग्यं तस्याः पुण्यं हेतुत्वेनाहुः । अनया हरिर्नूनमाराधितः । यद्यप्यस्माभिरप्याराधितः, तथापि नूनं नाराधितः । भगवदनाराधकैरपि फलत्वात् भगवतः सम्बन्धसम्भवात् । आराधिते तु फलं स्ववशे भवति । तत्रापि तारतम्यम् । ननु तुल्यकर्मणां मध्ये कथं अवान्तरभेदः, तत्राह भगवानिति । सामग्रीभेदात् कर्माणि सर्वत्र विलक्षणानि भवन्ति । तदवान्तरवैलक्षण्यं स एव जानाति । अतस्तथा फलनिरूपको जातः । ननु तथापि वयं तथा न ज्ञापनीयाः, दुःखसाधकत्वादिति चेत्, तत्राहुः हरिरिति । स हि सर्वदुःखहर्ता, वैलक्षण्यज्ञापनार्थं तथा बोधितवान् । ननु भक्तिः तुल्येति कथं भक्त्यनुसारेण तुल्यं फलं न कृतवान्, तुल्यफलत्वेन कर्म कुतः स्वीकृतवान्, तत्राहुरीश्वर इति । कदाचिद्भक्तिमुररीकरोति, कदाचित्कर्म, कदाचित् स्वेच्छाम् । न हीश्वरो नियन्तुं शक्यः । अस्मान् भक्तिमार्गे योजयति, न कर्ममार्ग इति । अत एव नः अस्मान् विहाय गोविन्दः साधारणेन्द्रोऽपि रहः एकान्ते प्रीतः सन् तामेवानयत् । कामरसः स्त्रीसमूहापेक्षयाप्येकस्यामेव मुख्यतयोत्पद्यते । तथा करणे प्रीतिर्हेतुः, प्रीतौ भक्तिः, कर्म वा ॥२८॥

एवं तस्या भाग्यमभिनन्द्य मात्सर्येऽपि गूढे तथा वचनं भवतीति स्वभाग्याभिनन्दनमप्याहुः धन्या इति ।

धन्या अहो अमी आल्यो गोविन्दाङ्घ्र्यब्जरेणवः ।
यान् ब्रह्मेशो रमा देवी दधुर्मूर्ध्न्यघनुत्तये ॥२९॥

अहो आश्चर्ये, हे आल्यः सख्यः, अमी अंघ्रिरेणवो धन्याः । मात्सर्याभावार्थं चैतदुच्यते । यथा रेणवः, तथा सेति । विश्वासार्थं अप्रतारणार्थं च सम्बोधनम् । अनेन

रेणूत्कर्षेण रेणव एव धार्याः स्वदोषनिवृत्त्यर्थमित्युक्तं भवति। पूर्वमत्रैव ते रेणवः स्थिताः, न तदा तेषामुत्कर्षः, यदा पुनश्चरणसम्बद्धाः, तदा धनमर्हन्तीति । धनं कृष्णः, यथेन्द्रो देवानाम् । यथा धनेन सर्वविषयप्राप्तिः, एवं प्रभुणापि। तेषां धन्यत्वमुपपादयन्ति यानिति । ब्रह्मा ईशो रमा च देवतारूपा पालिका शक्तिः । तेषां स्वस्वाधिकारे दोषसंभवात् तन्निवृत्त्यर्थं मूर्ध्नि दधुः । ब्रह्मानन्दरूपाया निवृत्त्यर्थं देवतापदम् । अतः कारणादेतद्धारणेन वयमपि निर्दुष्टाः नीयमानगोपिकातुल्या भविष्याम इति ॥२९॥

अन्या रजःप्रकृतय आहुः तस्या इति ।

तस्या अमूनि नः क्षोभं कुर्वन्त्युच्चैः पदानि यत् ।
यैकापहृत्य गोपीनां रहो भुङ्क्तेऽच्युताधरम् ॥३०॥

भगवंश्चरणारविन्दरजस्तथैव, परमस्याः गोपिकायाः अमूनि पदानि सङ्गे गच्छन्त्याः नोऽस्माकं क्षोभं कुर्वन्ति । तत्राप्युच्चैरत्यर्थम् । नन्वेकाकी भगवान् गच्छेत्, तदपेक्षया ससहायो भक्तिमार्गे युक्त इति चेत्, तत्राहुः । यद्यस्मात् गोपिकानां सर्वासामेव भागरूपमच्युताधरं ता विहाय एकैवोपभुङ्क्ते । तत्रापि रहः एकान्ते तासामनुज्ञाव्यतिरेकेण । ननु विरतो भगवान् बहुस्त्रीसम्बन्धाद्भविष्यति, कुतः सा भोक्ष्यते, तत्राहुः अच्युतेति । स हि पूर्णकाम एव, न तस्य च्युतिरस्ति ॥३०॥

अन्याः पुनस्ततोऽपि खेदं कृतवत्य इत्याह न लक्ष्यन्त इति ।

न लक्ष्यन्ते पदान्यत्र तस्या नूनं तृणाङ्कुरैः ।
खिद्यत्सुजाताङ्घ्रितलामुन्निन्ये प्रेयसीं प्रियः ॥३१॥

अहो किमिति विचार्यते । अधरामृतं पिबतीति । एतावद्दूरे समागतानि तस्याः पदानि अग्रे न लक्ष्यन्ते । न च वक्तव्यं समीचीनं जातमिति, तत्राहुः । तस्याः तृणाङ्कुरैः खिद्यत् पादतलं जातम् । तदा तादृशीमुन्निन्ये, ऊर्ध्वं नीतवान् । कटिभागे स्कन्धभागे वा । वस्तुतस्तु हस्ताभ्यामेवोद्धृतवानिति सुतरां खेदे हेतुः । ननु कथमेवं करिष्यतीत्याशङ्क्याहुः प्रेयसीमिति । साप्यत्यन्तं प्रिया, स्वयमपि तस्याः प्रियः । अतो ज्ञायते न सा स्कन्धमारूढा, किन्तु केवलमुन्निन्ये ॥३१॥

किञ्च । तेन प्रकारेण न बहुदूरे गमनं सम्भवति । अतः क्वचिद्विश्रम्य पुष्पावचयमपि तदर्थे करोतीत्याहुः अत्रेति ।

अत्रप्रसूनावचयः प्रियार्थे प्रेयसा कृतः ।
प्रपदाक्रमणे एते पश्यतासकले पदे ॥३२॥

प्रसूनानामवचयो वृक्षादुत्तारणम् । न च स्वार्थं भविष्यतीति शङ्कनीयम् । सा हि श्रान्ता । अतः प्रियार्थं एव । सा तु कर्तुमशक्तैव । तदाहुः प्रेयसा कृत इति । सा हि भगवदपेक्षया खर्वा प्रपदाभ्यामुत्थातुमप्यशक्ता । अतः प्रेयसैव कृतः । यतः प्रपदाक्रमणे पादाग्राभ्यामेवाक्रमणं ययोः । अत एवासकले, पार्ष्णिभागो नाभिव्यक्त इति । पश्यतेति सन्देहाभावार्थं वचनम् ।३२।।

ततोप्यन्या अधिकमेव सूचयन्त्य आहुः केशप्रसाधनमिति ।

केशप्रसाधनं त्वत्र कामिन्याः कामिना कृतम् ।
तानि चूडयता कान्तामुपविष्टमिह ध्रुवम् ।।३३।।

नखैरेव केशानां प्रसाधनम्, वेण्याकारेण आपीडाकारेण वा । तुशब्दोऽन्यथापक्षं व्यावर्तयति । न ह्यत्र ज्ञानोपदेशः सम्भवति । तदाहुः कामिन्याः कामिना कृतमिति । एतत् उत्थायापि भवति । चूडायां पुष्पप्रवेशनं तु उत्थिते न भवति । क्रोडे पुष्पाणि स्थापयित्वा क्रमेण तानि निवेशनीयानि । अतः तानि चूडयता इहोपविष्टम् । ध्रुवमिति सत्यम् । कान्तामुप कान्तासमीपे । कान्तामुद्दिश्य वा । तथैवाकृतिर्दृश्यत इति ।।

एवं रसार्थं तस्यानयनं सामग्रीसम्पादनमलङ्करणं चोक्तम् । यदर्थमेतावत्तदाहुः रेम इति ।

रेमे तया चात्मरत आत्मारामोऽप्यखण्डितः ।
कामिनां दर्शयन् दैन्यं स्त्रीणां चैव दुरात्मताम् ।।३४।।

पुष्टत्वात् कामस्य आत्मरतः तया च सह रेमे । चकारात् लक्ष्म्या च । अन्तःप्रविष्टाभिर्वा । सापि रेम इति वा । आत्मन्येव रतिर्यस्य । तेन निष्काम एव तस्या यथेच्छं कामं पूरितवान् । अस्यामपि दशायामात्मरत एव, रसाधारत्वाय तस्यामात्मानं स्थापितवान् । आत्मन्येव मुख्या रति : आत्मन्येव रमणं क्रीडा च यस्य । यतः अखण्डितः इन्द्रियैरन्तःकरणैर्विषयैर्वा । यदि स्वानन्दोऽन्यत्र गच्छेत्, तदान्यत्र रतो भवेत् । ननु कथमेवमसमीचीनस्थाने एतावता प्रयासेन एवं रमणं कृतवानिति, तत्र प्रयोजनमाहुः कामिनां दर्शयन् दैन्यमिति । कामिनस्त्वेवमेव दीना भवन्ति । 'कामार्ता हि प्रकृतिकृपणा' इति तेषामनुकरणं करोति । अन्यथा तेषां निरोधो न स्यात् । प्रयोजनान्तरमप्यस्तीत्याहुः स्त्रीणामिति । स्त्रीणां च दुरात्मता प्रदर्शिता । न तासां काचिदशक्तिरस्ति, नापि सौकुमार्यम्, किन्तु वशीकृते पुरुषे दौष्ट्यमेव कुर्वन्ति । 'शालावृकाणां हृदयान्येता' इति । अत उभयबोधनार्थमेवं रेमे ।।३४।।

एवं सर्ववस्तुयाथात्म्यस्फुरणं भगवदावेशात्तासां निरूपितमुपसंहरति इत्येवमिति ।

श्रीशुक उवाच— **इत्येवं दर्शयन्त्यस्ताश्चेरुर्गोप्यो विचेतसः ।**

एवंप्रकारेण भगवल्लीलाः प्रदर्शयन्त्यः चेरुः गतिं कृतवत्यः । तासामनेकविधत्वे हेतुमाह गोप्य इति । न हि ताः शास्त्रेण भगवदीया जाताः , किन्तु स्वभावेन । स्वभावस्त्वनेकविध इति सर्वमुपपद्यते । किञ्च, नहि ताः किञ्चित् ज्ञात्वा वदन्ति, किन्तु विचेतस एव । अथवा । एवं दर्शयन्त्यो विचेतसो जाताः । प्रकारत्रयस्यापि समाप्तत्वात् । अतस्तासां नाग्रे गतिर्न वचनानि ।

एवमेतासां स्वरूपं निरूप्य, तस्याः स्वरूपं निरूपयति यां गोपीमिति सार्धैः त्रिभिः ।

यां गोपीमनयत् कृष्णो विहायान्याः स्त्रियो वने ॥३५॥

सा च मेने तदात्मानं वरिष्ठं सर्वयोषिताम् ।
हित्वा गोपीः कामयाना मामसौ भजते प्रियः॥३६॥

ततो गत्वा वनोद्देशं दृप्ता केशवमब्रवीत् ।
न पारयेऽहं चलितुं नय मां यत्र ते मनः ॥३७॥

एवमुक्तः प्रियामाह स्कन्धमारुह्यतामिति ।
ततश्चान्तर्दधे कृष्णः सा वधूरन्वतप्यत ॥३८॥

दोषोऽभिमानवचनं वचनोत्तरमेव च ।
पूर्ववच्च तिरोभावो विज्ञेयं दोषदर्शने ॥१॥

यां गोपीं पूर्वमजातदोषां अनयत् । यतः कृष्णः सदानन्दः, तस्यामानन्दं स्थापयितुम् । अन्यास्तु स्त्रियो जाताः । सा तु मुग्धैव गोपी । अतस्ता वने विहाय तामनयत् । वनस्थानां विवेको भवतीति ॥३५॥

स्वयं त्वयुक्तकरणात् प्रकृत्याद्यधिकारिणः ।
बुद्धिं स्म नाशयामासुः साप्यन्येवाभवत्ततः ॥१॥

तदाह । सा च तदा सर्वयोषितां मध्ये वरिष्ठं मेन इति । चकारः पूर्वसमुच्चयार्थोऽप्यर्थे । तदेति । पूर्वं तस्यास्तथात्वं न जातमिति । अनेन समुदायदोषेण न भगवांस्त्यजति, किन्तु प्रत्येकदोषेणेति ज्ञापितम् । तस्यास्तथा दोषे हेतुः हित्वेति । कामयाना अपि सर्वाः गोपीः हित्वा असौ मां भजत इति । तत्रापि प्रियः, यथैव मम प्रीतिर्भवति, तथैव करोति । न तु क्वचिदप्यप्रियविषयः । अतोऽहं वरिष्ठा । अन्यथानुपपत्त्या तथात्वं कल्प्यते ॥३६॥

दोषाभावेनैवोत्तमता, न तु धर्मान्तरेण, अतस्तस्या भ्रमः, भ्रान्ताया वाक्यमाह ततो गत्वेति । ततो भोगस्थानादग्रे गत्वा । वनोद्देशमतिरमणीयम् । स्वार्थमयं गच्छति, न तु मदर्थम् । ततश्चान्यार्थं मया कथं खेदः प्राप्तव्य इति दृप्ता । तादृशभगवत्कृपायामनधिकारिणी प्राप्तप्रसादेन जाताजीर्णा ब्रह्मादिभ्योऽपि मोक्षदातारं देहेन्द्रियादिसर्वरहितं परमानन्दरूपं केशवमब्रवीत् । तस्या वाक्यमाह न पारय इति । अहं चलितुं न पारये । तथापीष्टदेशं गन्तव्यमिति चेत्, तत्राह । यत्र ते मनः, तत्र मां त्वमेव नय ॥३७॥

तदा भगवानतिचतुरः तद्वाक्यस्योत्तरमाह एवमुक्त इति । प्रियेति कृत्वा उत्तरमुक्तवान् । उत्तरमाह स्कन्धमारुह्यतामिति । एषा हि नृत्यं कर्तुं वाञ्छति । स्वान्तर्गतं रसमभिनेतुम् । तद्भूमौ पदस्थापने ऊर्ध्वभावाभावात् रसः च्युतो भवेत् । अतः स्वस्कन्धमेवारुह्यतामिति । स एवात्यन्तं नटवटुः यः स्वस्कन्धमारुह्य नरीनर्ति । अशक्यं ह्युपदिशति । प्रार्थितं तथेति । भगवतो हि मनः अलौकिकरसाभिनयने, तद्भूमौ पदस्थापने न भवति । अशक्ता चेत् कथं वदेत् । अतो मम तत्रैव मनः । यदि तथा करिष्यति, तदा नेष्यामीति । नह्यनधिकारी नेतुं योग्यः । भगवांस्तु नान्यथा वदतीति न स्वस्कन्धसम्भावना । तया तु मोहवशात् तथैव बुद्धम् । ततो मोहवशात् तथा चिकीर्षमाणां तां दृष्ट्वा ततोऽप्यन्तर्दधे । यतोऽयं कृष्णः सदानन्दः । ततः पूर्ववदेव सापि जातेत्याह सा वधूरन्वतप्यतेति । वधूरिति सा अनन्यपूर्वा व्रतमध्यस्था । तत्रापि गुणातीता । अतः अन्वतप्यत, अनुतापं कृतवती ॥३८॥

न केवलमन्तरनुतापः, किन्तु तज्जनितो बहिरपि विलापो जात इत्याह हा नाथेति ।

हा नाथ रमण प्रेष्ठ क्वासि क्वासि महाभुज ।
दास्यास्ते कृपणाया मे सखे दर्शय सन्निधिम् ॥३९॥

हा इति पश्चात्तापे । अयुक्तं कृतमिति । तथापि हे नाथ, त्वमेव स्वामी । अतो दोष एव दूरीकर्तव्यः, न तु त्यक्तव्या । ननु दूरे स्थित्वा पालनं करिष्यामीति चेत्, तत्राह रमणेति । त्वमेव रतिवर्धको भोक्ता, भोग्यरूपाश्च वयम् । अतो निकट एव स्थातव्यमिति भावः । नन्वनुरोधेन केवलं पालनं करिष्यामि, भोक्तुरिच्छाभावात् । न हि भोग्येच्छया भोक्ता भुङ्क्ते, तत्राह प्रेष्ठेति । न ह्यन्यः प्रीतिविषयोऽस्ति येन जीविष्यामि । अत्यन्तं व्याकुलाया वचनमाह क्वासि क्वासीति । मोहवशात् अन्धा पतिता च जाता, तत उत्थापनार्थं संबोधयति महाभुजेति । महान् भुजो यस्य । महती क्रियाशक्तिः । अतो दोष एव दूरीकर्तव्यो, नत्वहम् । यतोऽहं दासी, तत्रापि ते तवैवाहं दासी, स्वभावत एवाहं कृपणा, अनालोचितयाचिका, अतो मद्वचनान्नान्यथाभावः कर्तव्यः । एवं प्रार्थनायां परमकृपालुस्तामुत्थाप्य स्वस्थां कृतवान्,

अदृश्यरूपेणैव । तदा पुनराह । हे सखे, स्पर्शेन स्वधर्मारोपात्स्वसंनिधिं दर्शय । वर्तसे निकटे, तथापि यथा सान्निध्यं दृष्टं भवति, तथा कुरु । एवमेव वदन्ती स्थिता । भगवानपि तत्रैव स्थितः ॥३६॥

ततो यज्जातं तदाह अन्विच्छन्त्य इति ।

अन्विच्छन्त्यो भगवतो मार्गं गोप्यो विचेतसः ।
ददृशुः प्रियविश्लेषमोहितां दुःखितां सखीम् ॥४०॥

पूर्वोक्ता गोप्यः भगवन्मार्गमन्विच्छन्त्यः अविदूरत एव तां ददृशुः । तासां क्रोधाभावायाह दुःखितामिति । न हि दुःखितायां क्रोधो भवति । दुःखे हेत्वन्तर-निराकरणायाह प्रियविश्लेषमोहितामिति । भगवत एव विश्लेषेण परममोहं मूर्च्छां प्राप्ताम् । सापि तासां सखी । अतः सख्यभावेन बह्वयः तां प्रबोधितवत्यः । 'न दुःखं पञ्चभिः सहेति' ॥४०॥

पूर्वमेताः भगवानेवमेव कौतुकार्थं गतः, न त्वस्मद्दोषेणेति ज्ञातवत्यः । अन्यथा दोषनिराकरणार्थमेव यत्नः कृतः स्यात् । स्वदोषपरिज्ञानं च भगवत्कृपयैव भवति, न स्वत इति ज्ञापयितुं सा नीता, पश्चात् त्यक्ता कथनार्थमेव, अतो भगवदिच्छया सर्वं कथितवती । तत्र वक्तव्ये यत्प्रयोजकं तदाह तया कथितमिति ।

तया कथितमाकर्ण्य मानप्राप्तिं च माधवात् ।
अवमानं च दौरात्म्याद्विस्मयं परमं ययुः ॥४१॥

मानप्राप्तिं च माधवात्, अवमानं च दौरात्म्यादिति । तया कथितं यद्यपि बह्वेव श्रुतम्, तत्रैतावानर्थो निर्धारितः । सन्माननं यत्प्राप्तम्, तन्न स्वगुणैः, किन्तु लक्ष्मीपतेरेव गुणैः, लक्ष्म्यंशा एता इति । दौरात्म्यात्स्वधर्मादेव अवमानम् । चका-रात् खेदभ्रमादयः । एवं भगवतः अलौकिकं सामर्थ्यं दृष्ट्वा परमं विस्मयं प्राप्ताः । एवं तद्वाक्यैः पदार्थनिर्धारो जातः । अन्वेषणादिना भगवान् न प्राप्तव्य इति ॥४१॥

अतः परं भगवत्प्रसादे को हेतुरिति विचार्य, सर्वपरित्यागेन देहपरित्यागपर्यन्तं साधनमिति निश्चित्य, तथा कृतवत्य इत्याह तत इति ।

ततोऽविशन् वनं चन्द्रज्योत्स्ना यावद्विभाव्यते ।
तमः प्रविष्टमालक्ष्य ततो निववृतुर्हरेः ॥४२॥

ततो वनमविशन् । मोहनिवृत्त्यर्थं वनप्रवेशः । वनं गतानामपि चेन्मोहः, तदा किं वनप्रवेशेनेति । चन्द्रज्योत्स्ना यावद्विभाव्यते, तावद्दूरमेव गताः । अतिनिबिडवनं

तु न प्रविष्टाः । यदा पुनर्गाढे वने अन्तश्चन्द्रकिरणा न प्रविशन्ति, तदा तत्र तमः प्रविष्टमालक्ष्य, ततो निवव्रृतुः निवृत्ता जाताः । ननु प्रथमं यदुद्योगेन वनं गताः, तदकृत्वा कुतो वा निवृत्ता इत्याशंक्याह हरेरिति । हरेः सकाशात् हरेः सम्बन्धिन्यो वा । ततः अन्धकारान्निवृत्ताः । न हि भगवदीया अन्धकारं प्रविशन्ति । भगवतैव निवर्तिताः ॥४२॥

निवृत्ताः चेत्, गृहं गताः भविष्यन्तीत्याशंकायामाह तन्मनस्का इति ।

तन्मनस्कास्तदालापास्तद्विचेष्टास्तदात्मिकाः ।
तद्गुणानेव गायन्त्यो नात्मागाराणि सस्मरुः ॥४३॥

ता नात्मागाराणि सस्मरुः । आत्मानं देहम् । अगारं गृहम् तत्सम्बन्धीनि च वस्तूनि स्मृतवत्य एव न, कुतो गमिष्यन्ति । अस्मरणे हेतवः । तन्मनस्का इत्यादिभिः पञ्चभिः पदैः पञ्च निरूप्यन्ते । स्मृतिर्मनसि जायते, तन्मनस्तु केवलं भगवत्येव, अतस्तन्मनस्काः भगवन्मनस्का न सस्मरुः । अन्यद्वाराप्यस्मरणार्थमाह तदालापा इति । अन्या अपि चेदन्यवार्तां कुर्युः, तदा तत्प्रसङ्गात् गृहादिस्मरणं भवति । सर्वा एव तस्मिन् भगवत्येवालापो यासाम् । अतोऽन्यतोऽपि न स्मरणम् । ननु दैहिकी क्रिया क्षुत्पिपासाकृता आवश्यकी, तया देहादिस्मरणं भविष्यतीति चेत्, तत्राह तद्विचेष्टा इति । तस्यैव भगवतः पूर्ववच्चेष्टाविष्टाः । ननु तथापि सर्वज्ञानेष्वात्मांशः स्फुरति, घटमहं जानामि, पटमहं जानामीति । अतः कथमात्मास्फूर्तिः, तत्राह तदात्मिका इति । स एवात्मा यासाम् । सर्वदा कृष्णात्मभावनैव चित्ते सहजा तासाम् । अत आत्मत्वेन भगवानेव स्फुरति इति न देहादिस्फुरणम् । ननु 'सदृशादृष्टचिन्ताद्याः स्मृतिबीजस्य बोधका' इति अदृष्टवशात् कथं न स्मृतिः, तत्राह तद्गुणानेव गायन्त्य इति । यदि तूष्णीं तिष्ठेयुः, भवेदपि स्मृतिः, अन्यासक्तास्तु ताः कार्यान्तरपराः । यतस्तस्य भगवतो गुणानेव गायन्ति । गुणैः कृत्वा दुरदृष्टं च नश्यति । अतो नादृष्टद्वारापि स्मृतिबोधः ॥४३॥

तर्हि किं जातमित्याकाङ्क्षायामाह पुनः पुलिनमागत्येति ।

पुनःपुलिनमागत्य कालिन्द्याः कृष्णभावनाः ।
समवेता जगुः कृष्णं तदागमनकाङ्क्षिताः ॥४४॥

इति श्रीभागवतमहापुराणे दशमस्कन्धपूर्वार्धे सप्तविंशोऽध्यायः ॥२७॥

पूर्वं पुलिने स्थिता यत्र, तत्रैव पुनरागताः । ननु विवेकरहिताः कथं तत्रागताः, तत्राह कृष्णभावना इति । कृष्ण एव भावना यासाम् । तेन भगवदिच्छया भगवत्प्रेरणया तत्रैव स्थाने भगवान् रतिं करिष्यतीति निश्चित्य, तत् स्थानमस्माकं हित-

करमिति तत्रैवागताः । ततः कस्या वा भाग्यात् स्नेहेन कृपया वा आगच्छेदिति संदेहात् समवेता जाताः । तदा साधनान्तरमलभमानाः कृष्णं सदानन्दं जगुः । दोषनिवारणे हरिगुणगानमेव साधनमिति । निवृत्ते पुनर्दोषे स्वयमेवायास्यतीति तदागमनकाङ्क्षया जगुः ॥४४॥

श्रीकृष्णगोपिकास्तत्र द्विविधा नवधा गुणैः ।
समुदायेन भिन्ना वा गतगर्वा असाधनाः ॥१॥

हरेर्गानं प्रियं मत्वा जीवनार्थमपि प्रियाः ॥
स्वसंदेहात्तु मिलिता जगुर्नानाविधैर्गुणैः ॥२॥

इति श्रीभागवतसुबोधिन्यां श्रीमल्लक्ष्मणभट्टात्मजश्रीमद्वल्लभदीक्षितविरचितायां दशमस्कन्धविवरणे सप्तविंशाध्यायविवरणम् ॥२७॥

श्रीकृष्णाय नमः ।

अष्टाविंशोऽध्यायः

अष्टाविंशे हरेर्गानं स्वभावादपराधतः ।
कृतावज्ञा गोपिका हि स्तोत्रं चक्रुरितीर्यते ॥१॥

एकोनविंशतिविधा गोप्यः स्वस्याधिकारतः ।
एकोनविंशतिविधां स्तुतिं चक्रुर्हरेः प्रियाम् ॥२॥

राजसी तामसी चैव सात्त्विकी निर्गुणा तथा ।
एवं चतुर्विधा गोप्यः पतिमत्यो निरूपिताः ॥३॥

तथैवानन्यपूर्वाश्च प्रार्थनामाहुरुत्तमाम् ।
गुणातीताः सात्त्विकीश्च तामसी राजसीस्तथा ॥४॥

कृष्णभावनया सिद्धा विशेषेणाह ताः शुकः ।
अनन्यपूर्विका एव पुनस्तिस्रो मुदा जगुः ॥५॥

सात्त्विकी तामसी चैव राजसी चेति विश्रुताः ।
सपूर्वाश्च ततस्तिस्रः तामसी राजसी परा ॥६॥

पुनस्ता एव त्रिविधा अटतीत्यादिभिस्त्रिभिः ।
राजसी तामसी चैव सात्त्विकीति विभेदतः ॥७॥

अनन्यपूर्वा द्विविधा राजसी सात्त्विकी तथा ।
तमसा तामसी तत्र नास्तीत्येकोनविंशतिः ॥८॥

अथवा प्रार्थनाद्यायाः सप्तान्ते द्विविधा पुनः ।
चतुर्थ्यस्तु समास्तत्र तत एकोनविंशतिः ॥९॥

तत्तद्वाक्यानुसारेण तासां भावो निरूप्यते ।
अन्यथाऽनेकता स्तोत्रे प्रकारैर्नोपयुज्यते ॥१०॥

तत्र प्रथमं राजस्यः काश्चन गोप्य आहुः जयतीति ।

श्रीगोप्य ऊचुः ।

जयति तेऽधिकं जन्मना व्रजः श्रयत इन्दिरा शश्वदत्र हि ।

दयित दृश्यतां दिक्षु तावकास्त्वयि धृतासवस्त्वां विचिन्वते ॥१॥

मङ्गलार्थोऽत्र जयशब्दः । यथा फलं साधयेत्स्तोत्रम्, तथा निर्विघ्नार्थः । अन्यथा क्रियामादौ न प्रयुंज्यात् । त्वदवतारेण व्रजः सर्वोऽपि कृतार्थः । वयमेव परमकृतार्था एवेति । यथा वयमपि कृतार्था भवामः, तथा यत्नः कर्तव्य इति वक्तुं व्रजस्य तवावतारेण सर्वोत्कर्षो जात इत्याहुः । ते जन्मना व्रजः अधिकं जयतीति । सर्वोत्कर्षेण स्थितिः जयः, अधिकजयो वैकुण्ठादप्युत्कर्षः । न हि वैकुण्ठे भगवानेवंविधां लीलां करोति । यद्यपि मथुरायां जन्म जातम्, तथापि तेन जन्मना न मथुरा सर्वोत्कर्षेण स्थिता, किन्तु व्रज एव । ननु भगवज्जन्मनः सर्वोत्कर्षहेतुत्वं न लोके प्रसिद्धम्, अनन्यत्वेनैकत्वात्, अतस्तादृश उत्कर्षहेतुर्वक्तव्यः, यो लोके प्रसिद्ध इति चेत् , तत्राह श्रयत इन्दिरा शश्वदत्र हीति । अत्र व्रज इन्दिरा सर्वदा श्रयते । हीनभावेनाश्रयं कुरुते । वैकुण्ठे तु सैव नियता भार्येति न तस्याः सर्वदा श्रयणं कर्तव्यं भवति । इह तु तादृश्यो वयमनेका इति तस्याः स्वास्थ्याभावात् कदा वा ममावसरो भविष्यतीति निरन्तरं सेवते । अतो लक्ष्मीस्थित्या लोका उत्कर्षं मन्यन्ते । सा पुनर्लक्ष्मीः गोकुलाश्रया जाता । हि युक्तश्चायमर्थः । पतिव्रता हि सा । यत्र पतिः स्वयमन्याधीनतया तिष्ठति, भक्तेषु कृपां ख्यापयितुम्, तदुक्तमुलूखलप्रकरणे, तत्र तद्भार्या सुतरामेवाश्रयत इति किमाश्चर्यम् । तव जन्मना व्रजस्य सर्वोत्कर्षः सर्वजनीनः । अतस्तव रमणे न कापि न्यूनता, न वा लक्ष्म्या मनसि विषादः, अङ्गीकृतत्वात् । अतः कारणादस्मदर्थमागतेन त्वया दृश्यतामिदं गोकुलमेकदा द्रष्टव्यम् । वाक्यार्थो वा कर्माग्रे वक्ष्यमाणः । तावकास्त्वयि धृतासवः दिक्षु त्वां विचिन्वत इति दृश्यताम् । एतादृशोऽर्थोऽनुचित इति अनुचितप्रदर्शनेन बोधयन्ति । लोका हि ब्रह्मादयः त्वमवतीर्णो व्रजे वर्तस इति निश्चित्य समायान्ति । व्रजस्थाः पुनरस्मदादयः दिक्षु विचिन्वन्ति । इयं महत्यनौचिती । ननु व्रजस्थानां भक्तिर्नास्ति, अन्यथा विरहे म्रियेरन्; अतः अभक्ता न पश्यन्तीति युक्तं इति चेत्, तत्राहुः त्वयि धृतासव इति । त्वदर्थमेव धृता असवः प्राणा यैः । यदैव त्वदनुपयोगं ज्ञास्यन्ति, तदैव त्यक्ष्यन्तीति भावः । अत एव त्वां विचिन्वते, प्राणानाश्वासयितुम् । अल्पविलम्बेऽपि प्राणा गमिष्यन्तीति । अन्यथा व्रजे गच्छेयुः, प्रातस्त्वमेवायास्यतीति अन्वेषणं व्यर्थमेव स्यात् । दिक्षु त्वदीयाः त्वयि सतीति महद्दैन्यम् । अत एकवारं त्वदीयाः पश्येति प्रार्थना । एवमेकया दर्शनं प्रार्थितम् । दयितेति सम्बोधनात् भर्तृदर्शनेन स्त्रीणां जीवनं न युक्तिमिति निरूपितम् । यद्यपि भगवाँश्चेत् पश्येत्, तदा न कोऽपि पुरुषार्थः सिध्येत् । तथापि दैन्यं दृष्ट्वा आत्मानमपि प्रदर्शयेदिति तथा प्रार्थना ॥१॥

एवं स्वदैन्यानौचित्यादिनिरूपणेन तस्या राजसत्वं निरूपितम् । तामसी तु वधाभावं प्रार्थयितुमदर्शनस्य वधसाधकत्वमाह शरदुदाशय इति ।

शरदुदाशये साधुजातसत्सरसिजोदरश्रीमुषा दृशा ।
सुरतनाथ ते शुल्कदासिका वरद निघ्नतो नेह किं वधः ॥२॥

शरत्कालीनो योऽयमुदाशयः पुष्करिणी, तत्र साधु सम्यक् प्रकारेण जातं यत्सरसिजं कमलं, तदन्तर्वर्तिनी या श्रीः, तामपि मुष्णातीति तादृग्रूपया दृशा दृष्ट्या, हे वरद, यो निहन्ति तस्य किं वधो न, अपि तु वधदोषो भवत्येव। येनैव साधनेन परस्य प्राणा गच्छन्ति, तत्सम्पादनसाधको घातकः दोषभाग्भवति । अनेन भगवद्दृष्टिः सर्वघातुका निरूपिता । 'आयुर्मनांसि च दृशा सह ओज आच्छे'दिति वाक्यात् । तथास्मानपि प्रायेण क्रूरदृष्ट्या पश्यसि । अन्यथा कथं प्राणबाधा स्यात् । रूपं त्वानन्दमयमिति तद्दृष्टौ तदेव जीवयेत् । अतस्तदभावात् केवलं घातयस्येव । किञ्च, न वयं वधार्हाः, यतो दासिकाः, कुत्सिता दास्यः । न हि स्त्रियः अप्रयोजिकाश्च हन्यन्ते । किञ्च, वयं शुल्कदासिकाः, त्वं च सुरतनाथः । सर्वपुरुषार्थसाधकत्वेन तव सम्बोधनानि यथाधिकारं नियतानि । यथा धर्ममार्गे, हे धर्मपालक, हे ब्रह्मण्य, हे यज्ञेश्वरेत्यादीनि । अर्थे, हे लक्ष्मीपते, सर्वसिद्धिदेत्यादीनि । तथा मोक्षे, हे मुकुन्द, हे योगेश्वर, हे ज्ञाननिधे इत्यादीनि धर्मार्थमोक्षार्थिभिरुच्यन्ते । एवमस्माभिरपि सुरतनाथेत्युच्यते । सुरतं सम्भोगः जगति यावानस्ति तस्य भवान् नाथः । त्वदाज्ञाव्यतिरेकेण सुरतं जगति न प्रवर्तते । अतो ब्रह्मणा कामेन वा लोके सुरतप्रवृत्त्यर्थं वयं शुल्करूपादासिका दत्ताः । शुल्कं मार्गनिर्वाहकं द्रव्यं प्रतिबन्धनिवर्तकम् । सुरतं चेत् भगवत्येव निरुद्धं तिष्ठेत्, तदा लोके रसो न भविष्यतीत्यस्मद्द्वारा त्वत्तः तल्लोके प्रसृतं भवत्विति वयमागताः । तत् कार्यं दूरत एव स्थितम्, प्रत्युतास्मान्मारयसि । एवं सति सर्वमेव कामशास्त्रं व्यर्थं स्यात् । तृतीयः पुरुषार्थश्च न भवेत् । अतः सर्वथा यदर्थं वयं प्रेषितास्तत्कर्तव्यम् । अथवा । यदा कदाचित्कर्तव्यम्, इदानीं जीवयितव्या रूपप्राकट्येन । दृशो मारकत्वमुपपादयन्ति श्रीमुषेति । यस्तु चोरो भवति, स घातकोपि भवति । यथा यथा चौर्ये नैपुण्यम्, तथा तथा घातकत्वम् । तदर्थमाहुः उदरश्रीमुषेति । तत्रापि ये दुर्गजाताः, ते अतिनिपुणाः । तत्रापि जलदुर्गजाः । तत्सरसिजम् । तत्रापि ते दुर्ग एव तिष्ठन्ति । तत्रापि ते साधुजाताः प्रभवः । तत्रापि प्रकाशवति काले शीताद्युपद्रवरहिते । एवं देशकालस्वरूपादिभिः अशक्यचौर्यादपि पुरुषात् तदुदरवर्तिसर्वस्वनेता अन्तःस्थितप्राणान् साधारणगोपिकादीनां नेष्यतीति किमाश्चर्यम् । चौर्यं हि क्रियते बलिष्ठेनापकीर्त्यभावाय । तदत्र तु न भविष्यतीत्युक्तं किं वधः न इति । अथवा । अदृशा अदर्शनेन दर्शनमदत्वा निघ्नतः किं वधो न । सुरतार्थमागताः, तद्गतं दूरे, अन्तरा मरणमुपस्थितम् ।

तथा सति सुरतस्याप्रकटितत्वात् नाथत्वमपि न स्यात्। न हि योगी अश्वनिर्माण-समर्थोऽप्यश्वपतिरुच्यते। प्रकटयति चेत्, तदा तथा। किञ्च, **अस्मद्वधे किमाश्चर्यम्** तवादर्शने लक्ष्मीरपि न तिष्ठेत्। तदाहुः श्रीमुषेति। **उदरस्थिता** श्रीश्चेद् बहिरानीता, तदैव म्रियते, अपुष्टत्वात् आमगर्भवत्। यद्यपि तस्याः जीवने कालद्रव्य देशवस्तूनि बहून्येव सन्ति, तथापि त्वद्दर्शने न जीवति, तथा वयमपि। किञ्च। त्वं सर्वेषां वरान् प्रयच्छसि, अस्माँस्तु मारयिष्यसीति महदाश्चर्यम्। वरदाता हि प्रत्यक्षो भवति। अथवा। ते वयममूल्यदासिकाः, धर्मदासिकाः। अतो न हन्तव्याः। एवमनेकविधक्रौर्यभावनया काश्चिद्भगवन्तं उपालभन्ते।

अन्तःस्थितो रसः पुष्टो बहिश्चेन्न विनिर्गतः।
तदा पूर्णो नैव भवेदिति वाग्निर्गमस्तथा ॥२॥

अन्याः पुनः कोमलाः बहुधा त्वया रक्षिताः, इदानीमपि पालयेत्याहुः विष-जलाप्ययादिति।

विषजलाप्ययाद्व्यालराक्षसात् वर्षमारुताद्वैद्युतानलात्।
वृषमयात्मजाद्विश्वतो भयादृषभ ते वयं रक्षिता मुहुः ॥३॥

बिषजलं कालीयह्रदजलम्, तत्पीत्वा सर्व एव बालकाः गावश्च मृताः, ते पुन-र्जीविताः। व्यालाः सर्पाः कालियसुदर्शनादयः, राक्षसाः तृणावर्तादयः, तेषामेक-वद्भावः। तस्मादपि रक्षिताः। वर्षमारुतादिन्द्रकृतात्। तत्रैव वैद्युतानि अनलो दवाग्निश्च, तयोरप्येकवद्भावः। वृषो योऽयं मयात्मजः व्योमासुरः, तस्मादपि रक्षिताः। न तासां भूतभविष्यद्विषयकपदार्थज्ञाननिर्बन्धोऽस्ति, सर्वज्ञत्वात्। किम्बहुना विश्वत एव भयात्। पालने हेतुः ऋषभेति। भर्ता हि पालयत्येव। अतः सर्वदा पालक इति इदानीमपि पालयेत्यर्थः। ते च मारका बाह्याः, इदानीन्त-नस्त्वान्तर इति सर्वथा पालनीयाः ॥३॥

अन्याः पुनः भगवतो महानुभावत्वं ज्ञात्वा तस्य स्वरूपं कीर्तयन्ति। ततश्च ज्ञानिभ्यो यथा मोक्षं प्रयच्छति, तथास्मभ्यमपि अस्मदुचितं मोक्षं दास्यतीति, तं स्तुवन्ति न खल्विति।

न खलु गोपिकानन्दनो भवानखिलदेहिनामन्तरात्मदृक्।
विखनसार्थितो विश्वगुप्तये सख उदेयिवान्सात्वतां कुले ॥४॥

भगवतो नन्दसूनुत्वे सर्वे उपालम्भा युक्ता भवन्ति। तदेव नास्ति इति सर्वम-युक्तमुपालम्भनम्। खल्विति निश्चये। नात्र तिरोहितमिव। गोपिकायाः यशोदाया नन्दनः पुत्र इति न। तथा सति यथा तया स्वाधीनः कृतः, ज्ञातो वा, तथा गोपि-

कानामपि भवेत् । गोकुलस्वामिपुत्रत्वात् । तुल्यतायामेव हि विद्यायोनिसम्बन्धः । किञ्च, न केवलं भवान् वैकुण्ठाधिपतिः पुरुषोत्तमः, किन्तु अखिलदेहिनां सर्वेषामेवास्मदादीनामन्तरात्मानं अन्तःकरणं पश्यतीति । यद्यस्मद्धृदये तादृशं तापं पश्येत्, तदा प्रसन्न एव भवेत् । अतो नास्मिन्वक्तव्यं किञ्चित् । किञ्च, आगतश्चास्मदादीनां परिपालनार्थमेव । यदि जानीयात् एता नश्यन्तीति, तदा परिपालयेत् । रक्षणार्थं च प्रार्थित एव, न तु स्वेच्छया समागतः, तदाह विखनसार्थित इति । विखना ब्रह्मा, विशेषेण खनतीति सर्वथा वेदार्थविचारकः । अत एव वैखानसं मतं ब्रह्मणा कृतं भगवद्भजनप्रतिपादकम्, तेनैव मार्गेण पूजां भगवान् गृह्णातीति वेङ्कटादौ तथैव पूजा । अतः सर्वेषां पूजामपि ग्रहीतुं ब्रह्मणा प्रार्थितो विश्वगुप्तये इति मुख्यं प्रयोजनम् । एवमन्तरात्मत्वात् सर्वेषामेव जीवानां भवान् सखा । तादृशः लोके सख्यं प्रकटयितुं सात्त्वतां यादवानां वैष्णवानां वा कुले उदेयिवान्, प्रादुर्भूतः । अत एतदर्थमेवागतः । पूर्वमपि सखा यथेच्छमेव प्रेरयसि, आगतस्य पुनर्विशेषो वक्तव्यः । स चात्मनिवेदनरूपो भवति । अतो वयं किं विज्ञापयामः । यथोचितमेव कर्तव्यमिति भावः ।

अन्याः पुनः सात्त्विकसात्त्विक्यः राजसप्रधानाभ्यो विशिष्टाः, अप्रार्थितं च भगवान् न दास्यतीति भगवत्करस्य स्वशिरःसंबन्धं प्रार्थयन्ति विरचिताभयमिति ।

विरचिताभयं वृष्णिधुर्य ते शरणमीयुषां संसृतेर्भयात् ।
करसरोरुहं कान्त कामदं शिरसि धेहि नः श्रीकरग्रहम् ॥५॥

हे स्वामिन्, हृदयं स्फुटति । अतः यथा सर्वाङ्गे अप्यायनं भवति, तथा शिरसि करसरोरुहं धेहि । शीतलं हि कमलं भवति । तत्रापि सरसि जातम् । तत्रापि कर एव सरःस्थानं सरसिजस्थानं च । अत उद्धरणादिना न रसालतापगमः । कान्तेति संबोधनम् । प्रथमतः शिरसि हस्तस्थापनेन स्वाधीनीकरणं द्योतितम् । किञ्च, न केवलं हस्तस्तापमेव दूरीकरोति, किन्तु कामदं च । अभिलषितं कामं प्रयच्छति । ननु भगवान् पुरुषोत्तमः, योगिध्येयः, कथं स्त्रीणां स्पर्शं करिष्यति इति चेत्, तत्राह श्रीकरग्रहमिति । श्रियाः करस्य ग्रहो ग्रहणं येन । अतो भगवान् गृहस्थ इति । यत्र लक्ष्म्या हस्तं गृह्णाति, तत्रास्मच्छिरोग्रहणे किं भविष्यतीति भावः । ननु लक्ष्मीर्विवाहितेति विधिवशात् तस्या हस्तग्रहणम्, भवतीनां ग्रहणे को हेतुरिति चेत् तत्राहुः संसृतेर्भयात् शरणमीयुषां विरचिताभयमिति । यथा विधिर्विवाहे, तथैव शरणागतपालनेऽपि । विवाहापेक्षया शरणागतरक्षा महती । स साधारणधर्मः अयमीश्वरधर्म इति । नन्वयं निषिद्धः प्रकार इति कथं पालनमिति चेत्, तत्राहुः हे वृष्णिधुर्येति । वृष्णिर्हि यदुवंशोद्भवः बहुस्त्रीकः बहुवंशकर्ता । तद्वंशेऽपि भवान्

धुर्यः श्रेष्ठः । तत्रापि स्त्रियः संसारभयात् समागताः । न हि संसारः स्वभावत एव दुष्टः, किन्त्वसह्यदुःखहेतुरिति । तथा वयमपि महत् दुःखं प्राप्नुम इति दृष्टादृष्टद्वारा भवांस्तन्निवर्तक इति । अनेनैव निर्भयतापि सूचिता । अतः कान्तसम्बोधनात् भवानेव भर्ता । अतः स्त्रीणां व्रतमनुस्मरन् वाञ्छितं कुर्वित्यर्थः ॥५॥

ततः तामसी किञ्चिद्वैलक्षण्येन धाष्टर्येन तमेवार्थं प्रार्थयति व्रजजनार्तिहन्निति ।

व्रजजनार्तिहन् वीर योषितां निजजनस्मयध्वंसनस्मित ।
भज सखे भवत्किंकरीः स्म नो जलरुहाननं चारु दर्शय ॥६॥

हे भगवन्, एता वक्तुं न जानन्ति । मया तु निर्धारितमुच्यते । हे सखे इति अप्रतारणार्थं संबोधनम् । नः अस्मान् भजेति हितोपदेशः । ननु कथमेवं धाष्टर्यं निषिद्धं च बोध्यते, तत्राहुः भवत्किंकरीरिति । 'ये यथा मां प्रपद्यन्ते' इति हि तव प्रतिज्ञा । अतो यथा किंकर्यो वयं भवन्तं भजामः, तथा भवानपि भजतु । किंकरीत्वं तव प्रतिज्ञा च प्रसिद्धेत्याहुः स्मेति । न केवलमस्मद्भजने तव सैवैका प्रतिज्ञा हेतुः, किन्तु अन्येऽपि हेतवः सन्ति । प्रथमं अवतारप्रयोजनम् । व्रजजनार्तिहन्निति । व्रजजनानां आर्तिं हन्तीति तथा । नातः परमन्या आर्तिरस्ति । सामान्यप्रयोजनमेतत् । विशेषप्रयोजनमाहुः योषितां वीरेति । कृष्णो भगवान् । वीरैर्हि शूरा निराकरणीयाः, अन्यगतकामादयः । तत्र मुख्यः कामः । स च बहुविधः । अन्तर्बहिःपदार्थेन पूर्णेन पूरयित्वाश्रयाभावान्निवारणीयः । अत एव लोके दातारः कीर्तिमन्तो भवन्ति वीरेभ्यः । अतो भवान् महावीरः । अन्तःस्थितेनानन्देन अतिदरिद्राणां ब्रह्मणापि पूरयितुमशक्यानामिच्छापूरकः । अयं चार्थस्तव सर्वजनीनः । अतः योषितां वीरेति सम्बोधनम् । न हि कृष्णादन्यो जगति कश्चिदेवं सम्बोधनमर्हति, अपूर्णकामत्वात् । अतोऽवतारसामान्यविशेषप्रयोजनाभ्यां च नो भज । ननु सत्यम्, तथापि भवतीनामभिमानदोषनिवृत्त्यर्थं भजनं न क्रियते इति चेत्, तत्राह निजजनस्मयध्वंसनस्मितेति । निजजनाः सेवकाः तेषां स्मयो गर्वः, तस्य ध्वंसनार्थं स्मितं यस्य । निजजनानां स्मयदूरीकरणार्थं परित्यागो नोपायः, किन्तु तदर्थं स्मितमेव कर्तव्यम् । स्मितं हि मन्दहासः । "हासो जनोन्मादकरी च माया' । तस्या मन्दत्वं भक्तेष्वप्रवर्तनम् । नहि मायामोहव्यतिरेकेण कस्यचित्स्मयो भवति । अत एव हास्यसंकोच एव साधनम् । निजजनानामपि धर्म एव दुष्टः, न तु धर्मी । अन्यथा निजजनत्वमेव न स्यात् । इत्यलौकिकोपायः । लौकिकेऽपि तव हास्येन ता अपि आत्मानं तुल्यं मन्यन्ते । यदा पुनर्हास्ये संकोचः, तदैव तासां गर्वो निवर्तते । किञ्च, अभिमानो हि दोषः । स तावदेव तिष्ठति, यावत्तव स्मितयुक्तमाननं न पश्यति । नहि काचित्तादृशमप्याननं दृष्ट्वा स्वाभिमानं पालयितुं शक्ता । नन्वेतल्लोके अप्रसिद्धं साधनत्वेनेति कथं ज्ञातुं शक्यत इत्याशङ्क्याहुः जलरुहाननं चारु

दर्शयेति । जलरूहं कमलम्, तत्सदृशमाननममृतस्त्रावि । नह्यमृते पीते कस्यचिद्दोषस्तिष्ठतीति युक्तिः । साधनत्वे चेत्संदेहः, एकवारं प्रदर्श्य पश्येत्यर्थः । किञ्च, अभिमानो हि मनोधर्मः, तव आननं तु चारु मनोहरम् । नहि धर्मिणि हृते धर्मस्तिष्ठति । सख्युः सखिभजनं युक्तमेव ॥६॥

राजसी तु तत उत्तमा तमेवार्थं प्रकारान्तरेण प्रार्थयते प्रणतदेहिनामिति ।

प्रणतदेहिनां पापकर्षणं तृणचरानुगं श्रीनिकेतनम् ।
फणिफणार्पितं ते पदाम्बुजं कृणु कुचेषु नः कृन्धि हृच्छयम् ॥७॥

ते पदाम्बुजं नः कुचेषु कृणु कृणुष्व । छान्दसो लोपः । स्थापय । तस्य प्रयोजनं कृन्धि हृच्छयमिति । हृदये चौरवत् स्थितं कामं कृन्धि । कुचेष्विति समुदायाभिप्रायेण बहुवचनम् । विरहेण भिन्नान् वा मन्यन्ते । शिरसि हस्तदानेन निकटे समानयनमुक्तम् । ततो भजनेन सम्बंन्ध उक्तः । अनेन विपरीतरस उच्यते, बंधविशेषो वा तिर्यग्भेदः । एकवचनात् । तावता हि हृदयस्थितः कामो गच्छति । स्त्रीणां समूहे लीलाशयने परितः स्थितानां तथा संबन्धो भवतीति वा । ननु कर्कशेषु स्तनेषु कथं कोमलचरणस्थापनमिति चेत्, तत्राहुः फणिफणार्पितमिति । नहि कालियफणात् क्रूरा अस्मत्स्तनाः । तत्र यथा चरणस्थानं कृत्वा तदन्तर्गतो दोषो दूरीकृतः, एवमत्रापि कर्तव्यः । अम्बुजपदेन च प्रत्यक्षतस्तापहारकत्वम् । ननु तथापि स्त्रीणां वक्षसि चरणस्थापनमयुक्तमिति चेत्, तत्राहुः श्रीनिकेतनमिति । लक्ष्म्याः स्थानं तत् । लक्ष्मीः किल तत्र स्पर्शमर्हति, अन्यासु कः संदेह इति । ननु भवत्यो मूढाः, कथं भवतीनां हितं कतर्व्यमिति चेत्, तत्राहुः तृणचरानुगमिति । तृणचरा गावः, तेषामप्यनुगं पश्चाद्गच्छति तद्धितार्थम्, ते किं भगवता प्रेर्यमाणा इति तृणं परित्यज्यामृतं भक्षयन्ति । तेषां तृणमेवामृतम्, तथास्माकमपि काम एवामृतम् । नैतावता परमकृपालोः कश्चनार्थः क्षीयते । ननु भवतीनां जितेन्द्रियत्वाद्यभावात् पापमस्ति, तदपगमे पश्चात्पदं स्थापयिष्यामीति चेत्, तत्राहुः प्रणतदेहिनां पापकर्षणमिति । वयं प्रकर्षेण नताः, नास्माभिः प्रकारान्तरेण निवर्तयितुं शक्यते, किन्तु तव चरणप्रसादादेव नम्राणां पापं गच्छति । तत्रापि देहिनः । प्रकर्षेण नतत्वेन धर्ममार्गादिपरित्याग उक्तः । देहाभिमानस्य विद्यमानत्वात् न ज्ञानमपि । प्रणतानां हि नाप्यधोगतिः । अतस्तव पदमेव तेषां पापनाशकम्, चिन्तितम्, दृष्टम्, स्पृष्टम् आलिंगितं वा ॥७॥

इममेवार्थं ततोऽप्युत्तमा प्रकारान्तरेण प्रार्थयते मधुरया गिरेति ।

मधुरया गिरा वल्गुवाक्यया बुधमनोज्ञया पुष्करेक्षण ।
विधिकरीरिमा वीर मुह्यतीरधरसीधुनाप्याययस्व नः ॥८॥

हस्तेन च स्वरूपेण पदा चोपकृतिर्मता ।
मुखेन चोपकारो हि कर्तव्य इति ता जगुः ॥१॥

पूर्वोक्तमपि सर्वं हि यावत्स्पष्टं न भाषते ।
तावत्सरसतां याति न कदाचिदिति स्थितिः ॥२॥

हे स्वामिन्, मधुरया गिरा मुह्यतीरिमा गोपीराप्याययस्व । मोहो हि मरणपूर्वावस्थारूपः । तासामाप्यायने हेतुः विधिकरीरिति । आज्ञाकारिणीः सेवाकारिणीर्वा । असामर्थ्यं तु तव नास्तीत्याहुः हे वीरेति । शौर्यं हि आर्तानामार्तिनिराकरणार्थम् । इमा इति प्रदर्शनेन क्षणमात्रविलम्बेन मरिष्यन्ति इति सूचितम् । ननु वाङ्मात्रेण कथं मोहनिवृत्तिरिति चेत्, तत्राहुः मधुरयेति । मोहो हि मायारूपः । स भवत्स्वरूपेणैव निवर्तते सच्चिदानन्दरूपेण । तत्र तव वाणी आनन्दरूपेत्याह मधुरयेति । मध्वसाधारणो रसः । तद्युक्ता मधुरा । वल्गु मनोहरं वाक्यं यत्र । वाक्यस्य मनोहरत्वं सत्यप्रियप्रतिपादकत्वेन । अतः सद्रूपता निरूपिता । बुधानां मनोज्ञा आह्लादकारिणी । अनेन ज्ञानरूपा निरूपिता । ते हि ज्ञानेनैव रता भवन्ति । मुखे नयने वर्तेते इति तयोरपि व्यापारं कृत्वैव वक्तव्यमित्याहुः पुष्करेक्षणेति । कमलवत् परतापापहारके ईक्षणे यस्य । किञ्च, अधरसीधुना अधरामृतेन च आप्याययस्व । वक्तव्याः द्रष्टव्याः पाययितव्या इति । मूर्छितानां हि मूर्छानिवारणार्थं महामन्त्राः पठ्यन्ते, कमलादीनि च शीतलद्रव्याणि स्थाप्यन्ते । सर्वथा असाध्ये अमृतमपि पाय्यते । अतिगोप्यान् वा रसान् पाययन्ति । इयं तु मूर्छा नाल्पेन निवारयितुं शक्येति वीरेति सम्बोधनम् । अनेनान्तिमावस्था प्रदर्शिता । पूर्वप्रार्थिताश्चार्थाः स्मारकत्वेनाधिकमूर्छाहेतवो जाताः । ॥८॥

एवं पदार्थचतुष्टयं संप्रार्थ्य तददाने स्वयमेव हेतुमाशङ्क्य परिहरन्ति तव कथेति ।

तव कथामृतं तप्तजीवनं कविभिरीडितं कल्मषापहम् ।
श्रवणमङ्गलं श्रीमदाततं भुवि गृणन्ति ते भूरिदा जनाः ॥९॥

ननु सर्वमिदं प्रार्थितं भक्तेभ्यो देयम्, नत्वभक्तेभ्यः । अभक्तत्व च विरहेऽपि जीवनादवसीयते । भगवांस्तु सर्वनिरपेक्षः । न तस्य भवज्जीवनेन कार्यम् । लक्ष्मीसदृश्यो यस्य कोटिशो दास्यः । 'अतस्त्वयि धृतासव' इत्यप्यसंगतम् । तस्माद्व्यर्थमेव प्रार्थनमित्याशङ्क्य परिहरति । नेदं जीवनमस्मत्कृतिसाध्यम्, किन्तु तव कथा विरहेण प्राणानां गमने प्रतिबन्धं करोति । कथायाः पुनः यथा तव सामर्थ्यं तथा । सापि षड्गुणात्मिका मोक्षदायिनी परमानन्दरूपा च, तदाहुः । तव कथा अमृतमिव । अमृतं भगवद्रसात्मकम् । सर्वेषां मरणादिनिवर्तकं यद्रूपं तदमृतशब्देनोच्यते । अतो

मोक्षदातृत्वं परमानन्दरूपता च सिद्धा। इदानीं षड्गुणान्निरूपयन्ति तप्तमित्यादि-षड्भिः पदैः। तप्ता ये संसारे तेषां जीवनं यस्मात्। अमृतं हि तापनिवर्तकं प्रसिद्धमेव। वैराग्यं च भगवतो ज्ञानं वा सर्वतापनिवर्तकम्। यत्संस्कारयोग्यं तत् ज्ञानेन नश्यति। यदयोग्यं तत्परित्यागेन। अत एव स्मार्तैः संस्काराशक्तैः परित्याग एव बोध्यते। अतो ज्ञानं वैराग्यं च तापनाशके भवतः। आपाततस्तापनाशकत्वं जलादावपि वर्तत इति तदर्थमाह कविभिरीडितमिति। कविभिः सर्वैरेव शब्दार्थरसिकैः ज्ञानिभिरीडितं ज्ञानं वैराग्यं वा। आपाततः स्त्रीषु तथात्वमस्तीति तद्व्यावृत्त्यर्थमाहुः कल्मषापहमिति। कल्मषं पापमपहन्तीति। 'ऐश्वर्यस्य समग्रस्य धर्मस्ये'त्यपि क्वचित्पाठः। अलौकिकसाधकं च वीर्यं महत् तद्धर्मरूपमेव भवति। धर्म्यं च पुनः कल्मषनिवर्तकं भवति। पूर्वोक्तधर्मविशिष्टं च। कथायाश्च तथात्वं सर्वत्र प्रसिद्धम्। प्रायश्चित्तादीनामपि आपाततस्तथात्वमस्तीति तद्व्यावृत्त्यर्थमाह श्रवणमङ्गलमिति। तद्गोमयादिलेपनात्मकमुपवासात्मकं च स्वरूपतोप्यमङ्गलम्। घोरात्मकत्वात् श्रवणेप्यमङ्गलम्। इदं तूदारचरितम्, श्रुतमेवानन्दं जनयतीत्यनुभवसिद्धत्वात् श्रवणमङ्गलम्। तेन कीर्तितुल्यता निरूपिता। पुत्रजन्मादिश्रवणस्यापि किञ्चिद्धर्मसाम्यात् श्रवणमङ्गलत्वमाशङ्क्य तद्व्यावृत्त्यर्थमाह श्रीमदिति। तद्धनव्ययसाधकम्, न तु धनसाधकम्। कथामृतं तु लक्ष्म्या अप्यपेक्षितत्वात् तद्युक्तं भवति। तेन श्रोतुर्वक्तुश्च तत्सिद्धिः। राज्यप्राप्तिश्रवणं तथा भवतीति तद्व्यावृत्त्यर्थमाह आततमिति। आ सर्वतः ततं व्याप्तम्। राज्यादिकं तु परिच्छिन्नम्। भगवत ऐश्वर्यं तु न तथा। अन्तर्बहिः सर्वेषां सर्वथा व्याप्तमिति। कथामृतं च पुनः सर्वलोकान् व्याप्य तिष्ठति, स्वसामर्थ्यं सर्वत्रैव सम्पादयति। तस्मात् स्वरूपतो धर्मतश्च भवत्सदृशी भवत्कथेति तया कृत्वा जीवनम्, न तु स्वतः। अनेनोत्कर्षोप्युक्तः। त्वं कदाचिन्मारयस्यपि, कथामृतं तस्मिन्नपि काले जीवयतीति। भगवान् स्वतन्त्रः, कथामृतं परतन्त्रमित्येतावान् विशेषः। त्वं च अवतारे ब्रह्मादिभिः प्रार्थित आगच्छसि, आगतोऽपि तिरोभवसि। कथा तु समागता न तिरोभवति। अत एव तादृशं कथामृतं ये भुवि गृणन्ति, त एव भूरिदाः बह्वर्थदातारः। य इति प्रसिद्धाः व्यासादयः। भूरिदाश्च ते अजनाश्च। ते केवलं भगवद्रूपाः। जननादिदोषरहिता वा। परं विरलममृतं केवलं मरणोपस्थितौ तान्निवर्तकमेवेति, न तु संभूयैकत्र रसजनकम्। रसपिण्डयोरिव तव कथायाश्च विशेषः। अन्यथा कथार्थमेव यत्नः कृतः स्यात्। परं विरहे मरणनिर्वतकत्वेन तदुपयोग इति भगवत्त्वेन स्तूयते। अतस्तैर्भगवत्कथाकथकैः बहु दत्तमिति तद्वशात् जीवनम्। एतत्सात्त्विक्याः ॥९॥

तामस्याः वचनमाह प्रहसितमिति।

प्रहसितं प्रिय प्रेमवीक्षितं विहरणं च ते ध्यानमङ्गलम्।
रहसि संविदो या हृदिस्पृशः कुहक नो मनः क्षोभयन्ति हि ॥१०॥

यद्यपि कथया स्थातुं शक्यते, यदि त्वदीयैर्धर्मैः क्षोभो नोत्पादितः स्यात् । यथा भगवति षड्गुणाः सन्ति, तथा षट् व्यामोहका अपि गुणाः सन्ति। अन्यथा कथयैव चरितार्थता स्यात् । तदर्थं भगवान् मायया कुहकलीलामपि करोतीति स्वस्वभावदोषात् भगवति तथा स्फूर्तिरिति । यथा ज्वरितस्य अन्ने विरसता-प्रतीतिः । अत आह । तव प्रहसितादिकं नो मनः क्षोभयतीति । प्रकर्षेण हसितम् । स्वभावत एव खिन्ना तां त्यक्त्वा अन्यया सह स्थित इति । ततश्चेत् समागत्य प्रकर्षेण हसति, सुतरां क्षोभं प्राप्नोति । प्रियेति सम्बोधनात् तव सम्बन्धोऽपि स्मृतः क्षोभजनको जायते । अत एव यासां न सम्बन्धः, तासां न क्षोभ । किञ्च, तव यत्प्रेमवीक्षितं प्रेम्णा वीक्षितं तदपि क्षोभयति । स्मृतं सत् । अन्यविषयकं वा विश्वासजनकत्वाद्वा अन्तःकपटरूपमिति क्षोभजनकम् । अन्यथा कार्ये विसंवादो न स्यात् । मनस उत्तोलकं वा । आशाजनकम् । आशया च श्रमः । तव विहरणमपि क्षोभजनकम् । विहरणं यच्चलनं वेणुवादनादिना । रसो भगवदीय आकाराद्बहिः स्थाप्यत इति विशेषेण हरणं यस्मादिति त्रिभङ्गललितादिकं भवति । तत्पूर्वम-स्माभिर्ध्यातमिति ध्यानं एव मङ्गलं त्वल्लक्षणं शुभफलं प्रयच्छतीति । तदपीदानीं क्षोभजनकम्, तिरोहितत्वात् । त इति सर्वत्र सम्बन्धः । अन्यन्माययापि करोतीति मुख्यतया अत्रोक्तिः । एवं रूपसम्बन्धे चतुष्टयं क्षोभकमुक्तम् । नामसम्बन्धि द्वयमाह रहसि संविद इति । या हृदिस्पृश इति । रहसि एकान्ते संविदो ज्ञानरूपाः भगवद्वाचः । ज्ञानान्येव वा शास्त्रजनितानि बन्धाद्यभिज्ञारूपाणि । तत्रापि या वाचो हृदिस्पृशः हृदयगामिन्यो भवन्ति । अस्मदनुगुणा एव बन्धसंविदो वा । न तु केवलं नायकानुगुणाः । अत एवमेते सुखहेतवोपि , भवान् वञ्चयति चेत् , तदा क्षोभं जनयन्ति । अयमर्थः सर्वानुभवसिद्ध इत्याह हीति ॥

राजस्या वचनमाह चलसीति ।

चलसि यद्व्रजाच्चारयन्पशून् नलिनसुन्दरं नाथ ते पदम् ।
शिलतृणाङ्कुरैः सीदतीति नः कलिलतां मनः कान्त गच्छति ॥११॥

अस्माकं तु स्नेहवशात् त्वद्विषयिकासमीचीनेऽपि खेदबुद्धिर्जायते, तव तु नास्मद्विषयिणी सत्यखेदेपि जायत इति न्यायविरोधमिवाह । यत् व्रजान्पशून् चारयन् चलसि । तत्र चलने नलिनापेक्षयापि सुन्दरं कोमलं, हे नाथ, ते पदं मार्ग-स्थितैः शिलतृणाङ्कुरैः, शिलाः पाषाणाः, तृणानि, अङ्कुराः दर्भादीनाम्, तामसानि सात्त्विकानि राजसानि । अथवा शिलारूपं यतृणं शिलतृणं कठिनतृणम्, तस्याङ्कुरैः अतिपरुषतीक्ष्णैः सीदतीति क्लेशं प्राप्नोतीति, वस्तुतो न प्राप्नोत्येव, तथापि हे कान्त भर्तः मनः कलिलतां गच्छति । व्रजादिति प्रातरारभ्य खेदः सूचितः । चलनादेव च खेदः । अतः प्रथमतस्तदेवोक्तम् । वस्तुतस्तु तव पदे अस्मत्स्थानं विहाय न गच्छतः,

तथापि भवानेव तथा चालयति । किञ्च, व्रजस्थिता गावः अरण्ये नीयन्ते, तासां चारणं न मार्गगमनेन भवति । अतः अमार्गेऽपि गन्तव्यम् । भूम्यादीनां अनुग्रहार्थं न पादुकाग्रहणम्, पाल्यानां चर्म च न परिधेयम् । अतो नलिनसुन्दरं पदमेव शिलतृणाङ्कुरैः सीदति । जले एव स्थातुं योग्यम् । जलपूर्णे वा । नलिनादपि सुन्दरं चेत्, लक्ष्म्यामस्मासु वा स्थातुं योग्यम् । नाथेति सम्बोधनात् बहव एवात्रार्थे नियोज्याः सन्ति, तथापि स्वयमेव गच्छसीति । वने हि त्रिविधा भूमिः, पर्वतरूपा अरण्यरूपा कच्छरूपा च । तत्र क्रमेणैकमेकत्र भवति, सर्वं वा सर्वत्र । अवसादः अशक्त्या एकत्र स्थितिः । तदा चिन्ता भवति । स्वयं गत्वा स्वहृदये स्थापनीयमिति । मनःकान्तेति च । तेन मनः स्थापितमपि न तिष्ठतीति ॥११॥

एवं सप्तविधा अनन्यपूर्वा निरूपिताः । चतस्रश्च ताः । अतः परं क्रमेण षट् ता एव निरूप्यन्ते । तत्र प्रथमं राजसतामस्या वचनम् । ता हि बहिर्गत्वा द्रष्टुमशक्ताः । अतो यदा संध्यायां भगवानायाति, तदा भगवन्तं दृष्ट्वा मनसि कामो भवति । ततो बन्धप्रार्थना अधरामृतप्रार्थना च रजसा सत्त्वेन च भविष्यतः । अनन्यपूर्वाणां तु नित्य एव कामः । दिनपरिक्षये इति ।

दिनपरिक्षये नीलकुन्तलैर्वनरुहाननं बिभ्रदावृतम् ।
धनरजस्वलं दर्शयत् मुहुर्मनसि नः स्मरं वीर यच्छसि ॥१२॥

दिनपरिक्षये संध्याकाले । क्षयोक्त्या दिने द्वेष्यत्वं ज्ञाप्यते । रजोगुणस्यायं समयः, कामस्य च कालः । नीलकुन्तला भ्रमरा इव रसबोधकाः । ये हि मुखकमललावण्यामृतं पिबन्ति, ते उद्बोधका भवन्ति । अतस्तैरावृतं वनरुहवत् कमलवत् आननं बिभ्रत्, हे वीर, नः मनसि स्मरं यच्छसि । (सन्ध्यायां नीलवर्णैरावृतत्वे तत्प्रभाव्याप्तत्वं भवतीति तदुक्त्या वनरुहोक्त्या च कुवलयाभत्वं ज्ञाप्यते । तथा च प्रियामुखेन्दुदर्शनेनोत्तरोत्तरमधिकविकासवत्त्वमितः पूर्वमतादृशत्वं च ज्ञाप्यते । तेन प्रियस्य सर्वास्वासक्तिः सूचिता भवति । अत एव जलपदं विहाय वनपदमुक्तम् । तेन वने यावस्था तां ज्ञापयितुं तान् धर्मान् बिभ्रदेवाननं दर्शयतीति ध्वन्यते ।) धनेन गोभिः रजस्वलम् । मुहुश्च प्रदर्शयन् । मध्ये मार्गं गच्छन् उभयतः स्थिता गोपीः पर्यायेण पश्यति । अतो मुहुः प्रदर्शनम् । अग्रे गच्छन् पुनः पुनर्व्याघुट्य पश्यतीति वा तथा । तादृग्दर्शनं स्वापेक्षाज्ञापकमिति स्मरजनकम् । निरन्तरदर्शनेन तत्रैव रसास्वादनमिति न स्मरोत्पत्त्यवसरः स्यात् । अतो वारंवारं प्रदर्शनं स्मराग्नेः संधुक्षणमिव भवति । तादृशं कृत्वा तत्पूरणार्थं तन्निराकरणार्थं वा युद्धमवश्यं कर्तव्यम् । तत्सूचयन्ति वीरेति । धनेन रजस्वलं च श्रमसूचकं भवति । श्रमनिवृत्तिश्चास्माभिरेव । वनरुहमिति । वन एवैतत्सर्वथा भोग्यम् । अतोऽत्रैव समागमनम् । अनेन गृहे रतिं दास्यामीति पक्षो व्यावर्तितः । बिभ्रदिति बलात्कारेण तामेवावस्थां स्थापयति ।

यदि मुखसंमार्जनं कृत्वा समागच्छेत्, तदा प्रसन्नमुखदर्शनात् ज्ञानं वा भवेत् । धनसम्बन्धि रज इति काम एव, न तु क्रोधः । यथा पात्रं धृत्वा तत्स्थितमन्नं भोगार्थं दीयते, तथा मुखं धृत्वा तत्रत्यो रसः कामात्मा मनसि स्थाप्यत इति मुखधारणस्य हेतुत्वम् । अतो भोगार्थं दत्त इति भोगः करणीयः । अयं काम आगन्तुक इति नास्यान्येन पूरणं भवति ॥१२॥

तत उत्तमा अनन्यपूर्वावत्स्तनयोश्चरणधारणं प्रार्थयन्ति प्रणतेति ।

प्रणतकामदं पद्मजार्चितं धरणिमण्डनं ध्येयमापदि ।
चरणपङ्कजं शन्तमं च ते रमण नः स्तनेष्वर्पयाधिहन् ॥१३॥

अत एव न पौनरुक्त्यम् । परं पूर्वापेक्षयात्र चरणमाहात्म्यमधिकम् । गुणाधायकमेतत् । पूर्वं तु दोषनिवर्तकम् । हे रमण रतिकर्तः । नः स्तनेषु चरणपङ्कजमर्पय । प्रयोजनमाहुः आधिहन् इति । आर्तिहन् इति वा । हृदयतापः चिन्ता च निवारणीया । दृष्टोपकारेणैव तापो गमिष्यति । अस्माभिर्हृदये स्थापितं न बहिः समायाति। अतस्त्वया बहिः स्थापनीयम्। चरणपङ्कजस्यापि भगवत इव षड्गुणानाह। तत्र प्रथममैश्वर्यम्। प्रणतकामदमिति। प्रकर्षेण ये नता अनन्यशरणाः तेषां कामदमभिलषितार्थदातृ । ईश्वर एव तथाविधो भवति । तत्रत्यः कामः स्तब्धैर्ग्रहीतुं न शक्यत इति प्रणतत्वमुक्तम्। पद्मजार्चितमिति। धर्मरूपता निरूपिता। ब्रह्मप्रार्थनयैवात्रागतमिति । कीर्तिरूपतामाह धरणिमण्डनमिति धरण्या मण्डनमलङ्करणरूपं श्रीरूपं वा। आपदि ध्येयं श्रीरूपं कीर्तिरूपं वा । पङ्कजसाम्यात् स्वरूपोत्कर्ष उक्तः। शन्तमं कल्याणतमम्। ज्ञानरूपम्। आर्तिहन्निति सम्बोधनात् ते चरणपङ्कजमिति सम्बन्धनिरूपणाद् वैराग्ययुक्तं च । रमणेतीष्टप्रापकः । आर्तिहन्नित्यनिष्टनिवारकः । अथवा । यल्लोके पञ्चविधमुपकारं करोति, तदस्मास्वेकमेव करोत्विति प्रार्थ्यते। प्रणतासु कामं ददाति। तत्पूर्वमुक्तं 'मनसि नः स्मरं वीर यच्छसी'ति। प्रकर्षेण नम्रेषु वा कामं द्यति खण्डयति। पद्मजेन पद्मजया वा अर्चितम्। ऐश्वर्यार्थं कामार्थं या पद्मजैः अर्चितम्। तत्तुल्यं वा। अन्यथा तानि चरणपङ्कजजन्म कथं प्राप्नुयुः। धरण्यपि स्त्री अनलङ्कृता न भुज्यत इति तस्यां पदस्थापनम्। भगवदपेक्षयापि चरणो महान्। आपदि ध्यानमात्रेणैवापदं दूरीकरोतीति । यथैतेषां सर्वोपकारकर्तृ, तथास्माकमपि करोत्विति प्रार्थना। अनेन सर्व एव सुरतबन्धा आक्षिप्ताः ॥१३॥

तदनन्तरं तत उत्तमाः प्रार्थयन्ते सुरतेति ।

सुरतवर्धनं शोकनाशनं स्वरितवेणुना सुष्ठु चुम्बितम् ।
इतररागविस्मारणं नृणां वितर वीर नस्तेऽधरामृतम् ॥१४॥

अधरामृतं वितरेति । अत्राप्यधरामृतं गुणाधायकम् । एतस्य चतुर्गुणत्वमेव विवक्षितम् । ज्ञानवैराग्ययोरत्रानुपयोगात् । तस्यैश्वर्यमाह सुरतवर्धनमिति । गोपिकासु परिच्छिन्नः कामः अपरिच्छिन्नेन सह संयोगे क्लिष्टो भवति । यथा रसाः क्षुदुद्बोधका भवन्ति, तथायं रसः कामोद्बोधकः । किञ्च, न केवलमयं काममेव पोषयति, किन्तु सर्वानिवान्तःकरणदोषान्निवारयति । अतः शोकनाशकत्वं ज्ञान-वैराग्यरूपता च निरूपिता । ऐश्वर्यधर्मरूपता च । यशोरूपतामाह । स्वरितो नादयुक्तो यो वेणुः, तेन सुष्ठु चुम्बितमिति । यशो हि नादज्ञैः कीर्त्यते । वेणुश्च परमभक्त इति तेनापि चुम्बितमेव । न तु पीतम् । इतररागविस्मारणमिति श्रियो रूपम् । सा हि सर्वं विस्मारयतीति । स्वतः पुरुषार्थत्वेन प्रमेयबलमुक्तम् । पूर्वेण प्रमाणबलम् । शोक-नाशनमिति फलबलम् । सुरतवर्धनमिति साधनबलम् । एवं चतुर्विधपुरुषार्थप्रदं स्वतः पुरुषार्थरूपम् । नृणामस्माकमधिकारिणां दुर्लभपुरुषार्थानां वा । यद्यपीदं देयं न भवति, तथापि वितरणगुणेन दातुं शक्यत इति वितरेत्युक्तम् । वीरेति सम्बोधनात् शौर्यं नान्यथा संभवतीति निरूपितम् ॥१४॥

एवं त्रिविधा निरूप्य, पुनस्तामस्यः त्रिविधा निरूप्यन्ते । देवनिन्दिकाः सात्त्विकतामस्यः । भगवन्निन्दिकाः तामसतामस्यः । स्वनिन्दिका राजसतामस्य इति । अटतीति ।

अटति यद्भवानह्नि काननं त्रुटिर्युगायते त्वामपश्यताम् ।
कुटिलकुन्तलं श्रीमुखं च ते जड उदीक्षतां पक्ष्मकृद् दृशाम् ॥१५॥

भवान् अह्नि काननं यदटति, तत्र दिवसे त्रुटिः युगायते । तत्र निमित्तं त्वाम-पश्यतामिति । यदा पुनः पश्यामः, तदा कुटिलकुन्तलं श्रीमुखं ते उदीक्षतां नोऽस्माकं यः पक्ष्मकृद् ब्रह्मा स जडः । यथा देवानां पक्ष्म न करोति, अलौकिकद्रष्टृत्वात्, तदपेक्षयाप्यत्यलौकिकद्रष्टृत्वादस्माकमपि पक्ष्मकरणमनुचितम् । अतोनुचितकरणात् जडः । देवा हि बहुकालं जीवन्ति, तथा वयमपि । त्रुटिर्युगायत इति । त्रुटिशब्दो-स्त्रियाम् । यदि सार्थकं गमनं भवेत्, तथापि न काचिच्चिन्ता । परमह्नि कानन-मेवाटति, न तु कानने कश्चन पुरुषार्थः । अस्माकं च न बहिर्गमनं संभवति । एवं देवत्वं भगवता संपादितम् । मूर्खो ब्रह्मा तादृशीनां पक्ष्मकृत् ॥१५॥

तदपेक्षया हीना आहुः पतीति ।

पतिसुतान्वयभ्रातृबान्धवानतिविलङ्घ्य तेऽन्त्यच्युतागताः ।
गतिविदस्तवोद्गीतमोहिताः कितव योषितः कस्त्यजेन्निशि ॥१६॥

हे अच्युत, स्वतः कामनिवृत्तिभयरहित । पतिः, सुताः, अन्वयो वंशः, भ्रातरः,

बान्धवाः संबन्धिनः, एते सर्वथा अविलङ्घ्याः, तानप्यतिविलङ्घ्य ते अन्ति समागताः । त्वं सर्वेषां गतिं जानासीति गतिवित् । सर्वैर्यावती गतिः संपाद्यते, तां भवानेव दास्यतीति । वयं वा गतिविदः । तेषां भजने भगवद्भजने च तारतम्यविदः । किञ्च, तव उद्गीतेन च मोहिताः । अतो मोहयित्वा समानीय उभयभ्रंशार्थं अरण्ये निशि योषितः कस्त्यजेत् । सर्वदैव स्त्रियो न त्याज्याः । सुतरामरण्ये । सुतरां निशि । यदर्थं वा समाहूताः, तदप्यदत्वेत्यभिप्रायेण सम्बोधनम् । कितवानां वयं संबन्धिन्यः । अतोस्माकं तेषु न प्रवेशः ॥१६॥

तत उत्तमाः आत्मानमेव निन्दन्ति रहसीति ।

रहसि संविदं हृच्छयोदयं प्रहसिताननं प्रेमवीक्षणम् ।
बृहदुरः श्रियो वीक्ष्य धाम ते मुहुरतिस्पृहं मुह्यते मनः ॥१७॥

नो मनः अतिस्पृहं सत् मुह्यत इति । तत्र कारणत्रयं गुणत्रयसहितम् ।

वाक्यं हास्यमुरश्चैव कामानन्दाधिकारिणः ।

रहसि एकान्ते या संविद् ज्ञानं वा । पूर्ववत् हृच्छयस्य कामस्य उदयो येन तादृशम् । प्रहसितयुक्तमाननं प्रेमपूर्वकं वीक्षणं च यस्मिन् । श्रियो धाम बृहदुरः । भगवद्रूपस्य वा षड्गुणत्वमुच्यते । रहसि संविदो यस्मादिति । एतादृशं त्वाम् । हृच्छयस्य उदयो यस्मात् । प्रहसितमाननं यस्य । प्रेमपूर्वकं वीक्षणं यस्य । बृहदुरः श्रीधाम च वीक्ष्य । प्रमाणादिबलरूपता भगवद्रूपे निरूपिता । वक्षसि च स्वस्थित्यर्थं यशः श्रीश्च निरूपिता । मुखदर्शनेनैव प्रहसितयुक्तत्वात् पूर्वस्थित्यभावः । ततः कामः । प्रेमवीक्षणेन च तस्य स्थिरीकरणम् । ततः स्वयोग्यता । ततो भोगचातुर्ये प्रथमविशेषणेन । एवं सर्वं भविष्यतीति अतिस्पृहायुक्तं मनः मुह्यते, केवलं मोहं प्राप्नोति, पदार्थालाभात् मुहुर्मूर्च्छा समायातीति जीवनमरणान्यतराभावात् धिग्जीवनमित्यर्थः ॥१७॥

पुनरनन्यपूर्वा एतावत्कालं मनोरथाभिनिविष्टा किञ्चित्प्रार्थयते व्रजवनौकसामिति ।

व्रजवनौकसां व्यक्तिरंग ते वृजिनहन्त्र्यलं विश्वमङ्गलम्
त्यज मनाक् च नस्त्वत्स्पृहात्मनां स्वजनहृद्रुजां यन्निषूदनम् ॥१८॥

इयं ते व्यक्तिः व्रजवनौकसां वृजिनहन्त्री पापनाशिका । विश्वस्याप्यत्यर्थं मङ्गलरूपम् । दोषनिवर्तकं विशेषाकारेणास्माकमेव । गुणाधायकं सर्वेषाम् । अत एतादृशं मनाक् त्यज । त्यागावश्यकत्वे हेतुः त्वत्स्पृहात्मनामिति । त्वय्येव स्पृहायुक्त आत्मा अन्तःकरणं यासाम् । किं त्यक्तव्यमित्याशङ्कायामाह स्वजनेति ।

स्वजनानां गोपिकानां हृद्रुजां हृदयरोगाणां कामरूपाणां यदेव निषूदनं भवति, नितरां सूदनं नाशनं यस्मात् । केषाञ्चित्पापनाशकः, केषाञ्चित्फलदाता, तादृशोस्माकं रोगनिवर्तको भवत्विति ॥१८॥

काचिद्राजसतामसी सखेदमाह यत्त इति ।

यत्ते सुजातचरणाम्बुरुहं स्तनेषु भीताः शनैः प्रिय दधीमहि कर्कशेषु ।
तेनाटवीमटसि तद्व्यथते न किंस्वित् कूर्पादिभिर्भ्रमति धीर्भवदायुषां नः ॥१९॥

इति श्रीभागवते महापुराणे दशमस्कन्धे अष्टाविंशतितमोऽध्यायः ॥२८॥

सुजातं यच्चरणाम्बुरुहं चरणकमलं भीताः सत्यः स्तनेषु शनैर्दधीमहि । शनैर्धारणे हेतुः कर्कशेष्विति । प्रियेति सम्बोधनात् स्नेहाद्धारणम् । सुजातमिति तथा महत् सम्यक्प्रकारोत्पन्नं शीतलं सुगन्धि तापनाशकं भवति । अतः स्तनेषु स्थापनम् । प्रियत्वात् धाष्टर्च्येन स्थापनम् । तेनैवातिकोमलेन अस्मान् त्यक्त्वा अस्मद्दोषेण इदानीमटवीमटसि । स्वयमदुःखेन स्थित्वा यद्यन्यस्मै दुःखं दातुं शक्नुयात्, तर्हि प्रयच्छेत्, न तु स्वयमपि दुःखं प्राप्य । तत्रास्माकं संदेहः, किं व्यथते, न वेति । स्विदित्युत्प्रेक्षायाम् । किं न व्यथते, अपि तु व्यथत एव । कूर्पादिभिः शर्करादिभिः । कूर्पशब्देन विषमाः शर्करा उच्यन्ते । तर्हि व्यथत एव, कथमुत्प्रेक्ष्यते, तत्राह भ्रमति धीरिति । बुद्धिः केवलं परिभ्रमति । यदि व्यथत इति निश्चयः स्यात्, तदा बुद्धिः शान्तैव भवेत् । पुनर्यदायाति तेन संदेहः । तत्र हेतुः भवदायुषामिति । भवल्लीलार्थमेवायुर्येषाम् । पूर्वं तु खेदेन मनःपीडा निरूपिता, इदानीं तु मूर्च्छा निरूप्यत इत्यन्तस्थितिः । एवं सर्वासां मूर्च्छापर्यन्तं स्थितिर्ज्ञातव्या । पुनर्लीलाप्रवेशे प्रलापः , पुनः स्वरूपस्थितौ गानमिति । एवं साधनपरीक्षयोर्यावत्, तावत्तासां तापो निरूपितः ॥१९॥

इति श्रीभागवतसुबोधिन्यां श्रीमल्लक्ष्मणभट्टात्मजश्रीमद्वल्लभदीक्षितविरचितायां दशमस्कन्धविवरणेऽष्टाविंशाध्यायविवरणम् ॥२८॥

श्रीकृष्णाय नमः

एकोनत्रिंशोऽध्यायः ।

एकोनत्रिंशकेऽध्याये प्रसादं भगवत्कृतम् ।
रोदनात् प्राप्य तुष्टास्ता निर्णयज्ञा इतीर्यते ॥१॥

नहि साधनसम्पत्त्या हरिस्तुष्यति कस्यचित् ।
भक्तानां दैन्यमेवैकं हरितोषणसाधनम् ॥२॥

सन्तुष्टः सर्वदुःखानि नाशयत्येव सर्वतः ॥
अतो निर्णयवाक्यानि भजनार्थं न्यरूपयत् ॥३॥

एवं पूर्वाध्यायान्ते तासां स्तुतिमुक्त्वा, ततः पूर्वाध्याये तासां प्रलापमुक्त्वा, उभयमप्युपसंहरन् तयोरसाधनतायां जातायां रोदनं कृतवत्य इत्याह इतीति ।

इति गोप्यः प्रगायन्त्यः प्रलपन्त्यश्च चित्रधा ।
रुरुदुः सुस्वरं राजन् कृष्णदर्शनलालसाः ॥१॥

पूर्वोक्तप्रकारेण सर्वा एव गोप्यः प्रगायन्त्यः प्रलपन्त्यश्च जाताः । अस्माभिरेकः प्रकार उक्तः । तास्तु चित्रधा विलापयुक्ता जाताः । यदा तयोरसाधनत्वं जातम्, तदा सर्वाः सम्भूय महद्रोदनं कृतवत्यः । रोदने निमित्तमाह कृष्णदर्शनलालसा इति । न तु स्वदेहरक्षार्थम् ॥१॥

ततो भगवान् ब्रह्मा विष्णू रुद्रश्च भूत्वा पुनः कृष्ण एव जात इत्याह तासामाविरभूदिति ।

तासामाविरभूत् शौरिः स्मयमानमुखाम्बुजः ॥
पीताम्बरधरः स्रग्वी साक्षान्मन्मथमन्मथः ॥२॥

तासां मध्य एव भगवानाविर्भूतः । मायाजवनिकां दूरीकृत्य भगवान् प्रकटो जातः । यतः शौरिः । शूरस्य पौत्रः । शौर्यमत्र प्रकटनीयमिति । सर्वेषां दुःखनिवारणार्थमेव यदुवंशेऽवतीर्ण इति । तदा तासां दोषनिवृत्त्यर्थं स्मयमानं मुखाम्बुजं यस्य । ईषद्धसन्मुखः । तासां वैक्लव्येन सन्तुष्टः । स्मितयुक्तं स्मयमानम् । स्मयमानाभ्यां वा सहितं मुखाम्बुजं यस्य । भक्तानां दोषः भक्तेभ्यो निर्गतः भक्तौ समायातीति ज्ञापनार्थम् । तदानीन्तनं रूपं वर्णयति पीताम्बरधर इति । पीताम्बरं हास्यसङ्कोचार्थं हस्ते धृत्वा तिष्ठति । अथवा । व्यापिवैकुण्ठरूपेण एतावत्कालं लक्ष्म्या सह

रमणं कृत्वा तेनैव रूपेण प्रादुर्भूतः । स्रग्वी वनमालायुक्तश्च । मध्ये ब्रह्मादिपूजां च गृहीतवान् । लक्ष्म्या वा । अतो विलम्ब इत्यपि सूचितम् । अत एव प्रथमश्लोके पूर्वाध्याये 'श्रयत इन्दिरे' त्युक्तम् । इदानीं तु उपेक्षा कर्तुमयुक्तेति प्रादुर्भूतः । अत आगमनमुक्तमग्रे । (यद्वा तत्र हेतुमाह विशेषणद्वयेन । इदानीमनाविर्भावे तु न रसो, न वा कीर्तिः । स्वयं त्वाच्छादनेन रसत्वसाधकपीताम्बरधरः कीर्तिमयस्रग्वाँश्च । अतः प्रकट इत्यर्थः । अन्यथा तु भक्तानां स्वरूपतिरोधाने उक्तोभयाभावः स्फुट इति भावः ।) ननु कन्दर्पेण कथं न वशीकृतः, स्वपृतना खिन्नेति, तत्राह । साक्षान्मन्मथस्यापि मन्मथः । आधिभौतिको मन्मथः देवतारूपः । तत आध्यात्मिकः सर्वहृदयेषु साक्षान्मन्मथः । तस्याप्ययं मन्मथः आधिदैविकः । सर्वस्यापि सर्वत्वात् । अतः कन्दर्पोपि मुग्धः । कन्दर्पस्याप्यशक्यमोहः । कन्दर्परूपश्च । अतस्तासां दैन्ये प्रादुर्भूते तन्निवारणार्थं कामरूपमेव प्रकटीकृतवान् । अतस्तेन पूर्ववत् कामसम्पन्नाः ताः कृताः ॥२॥

ततो यज्जातं तदाह तं विलोक्येति ।

तं विलोक्यागतं प्रेष्ठं प्रीत्युत्फुल्लदृशोऽबलाः ।
उत्तस्थुर्युगपत् सर्वास्तन्वः प्राणमिवागतम् ॥३॥

तमागतं विलोक्य युगपत् सर्वा उत्थिताः । पूर्वमाविर्भावमुक्त्वा अधुना यदागमनमुक्तम्, तद्विलोकनसमये स्वामिनीभावानुवादरूपम् । पूर्वमन्तःस्थितोऽधुना बहिरागत इति वा ज्ञापनाय तथोक्तिः । ननु किमाश्चर्यं भगवत्यागते उत्थिता इति । तत्र न ह्येताः सजीवाः स्थिताः, किन्तु निर्जीवा इति वक्तुं दृष्टान्तमाह । तन्वः करचरणाद्यवयवाः । प्राणमागतमिवेति । प्रयत्ने हि एकमेवाङ्गं व्यापृतं भवति, प्राणे तु सर्वाणि सम्भूय । अतो बहुवचनं युगपदुत्थानार्थम् । उत्थानं पञ्चानां भाव्यम्, देहेन्द्रियप्राणान्तःकरणजीवानाम् । तत्र जीवस्यान्याधीनमुत्थानम् । परं तस्मिन्नागते सर्वाण्युत्तिष्ठन्ति । स तु भगवति प्रविष्टः, भगवत्सङ्गे समागतः, भगवत्युत्थित एवोत्थितः । अन्तःकरणं तु उत्थितमित्यत्र हेतुमाह प्रेष्ठमिति । अत्यन्तं प्रियो भगवान् । तं दृष्ट्वा उत्थितम् । भगवति या प्रीतिस्तया कृत्वा उत्फुल्ला दृक् यासाम् । अनेन प्रीत्या इन्द्रियाणामुत्थानम् । (एतासां विलोकनार्थमेवागमनमित्यागमनमात्रेण विलोकनमादौ सम्पन्नम् । उत्फुल्लता तु ततो भिन्ना । तस्याः पुष्पधर्मत्वेन तदुक्त्या दृशां कमलत्वं व्यज्यते । तत्र प्रीतेर्हेतुत्वोक्त्या इयदवधि तत्कार्याभावेनाधुनैव तत्प्राकट्यं ज्ञाप्यते रवेरिव । विरहे सर्वतिरोधानादेतत्तिरोधानमप्यासीत् । अत एवाबलात्वमुक्तम् । कार्यमात्रे स्वसामर्थ्याभावज्ञापनार्थम् । दृष्टान्तेनैव प्राणानामुत्थानम् । प्राणानां भगवान् प्राण इति । शरीरं तु पूर्वोक्ताभिलषितपदार्थत्वेन निरूपणात् उत्थितमित्यत्र तमिति हेतुः) ॥३॥

एवमुत्थितानां भगवता सह स्थितानां कार्यमाह काचिदिति पञ्चभिः ।

काचित् करांबुजं शौरेर्जगृहेऽञ्जलिना मुदा ।
काचिद् दधार तद्बाहुमंसे चन्दनरूषितम् ॥४॥

काचिदञ्जलिनागृह्णात्तन्वी ताम्बूलचर्वितम् ।
एका तदङ्घ्रिकमलं सन्तप्ता स्तनयोरधात् ॥५॥

एका भ्रुकुटिमाबध्य प्रेमसंरम्भविह्वला ।
घ्नन्तीवैक्षत् कटाक्षेपैः सन्दष्टदशनच्छदा ॥६॥

अपराऽनिमिषद्दृग्भ्यां जुषाणा तन्मुखाम्बुजम् ।
आपीतमपि मातृप्यत्सन्तस्तच्चरणं यथा ॥७॥

तं काचिन्नेत्ररन्ध्रेण हृदि कृत्य निमील्य च ।
पुलकाङ्ग्युपगूह्यास्ते योगीवानन्दसम्प्लुता ॥८॥

पूर्वमनेकविधा अपि भगवत्याविर्भूते सप्तविधा एव जाताः । एको भगवान् सर्वार्थे प्रकटीभूतः । तत्र या अग्रे स्थिताः, ता अपि निकटस्थिता एव पूर्वमुच्यन्ते । शुद्धसात्त्विक्यः शुद्धरजोयुक्ता रजःसात्त्विक्यश्च, निर्गुणाश्च, शिष्टाः सप्तविधा गण्यन्ते । काचिदत्र शौरेः करांबुजं मुदा अञ्जलिना अगृह्णात् । एक एव हस्तो भगवता प्रसारितः । पीताम्बरधर इति द्वितीयेन हास्यनिवारणार्थं पीताम्बर-ग्रहणात् । बहुमानेन ग्रहणमञ्जलिना भवति । शौरेरिति वीरत्वज्ञापनाय । मुदेति पूर्वोक्तक्लेशव्यावृत्त्यर्थम् । अन्या पुनस्ततोप्यन्तरङ्गा भविष्यामिति तद्बाहुमंसे दधार । यथालिङ्गितैव भवति । अग्रे एतस्या विनियोगो वक्तव्यः । 'भुजमगरुसुगन्धं मूर्ध्न्यधास्यत् कदा नु' इति । अत एव तदीयो धर्मोन्तःस्थित-स्तस्या निरोधं साधयिष्यतीति चन्दनरूषितमित्युक्तम् । चन्दनेन रूषितं लिप्तम् । चन्दने हेतुः पूजा लक्ष्मीर्वा पूर्वोक्ता । तथा ताम्बूलेपि । एवं सामग्रीप्रकटनेन तासां देवोत्तमानां च कृत्यं प्रदर्शितम् । एता आरोढुकामाः, बेबोत्तमास्तु पूजका इति । अतः काचित्ताम्बूलचर्वितमञ्जलिना अगृह्णात् । तस्याः ताम्बूलयोग्यतामाह तन्वीति । कोमलाङ्गी । एका पुनर्बहिःस्थिता साक्षात्सम्बन्धमलभमाना, उत्थातुं वा अशक्ता, उपविश्यैव तदङ्घ्रिकमलं स्तनयोरधात् । अनुत्थाने धारणे च हेतुः सन्तप्तेति । सा ह्यत्यन्तं विरहातुरा एकेति । अन्या पुनर्दूरस्था तामसी तमसा भ्रुकुटिमाबध्य कटाक्षेपैः घ्नन्तीव ऐक्षत् । अत्र सवर्णे वर्णलोपः । कटाक्षक्षेपैरित्यर्थः । प्रेम्णा सहितो यः संरम्भः क्रोधः तेन विह्वला । सम्यक् दष्टः दशनच्छदो यया । तादृशी च जाता । भ्रुकुटिबन्धनेन चित्तकौटिल्यम् । प्रेमसहितसंरम्भेण इन्द्रियवैक्लव्यम् ।

सन्दंशेन देहक्षोभः। घ्नन्तीवेति प्राणैर्बलस्फूर्तिः। ज्ञानसाधनमपि तस्या विकृतम्। प्रान्तदृष्टिः कटाक्षः। तत्रापि आक्षेपभावः। यथा वाचावगुरणम्, तथा कटाक्षा एव आक्षेपरूपाः निरन्तरं प्रवृत्ताः। तादृशभावस्य पूर्णत्वाय कालनियमनार्थं वा भ्रुकुटि-भङ्गः। स्वभावनियमनार्थं च संरम्भः। लोभनाशार्थं दंशः। मोक्षाभावार्थं ज्ञान-वक्रता। प्रमाणनिराकरणार्थं हननमिति। यतो लौकिकी भक्तिः पुष्टा भवति। एतदर्थमेषा निरूपिता।

एवमतिपुष्टां निरूप्य अत्युत्तमां निरूपयति अपरेति। एषा हि भगवद्दर्शनेन गतदोषा, अतो ध्यानेन भगवन्तं हृदये स्थापयितुकामा नेत्राभ्यां नेत्रद्वारा भगवन्तं हृदि स्थापितवती। अत्र लावण्यामृतं पेयम्, मुखस्याम्बुजत्वोक्तेः। अनिमिष-दृग्भ्यामिति पानकरणम्। द्रवद्द्रव्यस्यान्तर्निवेशनं पानम्। मध्ये रसविच्छेदो भविष्यतीति अनिमिषदृग्भ्यां पानम्। नेत्रयोरञ्जलित्वं लावण्यामृतस्य विरलत्वात्। प्रीतिसेवनमत्राभिप्रेतम्। यद्यपि आसमन्ताद्धर्मसहितं सर्वमेवाभिनिविष्टं स्वाधीनं जातम्। यदैवेच्छति तदैव हृदये पश्यतीति तथापि नातृप्यत् अलंभावं न कृतवती। तत्र हेतुर्विषयसौन्दर्यम्। न तु प्रयोजनाभावः प्रतिबन्धकः। एतदर्थं दृष्टान्तमाह सन्तः तच्चरणं यथेति। सन्तो हि जातकार्याः। तथापि चरणारविन्दे सहजो रसः। न तु किञ्चित् प्राप्तव्यं निवर्तनीयं वा।

एका पुनर्दूरस्था अनया तुल्यशीला योगानुसारेण भगवन्तं गृहीतवतीत्याह तं काचिदिति। पूर्वं लौकिकी पश्चाद् भक्तिमार्गानुसारिणी निरूपिता। इयं योगानु-सारिणी। अतोऽस्याः सर्वावयवे दृष्टिः। उभयोरेकीकरणम्, अन्यथा दृष्टिभेदः स्यात्। पूर्वस्यास्तु दर्शनमेव प्रयोजनम्। एषा विरलेति काचिदित्युक्तम्। तं पूर्वोक्तम्। 'न खलु गोपिकानन्दनो भवानि'ति यया निरूपितम्। नेत्ररन्ध्रेणेत्येक-वचनं रूपप्रवेशार्थम्। हृदि कृत्येति। हृदि कृत्वा। असमासेऽपि ल्यप्। हृदिकृत्येत्य-लुक्समासो वा। ततोऽन्तःप्रविष्टो बहिर्मा गच्छत्विति निमीलनं कृतवती। न हि तस्या बुद्धौ भगवान् बहिरवशिष्टोऽस्ति। स्वकीयो वा भागस्तया गृहीत इति। चकारात् सर्वेन्द्रियनिवर्तनम्। ततोऽन्तरानन्दे पूर्णे पुलकाङ्गी जाता। केवलानन्देन पुलके गोपीत्वं न भविष्यतीति तदर्थं विशेषमाह उपगूह्यास्त इति। अयं रोमाञ्चः सात्त्विकभावे प्रविष्टः। अत एवान्तरुपगूह्यालिङ्ग्य आस्ते। तामेव स्थितिं धारितवती अवस्थान्तराभावाय। ननु तस्या उत्तरत्र कार्यम्, भगवता सह सम्भोगः कर्तव्यः, अलापाः, गृहे च गन्तव्यमिति कथं तामेवावस्थां स्थापितवती, तत्राह योगीवेति। योगी हि तयैवाग्रे सर्वं कार्यं साधयति, तथेयमपि तयैवावस्थया सर्वं साधनीयमिति स्थिता। किञ्च। आनन्दसम्प्लुता। आनन्दे निमग्ना। अत एव बहिःसंवदेनरहिता। संवेदनायामेव सत्यां कार्यानुसन्धानम्। न हि पूर्णे आनन्दे कश्चन कामोस्ति ॥८॥

एवं विशेषाकारेण कृत्यमुक्त्वा सर्वासां सामान्याकारेण प्रयोजनमाह सर्वास्ता इति ।

सर्वास्ताः केशवालोकपरमोत्सवनिर्वृताः ।
जहुर्विरहजं तापं प्राज्ञं प्राप्य यथा जनाः ॥६॥

यो हि बलिष्ठरजस्तमोभ्यां व्याप्तयोरपि फलसम्पादकः, तस्य क्षुद्रगुणक्षोभयुक्तानामासामुद्धारे कः प्रयास इति वक्तुं केशवेत्युक्तम् । तस्य योयमालोकः आलोकनं प्रकाशो वा अन्तर्बहिः । अत एव स एव परमोत्सवः । यथा लौकिकानां महाराज्यप्राप्तिः पुत्रोत्सवो वा । तेन निवृत्ताः सर्वा एव जाताः । एवं तासामिष्टसिद्धिरुक्ता । अनिष्टनिवृत्तिमाह जहुर्विरहजमिति । नन्वेवं सति मुक्ता एव ता भवेयुः । नहि संसारे निवृत्ते भगवत्साक्षात्कारेण परमनिर्वृतौ सत्यां कश्चन पुरुषार्थोऽवशिष्यते । तत्राह प्राज्ञं प्राप्येति । प्राज्ञः सुषुप्तिसाक्षी । स्वाप्यये भगवदाविर्भावो निरूपितः । तत्र च जीवानां प्रवेशो वासनासहितानाम् । तं प्राप्य यथा जनाः अधिकारिणो मनुष्याः पुनरायान्ति, एवमत्राप्यागमिष्यन्तीति भावः । यतो जनाः जायमानाः । न तु उत्तमाधिकारिणः । स्वसम्बन्धख्यापनार्थमेव परं भगवान् प्रकटः ॥६॥

एवं तासां कृत्यमुक्त्वा ताभिर्भगवत्कृत्यमाह ताभिरिति ।

ताभिर्विधूतशोकाभिर्भगवानच्युतो वृतः ।
व्यरोचताधिकं तात पुरुषः शक्तिभिर्यथा ॥१०॥

तासां सम्बन्धे प्राकृतीनां भगवतोऽन्यथात्वं शङ्क्येत, तन्निवर्त्यते । अन्यथा स्वार्थमेव भगवत्तिरोधानं स्यात् । 'स नैव व्यरमत्, तस्मादेकाकी न रमत' इति श्रुतेः । लोकोपि केवलं भगवन्तं पश्यन् न निर्वृतो भवति, किन्तु सर्वशक्तियुक्तं परम् । 'पुंसः स्त्रियाश्च रतयोः सुखदुःखिनोर्न'ति वाक्यात् । पूर्ववत् ता दुःखिताश्चेत्, तदोत्तमता न भवतीत्याह विधूतशोकाभिरिति । ताः पूर्वोक्ताः । गुणास्तासामुक्ता एव । सर्वथा प्रपन्ना इति । मध्ये शोकः समजनि । तस्मिन्निवृत्ते यथापूर्वमेव ताः । भगवांश्च षड्गुणैश्वर्ययुक्तः । तथापि प्राकृत इव यदि परिच्छिन्नकामः स्यात्, तथापि वैलक्षण्यात् न रोचेत । भगवाँस्तु पूर्णकाम इत्याह अच्युत इति । अतः ताभिर्वृतः अधिकं व्यरोचत सहजापेक्षया । उक्तार्थविश्वासेन हि श्रोता वक्तारं पुष्णातीव पितेव पुत्रं स्वार्थम् । अत एवाग्रेऽतिगुप्तार्थकथनेन वक्ता श्रोतारं सुखयति । अन्यथानधिकारिणं मत्वा न वदेदलौकिकमर्थम् । प्रकृते चास्मिन्नर्थे राज्ञो विश्वासं दृष्ट्वातिसन्तोषेण स्नेहेन च पितृत्वेन सम्बोधयति तातेति । नन्वेवं सति भगवत्कान्तेः तारतम्यात् सहजत्वं न स्यात् । अत आह पुरुषः शक्तिभिर्यथेति । यथायं प्राकृतोपि पुरुषः

सर्वसामर्थ्येषु लीनेषु लोकप्रतीत्या न रोचत इव, स चेत् क्रियाज्ञानादिशक्तीराविष्करोति, तदाधिको रोचते, तथा अयमपि भगवान् रोचमान एव प्रकटासु शक्तिषु गोपिकासु सर्वप्रतीत्या भावुकानामप्यन्तःकरणेन अधिकं व्यरोचत । अतिसौन्दर्यं प्राप्तवान् । ततो भगवान् परमानन्दयुक्तः स एव । 'एष ह्येवानन्दयाती'ति श्रुतेः ॥१०॥

तासामानन्दजननार्थं यत् कृतवाँस्तदाह ताः समादायेति ।

ताः समादाय कालिन्द्या निर्विश्य पुलिनं विभुः ।
विकसत्कुन्दमन्दारसुरभ्यनिलषट्पदम् ॥११॥

ताः सम्यक् आदाय समीचीने पुलिने निर्विश्योपविश्य विभुर्जातः । कालिन्दी कलिन्दकन्या । कलिं द्यतीति कलिन्दः । अतस्तस्याः पुलिने तासामन्योन्यं भगवता वा कलहो न भविष्यतीति ज्ञापितम् । पुलिनं वर्णयति क्रीडायोग्यत्वार्थं सार्धेन । सर्वत उपरि अधश्चेति । प्रथमतः सर्वतः सौभाग्यमाह । विकसन्ति कुन्दमन्दारपुष्पाणि तेषां सुरभ्यनिलः षट्पदा भ्रमराश्च यत्र । वायोस्त्रयो गुणा स्पष्टाः । मकरन्दोपि पुष्पेष्वधिकः । तेन मत्ता भ्रमरा अपि नादसाधकत्वेन गानादावुपयुज्यन्ते । विकासो वाय्वर्थ एव । कुन्दगन्धः शान्तः । मन्दारगन्धः पुष्टः । तेन गुप्तागुप्तकामयोरुद्बोधको निरूपितः । (शत्रन्तोक्त्या प्रभुनिवेशनसमये एव विकासारम्भो, न तु पूर्वमपीति ज्ञाप्यते । अन्यथा विकसितेति वदेत् । एवं सति यस्मिन् क्षणे यस्यार्थस्योपयोगः, तस्मिन्नेव क्षणे तत्कार्यं भवति, नान्यदेति लीलामात्रोपयोग्येवात्रत्यं सर्वमपि इति ज्ञापितं भवति । अन्यथा सार्धाध्यायत्रयोक्तलीलायां क्रियमाणायां भूयस्येव रात्रिरतीतेत्यधुनैव विकासे हेत्वन्तराभावात् स न भवेत्, अत एव न वदेदपि । एवं सत्येतादृक्कुन्दादिसम्बन्धित्वेनोक्तत्वादनिलादयोऽप्यधुनैव प्रवृत्ताः न पूर्वमपीति ज्ञेयम् ।) स्वतन्त्रतयापि सौरभ्यप्रतीत्यर्थं सुरभिरनिल उक्तः । एवं परितो जलं, परितः सुगन्धः, परितः पुष्पाणि, परितो वायुः परितो नाद इति निरूपितम् ॥११॥

उपर्युक्तमतामाह शरदिति ।

शरच्चन्द्रांशुसन्दोहध्वस्तदोषातमःशिवम् ।
कृष्णाया हस्ततरलाचितकोमलवालुकम् ॥१२॥

शरत्कालीना ये चन्द्रांशवः, तेषां ये सन्दोहाः समूहाः, तैर्ध्वस्तं दोषाया रात्र्यास्तमो यत्र । तेन अत्यन्तं शिवं कल्याणरूपम् । अन्धकारे गतेपि यदि भूताद्यभिनिर्विष्टं भवेत्, तथापि तदाप्यसमञ्जसमिति कल्याणरूपता निरूपिता । निर्विघ्न-

मग्निमेष्टकार्यसम्पादकत्वज्ञापनाय च । परितश्च निकृष्टाः पदार्थाः नोपर्यधश्च । अधस्तस्य पुलिनस्य गुणानाह कृष्णेति । सापि भगवत्सनाम्नी भूसंस्कारं कृतवती भगवद्रमणार्थम् । कृष्णाया हस्तरूपाः तरलास्तरङ्गाः तैः आचिताः कोमलवालुका यत्र । अन्यथा हस्तरूपताभावे समता न स्यात् । तेन शैत्यं कोमलत्वं समता चोक्ता । तादृशं पुलिनं निर्विश्य तत्र गत्वा वा स्थितः । उपवेशनमग्रे वक्ष्यति । भावेनैवोपवेशनम् ॥१२॥

ततो गोपिकानां कृत्यमाह तद्दर्शनाह्लादेति ।

तद्दर्शनाह्लादविधूतहृद्रुजो मनोरथान्तं श्रुतयो यथा ययुः ।
स्वैरुत्तरीयैः कुचकुङ्कुमाङ्कितैरचीक्लृपन्नासनमात्मबन्धवे ॥१३॥

शोके गतेपि कामस्तापात्मको वर्तत एव, सम्बन्धस्याजातत्वात् । यदा पुनस्तादृशस्थाने तदर्थं गतः, तदा तद्दर्शनेन तस्य तदवस्थामापन्नस्य दर्शनेन योऽयमाह्लादः भाव्यर्थनिश्चयात् तेन विधूताः हृद्रुजो यासाम् । एवं निवृत्ते दोषे तासां यज्जातं तदाह मनोरथान्तं ययुरिति । ताभिर्यथाकथञ्चित् सम्बन्धोऽभिलषितः। जातस्तु ततोऽनन्तगुणसामग्रीसहितः । अतो मनोरथस्याप्यन्तो यत्र तादृशं ययुः । नन्वनभिलषितं कथं प्राप्नुयुः, तत्राह श्रुतयो यथेति । श्रुतयो हि निरन्तरं भगवद्गुणवर्णनपराः । तेन धर्मेण, वाचः पूर्वरूपं यन्मनः, तस्यापि यदगम्यं भगवत्स्वरूपं, तत् प्राप्तवत्यः । 'यतो वाचो निवर्तन्ते अप्राप्य मनसा सहे'ति भगवदानन्दो मनोरथान्तो भवति । तत्प्रतिपादिकाः श्रुतयो जाताः । सर्वे च मन्यन्ते । 'तं त्वौपनिषदं पुरुषं पृच्छामि', 'अतोऽस्मि लोके वेदे च प्रथितःपुरुषोत्तम' इति, सर्वे वेदा यत्पदमामनन्ति' इत्यादिवाक्यैः ब्रह्मणि श्रुतयः प्रमाणमित्यध्यवसीयते । 'सर्ववेदान्तप्रत्यय' मिति न्यायाच्च । अलौकिको वेदार्थः । अलौकिका वेदशब्दाः। लोके च न सङ्केतः । तथापि निरन्तरं भगवत्कार्यं कथयन्तीति लोकाः तच्छ्रवणेन शुद्धान्तःकरणाः स्वयमेवालौकिकविषये सामर्थ्यं मन्यन्ते । श्रुतिश्च तत्प्रतिपादिका भगवदिच्छया । नात्र लौकिकं साधनमपेक्षते, युक्तिं वा । तथा एतासामपि मनोरथान्तप्राप्तिः । एवं परमपुरुषार्थदातुर्भगवतोऽन्यत्राभिनिवेशे आधारधर्मसम्बन्धात् स्वस्य कृतार्थता न भविष्यतीति पूजार्थमात्मनिवेदनार्थं च आसनं चक्रुरित्याह स्वैरुत्तरीयैरिति । तद्देशस्थानां स्त्रीवस्त्राणि त्रीणि भवन्ति । परिधानीयं, कुचपट्टिका, उपरिवस्त्रं च । सर्वाभिरेव स्वोपरिवस्त्राणि आसनार्थं दत्तानि । उपरिवस्त्राण्यपि द्विविधानि भवन्ति । सर्वदा परिधेयानि, भोगसमये च । तानि सूक्ष्माणि भवन्ति । तान्येव भगवते दत्तानीति ज्ञापयितुमाह कुचकुङ्कुमाङ्कितैरिति । शुष्काण्यपि कुङ्कुमानि क्रीडायामार्द्राणि भवन्ति । अतस्तेनाङ्कितानि उत्तरीयाणि, अचीक्लृपन् कल्पयामासुः । ननु स्वोपरिपरिधेयं कथमधः कल्पयाञ्चक्रुरित्याशङ्क्याह आत्मबन्धव इति ।

आत्मनः स एव बन्धुः, रक्षित आत्मा, तदर्थमेव देहः स्वात्मा च । अत उपर्याच्छादनमपि तदर्थमिति तस्यासनक्लृप्तिरुचिता ॥१३॥

ततो भगवान् तासु सर्वत्र निविष्ट इति ख्यापयितुं तद्दत्तासन उपविष्ट इत्याह तत्रोपविष्ट इति ।

तत्रोपविष्टो भगवान् स ईश्वरो योगेश्वरान्तर्हृदि कल्पितासनः ।
चकास गोपीपरिषद्गतोऽर्चितस्त्रैलोक्यलक्ष्म्येकपदं वपुर्दधत् ॥१४॥

भगवानिति तेषां कार्यसाधकत्वम् । ननूत्तरीयवस्त्रापगमे सभायां रसाभासो भवेत् । अतः कथमुपविष्ट इति चेत्, तत्राह स ईश्वर इति । सः पूर्वं प्रार्थितः । ईश्वरः सर्वकरणसमर्थः । अतस्तासां दिव्यानि वस्त्राणि सम्पन्नानीति बोधितम् । येषां जलक्रीडायां न वाससामार्द्रता । अतः सर्वकरणसमर्थः तत्रोपविष्टः सः प्रार्थितः । (यद्वा । पूर्वं वरदानसमये वस्त्रेष्वपहृतेषु सर्वथा तदभावे यस्य रमाभासो न जातः, तस्य केवलमुत्तरीयाभावे कथमधुनापि स भवेदिति वक्तुं स इत्युक्तवान् । ननु तदानीमपि कथं न रसाभास इत्यत आह ईश्वर इति । कर्तुं सामर्थ्यवत्त्वात् । यदि स भवेत्, तदा तथा न कुर्यादेव । अकर्तुं सामर्थ्यवत्त्वेन रसाभासहेतुत्वेऽपि तद्दत्तमासनं त्यक्तुमशक्यमेव । अन्यथाकर्तुं सामार्थ्यवत्त्वेन रसाभासप्रकारेणापि रसमुत्पादयितुं शक्तः । अतस्तादृशे न किञ्चिदनुपपन्नमिति भावः ।) ननु भगवान् अपवित्रे भोगादिलेपयुक्ते कथमुपविष्ट इति चेत्, तत्राह योगेश्वरान्तर्हृदि कल्पितासन इति । योगेश्वराणां हृदयं शुद्धम् । तत्राप्यन्तर्हृदयम् । तत्रापि कल्पितमेव भगवदासनम्, न तु क्लृप्तम् । मानसी मूर्तिस्तिष्ठति, न तु कदाचिदपि स्वयमुपविष्ट इति मुख्यमासनमेतदेव । अतश्चकास, परमशोभां प्राप्तवान् । पूर्ववद् गोपीनां परिषदं गतश्च जातः । परितो गोपिका उपविष्टा इत्यर्थः । सभापतिर्भगवान् । अतस्ताभिरर्चितः । ततो भगवान् तासामर्थे त्रैलोक्ये यावन्ति लक्ष्मीरूपाणि इन्द्रपदादीनि, तासां यदेकं पदं, यस्यांशविलासाः तत्तल्लक्ष्मीभोक्तारः, तादृशं वपुर्धृतवान् । अस्मिन्नर्थे देशकालादिभेदेन यावन्त उत्कृष्टा अर्था अपेक्ष्यन्ते, तान् प्रकटितवान्, तादृशवपुर्धारणेन ॥१४॥

एवं प्रसन्नं भगवन्तं दृष्ट्वा स्वान्तःकरणदोषदूरीकरणार्थं स्वकृतघ्नतां पूर्वं भगवति कल्पितवत्य इति तन्निराकरणार्थं लोकदृष्ट्या भगवति कृतघ्नतालक्षणो दोषोऽस्ति न वेति निर्णयार्थं किञ्चित् प्रष्टुमुद्यता इत्याह सभाजयित्वेति ।

सभाजयित्वा तमनङ्गदीपनं सहासलीलेक्षणविभ्रमद्भ्रुवा ।
संस्पर्शनेनाङ्कृताङ्घ्रिहस्तयोः संस्तुत्य ईषत्कुपिता बभाषिरे ॥१५॥

प्रश्नार्थं प्रथमतः सभाजनं स्तोत्रं कृत्वा । ननु किमनेन विचारेण साम्प्रतम्, जातं फलं भुज्यतामिति चेत्, तत्राह अनङ्गदीपनमिति । अनङ्गं दीपयति निरन्तरमेव । अङ्गाभावं सम्पादयतीति च ध्वनिः । अतो नैकेन भोगेन कार्यनिष्पत्तिः । पुनस्तेनापि भोगेनाग्रे अधिक एव खेदः स्यात् । स चेत् स्वदोषेण, तदा दोषो दूरीकर्तव्यः । भगवद्धर्मेण चेत्, वाङनिबधं कारयित्वा प्रार्थयित्वा वा फलानुभवः कर्तव्य इति भावः । अनङ्गदीपने साधनमाह सहासेति । साधनाभावार्थं वा प्रार्थनीय इति साधनकीर्तनम् । हासपूर्वकं यल्लीलेक्षणं, तेन विभ्रमन्ती या भ्रूः, तया अनङ्गं दीपयति । पञ्चात्र साधनानि । हासो लीला ईक्षणं विलासाः भ्रूश्चेति । पञ्च चेद्धेतवः कार्यमप्रतिहितं भवति । माया व्यामोहिका स्वरूपविस्मारणार्थम् । लीला स्वासक्तिं साधयति । ईक्षणं तत्र ज्ञानजनकम् । अन्यथा ज्ञानान्तरेण तन्निराकरणं स्यात् । विलासाः पोषकाः । भ्रूर्यमः नियन्ता काल इति । यावत्प्रसाददाता वा तत्रैव । ततः प्रश्नार्थं उपढौकनं कुर्वन्ति संस्पर्शनेनेति । अङ्के कृतः स्थापितो यो भगवदङ्घ्रिः, तत्सम्बन्धिनौ यौ हस्तौ, तयोः सम्यक्स्पर्शनेन सँल्लालयन्त्य इत्यर्थः । संस्पर्शनेन सहिताः । तत आभिमुख्यार्थं संस्तुत्य । एवं सर्वभावेन प्रपन्नानपि त्यजतीति भगवति दोषदृष्ट्या ईषत्कुपिताः। साधनैर्निवर्तितोऽपि दोषो न सम्यक् निवर्तते, यावद् भगवान्न निवर्तयतीति । अतो विवादमिव कुर्वन्त्यो बभाषिरे ॥१५॥

तासां प्रश्नमाह भजत इति ।

गोप्य ऊचुः —**भजतोऽनुभजन्त्येक एक एतद्विपर्ययम् ।**
नोभयांश्च भजन्त्येक एतन्नो ब्रूहि साधु भोः ॥१६॥

त्रयः पक्षाः सन्दिग्धाः, फलतः, स्वरूपतश्च, भजनाभजनाभ्याम् । तत्रैके ये यथा भजन्ति, ते तथा तानपि भजन्ति । एके पुनरभजतोऽपि भजन्ति । अन्ये तु उभयानपि न भजन्ति । तेषां त्रयाणां उभयोरपि प्रतियोगिनोः फलं वक्तव्यम् । ये भजनानुसारेण भजन्ति, ते किं कृतघ्नाः, आहोस्वित् धूर्ताः, आहोस्वित् समीचीना इति । केनचित् पादप्रक्षालनं कृतम्, सोऽपि चेत् करोति, तदा किं स्यात् । फलार्थकरणे फलं देयम् । तेनापि तदेव कर्तव्यमिति करणे तदेव कर्तव्यम् । निरपेक्षकरणे तु सन्देह एव । अभजतो भजने क्वचिद्दोषः स्यात् । यथा निष्कामे कामिनी । क्वचिदुपकारः, अपेक्षितश्चेदर्थः । क्वचित् स्नेहः । क्वचिद्धर्म इति । एकं फलं निर्धारितं वक्तव्यम् । यो वा न भजति पूर्वः, तस्य वा किं फलमिति । ये वा नोभयविधान् भजन्ति, तेषामुभयविधानां वा किं फलमिति। कृतस्य साधनस्य कुत्र वा उपयोगः एतत् सर्वं ब्रूहि । साधु यथा भवति तथा । भो इति सम्बोधनं सावधानार्थम् । भजतः पुरुषाननु तदनुसारेण भजन्ति । एके पुनः भजनव्यतिरेकेणैव भजन्ति । इत्युभये भजनकर्तारः । अन्ये तु भजनरहिता एव ॥१६॥

एतेषां भेदान् फलं चाह भगवान् मिथो भजन्तीति त्रिभिः ।

श्रीभगवानुवाच—**मिथो भजन्ति ये सख्यः स्वार्थैकान्तोद्यमा हि ते ।**
न तत्र सौहृदं धर्मः स्वार्थार्थं तद्धि नान्यथा ।।१७।।

तत्राद्यपक्षस्य निर्धारमाह । ये मिथो भजन्ति, ते स्वार्थैकान्तोद्यमाः । स्वार्थ एव एकान्तः एकं फलमुद्यमस्य । ते हि ज्ञात्वैवान्योन्यं भजन्ते । तरतमभावेन च भजनमनुवर्तयन्ति । अतो न तेष्वन्योन्यं वञ्चनापि सम्भवति । अतः स्वार्थमेव लौकिकार्थमेव तेषामुद्यमः । ननु उभये ब्राह्मणाः, अतोऽन्योन्यभजनेन धर्मः स्नेहो वा भवेत्, कथं स्वार्थ एवेत्याशङ्क्याह न तत्र सौहृदमिति । क्षणेनैव द्वितीयस्याभजनं ज्ञात्वा क्रोधकरणात् । अतो न सौहार्दम् । नापि धर्मः । 'सम्भोजनी नाम पिशाच-भिक्षा नैषा पितॄन् गच्छति नोत देवान् । इहैव सा चरति क्षीणपुण्या शालान्तरे गौरिव नष्टवत्से'ति । गुरुसेवायामपि यदि दृष्टार्थतोभयोः, तदापि न धर्मः । शास्त्रा-नुसारी चेत् , मिथोभजनाभावः । विद्या तु फलरूपा । सख्य इति सम्बोधनाद-प्रतारणा । य इति प्रसिद्धास्ते वणिज इव । स्वार्थ एव तेषां प्रवृत्तिः । यद्यपि धर्मा-दयोपि स्वार्था एव, तथाप्यन्योन्यभजने न ते सिध्यन्ति । तथा सौहार्दमपि, यद्यन्यमपेक्षेत । तस्य सावधनस्य विनियोगमाह स्वार्थार्थमिति । अन्यार्थमपि प्रतीयमानं स्वार्थमेव । एवं सेवादिदानेष्वपि । दुःखनिवृत्तिस्तत्र फलम् । अत्रार्थे सर्वोपि लोकः प्रमाणमिति हिशब्दः । अन्यथा परोपकाराय न । अन्यस्य हृदये तत्प्रती-कारार्थं चिन्ताजननात् । अतः फलं स्वार्थसिद्धिः लौकिकी । नाममात्रेणैव तेषां धर्मत्वम् , न तु वस्तुतः ।।१७।।

ये पुनः अभजतोऽपि भजन्ति , ते द्विविधा इत्याह भजन्तीति ।

भजन्त्यभजतो ये वै करुणाः पितरौ यथा ।
धर्मो निरपवादोऽत्र सौहृदं च सुमध्यमाः ।।१८।

ये अभजतोऽपि तूष्णीं स्थितान् भजन्ति, तत्र निमित्तद्वयम्, लौकिकं वैदिकं वा, स्नेहो विधिश्च । तत्र सौहार्दं धर्मश्च फलं क्रमेणैव । यः पूर्वः तस्य सौहार्दे अवसरे कर्तव्य एवोपकारः । अन्यथा कृतघ्नः स्यात् । धर्मशेषश्चेत्, प्रायश्चित्तं विधेयम् । तदीय एव धर्मः तद्द्वारा तेषु गच्छतीति । तत्र धर्मे यत्र कर्म प्रधानम्, यत्र वा देवता, तदुभयं न विवक्षितम् । प्रतियोगिनि भजनशङ्काभावात् । यत्र वा असमानता, गोः पङ्कोद्धारणवत्, तत्रापि तथा । यत्र पुनराधारे प्रत्युपकारः सम्भवति, तत्र प्रवृत्तौ, पूर्वस्याभजने, उत्तरभजने, निरपवादो धर्मः, सौहृदं च फलम् । अधिकारिविशेषणं तु एकत्र करुणा, अपरत्र दैहिकः सम्बन्धः । तदाह करुणाः पितराविति । अन्यत्रापि

दृश्यत इति तद्धर्मातिदेशमाह यथेति । ये संसारिणः क्रूराः, तेऽपि कदाचिद्दीनेषु भजनं कुर्वन्ति, स्निग्धा इव च भवन्ति । तेषां सङ्ग्रहार्थं यथेति । सम्बन्धस्तु जन्मान्तरीयोऽपि भवतीति उपमानोपमेययोरभेदादेकविधा एव । निरपवाद इति । एतदुपकारेण हि तस्यापवादः । तदभावान्निरपवाद एव । अत्र तादृशेऽर्थे । अनेन यत्र प्रत्युपकारसम्भावनापि न, तत्र धर्म इति सूचितम् । अत एव केचित् क्रियमाणमपि नाङ्गीकुर्वन्ति । सौहार्देपि धर्मोस्तीति चकारः । सुमध्यमा इति सम्बोधनमुक्तविश्वासाय । धर्मेणैव उत्तममध्यमता ॥१८॥

ये तु पुनः सर्वथैव न भजन्ति, भजनार्थं भजतः, सौहृदेन वा भजतः । धर्मार्थे तु न शङ्का । तानुभयविधानपि केचिन्न भजन्ति । अभजतो दीनान् धर्माधिकारिणश्च । तानपि न भजन्ति । तेषां स्वरूपमाह भजतोऽपीति ।

भजतोऽपि न वै केचिद् भजन्त्यभजतः कुतः ।
आत्मारामा ह्याप्तकामा अकृतज्ञा गुरुद्रुहः ॥१९॥

केचिन्महापुरुषा भजतोऽपि न भजन्ति, अभजतः कुतो भजिष्यन्ति । ते पूर्वोक्तन्यायेन चतुर्विधाः । तन्मध्ये उभये समीचीनाः, उभये न । ये धर्माधिकारिणस्ते अधमाः । ये लौकिकनिमित्तास्ते उत्तमा इति । तान् गणयति साङ्कर्याभावाय । आत्मारामा इति । आत्मन्येव रमन्त इति । अन्येन भजनीयो देहादिर्नापेक्षित इति भजनमेव न मन्यन्ते । तेषां भजनार्थं च साधनत्वेन स्वदेहादिकमपि न मन्यन्ते । तथा अन्ये आप्तकामाः । आप्तः प्राप्तः कामो यैः । यो भुक्तवन्तं ब्रूयात्, त्वं भुङ्क्ष्व, मा भुङ्क्ष्वेति वा । एकत्राप्रवृत्तिः । अपरत्र सिद्धसाधनत्वेनानुवादः । उभयथापि वैयर्थ्यम् । प्रवर्तमानस्य धर्मः सेत्स्यति । अज्ञानं वा । उभये तु अधमा इत्याह । ये कृतं न जानन्ति तदुपकारम्, ते प्रत्युपकारसमर्था अपि उभयविधानपि न भजन्ति । तेषामज्ञानमेव हेतुरभजने । ज्ञात्वा चेदभजनम्, गुरुद्रोहः । यः कश्चित् स्वस्य पुरुषार्थसाधकः स गुरुः, स पूज्यः । तस्यापदि स्वशक्तौ सत्यां तदुपेक्षायां तद्द्रोहः अनेनैव कृत इति गुरुद्रोहकर्ता भवति । एवं सर्वेषां गुणदोषा निरूपिताः ॥१९॥

गोपिकानां हृदये भगवानेतन्मध्ये क इति जिज्ञासायां अभजनकर्तृत्वाद् भजनसामर्थ्यस्यापि विद्यमानत्वान्मिथोभजनपक्षः अभजनभजनपक्षश्च व्यावर्तितः । ननु द्वितीये पक्षे गोपिकानां भजने स्नेहाद् भजनमस्तु, अतो भगवान् निरूपकत्वेन नैषामन्तर्भूतः । ईश्वरश्च नैषामन्तर्भवतीति कथमेवं विचार इति चेत्, मैवम् । गोपिका भोग्या इत्यविवादम् । ताश्च भोग्यसमर्पकत्व एवोपक्षीणाः । अतो भगवत एव विचारः कर्तव्यः । ईश्वरोऽपि फलार्थं सेव्यश्चेत्, न विचार्यः । व्यवहारे दृष्टार्थश्चेद्, दीयमानग्रहणाग्रहणाभ्यां विचार्य एव । पूर्वंगृहीतत्वात् नात्मारामता, नापि पूर्णकामता । प्रथमप्रवृत्त्या तृप्तावपि परित्यागो नोचितः । ततस्तृतीयपक्ष

एवाभिनिवेश उचितः । तदपि सर्वज्ञस्यानुचितम् । ईश्वराणां फलदातॄणां कदाचिदेवं भवतीति शङ्कायाः परिहारमाह नाहं तु सख्य इति ।

नाहं तु सख्यो भजतोऽपि जन्तून् भजाम्यमीषामनुवृत्तिवृत्तये ।
यथाधनो लब्धधने विनष्टे तच्चिन्तयान्यन्निभृतो न वेद ॥२०॥

तुशब्दस्तं पक्षं व्यावर्तयति । नापीश्वरभजनपक्षः शङ्कनीय इत्याह सख्य इति । गोपिकास्तु सख्यः । रसे तुल्याः । एकार्थाभिनिवेशाश्च । अहमिति भगवान्, न तु जीवः । तेन आत्मारामादिपक्षा व्यावर्तिताः । अहं राम एव, न त्वात्मारामः । ममात्मव्यतिरिक्तपदार्थाभावान्न व्यावर्त्यमस्ति । कामाभावादेव नाप्तकामत्वम् । अतो मम भिन्नैव व्यवस्था, न तु जीवतुल्यता । नाहं तु सख्य इति तामेव व्यवस्थामाह भजतोऽपि जन्तून् अहं न भजामि । तत्रान्य एव हेतुः । अमीषामनुवृत्तिवृत्तय इति । अमीषां जीवानाम् । जन्तुपदेन प्राणिमात्रम् । भगवतो न केनाप्युपयोगः । भगवान् फलरूप इति सर्वेषामेवोपयोगः । तथा सति तेषां भजनमेव इष्टमिष्टसाधनं वा । तत्राहं चेत् साधनत्वेन प्रविशामि, तदा भजनमेव नाशयामि । अग्रे भजनस्य प्रतिबन्धात् पूर्वभजनस्य च वैयर्थ्यापादनात् । चतुर्धा हि भगवदुपयोगः । भगवान् भोग्यो, भोक्ता वा । भोग्यपक्षे कामनापूरकत्वेन, स्वातंत्र्येण वा । भोक्तापि भक्त्या भक्तदत्तपदार्थस्वीकाराद् , विषयत्वेन भोगाद्वा । आद्ये भजनं नश्येत् । अल्पफलदानात् । स्वरूपतो महत्त्वेऽपि कालपरिच्छेदात् । द्वितीये तु तथात्वमतिभजनेन भवति । तद् गोपिकानां नास्तीति तत्सिद्ध्यर्थमभजनम् । अपेक्षाभावात् नाहं विषयन्यायेन भोक्ता । भक्त्यर्थं तु अभजनमेवेति सिद्धान्तसङ्ग्रहः । यथा अभजने अनुवृत्तिः सिध्यति, तथा प्रकारमाह यथाधन इति । पूर्वमधनः, पश्चाल्लब्धं धनं, तच्चेद्विनष्टं, तदा तच्चिन्तया व्याप्तः, निभृतः तदेकनिमग्नः सन्, अन्यन्न वेद । एतत्तु लोकप्रसिद्धम् । तथा गोपिकानामपि पूर्वमप्राप्तो भगवान् प्राप्तश्चेत्तिरोभवति, तदा निभृताः, तत्रैव मग्नचित्ताः न प्रपञ्चं स्मरिष्यन्ति । निभृतानां प्रयोजनं पूर्वमुक्तमेव ॥२०॥

एवं स्वस्याभजने हेतुमुक्त्वा प्रकृते तदभावमाह एवमिति ।

एवं मदर्थोज्झितलोकवेदस्वानां हि वो मय्यनुवृत्तयेऽबलाः ।
मया परोक्षं भजता तिरोहितं मासूयितुं मार्हथ तन्प्रियं प्रियाः ॥२१॥

यदुक्तं ताभिररण्ये स्त्रियो रात्रौ कथं त्यक्तव्याः । तदर्थमेवमुच्यते । द्वयमत्र कर्तव्यम् । भजनानुव्यावृत्त्यर्थमभजनम्, रात्रौ रक्षार्थं भजनं च । तत् परोक्षभजनेन सिध्यतीति मया परोक्षं भजता तिरोहितम्, भजने हेतुमाह

एवमिति । मदर्थमेव उज्झिता लोकवेदस्वा याभिः । वृथापरित्यागवृत्त्यर्थं मोक्षार्थ-परित्यागव्यावृत्त्यर्थं च मदर्थमुज्झितेत्युक्तम् । आद्ये त्यागोनिष्टहेतुः । द्वितीये न मम भारः । त्रयः पदार्थास्त्यक्तव्याः । लोको दुस्त्याज्यः । आर्यमार्गो वैदिकः । प्रकारस्तादृश इति । मयैव लोके तथैव प्रतीतिजननात् । पतिपुत्रादयो दुस्त्याज्याः । तत्रापि न मयि प्राप्ते, किन्तु मदर्थे मत्कामनायामेव । तदा मे विचिकीर्षितो भवतीति । 'सर्वधर्मान् परित्यज्ये'ति तादृश एव मम भाव इति त्रितयपरित्यागे मया भजनं कृतम् । (वस्तुतस्तु स्वपदं स्वात्मपरम् । अन्यथा पतिपुत्रादीनामपि लोकवेदमध्य-पातात्तेनैव तत्प्राप्तेः स्वपदमनर्थकं स्यात् । तथा च स्वात्मत्वेन स्नेहविषयत्वाभाव एव तत्त्यागः । एतासां भगवदर्थत्वेन प्रीतिविषयत्वादात्मादीनामिति सारम् ।) युक्तश्चायमर्थः । अनन्याः पालनीया इति । वः युष्मान् । मय्यनुवृत्तय इत्येकं फलम् । अवला इति सम्बोधनात् न सतामिव प्रत्यक्षेण भवतीनां भजनं सिध्यतीति ज्ञापितम् । परोक्षं भजता अतिरोहितं वा । भजनं भोगो वा । भोक्त्रैव मया भोगं कुर्वता तिरोहितम् । भवतिभिर्न दृष्ट इत्यर्थः ।अनेनाभजनपक्षो व्यावर्तितः । तस्मिन् सत्यसूया सम्भवति । अकृतज्ञत्वादिदोषारोपणेन मा मां असूयितुं नार्हथ । यतः प्रियम् । प्रिये दुष्टे स्वस्यापि तथात्वस्यावश्यकत्वात् त्यक्तुमशक्यत्वात् । किञ्च, प्रिया यूयम् । कृतज्ञत्वादयो हि धर्मा न प्रीतिविषये भवन्ति । औदासीन्यसामाना-धिकरण्यात् ॥२१॥

एवं तासां मनोमार्जनमुक्त्वा भक्तिमार्गविरोधं परिहर्तुं ताः स्तौति न पारये ऽहमिति ।

न पारयेऽहं निरवद्यसंयुजां स्वसाधुकृत्यं विबुधायुषापि वः ।
या माभजन् दुर्जरगेहशृङ्खलाः संवृश्च्य तद्वः प्रतियातु साधुना ॥२२॥

इति श्रीमद्भागवते महापुराणे दशमस्कन्धपूर्वार्धे रासक्रीडायां गोपीसान्त्वनं नाम एकोनत्रिंशोऽध्यायः ।

निरवद्यसंयुजां निर्दुष्टभजनयुक्तानाम् । स्वसाधुकृत्यं स्वप्रत्युपकारकरणम् । विबुधायुषा ब्रह्मायुषा । मन्वन्तरपरिमितायुषा वा । विशेषेण बुधानां ज्ञानिना-मनन्तायुषा वा । न पारये । भजनप्रत्युपकारयोर्वैसादृश्यात् । भवतीनां भजनं निष्कपटम् । अस्मद्भजनं सकपटमिति । न ह्यल्पजलस्यापि तुल्यं बह्वपि मरुमरीचि-काजलं भवति । सत्यभजनं तु ब्रह्मणोऽशक्यमेव, जीवधर्मत्वात् । तत्रापि विशेषमाह या माभजन्निति । दुर्जरा हि गेहशृङ्खला, या जीर्यतोऽपि न जीर्यत इति । तां संवृश्च्य छित्त्वा । याः भवत्यः प्रसिद्धाः । मा मामभजन् । यैः पूर्वं बद्धाः स्थिताः स्वार्थं तेषामर्थमात्मानं च मय्येव समर्पितवत्यः । बहिःशृङ्खला त्यक्तुमपि शक्या ।

न तु सर्वंत आवृते गृहं शृङ्खला । एवमलौकिककर्त्रीणां यद् भजनं तद् भवतीनामेव । साधुना । भावप्रधानो निर्देशः । साधुत्वेन प्रतियातु, प्रत्युपकृतं भवतु । साधवो हि महत् कर्म कृत्वा स्वयमेव तुष्यन्ति, न तु प्रत्युपकारमपेक्षन्ते । अतो मयि भजनं नास्ति । भजनस्य जीवधर्मत्वात् । अतोऽग्रेऽपि यदि स्वत एव सन्तुष्टाः, तदा भजत, नो चेत्, यथासुखं विधेयमिति भावः । न ह्यशक्यं कश्चित् कर्तुं शक्नोतीति ॥२२॥

इति श्रीभागवतसुबोधिन्यां श्रीमल्लक्ष्मणभट्टात्मज श्रीमद्वल्लभदीक्षितविरचितायां दशमस्कन्धविवरणे एकोनत्रिंशाध्यायविवरणम् ॥

श्रीकृष्णाय नमः ।

त्रिंशत्तमोऽध्यायः ।

त्रिंशत्तमे हरिः प्रीतो लीलां कामकृतामपि ।
इन्द्रादिदुर्लभां चक्रे स्वानन्दार्थमितीर्यते ॥१॥

अस्याः सर्वोपकाराय फलश्रुतिरुदीर्यते ।
लौकिक्यपि यदा दृष्टिस्तदा सिद्धान्त ईर्यते ॥२॥

रसात्मकस्तु यः कामः सोत्यन्तं गूढ एव हि ।
अतः शास्त्रं प्रवृत्तं हि तृतीयं भारतं तथा ॥३॥

अतोत्र भगवांश्चक्रे नृत्यं कारितवांस्तथा ।
सर्वाङ्गेषु तु यो लीनः स यथा व्यक्ततां व्रजेत् ॥४॥

जलं वायुश्च सामग्री श्रमात् शीताच्च जायते ।
अत्रैव लोके प्रकटमाधिदैविकमुत्तमम् ॥५॥

कामाख्यं सुखमत्कृष्टं कृष्णो भुङक्ते न चापरः ॥

एवं पूर्वाध्याये तासां सर्वभावेन प्रमाणेन प्रमेयेन दुःखं दूरीकृतवान् । तद् दुःखमज्ञानतश्चेत्, तदैव दूरीकृतं भवति । अन्यथा भगवतैव दुःखं दत्तं स्यात् । अतो भगवता त्यक्त्वा न गतमिति न भगवान् दुःखे हेतुः, किन्त्वज्ञानमेव । अतो भगवद्वाक्यादज्ञाने गते तन्मूलकं दुःखमपि गतमित्याह इत्थमिति ।

श्रीशुक उवाच—**इत्थं भगवतो गोप्यः श्रुत्वा वाचः सुपेशलाः ।**
जहुर्विरहजं तापं तदङ्गोपचिताशिषः ॥१॥

भगवतो वाचः श्रुत्वा विरहजं तापं जहुः । भ्रमादेवास्माकं विरहो जात इति । ननु वचनमात्रेण कथमज्ञाननिवृत्तिः, तत्राह भगवत इति । गोप्य इति विपरीतभावनानिवृत्त्यर्थम् । ननु ता वाचः कथं न मनसि सन्देहमुत्पादितवत्यः, तत्राह सुपेशला इति । अतिमनोहरा इति । मनसि विचिकित्सायामेव सन्देहः । शब्दस्वाभाव्यादेव मनसि सन्देहो न जातः । अतो विरहजं तापं जहुः, नास्माकं विरहो जात इति ज्ञातवत्यः । यथा स्वप्नादुत्थितः स्वाप्निकं दुःखं न मन्यते । तस्य भगवत अङ्गै रुपचिता आशिषो यासाम् । भगवत्कार्यव्यतिरेकेणैव भगवदवयवैरेव सर्वमनोरथाः पूरिताः ॥१॥

एवं दुःखाभावसुखयोः प्रतिबन्धकं रूपेण वाचा च निवार्य स्वकर्तव्यमारभते तत्रारभतेति ।

तत्रारभत गोविन्दो रासक्रीडामनुव्रतैः ।
स्त्रीरत्नैरन्वितः प्रीतैरन्योन्याबद्धबाहुभिः ॥२॥

गोविन्द इति । एतदर्थमेवेन्द्रो जातः । अतोऽसाधारणो भोगश्च तस्यावश्यक इति च । अनुव्रतैः स्त्रीरत्नैरन्वितः रासक्रीडामारभत । बहुनर्तकीयुक्तो नृत्यविशेषो रासः । रसस्याभिव्यक्तिर्यस्मादिति । रसप्रादुर्भावार्थमेष हि नृत्यम् । रासे क्रीडा लीला स्वस्य । क्रीडायां मनसो रसस्योद्गमः । नृत्ये देहस्य । कामस्तु भोक्तृनिष्ठ इति स्वप्राधान्यम् । समाजेनापि रस उत्पद्यत इति एकवचनम् । तदा हीक्षुरसवद् भक्तिरसवद्वा कामरसोऽप्युत्पद्यते । गोपिकानां रसयोग्यतामाह अनुव्रतैरिति । अनुव्रतं यासाम् तासामपि रसोत्पादनमावश्यकमिति । यादृशो भगवतोऽभिप्रेतः, तादृश एवेति च । नन्वयं रसः अलौकिकः, न लौकिकेषूत्पद्यते, अतो व्यर्थ आरम्भः । न हि सिकतासमूहात् तैलमुत्पद्यत इति चेत्, तत्राह स्त्रीरत्नैरिति । स्वभावतः स्त्रियस्त्रिविधाः, लोकभेदेन । तत्रापि मानुषीषु जातिभेदाश्चत्वारः, पद्मिन्यादयः । वासनाभेदाश्चतुर्दश अश्वप्रकृत्यादयः । सर्वास्वेवैता रत्नभूताः । स्वासाधारणधर्मैस्तद्धर्मप्रकाशिकाः । अतः सर्वभावेन रसोत्पत्तियोग्यता । तैरन्वित इति । स्वयं नायकमणिः । तद्योग्या एते मणय इति । एकरसत्वाय च मेलनम् । अनेन रसप्रकटनार्थं शुल्कदासिका भगवते दत्ता इति यदुक्तम्, तदपि समर्थितम् । नन्वेते जीवाः, भगवानानन्दमयः, कथं वैषम्याद्रसोत्पत्तिरिति चेत्, तत्राह प्रीतैरिति । ता अपि भगवत्सदृश्यो जाताः । सर्वतः प्रीता इति । तासामभिनिवेशप्रकारमाह अन्योन्याबद्धबाहुभिरिति । ताः परस्परमासमन्तादुभयतः बद्धौ बाहू यासाम् । न तु भगवता सह ॥२॥

भगवान् पुनः हस्तमण्डलाद्बहिःस्थितो यथा सम्बध्यते, तथा सन्निवेशमाह रासोत्सवः सम्प्रवृत्त इति ।

रासोत्सवः सम्प्रवृत्तो गोपीमण्डलमण्डितः ।
योगेश्वरेण कृष्णेन तासां मध्ये द्वयोर्द्वयोः ।
प्रविष्टेन गृहीतानां कण्ठे स्वनिकटं स्त्रियः ॥३॥

यं मन्येरन्, नभस्तावद्विमानशतसङ्कुलम् ।
दिवौकसां सदाराणामौत्सुक्यापहृतात्मनाम् ॥४॥

सर्वेषामेव गुणभावात् रसप्राधान्यात् रासोत्सव एव सम्यक् प्रवृत्तः । उत्सवो नाम मनसः सर्वविस्मारक आह्लादः । उत्सवत्वसम्पादनाय सजातीयानेकरसोत्पाद-

नार्थं विशेषमाह गोपीमण्डलमण्डित इति । गोपीनां मण्डलैरनेकविधैर्मण्डितः । उत्सवोऽप्यनेकविधैर्ब्राह्मणादिमण्डलैर्मण्डितो भवति । अत्रापि तुल्यस्वभावाः रसार्थमेकीकृताः पृथङ्मण्डलभाजः । तैरपि मण्डितः । पोषकाश्च रसास्तत उत्पादिता इति उत्तरोत्तरमण्डलैः पूर्वपूर्वरसः पोष्यत इति नायं रसोन्यत्र भवितुमर्हति । सम्यक्प्रवृत्तिर्निरन्तरमाविर्भावः । ननु कालकर्मस्वभावानां प्रतिबन्धकत्वादनेकत्र जायमानो रसः कथमेकीभवति, तत्राह योगेश्वरेणेति । स हि सर्वोपायवित् । सर्ववस्तुषु विद्यमानं भगवदैश्वर्यादिकं योग एवोद्घाटयतीति साधनेषु योगः प्रधानम् । तत्रैश्वर्ये सर्वत्रैव मूलभूतो रस उत्पादयितुं शक्यत इति सिद्धमेव । किञ्च । कृष्णोऽयमिति । स्वयमेव सदानन्दः । उद्गतोऽग्निः सर्वत्रैवाग्निं लीनं जनयितुं शक्नोति । तस्य भगवतस्तासु सन्निवेशप्रकारमाह तासां मध्ये द्वयोर्द्वयोरिति । मण्डलीकृता यावत्यो गोप्यः तासां द्वयं द्वयं भिन्नतया भावनीयम् । द्वित्वद्वयस्य नैकाधिकरणता भाव्या । अतो मण्डलमध्ये यत्र हस्तद्वयग्रन्थिः, तत्र भगवदुदरं यथा भवति, तथा भगवानुत्थितो जातः । तथोद्गतस्योभयत्र सम्बन्धमाह, द्वयोर्द्वयोर्मध्ये प्रविष्टेन भगवता कण्ठे गृहीतानामिति । हस्तद्वयेन पार्श्वस्थितयोः कण्ठे ग्रहणम् । एवं षोडशगोपिकानामष्ट कृष्णा भवन्ति । अन्यथा रसाभासः स्यात् । कृष्णद्वैविध्यप्रतीतेः । इममेवार्थमाह स्वनिकटं स्त्रियः यं मन्येरन्निति । स्वस्यैव निकटे, न त्वन्यासाम् । स्वसम्मुखस्थितगोपिकाकण्ठालिङ्गितभगवद्दर्शनमपि भगवदिच्छया तासां न जायत इति । प्रयोजनार्थं हि रूपकरणम् । तदर्धसङ्ख्ययैव प्रयोजनं भवतीति न समसङ्ख्या मृग्या । 'यावतीर्गोपयोषित' इत्यग्रे समसङ्ख्यायां भगवतो वक्ष्यति । यत्पुनः कैश्चिदुक्तं 'अङ्गनामङ्गनामन्तरे माधव' इति, तत्रापि सविसर्गः पाठो ज्ञेयः । द्विवचने बहुवचनप्रयोगश्च । अन्यदेव वा तन्मण्डलम्, न भागवतोक्तम् । मध्ये वेणुनादस्योक्तत्वात् अत्र तु रसार्थे नृत्यमिति । गानार्थमपेक्षायामपि देवैरेव तत्सिद्धिः । 'मध्ये मणीनां हैमाना'मित्यत्र तु दर्शनार्थमुक्तत्वात् गोपिकानां देवानां च दर्शनं तथैवेति नानुपपन्नं किञ्चित् । एवं रसार्थं सर्वसामग्र्यामुक्तायां स रसः प्रादुर्भूतः सर्वेषां भविष्यतीति देवादयः सर्वे अलौकिकज्ञानयुक्ता दर्शनार्थमागता इत्याह नभस्तावदिति । तावन्नभो विमानशतसङ्कुलमासीत् । मण्डपे हि नृत्यं रसजनकम् । अन्यथोपरि वैचित्र्यं न स्यात् । तदर्थमपि विमानशतेन सङ्कुलम् । यथा रसोत्पादनार्थं स्त्रियः पुरुषाश्च सम्बद्धाः नानाबन्धयुक्ताः चित्रे स्थाप्यन्ते । तदर्थं भगवता ते चित्रप्रायाः स्थापिताः । अत एवाग्रे 'औत्सुक्यापहृतात्मना'मिति वक्ष्यति । स्वलीलार्थं सर्वं तथा प्रेरयतीति न औत्सुक्येनान्यथासिद्धिः । तासां रसग्रहणार्थमागमनम्, भगवदिच्छा तु चित्रार्थम् । विमानस्थितान् तत्सम्बन्धिनो वर्णयति दिवौकसामिति । स्वर्ग एव स्थानं येषाम् । सदाराणामिति तेषां भावान्तरव्युदासार्थम् । स्त्रीणामुपसर्जनत्वं तासां भावार्थम् । स्वर्गस्थिता रसाभिज्ञा रसयोग्याश्च भवन्तीति ।

नन्वीश्वरलीला न द्रष्टव्येति कथं तेषां दर्शनार्थं प्रवृत्तिः, तत्राह औत्सुक्यापहृतात्मनामिति । औत्सुक्येन विचाररहितलीलाक्षिप्तमनसा अपहृत आत्मा स्वरूपं बुद्धिर्वा येषाम् । अतः स्वधर्मादिव प्रवृत्ताः, न तु भगवद्धर्मं विचारितवन्त : ।।४।।

ततो नृत्यारम्भे यद् भाव्यम् । तज्जातमित्याह तत इति ।

ततो दुन्दुभयो नेदुर्निपेतुः पुष्पवृष्टयः ।
जगुर्गन्धर्वपतयः सस्त्रीकास्तद्यशोऽमलम् ।।५।।

आदौ दुन्दुभिवादनम् । 'परमा वा एषा वाग् या दुन्दुभा'विति श्रुतेः । ततः प्रथमतः पुष्पवृष्टिर्मङ्गलार्था । पुष्पाञ्जलिः प्रसिद्धः । आगतो रसः तदधिष्ठाता वा पूज्यत इति । नानाविधानां पुष्पाणां भिन्ना वृष्टय इति बहुवचनम् । ततो गानं साधारणं जातमित्याह जगुर्गन्धर्वपतय इति । भगवान् श्रोष्यतीति उत्तमैरेव गानम् । गन्धर्वपतयो विश्वावसुप्रभृतयः । ते ह्यधिकारिण इति नटानामिव तेषां दर्शनं न दोषाय । अन्यथा भगवद्धस्तस्थितेन्द्रादीनामपि दोषत्वं स्यात् । 'अर्थद्रव्यविरोधेऽर्थो बलीया'निति न्यायात् । तथापि तेषामन्यथाबुद्धिः सम्भाव्येतेति विशेषणमाह। सस्त्रीका इति । वैषयिकदोषव्यावृत्त्यर्थमाह अमलं तद्यश इति । तद्धि मलनिवर्तकम् । अतो न तासां तेषां वा तत्कालोपयोगिपदार्थादतिरिक्तो भाव उत्पद्यते ।।५।।

एवं बाह्यगीतवाद्यादिकमुक्त्वा नृत्यमध्ये रसोपयोगिवादित्राण्याह वलयानामिति ।

वलयानां नूपुराणां किङ्किणीनां च योषिताम् ।
सप्रियाणामभूत् शब्दस्तुमुलो रासमण्डले ।।६।।

स्थानत्रये हि वादित्राण्यपेक्ष्यन्ते । नीचस्थाने भूमाविव मध्ये उपरि च । तथैव तालभेदाः । अतोऽत्रापि उपरि वलयानां शब्दः । अधो नूपुराणाम् । मध्ये किङ्किणीनाम् । अन्योन्याबद्धबाहव एव मध्ये मध्ये हस्तद्वयं योजयन्तीति वलयानां शब्दः । अथवाग्रे शब्दोत्पत्त्यर्थं प्रकारं वक्ष्यति 'पादन्यासै' रिति । सप्रियाणां कृष्णसहितानाम् । अत एव सर्वलास्यसम्पत्तिः सर्वासां भगवत्सम्बन्धार्थम् । चकारात् अन्येऽपि कूजितशब्दा मुखशब्दाश्चोक्ताः । सर्वः एकीभूय तुमुलो भूत्वा यथा दूरस्थानामवान्तरग्रहणं न भवति। तथा सति किं स्यात्, अत आह रासमण्डल इति । रसानां समूहमण्डले यथानधिकारित्वेन शूद्रस्य वेदश्रवणे तदध्येतुर्मन्त्रस्य च शक्तिह्रासः, शूद्रे च पापसम्भवः, तथैतद्भक्तातिरिक्तानामेतच्छ्रवणेऽप्यनधिकारादस्य रसस्यालौकिकत्वादेतच्छ्रवणे मण्डले सर्वेषां रसो गच्छेत् । श्रवणे सति तदन्वेषणपरत्वं स्यात् । तत्तेषामेवानिष्टकरमिति तदेव पापरूपम् ।।६।।

एवं नृत्यमध्ये प्रविष्टो भगवान् गुणभावात् कदाचिन्न भासेतेत्याशङ्क्य सर्वजनीना भगवच्छोभा तदा ता जातेत्याह तत्रेति ।

तत्रातिशुशुभे ताभिर्भगवान् देवकीसुतः ।
मध्ये मणीनां हैमानां महामरकतो यथा ।। ७ ।।

स्वभावशो भातोऽप्यतिशयेन शुशुभे । तदुक्तं 'शक्तिभिः सहितोऽधिकां शोभां प्राप्नोती'ति । कदाचित् स्वत एव शोभां प्रकटयेदिति तद्व्यावृत्त्यर्थं ताभिरित्युक्तम् । ननु सहजशोभायुक्तस्य कथं ताभिरतिशोभा, तत्राह भगवानिति । यथा गुणैः । ननु गुणाः सर्वोत्तमाः, न तथैता इति चेत्, तत्राह देवकीसुत इति । भक्त्या यथा देवक्या अपि पुत्रो जातः । स्त्रीणामेवोपकारायाविर्भूतः । अतस्तास्वपि स्वसामर्थ्यमेव दत्वा शोभां प्राप्तवान् । सहजस्य कृत्रिमैः शोभा न भविष्यतीत्याशङ्क्य दृष्टान्तमाह मध्ये मणीनामिति । महामारकतो गरुडोद्गारी स मणिः सहजः । सुवर्णमणयः कृत्रिमाः । तथापि ते परितः क्लृप्ताः सहजमणिमप्यतिशोभयन्ति ।।७।।

एवं पूर्वपीठिकामुक्त्वा मुख्यं नृत्यमाह पादन्यासैरिति ।

पादन्यासैर्भुजविधुतिभिः सस्मितैर्भ्रूविलासैः ।
भज्यन्मध्यैश्चलकुचपटैः कुण्डलैर्गण्डलोलैः ।

स्विद्यन्मुख्यः कबररशनाऽग्रन्थयः कृष्णवध्वो
गायन्त्यस्तं तडित इव ता मेघचक्रे विरेजुः ।।८।।

पादन्यासाः सर्व एव चारीकरणरूपाः । भुजानां विधुतयश्च सर्वहस्तकभेदाः । एकेनावयवेन शिष्टावयवाः तथा संविधानयुक्ता इति ज्ञेयम् । मन्दहाससहिताः सर्व एव कटाक्षा उक्ताः । भ्रूभेदाश्च । तत्तद्रसे हृदयाविष्टे तथैव भवन्तीति । भज्यद् भङ्गयुक्तानि मध्यानि उपरिभागपरिवर्तनात्मकानि । रसाभिनिविष्टानां तासां सर्वावयवातिभ्रमणेन रस एकीभवतीति । परिवर्तनादिभिरेव वा चलेषु कुचेषु पटा इति सर्वाण्येव कम्पनान्युक्तानि । कुण्डलैर्गण्डलोलैरिति । सर्व एव शिरोभेदा उक्ताः । शिरोभेदेष्वेव वक्तव्येषु कुण्डलानां यच्चलननिरूपणम्, तद्विद्युतामिव शोभार्थम् । गण्डलोलैरिति सर्वा कान्तिस्तत्रोपक्षीणेति ज्ञापनार्थम् । गण्डे हि केवलो रसः । पेयो रसस्तत एव पीयत इति । विद्योतनं तस्यैवाभिव्यक्त्यर्थम् । ततोऽन्तःस्थितो रसः पुष्टोऽभिव्यक्त इति ख्यापनार्थमाह स्विद्यन्मुख्य इति । स्विद्यत् स्वेदयुक्तानि मुखानि यासामिति । कबररशनासु च अग्रन्थयो जाताः । रसेन सर्वावयवस्थेन एकीभूतेन देहःसूक्ष्मतामापन्नः । अतः केशपाशे रशनायां च ग्रन्थिः शिथिलः । नन्वेवं कथं श्रमः, तत्राह कृष्णवध्व इति । सदानन्दस्य हि फलस्य ता उपभोक्त्र्यः । अतः क्रियायां

श्रमो भवत्येव। एतादृश्योऽप्यन्तःसन्तोषेण गायन्त्यो जाताः। एवं कायादिश्रमैरपि ता विरेजुः। अतिशोभायुक्ता जाताः। ननु लोकानां दर्शनसापेक्षा शोभा, तास्तदा कथं सर्वैर्दृष्टा इति, तत्राह तडित इव ता इति। नहि तडित् बहुकालं दर्शनयोग्या भवति। मेघचक्रे शोभामेव परं सम्पादयति। तथा कृष्णसमूहे भगवता आच्छादिताः। परितः कदाचिदेवोद्गताः केनचिदंशेन दृष्टा भवन्ति। अतस्तासां शोभा न दोषावहा जाता, किन्तु विशिष्टैव जाता ॥८॥

गाढनृत्यमुक्त्वा मध्यनृत्यमाह उच्चैर्जगुरिति।

उच्चैर्जगुर्नृत्यमाना रक्तकण्ठ्यो रतिप्रियाः।
कृष्णाभिमर्शमुदिता यद्गीतेनेदमावृतम् ॥९॥

नृत्यमाना नृत्यं कुर्वन्त्य एव उच्चैर्गानयुक्ता जाताः। अथवा आदावुच्चैर्जगुः। ततो नृत्यमाना नृत्यन्त्यो जाता। उभयत्र हेतुमाह रक्तकण्ठ्यो रतिप्रिया इति। रक्तः रञ्जकस्वरेण युक्तः कण्ठो यासामस्तीति। रतिरेव प्रिया यासामिति। गानेन व्यामोहनं नृत्येन च तासां प्रसिद्धम्। ननु पूर्वनृत्येन जातश्रमाः कथमेवं कृतवत्य इत्यत आह कृष्णाभिमर्शमुदिता इति। भगवतः अभितोमर्शः प्रोञ्छनादिविशेषरूपः, तेन मुदिताः अन्तःपूर्णानन्दाः। इतरविस्मारणार्थं नादाधिक्यमाह यद्गीतेनेद-मावृतमिति। यासां गीतेनेदं जगद् व्याप्तम्। अथवा। यदर्थमेतन्नृत्यादिकम्, तत् सफलं जातमित्याह यद्गीतेनेति। लोकैः क्रियमाणेन गीतेन एतत्प्रकाशकेन एतज्जगद् रसेन व्याप्तमित्यर्थः। लोके रसप्राकट्यार्थमेवैतत् कृतमिति। उत्पन्नस्य नादस्यामृतमयत्वाय भगवतापि नादः कृतः। स च मधुर एव कर्तव्यः। तेन च जगत् पूरणीयम् ॥९॥

ततोऽघटमानमेतदिति तदर्थमाह काचिदिति।

काचित् समं मुकुन्देन स्वरजातीरमिश्रिताः।
उन्निन्ये पूजिता तेन प्रीयता साधुसाध्विति॥
तदेव ध्रुवमुन्निन्ये तस्यै मानं च बह्वदात् ॥१०॥

मुकुन्देन समं अमिश्रिताः स्वरजातीः काचिदुन्निन्ये। काचित् सम्यग् भगवद्भावं प्राप्ता। भगवतो नादकरणे हेतुः मुकुन्देनेति। मोक्षदानार्थमेव उपनिषदि स्वनादं पूरितवान्। उभयोरेकता। नादे तुल्यता। मोक्षे कार्यद्वयम्। पूर्वसङ्घातान्निवर्तनं ब्रह्मप्रापणं च। तदर्थमितरनिवारणार्थमुपनिषदामुपयोगः। स्वराः षड्जादयः तेषां जातिभेदाः। यथा मयूरः षड्जं वदति। तथा अन्येऽपि पक्षिणः मनुष्या अन्ये जीवाः

षड्जं वदन्ति । तथापि तेषामवान्तरजातिरस्ति। ते चेद्यथाक्रमेण यथारसाभिव्यक्तिः यदभिप्रायेण सृष्टावुत्पादिताः, तथैव योजिताश्चेत्, तदा स्वरजातयः अमिश्रिताः भवन्ति। तद्भगवता कर्तुं शक्यम्, नान्येन। तासां चेदुन्नयनम्, तदा युक्त एव सन्तोषः। तदाह पूजिता तेन भगवतेति। स्वस्य ब्रह्मत्वात् स्वविचारितानुपूर्वीति स्वस्य तथा गानं नाश्चर्यहेतुः। अन्ये तु तत्स्वरूपमेव न जानन्ति, कुतः पुनः करिष्यन्तीति तेनैव पूजिता। किञ्च, कार्यमपि उन्नयनेन जातमिति। साधुसाध्विति। प्रीयता प्रीतीं कुर्वता भगवता। स्वरूपतः फलतश्च साधुत्वाय द्विरुक्तिः। प्रीतिश्च तुल्यत्वात् सर्वथा कार्यानुगुणत्वात्। अन्या पुनः उन्नीतमेव यावद् भगवता पुनर्गृह्यते, तावत्तथैवोन्नयनं कृतवतीत्याह तदेवेति। तदेवोन्नीतं ध्रुवं निश्चलं यथा भवति, तथा उन्निन्ये। तं नादं ध्रुवनादे योजितवती। ध्रुवनादः कारणनादः स्थायी स्वरः। 'यत्रोपविशते रागः स्वरः स्थायी स कथ्यते'। भगवन्नाद् एव वा। भगवता तथैव गीतमिति। ध्रुवतालादिषु योजितवतीति केचित्। तन्न विचारक्षमम्। एवं ध्रुवयोजनायां भगवाँस्तस्यै बह्वेव सन्मानमदात्। चकारादभीष्टमपि। एवं तासामन्तःसामर्थ्यं जातमिति बहिःसामर्थ्यं किं वक्तव्यमिति भावः। बह्विति सर्वगोप्यधिकम्। ऐश्वर्यवीर्यरूपे चैते निरूपिते। अन्याश्चतस्रः क्रमेण बोद्धव्याः ॥१०॥

कीर्तिर्हि भगवन्तमेवावलम्बते। अतः कायिकं व्यापारं द्वयोराह काचिदिति।

काचिद्रासपरिश्रान्ता पार्श्वस्थस्य गदाभृतः ।
जग्राह बाहुना स्कन्धं श्लथद्वलयमल्लिका ॥११॥

रासेन परितः श्रान्ता स्वस्यैकस्मिन् पार्श्वे विद्यमानस्य स्कन्धं स्वबाहुना जग्राह। गदाभृत इति भगवतः स्थिरत्वाय। अधिकप्रयत्ने अन्यथा क्रियमाणे रासो भज्येत। परिश्रमो रसाधिक्यात्। अन्यथा रसार्थं प्रवृत्तिर्न स्यात्। मण्डलपरित्यागे मण्डलसिद्ध्यर्थं भगवतापि हस्तग्रहणं सम्भवति। अत एकस्मिन् पार्श्वे भगवानेव। पार्श्वभागे विद्यमानस्य भगवतः कण्ठग्रहणं वृक्षाधिरूढालिङ्गनं भवति। भगवता पूर्वं कण्ठे सा गृहीता, तयापि भगवान् गृहीत इति मित्रवत् स्थितिः स्यादिति तन्निवृत्त्यर्थमाह श्लथद्वलयमल्लिकेति। श्लथन्ती वलयाकारा मल्लिका यस्याः। कबरे वलयाकारेण मल्लिकामाला बद्धा। सा च शिथिला जातेति वैकल्यं प्रदर्शितम्। आप्तता च प्रदर्शिता ॥११॥

तत्रैकांसगतं बाहुं कृष्णस्योत्पलसौरभम् ।
चन्दनालिप्तमाघ्राय हृष्टरोमा चुचुम्ब ह ॥१२॥

अन्या पुनः स्वस्य एकांसगतं बाहुं उत्पलापेक्षया अधिकपरिमलयुक्तं चन्दनेनालिप्तं बाहुमाघ्राय अन्तःप्रविष्टामोदा पूर्णानन्दा सती हृष्टरोमा बाहुमेव चुचुम्ब।

रूपस्पर्शौ पूर्वमेव स्थितौ। गन्धरसयोरप्यनुभवं कृतवतीति। हेत्याश्चर्ये। तत्रेति। तस्मिन्नेव समये, तत्रैव भगवति वा। उभयपार्श्वस्थयोर्गोपिकयोस्तथा सति विनियोग उक्तो भवति। एकांसगतमिति वा। सैव तथा कृतवतीति केचित्। सदानन्दत्वात् सर्वत्रैव समरसता। उत्पलं हि रात्रिविकासि। तत् स्त्रीणां मनोज्ञम्। आघ्राणे चन्दनजसौरभमेव न हेतुः, किन्तु ततोऽपि विलक्षणं साधारणजनावेद्यं तदपेक्षयापि सौरभयुक्तत्वेनात्यलौकिकभाववतीनामेव वेद्यम्। सहजसौरभमित्यपि ज्ञापनायेदं विशेषणम्। चन्दनालेपः विवेकधैर्यनाशनार्थः। घ्राणेनान्तःप्रवेशनमस्या विशेषः। एषा श्रीरूपा ॥१२॥

कयाचिद्भगवद्गृहीतताम्बूलं ज्ञानवद्गृहीतमित्याह कस्याश्चिदिति।

कस्याश्चिन्नाट्यविक्षिप्तकुण्डलत्विषमण्डितम्।
गण्डं गण्डे सन्दधत्या अदात्ताम्बूलचर्वितम् ॥१३॥

कस्यैचित् ताम्बूलचर्वितमदादिति। स्वगण्डं भगवद्गण्डे सन्दधत्या इति तस्या अपेक्षा लाघवं च सूचितम्। सम्मुखत्वाभावेऽपि लाघवेनैव प्रादात्। अनेन तस्यै स्वविद्या दत्तेति ज्ञापितम्। तेनेयमेवोपदेष्ट्री भगवदसन्निधाने सर्वासां भविष्यति। तस्याः विद्यायोग्यतां वक्तुं लौकिकक्रियाज्ञानशक्तिमत्त्वमाह नाट्यविक्षिप्तकुण्डलत्विषमण्डितमिति। नाट्येन विक्षिप्तस्य कुण्डलस्य त्विषा मण्डितं गण्डम्। नाट्ये क्रियाशक्तिः प्रतिष्ठिता। कुण्डले ज्ञानशक्तिः। क्रियाशक्त्या विक्षेपोऽत्यभ्यासः। योगात्मकत्वात् साधनानि वा। तस्य कान्तिरनुभवः। तेनालङ्कृता भक्तिः। भगवत्प्रेम्णा सम्बद्धा। यथा सा भगवति रता, एवं तस्यामपि भगवान् रतः। तत्रापि गण्डमिदं साध्यरूपा भक्तिरुच्यते। तां लक्ष्मीं प्रति मूलपर्यटनमिति। लक्ष्मीवन्तं प्रति पुनः पुनरावर्तत इति ज्ञानताम्बूलयोस्तुल्यता। चर्वितमिति साधनप्रयासाभावेन सिद्धदानम् ॥१३॥

अपरा पुनः वैराग्यात्मकं क्रियारूपमच्छिद्रं ज्ञाने सहायार्थं भगवद्धस्तं स्वहृदये स्थापितवतीत्याह नृत्यतीति।

नृत्यती गायती काचित् कूजन्नूपुरमेखला।
पार्श्वस्थाच्युतहस्ताब्जं श्रान्ताधात् स्तनयोः शिवम् ॥१४॥

सा नृत्यं गानं च कुर्वती स्थिता। तत्राभिनये यथान्यहस्तः स्थाप्यते, स्वहस्तो वा, तथा भगवद्धस्तमेव स्थापितवती। शाब्दं ज्ञानं तदर्थानुष्ठानं च तस्या वर्तत इति ज्ञापनार्थं नृत्यगानयोः कथनम्। कूजती नूपुरे मेखला च यस्याः। उपरि गानाभिनयनम्। पादयोर्नृत्यम्। अत एव नूपुरयोर्मेखलायाश्च शब्दः। स च

भावोद्दीपकः । अनेन तस्याः पूर्वस्थिता सर्वैव क्रियाशक्तिः सफलेति सूचितम् । एकस्मिन्नेव पार्श्वे विद्यमानस्य भगवतः श्रान्ता सती तत्तापहरणार्थं स्तनयोरधात् । तापहारकत्वमब्जस्य प्रसिद्धम् । श्रमो निर्वृतिसूचकः । स्वस्याः पूर्वक्रियापरित्यागः बाह्यत एवेति भगवत एकस्मिन् भागे स्थितिरुक्ता । भगवत्क्रियाशक्तेरक्षयत्व-सूचनायाच्युतेति । अग्रे सम्बन्धस्यापि करिष्यमाणत्वात् तदविघातार्थं च । तस्य पुनः कामाद्युद्बोधकत्वेन तापानाशकत्वमाशङ्क्याह शिवमिति । तदेव कल्याण-रूपम्, आनन्दरूपत्वाच्च भगवतः ॥१४॥

एवं षण्णां स्वरूपमुक्त्वा स्वरूपेण सर्वासां साधारणीं लीलामाह गोप्य इति ।

गोप्यो लब्ध्वाच्युतं कान्तं श्रिय एकान्तवल्लभम् ।
गृहीतकण्ठ्यस्तद्दोर्भ्यां गायन्त्यस्तं विजह्रिरे ॥१५॥

अच्युतः कान्तो भगवानेव भवति । अन्तर्बहिश्च नित्यानन्ददायी । अत एव सर्वस्त्रीणां मूलभूतायाः श्रिय एकान्ततो वल्लभः परमः प्रियः । तादृशं लब्ध्वा तमेव गायन्त्यो विजह्रिरे । ननु परमानन्दे प्राप्ते क्रियाया अपगम एवोचितः, न तु पुनः क्रिया, तत्कथं विहार इति चेत्, तत्राह तद्दोर्भ्यां गृहीतकण्ठ्य इति । भगवत्क्रिययैव व्याप्ताः, न तु स्वक्रिया काचित् । कण्ठे क्रियायाः स्थापितत्वाद्गानं क्रिया च सम्भवतः । इयं क्रिया शक्तिरूपेति स्वातन्त्र्यं तासां निरूपितम् ॥१५॥

अतः परं राधादामोदरवदुभयोर्नृत्यमाह कर्णेति ।

कर्णोत्पलालकविटङ्कपोलघर्मवक्त्रश्रियो वलयनूपुरघोषवाद्यैः ।
गोप्यः समं भगवता ननृतुः स्वकेशस्रस्तस्रजो भ्रमरगायकरासगोष्ठ्याम् ॥

रासार्थमेवैतदपि, परं प्रत्येकं रस उत्पद्यत इति गोष्ठीमात्रमुक्तम् । उभयोर्गा-ढनृत्ये विनियोगात् । भ्रमरो गायकः । वाद्यं तु पूर्ववदेव भविष्यति । तदाह वलय-नूपुरघोषवाद्यैरिति । वलयानां नूपुराणां घोषशब्देन किङ्किणीनां शब्दा एव वाद्य-शब्दाः । अत्यन्तं नृत्याभिनिवेशार्थं स्वकेशात् स्रस्ताः स्रजो यासामित्युक्तम् । (यद्वा । गायकास्तु भ्रमरा निरूपिताः, ते च मकरन्दार्थिनः । स च पुष्पेष्वेव तिष्ठति । तानि च वियुक्तानि तद्रहितानि च भवन्तीति स्वनृत्यानुरूपगानकरणादति-प्रसन्नास्तेभ्यः स्रज एव दत्तवत्यः । अन्यथा रसार्थं स्वकेशेषु शोभाहेतुत्वेन धृतानां तासामुपेक्षा न भवेत् । तेन भ्रमराणां गाननैपुण्यं प्रभुप्रियाणां च तदभिज्ञत्वं च ध्वन्यते ।) नृत्यारम्भे तासां शोभामाह कर्णेति । अन्यथा पूर्वोक्तनृत्येन श्रान्तानां पुनर्नृत्यमनुचितमेव स्यात् । न वा रसालम् । कर्णे उत्पलस्थापनं तस्य अपातने चातुर्यार्थम् । तत्सहिता अलकाः भ्रमरा इव रसपातारः । तेषां विटङ्कः अलङ्करणरूपं

स्थानम् । एतादृशौ कपोलौ । तत्र यो घर्मः अन्तरुद्गतश्रमजलं नृत्याभिनिवेशाज्जातम् । तैः कृत्वा वक्त्रे श्रीरलौकिकी काचित् सम्पन्ना । यथा मुक्ताभिर्मण्डितं भवति कपोलद्वयम् । अनेन मुखे श्रमो निवारितः । ताभिः सह भगवतो नृत्ये अनुभावकश्च भवति । स्वतो वा । क्रीडानिवृत्तिरनेन सूचिता । गोप्य इति । भगवत एव तासामेतावत्त्वम्, न स्वत इति ज्ञापितम् । अतो भगवता समम्, यथा यथा भगवान् नृत्यति, तथा तथा ता अपि नृत्यन्तीति ॥१६॥

एवं प्रादुर्भूते रसे अत्यन्तोद्गमनार्थं साक्षात्कामशास्त्रोक्ताश्चेष्टा निरूपयति एवमिति ।

एवं परिष्वङ्गकराभिमर्शस्निग्धेक्षणोद्दामविलासहासैः ।
रेमे रमेशो व्रजसुन्दरीभिर्यथार्भकः स्वप्रतिबिम्बविभ्रमः ॥१७॥

आलिङ्गनादयस्तत्र निरूपिताः । एवमेव रसोद्गमनार्थं परिष्वङ्गः, आलिङ्गनम् । ततः कराभिमर्शः, तत्तदवयवेषु भगवद्धस्तस्पर्शः । ततः स्निग्धेक्षणं भावोद्गारि । तत उद्दामो विलासः, अमर्यादो भोगः । ततो हास्यानि पूर्णमनोरथानाम् । एवं परिष्वङ्गादिहासान्ताः सर्वासु । ननु प्राकृतीभिः कथं रेमे, तत्राह रमेश इति । रमाया ईशः । सर्वत्र तासु रमापि भगवदाज्ञया निविष्टा । ता अपि अधिष्ठानयोग्या इत्याह व्रजसुन्दरीभिरिति । नन्वात्मारामः कथमेताभी रेमे, लक्ष्मीस्तु ब्रह्मानन्द इति रमणमुचितमपि । एतास्वावेशोऽप्यनुचितः, ब्रह्मभावाभावादिति चेत्, तत्राह यथार्भक इति । बालको हि दर्पणजलादिकं पुरतः स्थापयित्वा, तत्र तत्रात्मानं पश्यन् रमते । तथा भगवानपि स्वसामर्थ्यं स्वरूपं वा तत्र स्थापयित्वा, ब्रह्म ब्रह्मानन्दं चाविर्भावयित्वा रेमे । नन्वेतदप्यनुचितम्. किमनेनेति चेत्, तत्राह यथार्भकः। यथा बाललीलां कृतवान् तथैतदपि कृतवानित्यर्थः । (यद्वा । कदाचित्प्रकारसाम्येऽपि नैतद्रसानुभवो लक्ष्म्यां भवितुमर्हति, किन्त्वेतास्वेवेति ज्ञापयति पदद्वयेन, रमेशो व्रजसुन्दरीभिरिति । रमाया ईशः स्वामी भर्तेति यावत् । एतास्तु व्रजसम्बन्धिन्योऽन्यसम्बन्धिन्यः सुन्दर्यो, न तु विवाहिता इति । रमारमणदशायां एतादृग्रसानुभवो नोभयोरपि सम्भवति । रसस्वरूपस्यैव तादृशत्वादिति भावः । नन्वीश्वरे नेदमुचितमित्यत आह यथार्भक इति । 'सम्मुष्णन् नवनीतमन्तिकमणिस्तम्भे स्वबिम्बोद्गमं दृष्ट्वे'त्यादिवाक्यनिरूपितमुग्धलीला वान्यथा निरूप्यते । पूर्णज्ञानोऽपि तद्रसस्वरूपस्य तथात्वात् । तथेहापि 'रसो वै स' इति श्रुतेरिदं सर्वं रसमध्यपातित्वेन स्वरूपात्मकमेवेति तदुच्यत इति नानुपपत्तिः काचित् । शङ्काया एवानुदयादिति भावः ।)एतेन यथा प्रभुस्तद्भावो वा, तथैता एतद्भावोपीति ज्ञापितं भवति । तथा प्रतिबिम्बस्वभावात् । अत्र रमणं बहूनामप्येकदा भवति द्वयोश्च । अग्रे तु प्रत्येकपर्यवसानं वक्ष्यति ॥१७॥

एवं सर्वभावेन भगवद्धर्मावेशे तासां देहादिविस्मरणपूर्वकं महारसाभिनिवेशमाह तदङ्गेति ।

तदङ्गसङ्गप्रमदाकुलेन्द्रियाः केशान् दुकूलं कुचपट्टिका वा ।
नाञ्जः प्रतिव्योढुमलं व्रजस्त्रियो विस्रस्तमालाभरणाः कुरूद्वह ॥१८॥

तस्य भगवत अङ्गसङ्गेन यः प्रकृष्टो मदः देहादिविस्मारको भाव उत्पन्नः । तेन आकुलानीन्द्रियाणि यासाम् । सर्वा इतिकर्तव्यतामूढा जाताः । ततः केशपाशं परिहितदुकूलं कुचपट्टिकां वा स्वयमञ्जसा सामस्त्येन प्रति सम्मुखतया विशेषेण वोढुमलं न जाताः । पुनरल्पेनैव तथाविधा जाता इत्यत्र हेतुमाह व्रजस्त्रिय इति । श्रमोऽपि जात इत्याह विस्रस्तमालाभरणा इति । आकुलेन्द्रियत्वान्न विचारो लौकिकः । गोपिकात्वान्न पारमार्थिकः । श्रमान्न दैहिकः । अत आद्यन्तमध्येषु तासु युक्ता भगवतैव धृताः, न ताभिरित्यर्थः । यद्यप्यन्यप्रतीत्या ध्रियमाणा इव, तथापि न स्वतो धारणम् । कुरूद्वहेति सम्बोधनमभ्रमाय विश्वासार्थं च ॥१८॥

एवं समुदायलीलां निरूप्य तस्याः परिज्ञानं केषामपि न जातमिति वक्तुं देवस्त्रीणां चन्द्रस्य च विस्मयमाह कृष्णेति ।

कृष्णविक्रीडितं वीक्ष्य मुमुहुः खेचरस्त्रियः ।
कामार्दिताः शशाङ्कश्च सगणो विस्मितोऽभवत् ॥१९॥

नहि कस्याश्चित् पतिः परमानन्दो भवति । नहि निरानन्देनानन्दो दातुं शक्यते । 'एष ह्येवानन्दयाती'ति श्रुतेः । एवकारेणेतरनिषेधश्च । तत्रापि विशेषेण क्रीडा । नहि जीवो विशेषक्रीडां जानाति । खेचराणां स्त्रिय इति तासां सर्वदर्शनार्थं भगवद्दत्तो वरो निरूपितः । स्त्रीणां च दर्शनं न दोषाय । तासां मोह एवोत्पन्नः । न तु परिज्ञानम् । रसो वा । लौकिकोऽपि चन्द्रो दृष्टवान् । सोमात्मकत्वात् देहस्य । 'सोमः प्रथम'इति श्रुतेश्च । साधारण्यश्च स्त्रियः । तथापि तस्य दर्शनं तस्यैव हितकारि न भवतीति निरूपयितुमाह शशाङ्क इति । स हि कलङ्की । आनन्दमयोऽपि । सगणो नक्षत्रसहितः । तेनोद्दीपनेऽपि न तस्यान्यासु चित्तसम्भवः । चकारात् सोऽपि मुमुहे । यथा पुनरेताः मोहनानन्तरं पुनःपुनर्दर्शने उद्बुद्धकामा जाताः । गत्वास्माभिरपि कामरूपतया क्रीडा कर्तव्येति कामार्दिता जाताः । तथा चन्द्रोऽपि भगवति निवेशनार्थं यत्नं कृतवान् । अतः कामार्दितो जातः । अनेनाग्रे निसर्गात् सुखमिति पक्षे उपपत्तिरुक्ता । अस्यैव चन्द्रस्य अंशास्ततो निर्वतिष्यन्त इति । अन्यथा 'सहस्रवणान्मुक्ति'रित्येतत्सूत्रं विरुध्येत । सहस्रवणाभावात् । किञ्च, सगणः स्वस्त्रीसहितोऽपि विस्मितो जातः । विस्मयरस एवोत्पन्नः, नान्यो रस इति ॥१९॥

एवमाधिभौतिकानामाधिदैविकस्य च भगवदुत्पादितरसाभिनिवेशमुक्त्वा 'नन्दगोपसुतं देवि पतिं मे कुर्वि'ति प्रत्येकप्रार्थनया व्रतं कृतमिति प्रत्येकं रेम इत्याह कृत्वेति ।

कृत्वा तावन्तमात्मानं यावतीर्गोपयोषितः ।।
रेमे स भगवाँस्ताभिरात्मारामोऽपि लीलया ।।२०।।

गोपजातीया योषितो यावत्यस्तावन्तमात्मानं कृत्वा तत्र तत्र मायोद्घाटनेन तथा तथा प्रकटो भवति । एतन्महासौरतम् । एवं करणे सामर्थ्यम्, यतः स भगवानिति । स इति तदर्थमेवावतीर्णः । अत्र तासां व्रतार्थं ताभिः सहैव रेमे । न त्वात्मारामता पूर्ववत् । इममर्थमाह आत्मारामोऽपीति । न त्वात्माराम एव चन्द्रप्रवेशाद् रमणं सम्भवति । अस्यामपि दशायामात्मारामत्वमेव । 'अधिकं तत्रानुप्रविष्टं न तु तद्धानि'रिति । तत्रापि आत्मरमण एव मुख्यतेत्याह लीलयेति । यथा महानपि लीलया विसदृशं करोति । स्वयं पदातिरिव मृगयायां गच्छति । यथा अन्या अपि अवतारलीलाः, तथैतामपि कृतवानित्यर्थः ।।२०।।

ततस्तासां सुरतान्तो जात इत्याह तासामिति ।

तासामतिविहारेण श्रान्तानां वदनानि सः ।
प्रामृजत् करुणः प्रेम्णा शन्तमेनाङ्ग पाणिना ।।२१।।

अतिविहारेणानेकबन्धैः सम्यक् श्रान्ता जाताः । ततोऽग्रिमलीलार्थं तासां वदनानि स्वहस्तेन प्रामृजत् । यतः स कृष्णः । तदर्थमेवावतीर्णः । सर्वत्रैव तथाविधं जातमिति ज्ञापयितुं बहुवचनम् । तथा करणे हेतुः करुण इति । करुणायुक्तः । सा करुणा उदासीना न भवतीत्याह प्रेम्णेति । मार्जने क्लेश एव निवर्तत इति ज्ञापयितुं शन्तमेनेत्युक्तम् । अङ्गेति सम्बोधनमप्रतारणाय । एवं तासां दुःखनिवारणपूर्वकं परमानन्दं स्थापितवान् ।।२१।।

ततोऽतिमुदितानां कृत्यमाह गोप्य इति ।

गोप्यः स्फुरत्पुरटकुण्डलकुन्तलत्विड्गण्डश्रिया सुधितहासनिरीक्षणेन ।
मानं दधत्य ऋषभस्य जगुः कृतानि पुण्यानि तत्कररुहस्पर्शप्रमोदाः ।।२२।।

गोप्यो मानं दधत्यः तत्कृतानि जगुः । गाने हि रजोगुणाभिनिवेशो हेतुः । तदर्थं सहजमेकं भगवत्कृतं च हेतुद्वयमाह । तत्र प्रथमं सहजं निरूपयति । स्फुरद्यत् पुरटं सुवर्णं दाहोत्तीर्णमुज्ज्वलीकृतं च, तस्य ये कुण्डले कुन्तलाश्च, तेषां त्विषा सहिता या गण्डश्रीः । उज्ज्वला गण्डश्रीः पीता वा । उज्ज्वला नीला चेतरे । एवं कान्तित्रयं

मूलभूतगुणकार्यरूपम् । तेनासां सर्वोत्कर्षयोग्यता । सुधित सुधामिव प्राप्तं यद्धास-पूर्वकं निरीक्षणम् । अत्राप्यन्तःस्थितो रागः निरीक्षणं हासश्चेति त्रितयमुक्तम् । भगवदीयमेतत् । अत उभाभ्यां सन्माननमभिमानं वा दधत्यः स्वहृदयकृतविपरीत-बुद्ध्या जातदोषनिराकरणार्थं तत्कृतानि जगुः । तेषां न केवलं पापनिवर्तकत्वम्, किन्तु पुण्यरूपत्वमपीत्याह पुण्यानीति । भगवता कृतानि पापनिवर्तकानि पुण्य-जनकानि च । अतस्तासां दोषाभावः । अग्रिमलीलायां पुण्योपचयश्चोक्तः । पूर्व-क्लेशविस्मरणार्थमानन्दाविर्भावमाह । तस्य भगवतः कररुहा नखाः, तेषां स्पर्शेन जातपीडया स्मृतसम्भोगाः प्रमुदिताः जाताः । अन्तःपूर्णानन्दा गानेनापि जाता इति अन्ते विशेषणम् ॥२२॥

ततस्ताभिस्तुल्याभिर्भगवान् जलक्रीडां कृतवानित्याह ताभिर्युत इति ।

ताभिर्युतः श्रममपोहितुमङ्गसङ्गघृष्टस्रजः स्वकुचकुङ्कुमरञ्जितायाः ।
गन्धर्वपालिभिरनुद्रुत आविशद्वाः श्रान्तो गजीभिरिभराडिव भिन्नसेतुः ॥

ताभिः सर्वाभिरेवः युतः । महारात्रसमये यमुनायां जलक्रीडार्थं प्रविष्टः । तत्र प्रयोजनं श्रममपोहितुमिति । तासां सर्वाङ्गश्रमं जलक्रीडयैव दूरीकुर्वन् । भगवतस्ताभिः सह गमने जायमानां शोभां वर्णयति स्रजः गन्धर्वपालिभिरनुद्रुत इति । यमुनाया वा विशेषणानि । गन्धर्वाणां रक्षकाः गन्धर्वपाः गन्धर्वोत्तमाः । ते च ते अलयश्च तैरनुद्रुतः । सङ्गे शीघ्रं गतः वाः आविशत् । आमोदस्य निवारणार्थं च तथाकरणम् । सम्भोगेन श्रमोदके पद्मिनीनां कमलरूपो गन्धो भवति । तदुपरोधेन च द्रुतपदविन्यास इत्यनुद्रवणम् । ते च भ्रमरा भगवदीया एवेत्याह । अङ्गयोः सङ्गेन घृष्टा या स्रक् तस्यास्ते । यस्यां वा स्रक् तादृशी । स्वा चासौ कुचकुङ्कुमरञ्जिता च । भगवत एव माला । कालिन्दी च कुचकुङ्कुमै रञ्जिता । तत्र देहामोदः पुष्पा-मोदः कुङ्कुमामोदश्चेति । स्वकीयत्वेनासाधारण्यं च । आधिदैविकास्ते भ्रमरास्तद्-गन्धभोक्तार इति विशेषणं गन्धर्वपेति । श्रान्तः इभराडिवेति अविचारे हेतुः । श्रान्त इति विशेषणं लीलया गमनार्थम् । प्रत्येकसम्भोगावधि भगवतोऽन्यो भावो निरूपित इति तदपगमात् श्रमलीलाप्याविष्कृता । गजीभिरित्यन्यश्रमो निवारितः । सेतवो बध्यन्ते जलरक्षार्थम् । ते सर्वे भिन्नाः तादृशगजेन भवन्ति । भगवतापि ब्रह्ममर्यादा आत्मारामत्वरूपा जीवानां च मर्यादा तथा सति निवृत्ता । कामरूपस्पर्शात् पर-दाराणामभिमर्षणाच्च । पूर्वं तासां भगवत्स्पर्श एव स्थितः, न तु भगवता ताः स्पृष्टा इति । कामाभावात् । देशकालमर्यादा च भग्ना । अतो हस्तिश्रेष्ठ एव जल-क्रीडार्थं जलदेवतां दूरीकृत्य, स्वयं तत्र प्रविष्ट इत्यर्थः ॥२३॥

तत्र जलक्रीडां च कृतवानित्याह स इति ।

सोऽम्भस्यलं युवतिभिः परिषिच्यमानः
प्रेम्णेक्षितः प्रहसतीभिरितस्ततोऽङ्ग ।
वैमानिकैः कुसुमवर्षिभिरीड्यमानो
रेमे स्वयं स्वरतिरत्र गजेन्द्रलीलः ॥२४॥

स पूर्वोक्तः स्त्रीसहितः । अम्भसि अलं युवतिभिः परिषिच्यमानो जातः । ततः प्रेम्णा ईक्षितश्च । प्रहसतीभिः कौतुकाभिनिविष्टाभिः इतस्ततः सिच्यमानः, यदभिमुखमेव व्रजति, तयैव सह रेम इति । एवं सर्वाभिः । यथा स्वयं माहात्म्यज्ञानपूर्वकं निर्भरस्नेहेन निर्दोषभावेन वदति शुकः, तथैव राजापि शृणोतीति ज्ञात्वा स्नेहेन स्वमध्यपातित्वं सूचयन् सम्बोधयति अङ्गेति । अतः एव तुभ्यमिमां लीलां वदामीति भावः । ननु देवैः कथं न निषिध्यते, तत्राह कुसुमवर्षिभिर्वैमानिकैरीड्यमान इति । सर्वे देवा अभिनन्दनमेव कुर्वन्ति, न तु निवारणमिति । अन्यथा लोके कामरसो न व्यक्तो भवेदिति । युवत्य इत्यविचारे । परिषेके वीररसो मा भवत्विति प्रेम्णैव ईक्षितः । स्वयमिति पदेन बलात्कारेण।पि तथेति सूच्यते । तदापि स्वस्मिन्नेव रतिर्यस्य । परं स्वीकृता गजेन्द्रलीला येन । यथायथा जलेनोक्षणम्, तथातथा सखमिति गजदृष्टान्तः । महासौरतं च ॥२४॥

ततः पुष्पावचयक्रीडामाह तत इति ।

ततश्च कृष्णोपवने जलस्थलप्रसूनगन्धानिलजुष्टदिक्तटे ।
चचार भृङ्गप्रमदागणावृतो यथा मदच्युद् द्विरदः करेणुभिः ॥२५॥

जलक्रीडानन्तरं कृष्णायाः यमुनाया उपवने जलस्थलप्रसूनानां ये गन्धाः तत्सम्बन्धिना वायुना जुष्टाः दिक्तटाः सर्वदिग्भागा यस्मिन् वने तत्र पुनश्चचार। भृङ्गैः प्रमदागणैश्चावृतः। पुनर्भृङ्गाणां गमने हेतुं दृष्टान्तेनाह। यथा मदच्युत् मदस्रावी गण्डयोरन्यत्र च । द्विरदो हस्ती करेणुभिः सहितो भवति, भ्रमरैश्च सहितः । सहज एवान्तःस्थितो रस आविर्भूत इति भ्रमराणामनुद्रवणम् । चचारेति सर्वत्र नानाविधलीला निरूपिता । क्वचिल्लतानां भङ्गः, क्वचिद् वृक्षशाखानाम् । तथा मर्यादामार्गः लौकिकश्चान्यथाकृत इति । एषा त्रिविधा लीला अत्यलौकिकी । तत अविचारेण रमणमिति ॥२५॥

एवं लीलामुक्त्वोपसंहरति एवमिति ।

एवं शशाङ्कांशुविराजिता निशाः ससत्यकामोऽनुरताबलागणः ।
सिषेव आत्मन्युपरुद्धसौरतः सर्वाः शरत्काव्यकथा रसाश्रयाः ॥२६॥

शशाङ्कांशुभिः चन्द्रकिरणैः लौकिकैः या विराजिता निशाः ता एवं रेमे। पूर्वोक्तप्रकारस्तु सर्वदा लीलारूपः। स केनापि न विरुध्यते। नन्वेवं रमणे को हेतुरिति चेत्, तत्राह ससत्यकाम इति। सत्यः कामो यासां ताः सत्यकामाः। ताभिः सहित इति ससत्यकामः। स इति तथा प्रार्थितो वा। एवमपि क्रीडायां कामः सत्य एव स्थितः, न तु क्षीणः, असद्विषयको वा जातः। अनुरता अबलागणा यस्य। सर्वथा रतासु नित्यसम्बद्धासु स्वविवाहितासु न कापि शङ्का, सर्वथा प्रपन्नासु च। अग्रे मर्यादाभङ्गो रसपोषाय। तदुक्तं 'शास्त्राणां विषयस्तावद् मन्दरसा नराः। रतिचक्रे प्रवृत्ते तु नैव शास्त्रं न च क्रम' इति। तथापि तासु सत्य एव कामः स्थापितः। यो मोक्षपर्यवसायी। स कामो भगवन्तं प्रापयिष्यत्येव। एवं निशाः सिषेवे। तदनन्तरमात्मन्येव उपरुद्धं सौरतं यस्य तथा जातः। न तु तासु रतिं स्थापितवान्। तथा सति तासु स्वस्मात् पुत्रा भवेयुः। सर्वा एव निशा एवं नीताः। शरदपि नीता। काव्यकथा अपि नीताः। काव्योक्तप्रकारेण गीतगोविन्दोक्तन्यायेनापि रतिं कृतवान्। तत्र हेतुः रसाश्रया इति। कामरसस्तेष्वेव प्रसिद्धः। यावत् पुरुषो रसे गौणभावं न प्राप्नोति, तावन्न रसिको भवतीति। शरद्वर्णनायां वा यत् काव्यम्, तत्र याः कथाः, तासां रसाश्रया इति। निशा एता न लोकप्रसिद्धाः, किन्तु काव्योक्ता एव। तत्र हि नियतिकृत्यादिराहित्यं ह्लादैकता अनन्याधीनता, तथा अन्येऽपि गुणाः। तथा भगवल्लीलारात्रयो जाता इत्यर्थः ॥२६॥

एवमेतां लीलां श्रुत्वा राज्ञः सन्देह उत्पन्नः। तन्निवारणार्थं शङ्कते संस्थापनायेति त्रिभिः।

राजोवाच— **संस्थापनाय धर्मस्य प्रशमायेतरस्य च।**
अवतीर्णो हि भगवानंशेन जगदीश्वरः ॥२७॥

अवतारविरुद्धं लोकवेदविरुद्धं प्रमेयविरुद्धं चेति। तादृशकरणे अवश्यं हेतुर्वक्तव्यः। तदभावेऽपि लीलायाः सिद्धत्वात्। तत्र प्रथममवतारविरोधमाह। धर्मसंस्थापनाय भगवदवतारः। 'धर्मसंस्थापनाय चे' ति वाक्यात्। अधर्मनिवृत्तये च। तदुभयार्थमेव भगवदवतारः। दैत्यादिवधो भूभारहरणं च अधर्मनिवृत्तये। एतदर्थमेवावतारः, नान्यार्थमिति हिशब्द आह। भगवानिति तस्य साधनम्। अन्यथा पूर्णकामस्यावतारो न घटेतेति। लोकोपकारश्च एताभ्यामेव। अंशेन बलभद्रेण। आगत्य तथाकरणे हेतुः जगदीश्वर इति। स हि सर्वरक्षकः। अतः पालनार्थमेवं कृतवान् ॥२७॥

किमतो यद्येवम्, एवमेतदित्याह स कथमिति।

स कथं धर्मसेतूनां कर्ता वक्ताभिरक्षिता।
प्रतीपमाचरद् ब्रह्मन् परदाराभिमर्शनम् ॥२८॥

धर्ममर्यादापालकानां निर्माता। स्वयं वक्ता च। उपघातेऽभिरक्षिता च। तादृशः प्रतीपं प्रतिकूलमाचरत्। धर्मो नष्टः, अधर्मः स्थापितः। अधर्मः कृतः उक्तः रक्षितश्च। अतः प्रतीपाचरणमयुक्तम्। तत्र हेतुर्वक्तव्य इति। ब्रह्मन्निति सम्बोधनम्। ये पञ्च-पदार्था उक्ताः, तेषां स्वरूपमेकत्रैवेति तन्निर्दिशति परदाराभिमर्शनमिति ॥२८॥

ननु कामात् करणमिति चेत्। तत्राह आप्तकाम इति।

आप्तकामो यदुपतिः कृतवान् वै जुगुप्सितम्।
किमभिप्राय एतं नः संशयं छिन्धि सुव्रत ॥२९॥

स्वत एवाप्ताः कामा येन। यदुपतिरिति विद्यमानायामपि कामनायामनेकस्त्री-प्राप्तिः। तादृशोऽपि भूत्वा जुगुप्सितं लोकनिन्दितं कृतवान्। तत्र करणे कोऽभिप्रायः। परस्परविरुद्धार्थत्वादुभयोर्ग्रहणं न सम्भवति। नैकतापि विरुद्धानाम्। विरुद्ध-सर्वधर्माश्रयत्वेऽपि प्रयोजनं वक्तव्यम्। नैतत् कर्म लोकहितम्, नापि स्वहितम्। स्वस्य पूर्णत्वात्। लोकस्य मर्यादैव हितकारिणी। तथा गोपिकानामपि। अन्तर्यामिण ईश्वरस्य न किञ्चिदसाध्यम्। अत एवं सति किमभिप्राय एतत् कृतवान्। कः अभिप्रायो यस्येति। एतं नोऽस्माकं सर्वेषामेव संशयं छिन्धि। किञ्च, सुव्रत हे सदा-चारलक्षणव्रतयुक्त। यदीदमसङ्गतमिव स्यात्, त्वया नोक्तं स्यात्। यदि वा अधर्मः स्यात्, तव रुचिर्न स्यात्। प्रतीयते च विपरीतम्, अतो निर्णयो वक्तव्य इत्यर्थः ॥२९॥

प्रथमतः अवतारविरुद्धं कृतवानिति यदुक्तम्, तत्रोत्तरमाह धर्मव्यतिक्रम इति।

श्रीशुक उवाच—**धर्मव्यतिक्रमो दृष्ट ईश्वराणां च साहसम्।**
तेजीयसां न दोषाय वह्नेः सर्वभुजो यथा ॥३०॥

किमेतदीश्वराणां चरित्रं न भवतीत्युच्यते। आहोस्विदन्यार्थमागतोऽन्यत् करोतीति। नहि किञ्चिद् घटनार्थमागतः किञ्चिन्न विघटयति। न ह्यन्यार्थमप्या-गतः स्वधर्मं परित्यजति। प्रकाशनार्थमागतो दीपः गृहेण स्पृष्टश्चेत् दहत्येव। अत ईश्वरधर्मोऽयम्। अन्यथा ईश्वर एव न भवेत्। नहि वणिजामिव प्रभोर्नियमोऽस्ति सर्वकर्मसु। ईश्वरधर्माश्चैते इति तान् गणयति धर्मव्यतिक्रमः साहसमित्यादयः। धर्मव्यतिक्रमो विद्यमानोल्लङ्घनम्। साहसमविद्यमानकरणम्। एतदुभयमीश्वरे दृष्टम्। 'नहि दृष्टे अनुपपन्नं नाम'। चकारादीश्वरसेवकानामपि, वीर्यादिमतां वा। एतदेव वा साहसम्, सहसा क्रियमाणत्वात्। नन्वेवं सति तत्कर्मफलं कथं न भवेदित्याशङ्क्याह तेजीयसामिति। अतितेजस्विनामेतन्नाधर्मजनकम्। विधिनिषेध-वाक्यानां नियोज्यविषयत्वात्। यथा लोके, तथा वेदेऽपि। अतितेजस्विनां सर्वकर्म-

दहनसमर्थानां न दोषजनकं भवतीत्यत्र दृष्टान्तमाह वह्नेः सर्वभुज इति। नहि सर्वान् दहन् वह्निर्वधभाग् भवति। सर्वं भक्षयन् अभक्ष्यभक्षको वा। तथा सर्वं पिबन् सर्वत्र प्रविशन् सर्वसम्बद्धः तत्तत्कारी भवति। मिथ्याज्ञानसलिलावसिक्तायामेवात्मभूमौ कर्मबीजं धर्माधर्माङ्कुरतामारभते, न तु तत्त्वज्ञाननिदाघनिष्पीतसलिलतयोषरायाम् ॥३०॥

ननु 'तेजीयसामपि ह्येतन्नसुश्लोक्य'मिति न्यायाद् 'यद्वृत्तमनुतिष्ठन् वै लोकः क्षेमाय कल्पत' इति विरोधाच्च कथमेतत् कर्तुं शक्यत् इति चेत्, तत्राह नैतत् समाचरेदिति।

नैतत् समाचरेज्जातु मनसापि ह्यनीश्वरः।
विनश्यत्याचरन्मौढ्याद्यथा रुद्रोऽब्धिजं विषम् ॥३१॥

एतदीश्वरकृतमनीश्वरो न समाचरेत्। ऐश्वर्यसमानाधिकरणमेवैतत् नानिष्टं करोति। अतः जातु कदाचिदपि औत्सुक्यादपि न समाचरेत्। किं बहुना मनसापि। ऐश्वर्यतुल्यमेव तेषां तत्कर्म। यथैश्वर्यकामनायामपि अनीश्वरो वधमर्हति। यथा महाराज्यानधिकारी तदिच्छां कुर्वन्। अतो मनसापि न समाचरेत्। विपरीते बाधकमाह विनश्यतीति। मौढ्यादैश्वर्यसहभावं तस्य कर्मणः अज्ञात्वा केवलं तत् कर्म आरचन् तेनैव कर्मणा नष्टो भवति। नन्वेकमेव कर्म कथं धर्मान्तरसहितं न नाशकम्, इतरथा नाशकमिति चेत्, तत्राह। अरुद्रः रुद्रव्यतिरिक्तः रुद्रसमानपराक्रमरहितः अब्धिजं विषं कालकूटमाचरन् आसमन्ताद् भक्षयन् विनश्यति तथेत्यर्थः। निन्दितं कर्मापि कालकूटवन्नाशकम्। तदीश्वरस्यैव शोभाकरम्, येन नीलकण्ठो भवति। तथैव गोपीजनवल्लभ इति ॥३१॥

ननूक्तं 'यद्वृत्तमनुतिष्ठ'न्निति, तत्राह ईश्वराणामिति।

ईश्वराणां वचस्तथ्यं तथैवाचरितं क्वचित्।
तेषां यत् स्ववचो युक्तं बुद्धिमाँस्तत् समाचरेत् ॥३२॥

ईश्वराणां वच एव तथ्यम्, न त्वाचरितम्। क्वचिदाचरितमपि वचनानुगुणं चेत्। ईश्वराणां बहवो धर्माः। यथैश्वर्यम्, तथा धर्मात्मत्वम्, तथा दया। तत्रैश्वर्यज्ञानवैराग्यैर्यत् करोति, तत् स्वच्छन्दचरितमित्युच्यते। बुद्धिमान् तन्न समाचरेत्। ते ह्यन्यथा न वदन्ति। अन्यार्थं कथनमन्याधिकारेणेति। अतस्तद्विरुद्धं न कथयन्तीति ॥३२॥

ननु यथान्यस्मै न कथयन्ति, तथा स्वयमपि कुतो न कुर्वन्ति, तत्राह कुशलाचरितेनेति।

कुशलाचरितेनैषामिह स्वार्थो न विद्यते ।
विपर्ययेण वानर्थो निरहङ्कारिणां प्रभो ॥३३॥

एषामीश्वराणां कुशलाचरितेन अर्थः प्रयोजनं न विद्यते, ततोऽप्यनन्तफलस्य प्राप्तत्वादेव । विपर्ययेण अकुशलाचरितेन अनर्थोऽपि न विद्यते । ईश्वराणामेव निषिद्धकर्मणा अनिष्टाभाव इति न, किन्तु ज्ञानिनामपीति ज्ञानवैराग्ययोस्तुल्यं स्वरूपमाह निरहङ्कारिणामिति : अहङ्काररहितानाम् । न केनापि किमपि, कर्तृत्वाभिमानाभावात् । प्रभो इति सम्बोधनमीश्वरस्य लोकविलक्षणत्वज्ञापनार्थम् ॥३३॥

यत्र ज्ञानसहकृतमेव तत्कर्म नानिष्टजनकम्, किं वक्तव्यमैश्वर्यसहकृतमित्याह किमुतेति ।

किमुताखिलसत्त्वानां तिर्यङमर्त्यदिवौकसाम् ।
ईशितुश्चेशितव्यानां कुशलाकुशलान्वयः ॥३४॥

ईश्वरस्य सेवकमारणे सेवकानामन्यथाकरणे च न काचित् शङ्का भवति । यथैहिकी, तथा पारलौकिकी । नियामकाद्धि शङ्का । भगवतो न नियामकोऽन्योऽस्तीत्याह । अखिलसत्त्वानां सर्वजीवानाम् । तिर्यङमर्त्यदिवौकसां गुणत्रयकार्याणां जीवजडानामप्राकृतप्राकृतानां वा सर्वेषामेव ईशितुः प्रभो : कृष्णस्य । चकारादात्मनश्च । ईशितव्यानां सेवकानां सम्बन्धी । तत्कृतगुणदोषाभ्यां कुशलाकुशलयोरन्वयः कुतः । नहि दासीभिः स्वात्मभूताभि सम्बन्धे अनियम्यस्य ऐहिके पारलौकिके वा कश्चनापकारः सम्भवति । अन्तरङ्गैरेव तथा ज्ञायत इति न सुश्लोक्यतानिवृत्तिः ॥३४॥

नापि कर्ममार्गविचारेण कर्मप्राधान्यपक्षेऽपि दोषःशङ्कनीयः । यथा 'परमेष्ठिनो वा एष यज्ञोऽग्र आसीत्' 'ब्रह्म वा इदमग्र आसीत्' 'स आत्मानमेवावैत्' इत्यादिश्रुतिषु यथाज्ञानकर्मभ्यामुत्कर्षः, एवमपकृष्टज्ञानकर्मभ्यामपकर्षोऽपि सम्भाव्यत इति, तत्राह यत्पादेति ।

यत्पादपङ्कजपरागनिषेवतृप्ता योगप्रभावविधुताखिलकर्मबन्धाः ।
स्वैरं चरन्ति मुनयोऽपि न नह्यमानास्तस्येच्छयात्तवपुषः कुत एव बन्धः ॥

नहि सर्वेषामेव जीवानां समानकर्मणा समानं फलमुपलभ्यते । अन्यथा शास्त्रवैफल्यापत्तिः । उत्कृष्टकर्मादौ प्रवृत्तो नापकृष्टकर्मणा कादाचित्केन अपकृष्टो भवति । तत्र मार्गत्रयम् । त्रिष्वपि प्रवृत्तो नापकर्षं यातीत्याह । तत्र प्रथमं भक्तिमार्गे

प्रवृत्तस्य, तत्र पुष्टस्य, न केनाप्यपकर्ष इत्याह । यस्य भगवतः पादपङ्कजस्य परागभूता ये सेवकाः तेषां निषेवो निषेवणं तेन तृप्ताः । भगवद्भक्तैः सह भगवद्‌गुणस्मरणेनैव स्मारितदृष्टश्रुतसुखलेशाभासाः स्वैरं चरन्ति । न तेषां कर्मोत्कर्षापकर्षौ साधकबाधकौ । तथा कर्ममार्गेऽपीत्याह योगप्रभावेति । योगो हि महान् धर्मः । 'अयं हि परमो धर्म' इति स्मृतेः । तस्य प्रभावः अणिमाद्यैश्वर्यसम्पत्तिः । ज्ञानादयश्च । तेनैव विशेषेण धुताः । पूर्वकर्मजनिता अपि अखिलकर्मबन्धाः विशेषेण धुता भवन्ति । तेऽपि स्वैरं चरन्ति । ज्ञानमार्गेऽप्याह मुनयोऽपि स्वैरं चरन्तीति । सर्व एव न नह्यमानाः अबध्यमानाः । णह् बन्धने । सर्वत्रैव असम्बध्यमानाः । यत्र भगवत्प्रवर्तितमार्गेष्वप्येषा व्यवस्था, तत्र भगवतः किं वक्तव्यमित्याह तस्येच्छयात्तवपुष इति । इच्छया भोगार्थं आत्तानि वपूंषि 'यावतीर्गोपयोषित' इति तावन्ति येन । तस्य कुत एव बन्धो भवेत् । यो हि तावद्रूपो भवति, कार्यं कृत्वा च तान्याच्छादयति, तस्य केन कर्मणा बन्धो भवेत् । कर्म हि प्रतिनियतं व्यवस्थितम् । तत्र यदि भिन्नो भिन्नो जीवः स्यात्, तदा तेन कर्मणा बन्धो वा भवेत् । आकाशवद् भगवद्रूपाणि प्रतिपदमन्यान्येव भवन्ति । यथान्नभेदेनाप्येकदेहव्यवहारः, एवं देशभेदेनापि भगवतः सर्वतः पाणिपादान्तस्य तावत्परिच्छेदेन प्रादुर्भावं इच्छयेति । स्वामिनीनां वा वपूंषि । अतः सर्वथा प्रमाणप्रमेयविचारेणापि न बन्धः सम्भवति ॥३५॥

ननु तथापि लोकमर्यादाया भग्नत्वात् 'यद्यदाचरति श्रेष्ठ' इति न्यायेन शब्दबलविचारेण बन्धो भवेत् । ते ह्यवधूतास्त्रयोऽपि, न ते व्यवहारनियामकाः । अतो विषमो दृष्टान्त इति चेत्, तत्राह गोपीनामिति ।

गोपीनां तत्पतीनां च सर्वेषामपि देहिनाम् ।
योऽन्तश्चरति सोऽध्यक्षः क्रीडनेनेह देहभाक् ॥३६॥

नहि स्वस्पर्शः स्वस्य क्वापि निषिद्धः । परा चासौ स्त्री च परस्य च स्त्री । उभयमपि न भगवति । यतः भगवान् गोपीनां तत्पतीनां च आत्मा । बान्धवाः सर्वे लौकिकाश्च न मन्यन्त इति चेत्, तत्राह । सर्वेषामपि देहिनामयमात्मेति । यो भगवान् अन्तश्चरति । आसन्यो जीवो वा । सर्ववादिसिद्धान्तसंग्रहाय सामान्यवचनं योऽन्तश्चरतीति । स एवायं भगवानध्यक्षः प्रत्यक्षः क्रीडनेन कृत्वा नटवत् पुरुषदेहं भजते । वस्तुतस्तु नायं पुमान्, न च स्त्री, नाप्यन्यः कश्चित् । 'न स्त्री न षण्ढो न पुमा'निति श्रुतेः । अतः केनापि विचारेण नास्य दोषसम्भवः ॥३६॥

ननु तथापि एवंकरणे कोऽभिप्राय इति चेत्, तत्राह अनुग्रहायेति ।

अनुग्रहाय भक्तानां मानुषं देहमास्थितः ।
भजते तादृशीः क्रीडाः याः श्रुत्वा तत्परो भवेत् ॥३७॥

भक्तानामनुग्रहार्थमेव भक्तसमानरूपं देहमास्थितः । विजातीये तेषां विश्वासो न भवेदिति । ततो यथा मनुष्यानुग्रहाय मानुषो देहः प्रदर्शितः, एवं गोपिकानामप्यनुग्रहाय स्वानन्दं गोकुले दातुं तादृशीः क्रीडाः भजते । तत्तद्धर्मप्रवेशव्यतिरेकेण तस्य तस्य दोषस्यानिवृत्तत्वात् । यद्वा । भक्तानां मानुषं देहं प्रति आस्था सञ्जातास्मिन्निति स तथा । तत्रापि महान् पूर्णकामः सर्वं दातुं शक्तः । न त्वेवं निषिद्धप्रकारेणात्मनं दातुमिति । अत एतां लीलां निरोधपूर्वकादेयदानरूपां यः श्रोष्यति, सः सर्वथा भगवत्परो भविष्यतीति भगवता तथाचरणं कृतम् । तदाह याः श्रुत्वा तत्परो भवेदिति ॥३७॥

ननु तथापि लोकव्यवहारे स्त्रियोऽन्याधीना इति अदत्तोपादानं गोपानां मनसि खेदः तैः क्रियमाणा अपकीर्तिश्च भवेदित्याशङ्क्याह नासूयन्निति ।

नासूयन् खलु कृष्णाय मोहितास्तस्य मायया ।
मन्यमानाः स्वपार्श्वस्थान् स्वान्स्वान्दारान् व्रजौकसः ॥३८॥

ते भगवन्तं नासूयन्, असूयया न दृष्टवन्तः । प्रथमतः प्रवृत्तिं ज्ञात्वापि भगवन्मायया मोहिता नासूयन् । अग्रे तु स्वपार्श्वस्थानेव स्वान् स्वान् दारान् मन्यमाना जाताः । यतो व्रजौकसः पूर्वापरानुसन्धानरहिताः । सर्वथाङ्गीकृता इति वा । एतादृशानां प्रभौ दोषारोपासम्भवादिति भावः । अयमर्थः सर्वजनीन इति खल्वित्युक्तम् । भगवत्सान्निध्येऽपि मोहार्थं तस्येति । बुद्धिरेव तेषां भ्रमात् । शिष्टं भगवत एवेति । मननमात्रेणैव सर्वदोषपरिहारः । अनेन तास्वपि दोषारोपो निवारितः ॥३८॥

एवं प्रासङ्गिकं परिहृत्य उक्तां लीलामुपसंहरति ब्रह्मरात्र इति ।

ब्रह्मरात्र उपावृत्ते वासुदेवानुमोदिताः ।
अनिच्छन्त्यो ययुर्गोप्यः स्वगृहान् भगवत्प्रियाः ॥३९॥

अरुणोदयो ब्रह्मरात्रम्, तस्मिन् उपावृत्ते सम्यक् जाते । तदन्तर्यामितया प्रविष्टो भगवान् गृहे गन्तव्यमितीच्छामुत्पादितवान् । ततः भगवतानुज्ञाताः । यतो भगवान् मोक्षदाता । ताश्चेत् आसन्ध्यमन्तःस्मरणं करिष्यन्ति, तदा मोक्षाधिकारिण्यो भविष्यन्तीति वासुदेवेनानुमोदिताः । यद्यपि तासामिच्छा न स्थिता, सर्वपरित्यागेन भगवद्भजनस्य कृतत्वात्, किं गृहेण लोकैर्वेति, तथापि गोप्य इति, विपरीतबुद्धिर्हठबुद्धिश्च तासां नास्तीति, स्वगृहान् ययुः । तथापि तासां न गृहाः प्रियाः किन्तु भगवानेव । नापि संसारभयम्, यतो भगवतः प्रियाः ॥३९॥

मोक्षार्थमिदं चरित्रमिति ज्ञापयितुं एतदुपाख्यानश्रवणस्य फलमाह विक्रीडितमिति ।

विक्रीडितं व्रजवधूभिरिदं च विष्णोः श्रद्धान्वितोऽनुशृणुयादथ वर्णयेद्यः ।
भक्तिं परां भगवति प्रतिलभ्य कामं हृद्रोगमाश्वपहिनोत्यचिरेण धीरः ॥

इति श्रीमद्भागवते महापुराणे दशमस्कन्धे पूर्वार्धे रासक्रीडावर्णनं नाम त्रिंशोऽध्यायः ॥

व्रजवधूभिः सह भगवत इदं विशेषेण क्रीडितं श्रद्धान्वितो भूत्वा सम्यक् कथ्यमानमुपशृणुयात् । अथवा वर्णयेत् । श्रवणानन्तरमेव कीर्तनमित्यथशब्दः । य इति नात्र वर्णादिनियमः, किन्तु यः कश्चन । भगवतो माहात्म्यश्रवणादेवमपि मोचयतीति । भक्तानां च सर्वथा प्रतिपत्तिश्रवणाच्च । भगवति परां भक्तिमुपगतः । ततो भक्त्या अन्तः स्थिरीभूतया हृदयस्य रोगरूपं काममाशु शीघ्रमेवापहिनोति । यः पूर्वं हृदयबाधकत्वेन स्थितः, शीघ्रमेव च बाधकर्ता, तमाश्वेव दूरीकरोति । श्रवणमात्रेणैव । ततः पूर्ववासनया पुनरुद्गमे अचिरेणैव धीरो भवति । अत इदं साभिप्रायं श्रोतव्यमिति फलप्रकरणत्वात् फलमुक्तम् ॥४०॥

इति श्रीभागवतसुबोधिन्यां श्रीमल्लक्ष्मणभट्टात्मजश्रीमद्वल्लभदीक्षितविरचितायां दशमस्कन्धविवरणे त्रिंशाध्यायविवरणम् ॥

श्रीकृष्णाय नमः ।

परिशिष्टम्

।। युगलगीतम् ।।

द्वात्रिंशोऽध्यायः

द्वात्रिंशेऽन्तर्गोपिकानां स्वानन्दं भगवान् हरिः ।
पूरयामास येनैव पूर्णानन्द इतीर्यते ।।१।।

अन्तःप्रविष्टो भगवान् मुखादुद्धृत्य कर्णयोः ।
पुनर्निवेश्यते सम्यक् तदा भवति सुस्थिरः ।।२।।

शब्दार्थयोर्मुख्यतात्र युग्माः श्लोकास्ततोऽत्र हि ।
सर्वेषु चैव मासेषु यत् करोत्युच्यते हि तत् ।।३।।
अतोऽत्र मासयुग्मा हि प्रक्रमः फलमेव च ।
आद्यन्ते चापरं युग्मं त्रयोदश भवन्ति तत् ।।४।।

एवं भगवता सह रात्रौ क्रीडामुक्त्वा, दिने तासां संसारप्रवृत्तिर्भविष्यतीत्याशङ्क्य, दिवसेषु भगवद्गुणवर्णनपरा जाता इति वदन्, गुणवर्णनाया आवश्यकत्वाय आरम्भे दुःखं, पर्यवसाने सुखमिति निरूपयन्, प्रथमं प्रथमप्रवृत्तावपि गोपिकानां दिवसेषु परमं दुःखं जातमित्याह गोप्य इति ।

श्रीशुक उवाच—**गोप्यः कृष्णे वनं याते तमनुद्रुतचेतसः ।**
कृष्णलीलाः प्रगायन्त्यो निन्युर्दुःखेन वासरान् ।।१।।

केवलपदात् पूर्वोक्ता ग्राह्याः । सदानन्दे वनं गते तमन्वेव द्रुतं चित्तं यासाम् । वस्त्वन्तरग्रहणाक्षमं चित्तं जातम् । द्रुतशब्दाद्विलय उक्तः । ततः सर्वतः प्रसृतं सूक्ष्मभावापन्नं सदानन्दस्य लीलां गृहीतवत् । अतः कृष्णलीलाः प्रगायन्त्यो जाताः । यथा स्वरूपं सदानन्दरूपम्, तथा तल्लीला अपीति तदात्मकत्वं च लीलानां ज्ञापयितुं पुनर्नामग्रहणं कृतम् । अन्यथा तत्पदमेव वदेत् । तथा सति तत्सम्बन्धित्वमात्रं प्राप्येत, न तूक्तरूपत्वम् । अवश्यं वाच्यं चैतत् । यतः स्वरूपवियोगे तदतिरिक्तस्य न जीवनहेतुत्वम्, ततो हीनत्वात् । ततो यथाकथञ्चिन्महता मानसदुःखेन वासरान् निन्युः । यदा पुनस्तच्चित्तं प्रकीर्णे भगवच्चरित्रे विलीनं सद् एकभावं प्राप्स्यति,

तदा पूर्णमनोरथा भविष्यन्ति । इदानीं सर्वा सामग्री विशकलितेति दुःखेन दिन-नयनम् । वासरपदाद् रात्र्यर्थं कथञ्चित् प्राणानां धारणं लक्ष्यते ॥१॥

सर्वोत्तमा हरेर्लीला वेणुनादपुरःसरा ।
हेतुः सर्वत्र वाच्येऽर्थे प्रथमेषे निरूप्यते ॥१॥

देवस्त्रियस्तथा गावः सरितः पादपा लताः ।
पक्षिणश्च तथा मेघा ब्रह्माद्या गोपिकास्तथा ॥२॥

हरिण्यो देवगन्धर्वा द्विधा च भगवान् हरिः ।
उत्तरेषु निरूप्यन्ते रसज्ञा वेणुवादने ॥३॥

जानाति भगवानेव जानात्येव हरिः स्वयम् ।
अतोऽन्ते भगवानुक्तो वारद्वयमनन्यधीः ॥४॥

अनुभावस्तु नादस्य स्त्रीषु पूर्वमुदीर्यते ।
त्रिविधासु ततः पुंसु ब्रह्मा गोपी तथा मृगी ॥५॥

त्रयोऽत्र त्रिविधाः प्रोक्ताः प्रकीर्णाः सकलाः सुराः ॥
सर्व एवानभिज्ञा हि वस्तुसामर्थ्यसंयुताः ॥६॥

एवं वेणुर्द्वादशधा फलतीति निरूपितः ॥

तत्र प्रथमं स्त्रीप्राधान्याद् देवस्त्रियो मुख्या इति तासु वेणुनादप्रभावं वक्तुं येन प्रकारेण वेणुनाद उत्तिष्ठति, तं प्रकारमाहुः वामबाहुकृतवामकपोल इति ।

वामबाहुकृतवामकपोलो वल्गितभ्रुरधरार्पितवेणुम् ।
कोमलाङ्गुलिभिराश्रितमार्गं गोप्य ईरयति यत्र मुकुन्दः ॥२॥

व्योमयानवनिताः सह सिद्धैर्विस्मितास्तदुपधार्य सलज्जाः ।
काममार्गणसमर्पितचित्ताः कश्मलं ययुरपस्मृतनीव्यः ॥ ३ ॥

यत्र मुकुन्दः अधरार्पितवेणुमीरयति, तत्र तस्मिन् क्षणे व्योमयानवनिताः कश्मलं ययुरिति सम्बन्धः । वेणुनादः पञ्चधा भवति। मुखस्य परितः समतया उपर्यधश्च धारणेन। तत्र स्त्रीणां कामोद्बोधकः वामपरावृत्तः। स्त्रीणां पुरुषाणां च दक्षिणः। देवानामुच्चैः। अधस्तिरश्चाम्। समतया सर्वेषामचेतनानां च। तत्र देवस्त्रीणां कामोद्बोधको वामपरावृत्त एवेति तथा निरूप्यते। मानुषभावाद्देवभावो महानिति मानुष-

नादेन देवस्त्रीणां भ्रमो न भविष्यतीत्याशङ्क्य, 'तद्भ्रूविजृम्भः परमेष्ठिधिष्ण्य'मिति वाक्याद्, भ्रूविलासं नादे योजितवान्। तदाह । वामबाहौ कृतो योजितो वामकपोलो येन। वल्गिता भ्रूर्यस्येति । भ्रूरत्र दक्षिणा। तथैवाभिनयभावात् । वल्गिता उच्चैर्गतियुक्ता । अधरः पूर्वं वर्णितः लोभात्मकः । तत्र चेत्समर्पितः, परमानन्दं न प्रयच्छति। काममेवोद्बोधयति। यतः श्रुत्वापि विरहजनितक्लेशमेव प्राप्नुवन्ति, नतु परमानन्दम्। तत्रापि क्रियाशक्तिः पुष्टा चेद् भवेत्, तदा लुब्धादपि फलं सिध्येत् । तदपि नास्तीत्याह। कोमलाङ्गुलिभिराश्रितो मार्गो यस्य। आदौ मन्दप्रकारेणैव वेणुनादस्योचितत्वात् । मार्गास्तस्य रन्ध्राः । तेषां गाढभावेन निष्पीडने तारो नादो भवति। मध्यभावे मध्यमः। कोमले मन्द इति। गोप्य इति सम्बोधनं सर्वानुभवसाक्षिकमेतदिति ज्ञापयितुम्। ईरणमत्र वादनम्। प्रयोजनमाह मुकुन्द इति। वेणुनादेन शुद्धं चेत् जगत्, तदा मोक्षं दास्यामीति। एवं हितार्थेऽपि वेणुवादने, ये मोक्षानधिकारिणः, तेषां काम एव जात इत्याहुः व्योमयानवनिता इति । व्योमयानाः विमानयानाः सर्वे देवयोनयः तेषां वनिताः। अधिकारित्वात् स्त्रीत्वाद् भोग्यत्वाच्च न मुक्त्यधिकारिण्यः। सिद्धैः सहिता अपि। भगवद्व्यतिरिक्तं सर्वमेव दातुं समर्थाः। स्वयमत्यन्तं गाने निपुणाः। आदौ वेणुनादं श्रुत्वा विस्मिता जाताः। ततोऽल्पकामोद्रेके तद्वेणुनादमुपधार्य सलज्जा जाताः। भर्तारो ज्ञास्यन्तीति। ततोऽत्यन्तमुद्रेके स्वात्मरक्षार्थं कामेन मरणशङ्कया काममार्गणेभ्यः समर्पितं चित्तं याभिस्तादृश्यो जाताः। यथा मारकाय मारणात् पूर्वं स्वयमेव समर्प्यते भीरुभिः। ततः कामेन पीडिताः कश्मलं मूर्च्छां ययुः। सा मूर्च्छा अत्यन्तविस्मारिकेत्याह। अपस्मृता नीवी कटिवस्त्रं याभिरिति। एवं वेणुनादोऽत्यन्तं कामबोधक इत्यस्माकं मूर्च्छादौ किमाश्चर्यमिति भावः ॥२॥३॥

गवामपि वेणुनादेन तथा जातमिति वक्तुं प्रकारान्तरेण वेणुरवोद्गममाहुः हन्त चित्रमिति ।

हन्त चित्रमबलाः शृणुतेदं हारहास उरसि स्थिरविद्युत्।
नन्दसूनुरयमार्तजनानां नर्मदो यर्हि कूजितवेणुः ॥४॥

वृन्दशो व्रजवृषा मृगगावो वेणुवाद्यहृतचेतस आरात्।
दन्तदष्टकवला धृतकर्णा निद्रिता लिखितचित्रमिवासन् ॥५॥

हे अबलाः, इदमाश्चर्यं शृणुत। यर्हि नन्दसूनुः कूजितवेणुः, तर्हि वृषा गावो दन्तदष्टकवला निद्रिता आसन्निति सम्बन्धः। कामः पशुषु सजातीय एव, नोत्कृष्टे नापकृष्टे। अश्वतरे त्वन्यैव व्यवस्था। हीनेषु महतो रमणार्थं सम्बन्धोऽपि रसाभासजनकः। अतः सम्भोगलक्षणं कामं निराकृत्य पशुष्वत्यावश्यकं भक्ष्यं निरुणद्धि ।

पूर्वोक्तं वामबाहुकृतवामकपोलत्वमनुवर्तते । तत्रैवावान्तरभेदो वक्तव्य : । हन्तेति खेदे । यत्र गवामपि सर्वक्रियानिवृत्तिः, तत्रास्माकं न निवर्तते इति चित्रम् । पूर्वापेक्षयाप्युत्कृष्टम् । देवस्त्रियो हि पुरुषोत्तमे कामुक्यो भवन्त्येव । इदं त्वत्याश्चर्यमिति । अबला इति सम्बोधनं गत्वा दर्शनाभावाय। इदं मया प्रोच्यमानं शृणुत। अत्र गोपिका नवविधाः । गुणातीते प्रकारत्रयमिति । कर्मज्ञानभक्तिभिः । वक्तृव्यवस्थैषा । प्रथमा राजस्यः । इयं राजसराजसी । अपेक्षितं पूर्वं सर्वमेवानुवर्तते सर्वत्र । आदौ भगवतः स्वरूपं शृणुतेति । तं चतुर्धा वर्णयति । हारवत् हासो यस्य । उरसि स्थिरा विद्युद् यस्य । नन्दस्य च सूनुः । आर्तजनानां सर्वेषामेव नर्मदः । तत्र हेतुरयमिति । अन्यथेदानीमग्रे प्रकटो न भवेत् । द्वित्तीये मुहूर्ते निर्गच्छन्तं वालक्ष्याह । तदा प्रतिमुहूर्तं युगलानि भवन्ति । सन्ध्यासन्ध्यांशयोरन्तरेण द्वादशैव मुहूर्ता इति सोमोत्पत्तौ निर्णयः । अन्येषां हास्यं किमीरितं भवति, रज्जुवत् । भगवतस्तु दन्तानां कान्त्या विभक्तो हासः मुक्ताहारवद् भवति । यथा रत्नैर्व्यवहिता मुक्ता इति। अनेन जगतः प्रपञ्चे मोहजनकत्वं स्थिरीकृतम् । स्नेहकलाभिर्माया विभक्तेति श्रुतार्थापत्तिरर्थनिरूपणे मूलं सर्वत्र । यथा दृष्टे नानुपपत्तिः । दृष्टानुसारेणैव सर्वं व्यवस्थाप्यते । 'नहि दृष्टे अनुपपन्नं नाम व्याघाता'दिति । लौकिकानामेषा व्यवस्था । सर्वथा दृष्टविरोधो नाङ्गीक्रियत इति । तथा वैदिकानां श्रुतिः । यावतैव बोध्यमानः पदार्थः स्थिरीभवति, तावांस्तदनुगुण उच्यत इति सर्वत्रैवैषा व्यवस्था । न केवलं संसारे पुत्राद्यासक्तिमेव स्थिरीकरोति, किन्तु धनासक्तिमपीत्याह । स्थिरा लक्ष्मीर्यत्रेति । एवं प्रमाणबलनिराकरणार्थं द्वयं विधाय प्रमेयबलनिराकरणार्थं द्वयं कृतवानित्याह । यतोऽयमेव नन्दस्य सूनूर्जातः । आर्तानां च स्वयमागत्य सुखं प्रयच्छति । परिदृश्यते च तथेति च प्रमाणम् । नहि महानेवं करोति । अतः इदमाश्चर्यम् । एतमेवार्थं प्रकटीकुर्वन् कूजितवेणुर्भवति । अथवा । पूर्वपेक्षया अधोवक्त्रलीलया वेणुर्वाद्यते । हारवद्धासो यस्मिन् उरसि । तस्य स्थिरता विभागस्थैर्यं चाश्चर्यम् । श्रीवत्सोप्यत्युकृष्ट इति शोभार्थं तस्य स्थिरत्ववर्णनम् । तादृशस्य नन्दसूनुत्वे स्नेहो वर्धते । तत्रापि स्वोपकारक इति । कूजितत्वं वादनविशेषधर्मः । सर्वेषामान्तरं प्राणधर्ममप्याकर्षति । यत्र पशूनामपि प्राणादिधर्महारी, तत्रान्येषां किं वक्तव्यमिति पशूनां निरूपयति । एकस्य तथात्वं हेत्वन्तरसिद्धमपि भवेत् । अत उक्तं वृन्दश इति । समूहशः । यत्रैव वेणुनादः प्रविष्टः, तेषां सर्वेषामित्यर्थः । व्रजस्थिता वृषाः ककुद्मिनो मत्ताः । उत्सृष्टवृषा इव शकटादिनेतारः । ते व्रजसमीप एव तिष्ठन्तीति ग्राम्यपशूपलक्षणार्थं व्रजपदम् । मृगा गावश्चारण्ये मिलिता भवन्ति । आरण्या ग्राम्याश्चैवं भवन्तीति ज्ञापनार्थं मृगपदम् । किं बहुना सर्व एव पशवो वेणुवाद्येन कृत्वा हृतचेतसो भवन्ति । नापि भगवत्समीपगमने समर्थाः । किन्तु हृतचेतसो दूरादेव भवन्ति । अनेन वेणुनादस्य स्वाभाविक एवायं धर्मो, न तु भगवत्समीप-

कृत इति । कवलास्तृणरूपाः, केवलं दन्तैर्दंष्टाः, न त्यागे, न च भक्षणे समर्थाः । दन्तदंशमात्रेण प्रयत्नो निवृत्त इति नादस्येतरकार्यनिवर्तकत्वमुक्तम् । पूर्वक्रियाया अत्यावश्यकत्वाय कवलपदम् । देवस्त्रीवन्मूर्छानिवृत्त्यर्थमाह धृतकर्णा इति । अन्यत् सर्वं परित्यज्य कर्णमेव साधनं धृतवन्तः । ततो बाह्यान्निवृत्ता इत्याह निद्रिता इति । ततो नादेन सर्वतो व्याप्ताः । लिखितं गवादीनां चित्रमिव पश्चात्ते जाताः । स्थावरापेक्षयापि स्थिरा जाताः । पूर्वोक्तार्थादधिकोर्थ इति चित्रता ।।५।।

वेणुनादेन नदीनामतिजडानामपि स्पृहा जायत इति वक्तुं पुनर्वेणुनादं वर्णयन्ति बर्हिण इति ।

बर्हिणः स्तबकधातुपलाशैर्बद्धमल्लपरिबर्हविडम्बः ।
कर्हिचित् सबल आलि सगोपैर्गाः समाह्वयति यत्र मुकुन्दः ।।६।।
तर्हि भग्नगतयः सरितो वै तन्पदाम्बुजरजोऽनिलनीतम् ।
स्पृहयतीर्वयमिवाबहुपुण्याः प्रेमवेपितभुजाः स्तिमितापः ।।७।।

आवेशो देववेशश्च पूर्वं निरूपितौ । लीलावेशोऽधुना निरूप्यते । निरन्तरक्रिया हि नदीनाम् । चेतनानां तु निद्रामूर्च्छादौ क्रियानिवृत्तिरपि दृष्टा । नदीनां तु न कदापि निवर्तते इति । तत्रापि महतीनाम् । बन्धोऽपि न तासां भवति । सापि वेणुनादेन निवृत्ता । बर्हिणो मयूरस्य । स्तबकाः गुच्छकाः पिच्छगुच्छानि । धातवो गरिकादयः । पत्राणि च । धातूनां वा पत्राकारेण लेखाः । कमलपत्राण्यपि आकारार्थं बध्यन्त इति । तैः कृत्वा मल्लानां परिबर्हः अलङ्करणं वेश इति यावत् । स्वयं स्तबकादिभिः बद्धो योऽयं मल्लपरिबर्हः तं विडम्बयति । विडम्बो वा बद्धः । अस्वाभाविकं विडम्बनमेव भवति । नटमल्लवत् । अनेनायं नादो नृत्योपयोग्येव निरूपितः । तेन क्रियाशक्तिरुद्गता नादस्था निरूपिता नदीनामाकर्षे हेतुर्भवति । कर्हिचिदिति । यदोत्साहः क्रियाशक्तौ । अत एव सबलः बलभद्रसहितः । आलीति सम्बोधनं गोप्यतयायमर्थो निरूपितः, अप्रतारणार्थं च । प्रायेणैषा तदा दर्शनार्थं गतवती स्नानादिव्याजेन । एवं सामग्रीं विधाय सोऽस्माकं भोक्ता वस्तुतो वा जातो वा, तादृश्यो गोपैः सहितः । अनेनात्र वैकुण्ठस्थितलीला सूचिता । अत्रापि लक्ष्मीरस्माभिः सहिता रात्रौ, गोपैः सहिता दिवसे तिष्ठतीति । अत एव सम्बोधनं रहस्यसूचकम् । तदा गाः समाह्वयति वेणुनादेनैव, प्रकरणित्वाद् । वेणुनाह्वयतीत्यग्रे वक्ष्यति । वेणुतुल्यतया निरूपणार्थं वा वेणोरग्रहणम् । गवामाह्वाने हेतुः मुकुन्द इति । मोक्षो हि ताभ्यो देय इति स्वतस्तासां साधनाभावादाकार्य प्रयच्छति । स्वरसं वा तत्र स्थापयितुम् । उद्गता क्रियाशक्तिर्महदेव कर्म करोतीति गवामाकारणमुक्तम् । तत्र योगार्थं ज्ञात्वा नद्योऽपि नित्यं गच्छन्तीति ताः स्थगिता जाता इत्याह तर्हीति । तत्क्षणमेव भग्नगतयो जाताः । नहि भगवदाज्ञा केनाप्युल्लङ्घ्या भवति । सरित इति

प्रवाहैकस्वभावत्वं निरूपितम् । तासां वैष्णवत्वकामना । तासां हि समुद्रोऽधिपतिः । यथा भगवान् पतिर्भूयात्, तदर्थं तत्पदाम्बुजरजः स्पृहयतीर्जाताः । स्पृहयन्त्यः । रजसः सम्बन्धार्थमुपायमाह अनिलनीतमिति । अनिलेन वायुना स्वार्थं नीतम् । तेन सह प्रत्यासत्तिः । जलार्थी सः । भगवदीया एव भगवत्सम्बन्धं प्राप्नुवन्तीति रजःकामना दूराभिप्राया । काम एवात्रोद्देश्यः देवतात्वान्नदीनाम् । अत एवाग्रे कालिन्दी तथा भविष्यति । इदानीं तथाभावे भाग्यं नास्तीत्याह अबहुपुण्या इति । न बहु पुण्यं यासाम् । यथा शीघ्रमेव गोरूपत्वम्, गोपालरूपत्वं दिवसे, रात्रौ स्त्रीरूपत्वमिति । पुण्यैर्विना समीहितार्थसिद्ध्यभावात् । कथं ज्ञायते तासामेवंभाव इति तत्राह वयमिवेति । यथा वयं अबहुपुण्याः । अन्यथा दिवसे गावो गोपा वा भवेम । अतः स्वदृष्टान्तेन ज्ञायते स्पृहामेव कुर्वन्ति, न तु तासां कार्यं सिध्यतीति । किञ्च । तासां सात्त्विकभावादपि हृद्गतो भावो लक्ष्यत इत्याहुः प्रेमवेपितभुजा इति । प्रेम्णैव भुजानां वेपनम्, न तु वायुवशात् । अतो विरहसन्तापयुक्ता इव लक्ष्यन्ते । किञ्च । स्तम्भोऽपि जात इत्याहुः स्तिमिताप इति । स्तिमिताः स्तब्धा आपो यासाम् । एवं रजोभेदास्त्रिविधा निरूपिताः ॥७॥

सत्त्वभेदान् निरूपयितुं भगवन्तमपि तथा वर्णयन्ति अनुचरैरिति त्रिभिः । लताविहङ्गममेषाः सात्त्विकाः । एते वेणुनादेन भक्तिपूर्णा जाताः । तत्र प्रथमं वृन्दावनस्था लतास्तरवश्च वैष्णवाः वेणुनादेन उद्गतप्रेमरसा जाता इति तदर्थं प्रकारान्तरेण वेणुनादमाह । तदर्थं प्रकारान्तरेण भगवानपि वर्णनीयः । स च भक्त्यनुसारेण, लोकवेदानुसारेण च वर्णनीयः । तत्र भक्त्यनुसारेण प्रथममाह ।

अनुचरैः समनुवर्णितवीर्य आदिपूरुष इवाचलभूतिः ।
वनचरो गिरितटेषु चरन्तीर्वेणुनाह्वयति गाः स यदा हि ॥८॥

वनलतास्तरव आत्मनि विष्णुं व्यञ्जयन्त्य इव पुष्पफलाढ्याः ।
प्रणतभारविटपा मधुधाराः प्रेमहृष्टतनवः ससृजुः स्म ॥९॥

अनुचरैः सेवकैर्गोपैः सम्यगनुवर्णितानि वीर्याणि यस्य । आदिपूरुष इव पुरुषोत्तम इव च अनुचरैर्वेदैः सम्यक् सर्वोत्तमत्वेन वर्णितानि जगत्कर्तृत्वादीनि वीर्याणि यस्य । लोकानुसारेण माहात्म्यमाह सर्वोत्कृष्टं आदिपूरुष इवाचलभूतिरिति । अचला विभूतिर्लक्ष्मीर्यस्य । अनुचरैः सर्वैरेव देवादिभिस्तथोक्तः । लौकिकाः स्वव्यवहार्यत्वात् पुरुषोत्तमतुल्यतामेवाहुः । अतो दृष्टान्तभावः । भिन्नतया वर्णनायां हेतुमाह वनचर इति । वृन्दावनचरः सात्त्विकभावापन्नः सत्त्वभूमौ प्रतिष्ठित इति । गिरितटेषु गिरिप्रान्तेषु चरन्तीः विषमस्थानात् समदेशे पशुहिते स्वयं तत्रत्यो भूत्वा समाह्वयति, लौकिकत्वाभावाय वेणुनैवाह्वयति । वेणुद्वारा तत्र प्रविष्ट इति

अग्रिमचरित्रेण ज्ञायते । अन्यथा वृक्षाणां तथात्वं न स्यात् । स इति येषु वनप्रदेशेषु रेमे, यदैवाह्वयत्, तदैव मधुधाराः ससृजुः स्मेति सम्बन्धः । युक्तश्चायमर्थः । अन्यथा वेणुनादाभिज्ञता तत्र च स्वनामसङ्केतो न स्यात् । अतस्तद्द्वारा भगवान् प्रविष्ट इत्यग्रेऽपि तथात्वं युक्तमेव ।

वनस्था लताः अस्मन्निकटे भगवांश्चरति स्वकीयांश्चाकारयतीति ज्ञात्वा तेषां भोगसिद्धयर्थं स्वस्मिन् विद्यमानमानन्दं प्रकटितवत्यः । तथा तरवश्च । यथा स्त्रियः पुरुषाश्च भगवदीयाः भगवति भगवदीयेषु च समागतेषु आनन्दयुक्ता भवन्ति, भोगार्थं स्वकीयं च प्रयच्छन्ति, तद्वदेतेऽपि । नन्वयं धर्मो जङ्गमानाम्, न स्थावराणामिति चेत्, तत्राह आत्मनि विष्णुं व्यञ्जयन्त्य इति । चेतनेष्वेव भगवतः क्रियाज्ञानशक्त्योराविर्भावः । सच्चिदानन्दरूपता च क्रमेणाविर्भवति । एतत् सर्वं भगवति निविष्टे भवति । सोऽपि निविष्टश्चेत् प्रकटीभवति तदैवं युज्यत इति । ते वृक्षादयः पञ्चधर्मयुक्ताः आत्मनि विष्णुं व्यञ्जन्त्य इव जाताः । तत्र प्रथमं क्रियाशक्त्याविर्भावमाह पुष्पफलाढ्या इति । यत्र हि भगवान् निविशते, तत्रावान्तरफलं परमफलं च भवति । अतः कार्यद्विचञ्जयन्त्य इव जाताः । पुष्पाण्यवान्तरफलरुपाणि । परमफलानि तु फलानि । तैः सर्वैराढ्या जाताः । भगवदर्थं सदाधिक्यमाह प्रणतभारविटपा इति । भारेणापि नमनं सम्भवतीति तन्निरासायादौ प्रणतत्वमुक्तम् । प्रकर्षेण नताः भारेण विटपाः शाखा येषाम् । प्रेमहृष्टतनव इति चिदुत्कर्षो ज्ञानरूपो निरूपितः । भक्ता एव हि प्रेम्णा हृष्टरोमाञ्चा भवन्ति । (पूर्वमहरितानामपि तदा हरितत्वं, पूर्वस्मात् स्थौल्यं प्रत्यवयवमुच्छूनत्वं प्रभाविशेषश्चात्र प्रेमहृष्टतनुत्वम् । अपरं च । वेणुनादनिष्ठसुधास्वादवत्यः स्वामिन्य इति तद्धर्मं परिचिन्वन्ति ता एवेति तदुक्तावन्यविचाराक्षमत्वं युक्ततरमिति नाधिकं लेखनीयमत्र ।) मधुधाराः स्वस्मिन् विद्यमानानन्दं भगवदर्थं यहिः प्रकटितवत्यः । एतत्सर्वपरिज्ञानमेव ज्ञानशक्तिः ॥९॥

पक्षिणामपि वेणुनादकार्यं जातमिति तत्रोपयोगिरूपं वेणुनादं च वर्णयन्ति दर्शनीयतिलक इति । यद्यपि पक्षिणो मुनयः, न तेषां गीतादिना भगवद्भावो भवति, किन्तु स्वभावत एव, तथापि लोकदृष्टया कदाचिदन्यथाबुद्धिर्भवेत्, अतो रूपनादाभ्यां तेषां भजनसिद्धिर्निरूप्यते । तत्र रूपं वर्णयति दर्शनीयतिलक इति ।

दर्शनीयतिलको वनमालादिव्यगन्धतुलसीमधुमत्तैः ।
अलिकुलैरलघुगीतमभीष्टमाद्रियन् यर्हि कूजितवेणुः ॥१०॥

सरसि सारसहंसविहङ्गाश्चारुगीतहृतचेतस एत्य ।
हरिमुपासत ते यतचित्ता हन्त मीलितदृशो धृतमौनाः ॥११॥

दर्शनीयानां मध्ये तिलकरूपोऽतिसुन्दरः । पक्षिणश्च रूपप्रधानाः, रूपभेदविदः । किञ्च । यो वेणुनादः स स्वहितकारी, स्वकीयानामपराधमपि न मन्यते । तदाह । वनमालादिव्यगन्धतुलसीमधुमत्तैरलिकुलैः कृतमलघुगीतमपि आद्रियन्, आदरं कुर्वन्नेव कूजितवेणुर्यतः । यथैव भ्रमरा झङ्कारं कुर्वन्ति, तथैव तन्नादमनुकुर्वन्नेव अनुरणनवदेव वेणुनादं करोति । पक्षिणां मध्ये अलयो हीना निकृष्टाश्च । तेषामपि कुलानि समूहाः नानाविधजातिभेदाः । तैरप्यलघु यथा भवति तथा गीतम् । तस्याप्यादरं कुर्वन् । तत्राप्यलयो मत्ताः । मदोऽपि येनानुचितः । नहि तुलसी पुष्पान्तरवन्मादहेतुः । तत्रापि दिव्यगन्धा । तत्रापि भगवद्वनमालागता । तेषामप्यादरं चेत् कुर्यात्, तदा सरोवरादिषु ये सरसा रसिकाः क्षीरनीरविवेकिनश्च तेषामादरं कथं न कुर्यादिति । वनमालायाः या दिव्यगन्धतुलसी तस्या मकरन्देन मत्तैः । किञ्च । आदरोऽपि भ्रमराणां यथाभीष्टं भवति, तथा वनमालायां समागतान् भ्रमरान्न दूरीकरोति । किन्तु ते यथा नोपद्रुता भवन्ति, तथैवादरं करोति । अतो यर्ह्येव आदरं कुर्वन्नेव कूजितवेणुः, तदैव सरसि विद्यमानाः जलवासिनः सारसाः सरसानां भक्तानां सम्बन्धिनः, हंसाः क्षीरनीरविवेकिनः ते च विहङ्गा उत्कृष्टगतियुक्ताः, पुरुषापेक्षया ते पुनर्भगवद्भजनाधिकारिण इति तान् विशिनष्टि चारुगीतहृतचेतस इति । चारु यथा भवति निःकामार्थं भगवद्गीतेनैव हृतं वशीकृतं चित्तं येषाम् । तदपि भजनं भक्तिमार्गानुसारेण । न तु स्थानस्थितानामन्तर्यामिरूपे ज्ञानरूपे वा । तदाह । एत्य आगत्य हरिं उप समीपे सेवमाना जाताः । यतस्ते भगवदुक्ता मुनयः । भजने भ्रमराद्विशेषमाह यतचित्ता इति । यतं नियतं चित्तं येषाम् । चित्तनैयत्येन भगवद्भजनं मुख्यम्, न तु विक्षिप्तचित्ततया । किञ्च । हन्त इति हर्षे । एतद्भाग्यमेतेषामेव भवतीति । बहिर्व्यापाररहिता भजने सर्वोत्तमाः । बहिर्व्यापारेषु च नेत्रे वाक् च नियम्याः । यस्यैतद्द्वयं नियतम्, वाक् नान्यं वदति, चक्षुश्च नान्यत् पश्यति, तदाह मीलितदृशो धृतमौना इति । मीलिता दृग् येषाम् । धृतं मौनं व्रतं यैः । साम्प्रतमेते नादपराः । अतो दृष्ट्या अन्यचित्तता भविष्यतीति नेत्रनिमीलनम् । एवमेतेषां भाग्यं सात्त्विकत्वान्निरूपितवत्यः ।

(अथवा । दर्शनीयतिलक इति । इदमत्राकूतम् । अतिरसिका एते मुनयः, स्वस्व पुरुषत्वेन लीलायामनुपयोगं मत्वा, पक्षीभूय, विविधस्वकूजनैर्भगवतो भक्तानां च रसोद्दीपनं कुर्वन्तः, स्वकृतार्थतां मन्वानाः, शब्दमेवाधिकमभीष्टं मन्यन्ते । अतः शब्दप्रधानकीर्तिरूपवनमालाधर्माणामेवात्रोपयोग उच्यते । 'यथा वृक्षस्य सम्पुष्पितस्य दूराद्गन्धो वात्येवं पुण्यकर्मणो दूराद्गन्धो वाती'ति श्रुत्या कीर्तेर्गन्धसाम्येन निरूपणं कृतम् । वनमालायाः कीर्तिरूपत्वात् तन्निरूपकाणि गीतान्यावश्यकानि । तानि च तद्रसास्वादं विना न सम्भवन्त्यतो गुणातीतभक्तिरूपवक्ष्यमाणरूपगन्धवती तुलसी, तन्मध्वत्यलौकिकभक्तिरसात्मकमितरविस्मारकम् ।

अतोऽतिमत्ताः स्वदेहाद्यनुसन्धानरहिता ईश्वरधर्माननुसन्धाना अपीति तन्निकट एवालघु गायन्ति । वस्तुतस्त्विदमेव महत्तमं समाराधनं प्रभोरलिभिः क्रियते । अत एव प्रभोरभित इष्टं तदेव गीतम् । अपरं च । चार्वादिपदानि विहाय तत्र भवनार्थकप्रत्ययवत्पदोक्त्या भगवद्वनमालास्थतुलसीगन्धस्य दिविभवत्वस्य बाधितत्वादग्रे स्वामिनीषु व्रजदेवीत्वस्य वक्ष्यमाणत्वाद् दिवुधातोः क्रीडावाचकत्वाच्च स्वामिनीभिः सह क्रीडाजनितोऽयं गन्ध इति समभिव्याहारादवगम्यते । एतेन यथा दिविभवोऽर्थो नेतरलोकस्थजनविषयः, तथायमन्तरङ्गतमलीलाप्रपञ्चस्थभक्तैकगम्य इति ध्वन्यते । अत एव प्रभोरपि भावोद्बोधस्तेनासीदिति ज्ञापनाय कूजनमुक्तम् । किञ्च, वनमालास्थपुष्पमध्वनुक्त्वा तुलस्या एव तद्यदुक्तं 'दयितगन्धतुलस्या' इति वाक्याद् 'बाहुं प्रियांस' इत्युपक्रम्य 'तुलसिकालिकुलैर्मदान्धैरन्वीयमान' इति वाक्याच्च तद्गन्धमध्वादिस्वरूपं प्रभुरेव वेत्तीति नान्यगम्यः स विशेषः । तद्बोक्तारोऽलयोऽपि न साधारणाः, किन्त्वितरेभ्यो विजातीया अत्युत्तमा इति ज्ञापनार्थमेव कुलपदमुक्तम् । अत एवालिपदमुक्तम् । अलंशब्दो हि पूर्णतावाची । तथा च तद्वानलिरित्यत्रोच्यते । रसो न लीयते, न नश्यति यत्र येन वा सोऽलिरित्युच्यते । यद्यप्यत्र दीर्घः सम्भवति, तथापि 'दशहूतो ह वै नामैषः । तं वा एतं दशहूतं सन्तं दशहोतेत्याचक्षते परोक्षेण । परोक्षप्रिया इव हि देवा' इति श्रुतिन्यायेन 'परोक्षं च मम प्रिय'मिति भगवद्वाक्याच्च स्वप्रियार्थस्य गोपनं प्रभोः प्रियमिति ज्ञायते । प्रकृते च स्वान्तरङ्गरसपोषकता एतेषु गोप्येति परोक्षेण ह्रस्वान्तं पदं प्रभुः प्रकटितवान् । एवं सत्येत एवालयोऽन्ये तु भ्रमरा एव । क्वचिदेतेष्वप्यन्यनामप्रयोगस्तात्पर्यविशेषेणेति ज्ञेयम् । तारत्वं बहुत्वं चानुक्त्वा लघुत्वाभाव एव य उक्तस्तेन तद्गीतरसभरं वोढुं नान्यः शक्तः प्रभुं विनेति ज्ञाप्यते । महत्त्वे इयत्ता नास्त्येवेत्यपि ज्ञापनाय तथोक्तिः । एवं सति तदादरं कथं न कुर्यात् । यर्हीति पदात्तद्गीतरसपानपरवशश्चिरं तूष्णीमेव तिष्ठति कदाचित्तद्रसभरेणैव कूजितवेणुर्भवतीति ज्ञाप्यते । अग्रे गीतोक्त्या पूर्वं तद्गीतोद्बुद्धभावेन स्वप्रियाणां भावोद्बोधनाय तथैवाकरोत् । ततो यदा पूर्णरसोऽभूत्, तदा जगाविति ज्ञाप्यते । अतिसुन्दरत्वनिरूपणे तिलकत्वोक्त्या तद्यथा भाग्यस्थाने भाले तिष्ठति, तथेदमपि स्वरूपं परमभाग्यवतीष्वेव तिष्ठतीति ध्वन्यते । अत्र कर्मधारयो ज्ञेयः । स्वामिनीनां हृदि प्रियातिरिक्ते दर्शनीयत्वास्फूर्तेः । अत्र यद्यप्युभयं मुख्यम्, तथापि नादे विशेषो निरूप्यते । अन्यथा मीलितदृक्त्वं नोच्येत । तत्र हेतुः । सरसि विद्यमानैरेव तैर्वेणुगीतं श्रुतम् । तच्च चारुत्वेन मनोहरणैकस्वभावम् । अतो नादाधीना एव निकटे समागताः । आदावेव नादहेतुभूतस्वरूपसौन्दर्यनिरूपणान्नादरस एव स्वरूपरसमप्यनुभवन्तीति ज्ञाप्यते । इदमप्यतिचित्रं यन्मत्तानां गीतानुरणनरूपेण गीतेन यतचित्तत्वं सर्वेन्द्रियवृत्तिनिरोधश्चेति । एतेषामियं गीतरसपानदशेत्येवंरूपतैवोपपद्यतेपि ।

एतज्जन्यत्वेनैतदुत्तरकालीनत्वान्नादस्य । अलिकुलानामपि तुलसीगन्धमधुपानदशा पक्षितुल्यैव । पश्चात्तत्स्वभाववशादुक्तरूपत्वं परमिति ज्ञायते । मुनित्वात् पक्षिणा-मग्रेऽप्यन्तरेव निरन्तरमेतद्रसमग्नतैवेति न मत्ततोक्ता । अथवा । प्रभुरसस्वभावाद-नुक्तसिद्धैवाग्रिमा सेति नोक्ता । तदैतेषामप्यलिकुलवद्दशा भविष्यति । वस्तुतस्तु उक्तरूपरसमत्तालिकुलालघुगीतमभीष्टत्वेन अतिचित्तनैयत्येनैवानुभवन् प्रभुर्वेणु-कूजनगाने करोतीति तच्छ्रवणे पक्षिणामपि तथात्वमेवोचिततरमावश्यकत्वादिति युक्तमुत्पश्यामः । तथाप्यादौ स्वरूपसौन्दर्यमेवोक्तमिति स्वस्य तद्दिदृक्षातिभरेण पक्षिणां तत्प्राप्तिदशायां तत्प्रतिबन्धस्मरणेन कश्चित् खेदोऽभूदिति हन्तेत्युक्तम्) ॥

मेघः सर्वहितकारी, तस्यापि वेणुनादजनितभावमाह पूर्ववत् । सहबल इति द्वाभ्याम् ।

सहबलः स्रगवतंसविलासः सानुषु क्षितिभृतो व्रजदेव्यः ।
हर्षयन् यर्हि वेणुरवेण जातहर्ष उपरम्भति विश्वम् ॥१२॥

महदतिक्रमणशङ्कितचेता मन्दमन्दमनुगर्जति मेघः ॥
सुहृदमभ्यवर्षत्सुमनोभिश्छायया च विदधत्प्रतपत्रम् ॥१३॥

हे व्रजदेव्यः, गोप्यः, व्रजदेवतारूपाः । अनेन विश्वासो भविष्यतीति निरूपितम् । यर्हि वेणुरवेण विश्वमुपरम्भति पूरयति तर्हि महदतिक्रमेण शङ्कितचेताः सुहृदं भगवन्तमभ्यवर्षत् । स्वदेहछायया च आतपत्रं विदधत् जातः । तद्वा कुर्वन् अभ्यवर्षत् । अयं नादो महाबलयुक्तः । विश्वगतान् सर्वानेव धर्मान् दूरीकृत्य स्वयमेव पूर्णः । तदाभासरूपोऽपि मेघः धूमादिसमूहात्मा विश्वं भगवतैव कृतार्थीभूतमिति स्वय-मुपचरितार्थोपि स्वजन्मसाफल्याय भगवन्तमेव ववर्ष । तत्र यादृशेन वेणुनादेनै-तद्भवति, तादृशकर्तारं भगवन्तं वर्णयति विशेषणचतुष्टयेन । अन्यथा उपरम्भण-मर्थवादरूपं स्यात् । तत्र क्रियाशक्तिः सम्पूर्णेति वक्तुं सहबलो बलभद्रसहित इति उक्तम् । सृष्टिकरणक्रियापेक्षयापीयं महती क्रियेति ज्ञापयितुम् । स्रग्रूपो योऽयमवतंसः कर्णाभरणं तत्र विलासो यस्येति लीला निरूपिता । माला कीर्तिमयी । दश विशः श्रोत्रम्, कीर्तिर्दिक्षु पूरिता यया सा भवत्येव सर्वोत्तमा । भगवत्कीर्तिप्रतिपादकं वा भागवतादिशास्त्रं सर्ववेदेष्वाभरणरूपं तत्र विलासयुक्ता तत्प्रतिपादिका च । एवं क्रियायाः स्वरूपतो गुणतश्च माहात्म्यं निरूपितम् । तस्याः सहकारिण्या इच्छाया माहात्म्यमाह । स्वयं जातहर्षः सर्वमेव च हर्षयन्निति । एवं वेणुनादस्य कारणभूत-क्रियोत्कर्षमुक्त्वा देशतोऽप्युत्कर्षमाह क्षितिभृतः सानुष्विति । सर्वाधारभूतां पृथिवीं ये बिभ्रति, तेषामप्युच्चस्थानेषु स नादो जायते इति कथं न विश्वं पूरयेत् । रवः अनुरणनमतिगम्भीरं उपरम्भति नादेन पूरयतीति मेघादप्यधिका क्रिया निरूपिता ।

तदैव मेघः महतो वासुदेवस्य उपरि गच्छन् भगवदतिक्रमणे शङ्कितचित्तो भूत्वा उपर्येव तिष्ठन् अग्रे गमनार्थमुद्यतः नीलमेघश्यामं विश्वजीवनं भगवन्तं स्वमित्रं ज्ञात्वा सुहृदमभ्यवर्षत्सुमनोभिः पुष्परूपैः स्वबिन्दुभिः । अर्थात् पुष्पैः पूजितवान् । न केवलं पूजामेव कृतवान्, किन्तु राज्यमपि दत्तवानित्याह आतपत्रं दधदिति । न केवलं राज्यमेव दत्तवान्, किन्तु आत्मनिवेदनमपि कृतवानित्याह छाययेति । सूर्ये अधःस्थिते उपरिस्थितेन न छाया भवतीति पृथक् छायानिर्देशः ॥१२॥१३॥

उत्तमांस्त्रिविधान् वक्तुं तेषामपि वेणुनादेन किञ्चिद् जातमिति वक्तुं वेणुनादं वर्णयति, भगवन्तं च, विविधगोपचरणेष्विति युग्मत्रयेण । सन्देहो मोहः सर्वपरित्यागश्च ज्ञानिनां श्रुतीनामरण्यवासिनां वेणुनादेन कृतः । तत्र ये विश्वगुरवो ब्रह्मादयस्तेषामपि सन्देहार्थं भगवतो वेणुनादं वर्णयति विविधेति ।

विविधगोपचरणेषु विदग्धो वेणुवाद्य उरुधा निजशिक्षाः ।
तव सुतः सति यदाधरबिम्बे दत्तवेणुरनयत् स्वरजातीः ॥१४॥

सवनशस्तदुपधार्य सुरेशाः शक्रशर्वपरमेष्ठिपुरोगाः ।
कवय आनतकन्धरचित्ताः कश्मलं ययुरनिश्चिततत्त्वाः ॥१५॥

लोके जायमानः अलौकिकप्रकारः सन्देहमुत्पादयति । ननु न तद्रूपमीश्वरे यन्न वेदे श्रुतमस्तीति सर्वविद्यास्थानानां ब्रह्मा अभिज्ञ इति कथं तस्य सन्देह इत्याशङ्क्याह वेणुवाद्य उरुधा निजशिक्षा इति । सुशिरभेदो वेणुः । तस्यापि प्रकाराः शास्त्रे निरूपिताः । ते ब्रह्मणा ज्ञायन्ते । एते तु प्रकाराः उरुधानेकधा । निजशिक्षाः निजेनैव शिक्षा शिक्षणं अभिव्यक्तिप्रकाश यासु । अनेन नादब्रह्म नित्यमिति निरूपितम् । तत्र क्रियाशक्तिः साधनमिति तस्य लौकिकत्वे कथं नादः अलौकिको भविष्यतीत्याशङ्क्य तस्याप्यलौकिकत्वायाह । विविधेषु गोपचरणेषु गोपानां सञ्चारविशेषेषु विदग्ध इति । गोपसञ्चारा न वेदोक्ताः, किन्तु लौकिकाः । ब्रह्माण्डान्तरस्थिता अपि भवन्ति । ते न लोकेऽन्यत्र प्रसिद्धाः, नापि वेदे । भगवांस्तु सर्वत्रैव विदग्धः । अतोऽयं ब्रह्मा यं प्रकारं न जानाति, तमेव प्रकारं कृतवान् । ननु ब्रह्मसृष्टावाविर्भूतः कथं ब्रह्मणोऽप्यज्ञातं करोतीति चेत्, तत्राह तव सुत इति । यशोदां प्रति वदन्ति स्त्रीमण्डले समागताम् । अत एवात्र न कामादिवार्ता, किन्तु अनिषिद्ध एवोत्कर्षो निरूपितः । यथा तव पुत्रोऽपि सन् तव मनसाप्याकलयितुमशक्यं करोति, तथा ब्रह्मणोऽपि ब्रह्माण्डे जातः । सतीति सम्बोधनं विश्वासार्थम् । अज्ञाने हेतुमाहुः अधरबिम्बे दत्तवेणुरिति । लोभात्मकोऽधर इति पूर्वमुक्तम्, अतो न लोके प्रसिद्धः । तस्य रसो भगवता न दत्त इति । तत्रापि बिम्बरूपः सूर्यवत् प्रकाशकः । न हि प्रकाश्याः प्रकाशकस्वरूपं विदुः । तत्र च स वेणुः स्थापितः ततोऽप्युत्तमत्वख्यापनाय । स्वरजातीः

षड्जादिस्वरजातिभेदान् । अनयत् नूतनत्वेनोत्पादितवान् यर्हि, तदा तत्परिज्ञानार्थं त्रिगुणप्रधाना अपि देवाः कालत्रयेऽपि समागत्य । सोऽपि कालः आधिदैविक इति ख्यापयितुं सवनपदम् । तं वेणुनादं सवनश उपधार्य । शक्रः सात्त्विकः, शर्वस्तामसः, परमेष्ठी राजस इति ते पुरोगमा येषां देवानाम् । सर्व एव देवास्त्रिगुणात्मका भवन्ति । कवयो निपुणा अपि नादे । इन्द्रो हि त्रैलोक्याधिपतिः सर्वदा नादपरः । शर्वस्तु नादशास्त्रकर्ता । परमेष्ठी तयोरपि गुरुः । अत एव परमेष्ठिपदम् । तेषामन्यचित्तताभावायाह आनतकन्धरचित्ता इति । आसमन्तान्नता कन्धरा बाह्याभिनयार्थं चित्तं च येषाम् । ग्राहकं चित्तम् । नमनमत्र सर्वतः । तेऽप्यनिश्चिततत्त्वा जाताः । नाप्यौदासीन्येन कियत्कालं विचार्य अज्ञाने तूष्णीं भूता इति मन्तव्यम् । यतः कश्मलं ययुः, चिन्तया मूर्च्छिताश्च जाताः । वेणुनादेन वा मोहिताः । अत एव आभासत्वपक्षोऽपि निराकृतः । अलौकिकरसोत्पादकत्वात् ॥१४॥ १५ ॥

अस्त्वन्येषां वार्ता । वेणुनादोऽस्माकमेवान्यथात्वं सम्पादयतीत्याहुर्द्वयेन पूर्ववत् निजपदाब्जदलैरिति ।

निजपदाब्जदलैर्ध्वजवज्रनीरजाकृतिविचित्रललामैः ।
व्रजभुवः शमयन् खुरतोदं वर्ष्मधुर्यगतिरीरितवेणुः ॥१६॥

व्रजति तेन वयं सविलासवीक्षणार्पितमनोभववेगाः ॥
कुजगतिं गमिता न विदामः कश्मलेन कबरं वसनं वा ॥१७॥

यर्हि ईरितवेणुः सन् व्रजति, तदा तेन नादेन कुजगतिं स्थावरत्वं गमिता वयं गोप्यः सर्वा एव कश्मलेन मूर्च्छया वसनं परिहितं केशपाशं वा न विदाम इति सम्बन्धः । अयं वेणुनादोऽस्मदर्थमेव जायत इति तस्य चेष्टया अनुभवाज्ज्ञायते । तत्र चेष्टाया गोकुलनिवासिनामेवार्थे जायते, तथा व्याप्तः कथमन्यकार्यं कुर्यात् । अतः प्रथमं भगवतो गोकुलहितकर्तृत्वमाहुः । निजस्य स्वस्यैव यत्पदाब्जद्वयं तस्य दलैः वशाङ्गुलीभिः तलभागैर्वा । व्रजभुवः निरन्तरं पश्वाक्रमणेन जातव्यथायाः व्रजभूमेः खुरैर्जातं तोदं शमयन्निति शनैः शनैर्लीलया भगवद्गतिर्निरूपिता । क्षतांशः गतिविलासेन पादस्पर्शेन निराकृतः । आध्यात्मिकाद्यंशस्तु ध्वजादिना । तामसः भौतिकः ध्वजेन निराक्रियते । राजस आध्यात्मिको वज्रेण । सात्त्विक आधिदैविकः नीरजाकृतिचिह्नेन । तान्येव विचित्राणि ललामानि पदेषु । तेन लौकिकालौकिकप्रकारेण व्रजभुवः खुरतोदप्रशमनम् । व्रजे तिस्रः प्रधानभूताः । भूमिः गावो गोप्य इति । तत्र भूमेर्दुःखनिवृत्तिं गत्या निरूप्य, गत्या कृत्या च गवां दुःखं निवारयतीत्याह वर्ष्मधुर्यगतिरिति । वर्ष्मधुर्यो महावृषभः ककुद्मी, स यथा लीलया मन्थरगतिः, तथा गच्छन् गवामपि दुःखहारीव निरूपितः । ईरितवेणुर्व्रजतीति । गोपिकानां

तदास्माकं वेणुनादेन जाते कामे स्थावरत्वमधिकं जातमित्याहुः तेनेति । स्वभावत एव वेणुनादेन जातः कामः । तत्रापि सविलासवीक्षणेन अर्पितो मनोभववेगो यासु । अतो वेगेन स्तम्भे जाते कुजगतिं वृक्षगतिं गमिता जाताः । तेषामन्तर्ज्ञानमस्तीति तदर्थमाहुः न विदाम इति । सुषुप्तावपि न जानन्तीति तद्व्यावृत्त्यर्थमाह कश्मलेनेति । कश्मलेन मूर्च्छया । स्त्रीणामत्यावश्यकं वसनज्ञानं कबरज्ञानं च । वेणुनादप्रस्तावे एवैतज्जातमिति गतिदृष्ट्यादिभिरपि कृतमत्र निरूप्यते ॥ १६ ॥ १७ ॥

हरिणीनां वेणुनादेन यथा जातं तद्वक्तुं पूर्ववद्वेणुनादं वर्णयन्ति मणिधर इति द्वाभ्याम् ।

मणिधरः क्वचिदागणयन् गा मालया दयितगन्धतुलस्याः ।
प्रणयिनोऽनुचरस्य कदांसे प्रक्षिपन् भुजमगायत यत्र ॥१८॥

क्वणितवेणुरववञ्चितचित्ताः कृष्णमन्वासत कृष्णगृहिण्यः ॥
गुणगणार्णवमनुगत्य हरिण्यो गोपिका इव विमुक्तगृहाशाः ॥१९॥

गवामाधिदैविकानि रूपाणि मणयः । तान् स्वस्मिन् बिभर्तीति मणिधरः । अभिज्ञानार्थं वा । स्वप्रियाणामभिज्ञापका मणयः । अतस्तैः कदाचित् गाः आसमन्ताद् गणयन् जातः । अनेन ताः तद्गतधर्माश्च भगवत्येव प्रतिष्ठिता इति तासां संसाराभावः सूचितः । अत एव गोपिकानामपि । अत एव हरिणीनामपि । पशुत्वाविशेषाद् ग्राम्याणां चेदुद्धारकः, विशेषत आरण्यानां भवष्यितीति युक्ता कृष्णपरता । मालया दयितगन्धतुलस्या उपलक्षितः । यथा भगवतो नीलं रूपं प्रियम्, स्पर्शः स्त्रीणाम्, शब्दो वेणोः, रसो नवनीतस्य , तथा गन्धस्तुलस्याः । तद्गतोत्तमता सात्त्विकानां केषाञ्चिदनुभवसिद्धा । तादृशी तुलसी । अतस्तस्या मालां बिभर्ति । अतो यदा वयमपि प्रिया भविष्यामः, तदा अस्मानपि अस्मद्धर्मान् वा धारयिष्यतीति कृष्णसारस्त्रीणां प्रवृत्तिः । कृष्णसारस्तु वेदे नियुक्त इति भक्तौ तासां विनियोगार्थं प्रवृत्तिः । किञ्च । प्रणयिनोऽतिप्रेमवतः, अनुचरस्य गोपस्यांसे भुजं प्रक्षिपन्निति । कदा कदाचित् । 'आशंसायां भूतवच्चे'ति वा कदा अगायतेति मध्ये गानाशंसा । यथा गोपालस्य तथा स्नेहसेवाधर्मयोः सद्भावे एवं भविष्यतीति गोपिकानामिव हरिणीनामपि तथात्वाय स्नेहभजनम् । देहास्फुरणात् न विजातीयत्वेन कामाभावः । तदैव क्वणितो यो वेणुः । आकस्मिकः शब्दविशेषो मनोहारी क्वणनात्मकः । स चेद्वेणोर्निगतः, तत्सम्बन्धादन्येऽपि शब्दाश्रित्तवञ्चका इति रवपदम् । शब्देन मृगाणां वशीकरणं सिद्धमेव । इदानीमेवोपयोगो भविष्यतीति प्रतीतिजननाद्वञ्चकत्वम् । अतो रवेण वञ्चितचित्ताः कृष्णमन्वासत । कृष्णसमीपे आसत उपविष्टा जाताः । यथा प्रायमुपविशति, एवं कृष्णमनूपविष्टाः । ननु

स्त्रियोऽन्यस्य कथमन्यस्य गृहेऽन्यस्य समीपे उपविष्टा इति, तत्राह कृष्णस्य कृष्णसारस्य गृहिण्य इति। कृष्ण इति तास्तस्य गृहिण्यो जाताः। वञ्चितचित्तत्वाद्वा रूपं विस्मृत्य शब्दमात्राभिनिविष्टा जाताः। वेणुनादेन वा सानुभावेन कृष्णसारेऽपि कृष्णमत्या कृष्णमेवान्वासत। ननु कृष्णसारेऽपि कृष्णभ्रमात् शब्दोऽपि वर्तत इति तं परित्यज्य कथमागता इत्यत आह गुणगणार्णवमिति। कृष्णसारे एको द्वौ वा गुणौ। अतो यत्रैव भगवान् गच्छति, तत्रैव तमनुगत्य सर्वा एव हरिण्यो विमुक्तगृहाशा जाताः। गृहं गमिष्याम इत्याशामपि त्यक्तवत्यः। (सान्निध्येन भगवद्रसः पीत इति लब्धस्वादुभावाः गोपिका इव तदेकपरा जाताः। एतन्नयनेषु स्वप्रियानयनसादृश्यदर्शनेन यादृशेन भावेन ताः पश्यति, तादृशेनैवैता अपि पश्यन्तीति, एतासामपि तत्सजातीयभावोत्पत्तिः, तथैव वेणुक्वणनं च। अत एवाग्निबीजामृतबीजात्मकं रवपदमुक्तम्। यतस्तच्छ्रवणेऽत्यार्तिस्तत्तापशमनं च सम्पद्यते। अतः स्वदृष्टान्तोक्तिर्युक्ता) ॥१८॥१९॥

एवं नवप्रकारेण वेणुनादं निरूप्य, गुणातीतप्रकारेण त्रिधा निरूपयन् वेणुनादेन भगवान् जगदेव वशीकृतवानित्याह कुन्ददामेति द्वाभ्याम्।

कुन्ददामकृतकौतुकवेशो गोपगोधनवृतो यमुनायाम्।
नन्दसूनुरनघे तव वत्सो नर्मदः प्रणयिनां विजहार ॥२०॥

मन्दवायुरुपवात्यनुकूलं मानयन् मलयजस्पर्शेन।
बन्दिनस्तमुपदेवगणा ये वाद्यगीतबलिभिः परिवव्रुः ॥२१॥

यर्हि भगवान् यमुनायां विजहार, तत्रापि पूर्वोत्तरदशायामपेक्षितो वेणुनादः परिगृह्यते, प्रकरणित्वात्, प्रकारविशेषाभावाच्च न पृथगुक्तः, तदा उपदेवगणाः परिवव्रुरिति सम्बन्धः। यमुनायामिति सामीप्यसप्तमी। अधिकरणसप्तमी वा। धर्मे गवां गोपालानां च जले स्थितिः सम्भवति। तत्र विहारो गोपैः सह जलक्रीडा। गवां प्रक्षालनादिः। सर्वतोद्वेगशान्त्यर्थं वेणुनादः सहकारी। तदानीमनलङ्कृतत्वमाशङ्क्य अलङ्कारमाह कुन्ददामेति। वस्त्राभरणाद्यलङ्कारा भविष्यन्त्येव, पुष्पालङ्कारा न भविष्यन्तीत्याशङ्क्य तदेव निरूप्यते। कुन्ददाम्ना कृतः कौतुकवेशो यस्य। दामान्यनेकप्रकाराणि। तैस्तथा वेशो निर्मीयते। यथा अत्यद्भुतो भवति। अत्र तु यथैव हास्यरस उत्पद्यते, तथैव निर्मीयत इति। नन्वेतादृशीं प्राकृतलीलां भगवान् कथं कृतवानित्याशङ्कायामाहुः नन्दसूनुस्तव वत्स इति। यया लीलया नन्दपुत्रो भवति, तयैव लीलया प्राकृतलीलामपि सम्पादयति। अनघ इति सम्बोधनं क्रोधाभावाय विश्वासार्थं च। तव च वत्सो जातः। अनेन त्वं गोरूपेति सर्वगुप्तरसानभिज्ञत्वं सूचितम्। अन्यथा उलूखलबन्धनलीलां न कुर्यात्। मध्ये

निर्दोषत्वेन सम्बोधनादुभयोर्निर्दोषत्वं ज्ञाप्यते। तादृश्या वत्सत्वेन भगवत्यपि तथा। पूर्णगुणत्वलक्षणमाधिक्यं चोच्यतेऽग्रिमविशेषणेन । किञ्च, प्रणयिनां नर्मदः । ये केचन स्नेहयुक्ताः, यथैव ते स्निग्धा भवन्ति, तथैव लीलां करोतीति । अनेन सर्वत्रैव हेतुरुक्तः । यत्रैव लीलासक्त्या क्रीडा, स विहारः । सोऽत्र जलक्रीडा नृत्यक्रीडा वेणुवादनक्रीडा च ज्ञेया । अन्यथा वाद्यादीनामुपयोगो न स्यात् । विद्यावन्तो हि वशीकर्तव्याः । तत्र विद्योत्पादको वायुः । देवाश्च तदाधारभूताः । तत्राप्युपदेवगणा बन्दिनश्च बहिर्विद्याप्रकटनपराः । अतोऽन्यापेक्षया तेषु विशेष उक्तः । प्रथमतः कारणभूतं वायुं निरूपयन्ति । मन्दो वायु अनुकूलं यथा भवति, तथा उपवातीति । अनुकूलं कुलसमीपे हितं च। अनेन शैत्यं निरूपितम् । मलयजस्पर्शेन सहित इति सौरभ्यम् । अनेन दाक्षिणात्योऽयं वायुरिति निरूपितम् । भगवत्स्वरूपे दत्तेन वा मलयजेन सहभावादधिकशैत्यनिरूपकत्वेन अनुकूलत्वम् । मलयजस्पर्शः मलयजस्येव वा स्पर्शः । तथा सति तत्रत्यानां सर्वेषामेव भगवद्भावं सम्पादयिष्यतीति । मानयन्निति । स्वकीयैस्त्रिभिर्गुणैः यथैव सन्माननं भवति, तथैव वातीत्यतिवश्यता । उपदेवगणाश्च गन्धर्वादयश्च बन्दिनः कीर्तिनिरूपका जाताः । गायकाश्च सन्तः । य इति भगवदीयाः । वाद्यगीतपूजासाधनैः तामसराजससात्त्विकैः सहिताः परिवव्रुः । सर्वत्रैवापेक्षितं कृतवन्तः ॥२०॥२१॥

एवं गुणातीते प्रकीर्णतां निरूप्य युगलद्वयेन केवलं भगवत एव चरित्रमाहुः वत्सल इति ।

वत्सलो व्रजगवां यदगध्रो वन्द्यमानचरणः पथि वृद्धैः ।
कृत्स्नगोधनमुपोह्य दिनान्ते गीतवेणुरनुगेडितकीर्तिः ॥२२॥

उत्सवं श्रमरुचापि दृशीनामुन्नयन् खुररजश्छुरितस्रक् ।
दित्सयैति सुहृदाशिष एष देवकीजठरभूरुडुराजः ॥२३॥

भगवान् यद् गोकुलं गोष्ठे समानयति, तत् कृपया । अन्यथा एकस्यामपि लीलायां व्यापृता गावो मुच्येरन् । तथा गोपिकाः । परं कृपयैव भजनानन्दानुभवार्थं तथा करोति । अत्र हेतुः यदगध्र इति । यद् यस्मात् कारणात् अगं पर्वतं धारयतीति । यदि भजनानन्दं न दद्यात्, तदा गोवर्धनोद्धरणं न कुर्यात् । एतद्भगवन्माहात्म्यं सर्वजनीनमिति ज्ञापयितुमाह पथि वृद्धैर्वन्द्यमानचरण इति । वृद्धाः सर्वतो निपुणाः । बहुज्ञैरेव भगवान् सेव्यो भवति । अतः कृत्स्नमेव गोधनमुपोह्य, ततः पृथक्कृत्य, उप समीपे समाहृत्य वा । दिनान्त इति । अग्रे वनस्थितेरयुक्तत्वात् । लीलान्तरस्य च चिकीर्षितत्वात् । गीतवेणुर्जातः । श्रमापनोदनार्थं व्रजस्थानां ज्ञापनार्थं च । अस्य नादस्याग्रे कार्यं वक्तव्यम् । गोपिका एव कृतार्थाः करोतीति न, किन्तु गोपानपीति ज्ञापयितुं तत्कृतस्तोत्रमाह अनुगेडितकीर्तिरिति । अनुगैः सेवकैरीडिता

कीर्तिर्यस्य । अनेन रात्रौ तेषामपि गानमुक्तं भवति । यथा दिवसे गोपिकानाम् । अन्यथा सर्वेषां निरोधो न भवेत् । एतादृशस्य कार्यं स्वयमेव जानातीति स्वयमेव करोतीत्याहुः उत्सवमिति । श्रमरुचा व्रजस्थदृशां उत्सवमुन्नयन् आशिषो दित्सया एतीति सम्बन्धः । श्रमयुक्ता रुक् कान्तिः । भगवतः श्रमाभावपक्षे प्रदर्शनमात्रपरत्वम् । अस्ति श्रम इति सिद्धान्तः । 'भर्ता सन् भ्रियमाणो बिभर्ति' 'एको देवो बहुधा निविष्टः' 'यदा भारं तन्द्रयते स भर्तुं निधाय भारं पुनरस्तमेतीति'श्रुतेः । सर्वधर्माश्रयत्वाच्च । विरुद्धसर्वधर्माश्रयत्वादश्रान्तोऽपि । न तु केवलमश्रान्त एव । श्रमः सुखकारक इत्यपरे । तत्सम्बन्धिनी रुक् श्रमरुक् । सा नायकगता स्त्रीणां न हितकारिणी । तथाप्यस्माकं हितकारिण्येव जातेत्याहुः दृशीनामुत्सवमुन्नयन्निति । दृशिर्दर्शनम् । यदि भगवान् श्रान्तो न भवेत्, तदा शीघ्रं गच्छेत् । तदा दृष्टीनां परमानन्दसन्ततिर्न स्यात् । ऊर्ध्वं नयन्निति संघाते दृष्टीनां य आनन्दः स्थितः यावान्, तदपेक्षयाधिकं कृतवानित्यर्थः । भगवत्कीर्तेः सर्वपुरुषार्थदातृत्वाय प्रकारं वदन् श्रममुपपादयति खुररजश्छुरितस्रगिति । गोखुररजोभिश्छुरिता व्याप्ताः स्रजो माला यस्य । वायुवशादुद्गतो रेणुः न स्थिरो, नापि नियतः । खुरजातस्तु तथा । खुराणामेव गोत्वात् प्रकृतत्वाच्च न गोग्रहणम् । 'पशवो वा एकशफा' इत्यत्र तथा निर्णयात् । अनेन धर्मोऽयमिति निरूपितम् । रजोऽर्थः । व्याप्तिः काम इति । आगमनस्य तु यत् कार्यं तदाहुः । सुहृदां सर्वेषामेव सम्बन्धिनामाशिषः सर्वा एव देया इति । उक्तं गोपिकाद्वारा सर्वेष्वानन्दप्रवेश इति । एष इति प्रदर्श्याहुः । यतः स्वस्मिन् लीला ज्ञापिता भवति । साधारण्येन सर्वेषां तापनाशकत्वाय भगवद्गतमसाधारणं धर्ममाहुः देवकीजठरभूरुडुराज इति । 'अदितिर्देवकी अदितिर्द्यौरदितिरन्तरिक्ष' मिति श्रुतेः अदित्यवतारत्वात् द्युरूपा सा । तस्यामवश्यं चन्द्रोदयोऽपेक्षित एव । सा पुनर्विशेषरूपं गृहीतवतीति चन्द्रोऽपि विशिष्टकार्यं करोति । लौकिकस्तापस्त्रिविधो भगवद्विरहजश्च । अयं त्रिविधमपि नाशयतीति पूर्वोक्तमानन्ददातृत्वमुपपादितम् । देवकीजठरे भवतीति देवकीजठरभूः । स एव उडुराजः । जायते, यथा उदयाद्रौ । पतिस्तु नक्षत्राणामेव भवति । तथा देवक्यां जातः, परं सुखदोऽस्माकमेव ॥

(अथवा, एतास्तु भगवद्विरहेणार्ता इति स्वाभिलषितप्रकारेण तदङ्गसङ्गव्यतिरेकेण नैतासामुत्सवो भवतीत्यार्ता एव स्थिताः । परं दृशीनां दर्शनं मुख्यमिति तेनैवोत्सवोन्नयनमुच्यते । तथा च आर्तानामस्माकं दृशीनामिति समासो ज्ञेयः । आर्तशब्दस्य ह्रस्वोऽपि छान्दसः । नहि दृशीनामेवार्तत्वमत्र विवक्षितम् । प्रकारान्तरेणापि तत्स्वरूपरसास्वादवत्यः स्वामिन्य इति सर्वेन्द्रियाणामेवार्तत्वसम्भवात् । तदैव सर्वत्रोत्सवे पुनराशिषोऽनभीप्सितत्वेनाग्रे तद्दित्सोक्तिरप्यनुपपन्ना स्यात् । दृशीनामुत्सवो बहिरेव । अन्तरुत्सवस्य त्वधिकरणं मनः, तस्यातृप्तत्वान्न

स इदानीम्, परमग्रे सम्भोगसामयिकदर्शने भविष्यतीति ज्ञापनायोर्ध्वमित्युक्तम् । यथा गोप्यो 'दिदृक्षितदृशोऽभ्यगमन् समेता' इत्यत्र दर्शनानन्तरमपि दृशां दिदृक्षितत्वम्, एवमत्रापि ज्ञेयम्। अत एव दृशीनामिति। सम्बन्धषष्ठ्याप्युत्सवस्य तत्सम्बन्धित्वमेव प्राप्यते। तत्रापि भगवत्कर्तृकनयनोक्त्या तासां बहिरुत्सवोऽपि प्रियप्रापित इति तद्दर्शनस्वभावान्न स्वत इति बोध्यते । अत एवोत्सवकरणत्वं श्रमरुचोऽपि युज्यते । अन्यथा चिरादुत्कण्ठितानामासां प्रियतमागतश्रमनिरीक्षणेनाग्रिमरसप्रतिबन्धशङ्कया न उत्सवः स्यात् । प्रत्युत पूर्वापेक्षयाधिकतरः खेद एव स्यात् । किञ्च, विनास्माभिरन्येन प्रियः श्रमापनोदनं न कारयति, वयमतःपरं करिष्याम इति श्रमरुचस्तथात्वं युक्तमेव । श्रमस्य कान्तित्वनिरूपणेनापि स्वमनोरथाप्रतिबन्धकत्वात्तथेति ध्वन्यते । श्रमोऽप्यन्यनायिकाविषयकश्चेत्, कथं दृशामुत्सव इति चेत्, तथा नेत्याहुः खुररजश्छुरितस्रगिति । यद्यप्यन्यनायिकाविषयकः स्यात्, तदा स्रजि तदङ्गराग एव स्यात्, न तु खुररजः। रजोऽप्यागमनसामयिकं चेत्, सम्भवेदपि तथा, परं चिरकालीनमिति ज्ञापनाय छुरितत्वमुक्तम् । अल्पकालेन तथात्वस्यासम्भवात् । किञ्च, तथा चेत्, स्रगपि न स्यात्, क्रीडान्तरायत्वात् । अतो ज्ञायते सुहृदामस्माकमाशिषो दित्सया एतीति । एतीत्यागमनक्रियायां कर्मानुक्त्यापि तथेति ज्ञाप्यते । अयं भावः । 'कर्तुरभीप्सिततमं कर्म' भवति । तेनात्र भगवत्कर्तृत्वात्तदभीप्सिततमत्वमस्माकमेव, नान्यस्य । अन्यथा व्रजमेतीत्युक्तं भवेत् । यद्यपि सर्वेषामेव निरोधश्चिकीर्षतो भगवत इति व्रजस्याप्यभीप्सिततत्वम्, तथाप्यभीप्सिततमत्वलक्षणोतिशयोऽस्मास्वेवेति तथोक्तम् । तन्निदर्शनमेवाहुः एष इति । अन्यथा कथमात्मानं प्रदर्शयेत् । दक्षिणनायकत्वेनान्तर्भाववैषम्याभावायाहुः देवकीजठरभूरिति । सर्वथा निर्दुष्टा हि देवकी । तदुदरे प्रकटस्तथेत्यर्थः । तादृशस्य भवतीषु को विशेष इत्यत आहुः उडुराज इति । यथा चन्द्रः सर्वेषां तापहारको दूरादेव, परं पतित्वेनातिनिकटे नक्षत्राणामेव, तथायमपि सर्वेषां तथा दूरादेव, परं पतित्वेनास्माकमेव तथेति भूयान् विशेषः सम्पद्यते । स यथा नक्षत्रमण्डले तिष्ठंस्तैरेव राजमानः सर्वतापनिवर्तकः, तथायमप्यस्मन्मण्डले तिष्ठन्नस्माभिरेव राजमानस्तथेत्युडुराजपदेन द्योत्यते ।) इदं सर्वं कार्यं वेणुनादसाध्यमिति प्रकरणितत्वात् ज्ञेयम् ॥२२॥२३॥

साधारणीं लीलामुक्त्वा गोपिकास्वेव वेणुकृतां भगवतैव जनितां लीलामाह मदेति ।

मदविघूर्णितलोचन ईषन्मानदः स्वसुहृदां वनमाली ।
बदरपाण्डुवदनो मृदुगण्डं मण्डयन् कनककुण्डललक्ष्म्या ॥ २४ ॥

यदुपतिर्द्विरदराजविहारो यामिनीपतिरिवैष दिनान्ते ।
मुदितवक्त्र उपयाति दुरन्तं मोचयन् व्रजगवां दिनतापम् ॥ २५ ॥

यदुपतिः मुदितवक्त्र उपयातीति । पूर्वोक्ता एव वेणुनादा अत्र ग्राह्याः । दश लीलाः पूर्वं निरूपिताः, ता सर्वा अस्मदर्थमेवेति दशधा भगवतं विशेषयन्ति । एक

एव भगवानुभयत्रेति युगलत्वेऽपि नात्यन्तं विभागः । सर्वत्रैव वेणुनादे रजोगुणो मुख्य इति सोऽस्मदर्थं फलित इत्याहुः । मदेन विघूर्णिते लोचने यस्येति । मदोऽत्र स्वानन्दस्थित्या पूर्णावबोधः । स ज्ञानमार्ग एवेति प्रकटयितुं सर्वविषयान् व्यावर्तयितुं विघूर्णितलोचनत्वमुक्तम् । अयं धर्मो भगवन्निष्ठो निरूपितः । स्वरूपस्थित्यर्थं तादृशोऽपीषन्मानदः, मानं प्रयच्छति । सन्माननां करोति । तेनास्माकं गम्यो भवतीति ज्ञायते । मानमभिमानं वा रजोगुणप्राकटयात्, प्रयच्छति, खण्डयति वा, ज्ञान-प्राकटयात्, प्रयच्छति मानं द्यति खण्डयति त्रिष्वपीषदेव तत्तत् कार्यम् । ननु पूर्णस्य भवतीष्वेवंकरणे को हेतुस्तत्राहुः स्वसुहृदामिति । स्वपदादसाधारण्यम् । तेन स्वस्यैव सुहृदस्ताः । महतोऽपि सुहृत्कार्यं कर्तव्यमिति । साधारणं कार्यमाह वन-मालीति । कीर्तिमयीं वनमालां प्रकटयतीति । बदरवत् पाण्डुवदन इति । बदरोऽत्र फलवाचकः । स हि धर्मेण प्रतिक्षणं विसदृशीं कान्ति करोति । तत्राप्यर्धपक्वः पाण्डुवर्णो भवति । अग्रे त्वारक्तः । तथेदानीमर्धरतः, अग्रे त्वत्यन्तं रतो भविष्यतीति ईषन्मान-दत्वाद्विशेषः । साधनं कीर्तिरिति मध्ये विशेषणान्तरम् । अथवा । अत्र पाण्डुशब्देन आरक्त एव गुण उच्यते । तदा वदनं वक्त्रं अधरामृतपानं लक्षितं भवति । वनवासिनां वा एतदुपभोग्यमिति वने गत्वा एतदुपभोग्यमिति सर्वाः ज्ञापयन्ति । ततोऽपि विशेषमाहुः कनककुण्डललक्ष्म्या मृदुगण्डं मण्डयन्निति । श्मश्रूद्गमाभावादानन्द-निधानत्वाच्च मृदुत्वं भोगार्थमुपपाद्यते । गण्ड एव रससमाप्तिरिति । कनकपदं वर्णान्तरज्ञापनार्थम् । उत्कृष्टेनापि परमानन्देनापि अस्मदर्थं कामरस एवोद्बोध्यत इति सर्वथास्मदर्थमेव भगवदागमनमिति निश्चीयते । अन्यथा शिरोभेदान-स्मत्समक्षं न कुर्यादिति । ननु यद्यपि महान्, तथापि बाल इति, नन्दसूनुरिति, कथमसाधारणीं लीलां करिष्यतीत्याशङ्कां वारयन्ति यदुपतिरिति । अयं यादवानां पतिः । ते हि बहुस्त्रीका भवन्ति । अमर्यादार्थं विशेषणान्तरमाहुः द्विरदराजविहार इति । महासुरते गजेन्द्र इव महान् । तेन विना न पूर्तिरिति । तदपेक्षयाप्यादौ पूर्वतापं दूरीकरिष्यतीत्याहुः यामिनीपतिरिवेति । सम्पूर्णाया यामिन्या अयं पतिः । अतस्तद्गतानां विशेषेण सुखदः । नन्वहर्पतिरपि, कथमुच्यते यामिनीपतिरिवेति, तत्राहुः एष इति । सर्वालङ्कारभूतस्तत्र तिष्ठति । अधुना तु श्रान्त इव । दिनान्ते एष यामिनीपतिरिव चन्द्र इव दूरादेव तापनाशकः साम्प्रतम् । अग्रे तु यामिनी-पतिरिव । इममर्थं ज्ञापयतीति लक्ष्यते, यतो मुदितवक्त्रः प्रसन्नवदनो भूत्वा उपयाति, समीपमागच्छति । अयं भावस्तासामेव हितकारीति पूर्वं साधारण्यमुक्तम्, उपसंहारे पुनराह मोचयन् व्रजगवामिति । व्रजस्य गवां च सम्पूर्णे दिवसे यावांस्तापः, तं सर्वमेव मोचयतीति ॥२४॥२५॥

एवं निरोधं स्त्रीणामुंपसंहरन् प्रकरणस्थानामेव तद्द्वारोपसंहरति एवमिति ।

श्रीशुक उवाच—**एवं व्रजस्त्रियो राजन् कृष्णलीलानुगायतीः ।**
रेमिरेऽहःसु तच्चित्तास्तन्मनस्का महोदयाः ॥२६॥

इति श्रीमद्भागवते महापुराणे दशमस्कन्धे द्वात्रिंशोऽध्यायः ॥

राजन्निति सम्बोधनं विश्वासार्थम् । व्रजगता अपि स्त्रियः एवं प्रकारेण अहस्सु भगवत्सम्बन्धरहितदशायामपि कृष्णलीला एव आनुपूर्व्येण बहुकालानुवृत्त्यर्थमनुगायतीः अनुक्रमेण गायतीः रेमिरे । स्वत आनन्दरूपा कीर्तिस्ताः प्रति जातेति तासां क्रियाशक्तिर्ज्ञानशक्तिश्च भगवन्निष्ठैव जातेत्याह तन्मनस्काः तच्चित्ता इति । चित्तं ज्ञानप्रधानम्, मनः कर्मप्रधानमिति । एवं सर्वप्रकारेण प्रपञ्चविस्मृतिर्भगवदासक्तिश्च निरूपिता । नन्वेवं कथं तासां निरोधः फलित इति, तत्रोपपत्तिमाह महोदया इति । महानेवाभ्युदयो भाग्यराशिर्यासामिति सर्वं सुस्थम् ॥२६॥

इति श्रीभागवतसुबोधिन्यां श्रीमल्लक्ष्मणभट्टात्मजश्रीमद्वल्लभदीक्षितविरचितायां दशमस्कन्धविवरणे द्वात्रिंशाध्यायविवरणम् ॥

इति दशमपूर्वार्धतामसफलप्रकरणम् ॥

BIBLIOGRAPHY

Bhāgavata Purāṇa. Śrīmadbhāgavatamahāpurāṇam (Mūlamātram). Gita Press, Gorakhpur. 1942 (and frequently reprinted).

———*Śrīmadbhāgavatam.* Nirnayasagar Press, Bombay. 1950.

———. Cf. also under Joshi, Sanyal, Telivala, Vallabhācārya, and Vasu.

Barz, Richard K. *The Bhakti Sect of Vallabhācārya.* Faridabad: Thomson Press (India), 1976.

Bhatt, G.H. *Śrī Vallabhāchārya and His Doctrines.* Preface by K.K. Shastri; avant. propos by Vachaspati Upadhyaya. Delhi : Butala, 1980.

Bhaṭṭa, R.K. *The Vedanta of Pure Non-dualism: The Heritage of the Philosophical Tradition of Shri Vallabhāchārya.* Translated by I.C. Sharma; revised and edited by Richard M. Fox. Virginia Beach, Va. (USA): Donning, c. 1979.

Dr. Sushil Kumar. *Early History of the Vaishnava Faith and Movement in Bengal.* Second Edition. Calcutta: Firma K.L. Mukhopadhyay, 1961 (Reprint 1986).

Dimock, Edward C. *The Place of the Hidden Moon.* Chicago: University of Chicago Press, 1966.

Glasenapp, Helmuth von. "Die Lehre Vallabhācāryas", *Zeitschrift für Indologie und Iranistik*, Band 9, Heft 3, Leipzig, 1934, pp. 268-330. Translated with the title *Doctrines of Vallabhācārya* by Ishverbhai S. Amin and Another: Shri Shuddhadvaita Samsada, Kapadwanj, 1959.

Goswamy, Shyam. *Sarvātmābhava kā Tulanātmaka Adhyayana.* Published in 13 parts in 13 consecutive numbers of the monthly *Śrīvallabhavijñāna*, beginning with Volume 11, Number 9, March 1972.

———(re-editor and publisher). *Ṣoḍaśagranthāḥ* (Full title *Mahāprabhu Śrīmadvallabhācāryaviracitāḥ Ṣoḍaśagranthāḥ*). In three volumes. Contains the Telivala/Sankalia editions of *Bālabodhaḥ* (in Vol. I), *Bhaktivardhinī* (in Vol. II), *Nirodhalakṣaṇam* (in Vol. III), and *Sannyāsanirṇayaḥ* (in Vol. III). Private printing. Bombay: 1980-1981.

———. *Śuddhādvaita aur uskā Sandarbha.* Written under the pen-name "Kṛṣṇakānt Sharmā". In two parts, in the August and September, 1972, issues of *Śrīvallabhavijñāna.*

———. *Śrīvallabhācārya ke Darśan kā Yathārtha Svarūpa.* English Title: *The Philosophy of Śrīvallabhācārya As It Is*

(A Critical Estimate of 'The Philosophy of Vallabhacarya', by Dr. (Mrs) M. I. Marfatia). 1974: Anand Prakashan, Varanasi-1. Cf. also under "Marfatia" below.

———(re-editor and publisher). *Tattvārthadipanibandha* (of Vallabhācārya). In three volumes. Private printing: Bombay. 1983-84.

Haberman, David L. *Acting as a Way of Salvation: A Study of Raganuga Bhakti Sadhana.* New York: Oxford University Press, 1988.

Hardy, Friedhelm. *Viraha-Bhakti: The Early History of Kṛṣṇa Devotion in South India.* Delhi: Oxford University Press, 1983.

Hawley, J.S. with Shrivatsa Goswami: *At Play with Krishna.* Princeton: Princeton University Press, 1988.

Hein, Norvin. *The Miracle-Plays of Mathurā.* Oriental Publishing House, Delhi. 1972.

Johanns, Rev. P., S.J. *To Christ Through the Vedanta: Part III: Vallabha* (A Synopsis in 100 pages). Third Impression. Catholic Mission Press, Ranchi, 1944 (first printed 1932).

Joshi, R.V. *Śrīrāsapañcādhyāyī-Sāṁskṛtika-Adhyayana.* Motilal Banarsidass: Delhi, Patna, Varanasi, c. 1968.

Lālūbhaṭṭa (also known as Bālakṛṣṇabhaṭṭa). *Prameyaratnārṇava.* Cf. under "Mishra" below.

Marfatia, Mrudula I. *The Philosophy of Vallabhācārya.* Munshiram Manoharlal, Delhi, 1967. Cf. also under "Goswamy" above.

Mishra, Kedarnath, Editor and Translator (into Hindi). *Prameya-Ratnārṇava of Śrī Bāla-Kṛṣṇa Bhaṭṭa.* Anand Prakashan, Varanasi-1. 1971.

———, Editor and translator (into Hindi). *Tattvārthadipanibandhaḥ—Śāstrārthaprakaraṇam* (*of Vallabhācārya*). With Vallabha's *Prakāśaḥ*. Varanasi: Bharatiya Vidya Prakashan, 1971.

Radhakrishnan, Sarvepalli. *The Principal Upaniṣads* (Edited with Introduction, Text, Translation and Notes). George Allen and Unwin Ltd., London, 1968 (first published 1953).

Sankalia, D.V. Cf. under "Telivala" below.

Sanyal, J.M. (tr.) *The Srimad-Bhagavatam* (Translated into English Prose). Second Edition in five volumes, Oriental

Publishing Company, Calcutta, undated. Reprinted in two volumes by Munshiram Manoharlal, Delhi, in 1973.

Shah, J.G. *Shrimad Vallabhacharya: His Philosophy and Religion.* Pushtimargiya Pustakalaya. Nadiad. 1969.

Sharma, Balabhadra (editor). *Bālabodhaḥ* (of Vallabhācārya), *Śripuruṣottamapraṇītayā vivṛtyā Samanugataḥ.* Bombay, Nirnayasagar Press, 1917. Out of print.

Shastri, D.K. (editior). *Śrimadbhāgavatamahāpurāṇam.* Varanasi: Śrīvidyāhitanidhisadasyāḥ (1965—). Contains Vallabha's *Subodhinī,* Puruṣottama's *Subodhinīprakāśaḥ,* and Giridharalala's *Bālaprabodhinī.*

Shastri, Harishankar Onkarji (editor). *The Tattvārtha-Dīpa-Nibandha (of Vallabhācārya) with Prakāśa.* Two Volumes. Trustees of Sheth Narayandas and Jethanand Asanmal Charity Trust, Bombay. 1943.

Shastri, M. G. (editor). *Kṛṣṇa: Ṣoḍaśagranthāḥ sakārikā rāsapañcādhyāyībeṇugopikāyugalabhramaragītasubodhinī.* Bombay, Nirnayasagar Press, 1930. All are works of Vallabhācārya.

Sheth, Noel. *The Divinity of Krishna.* Delhi: Munshiram Manoharlal, 1984.

Telivala, M.T., and Sankalia, D.V. (editors). *Bhaktivardhinī (of Vallabhācārya): Caturdaśavivṛtisametā.* Bombay: Nirnayasagar Press. 1921. Cf. under "Goswamy, *Ṣoḍaśagranthāḥ*" above.

———. *Nirodhalakṣaṇam (of Vallabhācārya): Ṣaḍvivaraṇasametam.* Bombay: Nirnayasagar Press. 1917. Cf. under "Goswamy, *Ṣoḍaśagranthāḥ*" above.

———. *Sannyāsanirṇayaḥ (of Vallabhācārya): Aṣṭavivaraṇasametaḥ.* Bombay: Nirnayasagar Press. 1918. Cf. under "Goswamy, *Ṣoḍaśagranthāḥ*" above.

———. *Śrī Subodhinī (of Vallabhācārya): Daśama-pūrvārdha-tāmasaphala-prakarṇam.* Bombay: Nirnayasagar Press. 1924. Out of print.

Thoothi, N.A. *The Vaishnavas of Gujarat,* Longmans, Green & Co., Ltd.: London, Bombay, Calcutta. 1935.

Vallabhācārya. *Bālabodhaḥ.* Cf. under "Goswamy, *Ṣoḍaśagranthāḥ*" and "Sharma" above.

———. *Bhaktivardhinī.* Cf. under "Goswamy, *Ṣoḍaśagranthāḥ*" and "Telivala" above.

———. *Nirodhalakṣaṇam.* Cf. under "Goswamy, *Ṣoḍaśagranthāḥ*" and "Telivala" above.

———. *Śrī Rāsapañcādhyāyī-Śrīsubodhinī.* Sanskrit text, with Hindi translation by Jagannath Chaturvedi. Varanasi: Chowkhamba Sanskrit Series Office, 1971.

———. *Sannyāshnirṇayaḥ.* Cf. under "Goswamy" *Ṣoḍaśagranthāḥ* and "Telivala" above.

———. *Ṣoḍaśagranthāḥ.* Cf. under "Goswamy" and "Shastri, M.G." above.

———. *Subodhinī.* Cf. under "Telivala" and "Shastri, D.K." above and "Vasu" below.

———. *Tattvārthadīpanibandha.* Cf. under "Mishra" and "Shastri M.G." above.

Vasu, Fatehchand (translator into Hindi). Volume Five ("*Pañcama Puṣpa*") i.e., the *Tāmasaphalaprakaraṇa*, of Śrī Subodhinī Granthamālā. Shri Subodhini Prakashan Mandal, Jodhpur. 1971.

Vyas, Ramnarayan. *The Bhāgavata Bhakti Cult and Three Advaita Ācāryas* (Śaṁkara, Rāmānuja, and Vallabha). Delhi: Nag Publishers. 1977.

White, Charles S.J. *Bhakti as a Religious Structure in the Context of Medieval Hinduism in the Hindi Speaking Area of North India.* Ph.D. Thesis for the University of Chicago Divinity School, Sept., 1964. Of special interest is Chapter III, "Devotion to Kṛṣṇa in Indian Literature and History with Emphasis on the Child Kṛṣṇa of Sūrdāṣ."

Wulff, Donna M. *Drama as a Mode of Religious Realization.* Chico, Calif.: Scholars Press, 1984.

Zaehner, R.C. *The Bhagavad-Gītā* (edited and translated with an introduction and extensive notes). London: Oxford University Press, 1969.

INDEX

NOTE : This index of important words and themes is intended to double as a glossary. Also, in the cases of several important themes (especially 'mood of love' and 'passion'), I have sometimes recorded references in which the subject matter, rather than the word itself, is mentioned.